THE ULTIMATE SUPER BOWL BOOK

THE ULTIMATE
SUPER BOWL BOOK

A COMPLETE REFERENCE TO THE STATS, STARS, AND STORIES BEHIND FOOTBALL'S BIGGEST GAME— AND WHY THE BEST TEAM WON

2ND EDITION

Bob McGinn

Foreword by Michael MacCambridge

MVP
BOOKS

To my mother, Catherine: You taught me how to keep score of my first basketball game on the radio, made sure newspapers always were around the house, took me to sporting events big and small, and made certain good writing and good grammar were priorities.

To my father, Denis: You were my hero. I'll never forget taking the train with you to my first NFL game on Sunday, October 4, 1959, at City Stadium in Green Bay.

First published in 2009 by MVP Books, an imprint of MBI Publishing Company, 400 First Avenue North, Suite 300, Minneapolis, MN 55401 USA.

This second edition published 2012.

© 2009, 2012 MVP Books

Text © 2009, 2012 Bob McGinn

Photograph copyrights as indicated with captions.

MVP Books titles are also available at discounts in bulk quantity for industrial or sales-promotional use. For details write to Special Sales Manager at Quayside Publishing Group, 400 First Avenue North, Suite 300, Minneapolis, MN 55401 USA.

To find out more about our books, visit us online at www.mvpbooks.com.

Library of Congress Cataloging-in-Publication Data
McGinn, Bob.
 The ultimate super bowl book : a complete reference to the stats, stars, and stories behind football's biggest game--and why the best team won / Bob McGinn ; foreword by Michael MacCambridge. -- 2nd ed.
    p. cm.
 ISBN 978-0-7603-4371-5 (hardback)
 1. Super Bowl--History--Statistics. 2. Super Bowl--Miscellanea. I. Title.
 GV956.2.S8M36 2012
 796.332'648--dc23

                              2012013087

Editors: Peter Bodensteiner and Josh Leventhal
Design Managers: Katie Sonmor and James Kegley
Layout Design: Greg Nettles and Trevor Burks
Front Cover Photo by Scott Boehm/Getty Images

Printed in China

FOREWORD

by Michael MacCambridge

*Shoat said it was too bad we would all have to miss it but the Super Bowl
halftime show was going to be even more spectacular than the pre-game show.*
   *He said there would be a water ballet in the world's largest inflatable
swimming pool, a Spanish fiesta, a Hawaiian luau, a parade stressing the
history of the armored tank, a sing-off between the glee clubs of all the military
academies, and an actual World War I dogfight in the sky with the Red
Baron's plane getting blown to pieces.*

Dan Jenkins, *Semi-Tough*

Dan Jenkins wrote that send-up of the absurdity of Super Bowl halftime shows in 1972—and he'd be the first to tell you that, by 1974, the real thing had already outstripped even his healthy capacity for imagination.

From the beginning, there has been so much excess and bombast surrounding the Super Bowl that many people have come to the understandable conclusion that all the hype, sizzle, commotion, and distraction is what the event is truly *about*.

The way the game is presented by the NFL makes a kind of historical sense. When the AFL-NFL World Championship game was created, as part of the 1966 merger agreement between the two rival leagues, pro football was still straining to prove its supremacy. The models it was attempting to emulate and, ultimately, surpass—the fall classic in baseball, and college football's New Year's Day bowl games—were based on tradition, pomp, grandeur.

So we got men flying around in jet packs at Super Bowl I, and Giant Robot–sized football monster floats in Super Bowl II. By Super Bowl IV, we had the daily double of hot-air balloons taking off from inside the stadium (and, in one case, crashing into the stands and injuring a beauty queen) during the pre-game festivities and a re-enactment of the Battle of New Orleans, complete with smoking muskets and fallen soldiers, at halftime—on the same field where the second half of the world championship football game was about to be played.

The Super Bowl contains multitudes; it has always exemplified America at its best, America at its worst, and more than anything else, America at its *most*.

I'm afraid that, as a group, the press corps covering the big week has grown less able to take the full measure of the event. Most of the writers in attendance spend Super Bowl week scheming to line up tickets for the commissioner's party, or complaining about not having enough free food and drink in the media lounge, or trying to figure out a way to get their picture taken with Jared from Subway or the Bud girls (usually the latter, to be honest).

But not Bob McGinn.

He remembers that whatever else this monstrosity may be—and make no mistake, the prelude has become a weeklong cluster of the first order—it also happens to be the occasion of the most important pro football game of the year.

McGinn has become an indispensable writer by observing the cardinal rule of the game: He keeps his eye on the ball. He has developed a loyal following, of Packers fans and football fans nationally, by asking smart questions of people who know the most: scouts, assistant coaches, team captains, and offensive linemen. He is relentless about getting the story.

To fully appreciate McGinn's yeoman brilliance, you probably have to understand the triviality of much of the Super Bowl press corps. The inanity has grown with its mushrooming numbers. Super Bowl media day has seen such infamous questions as "If you were a tree, what sort of tree would you be?" (asked of John Elway), "How long have you been a black quarterback?" (asked of Doug Williams), and "What's the stupidest question you've been asked?" (asked probably hundreds of times, often with the accompanying answer, "That one").

In late January 2009, I sat at a press conference in Tampa, in the midst of media events building up to Super Bowl XLIII. It was a packed room featuring the halftime concert attraction, Bruce Springsteen and the E Street Band. It was Springsteen's first press conference in more than a quarter-century and the first time, as far as I know, that the entire band was onstage with him for an open questioning. Once you got past the obligatory radio DJ questions like, "Why now?" and "What do you remember about Tampa?" there was really only one question begging to be asked: Springsteen's saxophonist, Clarence Clemons, *played college football at Maryland State*. That was the obvious angle, and Springsteen performed the courtesy of reminding the journalists of this as he introduced Clemons. As I sat in the back, I assured myself that somebody had to ask the Big Man about his football career.

Nobody asked. Blinded by the light, I guess.

What happened in the press conference never happens in the real game. Bob McGinn will ask the obvious questions and the ones that aren't obvious. He'll inquire and, ultimately, elucidate. That's how he's developed his reputation as the best game-story writer in the business.

The obstacles are formidable and worth considering. Even beyond the weeklong parade of celebrities, good causes, extravagant parties, and world-class traffic jams, the contest itself has to fight against being upstaged by its own pageantry. Every year, the Super Bowl is the game put on by the NFL that is *least* like an NFL game. Normally, teams fly in the day before a game. With the Super Bowl, both teams fly in nearly a week prior to kickoff. There is no home team. Even the start time is odd— 6:19 p.m. eastern standard time. The halftime, twice as long as for a regular-season game, has become an exercise in both technological efficiency and mission creep. Staging a major rock concert in the middle of a game is possible—just as holding a pheasant hunt in the middle of a wedding ceremony is theoretically *possible*—but it doesn't make a great deal of sense, unless you understand that in addition to being the biggest football game of the year, the Super Bowl also has to be the biggest TV event of the year.

Mr. Jagger, you're on. Mind the football players on your way out.

The best football teams are successful because they can impose their will on their opponents. Every year on Super Sunday, two teams that have managed to do so over the course of 20 weeks— each of the combatants convinced it alone is a team of destiny—come together under these extra-ordinary circumstances.

The team that is the least distracted and most able to perform that elusive task wins. And then the confetti cannons erupt, the network sends an anchor out to present the trophy, the commemorative T-shirts and caps are being sold on the way out of the stadium, the ticket stubs and game programs are being peddled on eBay, the MVP is flying to New York to be on the Letterman show, and when the next week's issue of *Sports Illustrated* or *The Sporting News* hits the newsstands, they're already speculating on what team will have the inside track *next* season.

All the while, the story of the monumental game that will define the careers and reputations of football players and coaches is still there for the taking. McGinn seizes it, researches it, and explains it for those of us who yearn to know how and why our hopes and dreams were just realized or destroyed.

He won't settle for the obvious answers, but digs beneath the surface to discover the causes for those answers. He understands that football is opaque, and that unless you get beyond the platitudes about establishing the run and stopping the long ball, you'll never really understand why one team prevailed. So his writing shows why the Vikings offensive line couldn't contain Curly Culp and Buck Buchanan in the middle, or why the Steelers defense was able to find an answer for the Cowboys' multiple offensive looks, or how the Ravens' defense forced the Giants out of their game plan.

It is, like the best writing, at once informative and entertaining and illuminating.

Now, don't get me wrong. Bob is not some one-track savant, some Rain Man with binoculars. At two different Super Bowl weeks, my girlfriend Ivy and I have broken bread with him and his lovely wife Pat (who typed in all the lineup and substitution information for this book, thus earning herself a special place in heaven). During these times, I have listened to Bob weigh in on a wide range of subjects entirely unrelated to pro football, from bicycling to gourmet cooking to penguins. He's good company.

But when we get back to the game—and we always, sooner or later, get back to the game—he is impervious to distraction. He doesn't care about the quarterback mooning the helicopter, or the wide receiver grabbing a cell phone out of the goalpost stanchion, or any of the other things that Super Bowl week can devolve into.

He cares about the game. This book is for people who care as deeply. For people who have had their hearts broken or their lives ineffably improved by the fortunes of a team on Super Sunday. For people who have invested a great deal of emotional capital in the fortunes of their favorite team. It's for people like us. We have learned that we can't control the outcome, no matter how many lucky jerseys we wear, or pre-game rituals we perform. But win or lose, we'd like to better understand it.

Thanks to Bob McGinn and *The Ultimate Super Bowl Book*, we can now do that.

Michael MacCambridge has written several books on football and other sports, including America's Game: The Epic Story of How Pro Football Captured a Nation *and* More Than a Game: The Glorious Present and Uncertain Future of the NFL, *written with Brian Billick. His biography of NFL pioneer Lamar Hunt is due to be published in the fall of 2012.*

PREFACE

It is true that the Super Bowl draws more coverage from print media than any sporting event in the world. It's also true, however, that much of the coverage is largely superficial.

The mood in the press box before kickoff on Super Sunday is convivial, to say the least. Then the game starts and the next however many hours to deadline make it a pressurized blur for the members of the pro football press corps.

Sportswriters, at least those working for newspapers east of the Rockies, are all trying to surmount the same challenge: too many stories to write and not enough time to write them.

More than half the seats in the press box are filled by writers pounding out so-called running game stories and columns because of East Coast and Midwest deadlines. These pieces must be filed by the conclusion of the game, if not before.

When I first started covering the Super Bowl in the mid-1980s, my newspaper didn't go to press until noon of the next day and hit the street later in the afternoon, so I could, and usually did, stay up all night crafting my stories. The first time I covered a Super Bowl, I bumped into a jubilant Al Davis as he congratulated one Raiders player after another inside the sweaty, cramped locker room at old Tampa Stadium in January 1984. In those days, there was enough time to interview players until there were no players left to interview, return to the hotel, and analyze both strategy and performance before beginning to write.

It wasn't long before the newspapers in Milwaukee merged, leaving only a morning edition, just like everywhere else in the country. When this happened, my coverage of the Super Bowl went from a reasoned dissection of why things happened to a hasty summation of what happened. That newspaper had to be on somebody's doorstep early the next morning.

I cannot remember the last Super Bowl in which I had time to walk down to the interview areas/locker rooms and actually do my job—namely, talk to players and coaches about why the game turned out as it did.

These days, portions of post-game interviews are piped live into the press box through television monitors. Later, a flood of "quote sheets" from player and coach interviews are rushed out to writers as they fight to hit their deadlines.

The next day, Super Bowl coverage is remarkably homogenized. Depending on their deadlines, beat writers may or may not have any quotes in their stories. Columnists are asked to tell readers what it all meant with little or no time for reflection. Some of the more blatant examples of overwriting emanate from Super Bowl press boxes.

After the traditional Monday-morning press conference with the winning coach and most valuable player, most writers leave town, never to write about that Super Bowl again. There's a parade to cover in one of the competing cities, a quiet locker room to cover in another, and a Super Bowl to forget everywhere else.

Not many of the players in the Super Bowl actually watch the game before scattering to their homes across the country. Some find time to get at the tape a few months later, while others, particularly those from the losing team, never do. Even some coaches, already weeks behind preparing for free agency and the draft, don't have an immediate opportunity to break down the Super Bowl tape as they would for any other game.

The objective of this book is to fill in the blanks on what really happened on the field in every Super Bowl game that has been played since 1967 and examine why each one was won.

The Super Bowl has become a national celebration, but at its core, it is just a football game.

As a beat writer covering the Packers since the late 1970s, my goal has been to provide one of the league's most knowledgeable and rabid fan bases with as much inside information on their team as possible. In this book, I have tried to provide the serious fan with a clinical account of the most important football game of the year.

The guts of the book comprise the hundreds of extended interviews that head coaches, assistant coaches, personnel people, and players generously granted me. After viewing at least some tape of every game, I asked specific questions about tactics, player performance, team performance, and individual plays. These interviews were an education unto themselves.

Given the luxury and advantage of time, some of the stories that couldn't be told in the newspapers at the time can now be told here.

It would have been impossible for me even to consider writing this book if a long list of scouts, coaches, and players hadn't repeatedly gone out of their way over the last 35 years to teach the game to someone who really didn't know if a football was blown up or stuffed. Their patience and considerateness enabled me to learn the game

Some of those scouts were Dick Corrick, Ron Wolf, Charley Armey, Tom Braatz, Jerry Angelo, John Butler, Ken Herock, Paul Wiggin, Jack Faulkner, Jeff Robinson, Joe Woolley, Ron Hughes, Rich Snead, Jerry Reichow, Dave Hanner, Rudy Feldman, Jeff Smith, John Dorsey, Trent Baalke, Bill McPeak, Jon Kingdon, Dick Steinberg, Bobby Riggle, Ted Thompson, A. J. Smith, Marc Ross, Mike Lombardi, Tim Rooney, Tom Modrak, Mark Hatley, Tom Boisture, Bill Polian, Reggie McKenzie, Phil Savage, Keith Kidd, Ron Nay, Phil Emery, Will Lewis, Dick Mansperger, Hal Hunter, Jon Jelacic, Reed Johnson, Mike Allman, Duke Tobin, Bruce Kebric, Walter Juliff, Bobby DePaul, Jesse Kaye, Tom Heckert, Blake Beddingfield, Bill Kuharich, Ellis Rainsberger, Brian Gaine, Mark Koncz, Sheldon White, John Brunner, Tony Softli, Mike McCartney, Jerry Hardaway, Bill Quinter, Jim Gruden, and Frank Smouse.

Some of those coaches were Fritz Shurmur, Larry Beightol, Tom Lovat, Tom Rossley, Scott O'Brien, Bobb McKittrick, Jerry Wampfler, Chuck Priefer, Bill Muir, Andy Reid, Ed Donatell, Bill Kollar, Ron Rivera, Dick Modzelewski, Tim Lewis, Brad Seely, Forrest Gregg, Paul Boudreau, Joe Philbin, Bob Hollway, Dick Rehbein, John Levra, Steve Mariucci, Dom Capers, Mike Holmgren, Ray Sherman, Steve Szabo, Sherman Lewis, Gary Zauner, Charlie Davis, Larry Peccatiello, Sylvester Croom, Jack Henry, Willy Robinson, Brian Baker, Shawn Slocum, Ray Horton, Bob Schnelker, Dave McGinnis, Mike Westhoff, Joe Whitt, Andre Patterson, Mike Sherman, Herm Edwards, Mike Stock, Vic Rapp, Keith Rowen, Jimmy Robinson, John Mitchell, John Teerlinck, Paul Alexander, Brett Maxie, Pat Jones, Tony Dungy, Howard Mudd, Pete Mangurian, Mike Trgovac, Geep Chryst, Ron Lynn, Dick Coury, Mike McCarthy, Harry Sydney, Pat Morris, Floyd Peters, Bruce DeHaven, and Fred von Appen.

And some of those players were LeRoy Butler, Brian Noble, Larry McCarren, Darren Sharper, Randy Wright, Ron Hallstrom, Lynn Dickey, Eugene Robinson, Bryce Paup, Ed West, Chuck Cecil, Aaron Kampman, Bernardo Harris, Ryan Pickett, James Lofton, Mark Murphy, Mike Flanagan, Doug Pederson, Mark Tauscher, George Koonce, Greg Koch, Ken Ruettgers, Mark Chmura, Rich Moran, John Anderson, Scott Wells, Ezra Johnson, Doug Evans, Na'il Diggs, Mark Lee, Antonio Freeman, John Jurkovic, Tim Harris, Rich Campbell, Nick Barnett, Jerry Holmes, and Santana Dotson.

To all of the above and many others, I owe you a debt of gratitude. My apologies to anyone whom I may have neglected to mention by name.

For some coaches and players, the Super Bowl was their finest hour.

For others, it was the game that they would most like to forget.

These are the stories of the plays and the coaching that drove the outcome of these Super Bowls.

ACKNOWLEDGMENTS

In addition to the players, coaches, and other football personnel who offered invaluable assistance in providing information and insight, many other people were instrumental in the creation of this book. I wish to offer my special thanks to the following individuals.

To my wife, Pat, not only for her inspiration, wisdom, and calming presence throughout this four-year project, but also for spending months contributing to the statistical elements of the book. She obtained jersey numbers, heights, and weights of starting players, then arranged and keyboarded the lineups for every game. She's a designer, not a football statistician, but you wouldn't know it by the high caliber of her work.

To my beloved children, Erin, Katie, Maggie, and Charlie, for their love and support.

To my sister, Barbara, who ran a library upstairs in our house and fostered my love of reading.

To my brother, Denny, a great all-around athlete and student of every game.

To Josh Leventhal of MVP Books, for believing in the project and always steering me in the proper direction.

To Michael MacCambridge, for introducing me to the world of book writing, for his counsel, and for coming through with a foreword in his inimitable style.

To the late Dick Corrick, my friend and confidant, whose opinion was the first that I sought for this project.

To Eric Goska, football historian par excellence, for providing names of the assistant coaches in the early games and computing a host of passer ratings.

To Danny Peary, whose extensive interviews with an important player from each of the first 31 Super Bowls proved to be a valuable resource.

To Patrick Pantano of NFL Films, for allowing me to see tapes of the games.

To Joe Horrigan and Saleem Choudhry of the Pro Football Hall of Fame, for providing a treasure trove of contact information and original play-by-plays.

To Ed Krzemienski, for doing the research at the Pro Football Hall of Fame.

To Mark Eckel, for serving as a valuable sounding board with his East Coast edge.

To Peter Bodensteiner, for a clean, helpful edit.

To Dan Verdick, for using his publishing expertise and making a convincing case for why there would be a market for this book.

To Gordy LeDuc, for teaching me lessons about the meaning of team and success that forever shaped my perspective on athletic competition.

To Ron Wolf, Mike Holmgren, and Bob Harlan, for showing me what a successful NFL organization was all about.

To Garry Howard, Chuck Salituro, and Len Wagner, who believed in me all the way.

To the public relations people around the league, the agents, and my colleagues in the beat-writing business, many of whom went out of their way to help me obtain interviews.

And again, to all the coaches, players, personnel men, owners, and scouts, for sharing the Xs and Os from some of the most joyous and disappointing days of their careers.

Ten Greatest Super Bowl Games

1. **Super Bowl XLII, Giants vs. Patriots:** The ugly duckling, Eli Manning, comes of age. . . . The Giants prove the Patriots are not invincible. . . . David Tyree makes his miraculous reception. . . . New York shows all-time pass rush led by Justin Tuck and Michael Strahan, who plays his final game.

2. **Super Bowl XXXVI, Patriots vs. Rams:** Bill Belichick contains St. Louis' "Greatest Show on Turf" with a lineup filled by cheap free agents. . . . Late heroics put young Tom Brady on the sporting landscape. . . . Adam Vinatieri's 48-yard field goal wins it as time expires.

3. **Super Bowl XXXIV, Rams vs. Titans:** Mike Jones tackles Kevin Dyson at the 1-foot line and the confetti rains down. . . . Kurt Warner is a deserving MVP, but Steve McNair's boldness on final possession leaves an indelible imprint.

4. **Super Bowl X, Steelers vs. Cowboys:** Terry Bradshaw out-duels Roger Staubach as the passing game reigns supreme for the first time in a Super Bowl. . . . Lynn Swann beats the young, spirited Cowboys almost by himself.

5. **Super Bowl III, Jets vs. Colts:** An upstart league and its underdog champion have their day in the sun. . . . Joe Namath guarantees victory over the Colts, then shows the way with a measured, unforgettable performance.

6. **Super Bowl XIII, Steelers vs. Cowboys:** Round 2 between the Steelers and Cowboys is one for the ages. . . . Bradshaw, Swann, and the "Steel Curtain" defense prevail once again in a wild shootout between heavyweights that will never be forgotten.

7. **Super Bowl XLIII, Steelers vs. Cardinals:** Few playoff games have had three more electrifying plays than those made by James Harrison, Larry Fitzgerald, and Santonio Holmes. . . . Quarterbacks Ben Roethlisberger and Kurt Warner cover themselves in glory.

8. **Super Bowl XXXII, Broncos vs. Packers:** The Broncos slay the mighty Packers, snapping the NFC's winning streak at 13 games. . . . Redemption is sweet for John Elway, whose whirlybird scramble galvanizes his teammates down the stretch.

9. **Super Bowl XXIII, 49ers vs. Bengals:** Maybe the least dominant of the 49ers' championship teams, but Joe Montana's strike to John Taylor gives the Super Bowl its first decisive touchdown pass in the final minute.

10. **Super Bowl XXXVIII, Patriots vs. Panthers:** Players wilt under the closed roof at Reliant Stadium as a frantic finish unfolds. . . . Once again, Brady and Vinatieri come through in spades as time runs out.

Honorable Mentions: Super Bowl XXV, Giants vs. Bills; Super Bowl XVI, 49ers vs. Bengals; Super Bowl XVIII, Raiders vs. Redskins; Super Bowl XLVI, Giants vs. Patriots; Super Bowl XXII, Redskins vs. Broncos; Super Bowl XX, Bears vs. Patriots.

GREEN BAY PACKERS 35, KANSAS CITY CHIEFS 10

January 15, 1967
Memorial Coliseum, Los Angeles, California

Attendance: 61,946
Conditions: 72 degrees, sunny and hazy, wind slight from E
Time of kickoff: 1:15 p.m. (PST)
Length of game: 2 hours, 37 minutes
Referee: Norm Schachter

MVP: Bart Starr, QB, Packers

For what seemed like an interminable span, each day for two weeks Vince Lombardi couldn't get away from the pressure. As coach of the Green Bay Packers, he had led the seemingly anachronistic franchise to three NFL championships in his first seven seasons. Now, fresh from a harrowing victory over the Dallas Cowboys in the NFL Championship Game, he was cast as the league's standard-bearer against the upstart Kansas City Chiefs in the first NFL-AFL World Championship Game at the Los Angeles Memorial Coliseum.

The scribes and networks had dubbed it the "Super Bowl," but it didn't feel so super to Lombardi. Installed as a 13-point favorite, the Packers were expected to uphold the honor and prestige of the 47-year-old NFL against the 7-year-old AFL, not only by winning but by winning big. Losing? Well, that was out of the question.

"Coach Lombardi wanted to win this game very, very badly and treated it like a personal mission, yet I didn't detect worry," his quarterback, Bart Starr, said years later. "It was never, 'What if we lose?' but was instead, 'We must win; we can't lose.' I don't know that I ever saw worry in him. That wasn't in his makeup. I'm sure there was inner concern. That may be what Frank Gifford, who was on CBS's broadcasting team, was describing when he said Lombardi was shaking when he interviewed him prior to the game."

The teams had exchanged three game tapes. From those, Lombardi detected the fatal weaknesses that the Packers would pounce upon for their ultimate victory. Only then would the petrified NFL owners, who sent telegrams to Lombardi with words of encouragement in the days leading up to the game, breathe a mighty sigh of relief.

The NFL crowd was more than just a little concerned at halftime. The big bad Packers were leading 14–10, but the Chiefs didn't seem the least bit intimidated. "We had done a real solid job up to that point," Kansas City defensive coordinator Tom Bettis said. "We had played toe-to-toe with them. We were feeling pretty good. We received the ball in the second half. We were moving it pretty good, too."

Chiefs coach Hank Stram had never coached against Lombardi, but he had seen him work several times. "I had watched Lombardi at a practice in 1955 when he was still a Giants assistant," he said. "I couldn't believe that one man could yell and scream and spout so much profanity."

The Chiefs went in relatively confident in what their multiple offense, featuring Stram's moving pocket, could do against Green Bay. "Like Vince Lombardi, they were a simple team, yet complicated," Stram said of the Packers. "One defensive alignment. Man-for-man coverage. Simple. Predictable. They did things right and with maximum force. Everyone went all-out every second. Still, I was sure we could move the ball on their conservative defense."

Kansas City arrived on the West Coast four days before the Packers and stayed in Long Beach. "We had come too early," Stram said. "They had been ready to play days earlier. On that long bus ride to Los Angeles for the first Super Bowl, the team was quiet and preoccupied. [Each player was] afraid of the game, of coming into the presence of greatness—the Green Bay Packers."

After a desultory first quarter, the Chiefs played an inspired second quarter. Rookie running

	1	2	3	4	Final
Kansas City Chiefs	0	10	0	0	10
Green Bay Packers	7	7	14	7	35

SCORING SUMMARY

1st Quarter
GB McGee, 37-yd. pass from Starr (Chandler kick)
2nd Quarter
KC McClinton, 7-yd. pass from Dawson (Mercer kick)
GB Taylor, 14-yd. run (Chandler kick)
KC Mercer, 31-yd. FG
3rd Quarter
GB Pitts, 5-yd. run (Chandler kick)
GB McGee, 13-yd. pass from Starr (Chandler kick)
4th Quarter
GB Pitts, 1-yd. run (Chandler kick)

back Mike Garrett broke tackles by all three linebackers on one 17-yard dump-off pass. Then Len Dawson, gaining ample time to throw after his exquisite play-action fakes, found Otis Taylor for 31 yards behind Wood. On the next play, Dawson hit running back Curtis McClinton wide open in the left corner for a 7-yard touchdown. The Chiefs finished off the first half with a 31-yard field goal by Mike Mercer.

In the Packers' cramped dressing quarters at halftime, Lombardi was remarkably calm and made no changes on offense. What he did was order his defensive mastermind, Phil Bengtson, to start applying some pressure. To Lombardi, blitzing was a sign of weakness, but when the Chiefs quickly gained a first down near midfield to open the third quarter, the Packers blitzed for the first time in the game, sending six rushers against five blockers. Left linebacker Dave Robinson and right linebacker Lee Roy Caffey broke through untouched. In the middle, defensive tackle Henry Jordan split a feeble double-team block from center Wayne Frazier and left guard Ed Budde, and he hit Len Dawson a split-second before his teammates did.

Tight end Fred Arbanas was open in the flat against safety Willie Wood's loose coverage and probably would have had the first down. Under the Packers' pressure, however, Dawson's pass wobbled and sailed behind Arbanas, where Wood intercepted it and returned it 50 yards to the 5. Dawson called it the turning point of the game.

"Suddenly, the conservative Packers, who never blitzed, blitzed," Stram said. "Lombardi had turned into a fox. We were the deception-and-speed team, yet the Packers had tricked us with the blitz. One play and it came apart." On the next play, left tackle Bob Skoronski pancaked defensive end Chuck Hurston, and Elijah Pitts surged through a massive hole and into the end zone, after stepping out of the grasp of defensive tackle Buck Buchanan in the backfield.

With the Chiefs trailing by 11 points, the Packers could ignore the Chiefs' run fakes and tee off on Dawson. To that point, Kansas City had 201 yards in 32 plays. After Wood's pick, the Chiefs had the ball 6 times, punted all 6 times, registered just 5 first downs, and gained merely 38 yards in 25 plays.

"Green Bay reminded me of the later Dolphin teams, so solid, so well coached," said Bobby Beathard, the West Coast college scout for the Chiefs at the time. "They never made mistakes and it was hard to find a weakness. Overall, [with their] depth and everything else, we weren't a match for Green Bay."

In terms of sheer power, the Green Bay title teams of 1965, 1966, and 1967 weren't as good as the championship clubs of 1961 and 1962, according to tackle Forrest Gregg. At the start of the decade, the Packers would pulverize opponents with their Power Sweep and the rest of their overwhelming ground game. Lombardi's teams totaled more rushing yards than passing yards in four of his first seven seasons. By 1966, Green Bay was far less balanced, averaging just 119.5 rushing compared to 185.9 passing.

Swashbuckling fullback Jim Taylor gained

> "I coached for 40 years, and Phil Bengtson was the best defensive coach I've ever known. He set the whole game plan. Phil always preached that we'd play our game.... We had a middle linebacker like [Ray] Nitschke who could keep people off him and make the plays."
>
> *Jerry Burns, Packers defensive backs coach*

just 705 yards in 1966, his lowest total since 1959. Halfback Paul Hornung, who missed most of the season and the Super Bowl due to a pinched nerve in his neck, had a long gain of 9 yards in 76 carries. His replacement, Pitts, averaged 3.4.

When Starr joined the Packers as a 17th-round draft choice in 1956, he was a poor passer. Perhaps no great quarterback improved more mechanically during his career than Starr, in terms of developing touch, accuracy, and arm strength. Starr wasn't a natural athlete. As a basketball player, he found it impossible to execute a layup going off his left foot; he jumped off his right foot every time. But he was extremely intelligent, very tough, and, by January 1967, far more than the Chiefs' vulnerable defense could handle.

Kansas City's linebacking corps of Bobby Bell, Sherrill Headrick, and E. J. Holub was fast, physical, and ornery. Largely because of them, Taylor and Pitts were held to 101 tough yards in 28 carries. The Chiefs also had a force with defensive tackle in the massive Buchanan, a stalwart defensive end in Jerry Mays, and smart, active safeties in Johnny Robinson and Bobby Hunt, a tandem that combined for 20 interceptions during the season.

"They were more talented than any team we'd ever faced," Wood said years later. "Bigger, stronger, and faster—but they weren't experienced. That game could have gone either way."

What the Chiefs lacked were capable cornerbacks. Future Hall of Famer Emmitt Thomas replaced Fred Williamson in 1967, but the rookie from tiny Bishop College was still making the transition from collegiate wide receiver to a full-time role on defense. Willie Mitchell was the other starter at cornerback until 1969, when Jim Marsalis arrived as a first-round draft choice. "Fred Williamson was a fairly decent player, but he'd never hit anybody," Bettis said. "Willie Mitchell gave you everything he had. We were outmanned at one or two positions, and a good team will take advantage."

KANSAS CITY CHIEFS (AFL, 11–2–1)			GREEN BAY PACKERS (NFL, 12–2)	
		Offense		
88	Chris Burford (6-3, 220)	WR	84	Carroll Dale (6-2, 200)
77	Jim Tyrer* (6-6, 292)	LT	76	Bob Skoronski* (6-3, 250)
71	Ed Budde* (6-5, 260)	LG	63	Fuzzy Thurston (6-1, 245)
66	Wayne Frazier (6-3, 245)	C	50	Bill Curry (6-2, 235)
64	Curt Merz (6-4, 267)	RG	64	Jerry Kramer (6-3, 245)
73	Dave Hill (6-5, 264)	RT	75	Forrest Gregg* (6-4, 250)
84	Fred Arbanas (6-3, 240)	TE	81	Marv Fleming (6-4, 235)
89	Otis Taylor* (6-2, 211)	WR	86	Boyd Dowler (6-5, 225)
16	Len Dawson* (6-0, 190)	QB	15	Bart Starr* (6-1, 200)
21	Mike Garrett* (5-9, 195)	RB	22	Elijah Pitts (6-1, 205)
32	Curtis McClinton* (6-3, 227)	RB	31	Jim Taylor (6-0, 215)
		Defense		
75	Jerry Mays* (6-4, 252)	LE	87	Willie Davis* (6-3, 245)
58	Andy Rice (6-2, 260)	LT	77	Ron Kostelnik (6-4, 260)
86	Buck Buchanan* (6-7, 287)	RT	74	Henry Jordan* (6-3, 250)
85	Chuck Hurston (6-6, 210)	RE	82	Lionel Aldridge (6-4, 245)
78	Bobby Bell* (6-4, 228)	LLB	89	Dave Robinson* (6-3, 245)
69	Sherrill Headrick (6-2, 240)	MLB	66	Ray Nitschke (6-3, 240)
55	E. J. Holub* (6-4, 236)	RLB	60	Lee Roy Caffey (6-3, 250)
24	Fred Williamson (6-3, 209)	LCB	26	Herb Adderley* (6-0, 210)
22	Willie Mitchell (6-1, 185)	RCB	21	Bob Jeter (6-1, 205)
20	Bobby Hunt (6-1, 193)	SS	40	Tom Brown (6-1, 190)
42	Johnny Robinson* (6-1, 205)	FS	24	Willie Wood* (5-10, 190)
* AFL All-Star Team			* NFL Pro Bowl selection	

SUBSTITUTIONS

Kansas City

Offense: WR - 80 Reg Carolan, 25 Frank Pitts; T - 72 Tony DiMidio; G - 61 Dennis Biodrowski, 60 Al Reynolds; C - 65 Jon Gilliam; QB - 10 Pete Beathard; RB - 23 Bert Coan, 45 Gene Thomas. *Defense:* DE - 87 Aaron Brown; LB - 52 Bud Abell, 56 Walt Corey, 35 Smokey Stover; CB - 17 Fletcher Smith, 18 Emmitt Thomas; S - 14 Bobby Ply. *Specialists:* K - 15 Mike Mercer; P - 44 Jerrel Wilson.

Green Bay

Offense: WR - 80 Bob Long, 27 Red Mack; T - 72 Steve Wright; G - 68 Gale Gillingham; C - 57 Ken Bowman; QB - 12 Zeke Bratkowski; RB - 33 Jim Grabowski, 37 Phil Vandersea, 44 Donny Anderson. *Defense:* DE - 78 Bob Brown; DT - 73 Jim Weatherwax; LB - 56 Tommy Crutcher; CB - 43 Doug Hart; S - 45 Dave Hathcock. *Specialists:* K/P - 34 Don Chandler. *DNP:* 88 Bill Anderson (WR), 5 Paul Hornung (RB).

The other defensive end, second-year man Hurston, had been Buffalo's 12th-round pick in 1965 before finding his way to Kansas City. Late in the season, he had become ill and lost weight. Listed at 6-foot-6 and 240 pounds, Bettis said Hurston lined up on Super Sunday weighing between 205 and 210. Defensive end Aaron Brown, a first-round pick in 1966, had been tried at fullback by coach Stram early in his rookie season. By the time the Chiefs put him back on defense, it was too late for him to be a contributor. Thus, Hurston had to battle down after down against Skoronski (6-foot-3, 250), the Packers' Pro Bowl left tackle.

"I knew we had sort of a mismatch with [Hurston] and Skoronski," Bettis said. "As a protection, we had the weak-side blitz. No fault of Chuck's. He did a good job all year. We tried to protect him all year, but people knew he was outweighed by every tackle he faced by a considerable amount."

The weak-side blitz, known as "Wanda" in the Kansas City playbook, was employed so that Starr—coming out from the shadow of Johnny Unitas to become the NFL's MVP in 1966 with a passer rating of 105.0—wouldn't have all day to scan the field. When the Chiefs called that blitz, Dave Robinson was forced to vacate his free safety position in the middle of the field and come up into the flat to cover the first running back out of the backfield.

"If I'm not mistaken, we blitzed only four times," Robinson said. "Max McGee caught three of them and I think the other one went to [Carroll] Dale. In defense of Willie, the three passes that were caught against him, he didn't have any help in the middle. I would have liked to have played that game

with me in the middle. That was our downfall."

On the second play from scrimmage, split end Boyd Dowler reinjured his right shoulder while making a crack-back block and was done for the day. That meant the 34-year-old McGee, with a mere four catches in the regular season, had to come off the bench to replace him. The rest, as they say, is history.

The Packers' first possession ended with consecutive sacks when Buchanan bowled over left guard Fuzzy Thurston and Mays whipped right tackle Gregg, but the Packers struck shortly thereafter on Starr's 37-yard touchdown pass to McGee. On third and 3, Bettis decided to blitz. Starr, McGee, and the rest of the seasoned offense were anything but rattled. "The Chiefs may not have realized that we loved when teams blitzed," Starr said. "We had a very good adjusting process for dogging linebackers and safeties. Guys like McGee could read a blitz and let us know it was coming, which gave us the time to exploit it. Our line allowed me to remain in the pocket, rather than bootlegging or scrambling."

Playing well off McGee and using an outside technique, Mitchell was in poor position when McGee ran a down-and-in route into the vacated wide-open middle of the field. Under pressure from Buchanan, Starr's pass was well behind McGee, but McGee reached back with his right arm, snagged the ball, and pulled it to his chest just as Mitchell dived in vain at where the ball had been. McGee eased into the end zone 20 yards away on a fast jog, and the Packers led, 7–0.

His catch, which would live on in Super Bowl annals as one of the most famous ever, took place at about 1:30 p.m. Six hours earlier, Starr had stepped off the elevator on his way to breakfast at the team's Sheraton West hotel when he encountered McGee straggling in. "He was returning from his big night out with a blonde from Chicago," Starr said. "He didn't worry about his late night out affecting his performance because, with his career winding down, he didn't expect to play at all."

Ninety miles up the coastline in Santa Barbara, where Lombardi had billeted the Packers for about a week, McGee was desperate for some fun but didn't have much success finding it in the semi-retirement community. Upon arrival in L.A., McGee met a few airline stewardesses and made plans to meet up with them in Beverly Hills after curfew Saturday night. Dave "Hawg" Hanner, the team's defensive line coach, had made the mistake of telling McGee on Friday night that he didn't intend to re-check his room after curfew.

"I was in bed under the sheets with my clothes on when they came around for bed check," McGee said. "As soon as they finished checking, I checked out. It was like getting out of jail. I wasn't a heavy drinker; I was just out enjoying myself. The next day, I didn't even bother to stretch out too much because I figured I'd just be sitting around watching anyway. I could barely stand up for the kickoff.

"The game had just started, and I was sitting on the bench with Hornung. We were sitting there planning his bachelor party when I heard Lombardi yell, 'McGee! McGee!' Boyd Dowler had gotten hurt. I had to scramble to my feet. I grabbed a helmet—I'm pretty sure it was someone else's—and I went in. It was one of the best days of my career, one of those days when I couldn't do anything wrong."

All seven of McGee's receptions came with Mitchell trying to cover him. In the third quarter, the Chiefs double-teamed McGee with Bell on a third-and-11, but Starr still managed to find him for 16 yards on a curl pattern. Four plays later, on another "Wanda," Mitchell made the terrible decision of trying to undercut another post pattern to McGee. This time, Starr's pass hit him right in the hands as he crossed the goal line near the wooden goalposts. It should have been a routine grab, but showing a flair for the dramatic, McGee juggled it for a stride or two before securing it for a 13-yard touchdown, making it 28–10.

In the fourth quarter, the Chiefs blitzed one more time. Mitchell gave McGee another huge cushion, and a third big completion to the post gained 37 yards. That set up the Packers' final touchdown, a 1-yard burst by Pitts.

"When you look at the film, you wonder how he caught the ball," said Bettis, also a one-time linebacker for the Packers and McGee's teammate from 1955 to 1961. "Max was a decent route runner and he had decent speed. He knew how to work people. But those catches were out of his ass. That's the way it was. Those

KANSAS CITY	TEAM STATISTICS	GREEN BAY
17	Total First Downs	21
4	Rushing	10
12	Passing	11
1	Penalty	0
239	Total Net Yardage	361
57	Total Offensive Plays	61
4.2	Avg. Gain per Offensive Play	5.9
19	Rushes	34
72	Yards Gained Rushing (Net)	133
3.8	Average Yards per Rush	3.9
32	Passes Attempted	24
17	Passes Completed	16
1	Passes Intercepted	1
6	Tackled Attempting to Pass	3
61	Yards Lost Attempting to Pass	22
167	Yards Gained Passing (Net)	228
3/13	Third-Down Efficiency	11/15
0/0	Fourth-Down Efficiency	0/0
7	Punts	4
45.3	Average Distance	43.3
3	Punt Returns	4
19	Punt Return Yardage	23
6	Kickoff Returns	3
130	Kickoff Return Yardage	65
0	Interception Return Yardage	50
1	Fumbles	1
1	Own Fumbles Recovered	1
0	Opponent Fumbles Recovered	0
4	Penalties	4
26	Yards Penalized	40
1	Touchdowns	5
0	Rushing	3
1	Passing	2
0	Returns	0
1	Extra Points Made	5
1	Field Goals Made	0
2	Field Goals Attempted	0
0	Safeties	0
10	Total Points Scored	35
28:35	Time of Possession	31:25

things happen. That's part of the game."

Another reason why Starr had a field day through the air was Stram's triple-stack linebacker alignment. Besides Headrick, either Bell or Holub was also situated inside the defensive ends to help stop the run. "There was no one to help a defensive back cover a receiver," Starr said, "so our plan was

INDIVIDUAL STATISTICS

KANSAS CITY

Passing	CP/ATT	YDS	TD	INT	RAT
Dawson	16/27	211	1	1	80.9
Beathard	1/5	17	0	0	41.3

Rushing	ATT	YDS	AVG	TD	LG
Dawson	3	24	8.0	0	15
Garrett	6	17	2.8	0	9
McClinton	6	16	2.7	0	6
Beathard	1	14	14.0	1	4
Coan	3	1	0.3	0	3

Receiving	NO	YDS	AVG	TD	LG
Burford	4	67	16.8	0	27
Taylor	4	57	14.3	0	31
Garrett	3	28	9.3	0	17
McClinton	2	34	17.0	1	27
Arbanas	2	30	15.0	0	18
Carolan	1	7	7.0	0	7
Coan	1	5	6.0	0	5

Interceptions	NO	YDS	LG	TD
Mitchell	1	0	0	0

Punting	NO	AVG	LG	BLK
Wilson	7	45.3	61	0

Punt Ret.	NO/FC	YDS	LG	TD
Garrett	2/0	17	9	0
E. Thomas	1/0	2	2	0

Kickoff Ret.	NO	YDS	LG	TD
Coan	4	87	31	0
Garrett	2	43	23	0

Defense	SOLO	AST	TOT	SK
Robinson	6	3	9	0
Bell	7	1	8	0.5
Holub	6	2	8	1
Mitchell	6	2	8	0
Mays	2	5	7	0.5
Buchanan	5	1	6	1
Rice	1	5	6	0
Hurston	0	3	3	0
Williamson	1	2	3	0
Headrick	1	1	2	0
Hunt	0	2	2	0
Ply	2	0	2	0
Abell	1	0	1	0
A. Brown	1	0	1	0
Corey	1	0	1	0
Garrett	1	0	1	0
Stover	0	1	1	0
TOTAL	**41**	**28**	**69**	**3**

GREEN BAY

Passing	CP/ATT	YDS	TD	INT	RAT
Starr	16/23	250	2	1	116.2
Bratkowski	0/1	0	0	0	39.6

Rushing	ATT	YDS	AVG	TD	LG
Taylor	17	56	3.3	1	14
Pitts	11	45	4.1	2	12
D. Anderson	4	30	7.6	0	13
Grabowski	2	2	1.0	0	2

Receiving	NO	YDS	AVG	TD	LG
McGee	7	138	19.7	2	37
Dale	4	59	14.8	0	25
Pitts	2	32	16.0	0	22
Fleming	2	22	11.0	0	11
Taylor	1	-1	-1.0	0	-1

Interceptions	NO	YDS	LG	TD
Wood	1	50	50	0

Punting	NO	AVG	LG	BLK
Chandler	3	43.3	50	0
D. Anderson	1	43.0	43	0

Punt Ret.	NO/FC	YDS	LG	TD
D. Anderson	3/0	25	15	0
Wood	1/1	-2	0	0

Kickoff Ret.	NO	YDS	LG	TD
Adderley	2	40	20	0
D. Anderson	1	25	25	0

Defense	SOLO	AST	TOT	SK
Caffey	5	2	7	0.5
Aldridge	4	2	6	0.5
Jordan	4	2	6	1
Nitschke	5	1	6	1
Jeter	3	1	4	0
Kostelnik	2	1	3	0
Da. Robinson	3	0	3	0
Wood	2	1	3	0
Adderley	2	0	2	0
T. Brown	1	1	2	0
Davis	1	1	2	2
Gillingham	2	0	2	0
Hathcock	1	1	2	0
Mack	2	0	2	0
B. Brown	1	0	1	1
Curry	1	0	1	0
Crutcher	1	0	1	0
Wright	0	1	1	0
Weatherwax	0	1	1	0
Vandersea	0	1	1	0
TOTAL	**40**	**16**	**56**	**6**

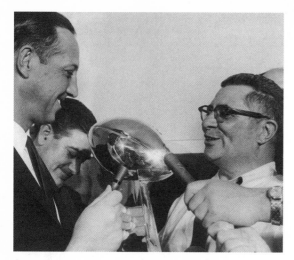

Coach Vince Lombardi (right) receives the victory trophy from Commissioner Pete Rozelle following Green Bay's 35–10 win over Kansas City in Super Bowl I. The trophy would later be renamed the Vince Lombardi Trophy in honor of the legendary coach. *Vernon Biever/NFL/Getty Images*

to isolate our wide receivers on their cornerbacks."

Williamson, a former Raider nearing the end of his eight-year career, bit on Starr's third-and-1 play fake a few plays later, and Dale raced by him for a 64-yard touchdown. Williamson was saved, however, when Skoronski was penalized for a false start, thus nullifying the touchdown, but Starr attacked him successfully later.

The Packers had done a slow burn early in the week when Williamson, nicknamed "the Hammer," had made disparaging remarks about some Packers and lipped off about the punishment he would mete out to their wide receivers. The only punishment involving Williamson was the knee to the head that he took from running back Donny Anderson in the waning minutes of the game, which knocked him cold.

Green Bay's post-game charter was delayed by fog and smog, so the team had to stay another night.

Jim Irwin, sports director for the ABC television affiliate in Green Bay, took the trophy with him from the Green Bay airport to the station when the team returned Monday to use it as a prop on the set that night. Irwin remembered to bring it back to the club's offices on Wednesday, but no one was concerned when he did. At the time, it was just another piece of hardware in the little city that by then was fond of calling itself "Titletown, U.S.A."

As the representative of the National Football League, the Packers had conveyed to the world of pro football that they were superior to the best team that the American Football League could offer. Many pundits sought to attach more far-reaching significance to the lopsided outcome. The truth was that the Lombardi Packers were a team for the ages.

Afterward, when the writers pressed into Lombardi's small office, they asked the question that everyone wanted answered: How did the great coach assess the Chiefs as compared to other teams in the NFL? "I have nothing to say about it," he replied. After several repetitions of the same line of questioning, however, Lombardi finally blurted out, "I don't think they are as good as the top teams in the National Football League. They're a good team with fine speed, but I'd have to say NFL football is tougher. Dallas is a better team, and so are several others. That's what you wanted me to say—now I've said it."

The AFL, as well as the Chiefs, would regain its self-respect in the not-too-distant future.

II

GREEN BAY PACKERS 33, OAKLAND RAIDERS 14

January 14, 1968
Orange Bowl, Miami, Florida

The defense of the Oakland Raiders in 1967 came to be known as the "Eleven Angry Men," and for good reason. Those Raiders led the AFL in defense and registered a total of 67 sacks on the season, which still stands as the club record more than 40 years later. In the AFL Championship Game, the Raiders defense allowed just 138 yards while pounding the Houston Oilers, 40–7.

Oakland's opponent in Super Bowl II, the Green Bay Packers, had 40 inspired men. The team was seeking a third straight championship, something that hadn't been done since the NFL inaugurated the playoff format and hasn't been done since. It also had the strong suspicion that Vince Lombardi, its legendary coach, was leading the team for the final time. That suspicion would prove to be correct 17 days after the 33–14 victory over the Raiders, when Lombardi officially stepped down as a coach. He remained in Green Bay as the team's general manager for another year before leaving to coach the Washington Redskins in 1969.

Some of the Packers didn't always enjoy playing under Lombardi, a man given to unsparing tirades and frequent acts of pettiness. Still, of the 40 players who took the field on a 68-degree afternoon at Miami's Orange Bowl, 9 had been with the Packers since Lombardi's first year in 1959 and had shared the glory of championships in 1961, 1962, 1965, and 1966. Six of them—Bart Starr, Forrest Gregg, Henry Jordan, Jerry Kramer, Max McGee, and Bob Skoronski—had been Packers in the pre-Lombardi era when the once-proud organization had struck rock bottom. If they didn't like or understand Lombardi, they certainly respected what he had done for them and the increasingly futile franchise.

Clearly, the Packers were starting to slip as they headed into the 1967 season. No one knew it at the time, but this would mark the end of the dynasty in Green Bay and the start of a generation

Attendance: 75,546
Conditions: 68 degrees, partly cloudy, wind W at 14 mph
Time of kickoff: 3:05 p.m. (EST)
Length of game: 2 hours, 34 minutes
Referee: Jack Vest

MVP: Bart Starr, QB, Packers

of losing. These players were particularly aware of Lombardi's intensity throughout the season, and the Packers seemed to win through his sheer force of will. That was especially true in the stark, brutal NFL Championship Game triumph over the Dallas Cowboys, known forever as the Ice Bowl.

"He was such a dominant force in our lives for the last 10 years," Kramer said several months after the Super Bowl. "He's been the only reason for our great success at Green Bay. I believe that, and I'm sure everyone else believes it. It's inconceivable to think that anyone would know it was Coach Lombardi's last game and just let it go as another game. I'm sure it was on everyone's mind, and they wanted to do the best they could and play the game as well as possible for him."

The Packers, a 14-point favorite, certainly weren't flawless on Super Sunday, just as they hadn't been during a discomfiting 9–4–1 regular season. Even against Oakland, said Kramer, "we made more mental mistakes than I can ever remember our team making in any other game." Then again, the Packers' standards were impossibly high. In the Super Bowl, they didn't fumble or throw an interception, and were penalized only once. Clearly what a Lombardi-coached team considered mistake-filled play would have been regarded as exquisite execution by many other clubs.

Just as the Kansas City Chiefs had done the previous year, the Raiders stuck with the vaunted Packers through the first half, or nearly so. The

	1	2	3	4	Final
Green Bay Packers	3	13	10	7	33
Oakland Raiders	0	7	0	7	14

SCORING SUMMARY

1st Quarter
GB   Chandler, 39-yd. FG
2nd Quarter
GB   Chandler, 20-yd. FG
GB   Dowler, 62-yd. pass from Starr (Chandler kick)
OAK   Miller, 23-yd. pass from Lamonica (Blanda kick)
GB   Chandler, 43-yd. FG
3rd Quarter
GB   Anderson, 2-yd. run (Chandler kick)
GB   Chandler, 31-yd. FG
4th Quarter
GB   Adderley, 60-yd. interception return (Chandler kick)
OAK   Miller, 23-yd. pass from Lamonica (Blanda kick)

Raiders trailed, 13–7, with 23 seconds left in the first half when Rodger Bird couldn't handle a towering, left-footed punt of 36 yards by Donny Anderson. Bird had led the AFL with a 13.3-yard punt-return average, but during the regular season, just 13 of Anderson's 40 punts had been returned, for a scant 22 yards.

Linebacker Dick Capp, the newest addition to the Packers' roster, recovered Bird's fumble at the Oakland 45. On Green Bay's next offensive sequence, defensive end Ike Lassiter put on a heavy rush on third and 10, but Starr managed to deliver a 9-yard sideline completion to Boyd Dowler under Willie Brown's too-soft coverage. On came Don Chandler, who kicked his third of four field goals, this one from the 43, and the Packers went to the dressing room with a 9-point lead.

"The Packers had dominated, but then we scored and the whole momentum had shifted in our favor," Raiders personnel director Ron Wolf recalled. "Then we gave it right back to them. After that punt, the wheels came off. I would say the reason that we lost was that fumbled punt."

Green Bay kept rolling in the third quarter with an 11-play, 82-yard touchdown drive that increased the lead to an insurmountable 23–7. Early in the push, on third and 1, Starr faked a handoff to Ben Wilson and found McGee all alone for a 35-yard gain. After so many years of being fooled, some NFL teams played Starr to pass in short yardage, but AFL clubs like the Raiders had not learned this lesson. McGee lined up close on the left side and was able to release quickly to the post when neither of the two defenders in front of him—Brown and free safety Howie Williams—slowed him up. There wasn't a Raider within 5 yards of McGee when he made the catch at the Oakland 33; he was dragged down at the 25. Starr hit Carroll Dale for 11 on third and 9, then Anderson for 12 on a rollout. Running off right tackle behind cleaving blocks by center Ken Bowman, tight end Marv Fleming, Jerry Kramer, and Ben Wilson, Anderson powered into the end zone standing up.

The long pass to McGee, who was getting the chance to play in another Super Bowl after another injury to Dowler, was the second of two bombs that changed the complexion of the game. The first, a 62-yard touchdown to Dowler, took place early in the second quarter. Unlike the Packers and most other NFL teams, the Raiders generally placed their cornerbacks—the excellent duo of Kent McCloughan and Brown—close to the line against wide receivers. In this case, Dowler was on the right side with McCloughan in press coverage. Thinking Bird would pick up Dowler deep, McCloughan offered merely a token jam. Dowler ran a quick post, took Starr's pass 20 yards downfield in the clear, and outran Bird to the end zone.

"The Packers were a pretty simple team," Raiders secondary coach Charlie Sumner said. "They just lined up and came at you pretty good. They did confuse us on a couple passes that hurt us more than anything else. We were a man-to-man

COACHING STAFFS

Green Bay
Head Coach: Vince Lombardi. *Offense:* Bob Schnelker (ends), Ray Wietecha (offensive line), Tom McCormick (backs). *Defense:* Phil Bengtson, Dave Hanner (defensive line), Jerry Burns (defensive backs).

Oakland
Head Coach: John Rauch. *Offense:* Ollie Spencer (offensive line), John Polonchek (backs). *Defense:* Tom Dahms (defensive line), John Madden (linebackers), Charlie Sumner (defensive backs).

team and were going to switch off when they brought the weak-side end in close." Dowler's touchdown had been a dropped coverage, caused by a mix-up between McCloughan and Bird. "We didn't want to get picked on it," Sumner continued, "so we were going to switch off on the pattern. We didn't get the switch in. The pass to McGee was the other one. They faked a run, and we bit on it and didn't get the switch in. We probably would have lost anyway, but they were big plays."

Starr, the MVP for the second straight time, finished the regular season with a passer rating of 64.4, his worst since 1958 and a dramatic downturn from his career-best mark of 105.0 the year before. Dogged by thumb and rib injuries during the exhibition season, he threw nine interceptions in the first two regular-season games and then missed two games with a shoulder injury.

At 34, Starr was also suffering from the absences of Jim Taylor (who left to play for New Orleans in 1967) and Paul Hornung (who retired because of a pinched nerve in his neck) in the backfield. Second-year man Jim Grabowski, the team's leading rusher with 466 yards, missed Super Bowl II with a knee injury, and the other starter, Elijah Pitts, was out with a torn Achilles tendon. Acquired from the Los Angeles Rams earlier in the year for a second-round draft choice, Wilson cut his weight from 240 to 225 and led all rushers in the Super Bowl with 62 yards in 17 carries.

"We were starting to age," Gregg said. "Experience only goes so far."

The Packers still were outstanding on the offensive line. Gregg and Kramer earned another trip to the Pro Bowl, quick-footed Bowman had re-established himself in the middle, and rugged Gale Gillingham had beaten out Fuzzy Thurston at left guard. "They were better in the offensive line than we were," Wolf said. "Gregg's in the Hall of Fame. Certainly, Gillingham should be in the Hall of Fame.

GREEN BAY PACKERS (NFL, 9–4–1)		Offense	OAKLAND RAIDERS (AFL, 13–1)	
86	Boyd Dowler* (6-5, 225)	WR	89	Bill Miller (6-0, 190)
75	Bob Skoronski (6-3, 245)	LT	76	Bob Svihus (6-4, 245)
68	Gale Gillingham (6-3, 255)	LG	63	Gene Upshaw* (6-5, 255)
57	Ken Bowman (6-3, 230)	C	00	Jim Otto* (6-2, 240)
64	Jerry Kramer* (6-3, 245)	RG	65	Wayne Hawkins (6-0, 240)
76	Forrest Gregg* (6-4, 250)	RT	79	Harry Schuh* (6-2, 260)
81	Marv Fleming (6-4, 235)	TE	33	Billy Cannon* (6-1, 215)
84	Carroll Dale (6-2, 200)	WR	25	Fred Biletnikoff* (6-1, 190)
15	Bart Starr (6-1, 190)	QB	3	Daryle Lamonica* (6-3, 215)
44	Donny Anderson (6-3, 210)	RB	40	Pete Banaszak (5-11, 200)
36	Ben Wilson (6-1, 230)	RB	35	Hewritt Dixon* (6-1, 220)
		Defense		
87	Willie Davis* (6-3, 245)	LE	77	Issac Lassiter (6-5, 270)
77	Ron Kostelnik (6-4, 260)	LT	53	Dan Birdwell (6-4, 250)
74	Henry Jordan (6-3, 250)	RT	74	Tom Keating* (6-2, 247)
82	Lionel Aldridge (6-4, 245)	RE	83	Ben Davidson* (6-7, 265)
89	Dave Robinson* (6-3, 240)	LLB	42	Bill Laskey (6-3, 235)
66	Ray Nitschke (6-3, 235)	MLB	55	Dan Conners* (6-1, 230)
60	Lee Roy Caffey (6-3, 250)	RLB	34	Gus Otto (6-2, 220)
26	Herb Adderley* (6-0, 200)	LCB	47	Kent McCloughan* (6-1, 190)
21	Bobby Jeter* (6-1, 205)	RCB	24	Willie Brown (6-1, 190)
40	Tom Brown (6-1, 195)	SS	20	Warren Powers (6-0, 190)
24	Willie Wood* (5-10, 190)	FS	29	Howie Williams (6-1, 186)
* NFL Pro Bowl selection			* AFL All-Star Team	

SUBSTITUTIONS

Green Bay
Offense: WR - 80 Bob Long, 85 Max McGee; TE - 88 Dick Capp; G - 63 Fuzzy Thurston; C - 50 Bob Hyland; QB - 12 Zeke Bratkowski; RB - 30 Chuck Mercein, 23 Travis Williams. *Defense:* DE - 78 Bob Brown; DT - 73 Jim Weatherwax; LB - 56 Tommy Crutcher, 55 Jim Flanigan; CB - 43 Doug Hart, 45 John Rowser. *Specialists:* K/P - 34 Don Chandler*. *DNP:* 33 Jim Grabowski (RB), 13 Don Horn (QB), 72 Steve Wright (T).

Oakland
Offense: WR - 84 Ken Herock, 88 Dave Kocourek, 81 Warren Wells; T - 78 Dan Archer; G - 70 Jim Harvey; C - 62 Bob Kruse; RB - 30 Roger Hagberg, 22 Larry Todd. *Defense:* DE - 85 Carleton Oates; DT - 73 Richard Sligh; LB - 50 Duane Benson, 48 Bill Budness, 52 John Williamson; DB - 21 Rodger Bird, 45 Dave Grayson. *Specialists:* K - 16 George Blanda; P - 11 Mike Eischeid. *DNP:* 23 Rod Sherman (WR).

I guess people argue whether Kramer should be. Starr was better than [Daryle] Lamonica. They had Dowler, and the guy that surprised us was Carroll Dale. I'm not sure he got his due because of all those great players around him."

On its first two possessions, Green Bay mixed 14 runs with 11 passes for 113 yards, leading to field goals by Chandler of 39 and 20 yards. Raiders coach John Rauch's defensive staff, which included John Madden as linebackers coach, made frequent use of a 5-2 alignment that helped limit AFL teams to just 80.6 yards rushing by taking away the middle. Despite ordinary backs, the Packers found room outside and off tackle for 160 rushing yards. "There wasn't any one defensive player who stood out, like Buck Buchanan, [Johnny] Robinson, E. J. Holub, and Bobby Bell had on Kansas City the year before," Kramer said. "They weren't of that caliber. We had run our offense for nine years, and it was unusual for us to make mental mistakes."

Still, the Raiders did have 67 sacks during the regular season, and they sacked Starr four times for 40 yards in losses. Their front four included AFL all-stars Ben Davidson at right end and Tom Keating at right tackle. Playing with a bad Achilles, Keating had two of the sacks, and Davidson had another. The Packers knew about the 6-foot-7 Davidson and his menacing handlebar mustache because he played 14 games for them in 1961. "We heard all the stories about how he killed quarterbacks," Gregg said. "We said, 'Well, Ben's a good football player, but I don't believe he's going to kill Bart.'"

Starr had to leave the game early in the fourth quarter with a bruised thumb when Davidson fell on him after a sack. By the time backup Zeke Bratkowski took his first snap, the Packers had increased their lead to 33–7 after cornerback Herb Adderley returned an interception 60 yards for another score. Lamonica said he didn't see the Hall of Fame cornerback, who played off Hall of Fame receiver Fred Biletnikoff and cut in front on a curl route. "Herb would back off far enough to invite the throw out there," Green Bay defensive line coach Dave Hanner said. "As soon as the ball was snapped he'd drive on you. He did that against the Cowboys a few times with Bob Hayes."

Although the Packers had allowed 4.3 yards per rush during the regular season (second worst

TEAM STATISTICS

GREEN BAY		OAKLAND
19	Total First Downs	16
11	Rushing	5
7	Passing	10
1	Penalty	1
322	Total Net Yardage	293
69	Total Offensive Plays	57
4.7	Avg. Gain per Offensive Play	5.1
41	Rushes	20
160	Yards Gained Rushing (Net)	107
3.9	Average Yards per Rush	5.4
24	Passes Attempted	34
13	Passes Completed	15
0	Passes Intercepted	1
4	Tackled Attempting to Pass	3
40	Yards Lost Attempting to Pass	22
162	Yards Gained Passing (Net)	186
5/16	Third-Down Efficiency	3/11
1/1	Fourth-Down Efficiency	0/0
6	Punts	6
39.0	Average Distance	44.0
5	Punt Returns	3
35	Punt Return Yardage	12
3	Kickoff Returns	7
49	Kickoff Return Yardage	127
60	Interception Return Yardage	0
0	Fumbles	3
0	Own Fumbles Recovered	1
2	Opponent Fumbles Recovered	0
1	Penalties	4
12	Yards Penalized	31
3	Touchdowns	2
1	Rushing	0
1	Passing	2
1	Returns	0
3	Extra Points Made	2
4	Field Goals Made	0
4	Field Goals Attempted	1
0	Safeties	0
33	Total Points Scored	14
35:54	Time of Possession	24:06

in the NFL), the Raiders weren't able to exploit the weakness. Clemon Daniels, Oakland's leading rusher since 1962, blew out his ankle in Week 9 and was replaced by handyman Pete Banaszak, who joined fullback Hewritt Dixon for a rather slow ball-carrying tandem behind Lamonica. "That didn't help," Wolf said. "If [Daniels were] playing today,

INDIVIDUAL STATISTICS

GREEN BAY

Passing	CP/ATT	YDS	TD	INT	RAT
Starr	13/24	202	1	0	96.2
Bratkowski	0/0	0	0	0	0.0

Rushing	ATT	YDS	AVG	TD	LG
Wilson	17	62	3.6	0	13
Anderson	14	48	3.4	1	8
Williams	8	36	4.5	0	18
Starr	1	14	14.0	0	14
Mercein	1	0	0.0	0	0

Receiving	NO	YDS	AVG	TD	LG
Dale	4	43	10.8	0	17
Fleming	4	35	8.8	0	11
Dowler	2	71	35.5	1	62t
Anderson	2	18	9.0	0	12
McGee	1	35	35.0	0	35

Interceptions	NO	YDS	LG	TD
Adderley	1	60	60t	1

Punting	NO	AVG	LG	BLK
Anderson	6	39.0	48	0

Punt Ret.	NO/FC	YDS	LG	TD
Wood	5/0	35	31	0

Kickoff Ret.	NO	YDS	LG	TD
Adderley	1	24	24	0
Williams	1	18	18	0
Crutcher	1	7	7	0

Defense	SOLO	AST	TOT	SK
Nitschke	5	4	9	0
Davis	7	0	7	3
Robinson	2	5	7	0
Wood	5	2	7	0
T. Brown	4	2	6	0
Caffey	4	2	6	0
Adderley	4	1	5	0
Jeter	2	2	4	0
Crutcher	2	1	3	0
Jordan	2	1	3	0
Aldridge	1	1	2	0
B. Brown	2	0	2	0
Capp	1	1	2	0
Bowman	1	0	1	0
Hyland	1	0	1	0
Kostelnik	1	0	1	0
Long	0	1	1	0
Rowser	0	1	1	0
Weatherwax	0	1	1	0
TOTAL	44	25	69	3

OAKLAND

Passing	CP/ATT	YDS	TD	INT	RAT
Lamonica	15/34	208	2	1	71.7

Rushing	ATT	YDS	AVG	TD	LG
Dixon	12	54	4.5	0	15
Todd	2	37	18.5	0	32
Banaszak	6	16	2.7	0	5

Receiving	NO	YDS	AVG	TD	LG
Miller	5	84	16.8	2	23t
Banaszak	4	69	17.3	0	41
Cannon	2	25	12.5	0	15
Biletnikoff	2	10	5.0	0	6
Wells	1	17	17.0	0	17
Dixon	1	3	3.0	0	3

Interceptions	NO	YDS	LG	TD
None	--	--	--	--

Punting	NO	AVG	LG	BLK
Eischeid	6	44.0	55	0

Punt Ret.	NO/FC	YDS	LG	TD
Bird	2/1	12	12	0
Wells	1/0	0	0	0

Kickoff Ret.	NO	YDS	LG	TD
Todd	3	63	23	0
Grayson	2	61	25	0
Hawkins	1	3	3	0
Kocourek	1	0	0	0

Defense	SOLO	AST	TOT	SK
Davidson	12	2	14	1
Conners	10	2	12	0
Birdwell	5	5	10	1
H. Williams	4	5	9	0
Bird	5	3	8	0
Keating	6	2	8	2
G. Otto	3	5	8	0
W. Brown	5	2	7	0
Lassiter	2	2	4	0
McCloughan	3	1	4	0
Benson	2	1	3	0
Kruse	2	0	2	0
Archer	2	0	2	0
Grayson	1	0	1	0
Kocourek	1	0	1	0
Laskey	1	0	1	0
Miller	0	1	1	0
Oates	0	1	1	0
Powers	1	0	1	0
Schuh	1	0	1	0
Todd	0	1	1	0
TOTAL	66	33	99	4

he'd be like [Edgerrin James]—that big and that fast. He was a 4.6-40 in gear before people were a 4.6-40 in gear. One thing the American Football League had [was] pretty good backs, but they never got the publicity."

Oakland's signature in the ground game was its sweeps, particularly with fleet rookie left guard Gene Upshaw leading the way. The Raiders had two problems. The first was dealing with Green Bay's linebacking corps of Dave Robinson and Lee Roy Caffey outside with Ray Nitschke in the middle. "They may be the best set of linebackers ever to play football," Cowboys coach Tom Landry said. According to Hanner, the 250-pound Robinson and the 245-pound Nitschke each could run 4.8. "We played some pretty good linebackers in the AFL, Willie Lanier and people like that," Wolf said. "I'm not saying that Nitschke was better, but to have a big guy that fast was a little different."

In order to pull both Upshaw and right guard Wayne Hawkins, the Raiders had to block Henry Jordan, the 243-pound defensive tackle who, according to Hanner, could keep up with Robinson and Nitschke in wind sprints. "One reason our sweeps didn't work was because we could pull only one guard," said Jim Otto, who played with double pneumonia. "The other had to stay back and take care of Jordan, who was so fast. Maybe we should have run right at 'em."

The Packers played a penetrating 4-3 defense, with Jordan and left end Willie Davis making most of the plays. The matchups were Jordan against Upshaw, who made All-AFL as a rookie, and Davis against another AFL all-star, right tackle Harry Schuh. "I don't think Upshaw blocked [Jordan] very many times," Hanner said. "Upshaw wasn't a big guy, either, and was a good athlete, too, but Henry gave him fits. Schuh had one or two decent years but I think Willie had a pretty good day against him."

That left it to Lamonica, a confident, if not brash, player whom the Packers had drafted in the 12th round in 1963 but never came close to signing. After four seasons backing up Jack Kemp in Buffalo, "the Mad Bomber" was traded to Oakland a few minutes before the start of the 1967 draft in exchange for starting quarterback Tom Flores and split end Art Powell, its leading receiver. Lamonica

was a big hit, leading the AFL in passing in 1967. "I didn't like the trade but, once again, Al [Davis] knew what he was doing," Otto said. "Lamonica had the league's strongest arm. Daryle was athletic, though not cerebral. He had difficulty seeing plays develop. He'd call the wrong formation at times, then through sheer athletic ability he'd pull off the play."

Biletnikoff averaged 21.9 yards per catch in 1967, the best mark of his career, but neither he nor journeyman Bill Miller had the speed to stretch the Packers' back seven and take the heat off the running game. "The Oakland receivers rely on moves rather than speed," Wood said. The Raiders receiver, Warren Wells, who did have sensational burst, was a little-used, second-year man who wouldn't emerge as a major force until the following season.

That year, the Packers held opposing quarterbacks to a regular-season passer rating of 41.5, the lowest during the Lombardi era. Adderley was in his prime, right cornerback Bob Jeter was adequate, and Wood, according to Hanner, "was the best safety that ever played."

The weak link on defense was the other safety, Tom Brown, and that's who the Raiders took advantage of for a pair of 23-yard touchdown passes using a creative double-wing formation. For the first, a corner route to Miller in the second quarter, Lamonica lobbed the ball over a deep-dropping Robinson at the 6, and Brown was late getting over to help. For the second touchdown, in the fourth quarter Brown was isolated on Miller in the deep middle and was inexplicably 3 yards away when the ball was caught a yard into the end zone.

"We were a really good football team," Wolf said, "but we hadn't probably swallowed the olive yet. We had enough personnel but there was the mystique of the Packers. It was a little hard for us because we only lost one game all year, then all of a sudden we were in the biggest game we had ever been in and we didn't play very well."

Said Sumner, Raiders secondary coach and a longtime NFL safety, "There might have been a small amount of intimidation there for some of the players and maybe some of the coaches. We were kind of a fledgling league. The first couple years the AFL wasn't quite ready. And Vince was a great coach."

Tormented by the workload associated with the dual role as coach and general manager, Lombardi had been thinking about quitting as coach for more than a year. "What's the matter with people?" Lombardi said to his wife, Marie, one day in 1967. "I have to go on that field every day and whip people. It's for them, not just me, and I'm getting to be an animal." Besides his wife, the other person to whom he confided his emotional and physical strain was Earl "Red" Blaik, his former boss at West Point.

Finally, he made the decision to walk away. "He told me that I had just seen him coach his next-to-last football game," his son, Vince Jr., related of a conversation they had during the car ride home after the Ice Bowl, two weeks before the Super Bowl. "I think I was one of the first people he told."

At halftime, the Packers were in control but had yet to extend dominance. Before they left the locker room, Kramer said just loud enough for most to hear, "Let's play the last 30 minutes for the old man."

And so they did. When it was over, off went Lombardi on the shoulders of Kramer and Gregg. One of the great dynasties in pro football history had ended, with five championships in seven years enduring as the Packers' legacy.

"I was out of Green Bay the day Lombardi announced that he was retiring," Kramer said later. "I can't say I was shocked but I did feel saddened. He was our most valuable player."

Top Ten Characters

1. **Max McGee, WR, Packers, I and II:** After an all-nighter with a blond from Chicago, McGee was stretched out on the bench relaxing. When Boyd Dowler went down on the second play of Super Bowl I, however, Vince Lombardi screamed for McGee to replace him. McGee had the game of his life.

2. **Jim McMahon, QB, Bears, XX:** Mooning news copters, ripping Bears management, carousing on Bourbon Street, flying in his own acupuncturist, allegedly insulting the residents of the Big Easy—each new day brought a new headline involving the punky passer.

3. **Joe Namath, QB, Jets, III:** The photos of Namath sitting poolside surrounded by writers and bathing beauties are enduring images of Super Bowl III. His guarantee of victory was the stuff of legend.

4. **Thomas Henderson, LB, Cowboys, X, XII, and XIII:** After filling up every reporter's notebook all week long, "Hollywood" snorted liquid cocaine during the game from an inhaler he had concealed in his uniform pants.

5. **Fred Williamson, CB, Chiefs, I:** Talked all week about the hell he would unleash on the Packers' receivers, but instead took a knee to the head from Donny Anderson in the fourth quarter and was out cold.

6. **Shannon Sharpe, TE, Broncos, XXXII and XXXIII; Ravens, XXXV:** Opinionated, arrogant, and loquacious, Sharpe was a charter member of the Super Bowl all-interview team.

7. **John Riggins, RB, Redskins, XVII and XVIII:** Ended an 18-month moratorium on interviews at Super Bowl XVII, dressed in camouflage pants and cracking one-liners.

8. **John Matuszak, DE, Raiders, XI and XV:** Left the team hotel in New Orleans on Wednesday night before Super Bowl XV and didn't return until after 3 a.m. Paid his $1,000 fine to coach Tom Flores and fell in with the rest of the Raiders' rabble.

9. **Duane Thomas, RB, Cowboys, V and VI:** At Super Bowl VI, he sat for almost half an hour surrounded by reporters and never said a word. Once referred to coach Tom Landry as "plastic man."

10. **Brett Favre, QB, Packers, XXXI and XXXII:** Regaled the press with stories of his partying days in Kiln, Mississippi. Those same reporters boarded buses in New Orleans during Super Bowl week and checked out his bayou stomping grounds for themselves.

III

NEW YORK JETS 16, BALTIMORE COLTS 7

January 12, 1969
Orange Bowl, Miami, Florida

The images from Super Bowl III are lasting: Joe Namath jogging off the field with his index finger pointing skyward; Jimmy Orr pleading helplessly for the ball near the goal line; Earl Morrall and Johnny Unitas, a pair of crewcut quarterbacks, bowing their heads in despair.

The New York Jets' 16–7 victory over the Baltimore Colts at the Orange Bowl in Miami was, without any question, one of the most stunning upsets in sports history.

Attendance: 75,377
Conditions: 73 degrees, overcast, threat of rain, wind N at 18 mph
Time of kickoff: 3:05 p.m. (EST)
Length of game: 2 hours, 44 minutes
Referee: Tommy Bell

MVP: Joe Namath, QB, Jets

Joe Namath came through on his bold prediction of victory in Super Bowl III against the heavily favored Baltimore Colts. Named the game MVP, Namath passed for 206 yards and soundly outplayed his Baltimore counterparts, Earl Morrall and Johnny Unitas. *Walter Iooss Jr./*Sports Illustrated/*Getty Images*

Namath was the MVP, and deservedly so. His performance, both as a composed field general and as a deadly accurate passer, inspired his teammates to play the game of their lives, just as it surely crushed the spirit of the heavily favored Colts. But, as Namath would say later, the award could have gone to several others.

Matt Snell handled the ball on 34 of 74 plays and gained 161 yards. To spring him, left tackle Winston Hill repeatedly caved in the aging right side of the Colts' defense. Converted guard Dave Herman shifted to right tackle and somehow neutralized the menacing Bubba Smith. Center John Schmitt played with pneumonia, yet fought on to the point of exhaustion by the fourth quarter. Split end George Sauer compensated brilliantly for gimpy flanker Don Maynard by catching eight passes for 133 yards. Jim Turner kicked three of five field goals, whereas his counterpart for the Colts, Lou Michaels, was zero for two. While the defense had no obvious standout, as a whole the unit played every bit as effectively as the offense and forced five turnovers.

"There will never be another Super Bowl played with the importance and tension of this one," Turner said years later. "I was in the AFL when everyone said the league stunk, and I'm proud to have been a part of pro football history when the AFL won the respect and recognition it deserved."

From coast to coast, newspaper headlines blared the shocking result:

	1	2	3	4	Final
New York Jets	0	7	6	3	16
Baltimore Colts	0	0	0	7	7

SCORING SUMMARY

2nd Quarter
NY   Snell, 4-yd. run (J. Turner kick)
3rd Quarter
NY   J. Turner, 32-yd. FG
NY   J. Turner, 30-yd. FG
4th Quarter
NY   J. Turner, 9-yd. FG
BAL   J. Hill, 1-yd. run (Michaels kick)

"Namath Wings Jets to Upset"—*The Boston Globe*

"They Believe Cocky Joe Now"—*Chicago Tribune*

"Pro Grid's Greatest Shocker"—*San Francisco Chronicle*

Without "Broadway Joe," Super Bowl III still would have been just a football game. With him, it became an allegorical event for the chaotic late 1960s—the clash between the haves and have-nots, the hawks and doves, the establishment and the anti-establishment.

Three days before the game, many of the sportswriters were attending a Super Bowl party at the Doral hotel, where Atlanta Falcons coach Norm "the Dutchman" Van Brocklin was holding court near a buffet line. "On Sunday," Van Brocklin said, "Joe Namath will be playing in his first pro game."

But an enterprising reporter from the *Miami Herald*, Luther Evans, was among the crowd of 600 at the Miami Touchdown Club dinner at which, for the first time, an AFL player, Namath, was to be honored by the group as its pro football player of the year. Namath had reluctantly agreed to leave a team barbeque on Miami Beach to attend. Riding in a turquoise Cadillac, he sipped Johnny Walker Red out of a paper cup en route.

After being teased by various speakers during the proceedings, he began a rambling acceptance speech by pointing out that all the single girls in New York City should be thanked equally with the players' wives. As Namath semi-slurred his words, a person described by Evans as a Colts fan yelled, "Sit down!" A short time later, Namath told the crowd, "The Jets will win Sunday. I guarantee it."

The next day, with the guarantee earning a headline in the *Herald*, Jets coach Weeb Ewbank mildly scolded Namath. Some of the linemen pointed out that he wasn't the one who had to block Bubba Smith, but no one really was too bent out of shape. The Jets had spent days watching the Colts on film. They were anywhere from an 18- to 19½-point underdog, but the more they watched, the more their confidence grew. "They looked slow, less inventive," Sauer said, "both offensively and defensively."

The Colts (15–1) seemed to the world to be a juggernaut after rolling over the Cleveland Browns, 34–0, for the NFL championship, but the Jets saw a lot of weaknesses. Frank Ryan had quarterbacked the Browns without distinction, just like Minnesota's Joe Kapp did in the Vikings' 24–14 divisional loss to Baltimore. "We had the type of offense that could score on anybody," Jets tight end Pete Lammons said. "Finally, I said [to offensive coach Clive Rush], 'If we keep watching these films, we'll get overconfident.'"

Before the Jets left Long Island for Florida, Namath told friends at a nearby watering hole to "bet the ranch" on the Jets with 7-to-1 odds. Cassius Clay had faced the same odds at the Miami Beach Convention Center in 1964 against Sonny Liston. At the heart of the matter—as it always is in pro football—was the matchup at quarterback. After a 27–23 victory over Oakland, Namath said the Raiders' Daryle Lamonica was better than Morrall. Later, on the flight to Miami, he told beat writers that not only was Lamonica better than Morrall, but so were AFLers Bob Griese and John Hadl. "You put Babe Parilli with Baltimore and Baltimore might have been better," said Namath. "Babe throws better than Morrall." Parilli was Namath's 38-year-old backup.

Of course, the Colts were enraged. Morrall, 34, had been player of the year in the NFL; his regular-season passer rating of 93.2 dwarfed Namath's 72.1. A few nights later, some Colts and Jets players, including Namath, ran into each other at Jimmy Fazio's Bar in Fort Lauderdale. According to Lou

Michaels, Namath told them, "We're gonna kick the s--- out of you, and I'm gonna do it." "That's the exact words he used," Michaels recalled. "God strike me dead." Michaels wanted to punch Namath's lights out in the parking lot, but cooler heads prevailed. Namath's own account portrayed Michaels as the instigator, with Namath placating him and eventually pulling out a $100 bill and paying for everyone's drinks.

The fact that the Jets felt good about their chances didn't mean the so-called experts did. In one poll of 55 writers, 49 picked the Colts. Curt Gowdy, the NBC-TV broadcaster, remembered bumping into Howard Cosell on the morning of the game. "Cowboy! This is going to be a slaughter," Gowdy, a Wyoming native, remembered Cosell saying. "The Colts'll kill 'em. I like Joe Willie Namath, but he may get a leg broken today." Tex Maule of *Sports Illustrated* wrote that the world championship already had been decided in Cleveland on December 29. When Packers coach Vince Lombardi was asked to quantify the Jets' chances, the great one said, "Infinitesimal."

One anonymous Colt told sports editor Bill Tanton of *The Baltimore Evening Sun*, "I think we'll beat the Jets, 50–0. Let me ask you. Who do you think has a better defense—the Jets or Cleveland? Cleveland, of course. And if we can hold Leroy Kelly's team scoreless, we should be able to hold anybody's scoreless."

The Colts were playing right into the Jets' hands. In his book, *My Story (and I'm Sticking to It)*, Colts backup receiver Alex Hawkins wrote, "After two days of watching the Jets' defense on film I came to one conclusion: Super Bowl III should be a rout. We should be able to score 50 against these people. I did not see one player in their defensive backfield who could make our team. Their linebackers were active but too small to be taken seriously. The front four were small and unable to rush the passer. All in all, I thought they were the poorest defensive unit I had seen in 10 years of pro ball."

So Namath wasn't the only

NEW YORK JETS (AFL, 11–3)			BALTIMORE COLTS (NFL, 13–1)	
		Offense		
83	George Sauer* (6-2, 195)	WR	28	Jimmy Orr (5-11, 185)
75	Winston Hill* (6-4, 280)	LT	72	Bob Vogel* (6-5, 250)
61	Bob Talamini (6-1, 255)	LG	62	Glenn Ressler (6-3, 250)
52	John Schmitt (6-4, 245)	C	50	Bill Curry (6-2, 235)
66	Randy Rasmussen (6-2, 255)	RG	71	Dan Sullivan (6-3, 250)
67	Dave Herman* (6-1, 255)	RT	73	Sam Ball (6-4, 240)
87	Pete Lammons (6-3, 223)	TE	88	John Mackey* (6-2, 224)
13	Don Maynard* (6-1, 179)	WR	87	Willie Richardson* (6-2,198)
12	Joe Namath* (6-2, 195)	QB	15	Earl Morrall* (6-2, 206)
32	Emerson Boozer* (5-11, 202)	RB	41	Tom Matte* (6-0, 214)
41	Matt Snell (6-2, 219)	RB	45	Jerry Hill (5-11, 215)
		Defense		
81	Gerry Philbin* (6-2, 245)	LE	78	Bubba Smith (6-7, 295)
72	Paul Rochester (6-2, 250)	LT	74	Billy Ray Smith (6-4, 250)
80	John Elliott* (6-4, 249)	RT	76	Fred Miller* (6-3, 250)
86	Verlon Biggs* (6-4, 268)	RE	81	Ordell Braase (6-4, 245)
51	Ralph Baker (6-3, 235)	LLB	32	Mike Curtis* (6-2, 232)
62	Al Atkinson* (6-2, 230)	MLB	53	Dennis Gaubatz (6-2, 232)
60	Larry Grantham (6-0, 212)	RLB	66	Don Shinnick (6-0, 228)
24	Johnny Sample (6-1, 204)	LCB	40	Bob Boyd* (5-10, 192)
42	Randy Beverly (5-11, 198)	RCB	43	Lenny Lyles (6-2, 204)
22	Jim Hudson (6-2, 210)	SS	20	Jerry Logan (6-1, 190)
46	Bill Baird (5-10, 180)	FS	21	Rick Volk (6-3, 195)
* AFL All-Star Team			* NFL Pro Bowl selection	

SUBSTITUTIONS

New York
Offense: WR - 30 Mark Smolinski, 23 Bill Rademacher, 29 Bake Turner; T - 71 Sam Walton, 74 Jeff Richardson; C - 56 Paul Crane; QB - 15 Babe Parilli; RB - 31 Bill Mathis. *Defense:* DE - 85 Steve Thompson; LB - 50 Carl McAdams, 63 John Neidert; CB - 43 John Dockery, 45 Earl Christy, 48 Cornell Gordon; S - 26 Jim Richards, 47 Mike D'Amato. *Specialists:* K - 11 Jim Turner*; P - 33 Curley Johnson.

Baltimore
Offense: WR - 25 Alex Hawkins, 27 Ray Perkins; TE - 84 Tom Mitchell; G - 75 John Williams, 61 Cornelius Johnson; C - 52 Dick Szymanski; QB - 19 Johnny Unitas; RB - 2 Timmy Brown, 34 Terry Cole, 26 Preston Pearson. *Defense:* DE - 85 Roy Hilton; LB - 55 Ron Porter, 64 Sid Williams; CB - 37 Ocie Austin, 47 Charles Stukes. *Specialists:* K/DE - 79 Lou Michaels; P - 49 David Lee. *DNP:* 16 Jim Ward (QB).

New York
Head Coach: Weeb Ewbank. *Offense:* Clive Rush (head offense), Joe Spencer (offensive line), George Sauer Sr. (backs). *Defense:* Buddy Ryan (defensive line), Walt Michaels (linebackers, defensive backs).

Baltimore
Head Coach: Don Shula. *Offense:* Dick Bielski (ends), John Sandusky (offensive line), Don McCafferty (backs). *Defense:* Bill Arnsparger (defensive line), Chuck Noll (defensive backs).

one who'd felt disrespected. A ton of Jets had an ax to grind against the NFL for real and imagined omissions and offenses. "Weeb let me in during the week and it was the weirdest practice I'd ever seen," Gowdy said. "There wasn't a word spoken. These were the maddest guys, the most insulted guys, I'd ever seen."

On the second play of the game, Namath audibled to a sweep and Snell powered for 9 yards. On the play, Snell's knee struck the helmet of safety Rick Volk and knocked him out. Volk later returned and played most of the game, but back in his hotel room afterward, he went into convulsions, began to swallow his tongue, and might have died had it not been for immediate medical intervention.

The Colts' vaunted defense, which allowed merely 144 points in 14 games, forced a punt. Morrall then directed an 11-play, 54-yard drive to the Jets 19 before he threw a pass that was dropped and another that was lousy and fell incomplete. He did well to avoid a sack by onrushing Jet defensive ends Gerry Philbin and Verlon Biggs, but then Michaels kicked and missed from the 27.

The Jets also had to punt on their second series, but what seemed like an innocuous incomplete pass on the fourth play proved significant. Maynard had run by cornerback Bobby Boyd and strong safety Jerry Logan, but Namath overthrew him. No one knew it before the game, but Maynard almost didn't play because of a pulled hamstring that had lingered since early December. It should have been a huge handicap for the Jets' long-ball offense; the future Hall of Famer had averaged 22.8 per reception and scored 10 touchdowns. But what that one play did was prompt the Colts to rotate their zone to

Maynard's side for the rest of the game, leaving right cornerback Lenny Lyles isolated against Sauer, one of the Jets' 11 AFL all-star selections. "Some writer later said that was the most important incomplete pass in Super Bowl history, which it was," Sauer said. Maynard didn't catch any of the five passes that Namath directed his way, but it didn't even matter.

In the waning seconds of the first quarter, the Colts' defense made its only big play when Lyles drilled Sauer after a 3-yard pass, causing a fumble that was recovered by linebacker Ron Porter at the Jets 12. On third and 4, Morrall backpedaled three steps and threw quickly into the end zone on a slant pass for tight end Tom Mitchell. It would have been a touchdown had middle linebacker Al Atkinson not made a great read and ticked the ball with his outstretched right hand. "It might have been thrown a little behind him," Colts coach Don Shula said. "It caromed off [Mitchell's] pads and right into their hands." The ball bounced off Mitchell and was intercepted by cornerback Randy Beverly in the end zone.

The feeling-out process was over. Starting from the 20, Namath called four straight runs to the left, and Snell piled up 26 yards. The Jets had detected weakness in right defensive end Ordell Braase, 36, right outside linebacker Don Shinnick, 33, and Lyles, 32. "It was a hot, sunny day, and that made it easier for Winston [Hill] to overpower [Braase]," Snell said. "Braase pretty much faded out. Once that worked, we could fake me running off-tackle and throw to Sauer."

At this point, the Colts started blitzing, but Namath reacted calmly and picked apart the openings in the defense. He found halfback Bill Mathis in the flat for 6 yards, zipped a 14-yard curl to Sauer with Lyles in soft coverage, and then took a short drop and hit Sauer on a square-out for 11 when Lyles missed the tackle. "We blitzed a lot," Shula said years later. "The blitz had been successful against everybody. Nobody had figured it out. Namath was the only guy to be able to beat our blitz that year."

Namath soon began calling a lot of plays at the line after seeing how the Colts had lined up. On this day, Namath was a thinking man's quarterback, as well as a physically gifted one. A 12-yard toss to Snell for a first down brought the Jets inside the 10, and then Snell ran right for a 5-yard gain. Finally, Snell followed Hill and halfback Emerson Boozer off left tackle for a 4-yard touchdown. It was the first time an AFL team led in a Super Bowl.

In its panicked effort to rally from behind, Baltimore squandered opportunity after opportunity. In the first half, the Colts reached the Jets 19-, 6-, 38-, 15-, and 41-yard lines, respectively, without scoring. During the game, they advanced into the red zone five times yet didn't score until 3:19 remained in the final quarter. "The key factor was, we didn't take advantage of our scoring opportunities in the first half," Shula said. "Then in the second half the Jets controlled the ball on us."

The Jets certainly weren't flawless. On the Colts' fourth possession, free safety Bill Baird missed a tackle on running back Tom Matte and a short pass turned into a 30-yard gain. One series later, strong safety Jim Hudson ducked his head as he tried to tackle Matte on a sweep, and what should have been a 5-yard gain ruptured into 58. But Michaels missed another field goal, this time from 46, and then Morrall threw late inside to Willie Richardson from the Jets 15 and cornerback Johnny Sample intercepted.

Shortly before the game, Orr had said to Hawkins, "Senor, don't let Earl wake up today. Just let him sleep for three more hours." Orr had recognized that the aging, modestly talented Morrall had been playing well beyond his capabilities for most of the season. He and the rest of the Colts had hoped Morrall's storybook season had one more happy chapter.

Seconds before the half, when Morrall failed to spot Orr for an easy touchdown on a flea-flicker and was intercepted by Hudson, the Colts' nightmare had come true. "Whether the disparaging remarks previously levied at Morrall by Namath came into the picture, I have no way of knowing, but some recollection of his past with four different teams must have flashed through his mind," Hawkins recalled in his memoir. "Jimmy Orr's and my own worst fear had been realized: Earl Morrall had awakened."

That fateful flea-flicker play from the Jets 42 started as a sweep to the right, when Matte sidestepped blitzing linebacker Larry Grantham and threw back to Morrall, who was waiting at the 50. The primary receiver, Orr, had been turned loose down the sideline by Beverly, had an arm raised, and

TEAM STATISTICS

NEW YORK		BALTIMORE
21	Total First Downs	18
10	Rushing	7
10	Passing	9
1	Penalty	2
337	Total Net Yardage	324
74	Total Offensive Plays	64
4.6	Avg. Gain per Offensive Play	5.1
43	Rushes	23
142	Yards Gained Rushing (Net)	143
3.3	Average Yards per Rush	6.2
29	Passes Attempted	41
17	Passes Completed	17
0	Passes Intercepted	4
2	Tackled Attempting to Pass	0
11	Yards Lost Attempting to Pass	0
195	Yards Gained Passing (Net)	181
8/18	Third-Down Efficiency	4/12
0/0	Fourth-Down Efficiency	1/2
4	Punts	3
38.8	Average Distance	44.3
1	Punt Returns	4
0	Punt Return Yardage	34
1	Kickoff Returns	4
25	Kickoff Return Yardage	105
9	Interception Return Yardage	0
1	Fumbles	1
0	Own Fumbles Recovered	0
1	Opponent Fumbles Recovered	1
5	Penalties	3
28	Yards Penalized	23
1	Touchdowns	1
1	Rushing	1
0	Passing	0
0	Returns	0
1	Extra Points Made	1
3	Field Goals Made	0
5	Field Goals Attempted	2
0	Safeties	0
16	Total Points Scored	7
36:10	Time of Possession	23:50

"Weeb [Ewbank] was an offensive coach. He was 100 years ahead of his time. [Linebacker] Larry Grantham made the calls himself on defense."

Buddy Ryan, Jets defensive line coach

NEW YORK

Passing	CP/ATT	YDS	TD	INT	RAT
Namath	17/28	206	0	0	83.3
Parilli	0/1	0	0	0	39.6

Rushing	ATT	YDS	AVG	TD	LG
Snell	30	121	4.0	1	12
Boozer	10	19	1.9	0	8
Mathis	3	2	0.7	0	1

Receiving	NO	YDS	AVG	TD	LG
Sauer	8	133	16.6	0	39
Snell	4	40	10.0	0	14
Mathis	3	20	6.7	0	13
Lammons	2	13	6.5	0	11

Interceptions	NO	YDS	LG	TD
Beverly	2	0	0	0
Hudson	1	9	9	0
Sample	1	0	0	0

Punting	NO	AVG	LG	BLK
Johnson	4	38.8	39	0

Punt Ret.	NO/FC	YDS	LG	TD
Baird	1/1	0	0	0

Kickoff Ret.	NO	YDS	LG	TD
Christy	1	25	25	0

Defense	SOLO	AST	TOT	SK
Atkinson	4	4	8	0
Baird	5	2	7	0
Hudson	3	3	6	0
Sample	5	0	5	0
Beverly	4	0	4	0
Biggs	4	0	4	0
Baker	3	1	4	0
Elliott	3	1	4	0
Grantham	3	0	3	0
McAdams	2	0	2	0
Philbin	2	0	2	0
Richards	2	0	2	0
Crane	1	0	1	0
D'Amato	1	0	1	0
Neidert	1	0	1	0
Snell	1	0	1	0
TOTAL	44	11	55	0

BALTIMORE

Passing	CP/ATT	YDS	TD	INT	RAT
Unitas	11/24	110	0	1	42.0
Morrall	6/17	71	0	3	9.3

Rushing	ATT	YDS	AVG	TD	LG
Matte	11	116	10.5	0	58
Hill	9	29	3.2	1	12
Unitas	1	0	0.0	0	0
Morrall	2	-2	-1.0	0	0

Receiving	NO	YDS	AVG	TD	LG
Richardson	6	58	9.7	0	21
Orr	3	42	14.0	0	17
Mackey	3	35	11.7	0	19
Matte	2	30	15.0	0	30
Hill	2	1	0.5	0	1
Mitchell	1	15	15.0	0	15

Interceptions	NO	YDS	LG	TD
None	--	--	--	--

Punting	NO	AVG	LG	BLK
Lee	3	44.3	51	0

Punt Ret.	NO/FC	YDS	LG	TD
Brown	4/0	34	21	0

Kickoff Ret.	NO	YDS	LG	TD
Pearson	2	59	33	0
Brown	2	46	25	0

Defense	SOLO	AST	TOT	SK
Lyles	11	2	13	0
Gaubatz	10	1	11	1
Shinnick	8	1	9	0
Miller	3	5	8	0
Bu. Smith	6	0	6	1
B. R. Smith	4	2	6	0
Volk	4	2	6	0
Curtis	5	0	5	0
Logan	3	1	4	0
Boyd	2	2	4	0
Hawkins	1	1	2	0
Porter	1	1	2	0
Michaels	0	2	2	0
Braase	0	2	2	0
Austin	1	0	1	0
S. Williams	1	0	1	0
TOTAL	60	22	82	2

was waving back to Morrall. Orr recalled, "I was open from here to Tampa."

Walt Michaels, the Jets defensive coach, maintained that Beverly, a 4.4 sprinter, would have been able to scramble back into the play and break

it up, but this proved to be irrelevant. Morrall inexplicably went to his fullback, Jerry Hill, deep on the right side, possibly because he was the first blue jersey in his line of vision. "I've wished thousands of times to do that game over again,"

Morrall said two years later, "because what went wrong was my fault."

The scenes at halftime told of deepening positions. Bubba Smith smoked one cigarette after another at his locker. "I think we even got to believing what the papers said—that we were going to win by 17, 18 points," he said. "It was a shock when the Jets got in front of us." And just how deep was the Jets' desire to win? Atkinson was begging the team doctor to let him play the second half, despite a separated shoulder that he had suffered at the end of the first half. "Let's get rid of the pain," said Atkinson, and the team doctor did so with a syringe full of xylocaine.

Biggs, whose 12 sacks trailed Philbin's total of 19 during the season, jumped on Matte from behind on the opening play of the second half and ripped the ball out, then left linebacker Ralph Baker recovered at the Colts 33. The drive bogged down and Turner kicked a 32-yard field goal. The only sack taken by Namath had come on second and 15 when he held the ball for too long. Bubba Smith, the 6-foot-7, 295-pound left end who had been the first pick in the 1967 draft, wrapped him up. "Not only was he big, he was strong and quick," said Herman, who had been a teammate of Smith's at Michigan State. "He was like a 1990s player back in 1969." Ewbank had benched right tackle Sam Walton and moved Herman outside before the AFL title game to oppose Oakland's Ike Lassiter, had liked the results, and had done it again in the Super Bowl.

Another clock-eating drive capped by another Turner field goal put the Jets ahead, 13–0. At that point, with 3:58 left in the third quarter, Shula benched Morrall and turned to the 34-year-old Unitas, who had been idling on the bench almost all season with a torn tendon in his passing elbow. "I kept a picture of Johnny U. over my bed," Namath said. "To me he meant one thing: toughness." Though he performed far better than Morrall, completing 11 of 24 passes for 110 yards, he was a mere shell of the Unitas of old. "He had no strength in his arm,

and was off-target and poorly timed-up with his receivers," Hawkins wrote. "It was painful to watch."

Namath completed his only long pass, a 39-yarder to Sauer behind Lyles, in the final minute of the third quarter to set up Turner's third field goal. That was Namath's final passing attempt of the game. On the Colts' next possession, Unitas drove the Colts down the field but couldn't get the ball to Orr on a deep post, and Beverly made his second interception in the end zone. Later, Unitas completed four passes measuring between 11 and 21 yards in an 80-yard drive that was capped by Hill's 1-yard touchdown run, and the Colts at last were on the board at 16–7.

There was a brief glimmer of hope for the old league when Sauer flubbed the recovery on Lou Michaels' onside kick, followed by Unitas hitting three passes in a row for a total of 25 yards to reach the Jets 19. The Colts' chances died there, however, as Unitas misfired on second, third, and fourth down, and the Jets simply ran out the clock from there.

"We had the best defense in the American Football League," said Buddy Ryan, a defensive assistant on Ewbank's staff, "but nobody remembers that because our quarterback wore white shoes. Elliott and Philbin and Biggs were all great ones. [Carl] McAdams went in and rushed the passer on third down for [Paul] Rochester. Atkinson was a great player. Grantham was undersized, but he could make plays. He made all the calls himself on defense; he studied hard. Hudson was tough and would hit you. Baird was smart. The corners played well. On defense, we knew we were going to play good. We always had. But nobody knew about us."

The Colts, a team that had posted seven more victories from 1963 to 1968 under Shula than even the two-time defending champion Green Bay Packers, had shown their age both on offense and defense. The average age of Baltimore's 40-man roster (27.33) was exactly one year older than New York's, but its 22 starters averaged 28.33, whereas the

"Maybe the secret of the whole thing is we stayed healthy. We played the entire season—offense, defense—with no more than 28 people. Your winners are the teams that stay healthy."

Walt Michaels, Jets defensive backs coach

Jets' starters (26.36) were nearly the same age as the entire team. "People don't realize that the Jets were a very good football team," Shula said. "Namath had been the Jets quarterback for four years and Earl had been my quarterback for four months. And Weeb was a great coach."

Nonetheless, Colts owner Carroll Rosenbloom looked almost beyond devastated as he sat in the press box among the writers. During the week, Rosenbloom had invited Ewbank, the two-time championship coach that he had fired in Baltimore after the 1962 season, to attend the team's anticipated victory party. Ewbank politely declined. The party went on at Rosenbloom's home at Golden Beach, but the mood was that of a funeral.

In 1984, Shula said, "During that offseason, [Rosenbloom] started to, in my mind, take a lot of heat from his golfing buddies about the loss. He became known as the first owner to lose to a team in the new league. I saw innuendos in the paper, talking about me and our relationship. And that's when I started to drift apart from him."

In 2005, he said, "I coached the following year but my relationship with Rosenbloom was never the same after that game. It changed the course of the NFL and it changed my life. He was an owner who was also a fan. A very intense guy. He wasn't used to losing at anything. That was one of the darkest moments of my career."

Shula was on target regarding the impact of the game. The lopsided results of the first two Super Bowls had led many to believe it would be a decade or more before the AFL teams could compete with NFL clubs. At a press conference two days before the game, NFL Commissioner Pete Rozelle had spoken about the possibility that the playoff format leading up to the Super Bowl might change after the merger in 1970, so that two NFL teams could play in the big game. After the Jets' stunner, such talk was tabled.

> "For us to be the first NFL team to lose to the upstart AFL meant we took all the more criticism. That's where the loss took on even more meaning. It gave them more credibility."
>
> *Don Shula, Colts head coach*

The vindicated Namath was somewhat prickly after the game with reporters representing NFL cities, letting them know that their widespread predictions of utter devastation for the Jets didn't quite come to pass. He rather quickly returned to his good humor and self-assured manner, however, and answered questions in full uniform for almost 45 minutes after the final gun. The roly-poly Ewbank, 61, was tossed fully clothed into the showers. Sample produced a clipping from his wallet from 24 months earlier that read: "Kansas City Not in Class with NFL Best—Lombardi." Said Maynard, "[The AFL] had been ridiculed by the other league for 10 years. Then we [got] to live with the victory for the rest of our lives."

At the Jets' team party that night, a group of Chiefs and Raiders stopped by, along with other AFL players. Chiefs defensive tackle Buck Buchanan, according to Turner, broke down and cried. "Buck Buchanan had to go around and shake everybody's hand and say, 'Thank you for redeeming us,'" Snell said years later. "So we started thinking that many of those guys appreciated what we did more than we did ourselves . . . and we've been reminded ever since."

Years later, Namath still received letters from high-school coaches who told him they used the Jets to inspire their players. "Maybe it motivated some other people, too," Namath said. "There are a lot of underdogs in the world. Maybe it meant something to the underdogs in life."

IV

KANSAS CITY CHIEFS 23, MINNESOTA VIKINGS 7

January 11, 1970
Tulane Stadium, New Orleans, Louisiana

When reflecting upon the matchups more than three decades later, it doesn't seem possible that the Minnesota Vikings went into Super Bowl IV on that chilly afternoon at Tulane Stadium as a 13-point favorite over the Kansas City Chiefs.

Kansas City's Len Dawson versus Minnesota's Joe Kapp at quarterback. Cornerbacks Jim Marsalis and Emmitt Thomas versus Earsell Mackbee and Ed Sharockman. Linebackers Bobby Bell, Willie Lanier, and Jim Lynch versus Roy Winston, Lonnie Warwick, and Wally Hilgenberg. The kicking game heavily favored the Chiefs, and one could argue that the Chiefs also were as good if not better than the Vikings in the offensive line, the defensive line, wide receiver, tight end, running back, and safety.

Jimmy "the Greek" Snyder, the Las Vegas oddsmaker, represented the widely held belief throughout the country that the NFL remained superior to the AFL, despite the Jets' defeat of the Colts the previous year. Snyder gave the Vikings 3 points for having "the greatest offensive line I've ever seen," 2 points for the better ground game, 1 point for the better quarterback, 3 points for a better defense, and 4 points for coaching (Minnesota's Bud Grant over Hank Stram) and the fact the game was being played in an NFL city.

All of that was nonsense, of course, but pro football was reported differently in those days. The people who knew the game best, namely the personnel directors and coaches, seldom were consulted. Electronic and print coverage was more superficial and personality-driven. The relative merits of players, teams, even entire leagues could easily be distorted.

Yes, the Chiefs had been steamrolled by Green Bay, 35–10, three years earlier, but the Chiefs had played that first Super Bowl with two voids at cornerback, two voids in the defensive line, and two voids in the offensive line. Defensive tackle Buck Buchanan warned the public that the Chiefs'

Attendance: 80,562
Conditions: 61 degrees, heavy overcast, humid and wet field, wind SW at 14–15 mph
Time of kickoff: 2:40 p.m. (CST)
Length of game: 2 hours, 40 minutes
Referee: John McDonough

MVP: Len Dawson, QB, Chiefs

defense was "80 percent stronger" than it had been in January 1967, and that the team was "50 percent improved" overall. Owner Lamar Hunt, never one to ruffle feathers, also agreed this team was superior to his 1966 club.

Just seven days separated the league championship games and Super Sunday, and the film exchange covered only the last three games. Feelings of uncertainty remained on both sides, although nowhere near the extent as before Super Bowl I. Publicly, the Vikings downplayed their role as prohibitive favorite, but Grant did say on the Thursday before the game, "Neither team is going to get knocked out of the ball park. Also, I expect a low-scoring game."

As expected, the participants pretty much knew the score. Jerry Burns, a Green Bay assistant in the first two Super Bowls, now found himself running Grant's offense in Minnesota and was expecting anything but a cakewalk. "We were not nearly as strong as Green Bay," Burns said. The Vikings personnel director, Jerry Reichow, studied the Chiefs from the team's headquarters at the Airport Hilton and recalled thinking how much better they were than most observers recognized. As for the Greek's overblown assessment of the Minnesota O-line, Reichow said, "We had a good offensive line. I don't think we had a great one."

Over at the Fontainebleau Hotel, the Chiefs were licking their chops. In fact, they had been waiting

	1	2	3	4	Final
Minnesota Vikings	0	0	7	0	7
Kansas City Chiefs	3	13	7	0	23

SCORING SUMMARY

1st Quarter
KC   Stenerud, 48-yd. FG
2nd Quarter
KC   Stenerud, 32-yd. FG
KC   Stenerud, 25-yd. FG
KC   Garrett, 5-yd. run (Stenerud kick)
3rd Quarter
MIN   Osborn, 4-yd. run (Cox kick)
KC   Taylor, 46-yd. pass from Dawson (Stenerud kick)

for this day for three years. Even if Lombardi had perhaps been goaded into his post-game comment that several NFL teams were better than Kansas City, his words had not been forgotten. "My main goal in football was to have a second opportunity to win a Super Bowl and erase Lombardi's cutting remark about our team and league," Dawson said. His players felt for Stram. "Absolutely, it was hard," Chiefs defensive coordinator Tom Bettis said years later. "It was tough for Hank to live [the loss] down."

In August 1967, the Chiefs played host to the Chicago Bears in an exhibition game, their first meeting with an NFL team since being pounded by the Packers. The Chiefs won that game, 66–24, and afterward Bettis, who played for Bears coach George Halas in 1963 and the Packers for seven years before that, remembered talking to one of the Bears' assistant coaches, Abe Gibron.

"He said, 'How could you guys do that to the Old Man [Halas]?'" Bettis said. "I said, 'Abe, if you'd have been in that locker room you would have understood exactly the emotion of our players.' Our kids had heard so much about the NFL and what they did to us in the first Super Bowl. They were bound and determined."

About Super Bowl IV, Bettis said, "We could have been a 40-point underdog. I still think they greatly exaggerated the strength of Minnesota.... In 1969 we were a much stronger team, particularly defensively."

Neither the final score (23–7) nor the yardage totals (273–239) reflected the one-sided tenor of the game. The most memorable freeze-frame moment was wide receiver Otis Taylor's remarkable 46-yard touchdown reception, as he shrugged off both Earsell Mackbee and safety Karl Kassulke in much the same way that the Chiefs had dismissed the Vikings. More than a minute remained in the third quarter and the Vikings' deficit was only 16 points, but the difference in talent, tactics, and motivation between the two sides made the fourth quarter all but irrelevant.

Even more memorable was the sideline audio of Stram captured by NFL Films. Stram, unbeknownst to his players, had agreed to wear a microphone. Dawson, however, knew something was amiss because Stram had been far chattier in the bench area than usual. After Taylor's touchdown, Stram is heard chirping, "That's it, boys; that's it, boys," meaning, the game was over. And it was.

"Lombardi was wrong," Stram said later. "The Chiefs and the other AFL teams could take on the NFL squads any time. Our styles were different only because the NFL had stood still for so long and resisted new approaches and ideas."

Before the Chiefs were able to dazzle and daze the Vikings, however, they had to endure a news flash that rocked the Super Bowl. On NBC's *Huntley-Brinkley Report*, a story broke linking Dawson and five other players to a Justice Department sting into widespread sports gambling. Dawson acknowledged having a casual acquaintance with a bookie in Detroit, whose address book included his phone number as well as Joe Namath's.

Very late on Tuesday night, after being questioned by NFL security, Dawson confronted the issue by reading a statement to reporters saying that he knew the bookie, Donald Dawson (no relation), but not well

> "I didn't know he was wired for sound. I don't think any of us did. In those days you had cords. We had cords tangled with guys' feet and I'm pulling it. He really didn't need me or anybody from upstairs because he was on a roll. Lenny [Dawson] and him called a hell of a game."
>
> *Tom Flores, Chiefs backup quarterback, on coach Hank Stram*

and hadn't seen him in years. In the end, Len Dawson was never subpoenaed, and the story died. "It was a tremendous distraction," the quarterback said years later. "My wife, who has since passed away, was ready for me to quit. She'd had enough because there had been so much pressure on the family."

With preparation time reduced to one week, the Vikings were in trouble whether they recognized it or not. On offense, they would have to contend with Kansas City's multiple shifts, formations, and motions. By contrast, their offense was so basic that they neither shifted nor put a man in motion even once—surely the last Super Bowl team ever to play the game without any pre-snap movement.

"Our whole influence was 'Bambi' [San Diego wide receiver Lance Alworth] and the things Sid Gillman was doing; the Raiders; and the Jets, when you got an arm like [Joe] Namath. That was our culture," Chiefs linebacker Jim Lynch said. "The NFL was different. Their culture was the Green Bay Packers." Lynch described the NFL method of football as "We're gonna line up and we're gonna run the Green Bay sweep. And you'd better stop us 'cause here we come." On defense, Minnesota had to get ready for the Chiefs' triple-stacking of linebackers and bump-and-run coverage from Marsalis, the AFL defensive rookie of the year, and Thomas, a fixture in the Pro Bowl.

"They hadn't seen it and didn't have much time to work on it," said Tom Flores, the Chiefs backup quarterback, who would go on to coach the Raiders in two Super Bowls. "It was won because we were a much better team than Minnesota and also because the Vikings were a vanilla team. They played a standard offense and the standard NFL 4-3 defense."

The Chiefs were even more diverse than usual, using their triple stack of linebackers on 95 percent of the snaps, according to Stram's estimate. Just as problematic for the Vikings was the Chiefs' decision to play an

MINNESOTA VIKINGS (NFL, 12–2)		KANSAS CITY CHIEFS (AFL, 11–3)	
	Offense		
84 Gene Washington* (6-3, 208)	WR	25 Frank Pitts (6-2, 199)	
67 Grady Alderman (6-2, 245)	LT	77 Jim Tyrer* (6-6, 275)	
63 Jim Vellone (6-3, 255)	LG	71 Ed Budde* (6-5, 260)	
53 Mick Tingelhoff* (6-2, 237)	C	55 E. J. Holub (6-4, 236)	
64 Milt Sunde (6-2, 250)	RG	76 Mo Moorman (6-5, 252)	
73 Ron Yary (6-5, 265)	RT	73 Dave Hill (6-5, 260)	
87 John Beasley (6-3, 230)	TE	84 Fred Arbanas (6-3, 240)	
80 John Henderson (6-3, 190)	WR	89 Otis Taylor (6-3, 215)	
11 Joe Kapp* (6-3, 208)	QB	16 Len Dawson* (6-0, 190)	
41 Dave Osborn (6-0, 205)	RB	21 Mike Garrett (5-9, 200)	
30 Bill Brown (5-11, 230)	RB	45 Robert Holmes* (5-9, 220)	
	Defense		
81 Carl Eller* (6-6, 250)	LE	75 Jerry Mays (6-4, 252)	
77 Gary Larsen* (6-5, 255)	LT	61 Curley Culp* (6-1, 265)	
88 Alan Page* (6-4, 245)	RT	86 Buck Buchanan* (6-7, 287)	
70 Jim Marshall* (6-3, 247)	RE	87 Aaron Brown (6-5, 265)	
60 Roy Winston (5-11, 226)	LLB	78 Bobby Bell (6-4, 228)	
59 Lonnie Warwick (6-3, 235)	MLB	63 Willie Lanier* (6-1, 245)	
58 Wally Hilgenberg (6-3, 231)	RLB	51 Jim Lynch (6-1, 235)	
46 Earsell Mackbee (6-0, 195)	LCB	40 Jim Marsalis* (5-11, 194)	
45 Ed Sharockman (6-0, 200)	RCB	18 Emmitt Thomas (6-2, 192)	
29 Karl Kassulke (6-0, 195)	SS	46 Jim Kearney (6-2, 206)	
22 Paul Krause* (6-3, 188)	FS	42 Johnny Robinson (6-1, 205)	
* NFL Pro Bowl selection		* AFL All-Star Team	

SUBSTITUTIONS

Minnesota
Offense: WR - 27 Bob Grim; TE - 89 Kent Kramer; G - 62 Ed White; QB - 15 Gary Cuozzo; RB - 35 Bill Harris, 26 Clint Jones, 21 Jim Lindsey, 32 Oscar Reed. *Defense:* DE - 74 Steve Smith; DT - 76 Paul Dickson; LB - 50 Jim Hargrove, 55 Mike McGill; S - 40 Charlie West, 49 Dale Hackbart. *Specialists:* K - 14 Fred Cox; P - 19 Bob Lee. *DNP:* 71 Doug Davis (T), 57 Mike Reilly (LB).

Kansas City
Offense: WR - 30 Gloster Richardson; TE - 32 Curtis McClinton; G - 60 George Daney; C - 65 Remi Prudhomme; QB - 10 Mike Livingston; RB - 38 Wendell Hayes, 6 Warren McVea, 14 Ed Podolak. *Defense:* DE - 82 Ed Lothamer; DT - 74 Gene Trosch; LB - 85 Chuck Hurston, 66 Bob Stein; CB - 20 Goldie Sellers, 22 Willie Mitchell; S - 24 Ceaser Belser. *Specialists:* K - 3 Jan Stenerud*; P - 44 Jerrel Wilson. *DNP:* 12 Tom Flores (QB).

Minnesota
Head Coach: Bud Grant. *Offense:* Jerry Burns (head offense), John Michels (offensive line), Bus Mertes (backs). *Defense:* Bob Hollway (head defense), Jack Patera (defensive line).

Kansas City
Head Coach: Hank Stram. *Offense:* Pete Brewster (ends), Bill Walsh (offensive line), John Beake (backs), Tommy O'Boyle (assistant backs). *Defense:* Tom Pratt (defensive line), Tom Bettis (defensive backs). *Strength:* Alvin Roy.

odd-man line, with either the imposing Buchanan or muscle man Curley Culp on the nose of center Mick Tingelhoff. Against NFL opposition, Tingelhoff was able to utilize his quickness and tenacity to cut off the middle linebacker. On this day, however, he was just trying to hang on for dear life. "With all due respect to Mick, he was not used to it," Flores said. "Our defensive line just overpowered their offensive line."

After averaging 132.1 yards on the ground during the season, Minnesota running backs Bill Brown, Dave Osborn, and Oscar Reed settled for 58 yards in 17 carries against Kansas City. The Vikings' game, as summarized by Reichow, was "pound and pound and pound. The colder the better. . . . We won a lot of games in those days by 10–7, 13–10. We weren't a big-play team at that time." Reichow also expressed surprise at how big the Chiefs were, referring mostly to Buchanan, who was two inches taller and 20 pounds heavier than any of Minnesota's offensive linemen. Compared to the Vikings' smallish blockers, right end Aaron Brown was a huge man as well.

Stram's team was also one of the first to mine the fertile feeding grounds of the Deep South. Buchanan was 1 of 13 Chiefs in Super Bowl IV who hailed from predominantly black colleges, whereas the Vikings had only 1. The starters in the group were Taylor and safety Jim Kearney from Prairie View A&M University, wide receiver Frank Pitts and running back Robert Holmes, both from Southern University, Buchanan from Grambling State, linebacker Willie Lanier from Morgan State, Marsalis from Tennessee State, and Thomas from

Bishop. "[Stram] didn't care what color, what creed, whatever," said linebacker Bobby Bell, one of seven Chiefs who made the All-AFL team. "If you could play football, and play it under his rules and regulations, that was cool."

The Vikings had to punt on their first two possessions of the game, going nowhere fast against the stout Chiefs. They did manage two first downs in the opening series and would have been three-and-out on their second possession if the Chiefs hadn't been penalized for roughing punter Bob Lee.

"I don't know if we were thoroughly prepared offensively or defensively," Burns said. "Every aspect of what they did was very good. We had a tough time running against them. We didn't get the job done from an offensive standpoint. Our actual game plan was pretty basic. If we made a substitution, it was to put in an extra tight end in a short-yardage play or inside the 10."

Unable to rush effectively, Kapp went with short passes that went nowhere when the determined Kansas City defenders kept coming up to make sure tackles. "Bobby Bell could outrun me," Chiefs safety Johnny Robinson said. "He was a 4.4 guy. We had Willie Lanier, another Hall of Fame linebacker. [Bell and Lanier] played their best game and just tore the Vikings apart."

Meanwhile, Kansas City scored on four of its first five offensive possessions, including three field goals of 48, 32, and 25 yards by Jan Stenerud to give the Chiefs an early 9–0 lead. The offense combined a workman-like run game with reverses by the big, fast Pitts and rhythmic passes into the flat. When Dawson rifled a quick hitch to Taylor in front of Mackbee, Stram said, "They can't cover that in a million years. No way in the world. That's like stealin' out there." When the Vikings' back seven was late to react on another completion, Stram blurted out, "Kassulke was running out there like it was a

> "Joe Kapp was a competitor is what he was. He got hurt a couple times in that game. He took some hellacious licks from our people."
>
> *Tom Bettis, Chiefs defensive backs coach*

Chinese fire drill. They look like they're flat as hell."

Minnesota's front four of Carl Eller, Alan Page, Gary Larsen, and Jim Marshall had accounted for 46 of the Vikings' 49 sacks during the regular season, and the foursome was headed to the Pro Bowl after the game. What Stram didn't want was the so-called Purple People Eaters teeing off against Dawson, who was vulnerable anyway because of a bad knee. So, Stram used three-step drops and a moving pocket to exploit the soft coverage. His offensive line, anchored by the longtime left side of Jim Tyrer and Budde, plus up-and-coming right guard Mo Moorman, had a dominating day. The Chiefs often double-teamed the Vikings' ends, keeping the defenders' hands down so that Dawson had clear passing lanes for his outside throws.

"Our weakness was the defensive backfield," Reichow said. "There were no great speed guys back there. The corners were lay-back guys. [Our philosophy was,] let that defensive line force the passer to throw it and make a mistake."

That's basically why free safety Paul Krause was able to intercept 81 passes in a 16-year career and why the Vikings led the NFL in 1969 with 30 picks. Krause stole a deep ball from Taylor early in the second quarter, perhaps the only mistake Dawson made all day in his MVP performance.

Stenerud's marksmanship and Jerrel Wilson's 48.5-yard average on four punts were not the extent of Kansas City's edge on special teams. Vikings kickoff returner Charlie West fumbled a boot from Stenerud midway through the second quarter and guard Remi Prudhomme recovered at the Minnesota 19. Marshall sacked Dawson for minus-8 on first down, but Wendell Hayes barged for 13 on a trap and Dawson found room to hit Taylor for 10 against Mackbee on third and 5.

On second and goal, the Vikings jumped into a six-man line, but Garrett slipped through a gaping hole off left tackle for a 5-yard touchdown. Moorman came across to trap Page, Budde won at the point of attack against backup defensive tackle Paul Dickson, and tight end Fred Arbanas broke through to the second level and wiped out Warwick. By then, it was 16–0, and it was apparent to everyone that the Jets' upset of the Colts in Super Bowl III hadn't been a fluke at all.

The Vikings finally showed a pulse on their

TEAM STATISTICS

MINNESOTA		KANSAS CITY
13	Total First Downs	19
2	Rushing	9
10	Passing	7
1	Penalty	3
239	Total Net Yardage	273
50	Total Offensive Plays	62
4.8	Avg. Gain per Offensive Play	4.4
19	Rushes	42
67	Yards Gained Rushing (Net)	151
3.5	Average Yards per Rush	3.6
28	Passes Attempted	17
17	Passes Completed	12
3	Passes Intercepted	1
3	Tackled Attempting to Pass	3
27	Yards Lost Attempting to Pass	20
172	Yards Gained Passing (Net)	122
3/9	Third-Down Efficiency	7/15
0/0	Fourth-Down Efficiency	0/0
3	Punts	4
37.0	Average Distance	48.5
2	Punt Returns	1
18	Punt Return Yardage	0
4	Kickoff Returns	2
79	Kickoff Return Yardage	36
0	Interception Return Yardage	24
3	Fumbles	0
1	Own Fumbles Recovered	0
0	Opponent Fumbles Recovered	2
6	Penalties	4
67	Yards Penalized	47
1	Touchdowns	2
1	Rushing	1
0	Passing	1
0	Returns	0
1	Extra Points Made	2
0	Field Goals Made	3
1	Field Goals Attempted	3
0	Safeties	0
7	Total Points Scored	23
25:27	Time of Possession	34:33

"Lenny looked like a China doll, but Lenny was tough."

Tom Bettis, on quarterback Len Dawson

MINNESOTA

Passing	CP/ATT	YDS	TD	INT	RAT
Kapp	16/25	183	0	2	52.6
Cuozzo	1/3	16	0	1	12.5

Rushing	ATT	YDS	AVG	TD	LG
Brown	6	26	4.3	0	10
Reed	4	17	4.3	0	15
Osborn	7	15	2.1	1	4t
Kapp	2	9	4.5	0	7

Receiving	NO	YDS	AVG	TD	LG
Henderson	7	111	15.9	0	28
Brown	3	11	3.7	0	11
Beasley	2	41	20.5	0	26
Reed	2	16	8.0	0	12
Osborn	2	11	5.5	0	10
Washington	1	9	9.0	0	9

Interceptions	NO	YDS	LG	TD
Krause	1	0	0	0

Punting	NO	AVG	LG	BLK
Lee	3	37.0	50	0

Punt Ret.	NO/FC	YDS	LG	TD
West	2/0	18	11	0

Kickoff Ret.	NO	YDS	LG	TD
West	3	46	27	0
Jones	1	33	33	0

Defense	SOLO	AST	TOT	SK
Hilgenberg	8	6	14	0
Warwick	8	5	13	0
Winston	4	6	10	1
Marshall	6	1	7	1
Page	4	3	7	0
Mackbee	6	0	6	0
Eller	3	3	6	1
Sharockman	4	0	4	0
Larsen	3	1	4	0
Krause	2	2	4	0
Tingelhoff	2	0	2	0
Hackbart	1	1	2	0
B. Brown	1	0	1	0
Dickson	1	0	1	0
Grim	1	0	1	0
Harris	1	0	1	0
Vellone	1	0	1	0
Kassulke	0	1	1	0
Lindsey	0	1	1	0
West	0	1	1	0
TOTAL	56	31	87	3

KANSAS CITY

Passing	CP/ATT	YDS	TD	INT	RAT
Dawson	17/22	142	1	1	90.8

Rushing	ATT	YDS	AVG	TD	LG
Garrett	11	39	3.5	1	6
Pitts	3	37	12.3	0	19
Hayes	8	31	3.9	0	13
McVea	12	26	2.2	0	9
Dawson	3	11	3.7	0	11
Holmes	5	7	1.4	0	7

Receiving	NO	YDS	AVG	TD	LG
Taylor	6	81	13.5	1	46
Pitts	3	33	11.0	0	20
Garrett	2	25	12.5	0	17
Hayes	1	3	3.0	0	3

Interceptions	NO	YDS	LG	TD
Lanier	1	9	9	0
Robinson	1	9	9	0
Thomas	1	6	6	0

Punting	NO	AVG	LG	BLK
Wilson	4	48.5	59	0

Punt Ret.	NO/FC	YDS	LG	TD
Garrett	1/0	0	0	0

Kickoff Ret.	NO	YDS	LG	TD
Garrett	1	18	18	0
Hayes	1	18	18	0

Defense	SOLO	AST	TOT	SK
Kearney	5	2	7	0
Buchanan	4	3	7	1
Lanier	3	4	7	0
Marsalis	4	1	5	0
Thomas	3	2	5	0
Culp	3	1	4	0
A. Brown	2	2	4	1
Mays	2	2	4	1
Bell	1	2	3	0
Belser	1	2	3	0
Robinson	2	0	2	0
Daney	1	0	1	0
Mitchell	1	0	1	0
Prudhomme	1	0	1	0
Stein	1	0	1	0
Taylor	1	0	1	0
TOTAL	35	21	56	3

opening possession of the third quarter, covering 69 yards in 10 plays. Dave Osborn fought his way over Lanier for a 4-yard touchdown, and it was a contest again at 16–7. But then, after the Chiefs picked up three straight first downs, Vikings defensive coach Jack Patera took a terrible gamble by rushing eight men on first and 10. Against any other play, it might have worked, since the Chiefs were blocking with only seven, but out of a Tight I formation Dawson had called another hitch to Taylor off a one-step drop. Dawson fired the pass without being hit. Mackbee raced forward and struck Otis Taylor, but the cornerback suffered a pinched nerve in his right shoulder and couldn't wrap up. Racing down the sideline, Taylor froze Kassulke with a stutter-step and then blew past him to the house (23–7).

"Otis was very strong," Flores said years later. "He didn't have a great career statistic-wise because he was never the featured guy. In today's game, he'd catch 100 balls. Easily. Otis was such a powerful guy, I don't think the Vikings were ready for that part. Maybe they didn't anticipate it or maybe they just couldn't play it."

As the Vikings' deficit mounted, so did the pressure on Kapp. Signed out of the Canadian Football League (CFL) in 1967 after general manager Jim Finks traded Fran Tarkenton to the New York Giants, Kapp fit Grant's model of toughness to a T. Boozing and brawling was a way of life for the 31-year-old Kapp, who finished his career with the 2–12 Boston Patriots in 1970. "Joe Kapp was probably the most competitive all-around player that I have ever been involved with," Burns said. "When you got behind there was no quit in him. He'd kill himself."

Early in the fourth quarter, Kapp threw down the middle to tight end John Beasley, but Lanier intercepted. On the next series, Robinson intercepted a long, wayward aerial by Kapp, prompting Stram to cackle, "That ball looked like it had helium in it."

Four plays into Minnesota's final series on offense, Kapp had to be replaced by Gary Cuozzo after suffering a shoulder injury on a sack by Aaron Brown, the defensive end. According to Bettis, Kapp

> "I was sorry to see us lose our identity as the AFL, to be honest with you. Those of us that were in the AFL since its inception would have liked to have stayed the AFL. But there were only about 20 of us."
>
> *Tom Flores, Chiefs backup quarterback*

wanted to stay in the game but knew he couldn't. "He was holding his throwing arm," said Bettis, "just a great competitor." On his fourth play behind center, Cuozzo's pass to wide receiver John Henderson was picked off by Thomas, giving the Chiefs half as many interceptions (10) in the postseason as they had allowed points (20).

The Chiefs weren't even the first-place team in the AFC Western Division, finishing 11–3 to Oakland's 12–1–1. In the playoffs, they went to Shea Stadium as a 4-point favorite over the defending champion Jets (10–4) and won, 13–6. The next week, they journeyed to Oakland, where they were a 4½-point underdog against the Raiders. The Chiefs triumphed again, 17–7, helped immensely by a defense that intercepted seven passes in the two playoff games.

In its 10-year history, the AFL would know ridicule and, in the end, respect. The Chiefs had suffocated the Vikings, a club that during the 1969 season had a 12-game winning streak, longest in the NFL since the Chicago Bears won 13 straight in 1934. With its victory in Super Bowl IV, the AFL finished 2–2 against the NFL. This was the last of the true Super Bowls, because the AFL as an independent entity would no longer exist after the merger of 1970. A hard-won feeling of equality burned brightly throughout the league.

"An insignia on your hat or jacket doesn't make any difference," Stram said after a victorious ride on the shoulders of his athletes. "Football is a game of people, not of emblems."

And the Chiefs had far, far too many good people for the Vikings.

Ten Most Significant Field Goals

1. **Adam Vinatieri, Patriots, XXXVIII:** When Vinatieri walked onto the field with nine seconds left, he had to overcome one missed field goal and one blocked attempt earlier in the game. Snapper Brian Kinchen was playing with a cut hand. Also, Scott O'Brien, Carolina's special-teams coach, was a master at blocking placements. But from 41 yards, with the game on the line, Vinatieri's kick was high and true.

2. **Adam Vinatieri, Patriots, XXXVI:** Coach Bill Belichick called Vinatieri New England's "best player." The boot was from 48 with seven seconds left. Vinatieri had been 12-for-13 on game-winning kicks in his six seasons, but none had been longer than 40 yards. The bull's-eye left Vinatieri 25-for-25 in domes.

3. **Jim O'Brien, Colts, V:** The rookie O'Brien had replaced popular veteran Lou Michaels in 1970. His only other action, an extra point in the second quarter, was blocked when the kicker hesitated in his steps. As he prepared for his straight-on attempt from the 32, Dallas players stood and screamed at him. Their taunts did no good. O'Brien called it the best kick of his life.

4. **Jan Stenerud, Chiefs, IV:** Field goals in the 1960s were almost a 50–50 proposition. Jan Stenerud began to change that when he joined the Chiefs in 1967. In the Super Bowl, he attempted a 48-yarder on Kansas City's first possession. He drilled it, and the underdog Chiefs were off and running.

5. **Steve Christie, Bills, XXVIII:** The Bills led the Cowboys 13–6 at halftime due in part to Christie's two field goals. His first, from 54 yards and a Super Bowl record, made it 3–3 in the first quarter.

6. **Don Chandler, Packers, II:** Six seconds remained when Chandler was summoned for his third field goal attempt of the first half. He had hit from 39 and 20, but this was from 43; only 2 of his 19 regular-season field goals had been longer than that. With Bart Starr holding, Chandler's kick was good.

7. **Jim Breech, Bengals, XXIII:** This was the first season of play at Miami's Joe Robbie Stadium, and not all kickers were well versed on prevailing wind currents. The wind was blowing so hard that Breech actually played the ball outside the uprights. The wind

Baltimore's Jim O'Brien leaps for joy after kicking the game-winning field goal with nine seconds left in Super Bowl V on January 17, 1971. *Tony Tomsic/Getty Images*

blew it back between the posts, and Breech's 41-yard field goal gave the Bengals a 6–3 third-quarter lead.

8. **Al Del Greco, Titans, XXXIV:** A 16-year veteran, Del Greco missed from 47 yards in the first quarter and had a 47-yard try blocked in the third quarter. With 2:12 left in the game, his kick from 43 was good and tied the game at 16. Two plays later, WR Isaac Bruce won it for St. Louis.

9. **Robbie Gould, Bears, XLI:** This was the first Super Bowl played in steady rain. When Gould lined up his 44-yard attempt late in the third quarter, the footing was slick and the Bears trailed, 22–14. His field goal got them within 5, but it turned out to be the end of the Bears' scoring.

10. **Jason Elam, Broncos, XXXII:** In four previous Super Bowl defeats, Denver kickers had gone 5-for-8 on field goals. Elam, a third-round pick in 1993, however, was a cut above predecessors Jim Turner, David Treadwell, and Rich Karlis. He drilled his only attempt against Green Bay, a 51-yarder, early in the second quarter.

V

BALTIMORE COLTS 16, DALLAS COWBOYS 13

January 17, 1971
Orange Bowl, Miami, Florida

It was an afternoon of crazy caroms and woeful execution, of squandered opportunities and slapstick play. It came down to a kicker, a rookie no less, to bring a measure of precision and ultimate closure to the high, but imperfect, drama that was Super Bowl V.

Just 9 seconds remained at the Orange Bowl and the Baltimore Colts were on the Dallas Cowboys' 25-yard line. Time was out. With his square-toed Riddell kicking shoe laced firmly in place, Baltimore's Jim O'Brien trotted onto the field to meet his date with destiny.

Just two minutes earlier, the Cowboys had been in Colts' territory at the 48 thinking this troubled season might end with their first NFL championship. Then a sack by defensive tackle Fred Miller, coupled with a holding penalty, put them 24 yards in arrears. Facing second down and 35 at his own 27, Dallas coach Tom Landry took a gamble that seemed out of character.

Landry had taken the play-calling responsibility away from Craig Morton, his sore-armed quarterback, with five games remaining in the regular season and the Cowboys (5–4) in danger of not making the playoffs. They hadn't lost again.

At this juncture, Landry told Morton to run the team's two-minute package. "Craig knew what plays I wanted," Landry said.

On the sidelines, Charlie Waters was just praying for overtime. The Cowboys' rookie safety, the interception leader for the "Flex" defense, which entered Super Sunday having allowed only one touchdown in the previous 25 quarters, was confident that the Colts wouldn't be able to score if it came to sudden-death overtime.

"They had the fluke play to [John] Mackey, but they hadn't moved it on us all day," Waters said years later. "Our defense was phenomenal. This was the peak of Doomsday I [defense]."

Attendance: 79,204
Conditions: 70 degrees, partly cloudy, wind NW at 10–15 mph
Time of kickoff: 2:00 p.m. (EST)
Length of game: 2 hours, 39 minutes
Referee: Norm Schachter

MVP: Chuck Howley, LB, Cowboys

From a spread formation, Morton sprinted out to the right, stopped, and floated a dangerous pass back inside to Dan Reeves, who had run a hook out of the slot right at the 40, 18 yards away from his quarterback. Morton had to loft his pass over the outstretched arms of Ted Hendricks, the Colts' 6-foot-7 outside linebacker.

The ball was high; Reeves leaped and got both hands on it, but the ball glanced off his hands to a point slightly above and behind him. "Certainly it was a catchable pass," Reeves said. As Reeves stretched back to pull it in, safety Jerry Logan drilled him in the small of the back, turning the halfback/coach into a pretzel. Having taken a deep drop in zone coverage, middle linebacker Mike Curtis was in position to cradle the interception, which he returned 13 yards to the Dallas 28.

"What are the odds of getting a first down there?" Waters insisted. "There's no way to make that first down. It just baffles everybody. We should have run a draw play, eaten some time off the clock, and punted the ball. I guess Coach Landry thought that was a safe play. It was the wrong philosophy. [We should have just played] the way our philosophy had been all season. The defense created turnovers and the offense tried not to make mistakes. It was so out of character for our team to lose that poise. Coach Landry prided himself on poise. Why [he] gambled is beyond me. I guess it was just human nature thinking they might be able to get the first and play for the victory right then. It was brutal."

	1	2	3	4	Final
Baltimore Colts	0	6	0	10	16
Dallas Cowboys	3	10	0	0	13

SCORING SUMMARY

1st Quarter
DAL Clark, 14-yd. FG
2nd Quarter
DAL Clark, 30-yd. FG
BAL Mackey, 75-yd. pass from Unitas (kick blocked)
DAL Thomas, 7-yd. pass from Morton (Clark kick)
4th Quarter
BAL Nowatzke, 2-yd. run (O'Brien kick)
BAL O'Brien, 32-yd. FG

Two carries by Norm Bulaich pushed Baltimore to the 25. The idea of having a net in the bench area for kickers to use to warm up hadn't come yet, so O'Brien could only stretch and follow through. The Colts stopped the clock with a timeout at the 9-second mark. When the Cowboys attempted to call another timeout, referee Norm Schachter denied it because the rule stated that two consecutive timeouts, regardless if they are called by different teams, couldn't be taken if the first timeout ran its full 90-second course, which the Colts' stoppage had.

O'Brien was an athlete who also happened to kick. As a three-year starting wide receiver at the University of Cincinnati, he set the National Collegiate Athletic Association (NCAA) record for yards per reception with 25.2 as a junior in 1968. He also made 20 of 44 field-goal attempts and was drafted as a kicker/wide receiver in the third round.

Veteran Lou Michaels had done all the placekicking for the Colts since 1964, but missed a short field goal (27 yards) in Super Bowl III and then made just 45.2 percent in 1969. Assigned jersey No. 80, O'Brien worked in camp as a receiver and kicked for a few minutes each day after practice.

"The fact that I was competing in camp with a popular player made things a bit difficult for me with some of the veterans," O'Brien said. "Lou Michaels was one of their buddies—and here comes this young kid. They were older and very conservative and most of them were married, and here I was young and single and feeling my oats, so to speak.

I exuded a lot of confidence and probably that was seen as my being brash or cocky. Also, I let my hair grow an inch longer than anybody else's."

Michaels was released, and O'Brien, nicknamed "Lassie" by defensive tackle Billy Ray Smith, made 55.9 percent of his 34 field-goal attempts during the season, including a 19-yarder in the final seconds that beat San Diego, 16–14, on opening day. Waters, who knew O'Brien from playing with him in a college all-star game, expected the worst even though the kick was anything but routine. "The biggest thing he had going for him, he was a cocky son of a buck," Waters said. "I knew that Jim was fearless. It never even crossed my mind that he was going to miss."

When O'Brien began lining up, the Cowboys screamed all kinds of potentially distracting words, yet, as he related later, his concentration was utterly complete. The snap from Tom Goode was true, the hold by Earl Morrall was sound, and the kick by O'Brien was dead-center perfect from 32 yards away. "It would have been good from 52 yards out," O'Brien said. "It was the best kick of my life."

The final score: Baltimore 16, Dallas 13.

As the Cowboys straggled off the field, the great Bob Lilly, their all-pro defensive tackle since 1961, flung his helmet high, high into the air. Finally, the helmet smashed down on the artificial turf and broke into pieces. For the Cowboys, it was the ultimate heartbreak, coming as it did after two NFL Championship Game losses to the Packers and two Eastern Conference playoff losses to Cleveland.

As bitter as defeat was for Dallas, victory was just as sweet for Baltimore. The Colts could feel a measure of vindication for having been humiliated by the Jets in the same stadium two years earlier.

"Our owner [Carroll Rosenbloom] took us over to the Bahamas for a week after the game," Hendricks said. "We left right from Miami. Wives, too. Two Dallas Cowboys made the mistake of getting on the same plane—Lee Roy Jordan and someone [else]."

The Colts were coached by the "Easy Rider," Don McCafferty, who had been an assistant in Baltimore since 1959. He was promoted by Rosenbloom after the 1970 draft, when Don Shula bolted for Miami. Rosenbloom demanded and received a first-round draft choice in 1971 for losing Shula.

"That kicks the genius coach theory into a cocked hat," Rosenbloom blustered after the title game victory over Oakland. "'Mac' took a team that looked like nothing last year [8–5–1], a team riddled with dissension and often hurt this season, and turned it into a champion. Here is a man who has no inner sanctum, no pretensions, no assistants—only associates. Everybody gets the credit except McCafferty. He is just a splendid man. What's more, he brought the fun back into the game of football for me."

Without injured running back Tom Matte, the Colts turned to rookie Norm Bulaich and fullback Tom Nowatzke. After beating the Raiders, Oakland coach John Madden had said of quarterback John Unitas, "I've never seen No. 19 play better." Unitas also was 37, however, and the truth was that he wasn't nearly the player that he had been in the mid-1960s. His backup, the hard-nosed Morrall, was 36.

The Cowboys had encountered some adversity of their own. During the season, a wire story alleged widespread drug use by their players. Wide receiver Lance Rentzel was arrested on a morals charge and left the team. Guard John Niland spent time in jail for fighting with police. Wide receiver Bob Hayes was benched for a time by Landry, who didn't settle on Morton over second-year man Roger Staubach until early October.

"We were a much better team than Baltimore," Cowboys linebackers coach Jerry Tubbs said years later. "[The Colts] had some problems. Unitas was old. We were just a better team and we blew it. We had several plays that were just terrible. The fumble on the goal-line by Duane Thomas cost us the ball game."

The first half, which ended with Dallas leading 13–6, was relatively uneventful with the exception of three plays.

Early in the second quarter, Unitas took a nine-step drop and threw about 25 yards downfield to wide receiver Ed Hinton. The pass tipped off Hinton's fingers at the Colts 42, grazed the fingers of Cowboys cornerback Mel Renfro

BALTIMORE COLTS (AFC, 11–2–1)		DALLAS COWBOYS (NFC, 10–4)
	Offense	
33 Eddie Hinton (6-0, 200)	WR	22 Bob Hayes (5-11, 185)
72 Bob Vogel (6-5, 250)	LT	73 Ralph Neely (6-6, 255)
62 Glenn Ressler (6-3, 250)	LG	76 John Niland* (6-3, 245)
50 Bill Curry (6-2, 235)	C	51 Dave Manders (6-2, 250)
75 John Williams (6-3, 256)	RG	61 Blaine Nye (6-4, 251)
71 Dan Sullivan (6-3, 250)	RT	70 Rayfield Wright (6-6, 255)
88 John Mackey (6-2, 224)	TE	84 Pettis Norman (6-3, 220)
87 Roy Jefferson (6-2, 195)	WR	88 Reggie Rucker (6-2, 190)
19 Johnny Unitas (6-1, 196)	QB	14 Craig Morton (6-4, 214)
36 Norm Bulaich (6-1, 218)	RB	33 Duane Thomas (6-1, 220)
34 Tom Nowatzke (6-3, 230)	RB	32 Walt Garrison (6-0, 205)
	Defense	
78 Bubba Smith* (6-7, 295)	LE	63 Larry Cole (6-4, 250)
74 Billy Ray Smith (6-4, 250)	LT	75 Jethro Pugh (6-6, 260)
76 Fred Miller (6-3, 250)	RT	74 Bob Lilly* (6-5, 260)
85 Roy Hilton (6-6, 240)	RE	66 George Andrie (6-6, 250)
56 Ray May (6-1, 230)	LLB	52 Dave Edwards (6-1, 225)
32 Mike Curtis* (6-2, 232)	MLB	55 Lee Roy Jordan (6-1, 221)
83 Ted Hendricks (6-7, 215)	RLB	54 Chuck Howley (6-2, 225)
47 Charlie Stukes (6-3, 212)	LCB	26 Herb Adderley (6-1, 200)
35 Jim Duncan (6-2, 200)	RCB	20 Mel Renfro* (6-0, 190)
20 Jerry Logan* (6-1, 190)	LS	34 Cornell Green (6-3, 208)
21 Rick Volk (6-3, 195)	RS	41 Charlie Waters (6-1, 193)

* Pro Bowl selection

SUBSTITUTIONS

Baltimore

Offense: WR - 27 Ray Perkins; TE - 84 Tom Mitchell; T - 73 Sam Ball; G - 61 Cornelius Johnson; C - 53 Tom Goode; QB - 15 Earl Morrall; RB - 17 Sam Havrilak, 45 Jerry Hill, 40 Jack Maitland. *Defense:* DE - 81 Billy Newsome; LB - 51 Bob Grant, 52 Robbie Nichols; CB - 30 Ron Gardin, 42 Tom Maxwell. *Specialists:* K- 80 Jim O'Brien; P - 49 David Lee. *DNP:* 28 Jimmy Orr (WR), 60 George Wright (DT).

Dallas

Offense: WR - 24 Dennis Homan; TE - 89 Mike Ditka; T - 78 Bob Asher; RB - 35 Calvin Hill, 30 Dan Reeves, 42 Claxton Welch. *Defense:* DE - 67 Pat Toomay; DT - 77 Ron East; LB - 60 Steve Kiner, 50 D. D. Lewis, 56 Tom Stincic; CB - 46 Mark Washington; S - 45 Richmond Flowers, 43 Cliff Harris. *Specialists:* K - 83 Mike Clark; P - 10 Ron Widby. *DNP:* 12 Roger Staubach (QB), 72 Tony Liscio (T).

at the 45, and was caught by Mackey at the 50. The Hall of Fame tight end ran in from there to complete a 75-yard touchdown. The Cowboys vehemently argued that the ball had been touched consecutively by two offensive players, which would have made the play illegal. But officials ruled, and replays later confirmed, that Renfro touched it between the two receivers.

Immersed in the confusion on the field, O'Brien had let his concentration wander before the extra point, his first kick of the game. "I hesitated a second too long and Mark Washington came in and blocked it with his chest," he said. "It was my fault more than anyone else's."

The second critical play of the half sent Unitas to the bench for the day. From the start, he had absorbed a pounding from the Dallas rush line, which included ends Larry Cole and George Andrie and tackles Jethro Pugh and Lilly. He had to ice his ribs after fumbling the ball away after a classic form hit by Lee Roy Jordan on a second-quarter scramble. Then he left the game for good with rib cartilage damage following a shot by Andrie on his second interception. "That probably hurt us," Waters said. "Morrall did pretty good."

Morrall, one of the goats of Super Bowl III before being replaced that day by Unitas, immediately led a 50-yard drive late in the half before the third key play of the half unfolded. After Bulaich failed to gain on three straight carries from the 2, McCafferty went for it on fourth down. Although McCafferty later insisted that the target, tight end Tom Mitchell, of Morrall's incomplete pass into the end zone had been held by linebacker Chuck Howley,

the fact remained that the rookie coach had shown a glaring lack of judgment in bypassing the field goal.

"If we had lost, it would have been the worst call I made this year," McCafferty said. "If it had worked, I would have been a hero."

Things went from bad to worse for the Colts on the second-half kickoff when James Duncan fumbled, 1 of 11 turnovers in the game. Alternating carries by rookie halfback Duane Thomas and veteran fullback Walt Garrison, who played despite ankle and knee injuries, the Cowboys swept 29 yards in five straight plays and reached the Baltimore 2. Already up by 7, the Cowboys could have all but clinched the game with another touchdown.

"I actually had this thought: I was trying to figure out whether I was going to get a size 10 or a size 11 on the Super Bowl ring," Waters said. "I still to this day remember that I had that thought." On first and goal, Dallas ran a simple off-tackle power play, Garrison leading and Thomas seeking daylight and a touchdown that would put the Cowboys ahead by 14. The 205-pound Thomas planted his left foot sharply at the 4 and crashed straight downhill toward the end zone. At the 1, he was met hard by one of the safeties, Rick Volk, and then the other, Jerry Logan. Thomas spun back to the inside but the ball had come free.

Years later, Thomas still resents being cast as a scapegoat. "Tom [Landry] got on me about losing the game," he said. "How about Dan Reeves? He tipped the damn ball into Mike Curtis' hands for the interception [at the end of the game]. At least I scored a touchdown in the game."

No one will ever know for sure what went on under that mass of human bodies. When the ball was fumbled, replays showed it heading toward Colts defensive tackle Billy Ray Smith. Yet when the players got up and referee Schachter signaled Baltimore ball, Dallas center Dave Manders had the football under his arm.

"Before they unpiled, Dave Manders was right on top of the ball," Morton said. "I screamed to the line judge on my side, 'Call the first thing! Call it, you son of a bitch!'" To this day, Dallas personnel director Gil Brandt's first memory of Super Bowl V was the name of that line judge, Jack Fette.

The Colts, who turned the ball over seven times,

reached the Dallas 11 to start the fourth quarter. On third and goal, Andrie beat left tackle Bob Vogel around the corner and slammed into Morrall just as he released a pass to Bulaich in the left corner. The ball was underthrown and easily intercepted by Howley in the end zone.

On Baltimore's next possession, the disappointment mounted. Pressured by defensive tackle Jethro Pugh, backup running back Sam Havrilak was unable to throw back to Morrall on a second-and-1 flea-flicker from the Dallas 30, so the one-time Bucknell University quarterback tried flinging it downfield to Mackey. Instead, the ball was caught by another Colt, Hinton, at the 22. As Hinton raced toward a tying touchdown, safety Cornell Green stripped him from behind near the 10. Dallas gained possession when the ball rolled out of the end zone.

Two plays later, on third and 7, Morton dropped back but his protection collapsed inside when Colts defensive end Roy Hilton trashed tackle Ralph Neely with a head slap and bore in. Morton's hurried pass was high, glanced off Garrison, was tipped by Duncan, and then was intercepted by Volk, who returned 30 yards to the Dallas 3. Nowatzke's 2-yard plunge tied the score, 13–13, with 7 minutes remaining.

After an exchange of punts later, the sequence of events leading to O'Brien's field goal began.

The soul-searching and gnashing of teeth in Texas would prompt longtime Dallas beat writer Steve Perkins to write a book, *Next Year's Champions: The Story of the Dallas Cowboys*. The Cowboys would have to live with that stigma for another year.

In Baltimore, the joy was unbridled. Two of their oldest pros, wide receiver Jimmy Orr and Bubba Smith, announced their retirements in the Orange Bowl's cramped locker room. The Colts had learned from their haughtiness in the days leading to Super Bowl III. Unlike in January 1969, these Colts didn't stay anywhere near the beaches (they were ensconced inland at the Miami Lakes Country Club) and an 11 p.m. curfew was in place all week.

"We walked out of the hotel that morning [of Super Bowl III] like the Jets were going to be too scared to show up," Bubba Smith said before Super

Bowl V. "The Jets stole our pride and everything else. We have to get it back."

No, the 1970 Colts weren't as awe-inspiring as they had been two years earlier. This team had only three players selected to the Pro Bowl, compared to eight in 1968. But in the end, despite all the blunders, Baltimore was back on top of the pro football world.

TEAM STATISTICS

BALTIMORE		DALLAS
14	Total First Downs	10
4	Rushing	4
6	Passing	5
4	Penalty	1
329	Total Net Yardage	215
56	Total Offensive Plays	59
5.9	Avg. Gain per Offensive Play	3.6
31	Rushes	31
69	Yards Gained Rushing (Net)	102
2.2	Average Yards per Rush	3.3
25	Passes Attempted	26
11	Passes Completed	12
3	Passes Intercepted	3
0	Tackled Attempting to Pass	2
0	Yards Lost Attempting to Pass	14
260	Yards Gained Passing (Net)	113
3/11	Third-Down Efficiency	1/13
0/1	Fourth-Down Efficiency	0/0
4	Punts	9
41.5	Average Distance	41.9
5	Punt Returns	3
12	Punt Return Yardage	9
4	Kickoff Returns	3
90	Kickoff Return Yardage	34
57	Interception Return Yardage	22
5	Fumbles	1
1	Own Fumbles Recovered	0
1	Opponent Fumbles Recovered	4
4	Penalties	10
31	Yards Penalized	133
2	Touchdowns	1
1	Rushing	0
1	Passing	1
0	Returns	0
1	Extra Points Made	1
1	Field Goals Made	2
2	Field Goals Attempted	2
0	Safeties	0
16	Total Points Scored	13
28:37	Time of Possession	31:23

BALTIMORE

Passing	CP/ATT	YDS	TD	INT	RAT
Morrall	7/15	147	0	1	54.0
Unitas	3/9	88	1	2	68.1
Havrilak	1/1	25	0	0	118.8

Rushing	ATT	YDS	AVG	TD	LG
Nowatzke	10	33	3.3	0	9
Bulaich	18	28	1.6	0	8
Unitas	1	4	4.0	0	4
Havrilak	1	3	3.0	0	3
Morrall	1	1	1.0	0	1

Receiving	NO	YDS	AVG	TD	LG
Jefferson	3	52	17.3	0	23
Mackey	2	80	40.0	1	75t
Hinton	2	51	25.5	0	26
Havrilak	2	27	13.5	0	25
Nowatzke	1	45	45.0	0	45
Bulaich	1	5	5.0	0	5

Interceptions	NO	YDS	LG	TD
Volk	1	30	30	0
Logan	1	14	14	0
Curtis	1	13	13	0

Punting	NO	AVG	LG	BLK
Lee	4	41.5	56	0

Punt Ret.	NO/FC	YDS	LG	TD
Gardin	4/3	4	2	0
Logan	1/0	8	8	0

Kickoff Ret.	NO	YDS	LG	TD
Duncan	4	90	30	0

Defense	SOLO	AST	TOT	SK
May	6	2	8	0
Hilton	4	3	7	2
B. R. Smith	4	3	7	0
Logan	6	0	6	0
M. Curtis	5	1	6	0
Miller	5	1	6	0
Bu. Smith	4	0	4	0
Volk	2	2	4	0
Stokes	3	0	3	0
Hendricks	1	2	3	0
Duncan	1	1	2	0
Gardin	1	0	1	0
Goode	1	0	1	0
Johnson	1	0	1	0
Maitland	1	0	1	0
Unitas	1	0	1	0
TOTAL	**46**	**15**	**61**	**2**

DALLAS

Passing	CP/ATT	YDS	TD	INT	RAT
Morton	12/26	127	1	3	34.1

Rushing	ATT	YDS	AVG	TD	LG
Garrison	12	65	5.4	0	19
Thomas	18	35	1.9	0	7
Morton	1	2	2.0	0	2

Receiving	NO	YDS	AVG	TD	LG
Reeves	5	46	9.2	0	17
Thomas	4	21	5.3	1	7t
Garrison	2	19	9.5	0	14
Hayes	1	41	41.0	0	41

Interceptions	NO	YDS	LG	TD
Howley	2	22	22	0
Renfro	1	0	0	0

Punting	NO	AVG	LG	BLK
Widby	9	41.9	49	0

Punt Ret.	NO/FC	YDS	LG	TD
Hayes	3/0	9	7	0

Kickoff Ret.	NO	YDS	LG	TD
Harris	1	18	18	0
Hill	1	14	14	0
Kiner	1	2	2	0

Defense	SOLO	AST	TOT	SK
Jordan	7	4	11	0
Adderley	6	0	6	0
Pugh	3	3	6	0
Edwards	4	1	5	0
Lilly	4	0	4	0
Howley	3	1	4	0
Renfro	3	1	4	0
Welch	3	1	4	0
Waters	3	0	3	0
Stincic	1	2	3	0
Cole	2	0	2	0
Flowers	2	0	2	0
Washington	2	0	2	0
Andrie	1	1	2	0
Green	1	1	2	0
Homan	1	0	1	0
Rucker	1	0	1	0
TOTAL	**47**	**15**	**62**	**0**

VI

DALLAS COWBOYS 24, MIAMI DOLPHINS 3

January 16, 1972
Tulane Stadium, New Orleans, Louisiana

Five times in five seasons the Dallas Cowboys had been to the pro football altar, and each time they had been denied. Then the team had to listen as fans castigated it as a loser instead of a cutting-edge organization and one of the great expansion franchises in professional sports history.

The false-start penalty against tackle Jim Boeke and Don Meredith's end-zone interception on the threshold of an NFL Championship Game victory against Green Bay in 1966. The unspeakable horror of permitting the Packers to traverse almost the entire length of Green Bay's Lambeau Field in minus-13-degree temperature in the Ice Bowl a year later. Back-to-back playoff defeats against Cleveland, as a three-point favorite in 1968 and as a six-point favorite in 1969. The self-destructive debacle against Baltimore in Super Bowl V. Defeat after heart-crushing defeat.

When the Cowboys stormed past Minnesota in a snowstorm and then San Francisco in the 1971 playoffs to reach the Super Bowl, there was little cause for celebration. The only thing that would satisfy the Cowboys and the football-mad state of Texas would be victory in the ultimate game.

"This was such an important game, not only for me but for the team," Dallas quarterback Roger Staubach said years later. "The Cowboys were tagged as a team that couldn't quite make it. Imagine what it would have been like since then if we hadn't won. It would have been a disaster."

Super Bowl VI—won 24–3 by Dallas over the Miami Dolphins on a 39-degree afternoon at Tulane Stadium—has gone down as one of the least compelling title games ever played. The MVP, Staubach, passed for only 119 yards and, by his own admission, didn't play very well. No running back for either team surpassed 100 yards, and no receiver had more than 40 receiving yards. The longest play of the day was a mere 27 yards.

Attendance: 80,591
Conditions: 39 degrees, sunny and cold, wind N at 9 mph
Time of kickoff: 1:35 p.m. (CST)
Length of game: 2 hours, 45 minutes
Referee: Jim Tunney

MVP: Roger Staubach, QB, Cowboys

None of that mattered, though. The wide smile emanating across the drawn features of coach Tom Landry as he was carried off the field on the shoulders of his players summed up the palpable feeling of joy and fulfillment. Three hundred sixty-four days after Bob Lilly flung his helmet skyward in frustration following Jim O'Brien's winning field goal in Super Bowl V, the albatross had flown away, leaving the Cowboys alone atop the NFL mountain.

"That game," said Jerry Tubbs, a Cowboys linebacker from 1960 to 1967 and then their linebackers coach for the next 21 years, "was more of a relief. Like being constipated. All of a sudden you get relief."

The Cowboys were favored by 6 points, and for good reason. Nine of their 22 starters had been regulars since that first championship loss to Green Bay, and 13 had been in the lineup since 1968. At 11–3 in 1971, they shared the NFL's best record with the Vikings, and they were on a nine-game winning streak that began when Landry decided at midseason to forget about alternating Staubach with Morton and to play only Staubach.

The Dolphins, on the other hand, had failed to win more than five games in their first four seasons before Don Shula replaced George Wilson in 1970. Shula had done an amazing job, driving Miami to a 10–4 turnaround in his first year and then 10–3–1 in 1971, including playoff victories over the two previous Super Bowl champions, the Kansas City Chiefs and the Colts. The Dolphins came from behind three

	1	2	3	4	Final
Dallas Cowboys	3	7	7	7	24
Miami Dolphins	0	3	0	0	3

SCORING SUMMARY

1st Quarter
DAL   Clark, 9-yd. FG
2nd Quarter
DAL   Alworth, 7-yd. pass from Staubach (Clark kick)
MIA   Yepremian, 31-yd. FG
3rd Quarter
DAL   D. Thomas, 3-yd. run (Clark kick)
4th Quarter
DAL   Ditka, 7-yd. pass from Staubach (Clark kick)

times to outlast the Chiefs in double overtime, proving beyond a doubt that they were Super Bowl–worthy. But in the end, it wasn't their time.

"They were a team of overachievers," Gil Brandt, the Cowboys' longtime personnel director, said of the Dolphins. "Ours was a team that was ready to smell the roses."

The bedrock trait of all great teams—the ability to run the ball and stop the run—carried the Cowboys. Dallas rushed 48 times for 252 yards, limited the Dolphins to 80 yards in 20 carries, while piling up almost a 2-to-1 margin in time of possession. That was nothing unusual for the Cowboys, who ranked third in rushing during the season (160.6-yard average) and were second against the run (81.7).

"They were the established team and we were the upstart," Shula recalled. "They played a great football game and we didn't play well. They were outstanding on offense with Staubach and Duane Thomas. And they were a great defensive team. Landry had been in a Super Bowl and didn't win. He was such a great coach. He finally got his reward."

The change from Morton, one of the goats in the previous Super Bowl, to Staubach was enormous. Staubach, 29 at the time, had just 15 starts under his belt. A 10th-round draft choice in 1964, he had to fulfill his obligation to the Navy before joining the Cowboys as a backup in 1969. Morton had more experience and a stronger arm, but Staubach could shake his shoulders in the open field and hurt defenses with his legs.

Bill Arnsparger, the Dolphins' defensive coordinator, designed his entire game plan around stopping Staubach's scrambling. He described Thomas as "a solid performer," but added, "The guy to me that was really the difference was Staubach. He was very difficult when he started scrambling."

Although Staubach rushed for only 18 yards, his presence alone prevented Dolphins' defenders from committing to the run. It also placed even more of a burden on middle linebacker Nick Buoniconti, the heart and soul of Miami's "No-Name Defense." Additionally, during the two-week run-up, player-coach Dan Reeves impersonated Buoniconti for the Cowboys' scout-team defense.

"I knew him backwards and forwards because I was responsible for giving a scouting report on their linebackers," Reeves said. "It was hard to tell somebody how he flowed real fast to the football, so I played Nick in practice. I knew we were going to do a good job against him because I got the hell beat out of me the whole week. I knew our players knew where Nick Buoniconti was all the time."

In the first half, Buoniconti flowed hard behind the line, hoping to intercept ball carriers, but Thomas, fullback Walt Garrison, and backup Calvin Hill kept cutting back. In the second half, after the Dolphins shifted their front 7 to account for the inside run and cutbacks, the Cowboys ran wide 7 times for 59 yards in an 8-play, 71-yard drive, capped by Thomas' 3-yard touchdown on an audible for a 17–3 advantage. On the big play of the drive—a 23-yard run by Thomas on a toss-sweep right—Buoniconti gambled by running through the middle and got caught up in the trash. On the touchdown, a toss-sweep left, Buoniconti ran in again but slid off Thomas' waist and Thomas scored standing up.

"Dallas' game plan proved to be correct," Buoniconti said. "Tom Landry and his offensive coaches decided they were going to put two guys on me every play. They had me going 10 different ways and I wasn't a factor in the game. None of our defensive guys were. We were overmatched psychologically as well as physically. . . . I'm not sure any of us expected to win the game—and we played like it."

Besides the change at quarterback, the Cowboys made two shrewd trades to solidify their offense. In May, they acquired aging wide receiver Lance Alworth from the San Diego Chargers for three players, including tackle Tony Liscio. Then, on November 19, they reacquired Liscio for a fifth-round draft choice when Ralph Neely, their two-time Pro Bowl left tackle, suffered a broken leg riding a dirt bike during an off-day hunting trip. Liscio started over Forrest Gregg, the Hall of Fame tackle in Green Bay who was playing one final season in Dallas. Said Gregg, "I'll say one thing. Tony Liscio really did a great job."

The Dolphins were a zone-coverage team with smart but slow-footed cornerbacks in Curtis Johnson and Tim Foley and two outstanding safeties, Dick Anderson and Jake Scott. With so much attention being paid to speedster Bob Hayes, Alworth had all kinds of opportunities on the weak side against Johnson. Staubach, however, kept bolting the pocket prematurely and running. He didn't have much success on the move and, by leaving early, wasn't able to exploit the Alworth-Johnson matchup.

Dallas drew first blood with Mike Clark's 9-yard field goal after Larry Csonka, who hadn't fumbled once all season, couldn't control a handoff from Bob Griese and Chuck Howley recovered near midfield. On Miami's next possession, defensive linemen Larry Cole and Lilly flushed Griese on a third-down stunt. When the quarterback kept circling backward, Lilly sacked him for a loss of 29 yards.

Later in the second quarter, Dallas opened up and went 76 yards in 10 plays for a touchdown. First, Staubach found Alworth inside Johnson on a turn-in for 21. Then, on first and goal from the 7, he gunned a quick out to Alworth at the left pylon, a matter of inches ahead of Johnson, for the score. "I never threw a pass any harder," Staubach said. "If I hadn't, Curtis Johnson would have got it with a clear field in front of him."

Trailing 10–0 late in the first half, Griese completed

DALLAS COWBOYS (NFC, 11–3)			MIAMI DOLPHINS (AFC, 10–3–1)	
		Offense		
22	Bob Hayes (5-11, 185)	WR	42	Paul Warfield* (6-0, 185)
64	Tony Liscio (6-5, 255)	LT	77	Doug Crusan (6-4, 250)
76	John Niland* (6-3, 245)	LG	67	Bob Kuechenberg (6-2, 247)
51	Dave Manders (6-2, 250)	C	61	Bob DeMarco (6-2, 250)
61	Blaine Nye (6-4, 251)	RG	66	Larry Little* (6-1, 265)
70	Rayfield Wright* (6-6, 255)	RT	73	Norm Evans (6-5, 252)
89	Mike Ditka (6-3, 213)	TE	80	Marv Fleming (6-4, 235)
19	Lance Alworth (6-0, 180)	WR	81	Howard Twilley (5-10, 185)
12	Roger Staubach* (6-3, 197)	QB	12	Bob Griese* (6-1, 190)
33	Duane Thomas (6-1, 205)	RB	21	Jim Kiick (5-11, 215)
32	Walt Garrison (6-0, 205)	RB	39	Larry Csonka* (6-2, 237)
		Defense		
63	Larry Cole (6-4, 255)	LE	70	Jim Riley (6-4, 250)
75	Jethro Pugh (6-6, 260)	LT	75	Manny Fernandez (6-2, 248)
74	Bob Lilly* (6-5, 260)	RT	72	Bob Heinz (6-6, 280)
66	George Andrie (6-6, 250)	RE	84	Bill Stanfill* (6-5, 250)
52	Dave Edwards (6-1, 225)	LLB	59	Doug Swift (6-3, 228)
55	Lee Roy Jordan (6-1, 221)	MLB	85	Nick Buoniconti (5-11, 220)
54	Chuck Howley* (6-2, 225)	RLB	57	Mike Kolen (6-2, 220)
26	Herb Adderley (6-1, 200)	LCB	25	Tim Foley (6-0, 194)
20	Mel Renfro* (6-0, 190)	RCB	45	Curtis Johnson (6-1, 196)
34	Cornell Green* (6-3, 208)	SS	40	Dick Anderson (6-2, 196)
43	Cliff Harris (6-1, 184)	FS	13	Jake Scott* (6-0, 188)

* Pro Bowl selection

SUBSTITUTIONS

Dallas
Offense: TE - 87 Bill Truax; C - 62 John Fitzgerald; RB - 35 Calvin Hill, 30 Dan Reeves, 42 Claxton Welch, 36 Joe Williams. *Defense:* DE - 85 Tody Smith, 67 Pat Toomay; DT - 77 Bill Gregory; LB - 50 D. D. Lewis, 56 Tom Stincic; CB - 37 Ike Thomas; S - 41 Charlie Waters. *Specialists:* K - 83 Mike Clark; P - 10 Ron Widby*. *DNP:* 14 Craig Morton (QB), 79 Forrest Gregg (T), 31 Gloster Richardson (WR).

Miami
Offense: WR - 89 Karl Noonan, 82 Otto Stowe; TE - 88 Jim Mandich; T - 79 Wayne Moore; C - 62 Jim Langer; RB - 31 Terry Cole, 32 Hubert Ginn, 22 Eugene Morris. *Defense:* DE - 86 Vern Den Herder; DT - 71 Frank Cornish; LB - 53 Bob Matheson, 56 Jesse Powell; CB - 26 Lloyd Mumphord; S - 48 Bob Petrella. *Specialists:* K - 1 Garo Yepremian; P - 20 Larry Seiple. *DNP:* 10 George Mira (QB), 74 John Richardson (DT).

COACHING STAFFS

Dallas

Head Coach: Tom Landry. *Offense:* Ray Renfro (passing, receivers), Jim Myers (offensive line), Dan Reeves (backs). *Defense:* Ernie Stautner (head defense), Jerry Tubbs (linebackers), Bobby Franklin (defensive backs). *Special Assistant:* Ermal Allen.

Miami

Head Coach: Don Shula. *Offense:* Howard Schnellenberger (head offense, receivers), Monte Clark (offensive line), Carl Taseff (backs). *Defense:* Bill Arnsparger (head defense, linebackers), Mike Scarry (defensive line), Tom Keane (defensive backs).

three passes for 39 yards to give the Dolphins a first down at the Dallas 24. Wide receiver Paul Warfield ran a sideline-and-up route and beat safety Cornell Green, but the pass was underthrown at the 5. That gave Green enough time to scramble back into the play and tip the ball away from Warfield.

Warfield had caught 12 passes for 187 yards for the Browns in Cleveland's two playoff victories over the Cowboys in the late 1960s. President Richard Nixon, an avid football fan who knew Shula, phoned the Dolphins coach the night the Super Bowl pairing was decided and suggested that a down-and-in to Warfield might work in New Orleans.

However, the Cowboys spent much of the game with Green behind cornerback Mel Renfro and over the top of Warfield. "They made sure that under any circumstances we wouldn't be able to catch that pass," said Warfield, who was limited to four receptions for 39 yards. Another reason why Dallas could double-cover Warfield was its confidence that former Packer Herb Adderley, who arrived via trade in 1970, would shut down receiver Howard Twilley. He had one catch for 20 yards.

"Think about the Yankees, how they used to bring in someone like Johnny Mize," Brandt said. "What takes place is players get the feeling that you're bringing in somebody special, that you're really trying to help them win. They saw us bring in Ditka, Alworth, Adderley, Gregg. Those guys were kind of the cream on a pretty good team."

Griese's play-action passes fooled no one because Miami's three-pronged ground game, ranked first in the NFL at 173.5 yards per game,

had been rendered null and void. Just as the Cowboys aimed to confuse on offense with their pre-snap shifting and constant motion, the Flex defense that Landry introduced in the 1960s also proved to be a problem for the Dolphins' relatively youthful offensive line. Described by Shula as "a revolutionary-type defense," the Cowboys would line up with one defensive lineman tight to the line, a second maybe a yard off, a third tight to the line, and a fourth maybe a yard off.

"The Flex is the reason why Csonka did nothing against us," safety Waters said. "It took us almost three years of playing the Flex before we finally understood just what our positions were . . . [and] those offensive guys had no clue how to defeat it. . . . There was no way [the Dolphins] were going to run the ball on us."

In modern football, analysts speak frequently of bringing one of the safeties into the box to build an eight-man front. Free safety Cliff Harris was the eighth man in the box on Super Sunday. "Because we could play man to man with Herb and Mel, two of the best cover corners in the history of the NFL, we could sometimes leave those guys isolated and let Cliff get involved in the running game," Waters explained. "Landry used Cliff like an extra linebacker because he was so aggressive. Cliff was a critical component in that ball game."

Seven starters on the Dallas defense that ranked third in 1971 had been starting for at least six seasons, including linemen Andrie and Lilly, linebackers Dave Edwards, Howley, and Jordan, and Renfro and Green. Given all that seasoning, the Cowboys hardly needed an extra edge, but they had one nevertheless.

Starting in the mid-1960s, Dallas became the first team to use computers in collegiate scouting. After developing and assigning specific numerical values for each position, the Cowboys relied on the computerized results to make some of their selections later in the draft. They also used the computers to break down their opponents with statistical analysis. With two weeks to dissect the club's primitive printouts, Jordan discerned that the Dolphins' wide receivers lined up six or seven yards closer in on runs than on passes. The predictability factor did the Dolphins' ground game no good.

"People more or less laughed at us," Brandt said. "The concept of computers was a million years away. But Tom was a great believer and utilized that tool. We had a much more comprehensive game plan than other people did."

Early in the fourth quarter, Howley baited Griese into a third-and-4 interception on a pass intended for running back Jim Kiick in the right flat. On two earlier third downs, Howley stayed back and watched as Kiick made the catch for less than the required yardage. This time, Howley played for that same route, intercepted easily, and should have had a 50-yard touchdown, but he staggered and fell at the 9.

Three plays later, Buoniconti blitzed up the middle, but Staubach stepped away to his right and zipped a 7-yard touchdown pass to Mike Ditka in the right corner.

About 10 minutes remained and the only drama was who would be chosen MVP. *Sport* magazine was in charge of the award, so one of its representatives polled a group of writers in the press box. One of them, Paul Zimmerman, would later write that Thomas was the overwhelming choice of the writers, yet Larry Klein, the editor of the magazine, announced that the winner was Staubach—no doubt because he didn't know how Thomas would behave at an awards shindig planned for New York. Unhappy with his $20,000 salary, Thomas had refused to speak to reporters all season after his July 30 trade to New England fell through and the Cowboys took him back.

"Probably Duane Thomas' attitude toward the media during Super Bowl week got me the MVP," Staubach said. "Duane was the guy Miami couldn't stop. He had a great game, but they probably said, 'Well, Roger did OK, so let's give it to him.'"

Thomas, who had 95 yards in 19 carries, shocked Tom Brookshier of CBS by deciding to break his silence in the hubbub of the locker-room celebration.

"Duane, you don't look that fast the way you run, but then you're able to outrun the defensive players," Brookshier said. "Are you really that fast?"

"Evidently," replied Thomas.

Two weeks later, Thomas was arrested for possession of marijuana. He pleaded guilty, received five years probation, and was traded to the Chargers on July 30.

TEAM STATISTICS

DALLAS		MIAMI
23	Total First Downs	10
15	Rushing	3
8	Passing	7
0	Penalty	0
352	Total Net Yardage	185
69	Total Offensive Plays	44
5.1	Avg. Gain per Offensive Play	4.2
48	Rushes	20
252	Yards Gained Rushing (Net)	80
5.3	Average Yards per Rush	4.0
19	Passes Attempted	23
12	Passes Completed	12
0	Passes Intercepted	1
2	Tackled Attempting to Pass	1
19	Yards Lost Attempting to Pass	29
100	Yards Gained Passing (Net)	105
7/14	Third-Down Efficiency	2/9
1/1	Fourth-Down Efficiency	0/0
5	Punts	5
37.2	Average Distance	40.0
1	Punt Returns	1
-1	Punt Return Yardage	21
2	Kickoff Returns	5
34	Kickoff Return Yardage	122
41	Interception Return Yardage	0
1	Fumbles	2
0	Own Fumbles Recovered	0
2	Opponent Fumbles Recovered	1
3	Penalties	0
15	Yards Penalized	0
3	Touchdowns	0
1	Rushing	0
2	Passing	0
0	Returns	0
3	Extra Points Made	0
1	Field Goals Made	1
1	Field Goals Attempted	2
0	Safeties	0
24	Total Points Scored	3
39:12	Time of Possession	20:48

"Duane Thomas was a very, very good running back," Brandt said. "He would have been a great player had he not gone off the deep end, so to speak."

But Thomas was just one part of the Cowboys' methodical, disciplined machine. It was the Cowboys' long-awaited day in the sun.

DALLAS

Passing	CP/ATT	YDS	TD	INT	RAT
Staubach	12/19	119	2	0	115.9

Rushing	ATT	YDS	AVG	TD	LG
D. Thomas	19	95	5.0	1	23
Garrison	14	74	5.3	0	17
Hill	7	25	3.6	0	13
Staubach	5	18	3.6	0	5
Ditka	1	17	17.0	0	17
Hayes	1	16	16.0	0	16
Reeves	1	7	7.0	0	7

Receiving	NO	YDS	AVG	TD	LG
D. Thomas	3	17	5.7	0	11
Alworth	2	28	14.0	1	21
Ditka	2	28	14.0	1	21
Hayes	2	23	11.5	0	18
Garrison	2	11	5.5	0	7
Hill	1	12	12.0	0	12

Interceptions	NO	YDS	LG	TD
Howley	1	41	41	0

Punting	NO	AVG	LG	BLK
Widby	5	37.2	47	0

Punt Ret.	NO/FC	YDS	LG	TD
Hayes	1/1	-1	1	0
Harris	0/2	0	--	0

Kickoff Ret.	NO	YDS	LG	TD
I. Thomas	1	23	23	0
Waters	1	11	11	0

Defense	SOLO	AST	TOT	SK
Harris	8	2	10	0
Jordan	5	1	6	0
Lilly	3	3	6	1
Green	4	1	5	0
Edwards	2	2	4	0
Cole	2	1	3	0
Lewis	1	2	3	0
Pugh	1	2	3	0
Howley	2	0	2	0
Renfro	2	0	2	0
Andrie	1	1	2	0
Waters	1	1	2	0
Adderley	1	0	1	0
Gregory	1	0	1	0
T. Thomas	1	0	1	0
Toomay	1	0	1	0
Welch	0	1	1	0
TOTAL	36	17	53	1

MIAMI

Passing	CP/ATT	YDS	TD	INT	RAT
Griese	12/23	134	0	1	51.7

Rushing	ATT	YDS	AVG	TD	LG
Kiick	10	40	4.0	0	9
Csonka	9	40	4.4	0	12
Griese	1	0	0.0	0	0

Receiving	NO	YDS	AVG	TD	LG
Warfield	4	39	9.8	0	23
Kiick	3	21	7.0	0	11
Csonka	2	18	9.0	0	16
Fleming	1	27	27.0	0	27
Twilley	1	20	20.0	0	20
Mandich	1	9	9.0	0	9

Interceptions	NO	YDS	LG	TD
None	--	--	--	--

Punting	NO	AVG	LG	BLK
Seiple	5	40.0	45	0

Punt Ret.	NO/FC	YDS	LG	TD
Scott	1/0	21	21	0

Kickoff Ret.	NO	YDS	LG	TD
Morris	4	90	37	0
Ginn	1	32	32	0

Defense	SOLO	AST	TOT	SK
Kolen	9	4	13	0
Anderson	8	4	12	0
Buoniconti	7	5	12	0
Fernandez	6	4	10	1
Heinz	4	5	9	0
Swift	2	7	9	0
Riley	5	2	7	1
Scott	2	5	7	0
Johnson	4	2	6	0
Foley	4	1	5	0
Stanfill	2	2	4	0
Mumphord	2	0	2	0
Den Herder	1	1	2	0
Matheson	1	1	2	0
TOTAL	57	43	100	2

"It meant so much to a team that couldn't win the big one for four years," Landry said. "I remember Dave Edwards came up to me and said, 'Hey, Coach, if we're not ready, we're never going to be ready.' Those players, for that game, they really knew they could win. And they went out and won."

VII

MIAMI DOLPHINS 14, WASHINGTON REDSKINS 7

January 14, 1973
Memorial Coliseum, Los Angeles, California

The seed for the Miami Dolphins' perfect season in 1972 had been planted 12 months earlier at Tulane Stadium after their crushing loss to the Dallas Cowboys in Super Bowl VI. Those beaten Dolphins, 18 of whom would start in Super Bowl VII against the Washington Redskins, remembered well what coach Don Shula had told them in the aftermath of the 24–3 rout in New Orleans.

"I think that's when we all came together for what was going to happen for the next two years," Shula recalled years later. "What I stressed in the locker room was that we wanted to make sure that this never happened again. Our goal the next year, and the following year, was not to get to the Super Bowl but to win the Super Bowl."

On the first day of training camp in 1972, Shula made his players watch the film of that Super Bowl defeat—not once, but twice.

"The commitment was made that we were going to go back to the Super Bowl and win it," wide receiver Paul Warfield said. "We had grown up—we were ready to win."

Shula had a brilliant coaching staff headed by defensive coordinator Bill Arnsparger and offensive line coach Monte Clark. His offense, a mix of Larry Csonka's two-arms-around-the-ball brute force and Warfield's breathtaking athleticism, was superb.

His so-called No Name Defense would go for weeks without making a single mistake.

With their 14–0 record in the regular season, these Dolphins won the American Football Conference (AFC) East Division by seven games over the New York Jets. They arrived at the Coliseum after tough playoff victories over Cleveland and Pittsburgh to find themselves as a 2-point underdog against the Redskins, which were 13–3 after dispatching Green Bay and Dallas with surprising ease.

Oddsmakers and many football people alike

Attendance: 90,182
Conditions: 84 degrees, sunny and hazy, wind E at 9 mph
Time of kickoff: 12:49 p.m. (PST)
Length of game: 2 hours, 40 minutes
Referee: Tommy Bell

MVP: Jake Scott, S, Dolphins

still clung to the belief that the established National Football Conference (NFC) was the better of the two conferences. Despite what the Jets and Chiefs had achieved a few years earlier, it wouldn't be until Super Bowl VIII that a team from the upstart AFC would enter a Super Bowl as the favorite.

"If we had lost the Super Bowl everything else we had accomplished would have been wasted," Shula said. "It was hard to ignore the fact that every time you heard the name 'Dolphins' people would label us 'losers' and 'chokers.'"

On a smoggy, 84-degree afternoon, the Dolphins weren't exceptional by any means. They turned the ball over twice and outgained the Redskins by merely 253–228, yet their 14–7 victory over Washington's "Over the Hill Gang" was never in doubt. Only the madcap attempted pass by Cypriot kicker Garo Yepremian, which led to a 49-yard fumble return for a touchdown by Redskin Mike Bass, denied Miami a shutout.

"It's ironic—in a 17–0 perfect season the score should have been 17–0," Shula would say later. "That game should have been a lot more [one-sided] than the score [14–7] indicated. We just completely dominated it. They didn't come close to scoring a touchdown."

The architect of this aging roster in Washington, George Allen, was hired in 1971 after Vince Lombardi died of stomach cancer. Although Allen posted a 49–19–4 record with the Los Angeles Rams from 1966 to 1970, Rams owner Daniel Reeves eventually fired Allen because he was high-maintenance and

	1	2	3	4	Final
Miami Dolphins	7	7	0	0	14
Washington Redskins	0	0	0	7	7

SCORING SUMMARY

1st Quarter
MIA   Twilley, 28-yd. pass from Griese (Yepremian kick)
2nd Quarter
MIA   Kiick, 1-yd. run (Yepremian kick)
4th Quarter
WAS   Bass, 49-yd. fumble recovery return (Knight kick)

deemed not worth the trouble.

Allen's mantra, "The future is now," went with him to the nation's capital after he was given carte blanche control by Redskins owner Edward Bennett Williams. According to Marv Levy, his special-teams coach, "Before the first draft he had traded away 22 draft choices covering several years." After each victory, Allen would lead his seasoned warriors in with "Hail to the Redskins," the team's fight song.

Based on Yepremian's season-long marksmanship, his field-goal try from 42 yards was about a 50-50 proposition. At that point, with just more than 2 minutes left, the Dolphins' minds were perhaps on their post-game party.

Howard Kindig's snap to holder Earl Morrall was low. The side-winding Yepremian hit the ball dead-on, but it went low and directly into the charging torso of Redskins defensive tackle Bill Brundige. It was the 15th placekick or punt blocked that season by the Redskins' special teams, ably coached by Levy.

The ball bounded back and slightly to Yepremian's right, where he fielded it on the second hop. With Brundige descending upon him and the ball plopped in his right hand like a loaf of bread, Yepremian attempted to heave a pass at some friendly helmet downfield. When the ball went nowhere but a few feet above his head, Yepremian batted it forward. Bass leaped to haul it in and sprinted down the sideline for a touchdown.

"Jokingly, we said, 'If we can just find a way to get the ball in Yepremian's hands again . . . ,'" Levy said 30 years later.

Yepremian had gained a measure of respect not normally granted to diminutive foreign-born kickers when he refused to cross the picket line in 1970, even though at the time he didn't have a job. Still, being well liked didn't earn Yepremian much of a reprieve.

"That one play took a team that was being totally dominated and put them back into contention. We should have shut them out, and he put them into position to ruin possibly the greatest season in the history of the NFL," middle linebacker Nick Buoniconti said. "I pictured this whole awful scenario where Washington was going to have the opportunity to tie the game. If I had a rope, I would have hanged Garo right then and there."

Now Allen had a decision: kick away or attempt an onside kick. With three timeouts remaining, Allen trusted his defense. Shula permitted Bob Griese to pass once, and his 11-yard completion to Warfield did generate a first down. But the Dolphins were soon forced to punt and Larry Seiple, the hero of the Pittsburgh Steelers playoff game with a 37-yard run from punt formation, was fortunate to get off a 40-yard boot against a heavy rush. The Redskins started from their 30 with 1:14 left.

A heavy blitz team, the Dolphins put aside their mediocre four-man rush and swarmed Billy Kilmer. Under pressure from end Bill Stanfill, the Dolphins' lone Pro Bowl defensive lineman, Kilmer threw incomplete on second down after a first-down swing pass also misfired.

Stanfill then corralled Larry Brown for a loss of 4 on a third-down completion. Then he roared around left tackle Terry Hermeling to sack Kilmer as time expired. Kilmer, with his single-bar helmet knocked from his head on the play, trudged off knowing the Redskins had failed to capture their first NFL championship since 1942.

"Thankfully, our defense played well at the end when they had to," said Shula.

Shula had coached two previous Super Bowl losers: the Colts team that had been shocked by the Jets in Super Bowl III, and the young Dolphins who had been outclassed by Dallas in Super Bowl VI. The experiences had been painful, but Shula had by this time learned how to deal with the unusual two-week gap and media-saturated buildup to the big game. Though he had been a short-tempered bundle of nerves in many of the Dolphins practices during the two-week run-up, Shula came across as being in complete control during his media appearances.

Allen, who had never coached in the Super Bowl, complained daily about the "distractions" that kept him from his feverish work schedule. The Redskins boss was so "uptight," to use one of Shula's words, that two days before the game he dispatched an associate to the Coliseum to check the angles and brightness of the sun at kickoff, which was to be at 12:30 p.m. local time.

"We got out there and had great practices up until Wednesday," defensive line coach LaVern "Torgy" Torgeson said years later, "but our players were stale by the time we played. We'd never been there before and didn't know quite how to handle it. The players became bored, I guess. We made a mistake by getting ready for the game too quick."

According to Arnsparger, the focus of Miami's defense was Larry Brown, a reckless, relentless runner who had been the NFC's leading rusher with 1,216 yards. The Dolphins weren't worried about Kilmer, an all-time competitor who didn't have a whole lot of talent. He had become the Redskins' spiritual leader, filling in for the injured Sonny Jurgensen. Bobby Beathard, the Dolphins' youthful director of player personnel who also contributed on game days by helping in the bench area with special teams, remembered being overjoyed that it was Kilmer and not the aging Jurgensen behind center.

"We were a younger, faster team," Beathard said. "Lloyd Mumphord was the one corner who could run, but everybody on defense was always in the right place at the right time. Arnsparger did such a great job preparing those guys. Buoniconti once told me that it was almost eerie when 'Arns' called the defense because it was like he knew what the play was going to be. . . . He said it was a great feeling to have someone like Arnsparger there."

It wasn't only near the goal

MIAMI DOLPHINS (AFC, 14–0)			WASHINGTON REDSKINS (NFC, 11–3)	
		Offense		
42	Paul Warfield* (6-0, 188)	WR	42	Charley Taylor* (6-2, 210)
79	Wayne Moore (6-6, 265)	LT	75	Terry Hermeling (6-5, 255)
67	Bob Kuechenberg (6-2, 248)	LG	73	Paul Laaveg (6-4, 250)
62	Jim Langer (6-2, 250)	C	56	Len Hauss* (6-2, 235)
66	Larry Little* (6-1, 265)	RG	60	John Wilbur (6-3, 251)
73	Norm Evans* (6-5, 250)	RT	76	Walter Rock (6-5, 255)
80	Marv Fleming (6-4, 232)	TE	87	Jerry Smith (6-3, 208)
81	Howard Twilley (5-10, 185)	WR	80	Roy Jefferson (6-2, 195)
12	Bob Griese (6-1, 190)	QB	17	Billy Kilmer* (6-0, 204)
21	Jim Kiick (5-11, 214)	RB	43	Larry Brown* (5-11, 195)
39	Larry Csonka* (6-2, 237)	RB	31	Charley Harraway (6-2, 215)
		Defense		
83	Vern Den Herder (6-6, 250)	LE	79	Ron McDole (6-4, 265)
75	Manny Fernandez (6-2, 250)	LT	77	Bill Brundige (6-5, 270)
72	Bob Heinz (6-6, 265)	RT	72	Diron Talbert (6-5, 255)
84	Bill Stanfill* (6-5, 250)	RE	89	Verlon Biggs (6-4, 275)
59	Doug Swift (6-3, 226)	LLB	32	Jack Pardee (6-2, 225)
85	Nick Buoniconti* (5-11, 220)	MLB	66	Myron Pottios (6-2, 230)
57	Mike Kolen (6-2, 220)	RLB	55	Chris Hanburger* (6-2, 218)
26	Lloyd Mumphord (5-10, 176)	LCB	37	Pat Fischer (5-9, 170)
45	Curtis Johnson (6-1, 196)	RCB	41	Mike Bass (6-0, 190)
40	Dick Anderson* (6-2, 196)	SS	23	Brig Owens (5-11, 190)
13	Jake Scott* (6-0, 188)	FS	22	Roosevelt Taylor (5-11, 186)

* Pro Bowl selection

SUBSTITUTIONS

Miami

Offense: WR - 86 Marlin Briscoe; TE - 88 Jim Mandich; T - 77 Doug Crusan; G/C - 54 Howard Kindig; QB - 15 Earl Morrall; RB - 32 Hubert Ginn, 28 Ed Jenkins, 23 Charles Leigh, 22 Eugene Morris*. *Defense:* DT - 65 Maulty Moore; LB - 51 Larry Ball, 53 Bob Matheson, 56 Jesse Powell; CB - 47 Henry Stuckey; S - 49 Charlie Babb. *Specialists:* K - 1 Garo Yepremian; P - 29 Larry Seiple. *DNP:* 82 Otto Stowe (WR).

Washington

Offense: WR - 81 Mack Alston, 85 Clifton McNeil; C - 58 George Burman; QB - 18 Sam Wyche; RB - 26 Bob Brunet, 25 Mike Hull, 28 Herb Mul-Key. *Defense:* DE - 68 Mike Fanucci; DT - 64 Manny Sistrunk; LB - 53 Harold McClinton, 67 Rusty Tillman; CB - 29 Ted Vactor; S - 13 Alvin Haymond, 48 John Jaqua, 44 Jeff Severson. *Specialists:* K - 5 Curt Knight; P - 4 Mike Bragg. *DNP:* 62 Ray Schoenke (G).

Miami

Head Coach: Don Shula. *Offense:* Howard Schnellenger (head offense, receivers), Monte Clark (offensive line), Carl Taseff (backs). *Defense:* Bill Arnsparger (head defense, linebackers), Mike Scarry (defensive line), Tom Keane (defensive backs).

Washington

Head Coach: George Allen. *Offense:* Boyd Dowler (receivers), Mike McCormack (offensive line), Ted Marchibroda (backfield), Charley Waller (backs). *Defense:* Charley Winner (head defense), LaVern Torgeson (defensive line). *Special Teams:* Marv Levy. *Special Assignments:* Joe Sullivan.

line where the Dolphins excelled. The Redskins' dynamic Brown was the MVP during the regular season, but would finish with just 72 yards in 22 carries that day, clearly representing a job very well done by Miami. His long gain was just 11 yards, and Kilmer's longest completion was only 15.

"Our problem was running," Allen said. "We thought we could run but couldn't. We had planned to throw some at Mumphord but we had to run first to do it. We did not seem to have the spark we had against Green Bay and Dallas. You have to get adjusted to the carnival atmosphere of the game."

Miami, with Csonka and Eugene "Mercury" Morris in the backfield, had become the first team in NFL history to have two 1,000-yard rushers. Csonka bulled 15 times for 112 yards, while Morris and Jim Kiick combined for 72 in 22 attempts against the aging Redskins defense.

The Dolphins rushed 37 times, compared to just 13 dropbacks for Griese, who hit 8 of 11 passes for 88 yards and was sacked twice. His only big completion came on a nine-step drop late in the first quarter, when Howard Twilley beat Pat Fischer on a post-corner route for a 28-yard touchdown.

That Miami offensive line protected Griese for 4.4 seconds on the touchdown pass. From left to right, starters Wayne Moore, Bob Kuechenberg, Jim Langer, Larry Little, and Norm Evans all had been released by other teams before being molded into a fiercely effective group by Clark, a great tackle in the 1960s who joined Shula's staff in 1970.

"Monte did a fabulous job," Beathard said.

"Larry Little was a hell of an athlete. Those three inside guys were especially good. Wayne was a better athlete than Norm but Norm was just a real steady right-tackle type. It was a smart, cohesive group."

Midway through the second quarter, a 47-yard touchdown strike from Griese to Warfield behind Fischer was wiped out when the wide receiver on the other side, Marlin Briscoe, was flagged for illegal procedure. That disappointment faded quickly, however, when the defense went back to work.

Using both 4-3 and 3-4 defenses, the Dolphins kept beating the Redskins' blockers to the punch. Manny Fernandez, a 250-pound defensive tackle, was too quick for center Len Hauss and ended up making 17 tackles. Many football people felt that Fernandez deserved the MVP award more than Jake Scott, whose two interceptions led to no points.

"It was the game of his life," Buoniconti said of Fernandez. "They were intent on blocking me with two men [assuming] they could handle Manny one-on-one. Manny was very quick and he'd get into their backfield before they could react and tackle Brown. He beat Hauss like a drum."

The Redskins were so neutralized offensively that they didn't cross the 50-yard line until roughly two minutes remained in the first half. With Washington facing third and 3, Arnsparger inserted No. 53, Bob Matheson, a combination linebacker-defensive end for whom the Dolphins' innovative "53" defense was named. Shortly after acquiring Matheson from the Browns for a second-round draft choice in September 1971, Arnsparger spent 7 to 10 days trying to make a full-time rush end out of him. Later, Arnsparger would convince Shula to play Matheson standing up on the line over the tight end in a 3-4 alignment.

"Bob Matheson's great ability gave us a whole new concept of defense that was very successful," Shula said. "He was big enough to effectively rush the passer and agile enough to drop off into coverage. He weighed 230, 235, and probably ran a 4.6, 4.7. He was a wonderful player."

As Matheson's career developed, Arnsparger played him more on the weak side with Doug Swift over the tight end, but the Dolphins' most effective rush in this Super Bowl came with Swift lined up inside and Matheson lined up outside. On the first play after the two-minute warning, this alignment led to a key turnover for the Dolphins.

On third and 3, Swift drove untouched through the A-gap to the inside of right guard John Wilbur, who was turned outside toward Matheson. Swift crashed into Kilmer just as he released a pass over the middle toward Brown. The pass went straight to Buoniconti, who returned 32 yards to the Redskins 27. That set up Kiick's 1-yard touchdown run, making it 14–0 at halftime.

"We were in a 1-coverage, which meant I had the tight end, Jerry Smith," Buoniconti said. "Because Smith was tied up, I was free to react to Kilmer and go with Brown. I should not have been there."

The Redskins played much better in the second half on both offense and defense, but they weren't able to make any plays in the red zone against a defense that wouldn't give away anything. According to Buoniconti, Arnsparger later told him the defense had an amazingly low 13 mental breakdowns for the entire season.

The Redskins' 10-play, 45-yard drive to open the third quarter ended when Fernandez sacked Kilmer and Curt Knight missed a field goal from the 32. The most critical play came a few plays earlier on a play-action pass from Kilmer at the 17. A stumbling Charley Taylor should have made the catch at the 3, but failed to do so.

Miami's only threat of the second half came after safety Roosevelt Taylor ducked his head and allowed Csonka to run over him for a 49-yard gainer to the Washington 16. Five plays later, Griese blew it on second and goal at the 5 by underthrowing tight end Marv Fleming in the end-zone corner, allowing safety Brig Owens to make a leaping interception.

The Redskins mustered a 79-yard, 14-play march in the fourth quarter that consumed 7½ minutes but produced no points. Jerry Smith appeared set to catch a 10-yard pass in the back of the end zone on second down, but Kilmer's pass clanged off the crossbar (the goalposts were positioned on the goal line) and fell incomplete.

Still shaking his head in disgust, Kilmer went back into the middle of the field on third down, even though Charley Taylor was covered stride-for-stride by Mumphord, and Stanfill was rushing into his face. As usual, Scott was free and Kilmer's awful throw went straight to him for the Dolphins'

third interception.

So the Dolphins' perfect season—17 victories, no defeats—was preserved. They were the first team in pro football to finish undefeated since 1948, when the Cleveland Browns went 14–0 in the All-America Football Conference (AAFC) and then beat Buffalo

MIAMI	TEAM STATISTICS	WASHINGTON
12	Total First Downs	16
7	Rushing	9
5	Passing	7
0	Penalty	0
253	Total Net Yardage	228
50	Total Offensive Plays	66
5.1	Avg. Gain per Offensive Play	3.5
37	Rushes	36
184	Yards Gained Rushing (Net)	141
5.0	Average Yards per Rush	3.9
11	Passes Attempted	28
8	Passes Completed	14
1	Passes Intercepted	3
2	Tackled Attempting to Pass	2
19	Yards Lost Attempting to Pass	17
69	Yards Gained Passing (Net)	87
3/11	Third-Down Efficiency	3/13
0/0	Fourth-Down Efficiency	0/1
7	Punts	5
43	Average Distance	31.2
2	Punt Returns	4
4	Punt Return Yardage	9
2	Kickoff Returns	3
33	Kickoff Return Yardage	45
95	Interception Return Yardage	0
2	Fumbles	1
1	Own Fumbles Recovered	1
0	Opponent Fumbles Recovered	1
3	Penalties	3
35	Yards Penalized	25
2	Touchdowns	1
1	Rushing	0
1	Passing	0
0	Returns	1
2	Extra Points Made	1
0	Field Goals Made	0
1	Field Goals Attempted	1
0	Safeties	0
14	Total Points Scored	7
27:29	Time of Possession	32:31

MIAMI

Passing	CP/ATT	YDS	TD	INT	RAT
Griese	8/11	88	1	1	88.5

Rushing	ATT	YDS	AVG	TD	LG
Csonka	15	112	7.5	0	49
Kiick	12	38	3.2	1	8
Morris	10	34	3.4	0	6

Receiving	NO	YDS	AVG	TD	LG
Warfield	3	36	12.0	0	18
Kiick	2	6	3.0	0	4
Twilley	1	28	28.0	1	28t
Mandich	1	19	19.0	0	19
Csonka	1	-1	-1.0	0	-1

Interceptions	NO	YDS	LG	TD
Scott	2	63	55	0
Buoniconti	1	32	32	0

Punting	NO	AVG	LG	BLK
Seiple	7	43.0	50	0

Punt Ret.	NO/FC	YDS	LG	TD
Scott	2/2	4	4	0
Anderson	0/1	0	--	0

Kickoff Ret.	NO	YDS	LG	TD
Morris	2	33	17	0

Defense	SOLO	AST	TOT	SK
Fernandez	6	4	10	1
Den Herder	4	5	9	0
Kolen	6	1	7	0
Anderson	5	2	7	0
Mumphord	4	2	6	0
Matheson	3	3	6	0
Stanfill	3	1	4	1
Ginn	3	0	3	0
Heinz	3	0	3	0
Buoniconti	2	1	3	0
Mandich	2	1	3	0
Johnson	2	0	2	0
Scott	2	0	2	0
Swift	2	0	2	0
Stuckey	1	0	1	0
Ball	0	1	1	0
TOTAL	**48**	**21**	**69**	**2**

WASHINGTON

Passing	CP/ATT	YDS	TD	INT	RAT
Kilmer	14/28	104	0	3	19.6

Rushing	ATT	YDS	AVG	TD	LG
Brown	22	72	3.3	0	11
Harraway	10	37	3.7	0	8
Kilmer	2	18	9.0	0	9
C. Taylor	1	8	8.0	0	8
Smith	1	6	6.0	0	6

Receiving	NO	YDS	AVG	TD	LG
Jefferson	5	50	10.0	0	15
Brown	5	26	5.2	0	12
C. Taylor	2	20	10.0	0	15
Smith	1	11	11.0	0	11
Harraway	1	-3	-3.0	0	-3

Interceptions	NO	YDS	LG	TD
Owens	1	0	0	0

Punting	NO	AVG	LG	BLK
Bragg	5	31.2	38	0

Punt Ret.	NO/FC	YDS	LG	TD
Haymond	4/0	9	7	0
Vactor	0/2	0	--	0

Kickoff Ret.	NO	YDS	LG	TD
Haymond	2	30	18	0
Mul-Key	1	15	15	0

Defense	SOLO	AST	TOT	SK
Biggs	5	1	6	1
Pardee	5	1	6	0
Hanburger	4	2	6	0
McDole	4	2	6	0
Owens	4	1	5	0
Pottios	4	1	5	0
Talbert	4	1	5	1
Fischer	3	0	3	0
Bass	2	1	3	0
R. Taylor	2	1	3	0
Sistrunk	2	0	2	0
Alston	1	0	1	0
Brunet	1	0	1	0
Harraway	1	0	1	0
Hermeling	1	0	1	0
Tillman	1	0	1	0
Wilbur	1	0	1	0
Vactor	0	1	1	0
TOTAL	**45**	**12**	**57**	**2**

in the championship game, 49–7.

In a prophetic summation, *Sports Illustrated*'s Tex Maule wrote, "No other team has ever gone undefeated for a season, and no other club is likely to do it again soon, either."

The Redskins would return to the Super Bowl 11 years later under Joe Gibbs. Meanwhile, the Dolphins were just getting started.

VIII
MIAMI DOLPHINS 24, MINNESOTA VIKINGS 7

January 13, 1974
Rice Stadium, Houston, Texas

Outmuscled. Outcoached. Out of the game right from the start.

"This should be the best Super Bowl game of all because the teams are so good and so evenly matched," Minnesota Vikings coach Bud Grant said 48 hours before the kickoff of Super Bowl VIII. In the end, the Vikings lacked the physical strength and the coaching creativity to compete against the Miami Dolphins. The Dolphins' 24–7 victory at Rice Stadium gave them back-to-back Super Bowl triumphs and validated Miami as one of the truly special teams in NFL history.

"We completely dominated," coach Don Shula said. "Csonka was unbelievable. The Minnesota offense with Fran Tarkenton never had the ball."

When the annihilation was complete, a number of Dolphins, including Hall of Fame players Nick Buoniconti, Paul Warfield, Larry Little, and Jim Langer, all said this team was even better than the 1972 Dolphins that went 17–0, even though it had lost to Oakland (12–7) in Week 2 and Baltimore (16–3) in Week 13 to post a 12–2 record in the regular season. Judged by statistics, the 1972 team had the advantage in both point differential and yardage differential, yet the 1973 squad had been more dominant in the playoffs, dispatching three foes by an 85–33 margin, compared to the 1972 playoff margin of 55–38. The personnel on the two teams was almost exactly the same.

"This team was better than the 17–0 team and should have gone undefeated also," Buoniconti said. "We killed Cincinnati and Oakland in the playoffs and then killed Minnesota in the Super Bowl. But I would never wear the ring for Super Bowl VIII, only the one from Super Bowl VII. The win in VIII was anticlimactic."

Buoniconti wasn't the only Dolphin who viewed this Super Bowl as almost a foregone conclusion. A 7-point favorite over the Vikings, the Dolphins

Attendance: 71,882
Conditions: 50 degrees, overcast and humid, wind NE at 6 mph
Time of kickoff: 2:30 p.m. (CST)
Length of game: 2 hours, 29 minutes
Referee: Ben Dreith

MVP: Larry Csonka, RB, Dolphins

possessed an air of invincibility that permeated the organization, yet it was almost impossible to be overconfident playing for Shula, who had paid a terrible price for overconfidence when he coached Baltimore against the Jets five years earlier. "Shula probably had his team more ready than our team," Vikings offensive coach Jerry Burns said. These Dolphins had paid the price to be good, knew they were good, and were convinced that neither the Vikings nor any other team could keep them from their appointed rounds.

"There were . . . all kinds of guys who had everyone's respect on both sides of the ball," said Langer, the 25-year-old center. "What it came down to was that nobody wanted to let anybody else down. . . . We had nobody who thought he was better than the team. If we did, we'd go to the coach and say, 'Get rid of this son of a bitch. He's a problem.' We policed ourselves; the coaches didn't have to worry.

"I'd been in games when we knew that the team we were playing was better and that our only chance was if they didn't play well. In 1973, we didn't have that feeling. We knew that if we played our game there was nobody we couldn't beat. As we went into the playoffs we were, to use the old cliché, peaking at the right time. We were just like a steamroller."

When did the Vikings know they were in trouble? "After the first few plays," answered Alan Page, the Hall of Fame defensive tackle who was one of many Minnesota defenders victimized by the Dolphins' beautifully choreographed game plan.

	1	2	3	4	Final
Minnesota Vikings	0	0	0	7	7
Miami Dolphins	14	3	7	0	24

SCORING SUMMARY

1st Quarter
MIA Csonka, 5-yd. run (Yepremian kick)
MIA Kiick, 1-yd. run (Yepremian kick)
2nd Quarter
MIA Yepremian, 28-yd. FG
3rd Quarter
MIA Csonka, 2-yd. run (Yepremian kick)
4th Quarter
MIN Tarkenton, 4-yd. run (Cox kick)

The Dolphins had opened their 34–16 divisional playoff victory over the Cincinnati Bengals by driving 80 yards in 11 plays for a touchdown. They then went 64 in eight plays to start the 27–10 rout with the Raiders in the AFC Championship Game. After the Vikings kicked off in the Super Bowl, the Dolphins did pretty much the same thing, mounting a 10-play, 62-yard drive capped by Csonka's 5-yard touchdown run. On the march, the Dolphins rushed eight times for 43 yards, and Bob Griese completed his two passes for 19 yards.

When the Vikings quickly went three and out, the Dolphins drove 56 yards in 10 plays to set up Jim Kiick, who catapulted over for a 1-yard touchdown. That second drive, almost a mirror image of the first, contained eight rushes for 35 yards and two-of-two passing by Griese for 21 yards. The first quarter still wasn't over, but for all intents and purposes, the game was.

"Our offensive linemen—guys like Jim Langer, Larry Little, and Bob Kuechenberg—just dominated the line of scrimmage against the Vikings' 'Purple People Eaters,'" Griese said. "Before the game, everyone was talking about Minnesota's defensive line, guys like Jim Marshall and Alan Page. If you look at it, our line was probably the heart of our team; our whole attack was structured around it. We ended up winning 24–7, but the score didn't really sum up how one-sided the game was."

The Vikings had caught a break in the NFC Championship Game when the Cowboys' Calvin Hill, the NFL's third-leading rusher with 1,142 yards, didn't play because of a dislocated elbow. Partly due to this, the Cowboys gained merely 80 yards on the ground, 92.7 below their average, and the Vikings, a 1-point underdog, rolled at Texas Stadium, 27–10. "Dallas was more of a finesse team," Vikings middle linebacker Jeff Siemon said. "We probably matched up a little bit better against them."

Left end Carl Eller, Page, and Siemon gave the Vikings three Pro Bowl players in the front seven. Page's quickness off the ball was superlative; Shula called him perhaps the best defensive lineman in football. Eller, another future Hall of Famer, had a team-high 11 sacks. Jim Marshall, the 36-year-old right end, also could run. Left tackle Gary Larsen had been to the Pro Bowl in 1969 and 1970. Roy Winston, 33, and Wally Hilgenberg, 31, had been starting together at outside linebacker since 1968.

The Vikings always pursued hard and ran to the football. "The Vikings were a very good, vicious team," Langer said. But the Vikings also were undersized up front. Based on Siemon's estimates, the Super Bowl weights would have been 250 for Eller, 250 for Page, 265 to 270 for Larsen, 230 for Marshall, 225 for Winston and Hilgenberg, and 236 for himself.

By no means was the Dolphins' offensive line overwhelming in size. Based on program weights, the group averaged 259. What Miami did have was more explosiveness. "[The Vikings] weren't a physically strong team and we were," Langer said. "By then all of our linemen were benching 400 pounds plus and the Vikings weren't really on a weight program yet. They were great players and had great hustle, but physically they couldn't match up to us on the line. It was obvious from the beginning that our offense could overpower their defense." A maverick in the coaching ranks, Grant never employed a strength coach during his 18 seasons in the Twin Cities.

At first, the Dolphins ran misdirection plays so the Vikings' eagerness and Page's burst off the line would work against them. They also ran so-called sucker plays in which Page wouldn't even be blocked, and then one of their three running backs would slice into the hole that he had just vacated. Miami's sophisticated offensive line, coached brilliantly by Monte Clark, also set up traps in an attempt to spring Mercury Morris and Kiick around the corner. Eller and Marshall would step inside to take on the trap block, and the Dolphins backs then would bounce outside them.

"They were a smaller front but had good leverage," Siemon said. "We were a bend-but-don't-break kind of a defense but we did give up some yards. Part of it was our lack of size and part of it was our predictability. Offenses knew what defensive line charge we were going to be in most of the time. We learned how to do it very well and effectively and, against most teams, we could prevail."

Anticipating correctly that the flummoxed Vikings would stay more at home in the second half, Shula went back to a meat-and-potatoes ground game featuring man-on-man blocking. An eight-play, 43-yard touchdown drive early in the third quarter made it 24–0. The final indignity for the Vikings was when the Dolphins killed the final 6:24 by running 11 straight times for 41 yards.

Wouldn't Grant and his defensive coordinator, Neill Armstrong, have been better served if they had moved an eighth defender, perhaps strong safety Jeff Wright, up to the line in an all-out attempt to stop the run? "They did have Paul Warfield and Marlin Briscoe, both of whom were fleet, outstanding receivers and had to be respected," Siemon said. "I think it would have been a little dangerous to show them an eight-man front, but maybe less dangerous in the final analysis. We were so basic in our philosophy."

Warfield pulled a hamstring in practice on the Wednesday before and played the Super Bowl at what he described as 50 percent efficiency. Griese threw just 31 passes in the postseason, including seven against Minnesota. He completed six for 73 yards, including a 27-yard deep sideline route to a diving Warfield behind cornerback Bobby Bryant to set up the third-quarter touchdown. Of the Dolphins' 61 plays from scrimmage, that pass was the only

MINNESOTA VIKINGS (NFC, 12–2)			MIAMI DOLPHINS (AFC, 12–2)	
		Offense		
84	Carroll Dale (6-2, 200)	WR	42	Paul Warfield* (6-0, 188)
67	Grady Alderman (6-2, 247)	LT	79	Wayne Moore* (6-6, 265)
62	Ed White (6-2, 262)	LG	67	Bob Kuechenberg (6-5, 262)
53	Mick Tingelhoff (6-2, 237)	C	62	Jim Langer* (6-2, 253)
66	Frank Gallagher (6-2, 245)	RG	66	Larry Little* (6-1, 265)
73	Ron Yary* (6-5, 255)	RT	73	Norm Evans (6-5, 250)
83	Stu Voigt (6-1, 255)	TE	88	Jim Mandich (6-2, 224)
42	John Gilliam* (6-1, 195)	WR	86	Marlin Briscoe (5-11, 175)
10	Fran Tarkenton (6-0, 190)	QB	12	Bob Griese* (6-1, 190)
44	Chuck Foreman* (6-2, 216)	RB	22	Eugene Morris* (5-10, 192)
32	Oscar Reed (6-0, 222)	RB	39	Larry Csonka* (6-2, 237)
		Defense		
81	Carl Eller* (6-6, 247)	LE	83	Vern Den Herder (6-6, 252)
77	Gary Larsen (6-5, 255)	LT	75	Manny Fernandez (6-2, 250)
88	Alan Page* (6-4, 245)	RT	72	Rob Heinz (6-6, 265)
70	Jim Marshall (6-4, 240)	RE	84	Bill Stanfill* (6-5, 252)
60	Roy Winston (5-11, 222)	LLB	59	Doug Swift (6-3, 226)
50	Jeff Siemon* (6-2, 230)	MLB	85	Nick Buoniconti* (5-11, 220)
58	Wally Hilgenberg (6-3, 229)	RLB	57	Mike Kolen (6-2, 222)
43	Nate Wright (5-11, 180)	LCB	26	Lloyd Mumphord (5-10, 176)
20	Bobby Bryant (6-1, 170)	RCB	45	Curtis Johnson (6-1, 195)
23	Jeff Wright (5-11, 190)	SS	40	Dick Anderson* (6-2, 196)
22	Paul Krause* (6-3, 200)	FS	13	Jake Scott* (6-0, 188)

* Pro Bowl selection

SUBSTITUTIONS

Minnesota
Offense: WR - 89 Doug Kingsriter, 82 Jim Lash; G - 68 Chuck Goodrum; RB - 30 Bill Brown, 49 Ed Marinaro, 41 Dave Osborn. *Defense:* DE - 75 Bob Lurtsema; DT - 69 Doug Sutherland; LB - 55 Amos Martin, 52 Ron Porter; CB - 40 Charlie West; S - 24 Terry Brown. *Specialists:* K - 14 Fred Cox; P - 11 Mike Eischeid. *DNP:* 85 Gary Ballman (TE), 65 Steve Lawson (G), 51 Godfrey Zaunbrecher (C), 17 Bob Berry (QB).

Miami
Offense: WR - 81 Howard Twilley; TE - 80 Marv Fleming; T - 77 Doug Crusan; G - 64 Ed Newman; C - 55 Irv Goode; QB - 15 Earl Morrall; RB - 21 Jim Kiick, 36 Don Nottingham. *Defense:* DT - 65 Maulty Moore; LB - 51 Larry Ball, 58 Bruce Bannon, 53 Bob Matheson; CB - 25 Tim Foley, 49 Charlie Babb; S - 48 Harry Stuckey. *Specialists:* K - 1 Garo Yepremian*; P - 20 Larry Seiple. *DNP:* 34 Ron Sellers (WR).

COACHING STAFFS

Minnesota
Head Coach: Bud Grant. *Offense:* Jerry Burns (head offense), John Michels (offensive line), Bus Mertes (backs). *Defense:* Neill Armstrong (head defense), Jack Patera (defensive line), Jocko Nelson (linebackers).

Miami
Head Coach: Don Shula. *Offense:* Bill McPeak (head offense), Monte Clark (offensive line), Carl Taseff (backfield). *Defense:* Bill Arnsparger (assistant head coach), Mike Scarry (defensive line), Tom Keane (defensive backs).

one longer than 16 yards. "Everybody says that Jerry Rice is the greatest receiver," Vikings personnel director Jerry Reichow said years later. "If Paul Warfield would have been in that same West Coast offense, he'd have had statistics that you wouldn't believe."

Csonka, a battering ram of a fullback, was listed at 237 pounds, but Siemon estimated his weight as closer to 255. Joe Thomas, the Dolphins' personnel director until his departure for Baltimore in 1972, had selected Csonka with the eighth pick in the 1968 draft. This was his third straight 1,000-yard season. "I depended a great deal—I'd say 85 percent—on my offensive line for my yardage," Csonka said. "You hear about second effort, but second effort doesn't count unless you get that first shot through the line, and that's what they gave." Langer, left tackle Wayne Moore, and Little, who owned Larsen all day long, each made the Pro Bowl. Kuechenberg, a third-year starter, would go on to make six Pro Bowl appearances.

Given the ball 33 times, Csonka thundered ahead for 145 yards two weeks after hitting the Raiders with 29 carries for 117 yards and a playoff record-tying three rushing touchdowns. "With a poorer line I think Csonka would have been a more average back," Siemon said. "He was with a perfect line because they could give him some space. Then he was brutal when he got into the secondary. He had a head of steam up and would devastate defensive backs." In the three playoff games, the Dolphins averaged 234.3 yards on the ground, running on 72.3 percent of their plays.

As the opening drive unfolded, it became clear that the Vikings' only chance to win was if quarterback Fran Tarkenton had an MVP-type performance. General manager Jim Finks had reacquired Tarkenton from the New York Giants before the 1972 season in exchange for two first-round draft choices, wide receiver Bob Grim, and quarterback Norm Snead. In the Vikings' first six seasons as an expansion franchise, and then five seasons with the Giants, the teams for which Tarkenton had played posted a 62–88–4 record and never once made the playoffs. After watching Joe Kapp flounder in Super Bowl IV and then Gary Cuozzo fail in 1970 and 1971, Finks knew he had to make a move for a quarterback and brought back the still wildly exciting Tarkenton.

In 1973, the scrambling Tarkenton had a passer rating of 93.2, the best of his 13 seasons in Minnesota, but he had never even been in a playoff game before. Wanting to draft Sam Cunningham with the 12th pick that year, Finks had to switch gears when New England took the USC fullback at No. 11. Finks instead took Chuck Foreman, a multipurpose halfback from Miami. With Foreman able to run and receive in ways that more traditional Vikings backs had not, Burns could direct a multidimensional attack with new-found pizzazz.

Against Dallas, the Vikings had used a misdirection running game to pile up 203 yards, yet against Miami's quick, smart, well-conceived scheme, they were limited to 72. Tarkenton's 182 yards in the air, stemming from his Super Bowl record of 18 completions, almost were inconsequential.

Minnesota had one first down and only 27 yards in its opening three possessions. On the fourth series, Tarkenton had time to pick out John Gilliam wide open in the middle against one of the Dolphins' customary zones for a 30-yard completion to the Miami 15. Trailing 17–0, Grant then made the decision to go for it on fourth and 1. Oscar Reed followed pulling left guard Ed White off right tackle and appeared to have the first down. However, Buoniconti made a hard and fast read and accelerated into the left side of Reed's body right where the ball was positioned. The ball came loose and safety Jake Scott pounced on the recovery.

The Vikings' woes went from bad to worse when Gilliam returned the second-half kickoff 65 yards to the Miami 34, only to have the ball brought back 45 yards when Stu Voigt was detected clipping.

Two plays later, on third and 8, Tarkenton sprinted out hard to his right, but nose tackle Manny Fernandez defeated the block of center Mick Tingelhoff and sacked him for minus-6. The Vikings punted, the Dolphins drove for a clinching touchdown, and the rest was academic.

"We had an experienced group of guys; they had won one and they wanted to get another one," said Bill Arnsparger, who left a few days after the game to coach the Giants. "The key to our three years of success is we had people that really prepared and took the thing seriously during practice. Had it not been for Bob Matheson, we would not have played the three-man line. They'd put an end on him and he had the ability to beat the end. But that opened up the middle for one of the inside backers, Nick [Buoniconti] or Mike Kolen, to be in the pocket quick."

The Dolphins had no turnovers and just one penalty. About the only snafu was a fourth-quarter punt in which they had just 10 men on the field. As luck would have it, though, Larry Seiple banged the punt 57 yards before it was downed at the Minnesota 3. "I was on the field helping with special teams," Miami personnel director Bobby Beathard said. "Shula could count faster than I could, and he comes running up to me and said, 'Ten f---ing men on the field.' The guy missing was Ed Newman, a chemistry major from Duke. If I [had] had a facemask, he would have grabbed it.

"When I was around Don Shula, I always had the impression people were on their toes—everybody in the organization—because there was a fear. You respected him, you liked him, but there was a fear. There was nothing guaranteed—and I think that's healthy."

Shula's world would be altered dramatically a few months later. "I can't tell you how good I felt after that second Super Bowl," he said years later. "We were a young team, with nowhere to go but up. Then one phone call and it all changed." The call informed Shula of the decision by Warfield, Csonka, and Kiick to sign futures contracts with the World Football League. The threesome played for an 11–3 Dolphins team in 1974 that was eliminated by Oakland (28–26) on a last-second touchdown pass in its first playoff game, then they departed in the 1975 off-season. The Dolphins wouldn't win another playoff game until January 1982.

TEAM STATISTICS

MINNESOTA		MIAMI
14	Total First Downs	21
5	Rushing	13
8	Passing	4
1	Penalty	4
238	Total Net Yardage	259
54	Total Offensive Plays	61
4.4	Avg. Gain per Offensive Play	4.2
24	Rushes	53
72	Yards Gained Rushing (Net)	196
3.0	Average Yards per Rush	3.7
28	Passes Attempted	7
18	Passes Completed	6
1	Passes Intercepted	0
2	Tackled Attempting to Pass	1
16	Yards Lost Attempting to Pass	10
166	Yards Gained Passing (Net)	63
8/15	Third-Down Efficiency	4/11
0/1	Fourth-Down Efficiency	1/1
5	Punts	3
42.2	Average Distance	39.7
0	Punt Returns	3
0	Punt Return Yardage	20
4	Kickoff Returns	2
69	Kickoff Return Yardage	47
0	Interception Return Yardage	10
2	Fumbles	1
1	Own Fumbles Recovered	1
0	Opponent Fumbles Recovered	1
7	Penalties	1
65	Yards Penalized	4
1	Touchdowns	3
1	Rushing	3
0	Passing	0
0	Returns	0
1	Extra Points Made	3
0	Field Goals Made	1
0	Field Goals Attempted	1
0	Safeties	0
7	Total Points Scored	24
26:15	Time of Possession	33:45

"People look back and say we only won two Super Bowls, but you need to look beyond the numbers," safety Dick Anderson said. "Bob Griese fractured his ankle in the fifth game in 1972, and for the next 11 games Earl Morrall was our quarterback. What would those Pittsburgh teams have done if they lost Terry Bradshaw? For that two-year

MINNESOTA

Passing	CP/ATT	YDS	TD	INT	RAT
Tarkenton	18/28	182	0	1	67.9

Rushing	ATT	YDS	AVG	TD	LG
Reed	11	32	2.9	0	9
Foreman	7	18	2.6	0	5
Tarkenton	4	17	4.3	1	8
Marinaro	1	3	3.0	0	3
B. Brown	1	2	2.0	0	2

Receiving	NO	YDS	AVG	TD	LG
Foreman	5	27	5.4	0	10
Gilliam	4	44	11.0	0	30
Voigt	3	46	15.3	0	17
Marinaro	2	39	19.5	0	27
B. Brown	1	9	9.0	0	9
Kingsriter	1	9	9.0	0	9
Lash	1	9	9.0	0	9
Reed	1	-1	-1.0	0	-1

Interceptions	NO	YDS	LG	TD
None	--	--	--	--

Punting	NO	AVG	LG	BLK
Eischeid	5	42.2	48	0

Punt Ret.	NO/FC	YDS	LG	TD
Bryant	0/1	0	**	0

Kickoff Ret.	NO	YDS	LG	TD
Gilliam	2	41	21	0
West	2	28	15	0

Defense	SOLO	AST	TOT	SK
Eller	8	0	8	0
Hilgenberg	7	1	8	0
Siemon	6	2	8	0
Winston	4	3	7	0
Marshall	5	1	6	0
Krause	4	2	6	0
Larsen	3	3	6	0
Bryant	3	2	5	0
Page	3	1	4	1
J. Wright	0	3	3	0
N. Wright	1	1	2	0
T. Brown	1	0	1	0
Gilliam	1	0	1	0
Kingsriter	1	0	1	0
Porter	1	0	1	0
Sutherland	1	0	1	0
Tingelhoff	1	0	1	0
TOTAL	**50**	**19**	**69**	**1**

MIAMI

Passing	CP/ATT	YDS	TD	INT	RAT
Griese	6/7	73	0	0	110.1

Rushing	ATT	YDS	AVG	TD	LG
Csonka	33	145	4.4	2	16
Morris	11	34	3.1	0	14
Klick	7	10	1.4	1	5
Griese	2	7	3.5	0	5

Receiving	NO	YDS	AVG	TD	LG
Warfield	2	33	16.5	0	27
Mandich	2	21	10.5	0	13
Briscoe	2	19	9.5	0	13

Interceptions	NO	YDS	LG	TD
Johnson	1	10	10	0

Punting	NO	AVG	LG	BLK
Seiple	3	39.7	57	0

Punt Ret.	NO/FC	YDS	LG	TD
Scott	3/1	20	12	0

Kickoff Ret.	NO	YDS	LG	TD
Scott	2	47	31	0

Defense	SOLO	AST	TOT	SK
Fernandez	5	3	8	1
Buoniconti	4	4	8	0
Matheson	7	0	7	0
Foley	3	2	5	0
Kolen	3	2	5	0
Anderson	0	4	4	0
Scott	3	0	3	0
Stanfill	2	1	3	0
Swift	2	1	3	0
Johnson	2	0	2	0
Den Herder	1	1	2	1
Newman	1	0	1	0
TOTAL	**33**	**18**	**51**	**2**

period, I think we were the best—ever."

It had been a wonderful ride for the Dolphins while it lasted. "Nobody would have beat the Miami club the way it played in this game," Finks said that humid Sunday in Houston, "whether it was the Packers or the '27 Duluth Eskimos." Certainly, the Vikings weren't even in the Dolphins' same league.

IX

PITTSBURGH STEELERS 16, MINNESOTA VIKINGS 6

January 12, 1975
Tulane Stadium, New Orleans, Louisiana

From 1969 to 1974, the Pittsburgh Steelers drafted 15 players who would go on to make a total of 71 Pro Bowl appearances. It was the overriding reason why the NFL's losingest franchise under the benevolent ownership of Art Rooney made the transformation from dormancy to dominance. Super Bowl IX was the coming-out party for the "Super Steelers," the first of their four championships over a span of six years that lifted them past the Dallas Cowboys for coronation as "team of the decade" for the 1970s.

All that talent descended upon the Raiders in the AFC Championship Game in Oakland when the Steelers, a 5½-point underdog, produced a smashing 24–13 victory. In many ways, their 16–6 triumph over the overmatched Minnesota Vikings was almost anticlimactic as far as some Steelers were concerned. "Without doubt, [the AFC Championship Game] was the pivotal game in our whole decade," said Franco Harris, the Super Bowl MVP with 158 yards in 34 carries. "That win over Oakland showed the league and the entire country how good we were. And we proved it to ourselves."

It was the third Super Bowl in six years for coach Bud Grant, his veteran staff, and the majority of his starters, so the Vikings' vast advantage in big-game experience over the youthful Steelers kept the point spread modest at Pittsburgh by 3.

"They were kind of like a mirror image of us in the sense that they had the Purple People Eaters and a powerful running game and a real powerful quarterback," Steelers director of pro personnel Tim Rooney said. "I viewed us as a very young team and them as a very mature team with a stoic coach in Grant. Containing [Fran] Tarkenton was going to be a real big factor."

Not only did the Steelers prevent Tarkenton from running (1 carry, no yards), but they also batted down four of his passes and pressured him into an 11-for-26,

Attendance: 80,997
Conditions: 46 degrees, cloudy and cold, wind N at 17 mph
Time of kickoff: 2:00 p.m. (CST)
Length of game: 2 hours, 56 minutes
Referee: Bernie Ulman

MVP: Franco Harris, RB, Steelers

102-yard day. As magnificent as the Steelers' league-leading pass defense was, their run defense was even better. The Vikings stubbornly tried to run the ball up the middle, but one of the greatest defensive units ever assembled made mincemeat out of that plan to the tune of 21 yards in 17 rushes.

"They kicked our ass offensively," Grant's offensive coordinator, Jerry Burns, said. "We couldn't get them blocked. They were tough as hell. We didn't get the job done."

Still, despite the destructiveness of their defense and the power of their 57-carry, 249-yard ground game, the Steelers couldn't celebrate early. Their lead was merely 9–6 with 10 minutes left, after Vikings' rookie linebacker Matt Blair broke through the right side of the line and blocked a punt by Bobby Walden. Safety Terry Brown collected the ball on the fourth bounce in the end zone for a touchdown.

The Steelers' special teams' snafus in the first half alone included a missed 37-yard field goal by Roy Gerela and a bungled hold by Walden that prevented Gerela from even attempting one from the 33. Coach Chuck Noll, a former defensive coach from Don Shula's staff in Baltimore, managed the special-teams units without seeking much help from his assistants. "There wasn't the emphasis on special teams in those days like there is today," defensive coordinator Bud Carson said. "Chuck did a nice job, but he just didn't have a lot of time to do it."

Shortly after the blocked punt, Terry Bradshaw took a seven-step drop on third and 2 and hurled a

	1	2	3	4	Final
Pittsburgh Steelers	0	2	7	7	16
Minnesota Vikings	0	0	0	6	6

SCORING SUMMARY

2nd Quarter
PIT   Safety, White downed Tarkenton in end zone
3rd Quarter
PIT   Harris, 9-yd. run (Gerela kick)
4th Quarter
MIN   T. Brown, recovered blocked punt in end zone (kick failed)
PIT   L. Brown, 4-yd. pass from Bradshaw (Gerela kick)

long pass on the right side to tight end Larry Brown. "It was a sail route," wide receivers coach Lionel Taylor said. "The tight end takes an inside release, goes up the field 10 to 12 yards and then breaks out on a 45-degree angle to the sideline where the flanker cleared out. Larry was a very good blocking tight end, but he came up with the catches when we needed them."

Brown, who later would be converted to tackle, made the catch 18 yards downfield when strong safety Jeff Wright cut underneath looking for the interception but didn't get it. Brown advanced to the 28, a gain of 30 yards and the longest in the game for either team. As Brown was landing on his backside, though, the ball was being ripped loose by cornerback Jackie Wallace.

A pair of officials in the six-man crew signaled Minnesota's ball. The call, however, was overturned when head linesman Ed Marion ruled Brown was down before the ball came out. "They said that he was down, which was not the case," said Vikings middle linebacker Jeff Siemon, who made the recovery. "He was hit and fumbled. We stopped them and had the ball."

Rocky Bleier, who complemented Harris with 65 yards in 17 rushes, gained 17 yards on a misdirection run to the Viking 16. Then on third and 5, Bleier circled left out of the backfield and Bradshaw hit him for 6 yards. Harris plowed for 2 to the 3, but then Siemon tackled him for minus-1 to set up third and goal from the 4. Bradshaw rolled right outside blown containment and, with the onrushing Siemon fast approaching, found Brown open in the middle of the end zone for the clinching touchdown. "Bradshaw drilled it," Taylor said. "Larry couldn't drop it if he wanted to."

Tarkenton's third and final interception, which sealed the Vikings' fate, came on the next snap from scrimmage when he threw deep for John Gilliam and was picked off by safety Mike Wagner. For the second year in a row, Tarkenton had failed to throw a touchdown pass in the Super Bowl.

"We were perfectly set up for Tarkenton," Carson said. "What he did was obviously outstanding, as he did it so often and for so long. But with L. C. Greenwood, it was going to be awful hard to sprint out and get that tackle [Ron Yary] to block L. C. on any kind of pass play to that side. We had Dwight White on the other side. . . . Even though they didn't run down Tarkenton, they got him changing direction so many times."

Greenwood, merely a 10th-round selection, and the great defensive tackle "Mean Joe" Greene both arrived in 1969, the same year that Art Rooney hired the 37-year-old Noll to replace Bill Austin as head coach. The Steelers found Greenwood at Arkansas-Pine Bluff and took Greene out of North Texas. White (fourth round) from East Texas State and Ernie Holmes (eighth round), the other defensive tackle from Texas Southern, were selected in 1971.

Those phenomenal drafts in Pittsburgh were masterminded by Art Rooney Jr., but a central figure in choosing all four was Bill Nunn, a team scout since 1968. "He was known throughout the black colleges and conferences as *the* black college scout," said wide receiver John Stallworth, the club's fourth-round pick from Alabama A&M in 1974.

Greenwood, 6 feet 6½ and 245, could run 40 yards in 4.75 seconds, according to Tim Rooney. "If [he] walked into an airport, somebody would say he was playing for the Celtics," said Rooney. "He's like a Simeon Rice of today. There was a joke after the game. One of the writers had said, 'Pass attempt by Tarkenton, defended by Greenwood.' I think he had as many [passes defensed] as the defensive backs."

Even more damaging for the Vikings was their inability to block Greene, Holmes, and middle linebacker Jack Lambert on running plays. Two weeks after gouging the Los Angeles Rams' top-ranked run defense for 164 yards in the NFC Championship Game, the Vikings were suffocated inside and out by the Steelers.

Before the title game against Oakland, defensive line coach George Perles convinced Noll, Carson, and linebackers coach Robert "Woody" Widenhofer that the team's run defense would be even more stifling if the defensive tackle to the tight-end side was offset from the outside shoulder of the guard to a cocked position angling directly into the center. "It's the only thing I ever came up with in football," Perles said. "Most of our plays and all of our defenses were 100 years old." Perles labeled it the "Stunt 4-3," and after being wildly successful against the Raiders (21 rushes, 29 yards) and Vikings, he employed it as his base defense for the rest of his coaching days in Pittsburgh and at Michigan State.

Instead of being uncovered and having a clear path to block the blood-and-guts rookie Lambert in the middle, undersized and aging Viking center Tingelhoff (34) had to deal with either Greene or Holmes on his nose down after down. Today, offenses use the strong-side guard and center to double-team the nose tackle and then have one of them scrape up to the middle backer. "But in those days there was no scoop blocking," Carson said. "The way our nose tackle played, he basically charged into the 'V' in the neck of the center in such a manner so the center could not reach him if it was a strong-side play. If you weren't prepared for it, it made the guard totally ineffective."

Years later, Tingelhoff appeared to have selective amnesia about the pounding he took, insisting it wasn't the case. "I've watched that damn game film," he said. "We just didn't play very well at all. We just never got started." This much

PITTSBURGH STEELERS (AFC, 10–3–1)			MINNESOTA VIKINGS (NFC, 10–4)	
		Offense		
43	Frank Lewis (6-1, 196)	WR	82	Jim Lash (6-2, 199)
55	Jon Kolb (6-3, 262)	LT	62	Charles Goodrum (6-3, 256)
50	Jim Clack (6-3, 250)	LG	66	Andy Maurer (6-3, 247)
56	Ray Mansfield (6-3, 260)	C	53	Mick Tingelhoff (6-2, 240)
72	Gerry Mullins (6-3, 244)	RG	62	Ed White (6-3, 268)
71	Gordon Gravelle (6-5, 250)	RT	73	Ron Yary* (6-6, 255)
87	Larry Brown (6-4, 229)	TE	83	Stu Voigt (6-1, 225)
25	Ron Shanklin (6-1, 190)	WR	42	John Gilliam* (6-1, 195)
12	Terry Bradshaw (6-3, 218)	QB	10	Fran Tarkenton* (6-0, 190)
20	Rocky Bleier (5-11, 210)	RB	44	Chuck Foreman* (6-2, 207)
32	Franco Harris* (6-2, 230)	RB	41	Dave Osborn (6-0, 208)
		Defense		
68	L. C. Greenwood* (6-6, 245)	LE	81	Carl Eller* (6-6, 247)
75	Joe Greene* (6-4, 275)	LT	69	Doug Sutherland (6-3, 250)
63	Ernie Holmes (6-3, 285)	RT	88	Alan Page* (6-4, 245)
78	Dwight White (6-4, 220)	RE	70	Jim Marshall (6-4, 240)
59	Jack Ham* (6-1, 225)	LLB	60	Roy Winston (5-11, 222)
58	Jack Lambert (6-4, 205)	MLB	50	Jeff Siemon (6-2, 230)
34	Andy Russell* (6-2, 225)	RLB	58	Wally Hilgenberg (6-3, 229)
24	J. T. Thomas (6-2, 196)	LCB	43	Nate Wright (5-11, 180)
47	Mel Blount (6-3, 205)	RCB	25	Jackie Wallace (6-3, 197)
23	Mike Wagner (6-1, 210)	LS	23	Jeff Wright (5-11, 190)
27	Glen Edwards (6-0, 185)	RS	22	Paul Krause* (6-3, 200)

* Pro Bowl selection

SUBSTITUTIONS

Pittsburgh

Offense: WR - 86 Reggie Garrett, 82 John Stallworth, 88 Lynn Swann; TE - 84 Randy Grossman, 89 John McMakin; T - 74 Dave Reavis, 73 Rick Druschel; G - 57 Sam Davis; C - 52 Mike Webster; RB - 35 Steve Davis, 46 Reggie Harrison, 26 Preston Pearson. *Defense:* DT - 77 Charlie Davis, 64 Steve Furness; LB - 38 Ed Bradley, 54 Marv Kellum, 51 Loren Toews; CB - 45 Jim Allen; S - 22 Richard Conn, 31 Donnie Shell. *Specialists:* K - 10 Roy Gerela*; P - 39 Bobby Walden. *DNP:* 17 Joe Gilliam (QB), 5 Terry Hanratty (QB), 62 Jim Wolf (DE).

Minnesota

Offense: WR - 80 Sam McCullum; TE - 84 Steve Craig, 89 Doug Kingsriter; T - 67 Grady Alderman; G - 65 Steve Lawson, 64 Milt Sunde; C - 56 Scott Anderson; RB - 30 Bill Brown, 49 Ed Marinaro, 33 Brent McClanahan, 32 Oscar Reed. *Defense:* DE - 75 Bob Lurtsema; DT - 77 Gary Larsen; LB - 59 Matt Blair, 55 Amos Martin, 54 Fred McNeill; CB - 24 Terry Brown; S - 29 Randy Poltl. *Specialists:* K - 14 Fred Cox; P - 11 Mike Eischeid. *DNP:* 78 Steve Riley (T), 85 John Holland (WR), 17 Bob Berry (QB), 21 Joe Blahak (CB).

was clear: only one of the Vikings' 21 carries gained more than 4 yards, and 13 resulted in a gain of 1 yard or less. Perles looked at the same film and saw Tingelhoff getting it handed to him. "The poor guy, you slap the ball and you'd like to have a chance to get a little breathing room, and Pow!" Perles said. "He was an excellent player, but when you have Joe Greene on your ear it's different."

Siemon can recall Tarkenton saying that 9 of the 11 Steelers on defense were Pro Bowl caliber. "That was a great, great crew of linebackers," Tim Rooney said. "Andy Russell was nearing the end of a great, great career. Lambert was just beginning his. And, by '74, [Jack] Ham was polished and a great player already. In '74, we could win a game, 9–7, and really be happy. It was a less sophisticated game and defenses could really thrive."

Due to injuries, the Vikings were forced to move left guard Charles Goodrum to left tackle and start journeyman Andy Maurer, who was with his third team, at left guard. "We were a little shaky on the left side," Vikings director of player personnel Jerry Reichow said. "Goodrum was a stopgap guy." Even when Lambert and Russell left for good in mid-game with injuries (ankle and leg, respectively), Noll said the defense didn't miss a beat with Ed Bradley in the middle and Loren Toews on the right side.

Another factor, at least in Carson's estimation, was the brutal weather for mid-January in New Orleans. It rained hard that morning and the artificial turf at old Tulane Stadium, substituting for the not-quite-finished Louisiana Superdome, was saturated and slick. The temperature was 46 degrees, but with the stiff wind it felt like 22. "I don't care what anybody says, it was one of the coldest games I was ever involved in, and I've been around a few," Carson said after he retired. "The offenses just weren't going to be able to throw the ball like they did during the year. Everybody had gloves on, the old-time gloves. . . . The weather helped us."

Ranked eighth in the league on offense, the Steelers had gone through turbulence at midseason when Noll benched quarterback Joe Gilliam and gave the ball to Bradshaw. That summer there had been a players' strike, and with Bradshaw and most of the veterans out, Gilliam starred during an unbeaten exhibition season.

Noll, however, had become increasingly concerned about what he regarded as Gilliam's lack of trustworthiness. Moreover, he felt Gilliam called too many pass plays. Thus, with the Steelers off to a 4–1–1 start, Noll decided to go with Bradshaw, the top pick in the 1970 draft who had started for most of his first four seasons. It was a potentially explosive situation, because Gilliam was one of the rare black quarterbacks of the time, but it didn't seem to create a racial divide.

Bradshaw began the game after a harrowing experience that, at least for him, magnified the significance of the Super Bowl. "Our path to the field had been roped off and fans were standing on either side of this path as we ran onto the field," he recounted in his book, *It's Only a Game*. "As I waited, a fan standing only a few feet from me collapsed and died instantly of a massive heart attack. This was a man probably in his forties, wearing no shirt and a plastic Vikings helmet with horns on it. The man dropped dead right in front of me—and it didn't stop the program for one second. Nobody hesitated. We didn't even mention it on the sidelines or in the huddle. That was when I realized the Super Bowl wasn't a life-or-death situation—it was much more important than that."

This perspective was exemplified by the inspirational figure of the game, Dwight White, who came down with pneumonia and spent most of the week leading up to the game in a hospital bed. "I lost 20 pounds in one week," White said. "I weighed 250, maybe 245 at the end of the season. I was probably around 220 by game time." He ended up playing the entire game and then spent 10 more days in the hospital.

In the first half, the Steelers penetrated Vikings territory four times but were turned back each time. "We had some weaknesses and they showed up against great teams," Siemon said, "but we were typically good enough to keep a team from going down the field against us. We had an older team. Perhaps what we gave up physically, we made up for with moxie and experience. Sometimes, though, you get to the tipping point where experience can only go so far. You need to have the physical capacity to beat the opponent."

The only score in the first half was a safety for the Steelers, when Tarkenton failed to handle the exchange from Tingelhoff cleanly and was late on a reverse pivot handing off-tackle to Dave Osborn. Tarkenton did well just to make a crawling recovery in the end zone. "I think the 'Stunt 4-3' screwed up that exchange," maintained Perles.

Late in the first half, Tarkenton took a deep drop on first down from the Steelers 25 and for once had time to scan the field. John Gilliam, a terrific deep threat, was open in the middle of the field at the 4. As Gilliam leaped to haul the ball in, safety Glen Edwards slammed both arms into his face. Gilliam went flying and so did the ball, which dropped into the arms of cornerback Mel Blount. "Glen Edwards made what was, in my opinion, one of the all-time hits," Blount said. "Pound for pound, there wasn't anybody who could hit like Glen Edwards on the football field. That was a turning point."

The second-half kickoff proved even more devastating for the Vikings. Gerela's plant foot went out from under him just as he struck the ball. The ball skidded along the slippery surface to the 28, where veteran fullback Bill Brown (who was playing his final game as a pro) couldn't control it, and rookie linebacker Marv Kellum recovered for Pittsburgh at the 30. "Anybody but Bill," Reichow said. "He just didn't fumble."

Two plays later, Harris followed left guard Jim Clack's booming block against Alan Page, shoved aside a pathetic attempt of a tackle by free safety Paul Krause, and roared 24 yards to the 6. After linebacker Wally Hilgenberg tackled Harris for minus-3, Harris trailed pulling guard Gerry Mullins around the left side for the touchdown to make it 9–0.

TEAM STATISTICS

PITTSBURGH		MINNESOTA
17	Total First Downs	9
11	Rushing	2
5	Passing	5
1	Penalty	2
333	Total Net Yardage	119
73	Total Offensive Plays	47
4.6	Avg. Gain per Offensive Play	2.5
57	Rushes	21
249	Yards Gained Rushing (Net)	17
4.4	Average Yards per Rush	0.8
14	Passes Attempted	26
9	Passes Completed	11
0	Passes Intercepted	3
2	Tackled Attempting to Pass	0
12	Yards Lost Attempting to Pass	0
84	Yards Gained Passing (Net)	102
6/17	Third-Down Efficiency	5/12
0/2	Fourth-Down Efficiency	0/0
7	Punts	6
34.7	Average Distance	37.2
5	Punt Returns	4
36	Punt Return Yardage	12
3	Kickoff Returns	3
32	Kickoff Return Yardage	50
46	Interception Return Yardage	0
4	Fumbles	3
2	Own Fumbles Recovered	1
2	Opponent Fumbles Recovered	2
8	Penalties	4
122	Yards Penalized	18
2	Touchdowns	1
1	Rushing	0
1	Passing	0
0	Returns	0
2	Extra Points Made	0
0	Field Goals Made	0
1	Field Goals Attempted	1
1	Safeties	0
16	Total Points Scored	6
38:47	Time of Possession	21:13

"One of the things that stands out is Page did nothing," Tim Rooney said. "We really had a very strong game against Page."

In 1974, Pittsburgh had six players make the Pro Bowl, but not one was from its squatty, muscular, and underrated offensive line. Also, at that stage of their development, the Steelers weren't a high-scoring

INDIVIDUAL STATISTICS

PITTSBURGH

Passing	CP/ATT	YDS	TD	INT	RAT
Bradshaw	9/14	96	1	0	108.0

Rushing	ATT	YDS	AVG	TD	LG
Harris	34	158	4.6	1	25
Bleier	17	65	3.8	0	18
Bradshaw	5	33	6.6	0	17
Swann	1	-7	-7.0	0	-7

Receiving	NO	YDS	AVG	TD	LG
Brown	3	49	16.3	1	30
Stallworth	3	24	8.0	0	22
Bleier	2	11	5.5	0	6
Lewis	1	12	12.0	0	12

Interceptions	NO	YDS	LG	TD
Wagner	1	26	26	0
Blount	1	10	10	0
Greene	1	10	10	0

Punting	NO	AVG	LG	BLK
Walden	6	40.5	52	1

Punt Ret.	NO/FC	YDS	LG	TD
Swann	3/0	34	17	0
Edwards	2/0	2	2	0

Kickoff Ret.	NO	YDS	LG	TD
Harrison	2	17	17	0
Pearson	1	15	15	0

Defense	SOLO	AST	TOT	SK
Lambert	4	2	6	0
Holmes	4	0	4	0
Russell	4	0	4	0
Bradley	3	0	3	0
Thomas	3	0	3	0
White	3	0	3	0
Greenwood	2	1	3	0
Wagner	2	1	3	0
Ham	2	0	2	0
Toews	2	0	2	0
Blount	1	1	2	0
Allen	1	0	1	0
Edwards	1	0	1	0
Garrett	1	0	1	0
Greene	1	0	1	0
Kellum	1	0	1	0
Shell	1	0	1	0
TOTAL	**36**	**5**	**41**	**0**

MINNESOTA

Passing	CP/ATT	YDS	TD	INT	RAT
Tarkenton	11/26	102	0	3	14.1

Rushing	ATT	YDS	AVG	TD	LG
Foreman	12	18	1.5	0	12
Tarkenton	1	0	0.0	0	0
Osborn	8	-1	-0.1	0	2

Receiving	NO	YDS	AVG	TD	LG
Foreman	5	50	10.0	0	17
Voigt	2	31	15.5	0	28
Osborn	2	7	3.5	0	4
Gilliam	1	16	16.0	0	16
Reed	1	-2	-2.0	0	-2

Interceptions	NO	YDS	LG	TD
None	--	--	--	--

Punting	NO	AVG	LG	BLK
Eischeid	6	37.2	42	0

Punt Ret.	NO/FC	YDS	LG	TD
McCullum	3/0	11	6	0
N. Wright	1/0	1	1	0
Wallace	0/1	0	--	0

Kickoff Ret.	NO	YDS	LG	TD
McCullum	1	26	26	0
McClanahan	1	22	22	0
B. Brown	1	2	2	0

Defense	SOLO	AST	TOT	SK
Siemon	10	5	15	0
Sutherland	6	6	12	0
Winston	6	6	12	0
Page	9	1	10	1
Eller	7	1	8	0
J. Wright	2	6	8	0
Hilgenberg	6	1	7	0
Krause	5	2	7	0
Marshall	4	1	5	0
Wallace	4	1	5	0
Blair	2	0	2	0
Lurtsema	1	1	2	1
Kingsriter	1	0	1	0
Larsen	1	0	1	0
Poltl	1	0	1	0
Martin	1	0	1	0
McClanahan	1	0	1	0
Tingelhoff	1	0	1	0
Yary	1	0	1	0
TOTAL	**69**	**31**	**100**	**2**

outfit. Frank Lewis and Ron Shanklin started at wide receiver, but Stallworth and fellow rookie Lynn Swann generally rotated in during the second and fourth quarters. The team's cumulative passer rating during the regular season was an abysmal 49.0. "Bradshaw was just coming on," Reichow said, "but they were pretty close to a great team, if they weren't [already one yet]." Pittsburgh ranked just 21st among the 26 teams in passing yards. "We did what we had to do," Taylor said. "We could have been a lot better if we had to be."

Early in the fourth quarter, Krause recovered a fumble by Harris near midfield. On the next play, Tarkenton threw the ball with all his might (it carried 52 yards in the air) to John Gilliam, and Wagner was penalized 42 yards for pass interference when he didn't turn back for the ball on the sideline. From the 5, Tarkenton quickly faked a toss and tried a reverse-pivot inside handoff to Foreman, but placed the ball too high into his chest. The ball slipped out, and Greene recovered at the 7. Noll referred to that fumble as the turning point. Only the blocked punt saved the Vikings from being the first team to be shut out in the Super Bowl.

"It was a solid game, where if you make a play you might win, one of those deals," Reichow said.

"The funny thing about the four Super Bowls—I never felt like in any of them we played our best game. The only thing that keeps sticking in my mind is clinching it too early. With two or three games to go we always had it clinched. . . . It seemed to be we could never regain that level of play we had all year."

Afterward, in his role as defensive captain, Russell was preparing to present the game ball to the most outstanding player on an outstanding defense, but he couldn't stop thinking about the Steelers' futile history. Then he noticed the 73-year-old Rooney, the team's beloved owner, minding his own business off to the side.

"I'm standing there and I see 'the Chief,' and then it hit me," Russell recalled. "I had to give [the game ball] to him. He was the man. It was the right thing to do."

Commissioner Pete Rozelle presented Mr. Rooney with the Vince Lombardi Trophy. The Steelers had arrived. They wouldn't be leaving for a while, either.

Top Ten Coaches

1. **Chuck Noll (4–0):** A very private man in a very public business, Noll always did things his own special way.
2. **Bill Walsh (3–0):** Walsh won his first Super Bowl without much talent, his second with a ton of talent, and his third when it didn't look good for much of the season.
3. **Tom Coughlin (2–0):** Defeated the great Bill Belichick twice as an underdog, both times not long after his days appeared to be numbered in New York. Amazing ability to focus.
4. **Weeb Ewbank (1–0):** Ewbank had coached the Colts for nine seasons, knew the players, and recognized some were in decline. Buddy Ryan, Ewbank's defensive-line coach with the Jets, called him "100 years ahead of his time."
5. **Mike Shanahan (2–0):** Bobb McKittrick, the 49ers' distinguished O-line coach, once said Shanahan had the best football mind of any coach he had ever worked with. Green Bay found that out in Super Bowl XXXII.
6. **George Seifert (2–0):** A native San Franciscan, Seifert

stepped into those very large shoes left by the retirement of Bill Walsh and won not one, but two Super Bowls.

7. **Tom Flores (2–0):** A three-point underdog against the Eagles in Super Bowl XV and the Redskins in XVIII, Flores' Raiders dominated both opponents. It wasn't close to being all about Al Davis.
8. **Vince Lombardi (2–0):** Fourteen other owners couldn't have been happier that Lombardi was the NFL's standard-bearer in Super Bowl I against the AFL. He didn't let the Old Guard down, and he was again carried off the field after Super Bowl II.
9. **Joe Gibbs (3–1):** Just a brilliant offensive strategist who wasn't too proud to let others coach the defense and find the players. The only blemish was that bad night in Tampa in Super Bowl XVIII.
10. **Bill Belichick (3–2):** Was one win away from joining Chuck Noll with four wins before his old team, the Giants, interrupted his victory parade. His ambush of St. Louis in Super Bowl XXXVI won't soon be forgotten.

X

PITTSBURGH STEELERS 21, DALLAS COWBOYS 17

January 18, 1976
Orange Bowl, Miami, Florida

Defense. Defense. And then more defense. That's how the Pittsburgh Steelers dug themselves out from under almost four decades of lousy football. To become a pro football team for the ages, however, the Steelers had to execute a multidimensional offense—and that's precisely what they did for Super Bowl X.

The Steelers' 21–17 victory over the Dallas Cowboys at the Orange Bowl whet the public's appetite for what the NFL would become in the not too distant future. Too often, the first nine Super Bowls had been dreary, mistake-filled, lopsided affairs. This game, which was decided by Terry Bradshaw's last pass to Lynn Swann and Cowboys' Roger Staubach's last-second pass into the end zone, didn't need an overblown script by NFL Films or dramatic narration by John Facenda. It stood by itself near the top among the great playoff games in pro football history.

Swann, the MVP, gained 161 yards on only four receptions, three of which rank among the most memorable in Super Bowl annals. His final catch, a 64-yard touchdown strike from Bradshaw with 3:02 remaining—destined to live forever in football lore—gave the Steelers a 21–10 lead and sufficient cushion to withstand one of Staubach's patented comebacks.

"This was where Bradshaw and the passing game started to really come into effect," said Tim Rooney, the Steelers' director of pro personnel. "That team was much better [than in 1974] because those kids on offense started to mature and the defense was still extremely good."

The Steelers, a 6½-point favorite, were nursing a 15–10 lead over the determined Cowboys as the clock was winding down in the fourth quarter. Dallas entered the fourth quarter up 10–7 after a field goal by Toni Fritsch early in the second quarter, but a punt blocked for a safety by backup running back Reggie Harrison and field goals of 36 and 18

Attendance: 80,187
Conditions: 57 degrees, clear, wind N at 17 mph
Time of kickoff: 2:14 p.m. (EST)
Length of game: 2 hours, 58 minutes
Referee: Norm Schachter

MVP: Lynn Swann, WR, Steelers

yards by Roy Gerela enabled Pittsburgh to go ahead by five points.

On third and 4 with about 3½ minutes remaining, Bradshaw figured the Cowboys would expect him to throw short. "That was the percentage play, the smart move," he said, "but I just hated to throw those dinky little passes." So Bradshaw called "68 Basic," a play in which he explained, "I was just going to throw it as far as I could and Lynn Swann was going to catch up to it."

The only problem for Bradshaw was that the Cowboys called one of their rare blitzes. Right linebacker D. D. Lewis broke free on Bradshaw's blind side, but couldn't quite contort his body enough to do more than graze the quarterback's left leg. Bradshaw instinctively stepped up in the pocket, pump-faked to give Swann more time to get downfield, and then let fly. "The ball traveled almost 70 yards in a parabolic arc—in a movie they would show a close-up of the ball spinning through the air in slow motion—and Swann caught it without breaking stride for what turned out to be the winning touchdown," Bradshaw said. "It was the play everybody spends his childhood dreaming about."

Unfortunately for Bradshaw, he had no idea what happened to the ball after it left his hand. When free safety Cliff Harris and defensive tackle Larry Cole came from the same side as Lewis, Harris slipped, staggered to his haunches, and was able to grab Bradshaw around the waist. Most of the heavy damage, however, was done by Cole, who had

	1	2	3	4	Final
Dallas Cowboys	7	3	0	7	17
Pittsburgh Steelers	7	0	0	14	21

SCORING SUMMARY

1st Quarter
DAL D. Pearson, 29-yd. pass from Staubach (Fritsch kick)
PIT Grossman, 7-yd. pass from Bradshaw (Gerela kick)
2nd Quarter
DAL Fritsch, 36-yd. FG
4th Quarter
PIT Safety, Harrison blocked Hoopes' punt through end zone
PIT Gerela, 36-yd. FG
PIT Gerela, 18-yd. FG
PIT Swann, 64-yd. pass from Bradshaw (kick failed)
DAL P. Howard, 34-yd. pass from Staubach (Fritsch kick)

a head of steam up and drove his helmet directly into the left side of Bradshaw's jaw. "I was out cold before I hit the ground," Bradshaw said. "If you like big marching bands, you would have enjoyed being inside my head. Never saw the pass, never saw the catch, never saw the touchdown. I definitely never saw the victory celebration at the end of the game."

On the left side, Swann ran a simple post pattern against cornerback Mark Washington, a 13th-round draft choice by Dallas in 1970 out of Morgan State who was in his first and only season as a full-time starter. "If you just do your job at corner and take the inside away, you are going to eliminate 90 percent of the completions," safety Charlie Waters said. "Mark failed to do it." In Washington's defense, Waters said, "Lynn Swann and Terry Bradshaw abused a lot of people. Poor Mark Washington. He will be remembered for that Super Bowl. Mark was a very good technique guy. It was uncharacteristic for him not to use technique properly."

Swann's first reception, for 32 yards, came in the first quarter on a fly pattern up the sideline with Washington again in man-to-man coverage. Washington was abreast of Swann and looking back for the ball, but Swann reacted first, vaulted to make the catch, and then tip-toed inside the boundary before tumbling out of bounds at the Dallas 16. Three plays later, the Cowboys bit on a third-and-1 run fake and Bradshaw zipped a 7-yard touchdown pass to tight end Randy Grossman.

Swann's second reception, for 53 yards, makes every highlight reel, but it didn't lead to any points because, in the waning seconds of the first half, Gerela missed a field goal attempt from 36 yards. On Bradshaw's pass to Swann, the ball carried 58 yards in the air and was slightly underthrown. Swann, covered one-on-one by Washington, went up first. The receiver said Washington tipped the ball up into the air before falling off the play, leaving Swann to cradle it to his chest as he crashed to the artificial turf. "I still don't know how I caught it," Swann said years later. "I don't know how I kept my concentration on the ball while I was going down."

The possibility that Swann, in just his second season, might not even take the field that day was very real. He had spent two days in a Pittsburgh hospital after suffering a concussion in a brutally physical AFC Championship Game victory over Oakland. After sitting out the week of practice at Three Rivers Stadium, Swann found himself unable to concentrate and dropped passes left and right when the team worked out in Miami.

"I'm not going to hurt anyone intentionally," Cowboys' safety Cliff Harris said a few days before the game, "but getting hit again while he's on a pass route must be in the back of Swann's mind. I know it would be in the back of my mind." Swann concluded that Harris was attempting to intimidate him and decided that he had no choice but to play. He revealed later, "When we took the field at the Orange Bowl I was questioning my own ability. I

COACHING STAFFS

Dallas
Head Coach: Tom Landry. *Offense:* Jim Myers (coordinator, offensive line), Ed Hughes (receivers, quarterbacks), Mike Ditka (tight ends, special teams), Dan Reeves (backs). *Defense:* Ernie Stautner (coordinator, defensive line), Jerry Tubbs (linebackers), Gene Stallings (defensive backs). *Conditioning:* Alvin Roy. *Special Assistant:* Ermal Allen.

Pittsburgh
Head Coach: Chuck Noll. *Offense:* Lionel Taylor (receivers), Dan Radakovich (offensive line), Dick Hoak (backfield). *Defense:* Bud Carson (coordinator), George Perles (defensive line), Woody Widenhofer (linebackers). *Strength:* Lou Riecke. *Flexibility:* Paul Uram.

wasn't sure if I'd be able to perform because of that brutal week of practice."

Down 21–10 and starting from their own 20 with 3 minutes left, it couldn't have looked more bleak for the Cowboys. Just 8–6 in 1974, coach Tom Landry compensated for the loss of running back Calvin Hill to the World Football League, plus the retirements of Bob Lilly, Cornell Green, and Walt Garrison, by keeping 12 rookies (plus two rookie free agents) from a phenomenal draft that would sustain the Cowboys' greatness for another decade. The team finished 10–4, won on the road as a distinct underdog in the playoffs against the Vikings (17–14) and Rams (37–7), and became the first wild-card team to reach the Super Bowl.

"The veterans saw we had good rookies and played better, and that's the influence our rookies had on this club," Landry said. "That [team] was the best group I had from the standpoint of character, morale, spirit, and teamwork. They were the type who gave you your greatest reward from coaching."

Staubach opened by finding Drew Pearson on the right sideline for 30 to the Pittsburgh 43 with cornerback J. T. Thomas in coverage. Three plays later, rookie free agent Percy Howard somehow managed to beat a stumbling Mel Blount on the left side, and Staubach threw the ball to him in the end zone for a 34-yard touchdown with 3:02 remaining.

Gil Brandt, the Cowboys' player personnel director, had unearthed the 6-foot-4 Howard playing basketball at Austin Peay State University. "Mel Blount and Glen Edwards were really killing our wide receivers to the point where they hurt Drew and seriously hurt Golden Richards," Staubach said. "His ribs were banged up, so Percy Howard had to come in. It was the only pass Percy ever caught with the Cowboys." Richards, a dangerous deep threat, was shut out.

DALLAS COWBOYS (NFC, 10–4)		PITTSBURGH STEELERS (AFC, 12–2)
	Offense	
83 Golden Richards (6-0, 183)	WR	82 John Stallworth (6-2, 185)
73 Ralph Neely (6-6, 260)	LT	55 Jon Kolb (6-3, 262)
66 Burton Lawless (6-4, 250)	LG	50 Jim Clack (6-3, 250)
62 John Fitzgerald (6-5, 255)	C	56 Ray Mansfield (6-3, 260)
61 Blaine Nye (6-4, 255)	RG	72 Gerry Mullins (6-3, 240)
70 Rayfield Wright* (6-6, 260)	RT	71 Gordon Gravelle (6-5, 255)
84 Jean Fugett (6-3, 226)	TE	87 Larry Brown (6-4, 230)
88 Drew Pearson (6-0, 180)	WR	88 Lynn Swann* (6-0, 180)
12 Roger Staubach* (6-3, 197)	QB	12 Terry Bradshaw* (6-3, 210)
26 Preston Pearson (6-1, 205)	RB	20 Rocky Bleier (5-11, 210)
44 Robert Newhouse (5-10, 200)	RB	32 Franco Harris* (6-2, 230)
	Defense	
72 Ed Jones (6-9, 260)	LE	68 L. C. Greenwood* (6-6, 245)
75 Jethro Pugh (6-6, 250)	LT	75 Joe Greene* (6-4, 275)
63 Larry Cole (6-5, 250)	RT	63 Ernie Holmes (6-3, 260)
79 Harvey Martin (6-5, 250)	RE	78 Dwight White (6-4, 255)
52 Dave Edwards (6-1, 255)	LLB	59 Jack Ham* (6-1, 225)
55 Lee Roy Jordan (6-1, 221)	MLB	58 Jack Lambert* (6-4, 220)
50 D. D. Lewis (6-1, 218)	RLB	34 Andy Russell* (6-2, 220)
46 Mark Washington (5-11, 186)	LCB	24 J. T. Thomas (6-2, 196)
20 Mel Renfro (6-0, 190)	RCB	47 Mel Blount* (6-3, 200)
41 Charlie Waters (6-4, 193)	LS	23 Mike Wagner* (6-1, 210)
43 Cliff Harris* (6-1, 190)	RS	27 Glen Edwards* (6-0, 185)

* Pro Bowl selection

SUBSTITUTIONS

Dallas

Offense: WR - 81 Percy Howard, 87 Ron Howard; TE - 89 Billy Joe DuPree; T - 67 Pat Donovan; G - 68 Herb Scott; C - 57 Kyle Davis; RB - 21 Doug Dennison, 30 Charley Young. *Defense:* DT - 77 Bill Gregory; LB - 53 Bob Breunig, 59 Warren Capone, 56 Thomas Henderson, 58 Cal Peterson, 54 Randy White; CB - 31 Benny Barnes, 45 Rolly Woolsey; S - 42 Randy Hughes. *Specialists:* K - 15 Toni Fritsch; P - 9 Mitch Hoopes. *DNP:* 78 Bruce Walton (T), 19 Clint Longley (QB).

Pittsburgh

Offense: WR - 86 Reggie Garrett, 43 Frank Lewis; TE - 84 Randy Grossman; T - 74 Dave Reavis; G - 57 Sam Davis; C - 52 Mike Webster; QB - 5 Terry Hanratty; RB - 44 Mike Collier, 33 Frenchy Fuqua, 46 Reggie Harrison. *Defense:* DE - 76 John Banaszak; DT - 64 Steve Furness; LB - 38 Ed Bradley, 54 Marv Kellum, 51 Loren Toews; CB - 45 Jim Allen; S - 36 Dave Brown, 31 Donnie Shell. *Specialists:* K - 10 Roy Gerela; P - 39 Bobby Walden. *DNP:* 17 Joe Gilliam (QB).

The Steelers recovered an onside kick at the Dallas 42 with 1:48 left and then tried three unsuccessful running plays, with the Cowboys calling a timeout after each one. On fourth and 9, backup quarterback Terry Hanratty went to the sidelines to confer with coach Chuck Noll, the assumption being that the Steelers would call on 37-year-old punter Bobby Walden to pin Staubach deep in the Dallas end of the field. There was 1:28 left and the Cowboys were out of timeouts.

Pittsburgh line coach George Perles said he wanted the Steelers to punt, so the defense would have more room, "and then I wouldn't have the monkey on my back." Perles recalled that Noll told him, "If we don't stop them, we don't deserve to win."

Hanratty rejoined the huddle.

"I'm looking at him and saying, 'What is it? What is it?'" running back Rocky Bleier recalled. "He shook his head but doesn't say anything. He says, 'All right, guys, here it is: 84 Trap, on 2.' I couldn't even concentrate on the play because I thought it was so ridiculous." Bleier plunged for 2, the clock stopped for the change of possession, and Dallas had 1:22 to travel 61 yards for a winning touchdown. Bleier said, "We all walked off the field shaking our heads, thinking, 'What kind of play was that?' It was the stupidest play ever, ever called in history."

Noll offered an explanation years later: "If they had needed a field goal, then it would have been different. But we had them in a must-pass situation, and I like for my defense to have a team in that kind of spot. Our defense did just what we thought it would do. They came up with a pass interception. I would prefer to turn a situation like that over to the defense instead of taking a chance on getting a punt blocked."

The Cowboys' first touchdown, a 29-yard pass from Staubach to Drew Pearson against a blown coverage by safety Mike Wagner, had been set up when Walden dropped a perfect snap in punt formation at the Pittsburgh 29. Later, Cliff Harris and linebacker Bob Breunig would come within inches of blocking two other punts.

It has been called the most audacious coaching decision in Super Bowl history. In effect, Noll was telling Staubach, "You're good, but my defense is better"—and, as it turned out, it was.

TEAM STATISTICS

DALLAS		PITTSBURGH
14	Total First Downs	13
6	Rushing	7
8	Passing	6
0	Penalty	0
270	Total Net Yardage	339
62	Total Offensive Plays	67
4.4	Avg. Gain per Offensive Play	5.1
31	Rushes	46
108	Yards Gained Rushing (Net)	149
3.5	Average Yards per Rush	3.2
24	Passes Attempted	19
15	Passes Completed	9
3	Passes Intercepted	0
7	Tackled Attempting to Pass	2
42	Yards Lost Attempting to Pass	19
162	Yards Gained Passing (Net)	190
3/14	Third-Down Efficiency	8/19
1/1	Fourth-Down Efficiency	0/3
7	Punts	4
35.0	Average Distance	39.8
1	Punt Returns	5
5	Punt Return Yardage	31
4	Kickoff Returns	4
96	Kickoff Return Yardage	89
0	Interception Return Yardage	89
4	Fumbles	4
4	Own Fumbles Recovered	4
0	Opponent Fumbles Recovered	0
2	Penalties	0
20	Yards Penalized	0
2	Touchdowns	2
0	Rushing	0
2	Passing	2
0	Returns	0
2	Extra Points Made	1
1	Field Goals Made	2
1	Field Goals Attempted	4
0	Safeties	1
17	Total Points Scored	21
30:30	Time of Possession	29:30

Staubach scrambled for 11. Then Staubach hit Preston Pearson for 12 yards to the Pittsburgh 38, but the clock kept running when the running back turned into the middle of the field rather than out of bounds. So Staubach fired incomplete into the end zone just to stop the clock with 12 seconds showing. "With 1:22 left, I felt we'd win," said Staubach, "but

INDIVIDUAL STATISTICS

DALLAS

Passing	CP/ATT	YDS	TD	INT	RAT
Staubach	15/24	204	2	3	77.8

Rushing	ATT	YDS	AVG	TD	LG
Newhouse	16	56	3.5	0	16
Staubach	5	22	4.4	0	11
Dennison	5	16	3.2	0	5
P. Pearson	5	14	2.8	0	9

Receiving	NO	YDS	AVG	TD	LG
P. Pearson	5	53	10.6	0	14
Young	3	31	10.3	0	14
D. Pearson	2	59	29.5	1	30
Newhouse	2	12	6.0	0	8
P. Howard	1	34	34.0	1	34t
Fugett	1	9	9.0	0	9
Dennison	1	6	6.0	0	6

Interceptions	NO	YDS	LG	TD
None	--	--	--	--

Punting	NO	AVG	LG	BLK
Hoopes	6	40.8	48	1

Punt Ret.	NO/FC	YDS	LG	TD
Richards	1/3	5	5	0

Kickoff Ret.	NO	YDS	LG	TD
P. Pearson	4	48	24	0
Henderson	0	48	48	0

Defense	SOLO	AST	TOT	SK
Harris	5	11	16	0
Jordan	6	8	14	0
Jones	7	3	10	0
Martin	8	1	9	0
Waters	4	4	8	0
Lewis	5	1	6	0
Pugh	4	2	6	0
Edwards	4	1	5	0
Breunig	4	0	4	0
Washington	3	1	4	0
Dupree	2	2	4	0
Gregory	1	3	4	0
Henderson	3	0	3	0
Renfro	3	0	3	0
R. White	2	1	3	2
Barnes	1	1	2	0
Cole	0	2	2	0
Capone	1	0	1	0
Neely	1	0	1	0
Woolsey	1	0	1	0
Davis	0	1	1	0
Hughes	0	1	1	0
Richards	0	1	1	0
TOTAL	65	44	109	2

PITTSBURGH

Passing	CP/ATT	YDS	TD	INT	RAT
Bradshaw	9/19	209	2	0	122.5

Rushing	ATT	YDS	AVG	TD	LG
F. Harris	27	82	3.0	0	11
Bleier	15	51	3.4	0	8
Bradshaw	4	16	4.0	0	8

Receiving	NO	YDS	AVG	TD	LG
Swann	4	161	40.3	1	64t
Stallworth	2	8	4.0	0	13
F. Harris	1	26	26.0	0	26
L. Brown	1	7	7.0	0	7
Grossman	1	7	7.0	1	7t

Interceptions	NO	YDS	LG	TD
Edwards	1	35	35	0
Thomas	1	35	35	0
Wagner	1	19	19	0

Punting	NO	AVG	LG	BLK
Walden	4	39.8	59	0

Punt Ret.	NO/FC	YDS	LG	TD
D. Brown	3/0	14	9	0
Edwards	2/0	17	10	0

Kickoff Ret.	NO	YDS	LG	TD
Blount	3	64	27	0
Collier	1	25	25	0

Defense	SOLO	AST	TOT	SK
Lambert	7	7	14	0
Ham	5	5	10	0
Furness	5	4	9	1
Russell	5	4	9	0
Greenwood	5	2	7	3
Holmes	4	3	7	0
D. White	2	4	6	3
Blount	3	2	5	0
Wagner	2	3	5	0
Thomas	3	1	4	0
Edwards	2	2	4	0
Greene	0	2	2	0
Allen	1	0	1	0
Bradley	1	0	1	0
Davis	1	0	1	0
Gerela	1	0	1	0
Kellum	1	0	1	0
Shell	1	0	1	0
Harrison	0	1	1	0
TOTAL	49	40	89	7

we ran a lousy two-minute drill. We got off only five plays in 82 seconds. I believe we rushed ourselves into thinking we had to hit a long gainer."

On the next play, Staubach unloaded the ball into the right end-zone corner toward Howard. J. T. Thomas mistimed his leap, but obscured Howard's vision just enough so the ball appeared as if it had glanced off the wide receiver's helmet as it fell incomplete. Staubach later claimed that the Steelers had interfered with Howard, "but the refs just weren't going to call it. The Steelers didn't have a single penalty called against them in that game. The defensive back just pulled him down by his shoulders. The ball was right there."

Three seconds remained when Staubach took a shotgun snap, pump-faked, and put up what was popularly coined by the press as a "Hail Mary" pass in the general vicinity of Drew Pearson. Edwards intercepted and the game was over.

"We played a very good football game against a very great football team," Staubach said. "Their defensive team, I think, was the best defense that's ever played in the NFL. And they intimidated us. I screamed at Jack Lambert, calling him every name in the book when I saw Lambert kick Preston Pearson. But we didn't retaliate against him. We let him get away with that, so they won the war of intimidation."

Lambert, in just his second season, finished with 14 tackles for a defense that harassed Staubach into three interceptions and sacked him seven times. Four of the sacks, for 29 yards, were registered by defensive end L. C. Greenwood, who helped make up for the second-half loss of defensive tackle Joe Greene, who suffered a pulled groin. The Steelers plugged in Steve Furness alongside their seven remaining Pro Bowl defenders and held the Cowboys to 270 yards and 14 first downs.

"'Mean Joe' and Greenwood, Dwight White, Lambert, Ham," said Dan Reeves, the Cowboys running backs coach at the time. "God, Mel Blount was as good a corner as there was. Edwards. They had so many great players and they were well coached by Bud Carson. I thought they were as good as we played against."

One area in which the Steelers didn't measure up was special teams. It was one reason why Landry went along with the urgings of special teams coach Mike Ditka to run a reverse on the opening kickoff. Gerela's boot floated down to Preston Pearson at the 3-yard line. Pearson, an ex-Steeler and the only player on the Cowboys' roster to have played for another NFL team, handed the ball at the 8 to fleet rookie linebacker Thomas "Hollywood" Henderson, who used his blazing speed to race 48 yards all the way to the Pittsburgh 44 before Gerela's shoulder-block tackle got him out of bounds. "I caught my knee on his ribs," Henderson said. "He definitely cracked some ribs on the play and it affected his kicking."

In addition to missing wide left from the 36 late in the first half, Gerela missed from 33 yards at the 10-minute mark of the third quarter and hit the left upright on a botched extra-point attempt after Swann's 64-yard touchdown. Harris, the key outside rusher, came close to blocking Gerela's third-quarter attempt and stood almost chest-to-chest with the 5-foot-10 kicker while watching the flight of the ball. When the officials signaled wide left, Harris tapped Gerela twice atop his helmet and then gave him a hug.

Lambert, one of the wing blockers, promptly latched on to Harris from behind and, without saying a word, threw him down directly in front of the referee. As Harris gestured at Lambert seeking a penalty or ejection, referee Norm Schachter moved Lambert away but didn't throw a flag. "That would have been a penalty on Lambert in today's day and age," Tim Rooney said. "I think it did incite us."

Waters, who years later worked side-by-side with Harris in the natural gas industry, agreed that it was a terrible decision by his teammate. "Cliff has died a thousand deaths over this," he said. "It just pissed off Lambert and it pissed off the whole Pittsburgh team. We couldn't match their intensity in the second half. I know the momentum changed at that point."

The Cowboys were unable to cross midfield on their first six possessions of the second half after breaching Steelers' territory four times in the first half. A mediocre ground game during the season with running backs Robert Newhouse, William Douglas Dennison, and Preston Pearson had been surprisingly effective before halftime. "What a great team we'd have had, had he stayed," Landry said years later, referring to Duane Thomas and his drug-related departure after the 1971 season. "If Duane Thomas would have stayed with us and Calvin Hill, too, if we had had the strength of those two players, we would have competed very strongly against Pittsburgh in the '70s."

As it was, Landry did one of his best coaching jobs. In addition to their pre-snap shifting and motioning, the Cowboys became the first team in that era to make regular use of the shotgun formation and situation substitution. "It was very confusing to a defensive team," Waters said. "This was the most creative year that Tom Landry had. He didn't have the weapons that he wanted, especially at running back. That was a great year from the Cowboys' perspective. The Cowboys went through a huge renaissance."

John Stallworth wouldn't make his first Pro Bowl until 1979, while the Steelers had fully integrated Swann into their attack in 1975. Bradshaw's early travails were a thing of the past. His passer rating of 88.2 was the finest of his 14-year career. With Franco Harris (1,246 yards) joining Bradshaw in the backfield, the Steelers had much more versatility on offense and were ever-dominant on defense.

"We improved over last year," said Dan Rooney, newly appointed as team president under his father, Art. "Last year was a victory of elation. This was a victory of accomplishment. They pointed for us all year. The team did what it had to do."

The Green Bay Packers and the Miami Dolphins now had the company of the third back-to-back Super Bowl champion in 10 years.

Ten Best Performances by a Wide Receiver

1. **Lynn Swann, Steelers, X:** Three of his catches, including a 64-yard bomb to win the game, are among the most memorable in Super Bowl history. He had suffered a concussion in the AFC Championship Game, dropped a ton of balls in practice, and was questionable to play.

2. **Jerry Rice, 49ers, XXIII:** Caught 11 passes for 215 yards, dominating Bengals CB Lewis Billups all day long. His 27-yard reception on a deep-over route set up the winning touchdown pass to John Taylor and was almost as important.

3. **Jerry Rice, 49ers, XXIV:** Set the tone early, shrugging off a kill shot from FS Steve Atwater for a 20-yard touchdown. Added touchdown receptions of 38 and 28 yards.

4. **Isaac Bruce, Rams, XXXIV:** Scored the winning touchdown with a sensational run on a 73-yard pass that was badly underthrown by Kurt Warner. Caught six passes for 162, a 27-yard average.

5. **Santonio Holmes, Steelers, XLIII:** Speared the game-winning touchdown in the corner on a laser shot from Ben Roethlisberger. Holmes secured the ball, then braced his fall while keeping his toes down. He caught nine for 131 and had two others for 41 wiped out by penalty.

6. **Deion Branch, Patriots, XXXVIII:** The MVP of Super Bowl XXXIX, Branch might have been better in XXXVIII. Ran a perfect third-down route for 17 yards just before the winning field goal, and got the Patriots on track with a sensational over-the-head, 52-yard catch late in the first half.

7. **Lynn Swann, Steelers, XIII:** Made one of the great catches in Super Bowl history by out-jumping Dallas FS Cliff Harris for an 18-yard touchdown that proved to be the winning margin. Swann caught seven for 124, and drew a 33-yard pass-interference penalty on CB Benny Barnes.

8. **Terrell Owens, Eagles, XXXIX:** Played 63 of a possible 72 snaps just six and a half weeks after leg surgery. Owens caught the Patriots off guard and reeled in nine receptions for 122 yards.

9. **Michael Irvin, Cowboys, XXVII:** The Bills opened in a two-deep shell before moving a safety up and putting their cornerbacks on islands. Irvin scored twice in less than 20 seconds during the final two minutes of the second quarter.

10. **Max McGee, Packers, I:** An unlikely hero, the 34-year-old McGee got the call after Boyd Dowler was injured on the game's second play. Had a field day, catching seven for 138 and two touchdowns.

XI
OAKLAND RAIDERS 32, MINNESOTA VIKINGS 14

January 9, 1977
Rose Bowl, Pasadena, California

Late on the Saturday night before Super Bowl XI, Oakland Raiders coach John Madden was relaxing with his assistant coaches when he asked them point-blank how the pending battle against the Minnesota Vikings would play out.

"One of the coaches, Lew Erber, said, 'I think we're going to beat them 40–0,'" receivers coach Tom Flores recalled, "and John about croaked. He looked at me and I said, 'I think we're going to win. I don't know about that score.' I said there's no way we should lose this game unless they do something on special teams. They did have good special teams. Sure as shooting, they block a damn punt and I said, 'I shouldn't have opened my mouth.'"

The Vikings had blocked 15 placements and punts en route to their fourth Super Bowl appearance in eight years. "We kind of did it with smoke and mirrors that year," middle linebacker Jeff Siemon admitted years later. Also in the opening sequences of Super Bowl XI, the Raiders' Errol Mann missed a 29-yard field goal, the Raiders were penalized for clipping on a return, and the great Ray Guy had the first punt of his NFL career blocked, with the Vikings taking over at the Oakland 3.

But the Vikings didn't score. In fact, they failed to score in the first half, just as they hadn't gotten a point in the first halves of their previous three Super Bowl defeats. Flores need not have fretted about the fickle hand of fate. The Raiders were so superior on both offense and defense that a couple of special-teams snafus could ultimately be laughed off as hiccups in an onslaught of the Silver and Black.

As the crowd of 103,438 departed the Rose Bowl, the scoreboards read "Oakland 32, Minnesota 14," but the score didn't begin to tell the story of how badly the Vikings had been outplayed.

"It was total domination," Flores said. "I think '83 was the best Raider team, but it was close with '76. It'd be a pretty good argument."

Attendance: 103,438
Conditions: 58 degrees, sunny and clear, wind NW at 5 mph
Time of kickoff: 12:47 p.m. (PST)
Length of game: 3 hours, 3 minutes
Referee: Jim Tunney

MVP: Fred Biletnikoff, WR, Raiders

Quarterback Fran Tarkenton's post-game assessment was brutally on point: "We didn't make a single play other than the blocked punt."

The Vikings' aging defense was manhandled by the Raiders' rushing attack to the tune of 266 yards in 52 attempts. Minnesota's famed front four mounted little or no pass rush, while its defensive backs and linebackers were schooled by quarterback Ken Stabler's crisp passes to wide receiver Fred Biletnikoff and tight end Dave Casper. Additionally, the tackling by the whole unit was feeble.

The offense didn't perform any better. With five minutes left in the third quarter and Oakland up 19–0, the Vikings had 4 first downs, 93 yards, 7 punts, and 1 lost fumble to show for their first 9 possessions. Stifling Tarkenton and multi-talented running back Chuck Foreman, the Raiders rendered the Vikings' offense null and void.

Defensive tackle Alan Page, one of seven Vikings who started in all four Super Bowls (three others played in each game), finally could stand it no longer. With about a minute and a half remaining and the outcome already decided, Page headed for the dressing room. "He just walked off and left," Siemon said years later. "He pulled a Randy Moss, basically. Football was a means to an end for him. He entered law school while he was playing. It was as though he was a little above the childishness of a pro football environment. Walking off the field may have been just a culmination of his general distaste for the culture of professional football."

	1	2	3	4	Final
Oakland Raiders	0	16	3	13	32
Minnesota Vikings	0	0	7	7	14

SCORING SUMMARY

2nd Quarter
OAK Mann, 24-yd. FG
OAK Casper, 1-yd. pass from Stabler (Mann kick)
OAK Banaszak, 1-yd. run (kick failed)
3rd Quarter
OAK Mann, 40-yd. FG
MIN S. White, 8-yd. pass from Tarkenton (Cox kick)
4th Quarter
OAK Banaszak, 2-yd. run (Mann kick)
OAK Brown, 75-yd. interception return (kick failed)
MIN Voigt, 13-yd. pass from Lee (Cox kick)

Page played the 1977 season and half of '78 before being traded to Chicago. Bud Grant's coaching career didn't end until after the 1985 season, but this was the last time he would be humiliated in a Super Bowl. "We just played them on the wrong day," Grant quipped afterward. "Next time we'll play them on a Wednesday."

The Vikings' director of player personnel, Jerry Reichow, whose career as a player and scout for the team spanned five decades, never had much chance to plumb the depths of Grant's disappointment. "We talked a little bit," Reichow said. "He doesn't discuss much with you. I did with [Jim] Finks. He agreed with me. I just never felt we played a real good Viking-type game in a Super Bowl."

Despite having the best record in the league at 13–1, the Raiders were not an overwhelming favorite at minus-4½. Forced early in the season to switch from a 4-3 to a 3-4 because of injuries on the defensive line, the Raiders ranked only 18th in total defense under quasi-coordinator Bob Zeman, while the Vikings ranked sixth. Oakland was coming off a 24–7 shellacking of the two-time defending champion Pittsburgh Steelers in the AFC Championship Game, but the Steelers were down to Reggie Harrison at running back that day with Franco Harris and Rocky Bleier injured. Besides, the oddsmakers still had never seen the Raiders win the big one. Since being crushed by Green Bay in

Super Bowl II, they had lost championship games in 1968, 1969, 1970, 1973, 1974, and 1975.

The game was scoreless and 10 minutes old when Viking linebacker Fred McNeill swooped in to block the punt by Guy. The snap, a bit low, caused the former first-round draft choice to chatter his steps. Still, the burden of blame fell mostly on one of his blockers, fullback Mark van Eeghen. "I really should have gotten a shoulder or arm on Fred McNeill as he rushed in," van Eeghen said, "but I couldn't get back to him in time because for some reason I had taken an extra step to the middle. When I heard that thud, I can't tell you how sick I felt."

On first and goal from the 3, Foreman tried the right side and gained 1. On second and goal, Brent McClanahan took Tarkenton's handoff on a play designed for him to follow Foreman through right guard. Phil Villapiano, the left outside linebacker, shot through a gap and hit McClanahan in the backfield. The ball came out, and linebacker Willie Hall made the recovery. "On the preceding play I went in high and was sandwiched by Ron Yary and Stu Voigt," said Villapiano, the Raiders' only Pro Bowl pick that year on defense. "On the second down, I went in low and when I came up there was McClanahan getting the ball. I hit the ball with my helmet."

The horrors of Super Bowls past flashed through the minds of the Vikings. It was their ninth fumble in the Super Bowl, their sixth lost, and their third lost inside the opponents' 10. Oscar Reed fumbled at the Miami 6 in Super Bowl VIII, Foreman fumbled at the Pittsburgh 5 in Super Bowl IX, and now McClanahan fumbled on the threshold. "That was a major, major play," Reichow said. "It killed us. It just took the steam out of us. All four of those games we had a major fumble. Every doggone one

> "I know we didn't play our best in all four of them. I don't know why. The only thing that keeps sticking in my mind is clinching it too early. With two or three games to go we always had it clinched. It seemed to me we could never regain that type of play we had done all year."
>
> *Jerry Reichow, Vikings director of personnel*

of them. They turned games around." Minnesota's turnover differential in the four Super Bowls was a debilitating minus-12.

Now the Raiders got busy. On third and 7, Stabler sent Casper to the left alongside tackle Art Shell and guard Gene Upshaw. Shell blocked right end Jim Marshall, Upshaw blocked Page, and backup fullback Pete Banaszak kicked out right linebacker Wally Hilgenberg. Right guard George Buehler pulled left and negated Siemon, and running back Clarence Davis was off to the races for 35 yards. The free safety, Paul Krause, didn't even make contact with Davis until he was 29 yards downfield.

Three plays later, Casper caught an 11-yard pass in the left flat and eluded Hilgenberg, strong safety Jeff Wright, and Siemon for a gain of 25. The Raiders settled for Mann's 24-yard field goal, but their 12-play, 90-yard drive had set the tactical and physical tone.

Davis amassed 137 yards, an amazing 105 of which came to the left, in just 16 carries (8.6 average), with van Eeghen adding 73 in 18. Most of the time, the Raiders lined up Casper right and jammed it down the throats of the Vikings on the other side, which was the weak side of the formation. "All game long we ran just two plays for Davis," van Eeghen said. "Minnesota's defense was very predictable. It was pure and simple: put Shell on Marshall, put me on Hilgenberg, put Upshaw on Page, put [center Dave] Dalby on Siemon. We're going to win those matchups."

Ron Wolf spent 1975 to 1977 as general manager in Tampa Bay, but knew well the personnel that he had helped assemble for owner Al Davis. "The most significant factor was how easily the offensive line of the Raiders handled the defensive line of the Vikings," Wolf said. "That was a great Raiders' line. Dalby wasn't as good as [Jim] Otto, but he was a very good player. Buehler was certainly not in the class

OAKLAND RAIDERS (AFC, 13–1)		Offense		MINNESOTA VIKINGS (NFC, 11–2–1)	
21	Cliff Branch* (5-11, 170)	WR	28	Ahmad Rashad (6-2, 200)	
78	Art Shell* (6-5, 265)	LT	78	Steve Riley (6-5, 258)	
63	Gene Upshaw* (6-5, 255)	LG	68	Charles Goodrum (6-3, 256)	
50	Dave Dalby (6-3, 250)	C	53	Mick Tingelhoff (6-2, 240)	
64	George Buehler (6-2, 270)	RG	62	Ed White* (6-2, 270)	
75	John Vella (6-4, 260)	RT	73	Ron Yary* (6-5, 255)	
87	Dave Casper* (6-4, 228)	TE	83	Stu Voigt (6-1, 225)	
25	Fred Biletnikoff (6-1, 190)	WR	85	Sammy White* (5-11, 189)	
12	Ken Stabler* (6-3, 215)	QB	10	Fran Tarkenton* (6-0, 190)	
28	Clarence Davis (5-10, 195)	RB	33	Brent McClanahan (5-10, 202)	
30	Mark van Eeghen (6-2, 225)	RB	44	Chuck Foreman* (6-2, 207)	
		Defense			
72	John Matuszak (6-7, 270)	LE	81	Carl Eller (6-6, 247)	
74	Dave Rowe (6-7, 271)	NT I LT	69	Doug Sutherland (6-3, 250)	
60	Otis Sistrunk (6-3, 273)	RE I RT	88	Alan Page* (6-4, 245)	
41	Phil Villapiano* (6-2, 225)	LOLB I RE	70	Jim Marshall (6-4, 228)	
58	Monte Johnson (6-5, 240)	LILB I LLB	59	Matt Blair (6-5, 229)	
39	Willie Hall (6-2, 225)	RILB I MLB	50	Jeff Siemon* (6-3, 237)	
83	Ted Hendricks (6-7, 220)	ROLB I RLB	58	Wally Hilgenberg (6-3, 229)	
26	Skip Thomas (6-1, 205)	LCB	43	Nate Wright (5-11, 190)	
24	Willie Brown (6-1, 210)	RCB	20	Bobby Bryant (6-1, 170)	
43	George Atkinson (6-0, 185)	SS	23	Jeff Wright (5-11, 190)	
32	Jack Tatum (5-11, 206)	FS	22	Paul Krause (6-3, 200)	

* Pro Bowl selection

SUBSTITUTIONS

Oakland
Offense: WR - 81 Morris Bradshaw, 49 Mike Siani; TE - 46 Warren Bankston; T - 70 Henry Lawrence; G - 66 Steve Sylvester, 79 Dan Medlin; QB - 11 David Humm, 15 Mike Rae; RB - 40 Pete Banaszak, 31 Carl Garrett, 29 Hubert Ginn, 36 Manfred Moore. *Defense:* DE - 61 Herb McMath, 77 Charles Philyaw; LB - 51 Rodrigo Barnes, 54 Rik Bonness, 52 Floyd Rice; CB - 20 Neal Colzie; S - 47 Charles Phillips. *Specialists:* K - 14 Errol Mann; P - 8 Ray Guy*.

Minnesota
Offense: WR - 26 Bob Grim, 80 Leonard Willis; TE - 84 Steve Craig; C - 57 Doug Dumler; QB - 19 Bob Lee; RB - 47 Ron Groce, 48 Sammy Johnson, 35 Robert Miller. *Defense:* DE - 77 Mark Mullaney; DT - 72 James White; LB - 55 Amos Martin, 54 Fred McNeill, 60 Roy Winston; CB - 20 Nate Allen; S - 27 Autry Beamon, 40 Windlan Hall. *Specialists:* K - 14 Fred Cox; P - 12 Neil Clabo. *DNP:* 17 Bob Berry (QB), 74 Bart Buetow (T).

of Upshaw, but he was squatty, square, a solid pro. John Vella was as good a pass protector as there was and a very good run blocker. He had a mean, nasty disposition. Shell was a great, great player, but John Vella was a Pro Bowl tackle who will never get his due."

Clarence Davis, a fourth-round pick in 1971, was another in the assembly line of tailbacks coming out of USC in that era. "He was 195, 200 maybe, but tougher than the dickens," Wolf said. "Really good speed. The hands are what kept him down. Van Eeghen had a really great first step. Superb hands. Average blocker."

Opposing the 290-pound Shell was the 39-year-old Marshall, who weighed 228 and didn't have a tackle in the game. Page was 245, and Hilgenberg, age 34, was in serious decline as an athlete. "They ran to the right [side of the defense], where Hilgenberg was," Vikings defensive line coach Buddy Ryan said. "We couldn't get it contained. They blamed Jim Marshall, but really the end is not responsible for containing." The cornerback on that side, 32-year-old Bobby Bryant, had been injured a lot and weighed only 170. "He'd come up and stick his head in there," one of the starters on the Vikings' defense said, "but he was ineffective as a tackler."

Krause, 34, had lost a few steps and was nearing the end of a career that would end with induction into the Hall of Fame, primarily on the basis of his astronomical interception total (81). A freelancing center fielder, he was less than courageous in run support. "We couldn't find him in the film, he played so deep," Ryan said. Krause's unwillingness to hit wasn't widely recognized by the press or fans

of that era, but his teammates and opponents knew the truth. "He played 15 yards deep. That's why we were able to run the weak side so well," Flores said. "Cripes, you'd run 10 yards before he'd show up. He just wasn't that kind of a player."

When Stabler wasn't handing off, he was throwing to all-time speed demon and Pro Bowl wide receiver Cliff Branch, Casper, and the crafty Biletnikoff, who was voted MVP. "Two are in the Hall of Fame and the other one should be," Wolf said, referring to Branch. "When he got even, he was leavin'. That's where that first got started. He ran so fast that he was by people before they realized it."

Ken "The Snake" Stabler, whose passer rating of 103.7 in 1976 ranked sixth best of all-time, found Casper for 19 in the second quarter. On the next play, backup running back Carl Garrett sliced for 13 on the left side after Bryant ducked his head and missed the tackle near the line. On first and goal, the Vikings jammed six defensive linemen into the middle to stop the run, so Stabler flipped the ball to the wide-open Casper for a 1-yard touchdown. "Kenny did not have a strong arm but he knew that he had to throw the ball early and throw it hard," Flores said. "He was so accurate. He was perfect for the change of the times, where[as] Lamonica wasn't. When they went to all the different zones, with Snake's quick release, that was his strength."

When the Vikings continued going nowhere, Oakland's Neal Colzie returned a punt 25 yards. Then Biletnikoff beat cornerback Nate Wright inside for a 17-yard completion to the 1, and Banaszak, the gritty goal-line runner, banged over for a 1-yard touchdown. Mann blew the extra point, but it didn't matter. The score stood at 16–0 well into the third quarter until another Mann field goal, this time from 40 yards, increased the Raiders' margin to 19–0.

Late in the third quarter, Neil Clabo punted for the eighth time and linebacker Ted Hendricks was penalized for running into him. "What got them their first score was I was called for roughing the punter," said Hendricks, "or else it would have been a zero game." Retaking the field, Tarkenton completed a flock of passes until the last one, an 8-yarder to Sammy White, beat Colzie in the left corner for a touchdown.

When the Vikings got the ball back early in

the fourth quarter, trailing 19–7, Tarkenton passed to White across the middle on third and 11 for an 18-yard gain to the Oakland 44. The NFL offensive rookie of the year paid for the catch, however, when free safety Jack Tatum smashed into him a split-second later. Tatum's helmet crashed underneath White's chin and White's headgear went flying, but he held onto the ball. "Everybody remembers that hit," Wolf said. "Tatum was 5-foot-10½, 210, and ran 4.35. He was the fastest guy in that secondary and the toughest guy in that secondary. In all my time with the Raiders—which was darn near 25 years—he was the only rookie that never had to stand up and sing."

Three plays later, defensive end Otis Sistrunk and Hendricks broke loose on a stunt and flushed Tarkenton from the pocket. As Tarkenton scrambled to his left, nose tackle Dave Rowe and Hendricks took up the chase. It was third and 3 at the Oakland 37, clearly four-down territory for the Vikings. The play for any quarterback, particularly one with the experience of Tarkenton, was to throw the ball away.

Instead, Tarkenton committed a cardinal sin by putting up a floater back into the middle of the field in the general direction of Foreman. Hall stepped up, picked it off, and returned 16 yards to near midfield. "For whatever reason, [Tarkenton] didn't have any of his top games in the three Super Bowls he played for us," Reichow said.

It didn't take long for the Raiders to build an insurmountable lead at 26–7. On third and 6 at the 50, Biletnikoff found himself alone in the middle at the 35. "I loused up the coverage," Krause said. "I called one coverage to [Nate] Wright and played another. It gave Biletnikoff practically the whole field." Biletnikoff's glaring lack of speed—"I don't think Fred ever ran a 4.6," Flores said—was never more evident when he couldn't outrun the Vikings before settling for a 48-yard gain. Banaszak then plowed over from the 2.

The finishing touches were applied by 36-year-old Willie Brown, a cornerback destined for the Hall of Fame. Tarkenton took a quick drop, threw to White on the left sideline, and watched as Brown cut in front for an interception that he returned 75 yards for a touchdown. Although Minnesota managed to score

TEAM STATISTICS

OAKLAND		MINNESOTA
21	Total First Downs	20
13	Rushing	2
8	Passing	15
0	Penalty	3
429	Total Net Yardage	353
73	Total Offensive Plays	71
5.9	Avg. Gain per Offensive Play	5.0
52	Rushes	26
266	Yards Gained Rushing (Net)	71
5.1	Average Yards per Rush	2.7
19	Passes Attempted	44
12	Passes Completed	24
0	Passes Intercepted	2
2	Tackled Attempting to Pass	1
17	Yards Lost Attempting to Pass	4
163	Yards Gained Passing (Net)	282
9/18	Third-Down Efficiency	6/17
0/1	Fourth-Down Efficiency	1/2
5	Punts	7
32.4	Average Distance	37.9
4	Punt Returns	3
43	Punt Return Yardage	14
2	Kickoff Returns	7
47	Kickoff Return Yardage	136
91	Interception Return Yardage	0
0	Fumbles	1
0	Own Fumbles Recovered	0
1	Opponent Fumbles Recovered	0
4	Penalties	2
30	Yards Penalized	25
4	Touchdowns	2
2	Rushing	0
1	Passing	2
1	Returns	0
2	Extra Points Made	2
2	Field Goals Made	0
3	Field Goals Attempted	0
0	Safeties	0
32	Total Points Scored	14
33:27	Time of Possession	26:33

"John [Madden] was very good on game day at implementing the game plan, and at motivation, obviously. He was always screaming and yelling."

Tom Flores, Raiders receivers coach

INDIVIDUAL STATISTICS

OAKLAND

Passing	CP/ATT	YDS	TD	INT	RAT
Stabler	12/19	180	1	0	111.7
Rae	0/0	0	0	0	0.0

Rushing	ATT	YDS	AVG	TD	LG
Davis	16	137	8.6	0	35
Van Eeghen	18	73	4.1	0	11
Banaszak	10	19	1.9	2	6
Garrett	4	19	4.8	0	13
Ginn	2	9	4.5	0	9
Rae	2	9	4.5	0	11

Receiving	NO	YDS	AVG	TD	LG
Biletnikoff	4	79	19.8	0	48
Casper	4	70	17.5	1	25
Branch	3	20	6.7	0	10
Garrett	1	11	11.0	0	11

Interceptions	NO	YDS	LG	TD
Brown	1	75	75t	1
Wil. Hall	1	16	16	0

Punting	NO	AVG	LG	BLK
Guy	4	40.5	51	1

Punt Ret.	NO/FC	YDS	LG	TD
Colzie	4/0	43	25	0

Kickoff Ret.	NO	YDS	LG	TD
Garrett	2	47	24	0

Defense	SOLO	AST	TOT	SK
M. Johnson	7	0	7	0
Villapiano	7	0	7	1
Atkinson	6	0	6	0
Hendricks	6	0	6	0
Sistrunk	4	0	4	0
Thomas	4	0	4	0
Wil. Hall	3	0	3	0
Matuszak	3	0	3	0
McMath	3	0	3	0
Rice	3	0	3	0
Rowe	2	0	2	0
Tatum	2	0	2	0
Brown	1	1	2	0
Barnes	1	0	1	0
Bradshaw	1	0	1	0
Colzie	1	0	1	0
Garrett	1	0	1	0
Ginn	1	0	1	0
Phillips	1	0	1	0
Philyaw	1	0	1	0
TOTAL	58	1	59	1

MINNESOTA

Passing	CP/ATT	YDS	TD	INT	RAT
Tarkenton	17/35	205	1	2	52.7
Lee	7/9	81	1	0	141.2

Rushing	ATT	YDS	AVG	TD	LG
Foreman	17	44	2.6	0	7
Johnson	2	9	4.5	0	8
S. White	1	7	7.0	0	7
Miller	2	4	2.0	0	3
Lee	1	4	4.0	0	4
McClanahan	3	3	1.0	0	2

Receiving	NO	YDS	AVG	TD	LG
S. White	5	77	15.4	1	29
Foreman	5	62	12.4	0	26
Voigt	4	49	12.3	1	15
Miller	4	19	4.8	0	13
Rashad	3	53	17.7	0	25
Johnson	3	26	8.7	0	17

Interceptions	NO	YDS	LG	TD
None	--	--	--	--

Punting	NO	AVG	LG	BLK
Clabo	7	37.9	46	0

Punt Ret.	NO/FC	YDS	LG	TD
Willis	3/0	14	8	0

Kickoff Ret.	NO	YDS	LG	TD
S. White	4	79	26	0
Willis	3	57	20	0

Defense	SOLO	AST	TOT	SK
Siemon	15	2	17	0
Page	10	1	11	1
Krause	6	2	8	0
Bryant	6	0	6	0
Blair	3	2	5	0
Eller	3	2	5	0
Hilgenberg	2	3	5	0
J. Wright	4	0	4	0
N. Wright	4	0	4	0
Sutherland	3	0	3	1
Beamon	2	0	2	0
Craig	2	0	2	0
Allen	1	0	1	0
Win. Hall	1	0	1	0
Martin	1	0	1	0
Miller	1	0	1	0
Winston	1	0	1	0
Yary	1	0	1	0
TOTAL	66	12	78	2

one more touchdown, there were only 23 seconds left on the clock and no chance for a comeback.

"He [Willie Brown] and Ted Hendricks would probably tie as the greatest defensive players ever to play for the Raiders," Wolf said. "I don't know if Willie is better than Herb [Adderley]. Herb would hit you and Willie wouldn't always hit you. But Willie was faster and could cover anybody." The Raider secondary also included cornerback Skip Thomas, who had ideal size (6-foot-1½, 210), 4.5 speed, and terrific coverage skills, as well as strong safety George Atkinson, an ex-cornerback who had to move inside because of back problems. He also was an intimidating hitter.

"That was the mainstay of our defense," Hendricks said. "Those guys could cover anything. Tatum was always sitting there waiting for someone to come in his territory. Skip Thomas could play man."

He continued with his thoughts of the Vikings: "Tarkenton was a hell of a player with his scrambling ability, but he really only had one wide receiver—Sammy White. Ahmad [Rashad] was kind of a graceful guy, but I think he was really intimidated by our defenders. I don't think the Vikings ever were a very physical team."

When the Vikings arrived in Pasadena, a column by Jim Murray in the *Los Angeles Times* greeted them. Not only were the Vikings 0–3 in the Super Bowl, but they were also eight-time champions of the NFC Central, a division in which no other team had a winning record from 1973 to 1976. The Purple Gang, mused Murray, should be protected under the rules of the Geneva Convention and by the Red Cross. All Raiders touchdowns should be worth four points, Murray wrote, Stabler ought to be made to pass right-handed, and commissioner Pete Rozelle should make Oakland play with 10 men.

The Vikings had an "obsession" to win a Super Bowl, according to Tarkenton, and offensive coordinator Jerry Burns believed the 1976 team was the best that represented Minnesota in a Super Bowl. "In the locker room that day I remember just how intense things were as we were getting ready to take the field," Siemon said. "I say that in the best sense of the word. It was as ready as I thought we ever were. But that was defused pretty quickly."

Grant, according to Siemon, became so biased toward players who wouldn't make mental mistakes that he stayed with veterans too long. The athletic McNeill, a first-round draft choice in 1974, remained a backup in his third season while watching an over-the-hill Hilgenberg get obliterated by the Raiders. "We didn't let him play that year, for some reason," Ryan said. In 1977, McNeill would begin an eight-year run as a Vikings' starter, but that was too late to save Minnesota in the Super Bowl.

In much the same vein, Grant made little or no adjustments to his weak-side run defense, even as it was getting torn asunder. "Minnesota had not changed since the Super Bowl when I played for Kansas City, other than they had Fran Tarkenton," Flores said. "They played their stuff because they had won 12, 13 games doing it. If it's not broke, don't meddle with it. Just play the scheme better. That was their whole philosophy.

"Bud was not the kind of guy you ever got to know because he never talked or visited, but I always liked him and respected him because he was a no-nonsense guy. That part of his coaching was consistent. That's why they won so many games; they were very, very disciplined."

In four Super Bowls, the Vikings were outscored 51–0 in the first half and 95–34 overall, out-rushed on average 215.5 to 56.8, and out-gained 323.5 to 237.3. Their average time of possession was just less than 25 minutes. Minnesota's leading rusher in any game was Foreman with 44 yards (in 17 carries) against the Raiders. In their last three Super Bowls, the Vikings allowed Larry Csonka to rush for 145, Franco Harris to rush for 158, and Davis to rush for 137.

"Bud would say, 'Well, this is how we got here, this is the way we're going to play,'" Reichow said. "It was, 'God, when are we ever going to play a good game?' It never happened."

The Raiders carried Madden off the field, Rozelle gritted his teeth before handing the Lombardi Trophy to Al Davis, and the Raiders danced the night away back at their hotel in Newport Beach.

"Oakland had a chance to be in so many Super Bowls," Hendricks said. "[We] finally made it to one and . . . won it. We completely dominated. The curse was lifted."

Ten Hardest Hits

1. **Ronnie Lott, S, 49ers, XXIII:** Furious at his team-mates for not playing better, Lott takes matters into his own hands. From deep in the middle, he charges up and crashes into Bengals RB Ickey Woods. "It was like a train wreck, or two rhinos hitting each other full force," 49ers CB Eric Wright said. "That hit set the standard for us."

2. **Jack Tatum, S, Raiders, XI:** Early in the fourth quarter, WR Sammy White hauls in an 18-yard pass from Fran Tarkenton. Tatum hits White under the chin with his helmet, sending White's helmet flying. White hangs on to the ball. "Tatum knocked him out," Oakland LB Ted Hendricks said. "I've got a great picture of that."

3. **Larry Cole, DT, Cowboys, X:** Terry Bradshaw's last pass is the game-winning 64-yard touchdown to Lynn Swann with 3:02 left. On the play, Cole drives his helmet into the left side of Bradshaw's jaw, and the quarterback is out before he hits the ground. Backup Terry Hanratty plays the last series for Pittsburgh.

4. **Glen Edwards, S, Steelers, IX:** Late in the first half, Fran Tarkenton throws on target 20 yards downfield to WR John Gilliam at the Pittsburgh 4-yard line. Edwards delivers a two-armed shot to Gilliam's head. When the tipped pass comes down, it's intercepted by CB Mel Blount.

5. **Nick Buoniconti, LB, Dolphins, VIII:** With a minute left in the first half, Vikings RB Oscar Reed tries to run off right tackle on fourth and 1 from the Miami 6. Buoniconti cuts inside of pulling guard Ed White, crushes Reed, and causes a fumble.

6. **Doug Swift, LB, Dolphins, VII:** On a Washington third down late in the first half, the Dolphins line up LB Bob Matheson outside and Swift inside. When the Redskins turn their protection toward Matheson, Swift shoots through untouched and buries QB Billy Kilmer, whose pass in the flat is intercepted by Nick Buoniconti.

7. **Martin Mayhew, CB, Redskins, XXVI:** Early in the fourth quarter, Jim Kelly scrambles to his right for 9 yards and is unloaded upon by Mayhew. Kelly appears to be out. He sits out a play and then returns, but his memory seems spotty after the game.

8. **Bob Sanders, S, Colts, XLI:** On a simple run up the middle by Bears RB Cedric Benson late in the first quarter, Sanders roars up from the deep middle and flattens Benson with a form tackle. The Colts recover the fumble, and it's the beginning of the end for the Bears.

9. **Aaron Brown, DE, Chiefs, IV:** With about five minutes left, Brown, a second-year starter, comes around the edge and slams Vikings QB Joe Kapp, causing a fumble that the Vikings recover. It is Kapp's final play of the game.

10. **Ken Norton, LB, Cowboys, XXVII:** On third and goal from the Dallas 1, Buffalo RB Kenneth Davis tries to run high against Norton, but the linebacker doesn't budge an inch. On the next series, Norton leaps over Thurman Thomas and hits Jim Kelly, forcing him from the game with a sprained knee.

Oakland safety Jack Tatum (No. 32) sent Sammy White's helmet flying with this crushing blow in Super Bowl XI. White held on to the pass from Fran Tarkenton for a first down, but Tatum's hit was one of many devastating blows inflicted by the Raiders' defense. *Richard Drew/AP Images*

XII

DALLAS COWBOYS 27, DENVER BRONCOS 10

January 15, 1978
Louisiana Superdome, New Orleans, Louisiana

The Dallas Cowboys of 1977 would have been a very good team even without Tony Dorsett. With him, Dallas became a great team, perhaps the finest of the Tom Landry era.

Dorsett was the missing link, the franchise running back that the Cowboys needed. With a newfound running dimension to go with Roger Staubach's lethal passing and scrambling, the Cowboys had too much offense in Super Bowl XII even for a defense as good as the Denver Broncos'. Combine that with the Cowboys' suffocating defense, spearheaded by an all-time front four, and it's a wonder the Broncos even managed to stay competitive in this Super Bowl.

Despite all their disadvantageous matchups and physical shortcomings, not to mention eight turnovers, the Broncos still were in the game until midway through the fourth quarter. That's when running back Robert Newhouse floated a perfect 29-yard touchdown pass to Golden Richards in the Cowboys' 27–10 victory at the Louisiana Superdome.

"That was the best football team that I played on," Cowboys safety Charlie Waters said. During his 11 seasons in Dallas, Waters played on five teams that reached the Super Bowl and four others that lost in the NFC Championship Game. "I'd put that team against any team of any era," he said. "There was no weakness on that team. We solved the problem at running back."

In early May, the Cowboys consummated a trade with the Seattle Seahawks to move up from the 14th to 2nd overall selection and draft Dorsett, the Heisman Trophy winner from the University of Pittsburgh. In return, the Cowboys gave Seattle three picks in the second round, two of which had been obtained in shrewd trades for defensive end Pat Toomay and quarterback Clint Longley. "Dallas and Seattle must be sleeping together," a miffed Bud Grant of Minnesota said. "I don't understand it at all."

In the two previous seasons, the Cowboys had tried to compensate for the loss of Calvin Hill by shuffling such pedestrian ball carriers as Preston Pearson, Doug Dennison, Scott Laidlaw, Charles Young, and Newhouse. Clearly, none of them was the answer. After the deal was consummated, general manager Tex Schramm called Dorsett the best running back to come along since O. J. Simpson. He would lead the Cowboys in rushing for the next decade.

"Tony was the first Cowboys player to get $1 million, but that didn't bother me at all," wide receiver Drew Pearson said. "And, quickly, Tony showed us he was special. That year we were 12–2 and scored over 340 points. We were a machine, and Tony was the game-breaking piece that we needed. He could turn a game around at any point at any time with just one quick hit up the middle."

Landry didn't start Dorsett over Drew Pearson until midseason. In Week 12, Dorsett gained a club-record 206 yards against Philadelphia. In one-sided playoff victories over Chicago

Attendance: 75,583
Conditions: 70 degrees, indoors
Time of kickoff: 5:17 p.m. (CST)
Length of game: 3 hours, 32 minutes
Referee: Jim Tunney

MVP: Randy White, DT, and Harvey Martin, DE, Cowboys

"Denver's team was all emotion that year. They had this 'Orange Crush' going for them and their fans were wild and crazy. And here our team was very methodical, just like Landry's personality. It was a great matchup."

Charlie Waters, Cowboys safety

	1	2	3	4	Final
Dallas Cowboys	10	3	7	7	27
Denver Broncos	0	0	10	0	10

SCORING SUMMARY

1st Quarter
DAL Dorsett, 3-yd. run (Herrera kick)
DAL Herrera, 35-yd. FG
2nd Quarter
DAL Herrera, 43-yd. FG
3rd Quarter
DEN Turner, 47-yd. FG
DAL Johnson, 45-yd. pass from Staubach (Herrera kick)
DEN Lytle, 1-yd. run (Turner kick)
4th Quarter
DAL Richards, 29-yd. pass from Newhouse (Herrera kick)

(37–7) and Minnesota (23–6), he carried 36 times for 156 yards and three touchdowns. "He had speed, and he was tough and could run inside," Staubach said. "He took a lot of the pressure off me. With him, we had a very balanced game. That year [wide receiver] Tony Hill also came, and when you have Tony and Drew, we were one heck of an offense."

The Cowboys were the first team to lead the NFL in both total offense and total defense since the undefeated Miami Dolphins of 1972. Yet, the spread of just 5½ points was a tribute to the respect that the upstart Broncos had earned in their 12–2 season, the best in the AFC. Outfitted in comical, vertically striped socks during their fledgling years, the Broncos didn't mount a single winning season in their first 13 years as a franchise. They went 9–5 in 1976 under coach John Ralston, a cheery disciple of Dale Carnegie, but after the season, a dozen players drafted an anti-Ralston statement and got him fired. The Broncos then hired Red Miller, an NFL assistant for 17 years who most recently had been offensive coordinator in New England.

As the Broncos drove toward their first playoff berth in club history and then the Super Bowl, Broncomania hit its peak. The only defeats for the "Orange Crush" during the regular season were 24–14 against Oakland at home in Week 7 and 14–7 at Dallas in Week 14. Taking advantage of the controversial "non-fumble" by Rob Lytle at the goal line, the Broncos eliminated the Raiders, 20–17, in the AFC Championship Game, and the fans at Mile High Stadium went wild.

"On paper, the Cowboys are a better team than we are, but we've faced that situation all year," Miller said a few days before the game. "What usually happened is that we outplayed teams and beat them. And we have that one big thing going for us in this game: motivation. Winning is in the mind of the player. We're a team of destiny."

To move the ball effectively against the powerful Cowboys, the Broncos needed crisp execution, big plays, a multidimensional attack, and the lead. What happened was they turned the ball over seven times in the first half, never had a gain longer than 21 yards, finished with 35 net yards through the air, and trailed after Dorsett opened the scoring late in the first quarter when Landry went for it on fourth-and-1 at the Denver 3. Landry called the wrong formation, but Staubach ran the play anyway out of a Power-I set, and Dorsett fought his way into the end zone.

Staubach said the team was "jittery" in the early going, partially as a result of what he described as almost unprecedented noise level in the Superdome. "This was the first Super Bowl played indoors, and teammates could hardly hear me in the huddle," said Staubach. "The roar made audibles almost impossible. The first quarter was a mess. Pure chaos."

The Cowboys had three of their six fumbles in the first few minutes, none of which were recovered by Denver. A critical missed opportunity for the Broncos occurred on their first punt, when Cowboys returner Tony Hill lost track of where he was and fumbled trying to field the ball at the 1. The first man down, Denver wide receiver John Schultz, couldn't make what should have been a routine recovery, and somehow Hill managed to get the ball back. "If we had recovered that first fumble on the punt . . . I think we would have won the game," Miller said a decade later.

Two plays after Dorsett's 3-yard touchdown, Broncos quarterback Craig Morton was pressured by defensive end Ed "Too Tall" Jones, and his pass was tipped by middle linebacker Bob Breunig to cornerback Aaron Kyle for an interception. Starting from the Denver 35, Dorsett skirted right end for 18. On third and goal, left inside linebacker Joe Rizzo flushed Staubach on a blitz and defensive end Lyle Alzado sacked him for minus-10. On came Efren Herrera to kick a 35-yard field goal.

With the first quarter almost over, the Cowboys led, 10–0. In the second quarter, they began four possessions in Denver territory and another at their own 43 as the Broncos' litany of mistakes continued.

By rights, the game should have been over by halftime, but despite advancing within the Denver 30 on each of those five possessions, all the bumbling Cowboys had to show for it was a 43-yard field goal by Herrera. Their Pro Bowl kicker also missed from the 43-, 32-, and 44-yard lines, and tight end Billy Joe Dupree fumbled away a reception at the Denver 12 when he carried the ball far too loosely and cornerback Steve Foley poked it out.

Early in the third quarter the Broncos failed to execute a fake punt on fourth and 4, but the Cowboys were penalized for having 12 men on the field. Wearing his customary black high-top shoes, 36-year-old Jim Turner drilled a 47-yard field goal, and it was 13–3. Then neither team went anywhere until, in the midst of the overall sloppiness, Butch Johnson made one of the most spectacular catches in Super Bowl history.

It was third and 10 from the Denver 45 when Staubach got the call from Landry. It was a pass designed to hit either Dupree or the fullback on the right side, or Johnson on an inside breaking route. "I said 'Butch, you just run a good post route, and I will throw it to you if [Bernard] Jackson is not back in his coverage,'" Staubach said. "We'd been watching a lot of film and I saw that Jackson, their weak safety, liked to gamble a lot. If I had called '83-Y Post' in the huddle, everybody would have said, 'Roger's going against the coach.'"

From shotgun formation, Staubach had time against a three-man rush and let it go long because Jackson was out of position. "[Johnson] got behind

DALLAS COWBOYS (NFC, 12–2)			DENVER BRONCOS (AFC, 12–2)	
		Offense		
86	Butch Johnson (6-1, 191)	WR	82	Jack Dolbin (5-10, 183)
73	Ralph Neely (6-6, 255)	LT	74	Andy Maurer (6-3, 265)
68	Herb Scott (6-2, 250)	LG	62	Tom Glassic (6-4, 220)
62	John Fitzgerald (6-5, 260)	C	52	Mike Montler (6-4, 250)
64	Tom Rafferty (6-3, 250)	RG	60	Paul Howard (6-3, 260)
67	Pat Donovan (6-4, 255)	RT	71	Claudie Minor (6-4, 280)
89	Billy Joe DuPree* (6-4, 226)	TE	88	Riley Odoms (6-4, 232)
88	Drew Pearson* (6-0, 183)	WR	31	Haven Moses (6-2, 200)
12	Roger Staubach* (6-3, 202)	QB	34	Craig Morton (6-4, 213)
33	Tony Dorsett (5-11, 192)	RB	24	Otis Armstrong (5-10, 197)
44	Robert Newhouse (5-10, 205)	RB	32	Jon Keyworth (6-3, 234)
		Defense		
72	Ed Jones (6-9, 265)	LE	79	Barney Chavous (6-3, 250)
75	Jethro Pugh (6-6, 250)	LT | NT	68	Rubin Carter (6-0, 254)
54	Randy White* (6-4, 245)	RT | RE	77	Lyle Alzado* (6-3, 250)
79	Harvey Martin* (6-5, 252)	RE | LOLB	51	Bob Swenson (6-3, 225)
56	Thomas Henderson (6-2, 220)	LLB | LILB	59	Joe Rizzo (6-1, 223)
53	Bob Breunig (6-2, 227)	MLB | RILB	53	Randy Gradishar* (6-3, 231)
50	D. D. Lewis (6-1, 215)	RLB | ROLB	57	Tom Jackson* (5-11, 224)
31	Benny Barnes (6-1, 195)	LCB	20	Louis Wright* (6-2, 195)
25	Aaron Kyle (5-10, 185)	RCB	43	Steve Foley (6-2, 190)
41	Charlie Waters* (6-2, 198)	SS	36	Bill Thompson* (6-1, 200)
43	Cliff Harris* (6-1, 192)	FS	29	Bernard Jackson (6-0, 181)

* Pro Bowl selection

SUBSTITUTIONS

Dallas

Offense: WR - 80 Tony Hill, 83 Golden Richards; T - 71 Andy Frederick, 70 Rayfield Wright, 66 Burton Lawless; G - 61 Jim Cooper. **Defense:** DE - 65 Dave Stalls; DT - 63 Larry Cole, 77 Bill Gregory; LB - 59 Guy Brown, 58 Mike Hegman, 57 Bruce Huther; CB - 20 Mel Renfro, 46 Mark Washington; S - 42 Randy Hughes. **Specialists:** K - 1 Efren Herrera*; P/QB - 11 Danny White **DNP:** 87 Jay Saldi (TE), 18 Glenn Carano (QB).

Denver

Offense: WR - 86 John Schultz, 80 Rick Upchurch; TE - 85 Ron Egloff; T - 73 Henry Allison, 65 Glenn Hyde; C - 50 Bobby Maples; QB - 14 Norris Weese; RB - 30 Jim Jensen, 41 Rob Lytle, 35 Lonnie Perrin. **Defense:** DE - 66 Brison Manor; DT - 70 Paul Smith, 63 John Grant; LB - 56 Larry Evans, 58 Rob Nairne, 55 Godwin Turk; CB - 40 Randy Rich; S - 21 Randy Poltl. **Specialists:** K - 15 Jim Turner; P - 10 Bucky Dilts. **DNP:** 12 Craig Penrose (QB), 67 Steve Schindler (G), 26 Larry Riley (CB).

TEAM STATISTICS

DALLAS		DENVER
17	**Total First Downs**	11
8	Rushing	8
8	Passing	1
1	Penalty	2
325	**Total Net Yardage**	156
71	Total Offensive Plays	58
4.6	Avg. Gain per Offensive Play	2.7
38	**Rushes**	29
143	Yards Gained Rushing (Net)	121
3.8	Average Yards per Rush	4.2
28	**Passes Attempted**	25
19	Passes Completed	8
0	Passes Intercepted	4
5	Tackled Attempting to Pass	4
35	Yards Lost Attempting to Pass	26
182	Yards Gained Passing (Net)	35
5/17	**Third-Down Efficiency**	1/12
1/1	**Fourth-Down Efficiency**	2/3
5	**Punts**	4
41.6	Average Distance	38.3
1	**Punt Returns**	4
0	Punt Return Yardage	22
3	**Kickoff Returns**	6
51	Kickoff Return Yardage	173
46	**Interception Return Yardage**	0
6	**Fumbles**	4
4	Own Fumbles Recovered	0
4	Opponent Fumbles Recovered	2
12	**Penalties**	8
94	Yards Penalized	60
3	**Touchdowns**	1
1	Rushing	1
2	Passing	0
0	Returns	0
3	**Extra Points Made**	1
2	**Field Goals Made**	1
5	Field Goals Attempted	1
0	**Safeties**	0
27	**Total Points Scored**	10
38:38	**Time of Possession**	21:22

our safety, Bernard Jackson, but not by much," defensive coordinator Joe Collier said. "Staubach just threw the damn ball as far as he could throw it." Johnson caught the ball in his fingertips as he tumbled to the artificial turf at the goal line, cradled the ball to his chest, and at some point lost it.

The Broncos argued that Johnson never had control of the ball, but replays showed that the touchdown call by the crew of referee Jim Tunney was correct. What made the catch even more amazing was that Johnson had suffered a broken right thumb while blocking in the second quarter, after being pressed into service as the second tight end for Jay Saldi, who wasn't in uniform because of a leg injury.

Johnson's touchdown made it 20–3, but Rick Upchurch returned the ensuing kickoff 67 yards to the Dallas 26 after Bruce Huther and Kyle missed tackles. When Morton flipped a screen pass on the next play that was nearly intercepted by Jones, coach Miller inserted scrambler Norris Weese, a 6-footer who had little or no track record since being drafted in the fourth round by the Los Angeles Rams in 1974. Four plays later, Lytle went over from the 1 and it was 20–10.

If their defense hadn't been so dominant, the Cowboys might have been in some trouble. Dorsett was well on his way to a 100-yard game when he suffered a knee injury on the final play of the third quarter and didn't return. Two plays later, Staubach suffered a fracture on the tip of his right forefinger

on a sack by linebacker Tom Jackson. The ball came free and Jackson recovered at the Denver 45. Staubach took a painkilling injection and returned, but his accuracy was compromised.

With just less than eight minutes remaining, Weese tried to get out of the way when Jones ran over right tackle Claudie Minor. As Weese moved

DALLAS

Passing	CP/ATT	YDS	TD	INT	RAT
Staubach	17/25	183	0	1	102.6
Newhouse	1/1	29	0	1	158.3
D. White	1/2	5	0	0	56.3

Rushing	ATT	YDS	AVG	TD	LG
Dorsett	15	66	4.4	1	19
Newhouse	14	55	3.9	0	10
D. White	1	13	13.0	0	13
P. Pearson	3	11	3.7	0	5
Staubach	3	6	2.0	0	5
Laidlaw	1	1	1.0	0	1
Johnson	1	-9	-9.0	0	-9

Receiving	NO	YDS	AVG	TD	LG
P. Pearson	5	37	7.4	0	11
DuPree	4	66	16.5	0	19
Newhouse	3	-1	-0.3	0	5
Johnson	2	53	26.5	1	45
Richards	2	38	19.0	1	29
Dorsett	2	11	5.5	0	15
D. Pearson	1	13	13.0	0	13

Interceptions	NO	YDS	LG	TD
Washington	1	27	27	13
Kyle	1	19	19	0
Barnes	1	0	0	0
Hughes	1	0	0	0

Punting	NO	AVG	LG	BLK
D. White	5	41.6	53	0

Punt Ret.	NO/FC	YDS	LG	TD
Hill	1/1	0	0	0

Kickoff Ret.	NO	YDS	LG	TD
Johnson	2	29	15	0
Brinson	1	22	22	0

DENVER

Passing	CP/ATT	YDS	TD	INT	RAT
Morton	4/15	39	0	4	0.0
Weese	4/10	22	0	0	47.9

Rushing	ATT	YDS	AVG	TD	LG
Lytle	10	35	3.5	1	16
Armstrong	7	27	3.9	0	18
Weese	3	26	8.7	0	10
Jensen	1	16	16.0	0	16
Keyworth	5	9	1.8	0	6
Perrin	3	8	2.7	0	4

Receiving	NO	YDS	AVG	TD	LG
Dolbin	2	24	12.0	0	15
Odoms	2	9	4.5	0	10
Moses	1	21	21.0	0	21
Upchurch	1	9	9.0	0	9
Jensen	1	5	5.0	0	5
Upchurch	1	-7	-7.0	0	-7

Interceptions	NO	YDS	LG	TD
None	--	---	--	--

Punting	NO	AVG	LG	BLK
Dilts	4	38.3	46	0

Punt Ret.	NO/FC	YDS	LG	TD
Upchurch	3/1	22	8	0
Schultz	1/0	0	0	0

Kickoff Ret.	NO	YDS	LG	TD
Upchurch	3	94	67	0
Schultz	2	62	37	0
Jensen	1	17	17	0

up in the pocket, left end Harvey Martin slammed into him from the side and Kyle recovered the fumble at the Denver 29. "I thought we'd started coming on," Miller said. "We had done that before. Norris' fumble kind of put it away."

What happened next caught Collier, who had studied two full seasons of Landry's offense before the game, and the Broncos by complete surprise. "That little stumpy fullback [Newhouse], he had never thrown a halfback pass during the season—in his career, probably," Collier said. "It was a play we had not anticipated."

On the Wednesday before, the Cowboys put in the option pass for Newhouse, who did throw a touchdown pass against Detroit in early 1975. "We ran it in practice about four times that week," Water: remembered. "I don't even think he threw a spira one time." Before the game, Landry told Newhouse to warm up his arm. When Newhouse spotted some Broncos staring down at him, he had to stop throwing After the Weese fumble, Landry sent in the play with Golden Richards as the primary receiver deep down the left sideline. "It was signature Landry," said Waters. "He went for the throat with a trick play." The fact that Staubach could no longer throw effectively also influenced Landry's choice of passers.

Newhouse had stickum smeared all over his hands to ward off fumbles. "What did I think when

INDIVIDUAL STATISTICS

DALLAS Defense	SOLO	AST	TOT	SK		DENVER Defense	SOLO	AST	TOT	SK
Henderson	5	2	7	0		Rizzo	6	3	9	0
Breunig	5	1	6	0		Carter	6	2	8	2
Waters	5	1	6	0		Gradishar	5	3	8	0
R. White	5	0	5	1		T. Jackson	7	0	7	1
Jones	3	2	5	0		Alzado	6	1	7	2
Lewis	3	1	4	1		B. Jackson	5	2	7	0
Barnes	3	0	3	0		Swenson	4	2	6	0
Pugh	3	0	3	0		Thompson	3	2	5	0
Harris	2	1	3	0		Wright	3	2	5	0
Hegman	2	1	3	0		Smith	2	1	3	0
Hughes	2	0	2	0		Chavous	2	0	2	0
Kyle	2	0	2	0		Grant	2	0	2	0
Martin	2	0	2	2		Foley	1	1	2	0
Washington	2	0	2	0		Poltl	1	1	2	0
Cole	1	0	1	0		Rich	1	1	2	0
Huther	1	0	1	0		Nairne	1	0	1	0
Renfro	1	0	1	0		Manor	1	0	1	0
Dennison	0	1	1	0		Minor	1	0	1	0
Stalls	0	1	1	0		Moses	1	0	1	0
						Odoms	1	0	1	0
						Perrin	1	0	1	0
						Howard	0	1	1	0
TOTAL	47	11	58	4		TOTAL	60	22	82	5

the pass play was called? I was shocked. I panicked," he said. "I've never eaten so much stickum in my life. I started wiping it off my pants and started licking my fingers." It is hard enough for a back to throw on the run, but in this instance the right-handed Newhouse was running to his left, requiring him to turn his body completely around to set up to throw. "Not only did he throw an absolutely perfect spiral," Waters said, "but it was just one inch from Foley tipping it. It was just a brilliant play."

The Cowboys finished with 325 total yards, including 143 rushing and 182 passing. Other than two beautifully executed, long scoring passes to Johnson and Richards, the Broncos' fierce, fast 3-4 defense probably played well enough to win. "The rest of the game was back and forth as far as our defense against their offense," said Collier, who served as the Broncos' coordinator from 1969 to 1988. "That was our best year on defense [in] all the years I coached there. Those particular plays were the turning points. Our offense had eight turnovers. That put us in poor field position."

Shortly after being named to replace Ralston, Miller and newly promoted general manager Fred Gehrke made four trades in an attempt to improve the offense. Center Mike Montler came from Buffalo for a second-round choice. Andy Maurer, who ended up starting all season at left tackle, arrived from San Francisco for a ninth-round selection. The Broncos also picked up backup running back Jim Jensen from Dallas for a sixth-round pick.

The key trade, however, was the acquisition of Morton from the New York Giants in exchange for quarterback Steve Ramsey, who had been the Broncos' starter in 1975–1976, plus a fifth-round choice. Morton, 34, had spent his first 11 seasons in Dallas as a backup to Don Meredith, then as the starter in 1969–1970 following Meredith's sudden retirement, and eventually as a frustrated understudy to Staubach for the majority of his final four seasons. After three spotty years starting for bad teams in New York, Morton arrived in Denver with little fanfare. He got married and lived a much slower lifestyle, and put up a passer rating of 82.1, fourth best in the NFL.

To say Morton's old teammates were confident playing against him would be an understatement. "With the Giants, he never once beat the Cowboys because we knew how to get to him," said Dallas cornerback Mel Renfro, who was the nickel back in the final game of his illustrious 14-year career. "We pressured him. Blitzed him. Went after him. Didn't give him time. He wasn't able to scramble because of his knees. We knew he wasn't mobile. . . . If we didn't give him time, we could pretty much shut him down." As Staubach put it, "They could have had Jim Thorpe at quarterback for Denver and he would have been in trouble. It wasn't Craig Morton's fault. Put Craig on the '77 Cowboys and me with Denver and I'll tell you what would have happened: Morton would have won. But Craig had no chance. Our defense overwhelmed him."

Morton entered the contest with a bad hip that further limited his mobility. The Broncos offense, which ranked 17th during the regular season, was by design an extremely conservative operation. The team's leading wide receiver, Haven Moses, caught just 27 passes. Despite running on 59 percent of their plays, the Broncos still gave up a whopping 50 sacks, the third highest total in the NFL.

Maurer, who at 29 was in his final NFL season, found himself starting at left tackle against right end Harvey Martin, the Associated Press Defensive Player of the Year who had recorded 23 sacks. Throughout the game, Martin destroyed Maurer. The other mismatch was Broncos left guard Tom Glassic against right defensive tackle Randy White. "If I could do anything over again, I'd have Tom Glassic healthy and have him weigh more than 220 pounds," said Miller, a consensus pick as NFL coach of the year. "We found out later that he was allergic to grass and that he had lost about 30 pounds during the course of the year. He was overmatched, because of the weight, against Randy White." A first-year starter, White made the first of his nine Pro Bowl appearances a week after the Super Bowl. His predecessor in Dallas, Bob Lilly, played in 11. "I never thought I'd see another Bob Lilly in my lifetime, but Randy White can be another Bob Lilly," Landry said before the game. Martin and White shared MVP honors.

Together with 13-year veteran Jethro Pugh at left tackle, Jones, and capable backups Larry Cole and Bill Gregory, the Cowboys' down linemen put unrelenting heat on Morton. "They just took away everything we had," Morton said. He threw four interceptions in 15 attempts for a passer rating of 0.0. The first pick occurred after Waters barged through a feeble block by fullback Jon Keyworth, and White tossed aside Glassic. After they struck Morton almost simultaneously, nickel back Randy Hughes had the first of his three takeaways (he also recovered two fumbles). The second was the tip by Breunig to Kyle. The third was a terribly underthrown long pass that was picked off by cornerback Benny Barnes, and the fourth was another downfield special that had nothing on it because Morton threw it with Jones draped all over his upper body.

"Our defensive line would guarantee they'd get to the quarterback in 3.2 to 3.4 seconds," said Waters. "Our defensive line was so damn dominant, we had ways to cover up our corners. A great defense is always distinguished by a defensive line. We had a monster of a defensive line."

In two Super Bowls, Morton completed 16 of 41 passes for 80 yards, 1 touchdown, and 7 interceptions for a rating of 15.7. "Morton was horrible, absolutely horrible," Cowboys personnel director Gil Brandt said. "He had a better Super Bowl for us against Baltimore."

With Breunig at middle linebacker, the Cowboys had found a talented replacement for retired Lee Roy Jordan. Breunig was a first-year starter who would go on to play in three Pro Bowls. Old pro D. D. Lewis was undersized but a great competitor on the weak side, while talented but erratic Thomas "Hollywood" Henderson manned the strong side. "Henderson was a spectacular type guy," Dallas linebackers coach Jerry Tubbs said. "He'd make a great play and then screw up. He was on drugs at the time but we didn't know. One time he said to me, 'Coach Tubbs, I sure have made you earn your money, haven't I?' It wasn't much fun."

Free safety Cliff Harris was an intimidating physical presence and, in his eighth season, was still exceptionally fast. Waters had decent speed and was so smart that coordinator Ernie Stautner allowed him to help draw up schemes. "We'd be at our defensive meetings," recalled White, "and it would be Charlie and Ernie Stautner talking to each other about what we were going to do." It was this formidable surrounding cast that prevented quarterbacks from exploiting Barnes and Kyle on the edges.

As the clock expired, Henderson stood squarely on the green carpet as hordes of orange-clad zealots roared a final tribute to their beaten but unbowed Broncos. The linebacker picked up an orange cup, crinkled it in his raised hand, and shouted, "There's your Orange Crush."

Comedy of errors or not, the Cowboys had won another Super Bowl in rather routine fashion.

Ten Worst Performances by a Quarterback

1. **Craig Morton, Broncos, XII:** Benched in the middle of a third-quarter series after nearly throwing a fifth interception, Morton finished the game with a passer rating of 0.0 against his former teammates. Pre-existing hip injury contributed to his lack of mobility.
2. **John Elway, Broncos, XXIV:** Longest completion was a 27-yard shovel pass before he was relieved in the middle of the fourth quarter. Scrambled for just 8 yards and had three turnovers. Was sick much of the week and during the game.
3. **Earl Morrall, Colts, III:** The 1968 NFL player of the year with a 93.2 passer rating, Morrall was yanked in favor of Johnny Unitas late in the third quarter with a rating of 9.3. Looked every bit his 34 years. Rival Joe Namath dissed him during the week.

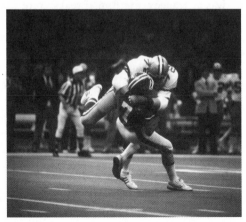

It was a tough evening all around for Denver quarterback Craig Morton during Super Bowl XII. Here he's getting leveled by Harvey Martin on one of the Cowboys' four sacks. Morton also threw four interceptions. *Vernon Biever/NFL/Getty Images*

4. **Kerry Collins, Giants, XXXV:** After playing the game of his life in the NFC Championship Game, Collins was humiliated by the Ravens' overpowering defense. He turned the ball over five times and posted a passer rating of 7.1.
5. **Jim Kelly, Bills, XXVI:** A pair of fourth-quarter touchdown passes lifted his passer rating to a deceivingly high 44.8. His four interceptions led to 17 points, and he also fumbled three times. Teammates didn't help, dropping nine passes.
6. **Rich Gannon, Raiders, XXXVII:** He called it the worst game of his 17-year career. Three of his five interceptions were returned long distances for touchdowns. His former coach, Jon Gruden, had his defense fully prepared.
7. **Fran Tarkenton, Vikings, IX:** Passed for 102 yards, failed to scramble for a single yard, threw three interceptions, and handled the ball poorly. Tarkenton was hemmed into the pocket and often couldn't see to throw downfield.
8. **Ron Jaworski, Eagles, XV:** Posted the best regular season of his 15-year career but was awful in the Super Bowl. He appeared to press, telegraphed his passes, and suffered three interceptions.
9. **Joe Theismann, Redskins, XVIII:** Rendered ineffective by the Raiders' bump-and-run cornerbacks and heavy pass rush. The regular-season MVP, he could muster only a 45.3 passer rating in the Super Bowl. His arm limitations showed up on a windy night.
10. **Billy Kilmer, Redskins, VII:** The unbeaten Dolphins were ecstatic that it was the overachieving Kilmer and not injured Sonny Jurgensen behind center. His longest completion was 15 yards and his passer rating was 19.6.

XIII

PITTSBURGH STEELERS 35, DALLAS COWBOYS 31

January 21, 1979
Orange Bowl, Miami, Florida

Attendance: 79,484
Conditions: 71 degrees, cloudy, rainy, and warm, wind W at
  20–25 mph
Time of kickoff: 4:15 p.m. (EST)
Length of game: 3 hours, 31 minutes
Referee: Pat Haggerty

MVP: Terry Bradshaw, QB, Steelers

For followers of professional football then and now, the matchups in Super Bowl XIII stir the blood. Peruse the starting lineups. Consider the two head coaches. Reflect upon the opposing quarterbacks. Remember that the Pittsburgh Steelers and Dallas Cowboys were the two finest organizations that the NFL had to offer in the 1970s.

In the world of pro football, Super Bowl XIII was a contest pitting elite against elite, Hall of Famer against Hall of Famer. It could be argued that the winning side should enter the conversation as the greatest team of all time. This was as good as it gets.

The Steelers prevailed, 35–31, in spectacular fashion at the Orange Bowl in Miami. In the end, Terry Bradshaw out-dueled Roger Staubach, adding the Super Bowl MVP trophy to go with his MVP honors for the regular season. Commissioner Pete Rozelle handed owner Art Rooney his third Super Bowl trophy in five years. Playing in their fifth Super Bowl in the span of only nine seasons, the defending champion Cowboys lost another to the Steelers by only four points.

"It was probably the hardest thing I had to deal with in my career," said strong safety Charlie Waters. "Roger, all of us, feel the same way. We all automatically start talking about Super Bowl XIII. We'd have about twice as many people in the Hall of Fame if we'd have won it. . . . We would have been the team of the 1970s. I might have gotten in the Cowboys Ring of Honor. You talk about ebb and flow. That was an incredible game."

Some said the turning point was the dropped touchdown pass by Cowboys tight end Jackie Smith late in the third quarter. Others maintain it was the pass-interference penalty on Cowboys cornerback Benny Barnes early in the fourth quarter. Steelers coach Chuck Noll kept going back to the flubbed kickoff that went to Dallas defensive tackle Randy White who, handicapped by a broken thumb, fumbled it away to set up Pittsburgh's winning touchdown. And Staubach still gets worked up about the interception he threw to cornerback Mel Blount late in the first half that helped put Pittsburgh ahead for good.

"This was the most disappointing game I ever played in because we had this great team," Staubach said. "I threw an interception, Randy White fumbled, the flag on the bogus interference call, and who got the hammer? Jackie, which was so unfair. It was a tragedy for him. Breaks were going to determine that game. No one dominated the other. To me, the '78 team was the best team we ever had in Dallas."

The Steelers would go on to win another Super Bowl the following season, but this was the seminal moment in their rightful claim to the title of "team of the 1970s." They were starting to show signs of age. Their once-vaunted rushing attack that had chewed up all comers for years mustered a mere 66 yards in this game and averaged just 143.6 in the regular season, their lowest mark since 1971. Their defense still was outstanding, of course, but with defensive tackle Mean Joe Greene in and out of the lineup because of chronic back problems, one-time running mate Ernie Holmes playing for New England, and end Dwight White reduced to part-time duty, the unit wasn't as dominant as in the past. Still, the Steelers found a way.

"I don't like to compare one game to another

	1	2	3	4	Final
Pittsburgh Steelers	7	14	0	14	35
Dallas Cowboys	7	7	3	14	31

SCORING SUMMARY

1st Quarter
PIT   Stallworth, 28-yd. pass from Bradshaw (Gerela kick)
DAL   Hill, 39-yd. pass from Staubach (Septien kick)
2nd Quarter
DAL   Hegman, 37-yd. fumble recovery return (Septien kick)
PIT   Stallworth, 75-yd. pass from Bradshaw (Gerela kick)
PIT   Bleier, 7-yd. pass from Bradshaw (Gerela kick)
3rd Quarter
DAL   Septien, 27-yd. FG
4th Quarter
PIT   F. Harris, 22-yd. run (Gerela kick)
PIT   Swann, 18-yd. pass from Bradshaw (Gerela kick)
DAL   DuPree, 7-yd. pass from Staubach (Septien kick)
DAL   B. Johnson, 4-yd. pass from Staubach (Septien kick)

center Mike Webster, remembering 1977.

The 1978 season marked significant rules changes that made it legal for offensive linemen to extend their arms while also opening their hands in pass protection. Defenders also were prohibited from chucking receivers more than five yards downfield. The Steelers, especially cornerback Mel Blount, saw this as legislation designed to soften their dominating style of defense. Although the Steelers allowed more passing yards per game (149.6) than they had since 1971, they finished third in total defense by being their usual stubborn selves against the run and competitive against the pass. "I think the rule changes hurt the Pittsburgh Steelers' defense, but [they] opened up the floodgates for our offense," safety Mike Wagner said.

Ultimately, Super Bowl XIII was won because the Cowboys were unable to stop Bradshaw and his sensational wide receivers, Swann and Stallworth. They combined for 10 of Bradshaw's 17 completions and 239 of his 318 passing yards. When the day was done, the Steelers' ability to pass vertically with a high degree of success was the most striking factor in their Super Bowl triumphs over Dallas.

Take the winning touchdown pass, which came with 6:51 remaining. On first down from the Dallas 18, Bradshaw fired high to the post, and Swann went up behind free safety Cliff Harris to snare the ball 6 yards deep into the end zone. "Man, alive," Waters said. "We had him double-covered, with Cliff inside and Aaron [Kyle] outside. Bradshaw should not have thrown it in there. Cliff, in his mind, thought the ball was out of the end zone. In reality, Lynn bounced off a trampoline and went up there and got it on his fingertips right behind Cliff. It should have

and say that one is more memorable," Steelers running back Franco Harris said, "but I think the most intense game I've ever been in was Super Bowl XIII. Two strong teams were on the field that day, each with so many great players. Usually you don't notice it or you try not to be affected by it, but there were 80,000 people in the Orange Bowl that day and the electricity was just amazing."

There are those in Pittsburgh who insist that the 1976 squad was the best team ever assembled by Noll in his 23-year tenure. "I think it was," said Tim Rooney, the team's director of pro personnel throughout the 1970s. "That year [1976] we had to start Mike Kruczek for seven, eight games. You'll be astonished to see that we gave up maybe 13 points in six games [actually, 28 points in the last nine games]. After that generation passed, the last two Super Bowls we had Bradshaw, Franco was still a power, and [John] Stallworth and [Lynn] Swann came into play. Now we had a big-play offense."

The 1976 team was crushed by Oakland, 24–7, in its attempt for a third straight Super Bowl, when both Harris and Rocky Bleier were sidelined by injury. The 1977 team, beset by injuries and contractual unrest, slumped to 9–5 and then absorbed a first-round playoff beating at the hands of the Denver Broncos. "We just didn't care enough for one another," said

> "We wanted Swann. The year [1974] he was drafted, [Pittsburgh] picked right ahead of us. You had the 15 minutes. We were ready to sprint up there with our Swann card. They took like 14:55 to make the pick. It was Swann. So we ended up taking Charlie Young."
>
> *Gil Brandt, Cowboys director of personnel*

been an interception."

Remarkable throws and catches such as this finally drove Cliff Harris to telephone Bradshaw and discuss what his reads were. "I asked him, 'What did you see? What were your primary reads—the free safety, the weak-side linebacker, or what?'" Harris said. "He said, 'Well, I'd look for Swann, and if he was covered I'd look for Stallworth, and if he was covered I'd look for Franco.' He was serious. I said, 'Oh no. There's got to be more to it than that.'"

There was more to it than that, of course—a lot more. But playing dumb has been the way Bradshaw has lived his life, first as a player and later as a broadcaster. By his ninth season, Bradshaw had become a thinking man's quarterback, yet this didn't stop Thomas "Hollywood" Henderson, the flamboyant Cowboys line-backer, from creating headlines during the week when he told a mob of reporters, "Bradshaw couldn't spell cat if you spotted him the C and the T." It is one of the most recognizable quotes in the annals of football. Noll's retort—"Empty barrels make the most noise"—was pretty good, too.

As usual, Bradshaw laughed off the insult in front of the press, but inside, he was seething, and so were the Steelers. "Dallas talks too much," Steelers defensive coordinator George Perles said. "We're out to get Henderson."

"Maybe some people thought it was clever; I thought it was nasty," Bradshaw said. He retaliated with one of the greatest games of his career. "I answered Henderson the best way possible: by halftime I had broken every significant passing record.

"Two decades later, I interviewed Henderson for the Fox show *NFL Sunday*. That week in 1979 had turned out to be the highlight of Henderson's professional football career. A

PITTSBURGH STEELERS (AFC, 14–2)			DALLAS COWBOYS (NFC, 12–4)	
		Offense		
82	John Stallworth (6-2, 183)	WR	80	Tony Hill* (6-2, 198)
55	Jon Kolb (6-2, 262)	LT	67	Pat Donovan (6-4, 250)
57	Sam Davis (6-1, 255)	LG	68	Herbert Scott (6-2, 252)
52	Mike Webster* (6-2, 250)	C	62	John Fitzgerald (6-5, 260)
72	Gerry Mullins (6-3, 244)	RG	64	Tom Rafferty (6-3, 250)
74	Ray Pinney (6-4, 240)	RT	70	Rayfield Wright (6-6, 260)
84	Randy Grossman (6-1, 215)	TE	89	Billy Joe DuPree* (6-4, 229)
88	Lynn Swann* (6-0, 180)	WR	88	Drew Pearson (6-0, 183)
12	Terry Bradshaw* (6-3, 215)	QB	12	Roger Staubach* (6-3, 202)
20	Rocky Bleier (5-11, 210)	RB	44	Robert Newhouse (5-10, 215)
32	Franco Harris* (6-2, 225)	RB	33	Tony Dorsett* (5-11, 190)
		Defense		
68	L. C. Greenwood* (6-7, 250)	LE	72	Ed Jones (6-9, 270)
75	Joe Greene* (6-4, 260)	LT	63	Larry Cole (6-5, 252)
64	Steve Furness (6-4, 255)	RT	54	Randy White* (6-4, 250)
76	John Banaszak (6-3, 244)	RE	79	Harvey Martin* (6-5, 250)
59	Jack Ham* (6-1, 225)	LLB	56	Thomas Henderson* (6-2, 220)
58	Jack Lambert* (6-4, 220)	MLB	53	Bob Breunig (6-2, 225)
51	Loren Toews (6-3, 222)	RLB	50	D. D. Lewis (6-1, 215)
29	Ron Johnson (5-10, 200)	LCB	31	Benny Barnes (6-1, 195)
47	Mel Blount* (6-3, 205)	RCB	25	Aaron Kyle (5-10, 185)
31	Donnie Shell* (5-11, 190)	SS	41	Charlie Waters* (6-2, 200)
23	Mike Wagner (6-2, 200)	FS	43	Cliff Harris* (6-1, 192)

* Pro Bowl selection

SUBSTITUTIONS

Pittsburgh

Offense: WR - 83 Theo Bell, 86 Jim Smith; TE - 87 Jim Mandich; T - 79 Larry Brown; G - 77 Steve Courson; C - 66 Ted Peterson; RB - 35 Jack Deloplaine, 39 Rick Moser, 38 Sidney Thornton. *Defense:* DE - 69 Fred Anderson, 78 Dwight White; DT - 65 Tom Beasley, 67 Gary Dunn; LB - 56 Robin Cole, 53 Dennis Winston; CB - 30 Larry Anderson; S - 21 Tony Dungy, 25 Ray Oldham. *Specialists:* K - 10 Roy Gerela; P - 5 Craig Colquitt. *DNP:* 89 Bennie Cunningham (TE), 15 Mike Kruczek (QB), 18 Cliff Stoudt (QB).

Dallas

Offense: WR - 86 Butch Johnson, 82 Robert Steele; TE - Jackie Smith; T - 71 Andy Frederick; G - 66 Burton Lawless, 60 Tom Randall; C - 61 Jim Cooper; RB - 24 Alois Blackwell, 36 Larry Brinson, 35 Scott Laidlaw, 26 Preston Pearson. *Defense:* DE - 65 Dave Stalls; DT - 76 Larry Bethea; LB - 59 Guy Brown, 58 Mike Hegman, 57 Bruce Huther; CB - 32 Dennis Thurman; S - 42 Randy Hughes. *Specialists:* K - 1 Rafael Septien; P - 11 Danny White. *DNP:* 18 Glenn Carano (QB), 75 Jethro Pugh (DT), 46 Mark Washington (CB).

year later, the Cowboys released him, and eventually he ended up in prison. He abused drugs and alcohol. As I sat opposite him during that interview, I certainly felt no animosity toward him."

Down by 18, the Cowboys swiftly drove 89 yards to make it 35–24 on Staubach's 7-yard touchdown pass to tight end Billy Joe Dupree. When Tony Dungy, a reserve safety, blew the recovery on Rafael Septien's onside kick, cornerback Dennis Thurman recovered for Dallas near midfield with 2:23 showing. "We'd held Dallas to only a field goal in the second half and they hadn't scored an offensive touchdown since the first quarter, and all of a sudden our coaches went to our 'prevent package,'" defensive end L. C. Greenwood said. "I didn't understand that." After finding Drew Pearson in the middle of a zone for 25 yards on fourth and 18, Staubach then hit Tony Dorsett for 9 and, finally, wide-open Butch Johnson in the end zone for a 4-yard touchdown with 22 seconds on the clock.

One of the Pittsburgh writers approached Perles after the game and said, "If the game had lasted 5 more minutes [the Cowboys] would have won." Perles pointed out that the Steelers went into a prevent defense to win the game. "If I hadn't gone into that," Perles said, "they couldn't score in a month of Sundays." No one will ever know, because another onside kick by Septien was recovered by Steelers running back Rocky Bleier, and the game was over.

Each team had three turnovers. All three by

Dallas led to scores, whereas just two of Pittsburgh's produced points. On the opening series, coach Tom Landry called a reverse pass by Drew Pearson to Dupree. The big tight end was wide open for what might well have been a 34-yard touchdown, but Pearson fumbled the handoff from Dorsett and defensive end John Banaszak recovered for Pittsburgh.

Seven plays later, Bradshaw had all day to throw and laid it up high to Stallworth in the left corner of the end zone for the 28-yard opening touchdown. Kyle made the mistake of letting Stallworth release outside, and Harris was unable to get over. "If Aaron would have just done his job and taken the position he was supposed to have taken, then Cliff's help coming over there would have eaten that play up," Waters said. "We changed our coverage in that game to protect our corners, but I'll be damned if our corner didn't even play that technique properly."

Late in the first quarter, defensive end Harvey Martin came off left tackle Jon Kolb as Bradshaw moved up in the pocket, and Martin forced a fumble that the other end, Ed "Too Tall" Jones, hopped on at the Pittsburgh 41. On third and 8, the Steelers blitzed eight against seven blockers, but Staubach stood tough and got the ball off before ducking out of the way of onrushing middle linebacker Jack Lambert and Wagner. The ball went on the left sideline to Tony Hill, who was open against slipshod man-to-man coverage by strong safety Donnie Shell. Hill made the catch at the 28 and slipped off down the boundary to the end zone for a 39-yard score.

Another stunning play occurred early in the second quarter when the Steelers were facing third and 10 from their 48. Bradshaw lost the ball against Harris' left hip as he tried to get out on a rollout. Bradshaw picked it up on one bounce, began to scramble right, and was grabbed by a blitzing Henderson. "He was trying to cover up, to cradle the ball and go down," said Henderson, "but I pinned both his elbows in the middle of his back and shook him, trying to make something happen." Nickel linebacker Mike Hegman arrived on the scene, ripped the ball out from behind Bradshaw's back, and set off on a 37-yard fumble return for a touchdown.

In a game when neither team was down for

long, the Steelers were back three plays later with a tying touchdown on a 75-yard pass to Stallworth. The Cowboys played mostly man-to-man in the first half, but got burned and fell back into more zones after that. Said Noll, "We didn't feel they could cover us in man." The touchdown to Stallworth came against another blitz from Dallas defensive coordinator Ernie Stautner. Bradshaw got the ball out quickly to Stallworth, who hooked about 12 yards downfield. Kyle, who was giving too much cushion, reacted late and failed to slow him down with an arm tackle around the waist. Kyle, who had replaced an aging Mel Renfro at left cornerback in 1977, had coverage skills but struggled adjusting to the ball, according to Cowboys personnel director Gil Brandt. Stallworth took off, cut back beautifully behind Waters, Barnes, and nickel back Randy Hughes, and ran majestically into the end zone.

The Steelers went to the locker room ahead, 21–14, after Bradshaw rolled right on third and 1 from the Dallas 7 and flipped to Bleier, who caught the ball in the end zone with linebacker D. D. Lewis the nearest defender. The five-play, 56-yard drive got underway after Blount made what he considers one of the top two interceptions of his 14-year career. "I saw Roger three months ago and he still remembers that play like it happened yesterday," Brandt said in September 2005.

The Steelers were in a three-deep zone against the Cowboys' two-minute offense. Staubach faked a run and threw to Drew Pearson in the middle near the Pittsburgh 15. "Staubach never saw me," Blount said. "He expected me to stay deep third. I came off and started moving toward the reception area where I anticipated Drew Pearson. Then Billy Joe Dupree clotheslined me and they tacked on a 15-yard penalty."

Pittsburgh had to play the rest of the way without Stallworth, who was suffering from a muscle cramp. He was replaced by Theo Bell, a fourth-round pick in 1976 who had only six catches in the regular season. Other than three big plays, the Steelers did little on offense in the second half. In the third quarter, they had just one first down in three possessions.

Meanwhile, the Cowboys were running effectively (Dorsett finished with 16 carries for 96 of the team's rushing total of 154) and Staubach

was sharp all day. Taking advantage of a short punt, they marched to the Pittsburgh 10, where it was third and 3. Landry sent in a goal-line pass without the proper personnel, and so Staubach called a timeout. Forced by rule to stick with their short-yardage people, the Cowboys were opposed by the Steelers' goal-line personnel. Dallas flooded the

TEAM STATISTICS

PITTSBURGH		DALLAS
19	Total First Downs	20
2	Rushing	6
15	Passing	13
2	Penalty	1
357	Total Net Yardage	330
58	Total Offensive Plays	67
6.2	Avg. Gain per Offensive Play	4.9
24	Rushes	32
66	Yards Gained Rushing (Net)	154
2.8	Average Yards per Rush	4.8
30	Passes Attempted	30
17	Passes Completed	17
1	Passes Intercepted	1
4	Tackled Attempting to Pass	5
27	Yards Lost Attempting to Pass	52
291	Yards Gained Passing (Net)	176
9/15	Third-Down Efficiency	8/16
0/0	Fourth-Down Efficiency	1/1
3	Punts	5
43.0	Average Distance	39.6
4	Punt Returns	2
27	Punt Return Yardage	33
3	Kickoff Returns	6
45	Kickoff Return Yardage	104
13	Interception Return Yardage	21
2	Fumbles	3
0	Own Fumbles Recovered	1
2	Opponent Fumbles Recovered	2
5	Penalties	9
35	Yards Penalized	89
5	Touchdowns	4
1	Rushing	0
4	Passing	3
0	Returns	1
5	Extra Points Made	4
0	Field Goals Made	1
1	Field Goals Attempted	1
0	Safeties	0
35	Total Points Scored	31
26:18	Time of Possession	33:42

PITTSBURGH

Passing	CP/ATT	YDS	TD	INT	RAT
Bradshaw	17/30	318	4	1	119.2

Rushing	ATT	YDS	AVG	TD	LG
F. Harris	20	68	3.4	1	22t
Bleier	2	3	1.5	0	2
Bradshaw	2	-5	-2.5	0	2

Receiving	NO	YDS	AVG	TD	LG
Swann	7	124	17.7	1	29
Stallworth	3	115	38.3	2	75t
Grossman	3	29	9.7	0	10
Bell	2	21	10.5	0	12
F. Harris	1	22	22.0	0	22
Bleier	1	7	7.0	1	7t

Interceptions	NO	YDS	LG	TD
Blount	1	13	13	0

Punting	NO	AVG	LG	BLK
Colquitt	3	43.0	52	0

Punt Ret.	NO/FC	YDS	LG	TD
Bell	4/0	27	12	0

Kickoff Ret.	NO	YDS	LG	TD
L. Anderson	3	45	24	0

Defense	SOLO	AST	TOT	SK
Cole	6	7	13	0
Lambert	6	6	12	0
Ham	7	3	10	0
Shell	5	3	8	0
Greenwood	5	1	6	1
Wagner	2	2	4	0
Johnson	3	0	3	0
Winston	3	0	3	0
Furness	2	1	3	1
Moser	2	1	3	0
Toews	2	1	3	0
Blount	2	0	2	0
Dungy	2	0	2	0
Banaszak	1	0	1	1
Deloplaine	1	0	1	0
Greene	1	0	1	1
Petersen	1	0	1	0
Stallworth	1	0	1	0
D. White	1	0	1	1
Oldham	0	1	1	0
TOTAL	53	26	79	5

DALLAS

Passing	CP/ATT	YDS	TD	INT	RAT
Staubach	17/30	228	3	1	100.4

Rushing	ATT	YDS	AVG	TD	LG
Dorsett	16	96	6.0	0	29
Staubach	4	37	9.3	0	18
Laidlaw	3	12	4.0	0	7
P. Pearson	1	6	6.0	0	6
Newhouse	8	3	0.4	0	5

Receiving	NO	YDS	AVG	TD	LG
Dorsett	5	44	8.8	0	13
D. Pearson	4	73	18.3	0	25
Hill	2	49	24.5	1	39t
Johnson	2	30	15.0	1	26
DuPree	2	17	8.5	0	10
P. Pearson	2	15	7.5	0	8

Interceptions	NO	YDS	LG	TD
Lewis	1	21	21	0

Punting	NO	AVG	LG	BLK
D. White	5	39.6	50	0

Punt Ret.	NO/FC	YDS	LG	TD
Johnson	2/1	33	21	0

Kickoff Ret.	NO	YDS	LG	TD
Johnson	3	63	23	0
Brinson	2	41	25	0
R. White	1	0	0	0

Defense	SOLO	AST	TOT	SK
Kyle	6	1	7	0
Barnes	5	2	7	0
Jones	5	2	7	0
Waters	5	1	6	0
Harris	3	3	6	0
Henderson	3	2	5	1
Breunig	3	1	4	0
R. White	1	3	4	1
Martin	3	0	3	1
Stalls	2	1	3	0
Huther	2	0	2	0
Lewis	2	0	2	0
Cole	1	1	2	0
Hegman	1	1	2	1
Hughes	1	1	2	0
Brown	1	0	1	0
D. Pearson	1	0	1	0
Thurman	1	0	1	0
Randall	0	1	1	0
TOTAL	46	20	66	4

right side with two receivers and Lambert blitzed up the middle. After carrying out a run fake from Staubach, running back Scott Laidlaw delivered a crushing block on Lambert and knocked him completely out of the play.

With Robert Newhouse covered, Staubach

looked immediately for the second tight end, Jackie Smith, who had been instructed to come off the right side and head for the back of the end zone in the middle of the field. Smith, 38, had retired because of a neck injury after the 1977 season, his 15th in St. Louis, but when the Cowboys lost tight end Jay Saldi for the season with a knee injury, Brandt sought out Smith. "Jackie had a bar in St. Louis," he said. "I called him and said, 'This is Gil Brandt, and we'd like to see if you'd like to play for us.'" Brandt says Smith thought the Cardinals' director of pro personnel, Larry Wilson, was playing games with him.

Even a harsh critic like Henderson was impressed by his new teammate after a few days of practice. "The man had iron hands," he said, alluding to Smith's power as a run blocker. "I felt like I had gone back two decades of football, like this was a real football player here."

After releasing off the line, Smith was wide open. "I'm saying, 'Oh my God, there is no one near Jackie Smith,'" Staubach said. "Now if he would have just stopped at the goal line, it would have been perfect. But that's not what he was told. I released the ball and took something off it because Jackie was not totally turned. I think it surprised him a little that the ball got to him that fast. And I threw it a little bit low, and he kind of slipped." The turf, sodden from an early-morning downpour, gave way under the wide-open Smith as he reached down for the ball. He tried to cradle the ball against his chest, but instead watched it bounce off his hip and fall to the grass incomplete as the entire Cowboys' sideline reacted in stunned agony.

Smith made no excuse after the game or in any of the interviews that he agreed to do in subsequent years. "What Jackie said is he just dropped it," Brandt said. "He's a s--- kicker, a guy from down in Louisiana. Those guys are no-excuse guys. Jackie didn't drop many passes, I'll tell you that. But that was a big play."

So Septien kicked a 27-yard field goal and the Cowboys still trailed, 21–17. Said Staubach, "We were still in charge. We dominated the whole third quarter." That score stood until the middle of the fourth quarter when the tide turned against Dallas on three plays, two of which involved the officiating

team headed by referee Pat Haggerty, and anothe because of the Cowboys' own malfeasance.

On second down, free safety Cliff Harri blitzed together with defensive tackle Larry Col and smashed Bradshaw just after he threw deep on the right side for Swann. The defender, Barnes never allowed Swann to pass him or even drav abreast up the sideline. With both players turning back for the ball, Swann seemed to run up the bac of Barnes' legs. Both players tumbled and the bal fell incomplete.

The official right next to the play, back judge Pat Knight, saw it as a no-call. From about 10 yard away, toward the middle of the field, field judge Fred Swearingen tossed a flag as he kicked his foot indicating tripping on Barnes. "Fred Swearingen— he operated a hardware store in Athens, Ohio, [and later became a referee," Brandt said. "There wasn' any contact. Both guys got their feet tangled."

Barnes cussed Swearingen, saying, "It was the closest I'll ever come to punching an official."

Said Swearingen, "It was a judgment call. The Pittsburgh receiver, in trying to get to the ball, wa tripped by the defender's feet." Swann wasn't sure what happened.

"Worst call in the history of football," said Staubach, still fuming years later. Not long after the game, Rozelle sent the Cowboys a letter conceding that an incorrect call had been made.

The 33-yard interference penalty set the Steelers up at the Dallas 23. On third and 4, Henderson roared in and sacked Bradshaw, but the play was ruled dead and the Steelers were penalized for delay of game. "When he sacked him, he kind of taunted Franco," Waters said. "Franco got pissed. Franco's a mild-mannered guy. Franco wasn't the toughest guy in the world but when he got pissed he could use that big ol' body and do some things pretty special." When the Steelers huddled, an enraged Harris told Bradshaw, "Give me the ball." It was third and 9 after the penalty, but Bradshaw went ahead and called "93 Tackle Trap," a play designed to get a few yards and shorten Roy Gerela's distance for a field goal.

Expecting a pass, the Cowboys' two cagey Pro Bowl safeties jumped into a blitz look in hopes of baiting Bradshaw into an interception. "It had worked against Jim Hart perfectly earlier in the year," Waters said. Bradshaw smelled out the ruse and refused to audible. "They could have been standing back there with shotguns and Franco was still getting the football," he said.

When Bradshaw handed to his now-ornery big back, Webster and right guard Gerry Mullins pancaked backup defensive tackle Dave Stalls in the hole. With the Cowboys in a dime defense, the only linebacker was Henderson. On Waters' instruction, Henderson vacated the middle to get a bump on tight end Randy Grossman, so that the only player between Franco Harris and the end zone was Waters. As the veteran safety moved up to take on Harris, he ran smack dab into the umpire, Art Demmas. A split-second later, right tackle Ray Pinney arrived on a short pull through the hole to wipe out Waters. When Kyle and Hughes dived at Harris near the 10 without effect, Harris pounded up the gut for a 22-yard touchdown. "I'm not saying we would have made the tackle," said Brandt, "but the umpire kind of got in the way."

Once again, the soggy Orange Bowl grass helped deliver a break for the Steelers. On the kickoff, Gerela's plant leg went out from under him. The ball bounced down the middle of the field all the way to the 24, where Randy White bobbled it for a second or two. (White had led the Cowboys with 16 sacks and went to the Pro Bowl for the second time, but Landry still had him playing special teams.) Two weeks earlier, White had suffered a fractured left thumb in the 28–0 blanking of the Rams in the NFC Championship Game and was playing with a cast. Just as Dungy swooped down to hit him, the ball slipped out of White's control as he attempted to transfer it to his broken left hand. A wild scramble ensued, and Pittsburgh linebacker Dennis "Dirt" Winston made the recovery at the Dallas 18.

Certainly, Landry had violated an old coaching rule by using a player with a cast on his hand at a position where he might have to handle the ball. "In hindsight, he shouldn't have been there," said Brandt. "We made a very bad error having Randy White on the kickoff return team. He was one of the up-backs in the four-man

When Dallas safety Charlie Waters (No. 41) collided with umpire Art Demmas midway through the fourth quarter, it cleared the way for Franco Harris to charge ahead for a 22-yard touchdown run. All the breaks seemed to go the Steelers' way that January day in 1979. *Al Messerschmidt/NFL/Getty Images*

[wedge] ahead of the two deep backs."

When Swann leaped over the wayward Cliff Harris for his 18-yard touchdown catch on the next play, the Steelers went up 35–17 for what turned out to be an insurmountable lead. Allowing 14 points in 19 seconds was too much for even the game Cowboys to overcome.

"It was like a Gatling gun—boom, boom, boom," Waters said. "Lynn Swann tripping over Bennie's foot. Randy White putting the ball into his cast hand. Me running into the official. Gimme a break. They were all in a row. It was like we were cursed."

Super Bowl XIII drew a Nielsen rating of 47.1, one of the most watched events in television history. More than 87 million people tuned in for what really was a clash of the titans.

"It was much bigger than Super Bowl X," Greenwood said. "In 1974 and 1975, we didn't have great football teams—we just had great players. But, in 1978, we were a great team."

A team for the ages, as it turned out.

XIV
PITTSBURGH STEELERS 31, LOS ANGELES RAMS 19

January 20, 1980
Rose Bowl, Pasadena, California

As the third quarter ended in Super Bowl XIV, the Pittsburgh Steelers were in trouble. Their opponent, the much younger and equally physical Los Angeles Rams, wasn't the least bit in awe. The crowd of 103,985 was given that message loud and clear when the Rams' entire offensive platoon sprinted more than 80 yards to the other end of the Rose Bowl at the quarter break, while the Steelers trudged the distance. The Rams weren't going to be put away easily.

Los Angeles, a 10-point underdog, amazingly enough had the lead. The Steelers had been unable to run on the Rams, and quarterback Terry Bradshaw had been intercepted twice in the third quarter. His favorite receiver, Lynn Swann, had been knocked from the game late in the third quarter with blurred vision and wouldn't return. In addition, Pittsburgh's aging "Steel Curtain" defense had proven incapable of unnerving Vince Ferragamo, the type of inexperienced quarterback whom the Steelers would have swallowed whole in the not too distant past.

"We went into the fourth quarter still ahead, 19–17," said Jack Youngblood, the Rams' great defensive end who was in his ninth season. "I'm thinking, 'Here we are on the verge of winning the Super Bowl. Let's do what we're doing just a little bit better for the final 15 minutes.' I was trying to encourage the team to keep up our good play and not give them something that could break our back. Which is what happened—right away."

The Steelers got the ball back at their 25 with 13 minutes remaining. Franco Harris, stymied all day long, plunged for 2 on first down. A screen pass was dropped by running back Sidney Thornton. Third and 8. Coach Chuck Noll always let Bradshaw call his own plays, but here Noll sent in "60 Prevent Slot Hook and Go." It was a play Noll had installed for this Super Bowl because he knew that Rams

Attendance: 103,985
Conditions: 67 degrees, sunny and clear, wind N-NW at 8–15 mph
Time of kickoff: 3:15 p.m. (PST)
Length of game: 2 hours, 57 minutes
Referee: Fred Silva

MVP: Terry Bradshaw, QB, Steelers

defensive coordinator Bud Carson, who had been his defensive mastermind in Pittsburgh from 1972 to 1977, would be double-covering John Stallworth with his innovative zone schemes.

Bradshaw didn't like the play; in fact, he almost changed it. The Steelers had tried the long pass about eight times in practice during the two-week run-up and failed to complete even one. Stallworth, however, thought it might work because the Rams had been doubling the wideouts with one defender inside and another defender outside. Lined up in the right slot as the primary receiver, Stallworth's mission was to come off hard into the middle, fake the hook, and haul ass deep. "When they double-cover you with a man in back, you can't do that," Stallworth said, "but with one on either side sometimes you can split them and get deep." The Rams had brought in an extra defensive back, Eddie Brown, a career backup who was playing for his third team in his sixth and final NFL season.

When Carson arrived in the NFL in 1972 after five seasons as head coach at Georgia Tech, he brought the Cover 2 scheme that was commonplace in college football, but almost non-existent in the pros, where three-deep zones were the norm. "You [wouldn't] believe how many great quarterbacks couldn't read that defense," said Carson.

The Steelers spread three receivers across the line; Carson responded with left cornerback Pat Thomas across from Jim Smith on the far left, right

	1	2	3	4	Final
Los Angeles Rams	7	6	6	0	19
Pittsburgh Steelers	3	7	7	14	31

SCORING SUMMARY

1st Quarter
PIT   Bahr, 41-yd. FG
LA   Bryant, 1-yd. run (Corral kick)
2nd Quarter
PIT   F. Harris, 1-yd. run (Bahr kick)
LA   Corral, 31-yd. FG
LA   Corral, 45-yd. FG
3rd Quarter
PIT   Swann, 47-yd. pass from Bradshaw (Bahr kick)
LA   R. Smith, 24-yd. pass from McCutcheon (kick failed)
4th Quarter
PIT   Stallworth, 73-yd. pass from Bradshaw (Bahr kick)
PIT   F. Harris, 1-yd. run (Bahr kick)

cornerback Rod Perry across from Stallworth in the slot, and free safety Nolan Cromwell across from the tight end on the far right. Eddie Brown was the safety behind Stallworth. Strong safety Dave Elmendorf, a nine-year veteran, was on the right hash mark.

Carson explained his team's method of deciding who would go in the hole and who would go over the middle as "one safety pointed to the other and told him, 'I'm going in the hole.'" Carson continued, "Dave Elmendorf was our seasoned guy who made the call. But instead of one coming over to double Stallworth, they both went in the hole." As Stallworth came off the line, Perry maintained outside leverage, expecting that a safety would have the inside blanketed. In this case, both Elmendorf and Eddie Brown remained stationary as Stallworth went blasting between them with Perry in pursuit. "I blew it," Brown said. "I should have gone to the inside but I took the outside receiver instead."

Bradshaw took a 10-yard drop as the four-man pattern developed, focusing on Stallworth when he saw the

two safeties stuck in the middle. With time to throw, he unloaded a bomb that carried 50 yards in the air. Stallworth caught the ball just beyond Perry's desperate dive that almost knocked the ball away. When Stallworth loped the remaining 33 yards to the end zone, the Steelers were back in front, 24–19.

"I go to my grave with this one," Carson said, calling it easily the most regrettable moment in his lifetime of coaching. "In fact, I spent the rest of the game chewing out a couple guys, so I probably missed the rest of the damn game after that. Without Swann, I knew Bradshaw was going to throw the ball to one guy: Stallworth. . . . It [was] an easy interception for a free safety who's doubling on Stallworth, but he's not back there. Hell, I could have intercepted it."

According to Carson, that play affected the entire team. "We lost steam on offense, too, after that," he said. "Emotionally, I thought the game was never the same. After that, they just ripped us. If ever a Super Bowl was thrown away, it was that one."

Blown coverage or not, Bradshaw's 73-yard thunderbolt to Stallworth could not have been more perfectly thrown. It was the turning point in the Steelers' 31–19 victory that gave them an unprecedented fourth Super Bowl crown in six years. Given what was at stake and the precarious situation, that touchdown pass from one Hall of Fame quarterback to one Hall of Fame wide receiver surely ranks among the greatest in Super Bowl history.

With victory secured, Bradshaw stepped away from the moment in the waning seconds and savored his second straight MVP performance. "There are few great moments [like this] in an athlete's life," he said. "Just this one time, Super Bowl XIV, I decided that this was my moment and I wanted to take it all in. I wanted to pack it away in my mind forever. I felt that for this bunch of Steelers the run was over, we would never be in this situation again. So I did just that. I stood there and absorbed that stadium."

> "Joe Greene was the enforcer. There wasn't anybody who monkeyed around with Joe. He was a violent guy when he got mad. He let nothing go. You didn't screw around with the trainer, the equipment guy. You didn't play that radio and disturb people. He was the captain and he enforced. . . . Always a gentleman off the field."
>
> *George Perles, Steelers defensive coordinator*

This was the end of the Steelers' dynasty. With their 22 starters averaging 29 years per man, the pernicious signs of aging were everywhere. "I think winning the championships in '79 and '80 was phenomenal," said Art Rooney Jr., the man who had drafted so many tremendous players for Noll. "Our players had gotten old and we had some real weak spots." The Rams did their best to expose the Steelers, limiting Franco Harris to a scant 46 yards in 20 carries. They also ran the ball effectively against a front four featuring Pro Bowlers Mean Joe Greene and L. C. Greenwood, both 33, and average players like John Banaszak, Gary Dunn, and Steve Furness.

"I could feel it," Greene said. "I wasn't as quick, wasn't as fast, wasn't as strong. Plays that I was making in the past I wasn't making anymore. Early on, 1974, 1975, 1976, we could play defense that was really truly stifling. In 1978 and 1979, we did play some stifling defense, but it was kind of hit or miss."

Not since Super Bowl IV had a team been favored by as many points as Pittsburgh. The Steelers went 12–4, finished second in defense, and led the league on offense, spearheaded by a passing attack that generated 228.4 yards per game, a club record that stood until 1995. After holding Houston's Earl Campbell to 15 yards in 17 carries in the AFC Championship Game, the Steelers were expected to manhandle a Rams team that had the worst regular-season record (9–7) of any Super Bowl entrant, until Arizona matched it in February 2009.

Almost no one saw a Super Bowl coming for the Rams. Their owner, Carroll Rosenbloom, had drowned while swimming in the Atlantic Ocean in early April. His wife, Georgia, became majority owner and quickly fired Steve

LOS ANGELES RAMS (NFC, 9–7)			PITTSBURGH STEELERS (AFC, 12–4)	
		Offense		
80	Billy Waddy (5-11, 180)	WR	82	John Stallworth* (6-2, 183)
77	Doug France (6-5, 268)	LT	55	Jon Kolb (6-2, 262)
72	Kent Hill (6-5, 260)	LG	57	Sam Davis (6-1, 255)
61	Rich Saul* (6-3, 243)	C	52	Mike Webster* (6-2, 250)
60	Dennis Harrah* (6-5, 251)	RG	72	Gerry Mullins (6-3, 244)
78	Jackie Slater (6-4, 269)	RT	79	Larry Brown (6-4, 255)
83	Terry Nelson (6-2, 241)	TE	89	Bennie Cunningham (6-5, 247)
88	Preston Dennard (6-1, 185)	WR	88	Lynn Swann (6-0, 180)
15	Vince Ferragamo (6-3, 207)	QB	12	Terry Bradshaw* (6-2, 215)
26	Wendell Tyler (5-10, 188)	RB	32	Franco Harris* (6-2, 225)
32	Cullen Bryant (6-1, 234)	RB	20	Rocky Bleier (5-11, 210)
		Defense		
85	Jack Youngblood* (6-4, 243)	LE	68	L. C. Greenwood* (6-7, 250)
79	Mike Fanning (6-6, 248)	LT	75	Joe Greene* (6-4, 260)
90	Larry Brooks* (6-3, 254)	RT	67	Gary Dunn (6-3, 247)
89	Fred Dryer (6-6, 230)	RE	76	John Banaszak (6-3, 244)
53	Jim Youngblood* (6-3, 231)	LLB	53	Dennis Winston (6-0, 228)
64	Jack Reynolds (6-1, 231)	MLB	58	Jack Lambert* (6-4, 220)
59	Bob Brudzinski (6-4, 231)	RLB	56	Robin Cole (6-2, 220)
27	Pat Thomas (5-9, 184)	LCB	29	Ron Johnson (5-10, 200)
49	Rod Perry (5-9, 177)	RCB	47	Mel Blount* (6-3, 205)
42	Dave Elmendorf (6-1, 196)	SS	31	Donnie Shell* (5-11, 190)
21	Nolan Cromwell (6-1, 197)	FS	24	J. T. Thomas (6-2, 196)

* Pro Bowl selection

SUBSTITUTIONS

Los Angeles

Offense: WR - 87 Drew Hill, 84 Ron Smith; TE - 86 Charle Young; T - 73 Gordon Gravelle; G - 62 Bill Bain; C - 54 Dan Ryczek; RB - 24 Eddie Hill, 43 Jim Jodat, 30 Lawrence McCutcheon. *Defense:* DE - 71 Reggie Doss, 70 Jerry Wilkinson; LB - 52 George Andrews, 51 Joe Harris, 57 Greg Westbrooks; CB - 33 Dwayne O'Steen, 25 Ivory Sully; S - 25 Eddie Brown, 20 Jackie Wallace. *Specialists:* K - 3 Frank Corral; P - 13 Ken Clark. *DNP:* 19 Bob Lee (QB), 8 Jeff Rutledge (QB), 28 Ken Ellis (CB).

Pittsburgh

Offense: WR - 83 Theo Bell, 86 Jim Smith; TE - 84 Randy Grossman; T - 66 Ted Peterson; G - 77 Steve Courson; C - 63 Thom Dornbrook; RB - 33 Anthony Anderson, 27 Greg Hawthorne, 39 Rick Moser, 38 Sidney Thornton. *Defense:* DE - 65 Tom Beasley, 78 Dwight White; DT - 64 Steve Furness; LB - 50 Tom Graves, 51 Loren Toews, 54 Zack Valentine; CB - 30 Larry Anderson, 49 Dwayne Woodruff. *Specialists:* K - 9 Matt Bahr; P - 5 Craig Colquitt. *DNP:* 15 Mike Kruczek (QB), 18 Cliff Stoudt (QB); 59 Jack Ham* (LB).

Los Angeles
Head Coach: Ray Malavasi. *Offense:* Lionel Taylor (receivers), Jack Faulkner (backfield, special assistant). *Defense:* Dan Radakovich (coordinator), LaVern Torgeson (defensive line), Frank Lauterbur (linebackers), Bud Carson (defensive backs). *Strength:* Paul Lanham, Clyde Evans. *Administrative Assistant:* Bill Hickman.

Pittsburgh
Head Coach: Chuck Noll. *Offense:* Tom Moore (receivers), Rollie Dotsch (offensive line), Dick Hoak (backfield). *Defense:* George Perles (coordinator), Woody Widenhofer (linebackers), Dick Walker (assistant). *Strength:* Lou Riecke. *Administrative Assistant:* Paul Uram.

Rosenbloom, her stepson and a popular executive with the team. Additionally, the coach, Ray Malavasi, was hospitalized around the same time for hypertension a year after undergoing quadruple bypass surgery.

"In all honesty, the Rams were probably a better football team between 1973 and 1978 than we were in 1979," Jack Youngblood said. "We had a more dominating defense and a stronger running game." Under coaches George Allen, Tommy Prothro, Chuck Knox, and Malavasi from 1967 to 1978, the Rams had posted 11 winning seasons and reached the playoffs eight times. They were 4–8 (5–6–1 against the spread) in those playoff games, losing as a favorite at Green Bay in 1967 and as a substantial favorite at home against Dallas in 1975. His frustration deepening, Carroll Rosenbloom fired Knox after the Rams lost to the Vikings, 14–7, as a 9-point favorite in 1977, hired Allen, and then promptly fired him after the second exhibition game in 1978. Malavasi, a longtime coordinator on both sides of the ball, was handed the job.

The Rams were 5–6 and being booed vociferously in their final year playing at the Coliseum before they moved to Anaheim in 1980. After quarterback Pat Haden went out with a fractured pinky on his right hand and both veteran Bob Lee and rookie Jeff Rutledge proved lacking, Malavasi called upon Ferragamo in Week 12. Ferragamo, a fourth-round draft choice in 1977 who only recently had recovered from a broken hand, wasn't impressive

statistically (48.8 passer rating), but the Rams finished 4–1 under him and then stunned Dallas, 21–19, in the divisional playoffs on his late 50-yard touchdown pass to Billy Waddy. The Rams blanked Tampa Bay, 9–0, in the NFC Championship Game.

Noll and his players had reason to fear the Rams. Not only was Carson on Malavasi's staff, but so were offensive coordinator Lionel Taylor, who had coached wide receivers in Pittsburgh from 1970 to 1976, and offensive line coach Dan Radakovich, the Steelers' line tutor from 1974 to 1977. "There was no question they knew everything we would do," Noll said. Furthermore, the Rams had beaten the Steelers in 1975 (10–3) and in 1978 (10–7). "At that point, I thought we were a better defense than Pittsburgh," Carson said. "L.A. was a good football team, it really was. Dallas kept them from going to the Super Bowl a lot of years."

The Steelers opened the scoring with rookie Matt Bahr's 41-yard field goal. What was significant about that 10-play, 55-yard drive was the fact that 8 running plays gained merely 23 yards. Carson's front seven included Pro Bowlers Larry Brooks at tackle, Jack Youngblood at end, and Jim Youngblood (no relation) at outside linebacker, plus middle linebacker Jack "Hacksaw" Reynolds. Reynolds, said Carson, "was one of the better leaders I had ever been around." Jack Youngblood had suffered a hairline fracture of his left fibula against Dallas and played the Super Bowl at about 60 percent efficiency. "It felt like a bunch of knives being stabbed into [my] leg, but I wasn't going to do more damage to a broken leg," Jack Youngblood said. "I just tried to minimize the pain and go."

Meanwhile, the Rams went right at the Steelers' defense with their young, aggressive offensive line. On the Rams' second possession, 1,000-yard rusher Wendell Tyler, who didn't become a starter until Week 5, took advantage of missed tackles by cornerback Mel Blount and safety J. T. Thomas near the line and dashed 39 yards to the 14. Then the Rams rammed the ball at the Steelers six straight times on the ground before 234-pound Cullen Bryant plowed over from the 1 to give the Rams the lead. Answering back, a 45-yard kickoff return by the Steelers' Larry Anderson, who set a Super Bowl record with 162 yards on five runbacks, led to

Harris' 1-yard touchdown run. But two field goals in the second quarter by Frank Corral sent the confident Rams to the locker room leading, 13–10.

Anderson returned the second-half kickoff for 37 yards, and five plays later the Steelers regained the lead on Bradshaw's 47-yard touchdown pass to Swann. Bradshaw took a deep drop and absorbed a nasty frontal shot from the blitzing Reynolds just after releasing the ball. "[We] were supposed to set at 7 [yards], but by that time Bradshaw was setting at 10 or 11 yards because he had the great arm to compensate," former Steelers pro personnel director Tim Rooney said. "He just let Swann and Stallworth go get the ball. It didn't matter if you were in a zone or not. Those guys outran a zone, and Terry would put it up over the top."

Swann had a step or two on Perry, and then, when Cromwell ranged over to help, Swann outleaped the talented, young free safety and tumbled into the end zone for the go-ahead score. "Nolan was also in the air but he barely mistimed his jump," Jack Youngblood said. "Nolan makes that play 9 times out of 10. But Terry stood in there and didn't flinch at the heat and delivered the ball perfectly 45 yards downfield."

Undaunted, the Rams struck for a 50-yard completion on third and 7 when Waddy came back for Ferragamo's underthrown pass and took it away from second-year cornerback Ron Johnson. On the very next play, the Rams ran what looked like a sweep to the right that brought Johnson flying up in run support. Running back Lawrence McCutcheon, a wonderful athlete, stopped and threw a strike over Johnson's head to Ron Smith for a 24-yard touchdown. But Corral's extra point sailed wide left, so the Rams' lead was two points, 19–17.

Bradshaw, who unloaded 25 interceptions during the regular season compared to 26 touchdowns, was intercepted three times and should have been picked on a fourth. Three plays after the Rams reclaimed the lead, Bradshaw misread a coverage and went to Swann in the middle of the field. The pass hit Cromwell squarely in the chest, but he didn't look the ball in and dropped it. "Nolan Cromwell was the best athlete I ever played with in 14 years," Jack Youngblood said. "He had nobody in front of him and that would have given us a 9-point lead. Believe

me, Nolan still sees that one in his dreams."

Things went from bad to worse for Bradshaw when he panicked under pressure from Brooks and threw back inside to Swann, who took a nasty lick from Thomas and couldn't continue. On third and 9, Bradshaw threw a wobbly, long pass to Jim Smith and Brown picked it off. Later in the third quarter,

TEAM STATISTICS

LOS ANGELES		PITTSBURGH
16	Total First Downs	19
6	Rushing	8
9	Passing	10
1	Penalty	1
301	Total Net Yardage	393
59	Total Offensive Plays	58
5.1	Avg. Gain per Offensive Play	6.8
29	Rushes	37
107	Yards Gained Rushing (Net)	84
3.7	Average Yards per Rush	2.3
26	Passes Attempted	21
16	Passes Completed	14
1	Passes Intercepted	3
4	Tackled Attempting to Pass	0
42	Yards Lost Attempting to Pass	0
194	Yards Gained Passing (Net)	309
5/14	Third-Down Efficiency	9/14
1/2	Fourth-Down Efficiency	0/0
5	Punts	2
44.0	Average Distance	42.5
1	Punt Returns	4
4	Punt Return Yardage	31
6	Kickoff Returns	5
79	Kickoff Return Yardage	162
21	Interception Return Yardage	16
0	Fumbles	0
0	Own Fumbles Recovered	0
0	Opponent Fumbles Recovered	0
2	Penalties	6
26	Yards Penalized	65
2	Touchdowns	4
1	Rushing	2
1	Passing	2
0	Returns	0
1	Extra Points Made	4
2	Field Goals Made	1
2	Field Goals Attempted	1
0	Safeties	0
19	Total Points Scored	31
29:31	Time of Possession	30:29

LOS ANGELES

Passing	CP/ATT	YDS	TD	INT	RAT
Ferragamo	15/25	212	0	1	70.8
McCutcheon	1/1	24	1	0	158.3

Rushing	ATT	YDS	AVG	TD	LG
Tyler	17	60	3.5	0	39
Bryant	6	30	5.0	1	14
McCutcheon	5	10	2.0	0	6
Ferragamo	1	7	7.0	0	7

Receiving	NO	YDS	AVG	TD	LG
Waddy	3	75	25.0	0	50
Bryant	3	21	7.0	0	12
Tyler	3	20	6.7	0	11
Dennard	2	32	16.0	0	24
Nelson	2	20	10.0	0	14
D. Hill	1	28	28.0	0	28
R. Smith	1	24	224.0	1	24
McCutcheon	1	16	16.0	0	16

Interceptions	NO	YDS	LG	TD
Elmendorf	1	10	10	0
Brown	1	6	6	0
Perry	1	-1	-1	0
Thomas	0	6	6	0

Punting	NO	AVG	LG	BLK
Clark	5	44.0	59	0

Punt Ret.	NO/FC	YDS	LG	TD
Brown	1/0	4	4	0

Kickoff Ret.	NO	YDS	LG	TD
E. Hill	3	47	27	0
Jodat	2	32	16	0
Andrews	1	0	0	0

Defense	SOLO	AST	TOT	SK
Cromwell	5	7	12	0
Brudzinski	8	3	11	0
Reynolds	8	3	11	0
Elmendorf	5	5	10	0
Ji. Youngblood	5	3	8	0
Brooks	4	3	7	0
Fanning	4	3	7	0
P. Thomas	4	2	6	0
Jodat	1	2	3	0
Ja. Youngblood	1	2	3	0
Corral	2	0	2	0
Perry	2	0	2	0
E. Brown	1	1	2	0
Dryer	1	1	2	0
Harris	1	0	1	0
O'Steen	1	0	1	0
Ryczek	1	0	1	0
Saul	1	0	1	0
Wallace	1	0	1	0
Andrews	0	1	1	0
TOTAL	56	36	92	0

PITTSBURGH

Passing	CP/ATT	YDS	TD	INT	RAT
Bradshaw	14/21	309	2	3	101.9

Rushing	ATT	YDS	AVG	TD	LG
Harris	20	46	2.3	2	12
Bleier	10	25	2.5	0	9
Bradshaw	3	9	3.0	0	6
Thornton	4	4	1.0	0	5

Receiving	NO	YDS	AVG	TD	LG
Swann	5	79	15.8	1	47t
Stallworth	3	121	40.3	1	73t
Harris	3	66	22.0	0	32
Cunningham	2	21	10.5	0	13
Thornton	1	22	22.0	0	22

Interceptions	NO	YDS	LG	TD
Lambert	1	16	16	0

Punting	NO	AVG	LG	BLK
Colquitt	2	42.5	50	0

Punt Ret.	NO/FC	YDS	LG	TD
Bell	2/0	17	11	0
Smith	2/0	14	7	0

Kickoff Ret.	NO	YDS	LG	TD
L. Anderson	5	162	45	0

Defense	SOLO	AST	TOT	SK
Lambert	10	4	14	0
T. Thomas	5	4	9	1
Cole	7	1	8	1
Shell	5	3	8	0
Winston	5	2	7	0
Moser	3	2	5	0
Blount	4	0	4	0
Toews	3	1	4	0
White	3	0	3	0
Furness	2	1	3	1
Greenwood	2	1	3	0
Mullins	2	0	2	0
A. Anderson	1	0	1	0
Banaszak	1	0	1	1
Johnson	1	0	1	0
Stallworth	1	0	1	0
Valentine	1	0	1	0
Woodruff	1	0	1	0
Bell	0	1	1	0
Dunn	0	1	1	0
TOTAL	57	21	78	4

Bradshaw made another boneheaded mistake after the Steelers moved 57 yards in nine plays to the L.A. 16. On third and 10, he forced a pass to Stallworth into traffic, and the tipped ball was intercepted by Perry. Bradshaw did bounce back early in the fourth quarter with his touchdown bomb to Stallworth, but the Rams were not going to bow out lightly.

Ferragamo's passer rating of 70.8 paled in comparison to Bradshaw's 101.9, but there are those who maintain that he played the better game. Ferragamo's spotty career flamed out quickly in the mid-1980s. He had a good arm and a heap of talent, but was anything but a quick study and frequently exercised lousy judgment. "In my opinion, the key ingredient we were missing in those years was a dominant quarterback," Jack Youngblood said. "Vinny wasn't dominating . . . but he had an aura of luck about him. He would do things that were fundamentally unsound and not only get away with it, but make big plays. So we started rallying around this luck: 'All right, Vinny, pull one more rabbit out of the hat.'"

Trailing by five points and starting from their 16 with 8:29 remaining, the Rams moved to the Pittsburgh 32 as Ferragamo hit three of four passes for 47 yards. On first down, Ferragamo faked a run and threw toward Ron Smith about 20 yards away in the middle of the field. High up in the press box, the L.A. coaches were yelling at him to throw it to an open Waddy deep along the sidelines. "It was a good old-fashioned dig pattern," Taylor said, "the double in. One inside receiver going inside and the outside receiver coming in. Front and back door. Sometimes in play-action you take your eye off the defense for a second. Sometimes you don't come back and recognize it quick enough. It will always live with me. To me, that was the killer."

Lambert intercepted at the 14 and made a 16-yard return. "He made the throw against Cover 2," Steelers assistant head coach George Perles said. "He tried to get it 18 yards down the middle. That's the weakness of that defense, but Lambert had great speed and got deep enough to pick it off."

The Steelers ran two running plays that went nowhere, leaving them with third and 7 and about four minutes left. "Knowing Bud, he always wanted to get you in a third-and-long situation," Noll said.

"Then they would make sure they jumped on your short routes. So every time we got in third-and-long we went deep and Terry would find [the receivers]. That was Terry's strength—his ability to go deep and accurately."

Noll sent in the same hook-and-go play. This time, Elmendorf stayed back and helped Perry bracket Stallworth, but it made no difference. Stallworth ran by them both and Bradshaw was dead-on target once again for a 45-yard completion. Two plays later, the Rams bitched to no avail about a 21-yard penalty for pass interference against Perry in the end zone. Then Harris powered over for another 1-yard touchdown and the game was over.

The Rams called out and reacted smartly to the Steelers' audibles all day, rendered Pittsburgh's trap-style running game null and void, and took back the lead three times in one of the most entertaining Super Bowls. Despite having a quarterback making just his eighth NFL start, the Rams stood toe-to-toe with possibly the finest defense in pro football history, turned the ball over just once, and committed only two penalties.

"Football fans will always know that the Steelers beat a very good team in the '79 Rams," Jack Youngblood said. "I'm not sure how dignifying losing is, even to the world champion Pittsburgh Steelers. But I know our effort was dignified and showed that we could play any team, any time, anywhere."

The Steelers lost the turnover battle (3–1) because Bradshaw made more poor throws and decisions than he had in three previous Super Bowls combined, but still had been good enough to earn the MVP trophy. "They seldom give such awards to quarterbacks who throw three interceptions," said Bradshaw. Then again, there haven't been many quarterbacks that threw bull's eyes for 47, 73, and 45 yards in one half when his team needed them the most.

"God-given ability," Steelers center Mike Webster said. "You just can't beat it. Terry had enough ability to overcome the mistakes, the three interceptions. He had the courage to go with that long stuff."

In the end, talent won out. The Packers had set the standard for NFL excellence in the 1960s, and the Steelers matched it in the 1970s.

Ten Best Performances by a Linebacker

1. **Jack Lambert, Steelers, XIV:** Lambert helped clinch victory over the Rams by getting great depth in Cover 2 and intercepting a Vince Ferragamo pass down the middle. He also was a fiery presence against the run, totaling 14 tackles.

2. **Rod Martin, Raiders, XV:** Overcame a lack of height with his great strength and speed. Martin also had tremendous instincts in coverage, evidenced by his three interceptions of Ron Jaworski passes.

3. **Ray Lewis, Ravens, XXXV:** By 2000, his fifth season, Lewis had bulked up to 253 pounds without any loss of speed. He went sideline to sideline against the Giants and also broke up four passes.

4. **Otis Wilson, Bears, XX:** Wilson was somewhat overshadowed by fellow linebackers Mike Singletary and Wilber Marshall. Against the Patriots, however, it was Wilson who was most productive, with two sacks and four knockdowns.

5. **Willie Lanier, Chiefs, IV:** Lanier was in just his third season when the Chiefs hammered the Vikings. With seven tackles, an interception, and a pass defensed, he was too much for Minnesota.

6. **James Harrison, Steelers, XLIII:** Harrison will be remembered always for his 100-yard interception return, but he also rushed the passer relentlessly and drew a pair of holding penalties on Arizona LT Mike Gandy.

7. **Cornelius Bennett, Bills, XXVI:** Posted six tackles in a losing effort. "I remember looking at him," Redskins offensive-line coach Jim Hanifan said. "I thought, 'Boy, what a warrior this guy is.' He played his heart out."

8. **Wilber Marshall, Redskins, XXVI:** The Redskins kept bringing five rushers to make Bills RB Thurman Thomas pick up the blitz. Marshall used his great speed and explosion to notch 11 tackles, two forced fumbles, a sack, and a pass defensed.

9. **Jack Reynolds, Rams, XIV:** "Hacksaw" had 11 tackles, a pass defensed, and a punishing knockdown of Steelers QB Terry Bradshaw. "One of the better leaders I was ever around," Rams coordinator Bud Carson said. "Not a real talented guy, but . . . very effective against the run."

10. **Jonathan Vilma, Saints, XLIV:** Defensive coordinator Gregg Williams gave Vilma complete freedom against Peyton Manning. He stayed one step ahead of the Colts great, checking 60 percent of Williams' calls at the line. Plus, he made a number of key plays.

Honorable Mentions: Brandon Spikes, Patriots, XLVI; Bill Romanowski, Broncos, XXXIII; Mike Vrabel, Patriots, XXXVIII; Mike Singletary, Bears, XX; Adalius Thomas, Patriots, XLII; Jack Lambert, Steelers, X.

Pittsburgh linebacker Jack Lambert was a dominating presence in all four of his Super Bowl appearances. He peaked in Super Bowl XIV, amassing 14 tackles and one interception against Vince Ferragamo and the Rams. He totaled 46 tackles in the four games. *Heinz Kluetmeier/ Sports Illustrated/Getty Images*

XV
OAKLAND RAIDERS 27, PHILADELPHIA EAGLES 10

January 25, 1981
Louisiana Superdome, New Orleans, Louisiana

Not a point has been scored in any Super Bowl before the ball had been kicked. There have been times, however, when one of the teams has staked a motivational claim in the days and weeks leading up to Super Sunday that, participants acknowledged then and years later, have played an extremely significant role in the eventual outcome.

Super Bowl XV at the Louisiana Superdome, in which the Oakland Raiders crushed the Philadelphia Eagles, 27–10, was one of those games.

Jim Plunkett, coming from the dark side of oblivion, was selected MVP after passing for 261 yards and three touchdowns. Teammate Rod Martin, the least well-known of the Raiders' heralded crew of linebackers, could have been MVP with his record three interceptions. The Raiders' defense pressured Eagles quarterback Ron Jaworski all day long and rendered his running game worthless.

Nevertheless, when viewed through the prism of introspection, much of what occurred on the field in New Orleans shouldn't have been a surprise. The Eagles might have been a three-point favorite and the wild-card Raiders might have been an underdog for the fourth straight playoff game, but Oakland was the better team and all the psychological factors were on its side.

As it turned out, the Eagles were seriously outplayed on both the offensive and defensive lines. Since it's rather hard to win if the team cannot block and cannot rush the passer, the two teams could have played a dozen games and the Raiders might have emerged victorious every time. "They beat us soundly," Eagles coach Dick Vermeil said after the game. "They dominated us. For some reason, I didn't think we were flying around the field like we usually do, but maybe that's a misjudgment."

Two weeks earlier, the Eagles defeated the Dallas Cowboys, 20–7, in the 17-degree chill of Veterans Stadium for the NFC championship. From

Attendance: 76,135
Conditions: 72 degrees, indoors
Time of kickoff: 5:16 p.m. (CST)
Length of game: 3 hours, 13 minutes
Referee: Ben Dreith

MVP: Jim Plunkett, QB, Raiders

December 1967 to November 1979, the Eagles had gone 2–21 against the Cowboys. In 1980, the two teams split a pair of regular-season games and finished atop the NFC East at 12–4, with the Eagles taking the division crown on the basis of the scoring differential tiebreaker. During the season, the Cowboys had scored 454 points, and all the Eagles needed to do in the regular-season finale against Dallas was not lose by more than 25 points. When the Cowboys won by just 8 points, 35–27, and the Eagles were declared NFC East champions, owner Leonard Tose delivered Dom Pérignon to his players in the Texas Stadium locker room.

For the Eagles, just making the playoffs was cause for joyous celebration. This was their first postseason appearance since the victory over Green Bay in the NFL title game in 1960. When Vermeil guided the Eagles to a 9–7 mark in 1978, his third year after leaving UCLA, it was the franchise's first winning season since 1966. Billeted in sunny Tampa for a week to prepare for the rematch with the Cowboys, Vermeil and his players did a masterful job of poor-mouthing their chances, never letting on just how much this game meant to all of them.

"When we came down through the tunnel, I had never, ever, in all my days, absolutely knew we were going to win a game," Eagles inside linebacker Bill Bergey said. "Dick Vermeil reached for everything that he could possibly find to let Dallas feel like they were going to kick our ass. Meanwhile, he was challenging every player. It was the most incredible

	1	2	3	4	Final
Oakland Raiders	14	0	10	3	27
Philadelphia Eagles	0	3	0	7	10

SCORING SUMMARY

1st Quarter
OAK Branch, 2-yd. pass from Plunkett (Bahr kick)
OAK King, 80-yd. pass from Plunkett (Bahr kick)
2nd Quarter
PHI Franklin, 30-yd. FG
3rd Quarter
OAK Branch, 29-yd. pass from Plunkett (Bahr kick)
OAK Bahr, 46-yd. FG
4th Quarter
PHI Krepfle, 8-yd. pass from Jaworski (Franklin kick)
OAK Bahr, 35-yd. FG

week of preparation that I ever went through. . . . Everything was focused on the Cowboys."

Wilbert Montgomery kept running isolation play after isolation play straight into the heart of the Dallas Doomsday defense until he had gained 194 yards, 2 shy of Steve Van Buren's playoff record set in 1949. "I think we had 19 or 21 free agents on that squad, and we played the year a lot on emotion," Eagles offensive line coach Jerry Wampfler said. "The only team that I can remember that we really dominated was Dallas in the NFC Championship Game." As Vermeil put it, "We should have beaten them worse than we did."

As the euphoria of beating the mighty Cowboys began to wear off, the thought occurred to many Eagles that they had another game to play. In two weeks, the Eagles would be in the Super Bowl against the Raiders, a team they had already beaten, 10–7, on November 23 in an eight-sack wipeout of Plunkett at the Vet.

"After the Dallas game, it was almost like, 'We did it, we did it. Oh, by the way, we have one more game and they happen to call it the Super Bowl,'" Bergey remembered. "I don't want to say that Dallas was our Super Bowl, but you know something? Dallas was our Super Bowl. If you can't get ready for a world championship game what the hell can you get ready for? But the thing of it was, we had put so much mentally and physically into that Dallas game, and guess what? We couldn't get back, not even close, to that level."

When the teams arrived in New Orleans on Monday, strict disciplinarian Vermeil bused his players directly to the practice field, whereas Raiders coach Tom Flores all but turned his cast of characters loose on Bourbon Street. Acting on the advice of his captains, Flores instituted an 11 p.m. curfew on Tuesday for the rest of the week. Nevertheless, Raiders defensive end John Matuszak was seen on Wednesday, his normal party night out, still going strong sometime after 3 a.m. "The next day I bring him in," Flores said years later. "He said, 'Coach, I was just out making sure everybody else was getting in.' I did everything I could to keep from smiling and laughing. I said, 'Get out of here. Behave.' He said, 'It won't happen again. It was my night out, Coach.' So I fined him, and that was the end of it."

A day later, Vermeil seemed incredulous that such shenanigans could happen four days before a Super Bowl. "If I had a player who broke curfew," said Vermeil, "he'd be home now." Retorted guard Gene Upshaw, a Silver and Black mainstay for 14 years: "If Tom Flores sent home every guy on this football team who screwed up, he'd be the only guy on the sideline." On Saturday, after a 25-minute workout in the Superdome, Vermeil told the pool reporter: "I get the feeling that the [Eagles] are getting a little uptight. I can't put my finger on it, but they are not as loose and as relaxed as they were Friday."

Wampfler, a longtime NFL assistant, got a sick feeling as he walked among the Eagles during pre-game warmups. "I noticed the Raiders were loosey-goosey as can be," he said years later. "We were tight as hell, tight as banjo strings. We went in, and the tension, you could have cut it with a knife. I tried to say a couple things to loosen these guys up and there was no response. Nothing." Running back onto the field, one of Wampfler's new coaching shoes got caught in the Astroturf and he went flying "ass over belly button and took about three players down with me. You never saw a guy get off the ground as fast in your life."

As both teams congregated in the end zone before introductions, Plunkett detected much the same thing. "I sensed that the Eagles were tense, which may have been the result of being sequestered all week," he said. "They looked dour, with glazed eyes. Our guys seemed much looser. I shook Ron Jaworski's hand. He seemed jittery."

The Eagles opened with two rushes for 11 yards and a first down. Jaworski then faked to Montgomery, took a five-step drop, and attempted the first pass. Harold Carmichael went deep up the left sideline on a clear-out route, while the tight end, John Spagnola, ran a 10-yard square-out with inside linebacker Bob Nelson trailing in coverage. The Eagles' expected that Martin, the outside linebacker o[n] that side in the Raiders' 3-4 defense, would have t[o] move up from his zone drop to honor Montgomer[y] in the flat. When Montgomery got tied up with de[-] fensive end Dave Browning, though, Martin was ab[le] to stay back and easily intercep[t] Jaworski's pass to Spagnol[a.] "Just misread it," Vermeil sai[d.] "Ron had a tough day. He wa[s] very competitive and tryin[g] too hard."

"When we looked at th[e] film, Ron normally wouldn['t] have done that," Wampfler sai[d,] harkening back to the pick[.] "Threw it right to the defende[r.] I really think it was a tensio[n] thing where he was trying s[o] damn hard."

Martin's 17-yard retur[n] put the Raiders in business a[t] the Philadelphia 30. A third[-] and-8 pass from Plunkett t[o] running back Kenny King fe[ll] incomplete, but Eagles defensiv[e] end Carl Hairston was offsides[.] "That right there," Bergey said[,] "was a big part of the game." Mark van Eeghen pounde[d] for 4 and the first down, the[n] Plunkett hit Cliff Branch fo[r] 15 to the 5 and finally for 2 an[d] the touchdown.

Later in the first quarte[r] the Eagles anguished a littl[e] more. On third and 10[,] Jaworski scrambled right an[d] threw a bomb in the end-zon[e] corner to backup wide receive[r] Rodney Parker for an apparen[t] 40-yard touchdown—excep[t] Carmichael, one of the Eagles['] four Pro Bowl selections, wa[s] penalized for illegal motion[.] "Even more than tying the[] game, think what it [would have]

OAKLAND RAIDERS (AFC, 11–5)			PHILADELPHIA EAGLES (NFC, 12–4)	
		Offense		
21	Cliff Branch (5-11, 170)	WR	17	Harold Carmichael* (6-8, 225)
78	Art Shell* (6-5, 280)	LT	75	Stan Walters (6-6, 275)
63	Gene Upshaw (6-5, 255)	LG	62	Petey Perot (6-2, 261)
50	Dave Dalby (6-3, 250)	C	50	Guy Morriss (6-4, 255)
65	Mickey Marvin (6-4, 270)	RG	69	Woody Peoples (6-2, 260)
70	Henry Lawrence (6-4, 270)	RT	76	Jerry Sisemore (6-4, 265)
88	Raymond Chester (6-4, 235)	TE	84	Keith Krepfle (6-3, 230)
85	Bob Chandler (6-1, 180)	WR I TE	88	John Spagnola (6-4, 240)
16	Jim Plunkett (6-2, 205)	QB	7	Ron Jaworski* (6-2, 196)
30	Mark van Eeghen (6-2, 225)	RB	31	Wilbert Montgomery (5-10, 195)
33	Kenny King* (5-11, 205)	RB	20	Leroy Harris (5-9, 230)
		Defense		
72	John Matuszak (6-8, 280)	LE	68	Dennis Harrison (6-8, 275)
82	Reggie Kinlaw (6-2, 250)	NT	65	Charlie Johnson* (6-3, 262)
73	Dave Browning (6-5, 245)	RE	78	Carl Hairston (6-3, 260)
83	Ted Hendricks* (6-7, 225)	LOLB	95	John Bunting (6-1, 220)
55	Matt Millen (6-2, 260)	LILB	66	Bill Bergey (6-3, 245)
51	Bob Nelson (6-4, 230)	RILB	55	Frank LeMaster (6-2, 238)
53	Rod Martin (6-2, 210)	ROLB	56	Jerry Robinson (6-2, 218)
37	Lester Hayes* (6-0, 195)	LCB	43	Roynell Young (6-1, 181)
35	Dwayne O'Steen (6-1, 195)	RCB	46	Herman Edwards (6-0, 190)
36	Mike Davis (6-3, 200)	SS	41	Randy Logan* (6-1, 195)
44	Burgess Owens (6-2, 200)	FS	22	Brenard Wilson (6-0, 175)

* Pro Bowl selection

SUBSTITUTIONS

Oakland

Offense: WR - 81 Morris Bradshaw, 89 Rich Martini; TE - 84 Derrick Ramsey; T - 79 Bruce Davis; G - 71 Lindsey Mason, 66 Steve Sylvester; RB - 46 Todd Christensen, 31 Derrick Jensen, 43 Ira Matthews, 22 Arthur Whittington. *Defense:* DE - 77 Joe Campbell, 86 Cedrick Hardman, 90 Willie Jones; DT - 74 Dave Pear; LB - 56 Jeff Barnes, 52 Mario Celotto, 57 Randy McClanahan; CB - 42 Monte Jackson, 23 Odis McKinney, 26 Keith Moody. *Specialists:* K - 10 Chris Bahr; P - 8 Ray Guy*. *DNP:* 6 Marc Wilson (QB).

Philadelphia

Offense: WR - 89 Wally Henry, 83 Rodney Parker, 85 Charles Smith; T - 73 Steve Kenney; G - 63 Ron Baker; C - 61 Mark Slater; RB - 37 Billy Campfield, 33 Louie Giammona, 35 Perry Harrington. *Defense:* DE - 97 Thomas Brown, 87 Claude Humphrey; NT - 71 Ken Clarke; LB - 59 Al Chesley, 52 Ray Phillips, 51 Reggie Wilkes; CB - 27 Richard Blackmore; S - 24 Zac Henderson, 21 John Sciarra. *Specialists:* K - 1 Tony Franklin; P - 4 Max Runager. *DNP:* 16 Rob Hertel (QB), 9 Joe Pisarcik (QB), 39 Rob Torrey (RB).

Oakland
Head Coach: Tom Flores. *Offense:* Lew Erber (receivers), Sam Boghosian (offensive line), Ray Willsey (backfield). *Defense:* Earl Leggett (defensive line), Charlie Sumner (linebackers), Chet Franklin (defensive backs). *Special Teams:* Steve Ortmayer. *Special Assistant:* Willie Brown. *Strength:* Bob Michak.

Philadelphia
Head Coach: Dick Vermeil. *Offense:* Dick Coury (receivers), Lynn Stiles (tight ends, special teams), Jerry Wampfler (offensive line), Ken Iman (offensive line), Sid Gillman (quarterbacks, research and development), Billy Joe (running backs). *Defense:* Marion Campbell (coordinator), Chuck Clausen (defensive line), George Hill (linebackers), Fred Bruney (defensive backs).

lone] to the confidence level," Wampfler said. "It changed the momentum of the game."

The Eagles punted, and then two plays later, on third and 4, came the play of the game. From deep in the pocket, Plunkett looked for one of three receivers streaking vertically up the field. "Our reads then were deep, middle, and short," Flores said. With everyone covered but under no pass-rush pressure, Plunkett scrambled to the left, hoping that one of his receivers would come free. "Kenny King was supposed to come out of the backfield and run a few yards downfield to clear out or maybe catch a dump-off if nobody was open deep," Plunkett said. "All good receivers are taught to scramble with the quarterback and go to the side he's on and try to help him out, so both Kenny and Bobby [Chandler] went to the left."

King broke up the field and the Eagles cornerback, Herman Edwards, reacted back toward King a little too late. Plunkett floated the ball to King just over the outstretched fingers of Edwards at the Oakland 39 right in front of Flores, who stood impassively with hands on hips. From there, King easily won a footrace down the sideline to complete an 80-yard touchdown. "King was incredibly fast," Flores said. "No one was going to catch Kenny King."

On the play, the Eagles blitzed linebacker Jerry Robinson off their right side and looped Hairston from right end into the middle as part of a four-man rush. Today, it's likely the play would be called

back on a holding penalty. Upshaw fanned back and blocked Robinson, but his hands were outside the frame of the linebacker's body as they tumbled to the ground. On the inside, Hairston spun into right guard Mickey Marvin and was taken down to the ground as well. "They grabbed my right end [Hairston], who was going to sack the quarterback, by the face mask and pulled him to the ground," said Vermeil, remembering 25 years later the details of the critical play.

The Eagles drove 61 yards for barefoot Tony Franklin's 30-yard field goal, making it 14–3. Even with that, Bergey later would admit that the die had been cast. When the 12-year veteran, a five-time Pro Bowl choice, tried to inspire his teammates a short time later, he found their reaction depressingly negative. "Everybody was like zombies," Bergey said. "I just said, 'This game is over. There is just no way we're going to win this game.'"

A good-looking drive of 62 yards carried to the Oakland 11 in the final minute of the first half. On third and 10, Parker beat press coverage by nickel back Odis McKinney at the line and was about as wide open as a wide receiver can be on a fade route in the corner of the red zone, but Jaworski's overthrown pass wasn't even close. Franklin then drilled a 28-yard field-goal attempt so low that 6-foot-7 linebacker Ted Hendricks didn't even have to leap before the ball banged into his left hand. "That was one of the things I picked up when I played for the Colts with Bubba Smith," Hendricks said. "Get a good push on one of the weakest linemen and bring two other guys with you. If Willie Jones had any hands at all he would have recovered and ran it for a touchdown."

Coordinated by Marion Campbell, the Eagles' uncomplicated defense ranked second in the NFL. "We were a bunch of overachieving sons of a gun," said Bergey. Raiders right tackle Henry Lawrence, who had been embarrassed by pass-rushing defensive end Claude Humphrey for three and a half sacks in their first meeting, played far better in the Super Bowl, and the Raiders also picked up Campbell's frequent blitzes. "Their scheme was really unique," Flores said. "It was very disciplined and very effective. They'd zone one side and man the other. You could beat it, but you had to have time to do it. We used play-action to buy some time."

At halftime, Eagles officials got word that Joe Kuharich, their coach from 1964 to 1968, had died back in Philadelphia earlier in the day at age 63. "This was a day of bad news," longtime Eagles broadcaster Merrill Reese said.

Early in the third quarter, Plunkett had all kinds of time and completed a 32-yard pass deep to Bob Chandler on the left side against rookie cornerback Roynell Young. Two plays later, Plunkett faked a run and took another seven-step drop. "I was fooled and I misread the coverage," said Plunkett. "I thought it was man-to-man but they ended up backing off into a zone, which I kind of threw into the heart of." The intended receiver, Branch, had to come back slightly for the ball at the 2 because Young was sinking and had a better angle to it. "Cliff was so quick that he slipped in front of Young and made a great catch," Plunkett said. "He jumped and tore it away from Young."

The 29-yard scoring strike extended the Raiders' lead to 21–3, but the Eagles weren't about to abandon their ground game altogether. Their problem, as Vermeil later summarized it, was "the physical matchups. They were a bigger, stronger team than we were." Wampfler called right tackle Jerry Sisemore the best technician he had in 20 years as an NFL line coach, but on this day he was outmuscled by the 6-foot-8, 290-pound Matuszak. Guy Morriss was in his eighth season as the starting center, but Wampfler admitted that Reggie Kinlaw, the Raiders' cat-quick but undersized nose tackle, clearly got the best of him. "Kinlaw was big in that game," said Raiders linebackers coach Charlie Sumner, who also called and coordinated the defense. "We just moved him off the ball a little bit so nose-to-nose they couldn't push him off. He stopped the run pretty good by himself."

Another reason why the Eagles gained merely 69 yards in 26 carries was Sumner's decision to walk up inside linebackers Matt Millen and Nelson almost to the line of scrimmage. "We were a zone blocking team, and that fouled up our zone-blocking schemes," Vermeil said. "They had big, strong guys."

With Montgomery effectively contained, the onus fell on the 29-year-old Jaworski to carry the offense. His passer rating of 91.0, which led the NFC, was almost 15 points higher than he posted

TEAM STATISTICS

OAKLAND		PHILADELPHIA
17	Total First Downs	19
6	Rushing	3
10	Passing	14
1	Penalty	2
377	Total Net Yardage	360
56	Total Offensive Plays	64
6.7	Avg. Gain per Offensive Play	5.6
34	Rushes	26
117	Yards Gained Rushing (Net)	69
3.4	Average Yards per Rush	2.7
21	Passes Attempted	38
13	Passes Completed	18
0	Passes Intercepted	3
1	Tackled Attempting to Pass	0
1	Yards Lost Attempting to Pass	0
260	Yards Gained Passing (Net)	291
6/12	Third-Down Efficiency	5/12
0/0	Fourth-Down Efficiency	1/1
3	Punts	3
42	Average Distance	36.3
2	Punt Returns	3
1	Punt Return Yardage	20
3	Kickoff Returns	6
48	Kickoff Return Yardage	87
44	Interception Return Yardage	0
0	Fumbles	1
0	Own Fumbles Recovered	0
1	Opponent Fumbles Recovered	0
5	Penalties	6
37	Yards Penalized	57
3	Touchdowns	1
0	Rushing	0
3	Passing	1
0	Returns	0
3	Extra Points Made	1
2	Field Goals Made	1
3	Field Goals Attempted	2
0	Safeties	0
27	Total Points Scored	10
29:49	Time of Possession	30:11

in any other season of his 15-year career. In the 1980 playoff run, however, his rating was only 38.3, including 49.3 in the Super Bowl, compared to 145.0 for Plunkett.

Jaworski's second interception, midway through the third quarter, ended a drive of 51 yards. It was third and 3 when he threw behind Spagnola

OAKLAND

Passing	CP/ATT	YDS	TD	INT	RAT
Plunkett	13/21	261	3	0	145.0

Rushing	ATT	YDS	AVG	TD	LG
Van Eeghen	18	75	4.2	0	8
King	6	18	3.0	0	6
Jensen	4	17	4.3	0	6
Plunkett	3	9	3.0	0	5
Whittington	3	-2	-0.7	0	2

Receiving	NO	YDS	AVG	TD	LG
Branch	5	67	13.4	2	29t
Chandler	4	77	19.3	0	32
King	2	93	46.5	1	80t
Chester	2	24	12.0	0	16

Interceptions	NO	YDS	LG	TD
Martin	3	44	25	0

Punting	NO	AVG	LG	BLK
Guy	3	42	44	0

Punt Ret.	NO/FC	YDS	LG	TD
Matthews	2/1	1	2	0

Kickoff Ret.	NO	YDS	LG	TD
Matthews	2	29	21	0
Moody	1	19	19	0

Defense	SOLO	AST	TOT	SK
Owens	7	2	9	0
Millen	5	2	7	0
Davis	4	2	6	0
Nelson	3	3	6	0
Martin	5	0	5	0
Kinlaw	3	2	5	0
Browning	4	0	4	0
O'Steen	2	2	4	0
Hayes	3	0	3	0
Hendricks	3	0	3	0
Barnes	2	0	2	0
Campbell	2	0	2	0
Matuszak	0	2	2	0
McKinney	2	0	2	0
Pear	2	0	2	0
Bahr	1	0	1	0
W. Jones	1	0	1	0
Jensen	1	0	1	0
Bradshaw	0	1	1	0
Hardman	0	1	1	0
TOTAL	50	17	67	0

PHILADELPHIA

Passing	CP/ATT	YDS	TD	INT	RAT
Jaworski	18/38	291	1	3	49.3

Rushing	ATT	YDS	AVG	TD	LG
Montgomery	16	44	2.8	0	8
Harris	7	14	2.0	0	5
Giammona	1	7	7.0	0	7
Harrington	1	4	4.0	0	4
Jaworski	1	0	0.0	0	0

Receiving	NO	YDS	AVG	TD	LG
Montgomery	6	19	3.2	0	25
Carmichael	5	83	16.6	0	29
Smith	2	59	29.5	0	43
Krepfle	2	16	8.0	1	8t
Spagnola	1	22	22.0	0	22
Parker	1	19	19.0	0	19
Harris	1	1	1.0	0	1

Interceptions	NO	YDS	LG	TD
None	--	--	--	--

Punting	NO	AVG	LG	BLK
Runager	3	36.7	46	0

Punt Ret.	NO/FC	YDS	LG	TD
Sciarra	2/0	18	12	0
Henry	1/0	2	2	0

Kickoff Ret.	NO	YDS	LG	TD
Campfield	5	87	21	0
Harrington	1	0	0	0

Defense	SOLO	AST	TOT	SK
Bergey	6	5	11	0
Johnson	7	2	9	1
Robinson	4	3	7	0
LeMaster	5	1	6	0
Hairston	4	2	6	0
Bunting	3	2	5	0
Young	4	0	4	0
Humphrey	3	1	4	0
Logan	3	1	4	0
Edwards	3	0	3	0
Harrison	1	2	3	0
Clarke	1	1	2	0
Wilkes	1	1	2	0
Wilson	1	1	2	0
Baker	1	0	1	0
Campfield	1	0	1	0
Giammona	1	0	1	0
Montgomery	1	0	1	0
Sciarra	1	0	1	0
TOTAL	51	22	73	1

on the left sideline and Martin intercepted in man coverage. "Jaworski looked at Spagnola the whole way," Sumner said. "I remember Martin just came out of nowhere and stepped right in front of him."

Perhaps Jaworski's best throw came after the Raiders went up 24–3 with a field goal by Chris Bahr late in the third quarter. With blitzing safety Mike Davis leaping right in his face, the "Polish Rifle" escaped beautifully and, on the dead run to his right, unloaded a 43-yard strike to Charles Smith. The starting wide receiver opposite Carmichael, Smith was able to play only sparingly due to the effects of a broken jaw suffered in Week 16. "Then my number-three receiver, Scott Fitzkee, was out with a stress fracture," Vermeil said years later. "We didn't have our second and third wide receivers against a team that played press man coverage. Those are not excuses. They're facts. I'm too old to have excuses." This time, the Eagles converted on Jaworski's third-down touchdown pass of 8 yards to tight end Keith Krepfle.

Fourteen minutes remained and it was a 14-point game when the Eagles basically packed it in. A full second after Plunkett completed a short pass to tight end Raymond Chester, Humphrey grabbed Plunkett by the shoulders and swung him to the ground. When one of the officials dropped a flag for roughing the passer, Humphrey picked it up and threw it back at the official, who perhaps too kindly walked away. "I talked to Marion Campbell after the game," Bergey said. "Defensively, we probably made 15 to 20 just flat mental mistakes. People going the wrong way. Jumping offsides. . . . In a normal game? We'd have five at most."

Only a tremendous breakup by Edwards on an end-zone toss to Chandler prevented Plunkett from having a fourth touchdown pass. Bahr's 35-yard field goal completed the scoring, but Jaworski still had two more turnovers in him. The third was his bungled center exchange with Morriss that was recovered by Jones, and the fourth was a forced throw into zone coverage that was picked off by Martin.

The Eagles' plan, according to Jaworski, had been to stay away from Hendricks because of the

problems that his gigantic wingspan, unpredictabl[e] blitzing patterns, and almost impenetrable low block shield presented. "I didn't get but three play[s] run my way," Hendricks recalled. That left it u[p] to Martin on the other side, who was up for th[e] challenge. "He's one of those stories that is real[ly] nice," Raiders personnel man Ron Wolf said. "H[e] was a 12th-round draft choice from the Universit[y] of Southern California. He was small and real fas[t]. What happened was, he built himself up and was i[n] the Pro Bowl a couple years. His hands were like [a] vise, so big and so strong for a little guy."

Up and down the roster, the Raiders ha[d] characters with ability. Oakland was just 2–[3] when Dan Pastorini, acquired from Housto[n] in the offseason in a trade for Ken Stabler, wen[t] down with a broken leg. Plunkett had thrown 8[0] touchdown passes compared to 117 interception[s] in seven unfulfilled seasons for New England an[d] San Francisco. Signed in 1978 by owner Al Davi[s], Plunkett had attempted merely 15 passes in tw[o] seasons before getting the call. "I know of no athlet[e] in the history of sport who has made a greate[r] comeback than Jim Plunkett," NFL Commissione[r] Pete Rozelle said. He made this remark onl[y] moments after presenting the Lombardi Trophy t[o] Davis, who was embroiled in a nasty $160 millio[n] lawsuit against the league for the right to move th[e] franchise to Los Angeles. "I remember Rozelle wa[s] a lot warmer than Al," Sumner said, "but neithe[r] one of them did anything wrong." The pair o[f] antagonists did not shake hands.

"It was hard to believe that we could win wit[h] the group of guys we had," Plunkett said, "but i[f] guys had been out drinking at night, they wouldn'[t] try to get out of practice by saying they had ba[d] hamstrings when they really had hangovers. W[e] had a crazy bad-boy reputation and sometimes th[e] guys tried to live up to it, but I never ran aroun[d] with a team that had such strong camaraderie. W[e] would be a dominant team when we won the Supe[r] Bowl again in three years, but I was fonder of thi[s] Super Bowl because of the guys I played with an[d] how, with so many new players, we evolved from [a] mediocre team into a great team."

XVI

SAN FRANCISCO 49ERS 26, CINCINNATI BENGALS 21

January 24, 1982
Silverdome, Pontiac, Michigan

By the mid-1980s, the San Francisco 49ers would become one of the greatest football machines ever assembled. Eddie DeBartolo's open-checkbook ownership. Bill Walsh's cutting-edge coaching. The magnificent passing combination of Joe Montana to Jerry Rice, in conjunction with a powerful running game. Rock-ribbed defenses masterminded by the likes of George Seifert and inspired by the incomparable toughness and leadership of Ronnie Lott.

In 1981, however, the 49ers were anything but a dominant outfit. That San Francisco became a championship team by beating the equally surprising Cincinnati Bengals, 26–21, in Super Bowl XVI at the Silverdome was a tribute to goal-line stands and squib kicks, not brilliant plays or stifling defense. This was a game in which some unknown 49ers, particularly linebacker Dan Bunz, had as much impact on the final outcome as the club's budding young superstars.

"We didn't have a great team in '81," Walsh said years later. "We lacked depth and our running game didn't meet NFL standards. . . . Looking back, I'd have to say that it was my most satisfying season, because we had been down so far and suddenly we were on top of the football world."

When the decade opened, the 49ers had lost 31 of their last 35 games. Walsh's first team went 2–14 in 1979, then 6–10 the next year. With the modest goal of regaining respectability after the destructive reign of general manager Joe Thomas, in 1981 the 49ers won the NFC West for the first time since 1972 with a 13–3 record. They proceeded to whip the New York Giants, 38–24, in the divisional playoffs and then defeated the Dallas Cowboys, 28–27, in the NFC Championship Game on a late touchdown pass from Montana to Dwight Clark that became known forevermore as "the Catch."

The Bengals arrived in Pontiac, Michigan, having followed a similar route. They also had been 6–10 in 1980. This was their first divisional title since

Attendance: 81,270
Conditions: 72 degrees, indoors
Time of kickoff: 4:20 p.m. (EST)
Length of game: 3 hours, 21 minutes
Referee: Pat Haggerty

MVP: Joe Montana, QB, 49ers

1973. Neither the Bengals nor the 49ers had even a single player selected for the Pro Bowl in 1978, 1979, or 1980. Cincinnati was coached by Forrest Gregg, the Vince Lombardi disciple who took over in 1980 after Bill Johnson and then Homer Rice flopped as Paul Brown's successors.

"Forrest Gregg came along at a good time for us," quarterback Ken Anderson said. "When he became our head coach in 1980, we were a team that wasn't disciplined, wasn't necessarily in great physical shape, and wasn't very strong. Forrest grabbed us by the back of the neck and shook us and made us a tough football team, physically and mentally. . . . Certainly that wasn't the Paul Brown style, but Paul let Forrest coach the team his way and he got results. We had good coaches, we had chemistry. We were an excitable, emotional team, and we had talent."

It didn't look that way, though, after the first half, which ended with the 49ers leading, 20–0. A 1-point favorite, the Bengals had been outgained, 208–99. Anderson was intercepted at the San Francisco 5 in the first quarter and wide receiver Cris Collinsworth lost a fumble at the San Francisco 8 in the second quarter. When kickoff returners David Verser and Archie Griffin misplayed bouncing boots by Ray Wersching, he turned their miscues into field goals of 22 and 26 yards just before halftime.

"It really looked bad in the first half," Gregg said years later. "We gave the ball away three times and we weren't playing well at all. In the locker room, we

	1	2	3	4	Final
San Francisco 49ers	7	13	0	6	26
Cincinnati Bengals	0	0	7	14	21

SCORING SUMMARY

1st Quarter
SF   Montana, 1-yd. run (Wersching kick)
2nd Quarter
SF   Cooper, 11-yd. pass from Montana (Wersching kick)
SF   Wersching, 22-yd. FG
SF   Wersching, 26-yd. FG
3rd Quarter
CIN   Anderson, 5-yd. run (Breech kick)
4th Quarter
CIN   Ross, 4-yd. pass from Anderson (Breech kick)
SF   Wersching, 40-yd. FG
SF   Wersching, 23-yd. FG
CIN   Ross, 3-yd. pass from Anderson (Breech kick)

just talked about doing what we do well. Don't worry what the score is, the score at the end is what counts. I never will forget. We were just getting ready to go back out on the field and Reggie Williams jumped up and said, 'You just gotta believe that we can do this.' We came out and roared."

The Bengals marched 83 yards to open the third quarter, scoring on a third-and-4 scramble by Anderson from the 5 after he eluded the pass rush of defensive end Lawrence Pillers. Then the much more aggressive defensive calls of coordinator Hank Bullough helped force the 49ers into three-and-outs on their first two possessions. "Once they started blitzing we really couldn't handle it," Walsh remembered. "We were opportunistic early and got in the end zone, but in the second half we were really struggling because he was bringing everybody, and his corners were really fine coverage guys. In a sense, I felt sort of helpless. Their defense was sort of overwhelming us at that point."

On the left side, a pair of second-round selections in the 1981 draft battled throughout the afternoon. Cornerback Eric Wright, the 40th overall choice from Missouri, had won the first round with his second-quarter strip of Collinsworth, the 37th overall choice from Florida. "It was just a big heavyweight fight on this guy," Wright said. "I'll be very blunt. For a white guy playing receiver he was one of the fastest

you'd ever want to see. We always saw him make big plays getting behind guys, because guys never played him true and never respected his speed. Ray Rhodes [assistant secondary coach] preached that. He said 'When you relax, he'll go by you.'"

Midway through the third quarter, the Bengals faced a third and 23 from their 37. Chuck Studley, the Bengals' defensive line coach from 1969 to 1978 who now was coordinating the 49ers' defense, called a soft zone coverage designed to prevent the long pass. Collinsworth set up Wright and burst past him when the rookie cornerback failed to heed the warning of his coaches. "Caught me sleeping," Wright said. Anderson, the league's MVP and the NFL leader in passer rating at 98.5, lofted a home-run ball that Collinsworth hauled in for a 49-yard gain.

"It was one of those real high, deep balls that comes right down over [the receiver's] head and they have to bend their head back. Kenny laid it right in there," Bengals tight ends and special-teams coach Bruce Coslet said. "It was a tremendous catch. Collinsworth had everything. He only played eight years because his legs just went. He lost his speed and then he couldn't play. But [in] his rookie year he was phenomenal."

A few plays later, the Bengals decided to go for it on fourth and 1 at the 5. Fullback Pete Johnson, their 249-pound battering ram, piled ahead for 2 yards against a defense missing one of its 11 players. Linebacker Keena Turner was standing next to Studley on the sidelines, thinking the coordinator

COACHING STAFFS

San Francisco
Head Coach: Bill Walsh. *Offense:* Milt Jackson (receivers, special teams), Bobb McKittrick (offensive line), Sam Wyche (quarterbacks), Billie Matthews (running backs). *Defense:* Chuck Studley (coordinator), Bill McPherson (defensive line), Norb Hecker (linebackers), George Seifert (defensive backs). *Strength:* Al Vermeil.

Cincinnati
Head Coach: Forrest Gregg. *Offense:* Lindy Infante (receivers, quarterbacks), Bruce Coslet (tight ends, special teams), Jim McNally (offensive line), George Sefcik (running backs). *Defense:* Hank Bullough (coordinator), Dick Modzelewski (defensive line), Dick LeBeau (defensive backs). *Strength:* Kim Wood.

ad called for the "giant" defense rather than the "goal-line" defense. With the ball on the 3, Turner rushed on the field late for the first of what would turn out to be the decisive four downs of the game.

Studley's goal-line unit was aligned in a 6-4-1 configuration. "We had four linemen inside between the tight ends," Studley explained. "I used to line up defensive ends outside the tight ends and just grind them down hard to the inside. [Dwaine] Board and [Fred] Dean, boy, they'd line up, angle in and just come roaring. They didn't have run force. That was the reason people used to have the quarterback fake action away and bootleg out, figuring they could negotiate the defensive end coming down. I remember going over it on the board before the game. Then we had four linebackers in man-to-man coverage."

Early in the season, one of the 49ers' defensive tackles was injured and Studley handed the vacancy in the goal-line defense to John Choma, a backup offensive lineman. On first down, the Bengals attempted to use Choma's lack of experience against him. "They double-teamed Archie Reese but didn't block Choma and ran right at the double team," Studley said. "They figured Choma would overpenetrate. What they didn't know is we worked our tails off all week on that play, too."

Choma shot forward; when he realized he wasn't being blocked, he put both hands on the turf to halt his momentum and grabbed Johnson by the waist as he entered the hole. As Choma slipped down to Johnson's ankles, Bunz arrived to finish him off after a gain of 2 to the 1. "It was a sucker play," San Francisco defensive line coach Bill McPherson said. "As far as I know, [Tom] Landry with Dallas was the guy that started that in the NFL. You didn't see it very often. It was always a tough play for a defensive tackle, especially

SAN FRANCISCO 49ERS (NFC, 13–3)		CINCINNATI BENGALS (AFC, 12–4)	
	Offense		
87 Dwight Clark* (6-4, 210)	WR	80 Cris Collinsworth* (6-5, 192)	
61 Dan Audick (6-3, 253)	LT	78 Anthony Muñoz* (6-6, 278)	
68 John Ayers (6-5, 260)	LG	62 Dave Lapham (6-4, 262)	
56 Fred Quillan (6-5, 260)	C	58 Blair Bush (6-3, 252)	
51 Randy Cross* (6-3, 250)	RG	65 Max Montoya (6-5, 275)	
71 Keith Fahnhorst (6-6, 263)	RT	77 Mike Wilson (6-5, 271)	
86 Charle Young (6-4, 234)	TE	89 Dan Ross (6-4, 235)	
88 Freddie Solomon (5-11, 185)	WR	85 Isaac Curtis (6-1, 192)	
16 Joe Montana* (6-2, 200)	QB	14 Ken Anderson* (6-3, 212)	
32 Ricky Patton (5-11, 192)	RB	40 Charles Alexander (6-1, 221)	
49 Earl Cooper (6-2, 227)	RB	46 Pete Johnson* (6-0, 249)	
	Defense		
79 Jim Stuckey (6-4, 251)	LE	73 Eddie Edwards (6-5, 256)	
78 Archie Reese (6-3, 262)	NT	75 Wilson Whitley (6-3, 265)	
74 Fred Dean* (6-2, 230)	DT I RE	79 Ross Browner (6-3, 261)	
76 Dwaine Board (6-5, 250)	DE I LOLB	53 Bo Harris (6-3, 226)	
52 Bobby Leopold (6-1, 215)	LLB I LILB	55 Jim LeClair (6-3, 234)	
64 Jack Reynolds (6-1, 232)	MLB I RILB	50 Glenn Cameron (6-2, 228)	
58 Keena Turner (6-2, 219)	RLB I ROLB	57 Reggie Williams (6-0, 228)	
42 Ronnie Lott* (6-0, 199)	LCB	34 Louis Breeden (5-11, 185)	
21 Eric Wright (6-1, 180)	RCB	13 Ken Riley (6-0, 183)	
27 Carlton Williamson (6-0, 204)	SS	26 Bobby Kemp (6-0, 186)	
22 Dwight Hicks* (6-1, 189)	FS	27 Bryan Hicks (6-0, 192)	

* Pro Bowl selection

SUBSTITUTIONS

San Francisco

Offense: WR - 84 Mike Shumann, 85 Mike Wilson; TE - 80 Eason Ramson; T - 66 Allan Kennedy; G - 60 John Choma; C - 62 Walt Downing; RB - 38 Johnny Davis, 20 Amos Lawrence, 30 Bill Ring. **Defense:** DE - 65 Lawrence Pillers; DT - 75 John Harty; LB - 57 Dan Bunz, 59 Willie Harper, 53 Milt McColl, 54 Craig Puki; CB - 28 Lynn Thomas; S - 24 Rick Gervais. **Specialists:** K - 14 Ray Wersching; P - 3 Jim Miller. **DNP:** 7 Guy Benjamin (QB), 31 Walt Easley (RB), 35 Lenvil Elliott (RB), 29 Saladin Martin (CB).

Cincinnati

Offense: WR - 84 Don Bass, 86 Steve Kreider, 81 David Verser; TE - 83 M. L. Harris; T - 68 Mike Obrovac; C - 60 Blake Moore; RB - 45 Archie Griffin, 36 Jim Hargrove. **Defense:** DE - 67 Gary Burley, 72 Mike St. Clair; NT - 71 Rod Horn; LB - 52 Tom Dinkel, 49 Guy Frazier, 51 Rick Razzano; CB - 44 Ray Griffin, 25 John Simmons; S - 21 Oliver Davis, 42 Mike Fuller. **Specialists:** K - 10 Jim Breech; P - 87 Pat McInally*. **DNP:** 15 Turk Schonert (QB), 12 Jack Thompson (QB), 74 Glenn Bujnoch (G).

[Choma] because he wasn't experienced."

On second down, the Bengals ran Johnson between left tackle Anthony Muñoz and left guard Dave Lapham. Anderson called an audible at the line, telling Verser, who was lined up tight on the right side, to block linebacker Craig Puki on the left side just outside Muñoz after he came across in motion. Verser did go in motion, but he missed the change in his blocking assignment because of the din of the crowd, and instead went wide beyond the tight end. The lead blocker, Charles Alexander, was stuffed by Bunz in the hole.

The unblocked Puki also got a piece of Johnson, but the big back still might have scored had it not been for Jack Reynolds. He reacted so quickly that Blair Bush couldn't get out on him before Reynolds slammed into Johnson chest-to-chest with all his might, halting him for no gain. "That was probably the play right there that hurt us the most," Gregg said. "David [Verser] was a good blocker but the noise was so great he didn't hear the call. David blocked the wrong man, leaving a linebacker free in the hole."

The 49ers had signed Reynolds as a free agent that spring after he was released by the Los Angeles Rams following 11 seasons in which he made the Pro Bowl twice. Reynolds acquired his nickname "Hacksaw" when, in a fit of anger after a galling loss late in his senior season at the University of Tennessee, he took a day and a half to saw a '53 Chevrolet in half with a cheap K-Mart hacksaw and 13 blades. "'Hacksaw' Reynolds possessed more inherent football knowledge than any former player I'd worked with," said Walsh, who had Reynolds on his staff as an assistant for a brief time in 1985. "Jack was absolutely the most competitive player I've ever known."

Whether the 49ers were at home or on the road, Reynolds's game-day routine was one of a kind. "Tight as a drum to begin with," Studley said. "He didn't keep an apartment; he just scrounged off the other players. He went to the pre-game meeting and meal completely dressed in his uniform. Shoulder pads, helmet, the whole bit. I've never seen it before or since. From the moment he got up on game day he was nothing but total business. He didn't want anybody talking to him."

On third down, Anderson faked to Johnson, rolled right, and threw a pass into the right flat

TEAM STATISTICS

SAN FRANCISCO		CINCINNATI
20	Total First Downs	24
9	Rushing	7
9	Passing	13
2	Penalty	4
275	Total Net Yardage	356
63	Total Offensive Plays	63
4.4	Avg. Gain per Offensive Play	5.7
40	Rushes	24
127	Yards Gained Rushing (Net)	72
3.2	Average Yards per Rush	3.0
22	Passes Attempted	34
14	Passes Completed	25
0	Passes Intercepted	2
1	Tackled Attempting to Pass	5
9	Yards Lost Attempting to Pass	16
148	Yards Gained Passing (Net)	284
8/15	Third-Down Efficiency	6/12
0/0	Fourth-Down Efficiency	1/2
4	Punts	3
46.3	Average Distance	43.7
1	Punt Returns	4
6	Punt Return Yardage	35
2	Kickoff Returns	7
40	Kickoff Return Yardage	52
52	Interception Return Yardage	0
2	Fumbles	2
1	Own Fumbles Recovered	0
2	Opponent Fumbles Recovered	1
8	Penalties	8
65	Yards Penalized	57
2	Touchdowns	3
1	Rushing	1
1	Passing	2
0	Returns	0
2	Extra Points Made	3
4	Field Goals Made	0
4	Field Goals Attempted	0
0	Safeties	0
26	Total Points Scored	21
30:34	Time of Possession	29:26

to Alexander. Tight end Dan Ross was crossing from the right side to the left corner and was in the clear, but the play was designed for Alexander and Anderson looked for him all the way. The ball was thrown ever so slightly behind Alexander, who made the catch one foot from the goal line before being driven to the turf on his back at that exact

SAN FRANCISCO

Passing	CP/ATT	YDS	TD	INT	RAT
Montana	14/22	157	1	0	100.0

Rushing	ATT	YDS	AVG	TD	LG
Patton	17	55	3.2	0	10
Cooper	9	34	3.8	0	14
Montana	6	18	3.0	1	8
Ring	5	17	3.4	0	7
Davis	2	5	2.5	0	4
Clark	1	-2	-2.0	0	-2

Receiving	NO	YDS	AVG	TD	LG
Solomon	4	52	13.0	0	20
Clark	4	45	11.3	0	17
Cooper	2	15	7.5	1	11t
Wilson	1	22	22.0	0	22
Young	1	14	14.0	0	14
Patton	1	6	6.0	0	6
Ring	1	3	3.0	0	3

Interceptions	NO	YDS	LG	TD	
Hicks	1	27	27	0	
Wright	1	25	25	0	

Punting	NO	AVG	LG	BLK	
Miller	4	46.3	50	0	

Punt Ret.	NO/FC	YDS	LG	TD	
Hicks	1/0	6	6	0	
Solomon	0/1	0	--	0	

Kickoff Ret.	NO	YDS	LG	TD	
Hicks	1	23	23	0	
Lawrence	1	17	17	0	

Defense	SOLO	AST	TOT	SK
Leopold	6	1	7	1
Reynolds	6	1	7	1
Harper	6	0	6	0
Reese	5	1	6	0
Williamson	5	0	5	0
Wright	5	0	5	0
Lott	4	1	5	0
D. Hicks	2	3	5	0
Stuckey	3	1	4	1
Board	2	1	3	0
Gervais	2	1	3	0
Harty	2	0	2	0
Turner	2	0	2	1
Bunz	1	0	1	0
Cross	1	0	1	0
Dean	1	0	1	1
Lawrence	1	0	1	0
McColl	1	0	1	0
Puki	0	1	1	0
TOTAL	55	11	66	5

CINCINNATI

Passing	CP/ATT	YDS	TD	INT	RAT
Anderson	25/34	300	2	2	95.2

Rushing	ATT	YDS	AVG	TD	LG
Johnson	14	36	2.6	0	5
Alexander	5	17	3.4	0	13
Anderson	4	15	3.8	1	6
A. Griffin	1	4	4.0	0	4

Receiving	NO	YDS	AVG	TD	LG
Ross	11	104	9.5	2	16
Collinsworth	5	107	21.4	0	49
Curtis	3	42	14.0	0	21
Kreider	2	36	18.0	0	19
Johnson	2	8	4.0	0	5
Alexander	2	3	1.5	0	3

Interceptions	NO	YDS	LG	TD
None	--	--	--	--

Punting	NO	AVG	LG	BLK
McInally	3	43.7	53	0

Punt Ret.	NO/FC	YDS	LG	TD
Fuller	4/0	35	17	0

Kickoff Ret.	NO	YDS	LG	TD
Verser	5	52	16	0
Frazier	1	0	0	0
A. Griffin	1	0	0	0

Defense	SOLO	AST	TOT	SK
Browner	10	0	10	1
Breeden	7	0	7	0
Kemp	6	0	6	0
Williams	5	1	6	0
Razzano	4	0	4	0
Riley	4	0	4	0
Cameron	3	1	4	0
B. Hicks	3	1	4	0
B. Harris	2	2	4	0
Le Clair	1	2	3	0
St. Clair	1	2	3	0
Edwards	2	0	2	0
Griffin	1	0	1	0
Hargrove	1	0	1	0
Montoya	1	0	1	0
Whitley	1	0	1	0
Wilson	1	0	1	0
Dinkel	0	1	1	0
TOTAL	53	10	63	1

point by the onrushing Bunz. "That was one of our basic goal-line plays," Coslet said. "When you throw that pass you want the catch to be for a touchdown. You don't want to have to break a tackle or run for it because you have your back turned to the defense. You want to make sure you get in the end zone on your pattern, and he didn't. He should have had the touchdown on the catch."

Drafted out of Long Beach State in the first round in 1978, Bunz started 64 games for the 49ers in the next seven seasons, a journeyman linebacker able to play both inside and outside. In this game, he played on the goal line and special teams only. "Bunz was an ordinary player," Studley said. "He was big, tough, strong. He was a tremendous competitor. You never had to worry about Danny Bunz being ready to play football. He was 230, maybe 235. But, God, you'd time him with a sun dial. He couldn't run at all. . . . Danny was a decent zone player but this was man-to-man. You put him in man-to-man coverage, and you were scared to death." How many times out of 100, Studley was asked, would Bunz have been able to tackle Alexander short of the end zone? "I would say Bunz would make that play one out of 100," he replied.

Only one minute remained in the third quarter, and the 49ers still led, 20–7. It was fourth down with a foot to go. The Bengals signaled for a timeout. "We said, 'If we're going to win this game, then we're going to have to run this play,'" Gregg said. "We ran the off-tackle slant. Reynolds, the old fox, sniffed it out and we didn't get in. Reynolds was basically unassigned. You hope you get enough push off the line of scrimmage where you can get into the end zone."

The handoff again went to Johnson to the right. Bunz took on the lead block by Alexander and didn't budge. Not only didn't right tackle Mike Wilson get movement, but he was also pushed backward by Pillers and Choma. "I saw the 49ers rise up at the snap of the ball," said Johnson. "I figured I could go under them. There just wasn't anything."

When Johnson reached the line, Reynolds, Bunz, and Lott converged on him simultaneously. There was no need to measure. He was a yard short. McPherson called it the greatest goal-line stand of his almost 50 years in football. "I just think they went to the well once too often," Studley said. "They

told me that the whole season long Pete Johnson had never been stopped down there." Said Walsh, "The Bengals were a very good team, but a very mechanical team."

The 49ers took possession, and Walsh tried three straight running plays, gained 8 yards, and punted out to the Cincinnati 47. The Bengals covered the distance in seven plays, slicing the deficit to 20–14 on Ross' 4-yard touchdown pass from Anderson. "I was really uneasy because we couldn't hold them off forever," Walsh said. "They had Kenny Anderson and any number of really fine offensive players. The Bengals, collectively, had better personnel than we had. Then one play changed the game and held it together for us."

Dan Audick, the 49ers' 245-pound left tackle who was acquired by Walsh before the season from San Diego for a third-round pick, promptly jumped offsides. On second and 15, and after having not recorded a first down in the second half, Walsh dug deep into his voluminous playbook. "It was a play we had prepared for difficult situations such as this," said Walsh. "It was what we called a 'drift' pass for Joe."

Montana dropped straight back, hesitated for a moment, and rolled to get away from the rush and give himself more time to throw. With the quarterback buying time outside the pocket, wide receiver Mike Wilson drove cornerback Louis Breeden off him, planted, and came back to make a 22-yard reception along the sideline.

"It was the biggest play of the game," said Walsh, "because it finally gave us some breathing room, improved our field position, and got us untracked."

With the ball near midfield, the 49ers turned to their 19th-ranked ground game for the next seven plays. Ricky Patton, who led the team in rushing that season with merely 543 yards, had five of the carries and gained 23 yards. In came Wersching to kick a 40-yard field goal, and the 49ers led, 23–14. "Ray Wersching had nerves of steel in the clutch," Walsh said. "Ray's kicking was the difference in four games that year, three of which we won by 3 points and one by just 2."

By now, the Bengals were fighting the clock with five and a half minutes remaining. Anderson tried a long sideline pass to Collinsworth against two-deep zone coverage on the first play of the possession.

but they weren't on the same page and the ball was intercepted by Wright. "Eric Wright's career was cut short by injury," said Seifert. "He probably was the best overall corner I ever coached." Wright returned the ball 25 yards, then tried to lateral the ball in traffic at the Cincinnati 22. "What I did was very stupid," he said. "Young player. Got caught up in the moment." Nevertheless, linebacker Willie Harper recovered for San Francisco, and six plays later Wersching delivered a 23-yard field goal with 1:57 remaining.

Anderson then completed six in a row for 74 yards, a drive capped by his 3-yard touchdown pass to Ross. Only 16 seconds were left because most of the completions had been in the middle of the field and the clock didn't stop. "The defense was designed so we'd buzz the outside linebackers outside the wide receivers," Studley said. "They had to run either curls or in routes, which they did. As a result, we consumed the clock. Then they tried the onside kick and didn't recover. That was it."

The Bengals outgained the 49ers, 356–275, but their 4–1 disadvantage in turnovers was telling. San Francisco's only giveaway occurred on the opening kickoff when Amos Lawrence fumbled on a hit by linebacker Guy Frazier and cornerback John Simmons recovered. But on third and goal on the ensuing drive, defensive end Jim Stuckey pressured Anderson on a slant to Isaac Curtis and free safety Dwight Hicks intercepted at the 5. "That was a really disappointing play because I'd only had 10 interceptions all season," said Anderson. "Dwight Hicks just jumped inside and made the play."

Hicks, who had been cut by Detroit and Philadelphia, joined the 49ers as a free agent in 1979. "Bill Walsh was a good friend of Dick Vermeil's, and he called him wanting to know if there was a defensive back out there unsigned," Studley said. "Dick told him about Dwight Hicks. He was working at an ice cream store in Minnesota."

Joining Hicks in the secondary were three of the 49ers' first four choices in the 1981 draft: Lott (the eighth pick overall), Wright, and strong safety Carlton Williamson (third round). The foursome combined for 23 interceptions, helping the 49ers to a phenomenal plus-23 turnover differential during the regular season. "We were just playin'," Wright said. "We didn't get caught up in the hype. We were just a bunch of young guys having fun and trying to establish ourselves in the league."

After the title game loss, Dallas coach Tom Landry said somewhat disparagingly of the 49ers, "There really is nothing else there except the quarterback." Montana, in his first full season as the starter, made the Pro Bowl but was not yet in his prime. The running game was deficient, and the receiving corps was far from overwhelming. But Walsh, the AP coach of the year, never stopped designing new plays. On the Saturday before the Super Bowl, Walsh came up with an unbalanced line that was used effectively on about 10 first-half snaps. Audick shifted to the right side between guard Randy Cross and tackle Keith Fahnhorst, keeping the Bengals on their heels during 49ers' touchdown drives covering 68 and 92 yards.

Cincinnati's statistical advantage was also mitigated by its awful field position brought on largely by its inability to handle Wersching's squib kicks. The 49ers got the idea to squib kick on opening day, when they had struggled trying to field low, bouncing kicks on the hard carpet at the Silverdome and lost to the Detroit Lions. "It was very, very cold outside, and somehow or another that ball did funny things," Gregg said. "That ball jumped all over the place." Verser returned five for a 10.4-yard average, and Griffin fumbled away another at the Cincinnati 4 late in the first half.

Given circumstances before the game, it was amazing that the 49ers didn't start poorly. The second of their two team buses became gridlocked in traffic caused by a motorcade for Vice President George Bush and didn't arrive until 2:40 p.m., an hour and 40 minutes before kickoff, but just 20 minutes before the pre-game warmup was to begin. Walsh kept it light, getting on the bus PA system and cracking jokes to relieve the tension. Earlier in the week, he donned a bellman's uniform at the team's hotel in snowy Southfield, Michigan, and helped several unknowing players lift their luggage before being discovered.

"After we won the Super Bowl, a half-million people turned out for a victory parade down Market Street and a rally at the San Francisco Civic Center," Walsh said. "But that was a long way off when we were 1–2. That was almost done by mirrors, Joe Montana being the mirror. And our defense played so well and so hard."

XVII

WASHINGTON REDSKINS 27, MIAMI DOLPHINS 17

January 30, 1983
Rose Bowl, Pasadena, California

M ost Super Bowls have been decided by gifted athletes making breathtaking plays, but Super Bowl XVII wasn't one of them. This game was about men of muscle and strength exercising their will against other men of muscle and strength.

The Washington Redskins' 27–17 triumph over the Miami Dolphins transported the crowd of 103,667 at the Rose Bowl back to a time when players wore woolen jerseys, high-top cleats, and leather helmets without face bars. The outcome was decided on one of the more memorable power plays in NFL history when John Riggins, a Mack truck wearing the burgundy-and-white No. 44 jersey, followed his offensive line, known collectively as "the Hogs," into football immortality.

"It was a hard-fought game," said Miami's Don Shula, who was coaching in his fifth Super Bowl. "That whole game boiled down to that one play. Two plays, really. The Riggins run and the [Joe] Theismann strip of [Kim] Bokamper on the interception."

Clinging to a 17–13 lead with just more than 10 minutes left, the Dolphins bowed their necks and held the Redskins to 9 yards in three running plays. Joe Gibbs, the Redskins' second-year coach, made a late decision to go for it on fourth and 1 from the Miami 43. Anticipating a punt, Shula called time out.

"The question was, are we going to go for it?" recalled Dan Henning, the Redskins' assistant head coach. "There really wasn't any decision on the play. It was the best play we had under those conditions, going to the best side we had."

The call was "70-Chip," the same play that Gibbs was going to run before the timeout.

"Two-back set, two tight ends and a wing," Henning explained. "The play was designed to go anywhere from over the left guard, all the way outside depending how the defense deployed itself." In the 70-Chip, he explained, the lead back would take on the linebacker while another player kicked

Attendance: 103, 667
Conditions: 61 degrees, sunny and clear, wind slight from NW
Time of kickoff: 3:17 p.m. (PST)
Length of game: 3 hours, 13 minutes
Referee: Jerry Markbreit

MVP: John Riggins, RB, Redskins

out on the support player, which would be a safety on the left side. The line would then block a solid zone concept. "The play was blocked exactly the way it was supposed to be blocked," he said. "There was one guy left. The job of the running back is to run him over. John ran him over."

The Dolphins were in a tight eight-man defensive front. Clint Didier, the Redskins' backup tight end, motioned from the left to the middle and then back again, where he blocked Glenn Blackwood to the outside as the strong safety crossed the line of scrimmage. Fullback Otis Wonsley, a squatty 214-pounder, stumbled a bit navigating over trash between left tackle Joe Jacoby and left guard Russ Grimm, but was still able to get on outside linebacker Earnest Rhone and send him pinwheeling off his feet. At the point of attack, both the 295-pound Jacoby and Grimm, a future four-time Pro Bowler, created movement.

The third-year cornerback to that side, Don McNeal, had mirrored Didier's movements but slipped a bit coming back. With all of his teammates cut down, it was left for McNeal, who weighed 192 pounds, to somehow prevent Riggins from breaking free.

No one could fault McNeal for not doing everything he could to stop Riggins. The problem was that McNeal took Riggins on too high; a back that enormous needed to be tackled below the waist.

"How much did he weigh? I'd be giving away secrets there," Henning said. "John was supposed to

	1	2	3	4	Final
Miami Dolphins	7	10	0	0	17
Washington Redskins	0	10	3	14	27

SCORING SUMMARY

1st Quarter
MIA Cefalo, 76-yd. pass from Woodley (von Schamann kick)
2nd Quarter
WAS Moseley, 31-yd. FG
MIA von Schamann, 20-yd. FG
WAS Garrett, 4-yd. pass from Theismann (Moseley kick)
MIA F. Walker, 98-yd. kickoff return (von Schamann kick)
3rd Quarter
WAS Moseley, 20-yd. FG
4th Quarter
WAS Riggins, 43-yd. run (Moseley kick)
WAS Brown, 6-yd. pass from Theismann (Moseley kick)

make a weight every week of about 237. He might have been there for about 5 minutes. I'm sure he was 250 or more."

McNeal crashed into Riggins' right side about a yard past the line of scrimmage and had his right arm fully across Riggins' chest before he started to slip off. As Riggins kept his knees pumping, McNeal frantically tugged with both hands at the side of his jersey. Finally, Riggins shoved McNeal on the side of his helmet, stepped away, and began his dead sprint to the end zone. At the end, the deceivingly fast Riggins was pulling away from the pursuing Glenn Blackwood.

This was the year of the so-called Super Bowl Tournament, a 16-team event that Commissioner Pete Rozelle devised after a 57-day players strike shortened the regular season to nine games. In four playoff victories, Riggins amassed 610 yards in 136 carries (4.5 average), including 166 in 38 cracks against Miami.

"If you took that over a season, that would be 2,400 yards and 600 carries," Henning said. "Nobody has ever done anything like that. Through that four-game stretch, to me, he was like Babe Ruth. He didn't fumble. He [had] charisma. John was a different guy beginning in the middle of December, when we made the playoffs, until we won the Super Bowl. . . . He was bound and determined."

The 43-yard touchdown run came at the expense of Bill Arnsparger, Shula's longtime aide who is regarded by many as one of the foremost defensive coaches of all time. "I was with him in Miami two years before that," said Henning. "I think he is one of the greats." Among the tens of thousands of defensive calls that Arnsparger made in his career, he considers this to be the most regrettable.

"Looking back, that's one call I wish I had never made," Arnsparger said years later. "It was a bad call. We talked it over and I called a short-yardage defense so [we] had six people committed to the run. . . . They did a good job blocking at the point of attack. I never should have put Don McNeal in that difficult situation where he had to tackle the ball carrier. I gambled, and I lost."

Fourth and 1 is a players' down more than a scheme down, and McNeal simply missed the tackle. "I've talked to Bill about this," Henning said. "He's being a little hard on himself. I mean, it's fourth and 1, everything that we had been doing had been up the middle. If he hadn't been committed to the inside, then maybe we would have stayed inside. The players have to make that call." If Riggins had been tackled at the 39, the Redskins still would have been a long ways away, needing a touchdown to go ahead.

"You've just got to give Riggins credit," Shula said. "We were in position to make the tackle and Riggins broke the tackle and goes for the big yardage. McNeal was there to make the play. Riggins was a big, powerful guy, and he broke a tackle in a critical situation."

Much to his jubilation, Riggins was named the MVP over quarterback Joe Theismann. The two had a considerable rivalry going on at the time and certainly weren't the best of friends.

"Riggins was a 100-yard state champ in Kansas," said Bobby Beathard, the Redskins' general manager. "When we went to training camp at Carlisle [Pennsylvania], I remember John between practices going out and running quarter-mile intervals. He could fly. He was kind of a freak. His thighs were the size of my waist. Like that long run in Pasadena. [Larry] Csonka couldn't have gotten outside like that."

Fully 10 minutes remained but the Dolphins were finished. Behind David Woodley, their athletic but overmatched quarterback, Miami went three-and-out one more time and punted. Starting from the Miami 41, the Redskins methodically marched down the field in 12 plays to set up Theismann's 6-yard clinching touchdown pass to Charlie Brown. "Joe [Gibbs] was convinced if we just took time off the clock and kept pushing, even if we had to settle for a field goal, he didn't believe they could score a touchdown," said Henning. "Our defense had shut them down cold. People don't remember, our defense in the second half didn't allow a pass completion."

With 1:55 left, Shula pulled Woodley and summoned Don Strock, but three straight incompletions ended the Dolphins' last chance. Miami finished with 96 yards rushing and just 80 yards passing for a total of 176, which paled in comparison to Washington's net of 400. "I don't know if there's been a stronger defensive effort in a Super Bowl," said Larry Peccatiello, who coached the Redskins' linebackers and worked side-by-side with coordinator Richie Petitbon on the game plan.

As Henning pointed out, the Redskins badly needed their running game at full force. Due to injury, the Redskins played without their best wide receiver, Art Monk, and their playmaking scatback Joe Washington. Thus, they had to make do with a motley collection of undersized wide receivers collectively nicknamed "the Smurfs," which included Brown, Virgil Seay, and Alvin Garrett. Nick Giaquinto replaced Washington as the third-down back, besides serving as the number-three quarterback.

"To be able to play the way we wanted to play, with John that was allowed by the fact our defense was so stout in the second half. Our defense dominated, I mean dominated," Henning said. "If we had to

MIAMI DOLPHINS (AFC, 7–2)		WASHINGTON REDSKINS (NFC, 8–1)
	Offense	
82 Duriel Harris (5-11, 176)	WR	89 Alvin Garrett (5-7, 178)
79 Jon Giesler (6-5, 260)	LT	66 Joe Jacoby (6-7, 295)
67 Bob Kuechenberg* (6-2, 255)	LG	68 Russ Grimm (6-3, 273)
57 Dwight Stephenson (6-2, 255)	C	53 Jeff Bostic (6-2, 245)
60 Jeff Toews (6-3, 255)	RG	63 Fred Dean (6-3, 255)
68 Eric Laakso (6-4, 265)	RT	74 George Starke (6-5, 260)
84 Bruce Hardy (6-4, 230)	TE	85 Don Warren (6-4, 242)
81 Jimmy Cefalo (5-11, 188)	WR	87 Charlie Brown* (5-10, 179)
16 David Woodley (6-2, 204)	QB	7 Joe Theismann* (6-0, 198)
22 Tony Nathan (6-0, 206)	RB	44 John Riggins (6-2, 250)
37 Andra Franklin* (5-10, 225)	RB | TE	88 Rick Walker (6-4, 235)
	Defense	
75 Doug Betters (6-7, 260)	LE	76 Mat Mendenhall (6-6, 255)
73 Bob Baumhower* (6-5, 260)	NT | LT	65 Dave Butz (6-7, 295)
58 Kim Bokamper (6-6, 250)	RE | RT	77 Darryl Grant (6-2, 265)
59 Bob Brudzinski (6-4, 230)	LOLB | RE	72 Dexter Manley (6-3, 240)
77 A. J. Duhe (6-4, 248)	LILB | LLB	55 Mel Kaufman (6-2, 218)
55 Earnest Rhone (6-2, 224)	RILB | MLB	52 Neal Olkewicz (6-0, 230)
50 Larry Gordon (6-4, 230)	ROLB | RLB	57 Rich Milot (6-4, 237)
48 Gerald Small (5-11, 192)	LCB	45 Jeris White (5-10, 188)
28 Don McNeal (5-11, 192)	RCB	32 Vernon Dean (5-11, 178)
47 Glenn Blackwood (6-0, 186)	SS	23 Tony Peters* (6-1, 190)
42 Lyle Blackwood (6-1, 188)	FS	29 Mark Murphy (6-3, 210)

* Pro Bowl selection

SUBSTITUTIONS

Miami

Offense: WR - 88 Vince Heflin, 89 Nat Moore; TE - 86 Ronnie Lee, 80 Joe Rose; T - 74 Cleveland Green; G - 61 Roy Foster; C - 63 Mark Dennard; QB - 11 Jim Jensen, 10 Don Strock; RB - 34 Woody Bennett, 33 Rich Diana, 31 Eddie Hill, 32 Tom Vigorito. *Defense:* DE - 83 Vern Den Herder; LB - 56 Charles Bowser, 53 Ron Hester, 54 Steve Potter, 52 Steve Shull; CB - 49 William Judson, 44 Paul Lankford, 41 Fulton Walker; S - 40 Mike Kozlowski. *Specialists:* K - 5 Uwe von Schamann; P - 3 Tom Orosz. *DNP:* 85 Mark Duper (WR), 72 Richard Bishop (NT), 76 Steve Clark (NT).

Washington

Offense: WR - 80 Virgil Seay; TE - 86 Clint Didier; T - 62 Donald Laster; G - 73 Mark May; RB - 30 Nick Giaquinto, 38 Clarence Harmon, 40 Wilbur Jackson, 39 Otis Wonsley. *Defense:* DE - 79 Todd Liebenstein, 78 Tony McGee; DT - 69 Perry Brooks; LB - 51 Monte Coleman, 54 Pete Cronan, 50 Larry Kubin, 56 Quentin Lowry; CB - 20 Joe Lavender, 46 LeCharls McDaniel; S - 22 Curtis Jordan, 21 Mike Nelms*, 47 Greg Williams. *Specialists:* K - 3 Mark Moseley*; P - 5 Jeff Hayes. *DNP:* 8 Bob Holly (QB), 17 Tom Owen (QB), 25 Joe Washington (RB), 71 Garry Puetz (T), 82 Rich Caster (TE).

Miami

Head Coach: Don Shula. *Offense:* John Sandusky (offensive line, running game), Wally English (quarterbacks), Carl Taseff (backfield, special teams). *Defense:* Bill Arnsparger (assistant head coach), Mike Scarry (defensive line, run defense), Tom Keane (defensive backs, punters). *Special Teams:* Steve Crosby.

Washington

Head Coach: Joe Gibbs. *Offense:* Dan Henning (assistant head coach), Joe Bugel (coordinator), Charley Taylor (wide receivers), Rennie Simmons (tight ends), Don Breaux (backs). *Defense:* Richie Petitbon (coordinator), LaVern Torgeson (defensive line), Larry Peccatiello (linebackers). *Special Teams:* Wayne Sevier. *Strength:* Dan Riley. *Administrative Assistant:* Billy Hickman.

open it up and play attack football against that defense that 'Arns' had, we wouldn't have been able to do it. We had the big offensive line, and Miami's defensive line was quick and agile. . . . We decided we'd try to get our big guys to push them around inside. Other than a few plays here and there, we pretty much dominated the front with the offensive line."

Miami's "Killer B's" defense, so-called because the last names of six starters began with the letter "B," led the NFL in total defense (256.8 yards) and pass defense (114.1). The key player was multidimensional A. J. Duhe, who had been a defensive tackle at Louisiana State but possessed the mobility and instincts to play inside and outside linebacker. Duhe intercepted three passes in the Dolphins' 14–0 victory over the Jets in the AFC Championship Game because quarterback Richard Todd was unable to recognize the innovative ways in which Arnsparger was utilizing Duhe.

"We started fooling around with the zone blitz," Arnsparger said. "We'd blitz the outside backer and the inside backer, and drop the end on that side. The end at that time was [Kim] Bokamper. We swapped him and Duhe around. That was our zone blitz." According to Henning, what Arnsparger was doing in the early 1980s would eventually lead to the wholesale zone blitzing 20 years later. "Bill was a teacher," said Shula. "He

look a lot of pride in preparation, putting players in positions where they had total confidence in what their responsibilities were and how they meshed with the other players on defense. It was a total understanding of a scheme."

Late in the third quarter, Duhe dropped from a down position into coverage and intercepted a confused Theismann, giving the Dolphins the ball at the Washington 47 with a chance to extend their 17–13 lead. "He surprised Joe," Henning said. "It looked like he was going to come and didn't come and got in a lane and picked it off." From the 39-yard line a few plays later, however, Woodley threw late on a deep post to Jimmy Cefalo, and the ball was tipped by cornerback Vernon Dean to free safety Mark Murphy for an interception.

"Mark Murphy was absolutely like a coach on the field," said Peccatiello. "He went to Colgate and Northwestern as [athletic director], and then to the Packers [as president]. We had to have a guy at that position who was real smart. Mark struggled to break 5-flat [in the 40-yard dash] but he wasn't smart. He was brilliant."

Woodley, the Dolphins' eighth-round draft choice in 1980, took over for Bob Griese as a rookie and held the starting job until Dan Marino came along in 1983. His passer ratings were 63.1 in 1980, 69.8 in 1981, 63.5 in 1982, and 59.6 in 1983. "Woodley was a very good athlete playing quarterback," said Shula. "We designed a lot of things where he'd fake the handoff and he'd keep the ball on an option run or pass outside the pocket. He was not a pure drop-back passer, although he did hit that first bomb to [Jimmy] Cefalo."

The Redskins structured their defensive plan to prevent Woodley from getting on the edge. "We felt Woodley's legs were more dangerous than his arm," Peccatiello said. "We had to cover Tony Nathan out of the backfield and they had a tight end they went to in Joe Rose. But, although the Dolphins were a formidable team, I think the quarterback position prevented them from being a great team."

The fact that the Dolphins, a 3-point favorite, scored even 17 points was somewhat remarkable. They opened the scoring when Woodley faked a pitchout, pump-faked, and threw a 25-yard sideline strike to Cefalo between cornerback Jeris White and strong safety Tony Peters. Cefalo turned it into a 76-yard touchdown.

Early in the second quarter, after the 31-yard field goal by Mark Moseley, Fulton Walker's 42-yard kickoff return set up Uwe von Schamann's 20-yard field goal. Then, after a 4-yard touchdown pass from Theismann to Garrett, Walker returned the following kickoff 98 yards for a touchdown.

"What I thought might lose it was when Fulton Walker ran the kickoff back," Beathard said. "Everyone was surely worried then. Up until that point, I thought we really had momentum."

Shortly after Walker's scoring jaunt, free safety Lyle Blackwood was penalized 30 yards for pass interference on a bomb to Giaquinto. On the next play, Theismann found Brown for 26 yards at the Miami 16 with 14 seconds remaining in the first half, and the Redskins called their final timeout. Instead of throwing into the end zone, Theismann erred by going short to Garrett, and Glenn Blackwood tackled him at the 7 before he could get out of bounds. "It was kind of a mistake on our part," said Henning. "We were going to set up for a field goal and we threw the ball underneath and time ran out."

Late in the third quarter, a leaping Duhe forced Theismann off his primary receiver to the right and into a hurried throw to the left. The 6-foot-6 Bokamper tipped the ball high into the air and was waiting for it to settle in his arms at the 3 for what probably would have been a touchdown. But, from out of nowhere, Theismann reentered the play. Springing at Bokamper with his right hand, the 6-foot Theismann knocked the ball away, denying Bokamper what could have been the game-winning interception.

"That's one of the great plays in Super Bowl history when you come to think of it," Shula said. "It was a quarterback doing something that was just instinctive." Added Peccatiello: "Theismann made one of the best plays that I was ever associated with in my entire life."

Twenty-six of the Redskins had been signed as free agents, including 14 who had not even been drafted. Beathard's never-ending hunt for players was most apparent on the offensive line, where center Jeff Bostic, right guard Fred Dean, and right tackle George Starke had all been released by other

teams. Jacoby had been a free agent, too. "We had Bostic as a long snapper only when we signed him out of Clemson," said Beathard. "Starke was part of the 'Over the Hill Gang' and still had something left and was smart. Jacoby couldn't move very well but boy, was he smart and had good footwork and just giant strength."

TEAM STATISTICS

MIAMI		WASHINGTON
9	Total First Downs	24
7	Rushing	14
2	Passing	9
0	Penalty	1
176	Total Net Yardage	400
47	Total Offensive Plays	78
3.7	Avg. Gain per Offensive Play	5.1
29	Rushes	52
96	Yards Gained Rushing (Net)	276
3.3	Average Yards per Rush	5.3
17	Passes Attempted	23
4	Passes Completed	15
1	Passes Intercepted	2
1	Tackled Attempting to Pass	3
17	Yards Lost Attempting to Pass	19
80	Yards Gained Passing (Net)	124
3/11	Third-Down Efficiency	11/18
0/1	Fourth-Down Efficiency	1/1
6	Punts	4
37.8	Average Distance	42.0
2	Punt Returns	6
22	Punt Return Yardage	52
6	Kickoff Returns	3
222	Kickoff Return Yardage	57
0	Interception Return Yardage	0
2	Fumbles	0
1	Own Fumbles Recovered	0
0	Opponent Fumbles Recovered	1
4	Penalties	5
55	Yards Penalized	36
2	Touchdowns	3
0	Rushing	1
1	Passing	2
1	Returns	0
2	Extra Points Made	3
1	Field Goals Made	2
1	Field Goals Attempted	2
0	Safeties	0
17	Total Points Scored	27
23:45	Time of Possession	36:15

INDIVIDUAL STATISTICS

MIAMI

Passing	CP/ATT	YDS	TD	INT	RAT
Woodley	4/14	97	1	1	50.0
Strock	0/3	0	0	0	39.6

Rushing	ATT	YDS	AVG	TD	LG
Franklin	16	49	3.1	0	9
Nathan	7	26	3.7	0	12
Woodley	4	16	4.0	0	7
Vigorito	1	4	4.0	0	4
Harris	1	1	1.0	0	1

Receiving	NO	YDS	AVG	TD	LG
Cefalo	2	82	41.0	1	76t
Harris	2	15	7.5	0	8

Interceptions	NO	YDS	LG	TD
L. Blackwood	1	0	0	0
Duhe	1	0	0	0

Punting	NO	AVG	LG	BLK
Orosz	6	37.8	46	0

Punt Ret.	NO/FC	YDS	LG	TD
Vigorito	2/1	22	12	0

Kickoff Ret.	NO	YDS	LG	TD
Walker	4	190	98t	1
L. Blackwood	2	32	17	0

Defense	SOLO	AST	TOT	SK
Brudzinski	10	5	15	0
Rhone	11	3	14	1
Baumhower	7	3	10	1
Gordon	8	0	8	1
Duhe	5	1	6	0
Betters	3	3	6	0
L. Blackwood	5	0	5	0
Bokamper	5	0	5	0
G. Blackwood	4	1	5	0
Den Herder	3	0	3	0
Kozlowski	3	0	3	0
Small	3	0	3	0
Diana	2	0	2	0
Heflin	2	0	2	0
McNeal	2	0	2	0
Shull	1	1	2	0
Hill	1	0	1	0
Judson	1	0	1	0
Potter	1	0	1	0
Lankford	0	1	1	0
TOTAL	77	18	95	3

WASHINGTON

Passing	CP/ATT	YDS	TD	INT	RAT
Theismann	15/23	143	2	2	75.1

Rushing	ATT	YDS	AVG	TD	LG
Riggins	38	166	4.4	1	43t
Garrett	1	44	44.0	0	44
Harmon	9	40	4.4	0	12
Theismann	3	20	6.7	0	12
Walker	1	6	6.0	0	6

Receiving	NO	YDS	AVG	TD	LG
Brown	6	60	10.0	1	26
Warren	5	28	5.6	0	10
Garrett	2	13	6.5	1	9
Walker	1	27	27.0	0	27
Riggins	1	15	15.0	1	15

Interceptions	NO	YDS	LG	TD
Murphy	1	0	0	0

Punting	NO	AVG	LG	BLK
Hayes	4	42.0	54	0

Punt Ret.	NO/FC	YDS	LG	TD
Nelms	6/0	52	12	0

Kickoff Ret.	NO	YDS	LG	TD
Nelms	2	44	24	0
Wonsley	1	13	13	0

Defense	SOLO	AST	TOT	SK
Murphy	5	1	6	0
Butz	5	0	5	0
Manley	4	1	5	1
Kaufman	2	3	5	0
Grant	4	0	4	0
Williams	4	0	4	0
Olkewicz	3	1	4	0
Milot	3	0	3	0
V. Dean	2	0	2	0
White	2	0	2	0
Brown	1	0	1	0
Coleman	1	0	1	0
Harmon	1	0	1	0
Jordan	1	0	1	0
McGee	1	0	1	0
Warren	1	0	1	0
Wonsley	1	0	1	0
TOTAL	41	6	47	1

It was during the 1982 season when line coach Joe Bugel gave his charges "Hogs" T-shirts, hoping to, as he put it, "develop an esprit de corps." Said Beathard, "Bugel really made those guys into not only real good individuals, but a unit. I've never been around anybody like Bugel."

Pressed for time because there wasn't an extra week of preparation between the title games and the Super Bowl, coaches on both sides worked longer hours than usual. Gibbs finally decided he would need more than just smash-mouth football to beat an Arnsparger-coached defense. He also concluded that his makeshift receiving corps wouldn't be able to get open without a gimmick or two. Working well past midnight Wednesday at their hotel in Anaheim, Gibbs and his staff hit upon a formation and personnel grouping known as the "Explode" package that they decided might just facilitate some big plays.

"Instead of just shifting one guy or two guys, or motioning one guy, we shifted all five receivers and put one in motion," Henning said. "We called that just 'exploding' to the formation. We caught [the Dolphins] off guard a little bit."

The short touchdown passes to Garrett and Brown occurred on two of the half-dozen plays in which the Redskins employed their new creation. Perhaps due to Explode, Miami cornerback Gerald Small arrived a step late in coverage on both of the touchdowns. Garrett, who had been drafted in the ninth round out of Angelo State by the San Diego Chargers in 1979 when Gibbs was their offensive coordinator, also gained 44 yards on a third-quarter reverse that set up the second of NFL MVP Mark Moseley's two field goals.

"He was not a little person. He was built," Henning said of Garrett. "He had some unusual talent. Because of his stoutness, it was very difficult to press him. We spent a lot of time trying to decide the best ways to use Alvin. He scored a couple touchdowns against Detroit in the playoffs."

At the same time, the Redskins' defense stayed a step ahead of Shula and his offensive coaches all game long. The Redskins didn't have great talent (Peters was the team's lone Pro Bowl defensive player), but they compensated with considerable multiplicity in their fronts and coverages. At times, the Redskins

simply would call "audible" in the defensive huddl meaning athletic middle linebacker Neal Olkewic was free to decide the front at the line and Murph then would shout out the coverage. "Olkewicz w so steady," said Beathard. "He wasn't a big-nam guy, but he always did the right thing."

"We always prided ourselves on having guy that were pretty smart," said Peccatiello. "Ove achievers, you might say. I don't know if we had on guy on that defense that would surely stand out as great football player, but they were smart."

Right end Dexter Manley, whose blind-sid sack of Woodley in the first quarter caused a fumbl and set up a field goal, was a feared pass rushe Defensive tackles Dave Butz and Darryl Gra were top-flight players as well. The other end, Ma Mendenhall, was adequate against the run.

"[Mel] Kaufman was a big hitter for a undersized guy," said Beathard. "[Rich] Milot ha good size and was fast and real smart. I'm not sayin they were great but they were really good. And w had a real good secondary. Richie Petitbon alway had the free safety make the calls. Mark Murph was great at that. Great leader back there. Jeris Whi could really run and was real tough, but couldn catch a cold. Tony Peters had a real good year.

"I thought that was a heck of a team. It might hav been [the Redskins' best]. We really had a lot going fo us. It would have been hard to beat that team."

In just his second season, Gibbs had brough the nation's capital its first NFL championship sinc 1942. A disciple of Don Coryell, Gibbs' club ha rebounded from a 0–5 start in 1981 to finish 8–8 and then had won it all a year later with an overal mark of 12–1.

It was duly noted that the Redskins' playo run had included victories over three Hall of Fam coaches: Bud Grant's Minnesota Vikings, Ton Landry's Dallas Cowboys, and Shula's Dolphins.

"The truly great people in this profession ar great for years and years," Gibbs said. "Let's see hov I am in 10 years."

By 1996, Joe Gibbs would stand alongside othe coaching legends with his induction in Canton Gibbs' active mind and steely leadership were to make the Redskins a frequent part of the Super Bow scene for a decade to come.

Ten Best Running Plays

1. **Marcus Allen, Raiders, XVIII:** Initially, the Redskins play the sweep left by Allen perfectly. The Raiders' left side is pushed back, and SS Ken Coffey is almost right next to Allen deep in the backfield. Allen then halts abruptly, executes a diagonal cutback, avoids a diving Coffey, and outruns everyone for a 74-yard touchdown on the final play of the third quarter.

2. **John Riggins, Redskins, XVII:** It's fourth and 1 at the Miami 43 with the Dolphins leading, 17–13, and 10 minutes left in the game. The Redskins call "70-Chip," a power play off the left side. After Washington's offensive line clears the way at the point of attack, Miami's 192-pound CB Don McNeal is left to take on the 250-pound Riggins, one-on-one. McNeal crashes hard into Riggins, but Riggins shrugs him off and then pulls away from SS Glenn Blackwood for the touchdown.

3. **Willie Parker, Steelers, XL:** On the second play of the second quarter, with Pittsburgh leading 7–3, the Steelers call "Counter Pike" against Seattle's nickel defense. When blocks are executed perfectly at the point of attack, it's Parker against SS Michael Boulware a few yards downfield. Boulware lunges and misses, and then Parker steps away from the diving FS Etric Pruitt. Parker sprints the rest of the way for a 75-yard touchdown.

4. **Emmitt Smith, Cowboys, XXVIII:** Early in the third quarter with the scored tied at 13, the Cowboys take over on their 36, determined to emphasize the ground game in the second half. Six consecutive runs by Smith gain 46 yards. After a 3-yard screen pass, it's third and 3 at the Buffalo 15. Bills NT Jeff Wright penetrates and hits Smith in the backfield, but the running back won't go down. Instead, he squirts through for the winning touchdown.

5. **Franco Harris, Steelers, XIII:** After Dallas LB Thomas "Hollywood" Henderson talks trash to Harris after roughing up QB Terry Bradshaw, Harris demands the ball from Bradshaw on the next play—even though it's third and 9 at the Dallas 22. With the Cowboys in a dime defense expecting the pass, SS Charlie Waters is the only man between Harris and the end zone. When Waters closes on the tackle, he runs into umpire Art Demmas, and Harris pounds in for the score.

6. **Dominic Rhodes, Colts, XLI:** The Colts are clinging to a 19–14 lead as they begin their second possession of the third quarter. On a sprint draw to the left, Rhodes freezes Chicago LB Hunter Hillenmeyer and then makes SS Chris Harris whiff on a tackle farther down the field. Rhodes gains 36 yards in all and sets up an Adam Vinatieri field goal.

7. **Larry Csonka, Dolphins, VII:** Miami's only scoring threat of the second half comes on Csonka's first-down run of 49 yards late in the third quarter. Csonka barges by DE Ron McDole and over FS Roosevelt Taylor before LB Jack Pardee and SS Brig Owens finally drag him down at the 16. (Miami QB Bob Griese then throws an interception in the end zone five plays later.)

8. **Marcus Allen, Raiders, XVIII:** The Raiders, comfortably ahead by 35–9 midway through the fourth quarter, toss the ball to Allen going right. He makes four Redskins defenders miss, all within the space of 4 yards, and then cuts back across the grain on a 39-yard run to set up a closing field goal.

9. **John Elway, Broncos, XXXII:** Facing third and 6 at the Green Bay 12 with the score tied at 17 late in the third quarter, Elway scrambles up the middle and veers right. As SS LeRoy Butler dives at his legs, Elway leaps into the air. He is struck in midair by safety Mike Prior and pinwheels to the ground at the 4 after a gain of 8. Terrell Davis plows over for the touchdown two plays later.

10. **Thurman Thomas, Bills, XXV:** It's the opening snap of the fourth quarter and the Giants are up, 17–12. In a strange 2-3-6 alignment, the Giants are playing pass on first and 10 when the Bills run a draw play. LG Jim Ritcher blocks LB Gary Reasons as Thomas ducks under FS Myron Guyton. After making nickel back Reyna Thompson miss, Thomas picks up Andre Reed's block against CB Everson Walls and strides across for a 31-yard touchdown.

XVIII

LOS ANGELES RAIDERS 38, WASHINGTON REDSKINS 9

January 22, 1984
Tampa Stadium, Tampa, Florida

On this one night, at windswept Tampa Stadium against an imposing opponent in Super Bowl XVIII, all the boasts, bravado, and braggadocio that have forever been associated with being a Raider rang true.

A 3-point underdog against the defending champion Washington Redskins, the Raiders unleashed a wondrous display of suffocating defense and quick-strike offense to turn what some expected to be a game for the ages into a 38–9 rout.

As Al Davis walked amid the cramped locker room to congratulate his players, he paused to consider this team's place in the history of the game that he had helped build.

"This is the greatest team we ever had, one of the greatest in history, hell, one of the greatest of all time in any professional sport," the Raiders owner-architect said. "There is nothing it lacks."

At the time, it was the most lopsided margin in Super Bowl annals, surpassing Green Bay's 35–10 mauling of Kansas City in the first Super Bowl. For sheer dominance, it brought to mind a frozen afternoon in 1961 when the Packers tore apart the New York Giants, 37–0, in the NFL Championship Game.

These Raiders, playing out of Los Angeles after a bitterly contested move from Oakland in 1982, will never be ranked among the legendary teams because they lost four games. There was a quarterback controversy between Jim Plunkett and Marc Wilson for three games at midseason, and coach Tom Flores' careless charges finished an astounding minus-12 in turnover differential, thanks to a whopping 24 interceptions and 25 lost fumbles compared to just 37 takeaways.

But the Raiders got it all sorted out in time for the playoffs and steamrolled their way through the AFC. By that time, it was a tough, talented, and intimidating force that descended on Tampa.

Attendance: 72,920
Conditions: 68 degrees, partly cloudy, wind NE at 20 mph
Time of kickoff: 4:45 p.m. (EST)
Length of game: 3 hours, 31 minutes
Referee: Gene Barth

MVP: Marcus Allen, RB, Raiders

The splendor of Marcus Allen. The daring of Mike Haynes and Lester Hayes. The aerial artistry of Cliff Branch and Plunkett. The brute strength and quickness of front-seven defenders Howie Long, Reggie Kinlaw, Lyle Alzado, Ted Hendricks, Matt Millen, Bob Nelson, and Rod Martin. The alertness of bit players Jack Squirek, Derrick Jensen, and Don Hasselbeck.

"I thought they played great in every area and whipped us in every area," Redskins coach Joe Gibbs said. "Would I like to play them again next week? That's a good question."

If a rematch had been possible, the Skins probably would have found a way to prevent Allen from rushing for 191 yards in just 20 carries. It is also hard to imagine that John Riggins, who had 1,347 yards and 24 touchdowns during the regular season, wouldn't have improved upon his mundane 26-carry, 64-yard showing.

Yet the Skins' overriding dilemma in another meeting would have remained: how could Gibbs, an offensive tactician and play caller of the highest order, organize an attack so his wide receivers would be able to free themselves of Haynes and Hayes?

Remember that Washington had scored 541 points, an NFL regular-season record that would last for 15 years until the Minnesota Vikings put up 556 in 1998. Quarterback Joe Theismann was the league's MVP, and the Skins had rattled off 17 points in the final 6:15 to overhaul the Raiders in early October and win at Robert F. Kennedy Memorial Stadium, 37–35.

	1	2	3	4	Final
Washington Redskins	0	3	6	0	9
Los Angeles Raiders	7	14	14	3	38

SCORING SUMMARY

1st Quarter
LA   Jensen, recovered blocked punt in end zone (Bahr kick)
2nd Quarter
LA   Branch, 12-yd. pass from Plunkett (Bahr kick)
WAS Moseley, 24-yd. FG
LA   Squirek, 5-yd. interception return (Bahr kick)
3rd Quarter
WAS Riggins, 1-yd. run (kick blocked)
LA   Allen, 5-yd. run (Bahr kick)
LA   Allen, 74-yd. run (Bahr kick)
4th Quarter
LA   Bahr, 21-yd. FG

The final piece of the puzzle for the Raiders came on November 10 when an out-of-court settlement was reached enabling them to acquire Haynes from New England in a trade for first- and second-round draft choices. Commissioner Pete Rozelle initially had voided the deal on the grounds it had been consummated minutes after the October 11 trading deadline.

"I'll tell you what the real difference was in that game," Skins general manager Bobby Beathard would say years later. "Mike Haynes and Lester Hayes were the two best corners in the league that year, and we couldn't get off the line of scrimmage. . . We had never played against someone like that. They changed our whole game plan."

The matchup with the Skins had been set for less than 48 hours when Charlie Sumner, the Raiders' de facto defensive coordinator, brought his players together for the first time.

"When we started the week, I said there were several things we could do," Sumner recalled. "Hayes and Haynes said, 'Don't worry about the wide receivers, you do what you want to with the other nine and we'll take care of them.' They got up on those little guys and they didn't know what the hell to do. They muscled them around and that was it. That made it real easy."

With the lithe Haynes hired to pair with the crouching, confrontational Hayes, the Raiders had not one but two shutdown corners. Their starting right cornerback before Haynes had been Ted Watts, a first-round draft choice in 1981 who was more of a nickel back or even a safety in terms of pure cover ability.

"Everybody knew how important corners were, but I think those kind of guys changed the game," Beathard said. "They were big, physical corners who could run. Those are two of the best that ever played the game. Those are still what prototype corners look like."

The Skins' first possession portended what was to come. On the first play, Kinlaw—the little nose tackle in Sumner's 3-4 defense—shed Pro Bowl center Jeff Bostic and tackled Riggins after a short gain. Sumner had moved Kinlaw off the line a slight distance to give him operating room against "the Hogs," Washington's O-line that also featured the Pro Bowl left side of tackle Joe Jacoby and guard Russ Grimm. Kinlaw kept making tackle after tackle.

"Marcus won the most valuable player award but Kinlaw should have won that," said Ron Wolf, the longtime top personnel man under Davis. "Kinlaw was little in stature but stronger than the dickens, had great natural leverage and was tough. Jeff Bostic was supposed to be the best center in the game but he had his butt handed to him in that game."

"Kinlaw dominated Bostic, and we knew he would," Long said. "He dominated [Mike] Webster and he dominated [Blair] Bush in the playoffs. He's my MVP." Kinlaw had been equally effective in Super Bowl XV against Philadelphia.

Because of Kinlaw, the Raiders didn't play their normal defense. They were able to align ends Long and Alzado farther outside than usual and

> "We shut down Riggins in the middle so they didn't have any running game. Theismann had to throw, and he had Lester Hayes and Mike Haynes covering his wide receivers. There was no way they were going to do anything."
>
> *Ted Hendricks, Raiders linebacker*

move the inside linebackers, Millen and Nelson, closer to the line and on the outside shoulders of the guards. Relieved of coverage responsibility because of the ability of Haynes and Hayes to smother the wide receivers, safety Mike Davis spent most of the game at the line. "Most of it was eight in the box," said Sumner, referring to how the Raiders blunted Riggins. That made the middle a bit vulnerable, but it also made it more difficult for Riggins to pound off-tackle or slide outside.

WASHINGTON REDSKINS (NFC, 14–2)		LOS ANGELES RAIDERS (AFC, 12–4)	
	Offense		
87 Charlie Brown* (5-10, 179)	WR	21 Cliff Branch (5-11, 170)	
66 Joe Jacoby* (6-7, 298)	LT	79 Bruce Davis (6-6, 280)	
68 Russ Grimm* (6-3, 275)	LG	73 Charley Hannah (6-5, 260)	
53 Jeff Bostic* (6-2, 250)	C	50 Dave Dalby (6-3, 250)	
73 Mark May (6-6, 288)	RG	65 Mickey Marvin (6-4, 265)	
74 George Starke (6-5, 260)	RT	70 Henry Lawrence* (6-4, 270)	
85 Don Warren (6-4, 242)	TE	46 Todd Christensen* (6-3, 230)	
81 Art Monk (6-3, 209)	WR	80 Malcolm Barnwell (5-11, 185)	
7 Joe Theismann* (6-0, 198)	QB	16 Jim Plunkett (6-2, 215)	
44 John Riggins (6-2, 235)	RB	32 Marcus Allen (6-2, 210)	
88 Rick Walker (6-4, 235)	TE I RB	33 Kenny King (5-11, 205)	
	Defense		
79 Todd Liebenstein (6-6, 255)	LE	75 Howie Long* (6-5, 270)	
65 Dave Butz* (6-7, 295)	LT I NT	62 Reggie Kinlaw (6-2, 245)	
77 Darryl Grant (6-1, 275)	RT I RE	77 Lyle Alzado (6-3, 260)	
72 Dexter Manley (6-3, 250)	RE I LOLB	83 Ted Hendricks* (6-7, 235)	
55 Mel Kaufman (6-2, 218)	LLB I LILB	55 Matt Millen (6-2, 250)	
52 Neal Olkewicz (6-0, 233)	MLB I RILB	51 Bob Nelson (6-4, 235)	
57 Rich Milot (6-4, 237)	RLB I ROLB	53 Rod Martin* (6-2, 225)	
28 Darrell Green (5-8, 170)	LCB	37 Lester Hayes* (6-0, 200)	
24 Anthony Washington (6-1, 204)	RCB	22 Mike Haynes (6-2, 190)	
48 Ken Coffey (6-0, 190)	SS	36 Mike Davis (6-3, 205)	
29 Mark Murphy* (6-3, 210)	FS	26 Vann McElroy* (6-2, 190)	

* Pro Bowl selection

SUBSTITUTIONS

Washington
Offense: WR - 89 Alvin Garrett; TE - 86 Clint Didier, 84 Mike Williams; G - 60 Roy Simmons, 61 Ken Huff, 67 Bruce Kimball; RB - 26 Reggie Evans, 30 Nick Giaquinto, 25 Joe Washington, 39 Otis Wonsley. *Defense:* DE - 71 Charles Mann, 78 Tony McGee; DT - 69 Perry Brooks; LB - 58 Stuart Anderson, 51 Monte Coleman, 54 Peter Cronan, 50 Larry Kubin; CB - 41 Brian Carpenter, 32 Vernon Dean; S - 22 Curtis Jordan, 47 Greg Williams. *Specialists:* K - 3 Mark Moseley; P - 5 Jeff Hayes. *DNP:* 83 Mark McGrath (WR), 80 Virgil Seay (WR), 8 Bob Holly (QB), 12 Babe Laufenberg (QB).

Los Angeles
Offense: WR - 28 Cle Montgomery, 82 Calvin Muhammad, 85 Dokie Williams; TE - 87 Don Hasselback, 31 Derrick Jensen; T - 64 Shelby Jordan; G - 66 Steve Sylvester; C - 72 Don Mosebar; QB - 11 David Humm, 6 Marc Wilson; RB - 27 Frank Hawkins, 34 Greg Pruitt*, 38 Chester Willis. *Defense:* DE - 68 Johnny Robinson, 93 Greg Townsend; DT - 71 Bill Pickel, 61 Dave Stalls; LB - 56 Jeff Barnes, 54 Darryl Byrd, 57 Tony Caldwell, 58 Jack Squirek; CB - 45 James Davis, 20 Ted Watts; S - 48 Kenny Hill, 23 Odis McKinney. *Specialists:* K - 10 Chris Bahr; P - 8 Ray Guy.

After Riggins rushed twice more for an opening first down, Theismann went to Art Monk in the left flat against coverage by Haynes. "I'll never forget the look on Theismann's face that first pass," Sumner said. "He liked to throw those quick passes with people playing off those little guys. Then they'd grab it and run. Haynes got up on [Monk]. I guess they didn't expect him to be up there. . . . Theismann took his three-step drop and threw it out there, and lucky for him Haynes dropped it. Hit him right in the hands. Stepped right in front of the guy. There just was complete surprise."

Then Theismann threw over the head of Monk on two deep fade routes with Haynes shadowing him. Against press coverage, the Skins' philosophy was to run fades and go for the touchdown. In subsequent years, Gibbs would change his system so the route called in the huddle was run whether it was press coverage or not.

A moment later, bad turned to worse for the Redskins when Jensen roared up the middle, leaped in front of punter Jeff Hayes, blocked the punt with outstretched hands, and dug out the recovery in the end zone for a touchdown. Washington's Otis Wonsley, a fullback in at left guard on the punt team, never expected Raiders special-teams

Washington
Head Coach: Joe Gibbs. *Offense:* Joe Bugel (assistant head coach), Charley Taylor (wide receivers), Rennie Simmons (tight ends), Jerry Rhome (quarterbacks), Don Breaux (backs). *Defense:* Richie Petitbon (assistant head coach), LaVern Torgeson (defensive line), Larry Peccatiello (linebackers). *Special Teams:* Wayne Sevier. *Strength:* Dan Riley. *Administrative Assistant:* Billy Hickman.

Los Angeles
Head Coach: Tom Flores. *Offense:* Sam Boghosian (offensive line), Ray Willsey (backfield). *Defense:* Earl Leggett (defensive line), Charlie Sumner (linebackers), Chet Franklin (defensive backs). *Special Teams:* Steve Ortmayer. *Assistants:* Joe Madro, Willie Brown, Bob Mischak.

coach Steve Ortmayer to go for a block five minutes in and his cursory bump was brushed off by Jensen. Normally, Jensen would have been picked up by tight end Clint Didier, the upback, but Didier stepped outside to block the onrushing Hayes, leaving Jensen a direct lane for the block.

The Achilles' heel for the Redskins in 1983 had been a secondary missing three starters from their Super Bowl–winning team of 1982. Strong safety Tony Peters was suspended for the year for conspiracy to distribute cocaine, cornerback Jeris White was a holdout, cornerback Vernon Dean was out with a shoulder injury, and nickel back Joe Lavender had retired.

Thus the Redskins, who ranked 28th (and last) in passing yards allowed (248.4), went into the Super Bowl with Anthony Washington at right cornerback. Acquired in mid-August from the Pittsburgh Steelers for a fourth-round draft pick, Washington was burned for touchdowns in both playoff games and then struggled in the Super Bowl.

"That was a weakness," Beathard said. "Oh God, we were scared to death of that the whole time." Allen's 74-yard touchdown run at the end of the third quarter made it clear to Beathard that lack of speed was the issue. "If you see the highlight, look at Anthony. Watch him chase [Allen]. He looked like an old man trying to run, and he was not physical at all. Without Vernon, that hurt. Vernon wasn't the fastest guy but he was always in position."

Plunkett went deep only three times, but one was a 50-yard completion to Branch between Washington and rookie Darrell Green. That drive was finished off when Washington, who was overplaying Branch to the inside, reacted woodenly to Branch's outside move and then let the speedy veteran cross his face back to the inside for an easy 12-yard touchdown.

On offense, Theismann got so sick of the Smurfs being blanketed that he spent much of the second and third quarters trying to isolate Didier on Davis, the strong safety. Didier did catch five passes for 65 yards, but there was no way he could beat the Raiders.

The Raiders also were able to blitz heavily, partially because Hayes and Haynes had the outside under control, according to Sumner. Gibbs tried to get the Raiders to check out of blitzes by using motion, but the Raiders made checks of their own and kept coming. "In those days, if you were blitzing, everybody was motioning and you'd check out of the thing," said Sumner, "but we always figured out a way not to have to check out of it. We might change from one [player] blitzing to the other one, going from Mike Davis to the other safety. But we went through with it anyway." Theismann was sacked six times, including four times by linebackers and defensive backs, and was forced to evacuate the pocket half a dozen other times.

"We got our rear ends handed to us on a platter," Theismann said. "We embarrassed ourselves."

Any chance the Skins had to make a game of it against the relentless Raiders essentially died in the waning moments of the first half in one of the more shocking turns of events in Super Bowl history.

Just 12 seconds remained and the Washington players were milling around in the end zone waiting to begin a possession from their 12. On the sideline next to Gibbs, defensive coordinator Larry Peccatiello remembered just wanting to get into the locker room with a 14–3 deficit and make some adjustments.

Instead, Gibbs called a screen pass to Joe Washington. Theismann was to look toward the three wide receivers on the right side of the field and then throw back to Joe Washington on the left. It was the same exact play—but to the other side—that Washington used to gain 67 yards late in the first half of the October 2 meeting against the Raiders to set up a score.

"I thought they were going to run the clock out," Sumner said. "I wasn't thinking too much about it, but then I looked up and saw Washington in there again and had a big flashback. I didn't change the defense. All I did was send Jack Squirek in for Matt Millen. I told Squirek just to go wherever Washington goes. . . . I remember Millen coming over mad as a hornet. He grabbed me. 'Don't ever take me out in front of 75,000 people.' And the next minute he picked me up and was hugging me and tossing me around."

Outside linebacker Hendricks, who had made the Pro Bowl for the seventh time, was nursing pulled stomach and groin muscles and played very little. Standing in the bench area near Sumner, he heard him instruct Squirek, "This guy is going to throw it right over there. You go over there and intercept it and take it in." Sure enough, Gibbs repeated the weak-side screen to Washington.

Trying to draw the pass rush to him, Theismann dropped back to the 1 before lofting a pass to Washington. The end on that side, Alzado, had smelled out the screen and was headed back toward Washington when Squirek leaped in front for the interception at the 5 and charged into the end zone.

"If you haven't done anything for 30 minutes, how are you going to drive 88 yards in the last 12 seconds?" Peccatiello said. "It's a call I'm sure Joe has second-guessed himself 1,000 times."

Beathard, who hired Gibbs in January 1981 from Don Coryell's staff in San Diego, was ever-understanding two decades later. "It was one of those plays," he said. "If it had worked, it would have been genius. But it was like the game was over." It had been downhill for the Skins since early afternoon. "God, the thrill of the week was when Bronco Nagurski came in our dressing room before the game," said Beathard. "I'll never forget it."

This Washington team, which had been apprehensive the year before in Pasadena, had already won a Super Bowl and beaten the Raiders. The players, according to Peccatiello, entered this Super Bowl "a little bit cockier." Early in the week, players from the two teams encountered each other. "They came into town and some of our guys ran into them," recalled Sumner. "They were wearing

combat fatigues. Looked like they were going to take everything by storm. They were so cocky."

Wolf, who grew up near Baltimore, found it surprising that the Redskins had so much public support entering the game. "It was so interesting to me," he said. "It was my first encounter with the East Coast media. . . . We were clearly a better team than

TEAM STATISTICS

WASHINGTON		LOS ANGELES
19	Total First Downs	18
7	Rushing	8
10	Passing	9
2	Penalty	1
283	Total Net Yardage	385
73	Total Offensive Plays	60
3.9	Avg. Gain per Offensive Play	6.4
32	Rushes	33
90	Yards Gained Rushing (Net)	231
2.8	Average Yards per Rush	7.0
35	Passes Attempted	25
16	Passes Completed	16
2	Passes Intercepted	0
6	Tackled Attempting to Pass	2
50	Yards Lost Attempting to Pass	18
193	Yards Gained Passing (Net)	154
6/17	Third-Down Efficiency	5/13
0/1	Fourth-Down Efficiency	0/0
8	Punts	7
32.4	Average Distance	42.7
2	Punt Returns	2
35	Punt Return Yardage	8
7	Kickoff Returns	1
132	Kickoff Return Yardage	17
0	Interception Return Yardage	5
1	Fumbles	3
0	Own Fumbles Recovered	1
2	Opponent Fumbles Recovered	1
4	Penalties	7
62	Yards Penalized	56
1	Touchdowns	5
1	Rushing	2
0	Passing	1
0	Returns	1
0	Extra Points Made	5
1	Field Goals Made	1
2	Field Goals Attempted	1
0	Safeties	0
9	Total Points Scored	38
31:18	Time of Possession	28:22

WASHINGTON

Passing	CP/ATT	YDS	TD	INT	RAT
Theismann	16/35	243	0	2	45.3

Rushing	ATT	YDS	AVG	TD	LG
Riggins	26	64	2.5	1	8
Theismann	3	18	6.0	0	8
J. Washington	3	8	2.7	0	5

Receiving	NO	YDS	AVG	TD	LG
Didier	5	65	13.0	0	20
Brown	3	93	31.0	0	60
J. Washington	3	20	6.7	0	10
Giaquinto	2	21	10.5	0	14
Monk	1	26	26.0	0	26
Garrett	1	17	17.0	0	17
Riggins	1	1	1.0	0	1

Interceptions	NO	YDS	LG	TD
None	--	--	--	--

Punting	NO	AVG	LG	BLK
Hayes	7	37.0	48	1

Punt Ret.	NO/FC	YDS	LG	TD
Green	1/0	34	34	0
Giaquinto	1/2	1	1	0

Kickoff Ret.	NO	YDS	LG	TD
Garrett	5	100	35	0
Grant	1	32	32	0
Kimball	1	0	0	0

Defense	SOLO	AST	TOT	SK
Olkewicz	10	1	11	0
A. Washington	7	1	8	0
Coffey	5	2	7	0
Grant	5	0	5	1
Murphy	5	0	5	0
Milot	4	0	4	0
Green	3	0	3	0
Liebenstein	3	0	3	0
Butz	2	0	2	0
Mann	1	1	2	0
Brooks	1	0	1	0
Coleman	1	0	1	1
Jordan	1	0	1	0
Manley	1	0	1	0
McGee	1	0	1	0
Wonsley	1	0	1	0
TOTAL	51	5	56	2

LOS ANGELES

Passing	CP/ATT	YDS	TD	INT	RAT
Plunkett	16/25	172	1	0	87.2

Rushing	ATT	YDS	AVG	TD	LG
Allen	20	191	9.6	2	74t
Pruitt	5	17	3.4	0	11
King	3	12	4.0	0	10
Willis	1	7	7.0	0	7
Hawkins	3	6	2.0	0	3
Plunkett	1	-2	-2.0	0	-2

Receiving	NO	YDS	AVG	TD	LG
Branch	6	94	15.7	1	50
Christensen	4	32	8.0	0	14
Hawkins	2	20	10.0	0	14
Allen	2	18	9.0	0	12
King	2	8	4.0	0	7

Interceptions	NO	YDS	LG	TD
Squirek	1	5	5t	1
Haynes	1	0	0	0

Punting	NO	AVG	LG	BLK
Guy	7	42.7	53	0

Punt Ret.	NO/FC	YDS	LG	TD
Pruitt	1/3	8	8	0
Watts	1/0	0	0	0

Kickoff Ret.	NO	YDS	LG	TD
Pruitt	1	17	17	0

Defense	SOLO	AST	TOT	SK
Millen	5	3	8	1
M. Davis	6	1	7	1
Kinlaw	6	0	6	0
Nelson	6	0	6	0
Martin	6	0	6	1
Long	4	1	5	0
McElroy	4	1	5	0
Barnes	2	1	3	1
J. Davis	2	1	3	0
Haynes	2	1	3	0
Squirek	2	1	3	0
McKinney	2	0	2	0
Willis	2	0	2	0
Townsend	1	1	2	1
Byrd	1	0	1	0
Christensen	1	0	1	0
L. Hayes	1	0	1	0
Muhammad	1	0	1	0
Pickel	1	0	1	1
Caldwell	0	1	1	0
Hill	0	1	1	0
Jenson	0	1	1	0
TOTAL	55	14	69	6

they were, yet the Raiders weren't given a chance to win that game."

Opening the second half, Washington appeared to have righted itself with a 70-yard drive capped by Riggins' 1-yard run, but Hasselbeck promptly bowled through Jacoby and blocked Moseley's line-drive extra-point attempt. The Raiders then pushed their lead to 28–9 on the next series with a 70-yard march capped by the first of Allen's three magical runs.

The big play was a 38-yard penalty for pass interference against Green on a long post pattern to Malcolm Barnwell. Seven plays later, Allen left free safety Mark Murphy grasping at air on a 5-yard touchdown run. On the final play of the third quarter, Allen reversed his field and exploded 74 yards for another touchdown, finishing one of the most unforgettable runs in football history.

"Of all the players I was ever around with the Raiders, Marcus Allen was the best player at any position," Wolf said. "Well, the best football player I was ever around was Warren Wells, but he didn't play long enough. Marcus Allen was a superb blocker and had just marvelous hands. He was as complete a back as you are probably ever going to find."

Allen swept left, but the Skins had penetration and strong safety Ken Coffey was already in the backfield. "We pushed the entire left side of the Oakland line up the field," Peccatiello said. "I mean, we dominated the point of attack. We were so far up the field that Allen couldn't go anywhere." Allen stopped abruptly, and then was able to locate a diagonal cut-back lane largely because defensive

end Todd Liebenstein was flattening down the line without regard to containment.

Eluding the diving Coffey, Allen suddenly cut up through the middle of the defense and outran everyone to the end zone.

"I had Bo Jackson go 80 yards on a toss sweep and Tony Dorsett went 94 yards against us one time," Peccatiello said years later. "But this was the greatest run that I ever had against a team that I coached in my 29 years in the NFL. That was seven points that should have been a 5-yard loss."

Finally, Allen made Murphy, Green, linebacker Rich Milot, and Anthony Washington all miss within the space of 4 yards on a 39-yard jaunt across the field to set up a closing field goal.

As the equipment men tidied up after the game, Davis didn't seem to want to leave. "We could have scored 50," he said. "This team will be great for years."

Despite a slew of young standouts, the Raiders won just four division crowns over the next 18 years and wouldn't reach another Super Bowl until February 2003. One reason was that they would spend much of the next two decades trying to find a quarterback with the steady professionalism and leadership of Plunkett, whose mercurial career had seen him pounded as a top draft pick in New England, left on the scrap heap in San Francisco, and at last reborn with the Raiders, whom he led to two Super Bowl triumphs.

In another corner of the now-empty stadium, Peccatiello and Richie Petitbon, the Skins' assistant head coach for defense, picked up their bags and walked the six or seven miles through the chilly Florida night back to the team hotel. It was the only time in Peccatiello's 40-year coaching career that he had forsaken the team bus. "Our wives wondered where we were," Peccatiello said.

"Had we lost the Dolphin game the year before, I don't think it would have been as traumatic as this was. We had such a good year. We had beaten them during the season. Then to get humiliated the way we were, Rich and I said, 'Screw it.' God forbid if anybody would have said, 'Redskins suck,' or anything like that. It was an ass-kicking, it really was."

> "We couldn't do anything that game. I don't know why. It just didn't seem there that day. Al Davis is one of the guys that got me into this game. I owe a lot to him. But we've never talked about this game."
>
> *Bobby Beathard, Redskins general manager*

Ten Best Performances by a Running Back

1. **Marcus Allen, Raiders, XVIII:** Reversing field and going 74 yards for a touchdown is the play that will live forever in the Super Bowl memory bank. A 5-yard TD run and a 39-yard gallop in which four Redskins missed within the space of 4 yards shouldn't be forgotten, either.

2. **Terrell Davis, Broncos, XXXII:** Gained 157 yards in 30 carries, despite sitting out the second quarter with blurred vision after being kicked in the head.

3. **John Riggins, Redskins, XVII:** Bulldozed through CB Don McNeal on fourth-and-1 en route to a 43-yard fourth-quarter touchdown, giving Washington its first lead. The ultimate workhorse, Riggins carried the team on his back to the first of three Super Bowl victories under coach Joe Gibbs.

4. **Matt Snell, Jets, III:** In colossal upset of the Colts, Snell handled the ball on 34 of the Jets' 74 snaps and gained 161 yards. He just kept hammering away, providing Joe Namath with play-action opportunities.

5. **Larry Csonka, Dolphins, VIII:** The hefty Csonka powered through Minnesota defense all day long, controlling the game. With both arms wrapped tightly around the ball, he thundered for 145 yards in 33 attempts.

6. **Roger Craig, 49ers, XIX:** The Dolphins tried to match their linebackers one-on-one with Craig and paid a terrible price. He scored three touchdowns, two receiving and one rushing. Miami couldn't tackle him in space.

7. **Franco Harris, Steelers, IX:** It was a day for the ground game, with the wind whipping and the turf at old Tulane Stadium rain-saturated and slick. Harris battered 34 times for 158 yards against the smallish Vikings defenders.

8. **Thurman Thomas, Bills, XXV:** Amassing 190 yards in a mere 20 touches, Thomas bolted 31 yards on a draw play for one fourth-quarter touchdown. Later, he went for 22 on a third-and-1 draw. Everson Walls' last-chance tackle prevented what would have been an 81-yard TD, which would have saved Scott Norwood from attempting the fateful field goal.

9. **Timmy Smith, Redskins, XXII:** The rookie made his first start in the Super Bowl and turned in an MVP-worthy performance with 204 yards in 22 carries. He did most of his damage on the counter trey, Washington's signature play. He never approached this form again.

10. **Emmitt Smith, Cowboys, XXVIII:** With Dallas trailing by 7 at halftime, Jimmy Johnson put the onus on Smith in the second half. Operating behind his prized offensive line, Smith slammed and slithered for 91 of his 132 yards and scored two touchdowns.

Honorable Mentions: Joseph Addai, Colts, XLI; Ottis Anderson, Giants, XXV; Eddie George, Titans, XXXIV; Clarence Davis, Raiders, XI; Larry Csonka, Dolphins, VII.

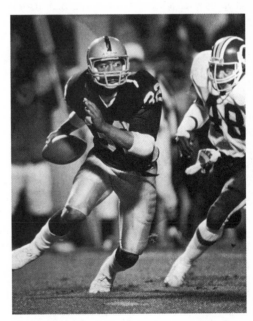

Marcus Allen's 74-yard touchdown run against the Redskins was perhaps the most dramatic moment of Super Bowl XVIII. He amassed a total of 191 yards in 20 carries, setting a record (since broken) for total rushing yards and average yards per carry in a championship game. *Rob Brown/NFL/Getty Images*

XIX

SAN FRANCISCO 49ERS 38, MIAMI DOLPHINS 16

January 20, 1985
Stanford Stadium, Stanford, California

Dan Marino against Joe Montana. Don Shula against Bill Walsh. Those were the marquee matchups in Super Bowl XIX—two quarterbacks and two head coaches destined for the Hall of Fame. But pro football always has been the ultimate team game, and the 1984 San Francisco 49ers might have been its ultimate team.

For six seasons Montana and Walsh had worked hand-in-hand, building for this moment. On a foggy night at old Stanford Stadium, each was as magnificent as could be. Montana, with 390 total yards and four touchdowns, earned his second MVP award. Walsh's masterpiece from the sidelines ended with him being carried off the field for his second Super Bowl ride in four years.

"We were a great team," Walsh said years later. "It was nearly a perfect game for us."

Another group of 49ers players and coaches left Stanford Stadium covered equally in glory. This defensive unit was far superior to what the Miami Dolphins had. What was expected to be a shootout between two evenly matched juggernauts became a 38–16 rout for San Francisco because one team played effective defense while the other did not.

"We went into the game thinking that we could score against anybody at any time," Shula said. "That was pretty much the story of that season. Nobody had figured out how to stop us. Then they did."

Despite their 15–1 record during the regular season and dominating playoff victories over New York Giants (21–10) and Chicago (23–0), the 49ers were just 3-point favorites. The Dolphins, 14–2, had blown past Seattle (31–10) and Pittsburgh (45–28) in the playoffs on the strength of Marino's seven touchdown passes. In just his second season, Marino had taken the league by storm. He would play another 15 seasons, but four of his statistical achievements in 1984 (5,084 passing yards, 64.2 percent completion mark, 48

Attendance: 84,059
Conditions: 53 degrees, clearing fog, wind NW at 3 mph
Time of kickoff: 3:19 p.m. (PST)
Length of game: 3 hours, 13 minutes
Referee: Pat Haggerty
MVP: Joe Montana, QB, 49ers

touchdown passes, 108.9 passer rating) would remain his career bests.

"His release was bar none," 49ers cornerback Eric Wright said. "Joe was Joe, but Marino had like a flick of the wrist. I'm talking about when a cobra strikes. Everybody hyped this game as Montana against Marino, their receivers against our defensive backs. We took this game very personal."

So did the 49ers' defensive linemen. Bill McPherson, who either tutored the defensive line or served as defensive coordinator in the team's five Super Bowls, said it was the finest collection of talent that he ever coached. On this day, Marino was sacked 4 times after having been sacked just 13 times in the previous 18 games. The most significant reason why his rating was just 66.9 in the Super Bowl, when it had been 90.6 against the Seahawks and 135.4 against the Steelers, was the constant pressure in his face, generally from a four-man rush. "We could substitute Pro Bowl football players whenever we chose," Walsh said. "Some of them were at the end of their career, but they could play 6, 8, 10 plays very, very well. That made a big difference. Marino was forced to make quick decisions and get rid of the ball very quickly."

Gary "Big Hands" Johnson had been an outstanding player for a decade with the San Diego Chargers but was unhappy with his contract. Four games into the 1984 season, San Diego traded him to the 49ers for fifth- and 11th-round draft choices. At 32, Johnson was the same age as Fred Dean, the exceptional

	1	2	3	4	Final
Miami Dolphins	10	6	0	0	16
San Francisco 49ers	7	21	10	0	38

SCORING SUMMARY

1st Quarter
MIA   Von Schamann, 37-yd. FG
SF   Monroe, 33-yd. pass from Montana (Wersching kick)
MIA   D. Johnson, 2-yd. pass from Marino (von Schamann kick)
2nd Quarter
SF   Craig, 8-yd. pass from Montana (Wersching kick)
SF   Montana, 6-yd. run (Wersching kick)
SF   Craig, 2-yd. run (Wersching kick)
MIA   Von Schamann, 31-yd. FG
MIA   Von Schamann, 30-yd. FG
3rd Quarter
SF   Wersching, 27-yd. FG
SF   Craig, 16-yd. pass from Montana (Wersching kick)

speed rusher whom the 49ers had obtained from the Chargers in 1981, and nine-year veteran Lawrence Pillers, who played his final game for the 49ers in this Super Bowl. In April 1984, the 49ers acquired another veteran defensive lineman, Manu Tuiasosopo, from Seattle for 4th- and 10th-round selections. Another ex-Charger, Louie Kelcher, contributed during the regular season but played sparingly in the Super Bowl, which was also his final game.

"The night before the game at the hotel, I told my guys, 'This game will be broadcast throughout the world. If we don't get to [Marino], everyone in the world is going to know how lousy you are,'" McPherson said. "We kind of had [Marino] talking to himself toward the end."

The game turned out to be all 49ers, although it really didn't start out that way. On the Dolphins' first play from scrimmage, running back Tony Nathan juked Wright in the flat and turned a swing pass into a 25-yard gain. "He came in my zone area and I missed the tackle," said Wright. "I'd been making that tackle all year. We were too hyper starting that game. We were very unsettled, and they were picking us apart." It led to the first of three field goals by Uwe von Schamann, who had made just 11 of 24 field goals in the first 18 games.

The 49ers dropped two passes on an unsuccessful first series, then scored on six of their next seven possessions. An eight-play, 78-yard drive was capped by Montana's 15-yard scramble and his 33-yard touchdown pass to running back Carl Monroe. Montana had rushed for just 118 yards during the regular season, but Walsh, after watching him take off eight times for 85 yards in the first two playoff games, wanted to see more. "Before the game I said to Joe, 'Now look. We know what they're going to do,'" Walsh said. "'If you see it, run with it.' I hadn't mentioned it to him because I didn't want him thinking about it all week."

When defensive end Kim Bokamper beat left tackle Bubba Paris on an inside charge and was threatening to sack him, Montana danced away for 15 yards to the Miami 33. It was his first of five carries that would net 59 yards. Said Montana, "In most cases, the coaches didn't make me run unless it was a necessity. Most of the time I ran on my own." On the next play, wide receiver Renaldo Nehemiah cleared out the right side and Monroe cut off him and then worked to the corner. Lyle Blackwood was a step behind Monroe at the 15 when Montana's bullet arrived. Monroe dashed to the end zone when Lyle Blackwood crashed into McNeal, knocking him off the tackle.

After the 49ers took a 7–3 lead, Shula stunned the crowd of 84,059 on the next series by having Marino call the plays at the line. "I don't remember if I'd seen an opponent use the no-huddle before that game," Montana said. Nathan began the six-play, 70-yard drive with a run for 5. In rapid-fire succession, Marino hit Mark Clayton for 18; Mark Duper for 11; Clayton for 13; tight end Dan Johnson for 21 on a simple release into the flat against strong-side linebacker Dan Bunz; and then Johnson behind inside linebacker Hacksaw Reynolds for a 2-yard

> "I think this team, as far as having a number of guys that could jump in and play, was our best defense. I talked to B.W. [Bill Walsh] about that and he thought the next one was the best. I might be going at it from the standpoint of what I had [on the defensive line]. All those guys were effective."
>
> *Bill McPherson, 49ers defensive line coach*

touchdown.

George Seifert, the 49ers' defensive coordinator, was an early proponent of situation substitution. The 49ers used the 3-4 as their base defense, but inserted a fourth lineman on passing downs. After seeing Bunz, Reynolds, and the other inside linebacker, Riki Ellison, get exploited by Marino, Seifert and Walsh made the dramatic decision to play with a nickel defense for the rest of the game. It meant that Bunz, Reynolds, and Ellison had to sit the bench.

Rookie Jeff Fuller, drafted out of Texas A&M as a safety, joined fleet-footed Keena Turner as the nickel linebackers. Safety Tom Holmoe was inserted as the extra defensive back. The front four consisted of Dwaine Board at left end, either Michael Carter or Jeff Stover at left tackle, Gary Johnson at right tackle, and Dean at right end. Board beat right tackle Cleveland Green around the corner for two sacks. Johnson had one sack, a tackle for a 3-yard loss, and numerous pressures, most at the expense of left guard Roy Foster.

"Our nickel defense was the most skilled defense that we had," Seifert said years later. "Danny Bunz and some others were very good base players but not as skilled in running and chasing. It really was key defensively in what happened. Fuller was awesome. I wouldn't say he was a blazer but he was so fluid and a beautiful athlete.

"Marino had an awesome, spectacular season, but our offense put pressure on them. Then they were just going to throw the ball and we got in our nickel and our athletes matched up with theirs and we got after them pretty good, actually."

Shula probably should have tried some more running plays against the 49ers' nickel defense, but the score got out of hand so quickly that Shula called just five runs compared to 27 passes

MIAMI DOLPHINS (AFC, 14–2)		SAN FRANCISCO 49ERS (NFC, 15–1)	
	Offense		
85 Mark Duper* (5-9, 187)	WR	87 Dwight Clark (6-4, 215)	
79 Jon Giesler (6-5, 260)	LT	77 Bubba Paris (6-6, 295)	
61 Roy Foster (6-4, 275)	LG	68 John Ayers (6-5, 265)	
57 Dwight Stephenson* (6-2, 255)	C	56 Fred Quillan* (6-5, 266)	
64 Ed Newman* (6-2, 255)	RG	51 Randy Cross* (6-3, 265)	
74 Cleveland Green (6-3, 262)	RT	71 Keith Fahnhorst* (6-6, 273)	
84 Bruce Hardy (6-5, 232)	TE	81 Russ Francis (6-6, 242)	
83 Mark Clayton* (5-9, 175)	WR	88 Freddie Solomon (5-11, 188)	
13 Dan Marino* (6-4, 214)	QB	16 Joe Montana* (6-2, 195)	
22 Tony Nathan (6-0, 206)	RB	26 Wendell Tyler (5-10, 200)	
34 Woody Bennett (6-2, 225)	RB	33 Roger Craig (6-0, 222)	
	Defense		
75 Doug Betters (6-7, 265)	LE	65 Lawrence Pillers (6-4, 250)	
73 Bob Baumhower* (6-5, 265)	NT	78 Manu Tuiasosopo (6-3, 252)	
58 Kim Bokamper (6-6, 255)	RE	76 Dwaine Board (6-5, 248)	
59 Bob Brudzinski (6-4, 223)	LOLB	57 Dan Bunz (6-4, 225)	
53 Jay Brophy (6-3, 233)	LILB	50 Riki Ellison (6-2, 220)	
51 Mark Brown (6-2, 225)	RILB	64 Jack Reynolds (6-1, 232)	
56 Charles Bowser (6-3, 235)	ROLB	58 Keena Turner* (6-2, 219)	
28 Don McNeal (5-11, 192)	LCB	42 Ronnie Lott* (6-0, 199)	
49 William Judson (6-1, 190)	RCB	21 Eric Wright* (6-1, 180)	
47 Glenn Blackwood (6-0, 190)	SS	27 Carlton Williamson* (6-0, 204)	
42 Lyle Blackwood (6-1, 190)	FS	22 Dwight Hicks* (6-1, 192)	

* Pro Bowl selection

SUBSTITUTIONS

Miami
Offense: WR - 81 Jimmy Cefalo, 88 Vince Heflin, 11 Jim Jensen, 89 Nat Moore; TE - 87 Dan Johnson, 80 Joe Rose; T - Ronnie Lee; G - 76 Steve Clark; C - 60 Jeff Toews; QB - 10 Don Strock; RB - 23 Joe Carter, 31 Eddie Hill. *Defense:* DE - 78 Charles Benson; DT - 71 Mike Charles, 70 Bill Barnett; LB - 77 A. J. Duhe*, 55 Earnest Rhone, 50 Jackie Shipp, 52 Sanders Shiver; CB - 41 Fulton Walker, 44 Paul Lankford, 45 Robert Sowell; S - 43 Bud Brown, 40 Mike Kozlowski. *Specialists:* K - 5 Uwe von Schamann; P - 4 Reggie Roby*. *DNP:* 46 Pete Johnson (FB).

San Francisco
Offense: WR - 83 Renaldo Nehemiah, 85 Mike Wilson; TE - 89 Earl Cooper; T - 66 Allan Kennedy, 67 Billy Shields; G - 62 Guy McIntyre; RB - 24 Derrick Harmon, 32 Carl Monroe, 30 Bill Ring. *Defense:* DE- 74 Fred Dean, 97 Gary Johnson, 79 Jim Stuckey, 72 Jeff Stover; NT - 95 Michael Carter, 94 Louie Kelcher; LB - 53 Milt McColl, 52 Blanchard Montgomery, 90 Todd Shell, 99 Michael Walter; CB - 43 Dana McLemore; S - 28 Tom Holmoe, 49 Jeff Fuller. *Specialists:* K - 14 Ray Wersching; P - 4 Max Runager. *DNP:* 6 Matt Cavanaugh (QB), 86 John Frank (TE), 29 Mario Clark (CB).

COACHING STAFFS

Miami

Head Coach: Don Shula. *Offense:* John Sandusky (head offense, offensive line), David Shula (receivers), Carl Taseff (backfield). *Defense:* Chuck Studley (head defense), Mike Scarry (defensive line, run defense), Tom Keane (defensive backs). *Special Teams:* Bob Matheson. *Strength:* Junior Wade.

San Francisco

Head Coach: Bill Walsh. *Offense:* Paul Hackett (receivers, quarterbacks), Bobb McKittrick (offensive line), Sherman Lewis (running backs). *Defense:* George Seifert (coordinator), Bill McPherson (defensive line), Norb Hecker (linebackers), Ray Rhodes (defensive backs). *Strength:* Jerry Attaway.

in the first half trying to keep up on the scoreboard. In all, the Dolphins rushed nine times for 25 yards. After averaging 138.5 yards rushing in the first two playoff games and 119.9 during the regular season, the inability of the Dolphins to sustain any ground game whatsoever placed too much of a burden on Marino. "He was a great, great player," Walsh said. "I think they depended too much on him over the years. Also, he never had a defense that could dominate."

Chuck Studley became Miami's defensive coordinator in 1984 when Bill Arnsparger went to LSU. Studley had held the same job in San Francisco from 1979 to 1982, which provided him with an insider's perspective of what the Dolphins' 19th-ranked defense could expect. "I wasn't surprised we lost the ball game, let's put it that way," Studley said years later. "Our defense was really suspect, particularly our secondary. We had some guys in the secondary that really shouldn't have been in pro football compared to the kids I had in San Francisco. It's unusual when you go to the Super Bowl not to have at least one all-pro player on defense. We had none."

In the secondary, Miami lined up with Don McNeal and William Judson at cornerback and the Blackwood brothers, Glenn and Lyle, at safety. "Our corners couldn't cover one-on-one and I was always forced to help them, either underneath with a linebacker or on top with a safety," Studley said. "You're always afraid to help on top with a safety because that means the safety has deep coverage, and the Blackwood brothers couldn't run that well.

They were tough against the run, but in my book defensive backs cover first."

The so-called Killer B's defense featured the undersized three-man front of left end Doug Betters, who had 14 sacks, Pro Bowl nose tackle Bob Baumhower, playing with knee and ankle injuries that required surgery a month later, and Bokamper. Nevertheless, the 49ers' robust offensive line of Paris, John Ayers, Fred Quillan, Randy Cross, and Keith Fahnhorst knocked them around. "After looking at the films we said, 'This is a Super Bowl defense?'" 49ers offensive line coach Bobb McKittrick said.

Paris outweighed Bokamper by a wide margin. Their matchup was one reason why the 49ers were able to pile up 211 yards in 40 carries and permit just one sack of Montana. "Our game plan was to run the ball and take them on physically," Cross said. "When you've got a 310-pound offensive tackle with a 50-pound weight advantage, you've got to be able to run with that matchup."

As mediocre as the Dolphins were both up front and in the back end, their linebacker corps—Bob Brudzinski and Charles Bowser outside, Jay Brophy and Mark Brown inside—was probably most to blame for the 49ers' 537-yard offensive explosion. The group sorely missed A. J. Duhe, a Pro Bowl selection who had to sit out with knee and shoulder injuries, which would require surgery in the offseason and end his career. Brudzinski, an eight-year veteran, was the only high-quality linebacker, according to Studley. Bowser, Brown, and Brophy were Dolphins' draft choices from 1982 to 1984 and had major deficiencies that would haunt Shula and Studley.

"We caught them in defenses that we could just take apart," said Walsh, who used to carpool to work with Studley. "They were playing a man-under style defense, so by bringing our backs through the line of scrimmage and crossing them, their inside linebackers had to try to cover them. They couldn't do it."

As confident as Walsh was watching films of the Dolphins, he felt even better during warmups. "As I walked through the Dolphins, I could see a distinct difference between the two squads," Walsh said. "We were a much more physical, more athletic football team than Miami. At that moment my confidence soared. We truly feared Dan Marino and his battery of receivers, but they were a one-dimensional team with no running attack to worry us, and I thought we could attack their defense effectively. It wasn't difficult to recognize that they didn't have outstanding speed and quickness. I realized that Don Shula had done it with mirrors because he didn't have the physical ability we had. For the Dolphins to have gone 14–2 and win two playoff games was a real tribute to Don."

Miami failed to gain a first down on its first three possessions of the second quarter. Reggie Roby, its all-pro punter, delivered three successive line-drive punts with averages of 38.7 yards (gross) and 26 (net). "It was the worst game of my life," said Roby, "counting high school, college, counting everything." Subsequently, the 49ers started drives at the Miami 47, their 45, and their 48. "On the sideline we were almost celebrating," Walsh said, "because, operating from midfield, we could use all the weapons in our arsenal."

It took just four plays for the 49ers to take a 14–10 lead, the touchdown coming when fullback Roger Craig beat Brophy inside on an 8-yard checkdown pass. Then they bumped the score to 21–10 on Montana's 6-yard scramble. "They blitzed and I stepped up to find a receiver and the hole was right in front of me," said Montana. "So I just took it."

Their lead swelled to 28–10 on Craig's 2-yard burst with 2:05 remaining in the half. Early in that drive, field judge Bob Lewis ruled that a pass to Freddie Solomon was incomplete. Replays, however, appeared to show that Solomon had made the catch. Lyle Blackwood made the hit, scooped up the apparent fumble, and was off to the 49ers' goal line when the play was blown dead. "We were dominated to the point where one play didn't make much of a difference," Shula said magnanimously.

Back came the Dolphins to score the final six points of the first half. A hurry-up 11-play, 72-yard march led to a field goal. Von Schamann then squibbed the kickoff to Guy McIntyre, a rookie guard playing in the wedge. McIntyre had the ball for two to three seconds, deciding what to do next while Monroe stood alongside coaxing him along. Finally, McIntyre careened forward, immediately fumbled on a hit by running back Joe Carter, and Dolphin Jim Jensen recovered at the San Francisco 12 with 4 seconds left. Von Schamann converted

TEAM STATISTICS

MIAMI		SAN FRANCISCO
19	Total First Downs	31
2	Rushing	16
17	Passing	15
0	Penalty	0
314	Total Net Yardage	537
63	Total Offensive Plays	76
5.0	Avg. Gain per Offensive Play	7.1
9	Rushes	40
25	Yards Gained Rushing (Net)	211
2.8	Average Yards per Rush	5.3
50	Passes Attempted	35
29	Passes Completed	24
2	Passes Intercepted	0
4	Tackled Attempting to Pass	1
29	Yards Lost Attempting to Pass	5
289	Yards Gained Passing (Net)	326
4/12	Third-Down Efficiency	6/11
0/0	Fourth-Down Efficiency	0/1
6	Punts	3
39.3	Average Distance	32.7
2	Punt Returns	5
15	Punt Return Yardage	51
7	Kickoff Returns	4
140	Kickoff Return Yardage	40
0	Interception Return Yardage	0
1	Fumbles	2
1	Own Fumbles Recovered	0
2	Opponent Fumbles Recovered	0
1	Penalties	2
10	Yards Penalized	10
1	Touchdowns	5
0	Rushing	2
1	Passing	3
0	Returns	0
1	Extra Points Made	5
3	Field Goals Made	1
3	Field Goals Attempted	1
0	Safeties	0
16	Total Points Scored	38
22:49	Time of Possession	37:11

again, this time from 30, and it was 28–16. "That ruined a perfect game," Walsh said. "That really troubled me."

Another so-so punt by Roby allowed the 49ers to begin from their 47 early in the third quarter. Mixing four runs with five passes, the 49ers this time settled for Ray Wersching's 27-yard field

MIAMI

Passing

Passing	CP/ATT	YDS	TD	INT	RAT
Marino	29/50	318	1	2	66.9

Rushing

Rushing	ATT	YDS	AVG	TD	LG
Nathan	5	18	3.6	0	16
Bennett	3	7	2.3	0	7
Marino	1	0	0.0	0	0

Receiving

Receiving	NO	YDS	AVG	TD	LG
Nathan	10	83	8.3	0	25
Clayton	6	92	15.3	0	27
Rose	6	73	12.2	0	30
D. Johnson	3	28	9.3	1	21
Moore	2	17	8.5	0	9
Cefalo	1	14	14.0	0	14
Duper	1	11	11.0	0	11

Interceptions

Interceptions	NO	YDS	LG	TD
None	--	--	--	--

Punting

Punting	NO	AVG	LG	BLK
Roby	6	39.3	45	0

Punt Ret.

Punt Ret.	NO/FC	YDS	LG	TD
Walker	2/0	15	9	0

Kickoff Ret.

Kickoff Ret.	NO	YDS	LG	TD
Walker	4	93	28	0
Hardy	2	31	16	0
Hill	1	16	16	0

Defense

Defense	SOLO	AST	TOT	SK
L. Blackwood	9	4	13	0
Brophy	5	7	12	0
M. Brown	8	2	10	0
Brudzinski	5	2	7	0
Betters	3	4	7	1
Bowser	3	3	6	0
McNeal	3	2	5	0
Bokamper	3	1	4	0
Baumhower	2	1	3	0
G. Blackwood	2	0	2	0
Charles	2	0	2	0
Heflin	2	0	2	0
Judson	2	0	2	0
Kozlowski	2	0	2	0
Sowell	1	1	2	0
Carter	1	0	1	0
Hardy	1	0	1	0
Hill	1	0	1	0
Shipp	1	0	1	0
TOTAL	56	27	83	1

SAN FRANCISCO

Passing

Passing	CP/ATT	YDS	TD	INT	RAT
Montana	24/35	331	3	0	127.2

Rushing

Rushing	ATT	YDS	AVG	TD	LG
Tyler	13	65	5.0	0	9
Montana	5	59	11.8	1	19
Craig	15	58	3.9	1	10
Harmon	5	20	4.0	0	7
Solomon	1	5	5.0	0	5
Cooper	1	4	4.0	0	4

Receiving

Receiving	NO	YDS	AVG	TD	LG
Craig	7	77	11.0	2	20
D. Clark	6	77	12.8	0	33
Francis	5	60	12.0	0	19
Tyler	4	70	17.5	0	40
Monroe	1	33	33.0	1	33t
Solomon	1	14	14.0	0	14

Interceptions

Interceptions	NO	YDS	LG	TD
Williamson	1	0	0	0
Wright	1	0	0	0

Punting

Punting	NO	AVG	LG	BLK
Runager	3	32.7	35	0

Punt Ret.

Punt Ret.	NO/FC	YDS	LG	TD
McLemore	5/0	51	28	0

Kickoff Ret.

Kickoff Ret.	NO	YDS	LG	TD
Harmon	2	24	23	0
Monroe	1	16	16	0
McIntyre	1	0	0	0

Defense

Defense	SOLO	AST	TOT	SK
Turner	4	2	6	0
Hicks	5	0	5	0
Holmoe	4	1	5	0
Williamson	2	3	5	0
Board	4	0	4	2
Johnson	4	0	4	1
Fuller	2	2	4	0
Bunz	2	1	3	0
Wright	2	1	3	0
McLemore	2	0	2	0
Tuiasosopo	2	0	2	1
Dean	1	1	2	0
Ring	1	1	2	0
Shell	0	2	2	0
Cooper	1	0	1	0
Ellison	1	0	1	0
Harmon	1	0	1	0
Lott	1	0	1	0
Monroe	1	0	1	0
Walter	1	0	1	0
Pillers	0	1	1	0
Reynolds	0	1	1	0
TOTAL	41	16	57	4

goal. Back-to-back sacks by Tuiasosopo and Board precipitated another punt by Miami, and on the next play halfback Wendell Tyler faked through the line and caught a short pass that he turned into a 40-yard gain. Once again, Brophy got lost in coverage.

The clinching touchdown, a 16-yard pass to Craig, came on a similar play when the second-year player slipped through the line on third and 10, ran away from Brown at the 15, and carried it across untouched. "We didn't worry too much about Tyler, but Craig was a great back," Studley said. "Frankly, it surprised me that he hurt us so much catching the ball, but he caught it short and then made us miss. Asking our linebackers to try to tackle that guy, it was really unfair."

For football historians, this would be the quintessential look at the classic West Coast split-back style of offense. "Many times guys would tell me, 'Goddamn, will you quit dinking the damn ball?'" Montana said. "My thing was, 'Hey, we're having a lot of success and aren't going to stop now.' Bill Walsh would have us run the same plays until they stopped us. I was the 'mailman' and it was up to the other guys to make the big plays after I delivered the ball to them."

Craig and Tyler combined for 270 yards, split evenly with 135 rushing and 135 receiving. "Bill Walsh just had a great game plan," McPherson said. "His offense won the game. Joe Montana was playing against a man-to-man."

All four members of the San Francisco secondary played in the Pro Bowl the following Sunday in Hawaii. In 19 games, the quartet of Ronnie Lott, Carlton Williamson, Dwight Hicks, and Wright intercepted 15 passes. Wright picked Marino's long pass for Clayton at the San Francisco 1 late in the third quarter, a throw that had touchdown written all over it. "That was the best play I ever made in my career," said Wright. "He ran a post-corner and was looking for me to overplay it. That was a pattern I always played well. If I hadn't been there, that was six and the momentum would have swung their way." In the fourth quarter, the desperate, frustrated Marino rolled right and threw back into the middle of the end zone for tight end Joe Rose, but the ball hung and was intercepted by Williamson.

Clayton, who had a record-setting 18 receiving touchdowns in the regular season, was fairly effective (6 receptions, 92 yards) but Duper was not

(1 reception, 11 yards). Under pressure for one c the only times all season, Marino didn't reac very well. Other than his brief flurry late in th first quarter, he passed like a mere mortal, an he showed almost no escapability when the rus drew near. "Body language. Different motion You could tell he was rattled," said Dean. "I'n not saying he became unsure of himself but h seemed shaken."

In the days leading up to the game, th operative question was whether any team could sto the Dolphins. "This week we are playing against th greatest passer of all time, as I understand it," sai Walsh, his voice dripping with sarcasm. There wa far more attention paid to Marino, the NFL MV than Montana, the implication being that Marin had more talent and Montana's only real advantag was mobility and experience. "When you heard al week 'Miami, Miami, Miami,' you had to think 'Hey, what about us?'" Montana said afterward.

The San Francisco quarterback more tha proved his point with a passer rating of 127.2 an another automobile as Super Bowl MVP.

"Marino had just a fair game, but he'll b back," Walsh said. "To me, Montana is the greates quarterback in football, the greatest quarterbac in some years. He is No. 1—his leadership assertiveness, and his quick feet."

For 23-year-old Marino and 55-year-old Shula there would not be another Super Bowl. "I hope w get another chance," Marino said after the game "You don't get here often." Truer words seldom hav been spoken.

For Montana and Walsh, there would be nary playoff victory in the next three seasons. "The 198 to 1984 era basically came to a close then, and w had to start rebuilding for the future," said Walsh In 1984, the only chink in the 49ers' armor was th lack of a genuine deep threat. The team's averag per catch was an astonishingly low 7.9 yards. Thre months after the Super Bowl, Walsh traded up t draft wide receiver Jerry Rice in the first round With Rice providing the final dimension, the 49ers passing game averaged no less than 11.9 yards pe completion from 1986 to 1994, a span during whic they were to win three more Super Bowls.

"When we won, we felt we were one of the grea

eams of all time," Walsh said. "Our only loss was a close, hard-fought game to Pittsburgh [October 14] decided by a phantom goal-line pass-interference call on Eric Wright. We missed a long field goal as the gun went off and lost, 20–17. Chuck Noll was very gracious about that later. He, too, questioned the call but told me, 'You're going to go all the way.' The loss may have sharpened us for the remaining games because it reminded us that anything could happen."

Ten Best Performances by a Quarterback

1. **Joe Montana, 49ers, XIX:** Sheer poetry in motion. Montana totaled 390 yards passing and running against the overmatched Dolphins. Dan Marino got most of the pre-game publicity, but Montana got the MVP and the victory.

2. **Joe Montana, 49ers, XXIV:** He just made it look so easy. Posted passer rating of 147.6 against two-deep looks out of a 3-4 defense employed by Denver coordinator Wade Phillips. The Broncos never had a chance.

3. **Steve Young, 49ers, XXIX:** Passed for 325 yards and a record six touchdowns, ran for 49 yards. Last Super Bowl appearance for Young, despite the fact that he played great for four more seasons.

4. **Phil Simms, Giants, XXI:** Coach Bill Parcells called it possibly the best game ever played by a QB. Simms came out red-hot and never cooled down. Of his three incompletions, only one came when he had ample time.

5. **Aaron Rodgers, Packers, XLV:** Confined to the pocket by Dick LeBeau's vaunted fire-zone system, Rodgers was precise, poised, and proficient. Three of his teammates' five dropped passes might have been TDs.

6. **Doug Williams, Redskins, XXII:** Threw for 228 yards and four touchdowns in a second-quarter explosion. After damaging his left knee late in the first quarter, he had to sit out two plays, but then came back and showed off his all-time deep-ball skills.

7. **Troy Aikman, Cowboys, XXVII:** Started slowly in his Super Bowl debut before firing three touchdown passes between 18 and 23 yards in the first half, with deadly accuracy off play-action fakes. Bills gambled and lost trying to play man-to-man coverage.

8. **Joe Montana, 49ers, XXIII:** The 10-yard touchdown pass from "Joe Cool" to John Taylor with 34 seconds left capped a 92-yard drive to beat the Bengals. Considered the best finish in first 23 Super Bowls.

9. **Tom Brady, Patriots, XXXVIII:** Completed four of five passes for 47 yards in last-ditch drive for victory over Panthers. Brady's red-zone interception a few minutes earlier didn't deter him in the clutch.

10. **Terry Bradshaw, Steelers, X:** Game-winning touchdown pass to Lynn Swann with 3:02 left traveled nearly 70 yards in the air; Bradshaw was hit and knocked cold after delivering the ball. A fitting end to what was the finest season of Bradshaw's 14-year career.

Joe Montana is one of only two quarterbacks (along with Terry Bradshaw) to win four Super Bowls. He was named MVP a record three times and holds the career marks for best passer rating (127.8) and most touchdown passes (11) in the Super Bowl. *Mickey Pfleger/*Sports Illustrated*/Getty Images*

XX

CHICAGO BEARS 46, NEW ENGLAND PATRIOTS 10

January 26, 1986
Louisiana Superdome, New Orleans, Louisiana

Few professional football teams have played the game better than the Chicago Bears did in 1985.

They marched through the regular season with a 15–1 record, their only defeat by a 38–24 count at the hands of Don Shula, Dan Marino, and the Miami Dolphins in early December on a Monday night at the Orange Bowl. They shut out their first two playoff opponents, the New York Giants and Los Angeles Rams. Needing an overwhelming triumph in the Super Bowl to validate their greatness, they punched it up a notch and annihilated the New England Patriots, 46–10, at the Louisiana Superdome.

"Dynasties are the ones that win two, three, four Super Bowls, like the Steelers and the Cowboys did. The one knock on us was we won one," coach Mike Ditka said years later. "But there is no such thing as the greatest football team of all time. I played on the '63 Bears. I played against all the great Green Bay teams. I was coaching in Dallas against the great Steeler teams in the 1970s. C'mon. Our defense was one of the most dominant defenses in the last 30 or 40 years, but you've got to have everything to win it. We had a very solid offense and good special teams, too. But I know that for one moment in time we probably enjoyed and did it as well as anybody."

As their season gained momentum, the frenzied popularity of "Da Bears" spread far beyond the Windy City. Much of it had to do with the release of the "Super Bowl Shuffle," a rap song recorded in late November that 25 players then had the audacity to film the day after their loss in Miami. The overwhelming sale of the video led *Time* magazine to feature the Bears on its cover. They were hip and they were fun, a team overflowing with brash personalities that captivated Chicago and the nation.

The Bears' specialty was devouring quarterbacks, but it was their own punky quarterback who had a stranglehold on the week of coverage leading

Attendance: 73,818
Conditions: 72 degrees, indoors
Time of kickoff: 4:21 p.m. (CST)
Length of game: 3 hours, 42 minutes
Referee: Red Cashion

MVP: Richard Dent, DE, Bears

to the game. Jim McMahon got started by blasting owner Michael McCaskey only a few hours after the team plane landed for his decision to bar McMahon's acupuncturist from boarding the charter flight. McMahon had suffered a bruised left buttock in the victory over the Rams and still needed his wife, Nancy, to help him put on his socks before departing Chicago on Monday.

After getting an earful from McMahon before practice on Tuesday, McCaskey changed his mind. Hiroshi Shiriashi arrived at the team hotel Wednesday and treated McMahon for several days. Shortly after McMahon's conversation with McCaskey, a local news helicopter buzzed the field during stretching and McMahon promptly mooned the camera. He went to bed early Tuesday night, but on Wednesday was seen walking down Bourbon Street with a drink in his hand and a woman on his arm shortly after 11 p.m.

By Thursday morning, McMahon found himself at the center of another controversy, this one not of his making. Buddy Diliberto, a New Orleans sportscaster, went on the air Wednesday night to report that McMahon had called the women of New Orleans "sluts" and the men "idiots" during an interview on a Chicago radio station at about 6:30 that morning. The story was later debunked and the apologetic Diliberto was suspended by his station for two weeks, but still the whole crazy scene was like nothing ever witnessed at a Super Bowl. Acting on Diliberto's suggestion, women showed up the next morning outside the Bears' hotel

	1	2	3	4	Final
Chicago Bears	13	10	21	2	46
New England Patriots	3	0	0	7	10

SCORING SUMMARY

1st Quarter
NE   Franklin, 36-yd. FG
CHI   Butler, 28-yd. FG
CHI   Butler, 24-yd. FG
CHI   Suhey, 11-yd. run (Butler kick)
2nd Quarter
CHI   McMahon, 2-yd. run (Butler kick)
CHI   Butler, 24-yd. FG
3rd Quarter
CHI   McMahon, 1-yd. run (Butler kick)
CHI   Phillips, 28-yd. interception return (Butler kick)
CHI   Perry, 1-yd. run (Butler kick)
4th Quarter
NE   Fryar, 8-yd. pass from Grogan (Franklin kick)
CHI   Safety, Waechter tackled Grogan in end zone

ready to lob rolls of toilet paper at McMahon.

A significant event actually did take place before kickoff. Late Saturday night, defensive coordinator Buddy Ryan was meeting with his players in a hotel banquet room. Although there had been rumors about the Philadelphia Eagles courting Ryan, it had been business as usual all week for a coach much beloved by many players. After handing out his customary reminder sheet, Ryan began to tear up. He said, "No matter what happens tomorrow, you'll always be my heroes," and walked out, leaving behind a room of stunned players and defensive line coach Dale Haupt to moderate one final reel of film.

"Dale says, 'Turn the damn lights out,'" defensive end Dan Hampton recalled. "But we had watched this film 10 times and were sick of it. Anyway, I just got up and I kicked the projector over, and [Steve] McMichael stood up and took a chair and impaled it into the chalkboard. The hair on the backs of our necks stood up. Holy s---. And we all looked at each other and walked out. Nobody said anything. It was like you know your folks are getting divorced but you're always hoping it ain't going to happen. But when Buddy said that, we knew it was over."

The Patriots were a wild-card team that finished third in the AFC East behind the Dolphins and the New York Jets with an 11–5 record. New England became the first team to reach the Super Bowl by winning three postseason games on the road, each time as an underdog. In order, they dispatched the Jets (26–14), Raiders (27–20), and Dolphins (31–14).

"We were very fortunate to get there," coach Raymond Berry said. "In Miami, I believed we used up a whole lot of whatever it is that keeps you sharp. I think our team physically was OK . . . but mentally we had lost something." Said cornerback Raymond Clayborn, "We kind of celebrated too much after winning in Miami for the first time in 20 years. [Actually, the first time ever.] We were very flat when we went there and ran into a very good Bear team that just wasn't going to be denied that year."

To say that the Bears were supremely confident would be an understatement. They were all about swagger. "We were down in Champaign [Illinois] practicing in the bubble the week before we left and I caught an interview with Tony Eason on TV," said Hampton. "Somebody said, 'The Bears had a pretty ferocious pass rush and had put out like seven quarterbacks this year. What do you think?' His answer, which was a bunch of mumbo-jumbo, was basically from a guy looking at the electric chair. You could tell by the look in his eyes that he was scared to death. It was kind of like stopping an avalanche. . . . I mean, you just couldn't block us."

With two weeks to prepare, Berry decided on an offensive plan unlike the one that had been wildly successful in the postseason. The Patriots, the NFL's sixth-ranked rushing team during the regular season, had become shockingly one-dimensional in the playoffs by averaging 49 runs and a mere 16 passes. Despite rushing for 510 yards in the three victories behind workhorse runners Craig James, Robert Weathers, and Tony Collins, New

> "I don't think there was a 46–10 difference in talent. The number one factor that was working in that game was the fact we put an A-B-C offense out there against a Ph.D. defense."
>
> *Raymond Berry, Patriots head coach*

England would pin its hopes on Eason pushing the ball downfield to talented wide receivers Stanley Morgan, Irving Fryar, and Stephen Starring.

"We had an excellent offensive line, Lin Dawson was a tremendous blocking tight end, and we had two sets of backs," said Berry. "We hardly threw the ball against the Raiders, and we had the ball [40] minutes against the Dolphins. But my thinking was Chicago had been studying our tendencies and so we'd do just the opposite. The running game got us there, but against the Chicago Bears that wasn't going to work."

<table>
<tr><td colspan="3">CHICAGO BEARS
(NFC, 15–1)</td><td></td><td colspan="3">NEW ENGLAND PATRIOTS
(AFC, 11–5)</td></tr>
<tr><td colspan="3"></td><td>Offense</td><td colspan="3"></td></tr>
<tr><td>83</td><td>Willie Gault (6-1, 183)</td><td></td><td>WR</td><td>86</td><td>Stanley Morgan (5-11, 181)</td></tr>
<tr><td>74</td><td>Jim Covert* (6-4, 271)</td><td></td><td>LT</td><td>76</td><td>Brian Holloway* (6-7, 288)</td></tr>
<tr><td>62</td><td>Mark Bortz (6-6, 269)</td><td></td><td>LG</td><td>73</td><td>John Hannah* (6-3, 265)</td></tr>
<tr><td>63</td><td>Jay Hilgenberg* (6-3, 258)</td><td></td><td>C</td><td>58</td><td>Pete Brock (6-5, 275)</td></tr>
<tr><td>57</td><td>Tom Thayer (6-4, 261)</td><td></td><td>RG</td><td>61</td><td>Ron Wooten (6-4, 273)</td></tr>
<tr><td>78</td><td>Keith Van Horne (6-6, 280)</td><td></td><td>RT</td><td>67</td><td>Steve Moore (6-4, 330)</td></tr>
<tr><td>87</td><td>Emery Moorehead (6-2, 220)</td><td></td><td>TE</td><td>87</td><td>Lin Dawson (6-3, 240)</td></tr>
<tr><td>85</td><td>Dennis McKinnon (6-1, 185)</td><td></td><td>WR</td><td>81</td><td>Stephen Starring (5-10, 172)</td></tr>
<tr><td>9</td><td>Jim McMahon* (6-1, 190)</td><td></td><td>QB</td><td>11</td><td>Tony Eason (6-2, 212)</td></tr>
<tr><td>34</td><td>Walter Payton* (5-10, 202)</td><td></td><td>RB</td><td>33</td><td>Tony Collins (5-11, 212)</td></tr>
<tr><td>26</td><td>Matt Suhey (5-11, 216)</td><td></td><td>RB</td><td>32</td><td>Craig James* (6-0, 215)</td></tr>
<tr><td colspan="3"></td><td>Defense</td><td colspan="3"></td></tr>
<tr><td>99</td><td>Dan Hampton* (6-5, 267)</td><td></td><td>LE</td><td>60</td><td>Garin Veris (6-4, 255)</td></tr>
<tr><td>76</td><td>Steve McMichael (6-2, 260)</td><td></td><td>LT | NT</td><td>72</td><td>Lester Williams (6-3, 272)</td></tr>
<tr><td>72</td><td>William Perry (6-2, 308)</td><td></td><td>RT | RE</td><td>85</td><td>Julius Adams (6-3, 270)</td></tr>
<tr><td>95</td><td>Richard Dent* (6-5, 263)</td><td></td><td>RE | LOLB</td><td>56</td><td>Andre Tippett* (6-3, 241)</td></tr>
<tr><td>55</td><td>Otis Wilson* (6-2, 232)</td><td></td><td>LLB | LILB</td><td>57</td><td>Steve Nelson* (6-2, 230)</td></tr>
<tr><td>50</td><td>Mike Singletary* (6-0, 228)</td><td></td><td>MLB | RILB</td><td>50</td><td>Larry McGrew (6-5, 233)</td></tr>
<tr><td>58</td><td>Wilber Marshall (6-1, 225)</td><td></td><td>RLB | ROLB</td><td>55</td><td>Don Blackmon (6-3, 235)</td></tr>
<tr><td>27</td><td>Mike Richardson (6-0, 188)</td><td></td><td>LCB</td><td>42</td><td>Ronnie Lippett (5-11, 180)</td></tr>
<tr><td>21</td><td>Leslie Frazier (6-0, 187)</td><td></td><td>RCB</td><td>26</td><td>Raymond Clayborn* (6-0, 186)</td></tr>
<tr><td>22</td><td>Dave Duerson* (6-1, 203)</td><td></td><td>SS</td><td>38</td><td>Roland James (6-2, 191)</td></tr>
<tr><td>45</td><td>Gary Fencik (6-1, 196)</td><td></td><td>FS</td><td>31</td><td>Fred Marion* (6-2, 191)</td></tr>
</table>

* Pro Bowl selection

SUBSTITUTIONS

Chicago
Offense: WR - 82 Ken Margerum, 89 Keith Ortego; TE - 80 Tim Wrightman; T - 71 Andy Frederick; G - 75 Stefan Humphries; C - 60 Tom Andrews; QB - 4 Steve Fuller, 18 Mike Tomczak; RB - 29 Dennis Gentry, 20 Thomas Sanders, 33 Calvin Thomas. *Defense:* DE - 73 Mike Hartenstine, 98 Tyrone Keys; DT - 70 Henry Waechter; LB - 54 Brian Cabral, 51 Jim Morrissey, 59 Ron Rivera, 52 Cliff Thrift; CB - 48 Reggie Phillips, 31 Ken Taylor; S - 23 Shaun Gayle. *Specialists:* K - 6 Kevin Butler; P - 8 Maury Buford.

New England
Offense: WR - 80 Irving Fryar*, 83 Cedric Jones; TE - 88 Derrick Ramsey; T - 70 Art Plunkett; G - 66 Paul Fairchild; C - 75 Guy Morriss; QB - 14 Steve Grogan; RB - 27 Greg Hawthorne, 30 Mosi Tatupu, 24 Robert Weathers. *Defense:* DE - 92 Smiley Creswell, 99 Ben Thomas; NT - 98 Dennis Owens; LB - 51 Brian Ingram, 52 Johnny Rembert, 95 Ed Reynolds, 54 Ed Williams; CB - 43 Ernest Gibson, 23 Rod McSwain; S - 28 Jim Bowman. *Specialists:* K - 1 Tony Franklin; P - 3 Rich Camarillo. *DNP:* 12 Tom Ramsey (QB).

Every underdog needs an early break to plant the seeds of doubt in the favorite. The Patriots got theirs on the game's second play when McMahon short-circuited and called the wrong formation on a weakside slant. Defensive end Garin Veris and linebacker Don Blackmon quickly appeared in the hole, Walter "Sweetness" Payton fumbled, and linebacker Larry McGrew recovered at the Chicago 19.

After faking an off-tackle run, Eason threw a crossing route to Dawson on first down. "We busted the first coverage," Ryan said. "I wouldn't want to say who blew the coverage—they know. That was the only plus thing [the Patriots] had all day, I think." As Dawson reached for the pass at the 8, the patellar tendon in his left knee ruptured and the ball fell incomplete. On second down, the Bears jumped into their signature "46" defense, and Eason threw a skinny post to Morgan. An overlooked reason why the 46 worked so brilliantly was the ability of middle linebacker Mike Singletary to cover like a safety. With his back to Eason, Singletary scrambled to where he figured Morgan would end up and grazed the ball just enough with his outstretched right hand so Morgan couldn't make

Chicago

Head Coach: Mike Ditka. *Offense:* Ed Hughes (coordinator), Ted Plumb (receivers), Dick Stanfel (offensive line), Johnny Roland (backs). *Defense:* Buddy Ryan (coordinator), Dale Haupt (defensive line), Jim LaRue (defensive backs). *Special Teams:* Steve Kazor. *Research and Quality Control:* Jim Dooley.

New England

Head Coach: Raymond Berry. *Offense:* Rod Humenuik (assistant head coach, offensive line), Les Steckel (wide receivers, quarterbacks), Harold Jackson (assistant wide receivers), Dante Scarnecchia (tight ends, special teams), Bobby Grier (backs). *Defense:* Rod Rust (coordinator), Ed Khayat (defensive line), Don Shinnick (linebackers), Jim Carr (defensive backs). *Strength:* Dean Brittenham. *Special Assistant to Head Coach:* John Polonchek.

he grab at the 6. "When you first looked at it, it looks like Stanley dropped the ball," said Berry. "But Singletary got a hand on it."

The Patriots sent in Starring as the third receiver on third down and flanked him wide right. When Eason took a deep drop, linebacker Otis Wilson beat Pro Bowl left tackle Brian Holloway around the corner and slammed into Eason from the blind side. Eason's pass into the end zone wasn't that close to Starring, but it was hardly the quarterback's fault. "The Bears came with an overload blitz, and Stephen Starring was supposed to make a quick inside fake and go deep," Berry said. "Well, Stephen Starring failed to read the blitz. Eason read the blitz and put the ball up on the go pattern and Starring is running the slant. Stephen Starring was not a real [smart] guy. If Stephen Starring had read that blitz, we [would have scored] because the corner jumped the slant. Eason was right on the money three times in a row and we were 0 for 3. It was that kind of day."

Tony Franklin's 36-yard field goal hurt the Bears more than anything the Patriots did all game, because their quest for a scoreless postseason was history. "That's what our goal was," said Ryan. "They wouldn't have ever scored if we hadn't fumbled on the first series. We were better off when we were on defense. The only time we screwed up was when we were on offense."

On first down, McMahon threw in the flat for

tight end Emery Moorehead. "It would have been a pick," Ditka said. "Jim's whole key throwing the ball was anticipation. He didn't have the strongest arm in the world. Not that his arm was weak. But he had to get the ball out in front of guys. He got it a little behind him there."

The pass was dropped by Blackmon after hitting him right in the chest. "Donnie was one of the best cover linebackers that I ever played with," said Clayborn. "He had the ball right in his hands ready to take it all the way to the house. After that, the rout was on." Blackmon had a lesser chance—but still a chance—for another interception five plays later, but flubbed that, too, and Kevin Butler followed with a 28-yard field goal to tie the score. It was set up on a 43-yard bomb to Willie Gault on an over route when cornerback Ronnie Lippett was out of position in zone coverage.

Berry came right back with three more passes on the next series. The first was thrown high over Starring's head, the second was dropped by Morgan, and the third never even got airborne. Eason held the ball too long and basically went into the fetal position for a 10-yard sack with defensive end Richard Dent, linebacker Wilber Marshall, and McMichael bearing down on him. The Patriots finally tried a running play to open their third possession but Singletary wasn't blocked and drilled James for no gain. "When we couldn't move the ball on our first run I thought, 'Where do we go from here? We can't pass, we can't run,'" right guard Ron Wooten said. "It was like trying to beat back the tide with a broom. It showed how completely demoralized we were."

The next play brought the first of the Patriots' six turnovers. (They had a plus-12 turnover margin in the first three playoff games.) McMichael, the muscular defensive tackle who entered the league in 1980 as New England's third-round draft choice, got there first, beating Wooten with an inside move. But the sack was credited to Dent, who zipped around Holloway and buried his helmet into Eason's back. The ball popped free, and Hampton recovered at the New England 13.

The Bears defense was the perfect blend of personnel, scheme, and coaching. Successful drafts engineered by Jim Finks and later Bill Tobin were responsible for procuring eight of the defensive starters, six of whom would make at least one Pro

Bowl during their careers in Chicago. Such was the depth of talent that when McCaskey played hardball and failed to sign two starters—end-turned-outside linebacker Al Harris and strong safety Todd Bell—the Bears were able to plug in high picks Marshall and Dave Duerson without missing a beat.

"Of that front seven in the Super Bowl, 'Fridge' [William Perry] was the only one who never made all-pro," said Hampton. "McMichael was a tremendous pass rusher, and Dent's as good a defensive end as I've ever seen. You pick one of the best running backs in the game with power and speed, that's what Wilber was. He was a 6-foot-1, 240-pound guy who could just run like the wind and knock the living s--- out of you. Otis was a man, 6-foot-2 and 235. And Singletary, obviously, was a hell of a player."

Hampton added that Perry had the potential to be an elite player as well. "Fridge was a terrific athlete who would kind of go through the motions," he said. "He could have been a Casey Hampton type guy, terrific on the nose. But in the latter part of '85 Buddy had ridiculed him to the point where he had gotten in somewhat shape at 320."

The secondary wasn't nearly as good, but Duerson did make the Pro Bowl that season and free safety Gary Fencik made it twice previously. Cornerbacks Leslie Frazier and Mike Richardson were vulnerable, to say the least, but Ryan knew it and pressured accordingly. "Our defense was designed to jump hot, meaning make the quarterback go to the second guy. In that split second it takes you to come off the primary and go to the second or third [receiver] is when we got there," Dan Hampton said. "Buddy would basically call us a bunch of rat bastards if we didn't get there within two seconds. . . . Thousand one, thousand two. By then, the quarterback's either going to be wrecked or somebody's in his face and he can't make a good throw."

In the three playoff games of 1985, the Bears defense yielded an average of 3.3 points, 144.6 yards, 10.3 first downs, and a third-down conversion rate of 8.3 percent. "The Chicago Bears defense I would say probably is in the top three all-time I've ever seen," said Berry, whose Hall of Fame career as a receiver with Baltimore began in 1955. "Their front seven compared very well to the great Steeler front,

which is saying a lot."

Chicago's base 4-3 alignment was powerful enough, but it was the 46 defense, which Ryan used an estimated 50 percent of the time, that made this defensive platoon one for the ages. Ryan developed it as a high-school coach in Gainesville, Texas, and then employed it with the Bears starting in the third game of the 1978 season, which was Ryan's first as coordinator under coach Neill Armstrong. It was a 4-1-6 alignment that the pair had used in Minnesota against passing formations. Ryan used a 5-1-5 defense for an entire game in mid-1981 before the classic 46 came into shape in 1984, when the Bears set an NFL record with 72 sacks and finished with 80 sacks over the 19 games.

"You had basically eight people around the line of scrimmage," said Ditka. "Now you have to make a determination on offense who's coming and who isn't. What people did in those days, they'd panic. There wasn't a lot of hot reads then, so they said 'We'll keep everybody in to block.' Well, that was the worst thing you could do. If the back who was supposed to block you stayed in, you went, too. You bring two from one side and you only got one guy to block, it's the hardest thing in football. If that back releases, one of those guys has to peel with them. But when you bring them both it's a complete mismatch because they can't do anything."

Dent led the team with 23 sacks on the year followed by Wilson with 14, McMichael with 9, Hampton with 7½, Marshall with 6½, Perry with 6, and Singletary with 4. Six of the sacks had come against Eason in a Week 2 game at Soldier Field won by Chicago, 20–7. "I felt sorry for Tony Eason in our first game," said Singletary. "When I looked into his eyes, I could see his desperation and confusion. Quarterbacks would get underneath the center with blood running from their noses and mouths and they had black eyes and they looked like they didn't want to play. And our guys would be barking and screaming at them—so it was a sad thing. It was 'I'm going to kill him next time.' That's the attitude our guys had. All game long."

In 1982, shortly after Armstrong was fired in the wake of a 6–10 season, Singletary said owner George Halas had plans to can Ryan and the entire defensive staff. The defensive players, however, collaborated on a letter to "Papa Bear" expressing their admiration for Ryan and his two longtime assistants, so Halas relented. "I think our action humbled Buddy," said Singletary. "He could see that he had a group of players that loved him. He then became a lot closer to his players." Still, Ryan always maintained an extremely high opinion of himself. Asked in 2008 if he considered himself the best defensive coordinator of all time, Ryan replied, "Well, I've been told that. I think there's a hell of a lot to it."

Several weeks after firing Armstrong, Halas hired Ditka after his nine-year stint on Tom Landry's staff in Dallas. Ditka—inducted into the Hall of Fame in 1988 as a rip-snorting tight end under Halas—was a volatile man of many moods. The relationship between Ditka and Ryan—who at 51 was five years the head coach's senior—was frosty, to say the least. He and Ryan co-existed for four years almost independently from each other, keeping their communication to the bare minimum.

"Ditka had great strengths," Hampton said. "Motivation was number one, and talent evaluation. It was great playing for Ditka, and I love him to death. But as far as like an offensive genius? No. Well, Buddy didn't respect Ditka because of that. He didn't understand why our offense was always so, you know, rudimentary when our defense was so high-tech. And he kind of resented it. One brother makes straight A's and the other one's a dumb ass. I'm not saying Ditka's a dumb ass but I'm just saying. Buddy has this, it wasn't a condescending attitude, but he didn't understand why they weren't able to play on a higher mental level."

Ryan cooked up something that he called "automatic front and coverage," which his players believed in. When the offense declared itself, Singletary made a call to determine positioning and assignment. The players trusted their pudgy, pompous little coordinator implicitly. But to make it work, Ryan campaigned loudly for experienced, intelligent players.

At the Super Bowl, the 46 included Hampton head-up on center Pete Brock, McMichael on the outside edge of Wooten, and Perry on the outside edge of left guard John Hannah. "Both tackles were playing like a wide-tackle three-technique," said Hampton. "The whole thing was predicated on you can't single-block Hampton. If the center tried to hook me, I basically threw him in a pile and would go make a play. So now they have to slide the line and try to take the gaps away. But when you start doing that you start having the linebackers coming outside free on a running back." Dent lined up five or six feet outside Holloway. Assuming it was a strong-right formation, Marshall would be on the outside shoulder of the tight end and Wilson would be on the inside shoulder of the tight end, leaving right tackle Steve Moore uncovered. Singletary was 5 yards deep directly behind Hampton.

The Bears ran six red-zone plays after the fumble by Eason, including two with Perry in the backfield, but had to settle for another field goal. But the offense was running right back onto the field after Dent assaulted Craig James, who was heading wide left on a pitchout from Eason. The ball came out and Singletary recovered at the 13. "Holloway was a fraud and Dent ate him on toast," said Hampton. "He tried to hook him, but Dent was very unorthodox. McMichael and I were textbook players. We never got hooked, we never got cut off. Richard played by the seat of his pants, but he was quick as a cat and could get up underneath a block. Before James knew what happened Dent kind of hit him and just slashed the ball away. Those two plays changed everything. My God, he was the most valuable player on the field." Using a two-back set, the play-calling Ditka gave it to fullback Matt Suhey for a 2-yard gain on first down and then an 11-yard touchdown on a pitchout to the right.

New England ran three plays on its fifth possession, including a reverse to Greg Hawthorne for minus-4 on third and 7, and still couldn't make a first down. After New England punted, the Bears covered 59 yards in 10 plays, McMahon keeping for the final 2 on an option in which the Patriots jumped outside in case the ball was pitched to Payton. That made it 20–3. After two more runs lost 2 yards and Eason was sacked by Wilson for minus-11, Berry went with veteran Steve Grogan for the rest of the game. "Eason did his job and I have a lot of respect for him," said Berry, "but it was obvious we were not able to protect him. I made the switch because Grogan wouldn't get sacked very often. We were in the first year of developing our offense and they were in their eighth year on defense. We didn't give the Bears anything to make them even one bit confused. The thing I had learned at that stage of my life was keep it as simple as I could the first year and let the athletes play. It served us well until we came up against that Bear defense."

The Bears wound up tying a Super Bowl record with seven sacks. On 10 other plays, Eason or Grogan absorbed shots a split-second after releasing the ball. Wilson meted out the most punishment with two sacks and four other knockdowns. "Our protection scheme was not adequate enough," Berry said, "and that was my responsibility." Eason's six-series stint included a total of 15 plays for minus-36 yards. Grogan passed for the Patriots' initial first down late in the half, which ended with New England at minus-19 in total offense and trailing, 23–3.

During the break, some of the Bears made noise about scoring 60 points, but by the start of the fourth quarter, McMahon was on the bench and Steve Fuller was in to hand off. Even so, each of Chicago's third-quarter possessions ended in touchdowns. The first was on a 1-yard sneak by McMahon, and the second was a 1-yard run by Perry in which he blew through McGrew and crashed 5 yards deep in the end zone. "I blacked that second half out," Clayborn recalled. "I was on the sideline waiting for the clock to run out when it got up to 37–3. I said, 'Let this end mercifully. Please.'" McMahon labeled the entire game a bore.

As the game dragged on (it lasted 3 hours, 42 minutes), attention was directed to the fact that Payton had not scored a touchdown. His best chance came early in the fourth quarter, but it was the Fridge, not Sweetness, who got the call from the 1. "We should have done something for him, and I'm partly at fault," said McMahon. "Ditka called for Perry to get the ball, and that's where I should have just given it to Wally and the hell with what Ditka wanted." Ditka expressed regret, but added that he had been oblivious to who was doing the scoring. Extremely agitated, Payton found a storage closet in the bowels of the Superdome and locked himself inside. Later, team officials talked him into coming out and participating in the remaining revelry and interviews.

TEAM STATISTICS

CHICAGO		NEW ENGLAND
23	Total First Downs	12
13	Rushing	1
9	Passing	10
1	Penalty	1
408	Total Net Yardage	123
76	Total Offensive Plays	54
5.4	Avg. Gain per Offensive Play	2.3
49	Rushes	11
167	Yards Gained Rushing (Net)	7
3.4	Average Yards per Rush	0.6
24	Passes Attempted	36
12	Passes Completed	17
0	Passes Intercepted	2
3	Tackled Attempting to Pass	7
15	Yards Lost Attempting to Pass	61
241	Yards Gained Passing (Net)	116
7/14	Third-Down Efficiency	1/10
0/1	Fourth-Down Efficiency	1/1
4	Punts	6
43.3	Average Distance	43.8
2	Punt Returns	2
20	Punt Return Yardage	22
4	Kickoff Returns	7
49	Kickoff Return Yardage	153
75	Interception Return Yardage	0
3	Fumbles	4
1	Own Fumbles Recovered	0
4	Opponent Fumbles Recovered	2
7	Penalties	5
40	Yards Penalized	35
5	Touchdowns	1
4	Rushing	0
0	Passing	1
1	Returns	0
5	Extra Points Made	1
3	Field Goals Made	1
3	Field Goals Attempted	1
1	Safeties	0
46	Total Points Scored	10
39:15	Time of Possession	20:45

INDIVIDUAL STATISTICS

CHICAGO

Passing	CP/ATT	YDS	TD	INT	RAT
McMahon	12/20	256	0	0	104.2
Fuller	0/4	0	0	0	39.6
Perry	0/0	0	0	0	0.0

Rushing	ATT	YDS	AVG	TD	LG
Payton	22	61	2.8	0	7
Suhey	11	52	4.7	1	11t
Sanders	4	15	3.8	0	10
Gentry	3	15	5.0	0	8
McMahon	5	14	2.8	2	7
Thomas	2	8	4.0	0	7
Fuller	1	1	1.0	0	1
Perry	1	1	1.0	1	1t

Receiving	NO	YDS	AVG	TD	LG
Gault	4	129	32.3	0	60
Gentry	2	41	20.5	0	27
Margerum	2	36	18.0	0	29
Moorehead	2	22	11.0	0	14
Suhey	1	24	24.0	0	24
Thomas	1	4	4.0	0	4

Interceptions	NO	YDS	LG	TD
Morrissey	1	47	47	0
Phillips	1	28	28t	1

Punting	NO	AVG	LG	BLK
Buford	4	43.3	52	0

Punt Ret.	NO/FC	YDS	LG	TD
Ortego	2/1	20	12	0

Kickoff Ret.	NO	YDS	LG	TD
Gault	4	49	18	0

Defense	SOLO	AST	TOT	SK
Phillips	7	0	7	0
Duerson	4	0	4	0
Marshall	4	0	4	0.5
Dent	2	1	3	1.5
Fencik	2	1	3	0
Hampton	2	1	3	1
Cabral	2	0	2	0
Rivera	2	0	2	0
Richardson	1	1	2	0
Singletary	1	1	2	0
Wilson	1	1	2	2
Gayle	1	0	1	0
Hartenstine	1	0	1	0
Ortego	1	0	1	0
Perry	1	0	1	0
Taylor	1	0	1	0
Gentry	0	1	1	0
McMichael	0	0	0	1
Waechter	0	0	0	1
TOTAL	**33**	**7**	**40**	**7**

NEW ENGLAND

Passing	CP/ATT	YDS	TD	INT	RAT
Grogan	17/30	177	1	2	57.2
Eason	0/6	0	0	0	39.6

Rushing	ATT	YDS	AVG	TD	LG
Collins	3	4	1.3	0	3
Grogan	1	3	3.0	0	3
Weathers	1	3	3.0	0	3
C. James	5	1	0.2	0	3
Hawthorne	1	-4	-4.0	0	-4

Receiving	NO	YDS	AVG	TD	LG
Morgan	6	51	8.5	0	60
Starring	2	39	19.5	0	24
Fryar	2	24	12.0	1	16
Collins	2	19	9.5	0	11
Jones	2	19	9.5	0	19
D. Ramsey	2	16	8.0	0	11
C. James	1	6	6	0	6
Weathers	1	3	3	0	3

Interceptions	NO	YDS	LG	TD
None	--	--	--	--

Punting	NO	AVG	LG	BLK
Camarillo	6	43.8	62	0

Punt Ret.	NO/FC	YDS	LG	TD
Fryar	2/0	22	12	0

Kickoff Ret.	NO	YDS	LG	TD
Starring	7	153	36	0

Defense	SOLO	AST	TOT	SK
S. Nelson	6	3	9	0
Blackmon	7	1	8	0
Marion	6	1	7	0
R. James	5	1	6	0
Tippett	5	1	6	0
McGrew	3	3	6	0
Lippett	5	0	5	0
Owens	4	1	5	2
Veris	3	2	5	0
Hawthorne	3	0	3	0
Adams	2	1	3	0
Clayborn	2	0	2	0
McSwain	2	0	2	0
Rembert	2	0	2	0
Thomas	2	0	2	1
Creswell	1	0	1	0
Gibson	1	0	1	0
Ingram	1	0	1	0
C. James	1	0	1	0
Morgan	1	0	1	0
Tatupu	0	1	1	0
TOTAL	**62**	**15**	**77**	**3**

In three playoff games, one of the game's all-time greats had been held to just 186 yards in 67 carries for a 2.8 average and no touchdowns. "I'm sorry that he was [mad]," Hampton said. "But their defense was pretty damn good, and they predicated everything on stopping him. . . . It kind of worked. They won the battle but lost the war. The novelty act of Fridge, it was too late to stop that. Walter's greatness shined so brightly, that's just one little pinhead of darkness." Payton died of a rare liver disease in 1999 at age 45.

As the clock wound down on Super Bowl XX, Hampton approached McMichael and told him, "As soon as this thing's over Dent and I are carrying Buddy off the field. If you don't want your boy, Ditka, to get his feelings hurt, you and Fridge need to carry him." According to Hampton, Perry was Ditka's draft pick, and he basically forced Ryan to play him. Hampton also said that Ryan wasn't overly impressed by McMichael, either. "Buddy said McMichael was a tough son of a bitch but said he wasn't a great player," Hampton said. "Buddy was just brutally honest like that. We had all these political rifts."

So that's precisely what happened at the final gun, two coaches riding off atop the shoulders of their favorite players. Three days later, Ryan was introduced as the new coach of the Eagles. Ditka's defensive coordinator for the last seven years of his tenure was Vince Tobin. "Ditka brought in good people after Ryan, but he was so dominating that he swallowed them up," said Singletary. "Meanwhile, Buddy had good people in Philadelphia, but not a Ditka. Both Ditka and Ryan needed someone like [each other] to share the power."

The next day, Berry was confronted by a story in *The Boston Globe* about reports of drug problems among the Patriots. Specifying cocaine as a drug involved, Berry said the organization knew of at least five players with a serious problem and five to seven others under strong suspicion. The players had met for two hours before voting to become the first NFL team to accept voluntary drug testing. The Patriots made the playoffs once in Berry's final four seasons before Bill Parcells and then Bill Belichick lifted them back to Super Bowl caliber.

That night, McMahon and his teammates went from room to room in the hotel, drinking beer and ripping the tightwad McCaskey. "A lot of guys were unhappy with the front office so we figured it was a good thing we won now because this thing could explode in another year," he said. The average age of Chicago's starters was just 26.1 years; of its nine Pro Bowl players, only the 31-year-old Payton was older than 28. There were boasts about returning to the Super Bowl again and again.

Alas, this would be the Bears' high-water mark. Even without Ryan, the defense continued to be highly effective. In fact, the 1986 unit gave up fewer points (187) than the 1985 unit did (198), but under Tobin's direction the group was never quite as intimidating. "Vince Tobin was a good guy," Hampton said, "but it was different as a T-bone steak and a banana split. There was nothing like playing for Buddy."

Leslie Frazier, the club's leader in interceptions every year from 1983 to 1985, suffered a torn anterior cruciate ligament (ACL) in the first half of the Super Bowl and never played again. That was a damaging blow, to be sure, but nothing like the crushing impact of McMahon's right shoulder injury in November 1986, caused by an illegal body slam by Green Bay nose tackle Charles Martin. His 13 games in 1985 were the most McMahon ever was healthy enough to play in a career that would last another 11 seasons. The bad shoulder reduced his arm strength and curtailed his devil-may-care scrambling ability. McMahon rushed for 252 yards in 1985 and 152 more in 1986 before the injury. His highest rushing total after that was 141 yards.

In five more postseasons under Ditka, the Bears were eliminated four times at Soldier Field, including three times as a favorite and once as a 1-point underdog against San Francisco. Ditka went 2–5 in the playoffs after his championship season.

"We did want to create some awe by playing the [New England] game as it had never been played before," Singletary said. "Despite the conflicts there was nothing that the 1985 Bears couldn't accomplish. So we won only one Super Bowl, but we did win one. And we did it convincingly."

XXI

NEW YORK GIANTS 39, DENVER BRONCOS 20

January 25, 1987
Rose Bowl, Pasadena, California

Even now, more than 20 years after the fact, Dan Reeves still is livid. Here it was, just a few minutes before the kickoff of Super Bowl XXI, and league officials were in his locker room telling him, the coach of the Denver Broncos, exactly how his players would have to be introduced before the crowd of 101,063 on a majestic afternoon at the Rose Bowl.

This was news to Reeves. Instead of having the bulk of his squad waiting on the field to greet the 11 to be introduced, the NFL people were telling him that, no, both teams would have to be in the bench area so other groups involved in the pre-game festivities wouldn't be disturbed.

Reeves didn't like it. The Broncos, like most teams, preferred the team approach to an exercise that focuses on the individual.

But he reluctantly agreed, telling the officials, "I don't agree with it, but if that's what we've got to do, we've got to do it." When the Broncos' intros were finished, out charged the New York Giants. Much to Reeves' dismay, the Giants massed in the middle of the field and stayed there until their starters were through being called.

"I mean, I'm hot," Reeves said. "I found out later that Bill Parcells said, 'The hell with it. If they want to fine me, fine, but I'm going to have my team out there.' That's what I should have done. That was one of the things that you always remember."

Something else stayed with Reeves that also had nothing to do with blocking or tackling. As the Broncos came out of the tunnel for the second half, Frank Sinatra's "The Theme from New York, New York," a sentimental staple at Giants Stadium, was booming throughout the Rose Bowl.

Few people expected it to be the Broncos' day. As a 9½-point underdog, the Broncos had John Elway and not much else. It's understandable that Reeves felt a little behind the eight-ball right from the start.

Attendance: 101,063
Conditions: 76 degrees, sunny, wind W at 2–5 mph
Time of kickoff: 3:13 p.m. (PST)
Length of game: 3 hours, 25 minutes
Referee: Jerry Markbreit

MVP: Phil Simms, QB, Giants

Against a superior opponent, the Broncos held a 10–9 lead at halftime that would have been substantially larger had it not been for missed field goals of 23 and 34 yards by barefoot Rich Karlis, plus a fruitless three-play sequence from the Giants 1. Having exhausted what little margin for error they might have had in the first half, the Broncos were worn down in the second half and ultimately crushed by the Giants, 39–20.

"We buried all the ghosts today," Parcells said. "They're all gone."

It was the first NFL championship in 30 years for one of the league's oldest franchises, a span during which the Giants could win neither the big one nor much of anything at all. Owner Wellington Mara, whose father, Tim, founded the team in 1925, became primarily responsible for its fortunes from 1930 until his death in 2005.

"Wellington would never come up to you and say, 'Hey, we've got to win this game,' or 'This is really a big game,'" said Bill Belichick, the Giants' 34-year-old defensive coordinator. "No, no, no. He was incredibly supportive to the team and everyone on it. . . . Whatever he said, it was always the right thing to say. He had a great presence of making you feel appreciated and good about your role. Whatever his words were, and he didn't have a lot of them, it was like, 'I know you did your best but we've got to do better next time.' He was awesome."

Just as the Giants had been castigated for years by their fans, so too had their quarterback, Phil

	1	2	3	4	Final
Denver Broncos	10	0	0	10	20
New York Giants	7	2	17	13	39

SCORING SUMMARY

1st Quarter
DEN Karlis, 48-yd. FG
NY Mowatt, 6-yd. pass from Simms (Allegre kick)
DEN Elway, 4-yd. run (Karlis kick)
2nd Quarter
NY Safety, Martin tackled Elway in end zone
3rd Quarter
NY Bavaro, 13-yd. pass from Simms (Allegre kick)
NY Allegre, 21-yd. FG
NY Morris, 1-yd. run (Allegre kick)
4th Quarter
NY McConkey, 6-yd. pass from Simms (Allegre kick)
DEN Karlis, 28-yd. FG
NY Anderson, 2-yd. run (kick failed)
DEN V. Johnson, 47-yd. pass from Elway (Karlis kick)

Simms. After arriving from obscure Morehead State University as the seventh overall selection in the 1979 draft, he had endured injuries and benchings, vicious name-calling, and merciless booing for the better part of six seasons.

By 1986, Simms was in his third consecutive season as a 16-game starter. Simms and Parcells, in his fourth year as coach, now were attached at the hip. During the regular season, Simms was merely a 55.3 percent passer with a passer rating of 74.6. In dominating playoff victories over San Francisco (49–3) and Washington (17–0), Simms completed a humdrum 48.5 percent of his 33 passes.

Those playoff games, however, had been played in the frigid, windswept Meadowlands. When Simms arrived in southern California after a hard week of preparation back in New Jersey, he sensed that this might really be his moment in the sun.

"The first day I came out here, I started throwing the ball well," Simms said. "These conditions are just about perfect to throw in. The ball carried better, and I could grip it any way I wanted. In New York, you can't do that."

With hardly a breeze at kickoff and the temperature at 76 degrees, Simms played as though he wished the game would never end. All the skepticism, ridicule, and contempt that Simms had lived through became a distant memory when he put on a show that would rival any in postseason football history.

Simms completed all 10 of his passes in the second half, including two for touchdowns, and was named MVP. By completing 22 of 25 for 88 percent—to go with a near-perfect passer rating of 150.9—he became the most accurate passer in NFL playoff history.

"That may be," said Parcells, "the best game a quarterback has played."

Simms mixed up his targets, finding running backs 9 times, wide receivers 8 times, and tight ends 5 times. On one of his incompletions, defensive end Rulon Jones hit him a split-second after he delivered the ball. Simms only missed one pass in which he had ample time. "I had a 20-yard out to Stacy Robinson that I was one yard short on because Karl Mecklenburg hit me as I threw it," said Simms. "I had a deep ball to Phil McConkey, who was open, and he got tripped and it should've been a penalty. And I had a deep ball to Mark Bavaro, who dropped it." All of his incompletions came on third downs in the second quarter.

"He was just a hot quarterback that day. He just couldn't miss," Broncos defensive coach Joe Collier said years later. "We were a big zone team. Always had been. Ron Erhardt devised a real good game plan

COACHING STAFFS

Denver
Head Coach: Dan Reeves. *Offense:* Mike Shanahan (coordinator, wide receivers), Alex Gibbs (offensive line, running game), Nick Nicolau (running backs, play-action passing game). *Defense:* Joe Collier (assistant head coach), Stan Jones (defensive line), Myrel Moore (linebackers), Charlie West (defensive backs). *Special Teams:* Chan Gailey. *Special Assistant:* Marvin Bass. *Strength:* Al Miller.

New York
Head Coach: Bill Parcells. *Offense:* Ron Erhardt (coordinator), Pat Hodgson (wide receivers), Mike Pope (tight ends), Fred Hoaglin (offensive line), Ray Handley (running backs). *Defense:* Bill Belichick (coordinator), Lamar Leachman (defensive line), Len Fontes (defensive backs). *Special Teams:* Romeo Crennel, Mike Sweatman (assistant). *Strength:* Johnny Parker.

against our type of defense. They found the holes and executed very well. He was the big difference in the game. It was one of the best performances I have ever seen."

Although the Giants had rushed the ball on 51.9 percent of their plays that season, Simms insisted everything stemmed from the passing game. The Broncos later expressed some surprise when Simms came out throwing (9 of 11 first downs in the first half), but that was all by design. With Collier's unit making adjustments at halftime to curtail the pass, Erhardt, who was in his fifth season as the Giants' offensive coordinator, called runs on 16 of 18 first downs in the second half.

"When I look back, I find it amazing that the press and the Bronco players didn't talk much about our passing game, because in the previous eight games going into the Super Bowl it had been just dominant," Simms said. "For two weeks we were about as hot in practice as any team I've been around. I audibled a lot during the year but I didn't need to audible once this entire game. I never once even got close to having a negative thought so I was never restricted physically or mentally. I was as free as a player ever could be."

The public's fascination was with Elway, the immense talent with the bazooka arm who had begun to fulfill his promise. His legerdemain had just produced "the Drive" in the AFC Championship Game victory in Cleveland. No one was more deep-ball dangerous or broken-play capable than Elway. But Simms later would say that he went into the Super Bowl thinking the better quarterback was playing for the Giants.

"The first factor you go to in that game was the perfection of Simms," said Tim Rooney, the Giants director of pro personnel, "and we really had Elway on the run. One of the

DENVER BRONCOS (AFC, 11–5)		NEW YORK GIANTS (NFC, 14–2)	
	Offense		
82 Vance Johnson (5-11, 185)	WR	86 Lionel Manuel (5-11, 175)	
70 Dave Studdard (6-4, 260)	LT	60 Brad Benson* (6-3, 270)	
54 Keith Bishop* (6-3, 265)	LG	67 Billy Ard (6-3, 270)	
64 Billy Bryan (6-2, 255)	C	65 Bart Oates (6-3, 265)	
63 Mark Cooper (6-5, 267)	RG	61 Chris Godfrey (6-3, 265)	
76 Ken Lanier (6-3, 269)	RT	63 Karl Nelson (6-6, 285)	
88 Clarence Kay (6-2, 237)	TE	89 Mark Bavaro* (6-4, 245)	
81 Steve Watson (6-4, 195)	WR	81 Stacy Robinson (5-11, 186)	
7 John Elway* (6-3, 210)	QB	11 Phil Simms (6-3, 214)	
23 Sammy Winder* (5-11, 203)	RB	20 Joe Morris* (5-7, 195)	
47 Gerald Willhite (5-10, 200)	RB	44 Maurice Carthon (6-1, 225)	
	Defense		
61 Andre Townsend (6-3, 265)	LE	75 George Martin (6-4, 255)	
71 Greg Kragen (6-3, 245)	NT	64 Jim Burt* (6-1, 260)	
75 Rulon Jones* (6-6, 260)	RE	70 Leonard Marshall* (6-3, 285)	
50 Jim Ryan (6-1, 218)	LOLB	58 Carl Banks (6-4, 250)	
77 Karl Mecklenburg* (6-3, 240)	LILB	55 Gary Reasons (6-4, 245)	
98 Ricky Hunley (6-2, 238)	RILB	53 Harry Carson* (6-2, 255)	
57 Tom Jackson (5-11, 220)	ROLB	56 Lawrence Taylor* (6-3, 255)	
20 Louis Wright (6-3, 200)	LCB	34 Elvis Patterson (5-11, 188)	
31 Mike Harden (6-1, 192)	RCB	23 Perry Williams (6-2, 203)	
49 Dennis Smith* (6-3, 200)	SS	48 Kenny Hill (6-0, 195)	
43 Steve Foley (6-3, 190)	FS	27 Herb Welch (5-11, 180)	

* Pro Bowl selection

SUBSTITUTIONS

Denver

Offense: WR - 80 Mark Jackson, 84 Clint Sampson; TE - 85 Joey Hackett, 87 Bobby Micho, 89 Orson Mobley; T - 74 Dan Remsberg; G - 62 Mike Freeman; QB - 8 Gary Kubiak; RB - 35 Ken Bell, 33 Gene Lang, 30 Steve Sewell. **Defense:** DE - 73 Simon Fletcher, 90 Freddie Gilbert; NT - 69 Tony Colorito; LB - 59 Darren Comeaux, 55 Rick Dennison, 52 Ken Woodard; CB - 36 Mark Haynes, 45 Steve Wilson; S - 22 Tony Lilly, 48 Randy Robbins. **Specialists:** K - 3 Rich Karlis; P - 2 Mike Horan.

New York

Offense: WR - 88 Bobby Johnson, 80 Phil McConkey, 87 Solomon Miller; TE - 84 Zeke Mowatt; T - 66 William Roberts, 68 Damian Johnson; C - 59 Brian Johnston; QB - 17 Jeff Rutledge; RB - 24 Ottis Anderson, 30 Tony Galbreath, Lee Rouson. **Defense:** DE - 77 Eric Dorsey; NT - 74 Erik Howard, 78 Jerome Sally; LB - 54 Andy Headen, 57 Byron Hunt, 52 Pepper Johnson, 51 Robbie Jones; CB - 25 Mark Collins; S - 28 Tom Flynn, 46 Greg Lasker. **Specialists:** K - 2 Raul Allegre; P - 5 Sean Landeta*.

quarterbacks played as if he was in a practice and the other played as if he was in a panic."

The two teams had played in late November, with the Giants winning, 19–16, at Giants Stadium. "Even though Denver had a competitive running game, we were a tough team to run against and felt we could handle that," Belichick said. "The big thing was Elway and the big plays down the field in the passing game. We were trying to keep him in the pocket." For the first three series, Elway and the 15th-ranked Broncos offense had every answer for the Giants' second-ranked defense. A 45-yard drive led to Karlis' 48-yard field goal. After the Giants scored on a 6-yard touchdown pass from Simms to tight end Zeke Mowatt, the Broncos responded with a 58-yard drive that culminated in Elway's 4-yard touchdown on a third-down quarterback draw.

With a 10–7 lead, the Broncos faced a third-and-12 from their 18 on their third possession. Elway took a shotgun snap 5 yards behind the line, dropped back 7 yards more, ran up 8 yards to the 14 as the pocket collapsed, and then heaved a bomb to Vance Johnson, who had outrun safeties Kenny Hill and Herb Welch, for a 54-yard gain. Elway's then completed third-down passes to tight end Orson Mobley and running back Steve Sewell, giving the Broncos a first down at the 1.

The Giants had a phenomenal set of linebackers in their 3-4 defense, and they were also much heavier than their program weights indicated. On the outside, Lawrence Taylor, the NFL's MVP in 1986 with 20½ sacks, weighed 255, according to Belichick, and Carl Banks was 250. On the inside, Harry Carson was 255 and Gary Reasons, who split time with 260-pound rookie Pepper Johnson, weighed 245. According to Belichick, Taylor always ran either 4.58 or 4.59 when the Giants timed their players in the 40-yard dash just before training camp.

In the Giants' goal-line defense, Taylor in effect played safety and Carson was the middle linebacker. "Taylor was the ultimate free safety on the goal-line," Belichick said. "When you have all six guys in front of you there's really nobody that could block him. He could just have a free run on pretty much everything without having any blockers. And he was fast. Harry was the perfect middle linebacker

TEAM STATISTICS

DENVER		NEW YORK
23	Total First Downs	24
5	Rushing	10
16	Passing	13
2	Penalty	1
372	Total Net Yardage	399
64	Total Offensive Plays	64
5.8	Avg. Gain per Offensive Play	6.2
19	Rushes	38
52	Yards Gained Rushing (Net)	136
2.7	Average Yards per Rush	3.6
41	Passes Attempted	25
26	Passes Completed	22
1	Passes Intercepted	0
4	Tackled Attempting to Pass	1
32	Yards Lost Attempting to Pass	5
320	Yards Gained Passing (Net)	263
7/14	Third-Down Efficiency	6/12
0/0	Fourth-Down Efficiency	1/2
2	Punts	3
41.0	Average Distance	46.0
1	Punt Returns	1
9	Punt Return Yardage	25
5	Kickoff Returns	4
84	Kickoff Return Yardage	53
0	Interception Return Yardage	-7
2	Fumbles	0
2	Own Fumbles Recovered	0
0	Opponent Fumbles Recovered	0
4	Penalties	6
28	Yards Penalized	48
2	Touchdowns	5
1	Rushing	2
1	Passing	3
0	Returns	0
2	Extra Points Made	4
2	Field Goals Made	1
4	Field Goals Attempted	1
0	Safeties	1
20	Total Points Scored	39
25:21	Time of Possession	34:39

on the goal line. He was usually on the strong side of the formation, where he had to read plays and take on plays."

On first down, Reeves called a bootleg to the right for Elway, but Taylor chased behind the line from the back side to make the tackle for minus-1. "Hell of a play," Reeves said. "We had hats on

INDIVIDUAL STATISTICS

DENVER

Passing	CP/ATT	YDS	TD	INT	RAT
Elway	22/37	304	1	1	83.6
Kubiak	4/4	48	0	0	116.7

Rushing	ATT	YDS	AVG	TD	LG
Elway	6	27	4.5	1	10
Willhite	4	19	4.8	0	11
Sewell	3	4	1.3	0	12
Lang	2	2	1.0	0	4
Winder	4	0	0.0	0	3

Receiving	NO	YDS	AVG	TD	LG
Johnson	5	121	24.2	1	54
Willhite	5	39	7.8	0	11
Winder	4	34	8.5	0	14
M. Jackson	3	51	17.0	0	24
Watson	2	54	27.0	0	31
Sampson	2	20	10.0	0	11
Mobley	2	17	8.5	0	11
Sewell	2	12	6.0	0	7
Lang	1	4	4.0	0	4

Interceptions	NO	YDS	LG	TD
None	--	--	--	--

Punting	NO	AVG	LG	BLK
Horan	2	41.0	42	0

Punt Ret.	NO/FC	YDS	LG	TD
Willhite	1/1	9	9	0

Kickoff Ret.	NO	YDS	LG	TD
Bell	3	48	28	0
Lang	2	36	23	0

Defense	SOLO	AST	TOT	SK
Woodard	8	3	11	0.5
Ryan	6	3	9	0
Hunley	7	1	8	0
Jones	4	2	6	0
Foley	5	0	5	0
Smith	5	0	5	0
Wright	5	0	5	0
Mecklenburg	2	3	5	0
Haynes	3	0	3	0
Wilson	3	0	3	0
Townsend	2	1	3	0
Micho	2	0	2	0
Gilbert	1	1	2	0.5
Lilly	1	1	2	0
Robbins	1	1	2	0
Kragen	0	2	2	0
Fletcher	1	0	1	0
Harden	1	0	1	0
Watson	1	0	1	0
Bell	0	1	1	0
Dennison	0	1	1	0
TOTAL	58	20	78	1

NEW YORK

Passing	CP/ATT	YDS	TD	INT	RAT
Simms	22/25	268	3	0	150.9

Rushing	ATT	YDS	AVG	TD	LG
Morris	20	67	3.4	1	11
Simms	3	25	8.3	0	22
Rouson	3	22	7.3	0	18
Galbreath	4	17	4.3	0	7
Carthon	3	4	1.3	0	2
Anderson	2	1	0.5	1	2t
Rutledge	3	0	0.0	0	2

Receiving	NO	YDS	AVG	TD	LG
Bavaro	4	51	12.8	1	17
Morris	4	20	5.0	0	12
Carthon	4	13	3.3	0	7
Robinson	3	62	20.7	0	36
Manuel	3	43	14.3	0	17
McConkey	2	50	25.0	1	44
Rouson	1	23	23.0	0	23
Mowatt	1	6	6.0	1	6t

Interceptions	NO	YDS	LG	TD
Patterson	1	-7	-7	0

Punting	NO	AVG	LG	BLK
Landeta	3	46.0	59	0

Punt Ret.	NO/FC	YDS	LG	TD
McConkey	1/1	25	25	0

Kickoff Ret.	NO	YDS	LG	TD
Rouson	3	56	22	0
Flynn	1	-3	-3	0

Defense	SOLO	AST	TOT	SK
Banks	10	0	10	0
Carson	7	0	7	0
Taylor	4	1	5	0
Patterson	3	2	5	0
Marshall	4	0	4	2
Welch	4	0	4	0
Collins	2	1	3	0
Flynn	2	0	2	0
P. Johnson	2	0	2	0
Reasons	2	0	2	0
Hunt	1	1	2	0
Dorsey	1	0	1	1
Headen	1	0	1	0
Hill	1	0	1	0
Jones	1	0	1	0
Lasker	1	0	1	0
Martin	1	0	1	1
Rouson	1	0	1	0
Williams	1	0	1	0
TOTAL	49	5	54	4

everybody and one extra blocker, but Lawrence Taylor came all the way across the field."

On second down, the Broncos tried to run Gerald Willhite inside behind a wham block by tight end Bobby Micho on backup nose tackle Erik Howard. Micho got his block, but Carson instinctively attacked the hole before guard Keith Bishop could cut him off and, when combined with defensive end Eric Dorsey's surge past right tackle Ken Lanier, stacked up Willhite for no gain. "Denver was a big trapping team with Reeves, like they did in Dallas with [Tom] Landry," said Belichick. "Harry [Carson] was all over it."

Then Belichick slanted his line for the third play in a row. Sammy Winder tried to sweep left end on a toss play, but outside linebacker Carl Banks swallowed him for a loss of 4. Then Karlis missed his first of his two chip shots as the air seeped from the Broncos.

"We started that series first and goal at the 1 and came away with no points," Reeves said. "That was huge. We could have been way ahead instead of just having the lead."

Said Belichick, "That was the critical juncture in the game. That kind of summed up the two teams in terms of the running game."

Later in the first half, with Denver backed up near its own goal line, defensive end George Martin beat Lanier around the corner and sacked Elway for a safety, making it 10–9. But the Broncos would have never been in that situation if Elway's pass to tight end Clarence Kay on the previous play had been ruled a catch instead of an incompletion. Subsequent replays showed conclusive proof that the ball had been caught. "Then the next play they got us on a safety," said Reeves. "If you complete that pass they don't get the safety. I thought we played well in the first half."

Karlis blew another gimme in the final seconds of the first half, negating a 42-yard drive and leaving the Broncos in a foul mood during the long intermission.

The game turned quickly in the third quarter. On fourth and 1, Parcells sent out backup quarterback Jeff Rutledge as part of the Sean Landeta–led punt team. "The play was 'Arapahoe,'" said Belichick. "A run, a pass, a hit on the enemy." Well aware that a fake was possible, Collier kept his 3-4 base personnel on the field. After a few seconds, Rutledge shifted underneath center Bart Oates. After a count lasting almost 10 seconds, during which the Broncos didn't jump into a short-yardage defense, Parcells nodded to Rutledge. When Oates and right guard Chris Godfrey, a pair of refugees from the United States Football League, applied a firm double-team on nose tackle Greg Kragen, Rutledge burrowed behind them on a sneak and made it by inches.

"It was a calculated gamble by Parcells," Reeves said. "We had worked on it all week, too, yet they executed it and made a first down. They played a great second half and that was the big play. Who knows what would have happened if they didn't make it."

Running the ball and stopping the run were the tenets of Parcells' coaching philosophy, but many times during his career he made bold moves on special teams. "Bill was always in favor of fakes but he never wanted the kicker to touch the ball," Rooney said. "That was not uncharacteristic of Parcells."

Simms subsequently found Morris underneath for 12 and running back Lee Rouson on a deep seam route for 23 against Mecklenburg. The go-ahead touchdown came on a 13-yard pass to Bavaro with backup safety Randy Robbins in coverage, making it 16–10.

Morris, who finished with 67 yards in 20 carries, was more effective in the second half. Many of his rushes came behind Bavaro's blocks against Tom Jackson, the Broncos' undersized right outside linebacker who retired in the offseason. To get that matchup, Erhardt had Bavaro shift shortly before the snap from one side of the line to the other. The Broncos didn't shift their linebackers in response to Bavaro's movement. "We always had a linebacker [Jim Ryan] that would be playing on the tight end," Collier said. "As soon as the tight end shifts then those two guys are playing different position because we didn't shift our linebackers with them. Not that they hadn't done it before because other teams had shifted tight ends, too. But it just changes you. You don't have quite the comfort zone."

Dubbed "the Suburbanites" because Parcells said all five resembled businessmen who caught the train into the city each morning, the Giants' offensive line of tackles Brad Benson and Karl Nelson, guards Billy Ard and Godfrey, and center Oates kept the Broncos' small but quick defense from penetrating. New York controlled the ball for 34:39 and piled up 399 yards.

"They were all good, tough guys, but they didn't have a great abundance of talent," Erhardt said. "Nothing like the next two Super Bowls. They were very coachable, like those people who live in the upper end of the community. Karl Nelson was a better physical player than people gave him credit for. He could handle certain big guys like a Rulon Jones. Jones was a bull.

"To be honest with you, we didn't have any household names. [Lionel] Manuel was a very good possession receiver. Stacy Robinson was sort of a backup type guy that we used in situations. In three or four wides we had [Phil] McConkey. He was in the Naval Reserve and made our team just on sheer guts. He's one of those guys that really could do a lot of average things, but every time you looked up McConkey was making yards. But I always had a great tight end, and Bavaro was one of them."

After their ground game was stuffed on the goal line, the Broncos didn't run again until the 8:50 mark of the fourth quarter—a stretch of 23 straight plays. The result was continuous pressure on Elway, who was sacked three times and flushed repeatedly.

"We had a great, great front seven," Rooney said. "Leonard Marshall didn't always have great years, but '86 was one of them. Marshall had to be prodded some, and our defensive line coach, Lamar Leachman, did that. George Martin wasn't real physical but was a real good athlete. He was a smaller version of L. C. Greenwood. Tight end in college [Oregon]. Parcells used to say the ball comes to him. One of those high-IQ guys. And, for a nose tackle, Jim Burt was a pretty damn good inside pass rusher."

The Giants released Burt in July 1989, and three months later he visited the San Francisco 49ers, for which he would play through 1991. As Burt watched film with the 49ers coaches, he would tell them how he'd counteract a certain blocking combination and the coaches would tell him that was impossible. "He was the best at reading blocking schemes as a nose tackle I ever had," Belichick said. "He was 6-foot, 255, small for a nose tackle. Real boxy kind of guy. Benched

the room. Probably 450, squatted maybe 760. Great technician with his hands. He was really outstanding."

New York's secondary, with Welch replacing injured Terry Kinard at free safety, wasn't great, but with a great pass rush (59 sacks), it didn't have to be. "Elvis Patterson was a smaller, stockier corner who had much better cover ability than people have given him credit for," said Rooney. "He was a street-fighter playing corner. Perry Williams was a taller guy with long arms who could run like hell. Kenny Hill was an Ivy League guy who kind of ran the whole thing, like Mike Wagner in Pittsburgh. Hill wasn't real fast, but Welch had really good speed. So there were three guys that could really run."

Elway would pass for 304 yards, including a 54-yard bullet touchdown pass to Johnson in the final 3 minutes that carried 48 yards with almost no arc, but the game was over by then.

Although Reeves, the master of the trick play, played this Super Bowl fairly close to the vest, Parcells dusted off a flea-flicker late in the fourth quarter. Morris pitched the ball back to Simms, who took advantage of free safety Steve Foley being out of position to find McConkey for 44 yards to the 1. On the next play Morris scored standing up and the rout was on.

Simms' 6-yard touchdown pass early in the fourth quarter actually was a perfect throw to Bavaro that ricocheted off his hands to a diving McConkey. "I hit him between the eyes, where I was supposed to throw it," said Simms. "If I throw that ball to Bavaro 1,000 times, he catches 999 balls."

On the Giants' next possession, Simms ran 22 yards on a bootleg to the Denver 2, and then Ottis Anderson dived across for the final touchdown. "They weren't expecting that," Erhardt said. "That was a little trick play. I set that up during the week. Phil hadn't bootlegged all year."

The game saw just one turnover, an interception by Patterson off a deflected pass by Elway. The underdog Broncos would have needed several takeaways and near-perfection across the board to beat a foe as powerful as the Giants and a quarterback who played as flawlessly as Simms.

"What's the secret to a quarterback playing well in the Super Bowl?" Simms said. "Play a defense that's not great. The Denver Broncos were a good team, but not a great one."

XXII

WASHINGTON REDSKINS 42, DENVER BRONCOS 10

January 31, 1988
Jack Murphy Stadium, San Diego, California

When the teams changed sides for the start of the second quarter of Super Bowl XXII, Doug Williams had a lot more on his mind than the social significance of being the first black starting quarterback in Super Bowl history.

For one, his mouth still ached from three hours of root canal work done on an abscessed molar the day before the game. For another, he had just limped off the field with a hyperextension of his surgically repaired left knee and was being taped and outfitted with a brace. His Washington Redskins trailed the Denver Broncos, 10–0, a substantial hole given the fact that no team in the first 21 Super Bowls had come back to win from a deficit of seven or more points. The Redskins were playing terrible football—dropping passes, fumbling the ball, and blowing assignments.

"I missed just two plays and was ready to go at the beginning of the second quarter," Williams said years later. "Pain? At that time it was no longer important. What I remember most in that whole game was what Joe Gibbs said just before we went back out for the second quarter: 'Just get in there; we're going to get this sucker running.'"

For the first 15 minutes of Super Bowl XXII, the Redskins could do nothing right. For the next 15 minutes at Jack Murphy Stadium, they could do nothing wrong.

Williams threw 11 passes in the second quarter and completed 9 for 228 yards and four touchdowns. Wide receiver Ricky Sanders caught 5 for 168 yards and 2 scores, and wide receiver Gary Clark caught a 27-yard pass for another score. Running back Timmy Smith carried 5 times for 122 yards and one touchdown. Possessing the ball for just 5 minutes and 47 seconds, the Redskins gained 356 yards in 19 plays, or 18.7 yards per snap. The Broncos turned the ball over twice and failed to score.

They could have played a 60-minute second half and it wouldn't have made any difference.

Attendance: 73,302
Conditions: 61 degrees, mostly cloudy, wind SW at 5 mph
Time of kickoff: 3:20 p.m. (PST)
Length of game: 3 hours, 40 minutes
Referee: Bob McElwee

MVP: Doug Williams, QB, Redskins

Twenty-five points in arrears after another Redskin touchdown late in the second quarter made it 35–10, the Broncos were finished physically, emotionally and every other way imaginable. The second half was as uneventful as the first half was historic. It ended 42–10, a fourth straight rout for the NFC and Denver's third one-sided Super Bowl defeat.

Shortly after Williams was named the game's MVP, he received a hug from his old Grambling State coach, Eddie Robinson. "He said that the proudest moment he ever had in football was to be at that game and watch me perform and be the Super Bowl MVP," Williams said. "Here's a guy who coached over 50 years, so what he said was really big time as far as I was concerned."

Across America, Williams was cheered—well, maybe not in Colorado, where the orange-clad zealots died a thousand deaths for the second Super Sunday in a row. Members of the Ku Klux Klan also couldn't have been thrilled by Williams' record shattering performance. Through a week of repetitious and often condescending questions, however, Williams had stood strong. He had overcome.

"Did I change history?" he said. "Well, I'm not going to the Hall of Fame. I like to think that I was part of history. Maybe I changed the way people looked at things. Maybe I changed things for the black quarterbacks who followed me.

"From an economic standpoint, not a lot happened from that Super Bowl," added Williams, who later served as head coach at his alma mater

	1	2	3	4	Final
Washington Redskins	0	35	0	7	42
Denver Broncos	10	0	0	0	10

SCORING SUMMARY

1st Quarter
DEN Nattiel, 56-yd. pass from Elway (Karlis kick)
DEN Karlis, 24-yd. FG
2nd Quarter
WAS Sanders, 80-yd. pass from Williams (Haji-Sheikh kick)
WAS G. Clark, 27-yd. pass from Williams (Haji-Sheikh kick)
WAS T. Smith, 58-yd. run (Haji-Sheikh kick)
WAS Sanders, 50-yd. pass from Williams (Haji-Sheikh kick)
WAS Didier, 8-yd. pass from Williams (Haji-Sheikh kick)
4th Quarter
WAS T. Smith, 4-yd. run (Haji-Sheikh kick)

and as an executive in the Tampa Bay Buccaneers personnel department. "I didn't get any Samsung commercials. You see Hall of Fame guys like Dan Marino, Jim Kelly, Dan Fouts, guys who got commercials and good pay, but they never won a Super Bowl. That's something I can always be proud of."

No one expected this kind of game. After all, the Broncos had John Elway, the NFL MVP in 1987. Elway's presence alone helped make the Broncos a 3½-point favorite. His counterpart, Williams, had started only two games during the regular season before getting the nod over Jay Schroeder heading into the playoffs. Furthermore, the Redskins no longer appeared capable of dominating a game on the ground, with aging running back George Rogers (who retired after this Super Bowl), and their defense ranked a lowly 20th in yards allowed.

"I don't think anybody thought there was that big of a difference between the two teams," Redskins general manager Bobby Beathard said years later. "They had John Elway. But everything we did went right. The difference in that game was Doug. I know Timmy ran for all that and probably the difference was we were able to run like that, but it couldn't have happened without Doug."

Denver kicked off, wide receiver Gary Clark dropped a third-and-6 pass, and Washington punted. On the Broncos' first play, Pro Bowl cornerback Barry Wilburn was caught napping

in zone coverage and Elway heaved the ball deep over his head to rookie Ricky Nattiel for a 56-yard touchdown. Clark, an all-pro selection with a 19-yard average, dropped another third-down pass, and the Redskins punted for a second time. Bronco Mark Jackson got a step on Darrell Green coming across the middle and turned a shallow crossing route into a 32-yard gain. On the next play, the Broncos struck on one of their renowned gadget plays when running back Steve Sewell threw back to Elway for 23 yards to the Washington 13. "They made a heck of a play to stop that from being a touchdown," Denver coach Dan Reeves said.

On third and 3 from the 6, Reeves called Elway's number on a quarterback draw. The year before, Elway ran one in from the 11 against the Redskins on the same play. It had been a tremendously successful play for the Broncos over the years. "They send out four wide receivers," recalled Larry Peccatiello, the Redskins' defensive coordinator who worked from the coaches' booth and was connected via headset with assistant head coach Richie Petitbon on the sidelines. "Generally, we match up with four corners. I told Richie, 'They're going four, let's stay base. Quarterback draw.'"

Washington's two defensive tackles, Dave Butz and Darryl Grant, ran a tackle-tackle stunt inside with Butz coming off first. Elway took the snap from shotgun formation, paused for a count, and then found Grant dead in his path as he bolted for the middle. When Elway tried to change direction, the 300-pound Butz was there to wrap him up for a 1-yard loss. Rich Karlis kicked a 24-yard field goal, but for the Redskins, the red-zone stop couldn't have been more resuscitating. "They could have checked out of it but they didn't," Peccatiello said. "Elway probably had a lot of confidence and figured he could do it anyhow. That and the next kickoff were the two most significant plays of the game."

Washington's return man, Sanders, was up-ended at the 16 by linebacker Bruce Klostermann and fumbled on a shot from Ken Bell as he hit the ground. "Up in the press box, it was obvious that Denver recovered," Peccatiello said. "I was just s---ting. But a scrum evolved. The officials are picking guys off the ball. We took the ball away somehow. I think Ravin Caldwell went in there and stole the ball out of somebody's arms. If they get that play, I think we lose the game."

Replays shed little light on what happened at the bottom of that pile. "I was in there on that," Broncos rookie cornerback Tyrone Braxton said. "Bruce Plummer, my roommate, had it and, boom, during the fight underneath some big guy took it from him. They're pulling guys off and you can't see what's going on. That saved them." Caldwell, a 6-foot-3, 229-pound linebacker, was credited with the recovery at the 16. Plummer, a cornerback, was 6-foot-1, 197. "We actually came out with the ball," said Reeves, "yet, they replayed it and ended up giving them the ball. The official who came over couldn't tell me why they overturned it. . . . It didn't make any sense."

Washington gained a measure of field position on Williams' 40-yard pass to Art Monk, but ended up having to punt again. The Broncos got to the Washington 30 on an 18-yard shovel pass to Sewell, but they were taken out of field-goal range when blitzing safety Alvin Walton sacked Elway for minus-18 to force a punt.

Nevertheless, the Redskins continued to flounder. A 25-yard burst by Smith was brought back by a holding penalty on tight end Don Warren. A few plays later, Williams dropped back on the soft turf and slipped; his right leg slid underneath him, and his left knee twisted as he hit the deck. (By then, some Redskins had changed to longer cleats, but to his good fortune Williams wasn't one of them and perhaps as a result escaped more serious injury.) Although Williams was already down on the ground, a half second later he was drilled by defensive end Rulon Jones.

Even before Jones made contact, Williams had flung the ball down amid the frustration of being sacked and injured. "There was a fumble," Reeves said. "They ruled that wasn't a fumble. We hit him pretty good on that play but we didn't get that." In his two

WASHINGTON REDSKINS (NFC, 11–4)	Offense	DENVER BRONCOS (AFC, 10–4–1)	
84 Gary Clark* (5-9, 173)	WR	82 Mark Jackson (5-11, 183)	
66 Joe Jacoby (6-7, 305)	LT	70 Dave Studdard (6-4, 260)	
63 Raleigh McKenzie (6-2, 262)	LG	54 Keith Bishop* (6-3, 265)	
53 Jeff Bostic (6-2, 260)	C	62 Mike Freeman (6-3, 256)	
69 R. C. Thielemann (6-4, 262)	RG	79 Stefan Humphries (6-3, 263)	
73 Mark May (6-6, 295)	RT	76 Ken Lanier (6-3, 269)	
86 Clint Didier (6-5, 240)	TE	88 Clarence Kay (6-2, 237)	
85 Don Warren (6-4, 242)	TE I WR	84 Ricky Nattiel (5-9, 180)	
17 Doug Williams (6-4, 220)	QB	7 John Elway* (6-3, 210)	
36 Timmy Smith (5-11, 216)	RB	23 Sammy Winder (5-11, 203)	
83 Ricky Sanders (5-11, 180)	WR I RB	33 Gene Lang (5-10, 196)	
	Defense		
71 Charles Mann* (6-6, 270)	LE	61 Andre Townsend (6-3, 265)	
65 Dave Butz (6-7, 295)	LT I NT	71 Greg Kragen (6-3, 245)	
77 Darryl Grant (6-1, 275)	RT I RE	75 Rulon Jones (6-6, 260)	
72 Dexter Manley (6-3, 257)	RE I LOLB	73 Simon Fletcher (6-5, 240)	
55 Mel Kaufman (6-2, 218)	LLB I LILB	77 Karl Mecklenburg* (6-3, 240)	
52 Neal Olkewicz (6-0, 233)	MLB I RILB	98 Ricky Hunley (6-2, 238)	
51 Monte Coleman (6-2, 230)	RLB I ROLB	50 Jim Ryan (6-1, 218)	
28 Darrell Green* (5-8, 170)	LCB	36 Mark Haynes (5-11, 195)	
45 Barry Wilburn (6-3, 186)	RCB	45 Steve Wilson (5-10, 195)	
40 Alvin Walton (6-0, 180)	SS	49 Dennis Smith (6-3, 200)	
23 Todd Bowles (6-2, 203)	FS	22 Tony Lilly (6-0, 199)	

* Pro Bowl selection

SUBSTITUTIONS

Washington
Offense: WR - 81 Art Monk, 80 Eric Yarber; TE - 82 Anthony Jones, 87 Terry Orr; G - 68 Russ Grimm, 61 Rick Kehr; QB - 10 Jay Schroeder; RB - 29 Reggie Branch, 24 Kelvin Bryant, 35 Keith Griffin, 38 George Rogers. *Defense:* DE - 64 Steve Hamilton, 74 Markus Koch; DT - 78 Dean Hamel; LB - 50 Ravin Caldwell, 54 Kurt Gouveia, 57 Rich Milot; CB - 34 Brian Davis, 31 Clarence Vaughn, 46 Dennis Woodberry; S - 32 Vernon Dean. *Specialists:* K - 6 Ali Haji-Sheikh; P - 12 Steve Cox.

Denver
Offense: WR - 82 Vance Johnson, 81 Steve Watson; TE - 46 Bobby Micho, 89 Orson Mobley; T - 72 Keith Kartz; QB - 8 Gary Kubiak; RB - 35 Ken Bell, 24 Tony Boddie, 30 Steve Sewell. *Defense:* DE - 65 Walter Bowyer, 90 Freddie Gilbert; LB - 56 Michael Brooks, 55 Rick Dennison, 97 Bruce Klostermann, 59 Tim Lucas; CB - 27 Kevin Clark, 28 Jeremiah Castille, 38 Bruce Plummer; S - 34 Tyrone Braxton, 48 Randy Robbins. *Specialists:* K - 3 Rich Karlis; P - 2 Mike Horan. *DNP:* 68 Larry Lee (G).

Washington
Head Coach: Joe Gibbs. *Offense:* Joe Bugel (assistant head coach, offensive line), Dan Henning (offensive assistant, receivers), Charley Taylor (wide receivers), Rennie Simmons (tight ends), Jerry Rhome (quarterbacks), Don Breaux (running backs). *Defense:* Richie Petitbon (assistant head coach), Larry Peccatiello (coordinator), LaVern Torgeson (defensive line), Emmitt Thomas (defensive assistant). *Special Teams:* Chuck Banker. *Strength:* Dan Riley, Joe Diange. *Administrative Assistant:* Bill Hickman.

Denver
Head Coach: Dan Reeves. *Offense:* Mike Shanahan (coordinator, quarterbacks), Chan Gailey (wide receivers, tight ends), Alex Gibbs (offensive line, running game), Nick Nicolau (running backs, play-action passing game). *Defense:* Joe Collier (assistant head coach), Stan Jones (defensive line), Myrel Moore (linebackers), Charlie West (defensive backs), Rubin Carter (assistant defensive line). *Special Teams:* Mike Nolan. *Strength:* Al Miller. *Special Assistant:* Marvin Bass.

naps, backup quarterback Jay Schroeder was sacked nd had a pass dropped by third-down back Kelvin Bryant. An exchange of punts later, Williams showed omething of the limp that would be noticeable for the est of the game as the Redskins opened the second quarter from their 20.

On the left side of the Denver defense, veteran ornerback Mark Haynes was playing bump-and-un coverage against Sanders. One play called for anders to run a 5-yard hitch, but with Haynes at he line Sanders converted the route to a fade. On quick count, Haynes gave up a too-easy release to he outside, and Sanders caught Williams' pass in tride at the Washington 48. Then Sanders easily utran the overmatched former Giant to the end one for an 80-yard touchdown.

A Denver punt after a three-and-out gave Washington the ball back just over a minute ater. Expecting a run on third and 1, the Broncos litzed. Instead of throwing to the tailback in the lat, Williams delayed to give Clark time to beat cornerback Steve Wilson on a corner route, and he connected for a 27-yard touchdown.

"That was a great blitz," said Dan Henning, who had been rehired by Gibbs as an offensive assistant in 1987 after four seasons as head coach in Atlanta. "I asked Doug later on about that. He said, 'I knew Gary was going to come open so I was going to wait.' He was big, strong, and capable of doing those types of things."

The Broncos kept moving the ball, gaining 26 on a shovel pass to running back Sammy Winder and 21 on a scramble by Elway. Then left tackle Dave Studdard, a starter since 1979, blew out his ACL on a pass dropped by Sewell. With free agent Keith Kartz replacing Studdard, Reeves generally deemed it necessary to keep a back in on that side for pass protection, thus limiting his offensive options. Karlis was wide left on a field-goal attempt from 43 yards, and the Redskins turned around to score two plays later on Smith's 58-yard run.

On this touchdown, the Broncos lined up in a version of the Bears' 46 defense, with defenders covering both guards and the center, and they were caught slanting the wrong way. Clint Didier blocked strong safety Dennis Smith, pulling guard Raleigh McKenzie blocked inside linebacker Ricky Hunley, and pulling tackle Joe Jacoby blocked outside linebacker Jim Ryan, all on the play side. Meanwhile, Timmy Smith shot through the hole and outran free safety Tony Lilly to the end zone.

The previous April, Beathard had drafted Timmy Smith in the fifth round from Texas Tech, where he had performed well as a sophomore, but was limited to five games as a junior due to a knee injury and then missed all but one game in 1986 with a broken ankle. Smith could run hard and had good speed. "Early that year we had a big argument about playing him," Beathard said. "Joe and his running backs coach, Don Breaux, wouldn't play him. He wasn't the easiest guy to coach, but he was talented and tough." Smith's first real chance came in the divisional playoffs in Chicago, when his 16 carries for 66 yards helped the Redskins overcome a 14–0 deficit to win, 21–17. He followed that up a week later with 13 carries for 72 yards in a 17–10 victory over Minnesota.

Before the team left for San Diego, Gibbs informed Williams that Smith would be making his first start, hopeful he would provide more of an outside threat than Rogers, but he never announced it. In the Super Bowl, Smith rushed for 204 yards on 22 carries, most coming on the counter trey, the Redskins' signature running play that featured the guard and tackle pulling to clear way for the running back.

Denver had suffered a major casualty in its first playoff victory (34–10 over Houston) when free safety Mike Harden, the team's best defensive back, broke his arm. His replacement was Lilly, a third-round pick in 1984 who lacked speed, size, and instinct.

On their next possession following their third touchdown of the second quarter, the Redskins called the same play that Timmy Smith had just carried to the house, only this time it was a play-action pass. Williams carried out his fake beautifully, Lilly took the bait, and Sanders was wide open behind him in the middle of the field for a 50-yard score.

"In all the time I've ever been around football, I've never seen a more perfect quarter," Henning said. "It was staggering. But if the safety makes the play on a few of those, maybe the game doesn't get out of hand." In Lilly's defense, he did suffer a badly bruised hip in the second quarter and was on crutches leaving the locker room after the game.

A few plays later, Elway was intercepted by the leaping Wilburn on a long ball to Nattiel. Running left this time, Timmy Smith followed guard R. C. Thielemann's trap block on inside linebacker Karl Mecklenburg for 43 yards on another counter trey. Once again, Hunley was buried at the point of attack. When Dennis Smith missed a tackle in the flat, Sanders broke a short pass into a gain of 21. Finally, Williams lobbed an 8-yard touchdown pass to Didier against loose coverage by Braxton and Wilson. The Broncos' quarter from hell ended when Elway completed three passes for 40 yards followed by a poor throw that was picked off by backup cornerback Brian Davis with seven seconds left.

From 1969 to 1988, Joe Collier coordinated the defenses in Denver. In an era of static 3-4 defenses and base 4-3s, Collier's scheme traditionally was as complex as it was multidimensional. The opposing offensive staff had to work overtime before playing the Broncos. "That's kind of the way we compensated for some weaknesses," said Collier. Their defense, which had been torn apart by the Giants in Super Bowl XXI, finished ninth that season in yards

TEAM STATISTICS

WASHINGTON		DENVER
25	Total First Downs	18
13	Rushing	6
11	Passing	10
1	Penalty	2
602	Total Net Yardage	327
72	Total Offensive Plays	61
8.4	Avg. Gain per Offensive Play	5.4
40	Rushes	17
280	Yards Gained Rushing (Net)	97
7.0	Average Yards per Rush	5.7
30	Passes Attempted	39
18	Passes Completed	15
1	Passes Intercepted	3
2	Tackled Attempting to Pass	5
18	Yards Lost Attempting to Pass	50
322	Yards Gained Passing (Net)	230
9/15	Third-Down Efficiency	2/12
0/0	Fourth-Down Efficiency	0/0
4	Punts	7
37.5	Average Distance	36.1
1	Punt Returns	2
0	Punt Return Yardage	18
3	Kickoff Returns	5
46	Kickoff Return Yardage	88
11	Interception Return Yardage	0
1	Fumbles	0
1	Own Fumbles Recovered	0
0	Opponent Fumbles Recovered	0
6	Penalties	5
65	Yards Penalized	26
6	Touchdowns	1
2	Rushing	0
4	Passing	1
0	Returns	0
6	Extra Points Made	1
0	Field Goals Made	1
1	Field Goals Attempted	2
0	Safeties	0
42	Total Points Scored	10
33:15	Time of Possession	24:45

allowed. The Broncos did rank 10th in 1987 but Collier said, "We weren't very strong that year. Ou defense was not as good as our offense."

Years later, Collier still searched for answer to why this sunny day in San Diego turned out t be the worst game of his career. "It was my 15 min utes of fame—the wrong way," he said. Two factor

WASHINGTON

Passing	CP/ATT	YDS	TD	INT	RAT
Williams	18/29	340	4	1	127.9
Schroeder	0/1	0	0	0	39.6

Rushing	ATT	YDS	AVG	TD	LG
Smith	22	204	9.3	2	58t
Bryant	8	38	4.8	0	15
Clark	1	25	25.0	0	25
Rogers	5	17	3.4	0	5
Griffin	1	2	2.0	0	2
Williams	2	-2	-1.0	0	1
Sanders	1	-4	-4.0	0	-4

Receiving	NO	YDS	AVG	TD	LG
Sanders	9	193	21.4	2	80t
Clark	3	55	18.3	1	27t
Warren	2	15	7.5	0	9
Monk	1	40	40.0	0	40
Bryant	1	20	20.0	0	20
Smith	1	9	9.0	0	9
Didier	1	8	8.0	1	8t

Interceptions	NO	YDS	LG	TD
Wilburn	2	11	11	0
Davis	1	0	0	0

Punting	NO	AVG	LG	BLK
Cox	4	37.5	42	0

Punt Ret.	NO/FC	YDS	LG	TD
Green	1/1	0	0	0
Yarber	0/1	0	--	0

Kickoff Ret.	NO	YDS	LG	TD
Sanders	3	46	16	0

Defense	SOLO	AST	TOT	SK
Bowles	5	0	5	0
Green	1	0	1	0
Vaughn	1	0	1	0
Davis	1	0	1	0
Walton	7	0	7	2
Wilburn	3	0	3	0
Coleman	0	0	0	0.5
Olkewicz	1	0	1	0
Kaufman	2	0	2	0
Butz	2	0	2	0
Mann	3	0	3	1
Manley	4	0	4	1.5
Grant	2	0	2	0
TOTAL	32	0	32	5

DENVER

Passing	CP/ATT	YDS	TD	INT	RAT
Elway	14/38	257	1	3	36.8
Sewell	1/1	23	0	0	118.8

Rushing	ATT	YDS	AVG	TD	LG
Lang	5	38	7.6	0	13
Elway	3	32	10.7	0	21
Winder	8	30	3.8	0	13
Sewell	1	-3	-3.0	0	-3

Receiving	NO	YDS	AVG	TD	LG
M. Jackson	4	76	19.0	0	32
Sewell	4	41	10.3	0	18
Nattiel	2	69	34.5	1	56t
Kay	2	38	19.0	0	27
Winder	1	26	26.0	0	26
Elway	1	23	23.0	0	23
Lang	1	7	7.0	0	7

Interceptions	NO	YDS	LG	TD
Castille	1	0	0	0

Punting	NO	AVG	LG	BLK
Horan	7	36.1	43	0

Punt Ret.	NO/FC	YDS	LG	TD
Clark	2/0	18	9	0

Kickoff Ret.	NO	YDS	LG	TD
Bell	5	88	21	0

Defense	SOLO	AST	TOT	SK
D. Smith	7	2	9	0
Mecklenburg	7	0	7	1
Fletcher	6	0	6	0
Gilbert	4	1	5	0
R. Jones	4	0	4	1
Lilly	4	0	4	0
Wilson	4	0	4	0
Haynes	3	0	3	0
Ryan	3	0	3	0
Townsend	3	0	3	0
Kragen	2	0	2	0
Castille	1	0	1	0
Dennison	1	0	1	0
Hunley	1	0	1	0
Robbins	1	0	1	0
TOTAL	51	3	54	2

contributed to this. One, the extra week gave Gibbs and his expert staff the time it needed to prepare. "I talked to Joe Bugel afterward," said Collier, referring to the Redskins' esteemed offensive line coach. "They just put up every defensive front and changes that we used and practiced their ass off against it. Consequently, when the game came up, nothing bothered them." Two, the Redskins' one-back, double–tight end offense forced the Broncos to play more straight-up defense. By doing so, their undersized front seven was more susceptible to the Redskins' physical offensive line known as "the Hogs."

"I think the two weeks were a disadvantage for them," agreed Henning. "We spent long hours saying, 'How can we set up so that we can eliminate confusion that this guy can cause with his defense?' Some of the formations and movements that we used were directly designed for that purpose. We also felt we were better than he was. We had a remarkable week of practice in San Diego.

"We were against an outstanding defensive coach with a group of feisty but little defensive people. As it turned out, I think Joe Collier tried to go overboard to take certain things away and, in turn, left other things open."

Petitbon and Peccatiello didn't do anything new on defense. They played man coverage against the "Three Amigos": Nattiel, the speedster; Jackson, a possession receiver; and Vance Johnson, who tried to play despite a severe groin pull and was shut out. Elway groused that his wide receivers were slow getting off jams in the bump zone. The Redskins almost always rushed five. The most effective blitzer probably was Walton, a ferocious hitter. "We had down who we felt was going to be the blitzer and they changed that up and came with somebody else," said Reeves. "They did a good job disguising their blitzes. You can't do that in a week."

It wasn't just the extra man that led to five sacks and constant pressure on Elway. The front four of Charles Mann, Butz, Grant, and Dexter Manley was better than the unit that put little heat on Jim Plunkett in Super Bowl XVIII. "That was a great front," Peccatiello said. "Butz and Grant really could push the pocket. We had two guys on the outside that had great athletic talent and speed and were tough guys. They gave everybody a bad matchup." Nick

Nicolau, who coached Denver's running backs, sa[id] the loss of center Billy Bryan, a 10-year starter wh[o] suffered a season-ending knee injury during a strik[e] replacement game, deprived the unit of its leader.

In the second half, Williams dropped back o[n] just nine plays while handing the ball off 25 time[s.] The Broncos were so dispirited on defense that the[y] couldn't even prevent Washington from killing th[e] final 9:11 on the clock even though 13 of the 14 play[s] in the 61-yard drive were runs. The only second half score was a 4-yard run by Timmy Smith on [a] counter trey that was set up by his 32-yard run o[n] the same type of play.

According to Gibbs, the Redskins "picked th[is] day to have our very best game of the season. Th[e] second quarter was the best I ever saw a Redski[n] team play. I was absolutely thrilled." The MVP awar[d] went to Williams but could just have easily gone t[o] Smith. "The crazy thing about that game, both th[e] stars never played [that well] again," Nicolau sai[d.] "But you just have to be good on that day."

Timmy Smith had scored 5 on the 50-questio[n] Wonderlic Personnel Test, tying for the lowes[t] score among the 50 running backs at the combin[e] in 1987. "Right after [the Super Bowl] his agen[t,] Steve Endicott, wanted Smith to be paid like th[e] top back in the league," Beathard said. "He wen[t] straight downhill after that game. We got all sort[s] of reports about cocaine and not working out. W[e] couldn't agree on a contract because nothing in th[e] world would satisfy him. He thought he had arrived[.] He told *Sports Illustrated* that I blackballed him[.] Blackball? Hell, I was the guy who was pulling fo[r] him the whole time. He hurt himself." Playing in 1[2] games (eight starts) in 1988, Smith gained 470 yard[s] and averaged only 3.0 per carry. His career ende[d] with one last game for the Dallas Cowboys in 1990[.] In 2006, he was sentenced to two and a half year[s] in federal prison for distribution of cocaine an[d] ordered to pay $88,000 in back child support.

Williams battled bad knees to start 10 game[s] for a Washington team that finished 7–9 in 1988[.] He missed four games because of an emergenc[y] appendectomy. His passer rating was 77.4. In 198[9] he started only two games behind Mark Rypien and then retired with a career passer rating of 69.4[.] "Hell, when people were open, there wasn't an[y] better passer that ever lived than Doug Williams, as far as being accurate and having leverage to throw the deep ball," Henning said.

Gibbs had served as the offensive coordinator in 1978 for Tampa Bay, where Williams played his rookie season. It was Gibbs, not Beathard, who was responsible for trading a fifth-round draft choice in August 1986 to obtain him from the Buccaneers. "I don't think Bobby was a big Doug Williams fan," Williams said. "He didn't think I worked hard; that's what he said. I didn't agree with him, but I liked that he was someone who was straightforward and didn't pull any punches."

Today, there is no greater supporter of Williams than the diminutive former general manager. "Thing about Doug, he really brought the team together," said Beathard. "Jay had all this physical talent and had a great year before that, but that kind of went to his head, in our minds. Doug was exactly what the team needed. He was the catalyst. When receivers were in there with Doug, they'd do anything for him. If it hadn't been for Doug we wouldn't have gone to the Super Bowl."

It could be argued that during his long career with the Redskins, Joe Gibbs had several teams better than the 1987 Redskins. But, on January 31, 1988, this squad played a single quarter better than any team ever did in NFL championship game history.

Top Ten Unexpected Heroes

1. **Timmy Smith, RB, Redskins, XXII:** Joe Gibbs played the right hunch, giving Smith his first start over the aging George Rogers. He broke loose for a Super Bowl–record 204 yards.

2. **Kurt Warner, QB, Rams, XXXIV:** Warner was a 28-year-old nobody when an injury to Trent Green during the 1999 exhibition season landed Warner the starting job. Playing for a base salary of $254,000, he was the MVP of the regular season and the Super Bowl.

3. **Jeff Hostetler, QB, Giants, XXV:** When Phil Simms went down with a season-ending foot injury in Week 14, the Giants turned to Hostetler. "He was an example of preparation and patience, of being ready when your number's called," said Bill Belichick, then the Giants' defensive coordinator.

4. **Terry Bradshaw, QB, Steelers, IX:** It was Bradshaw's fifth season in the league, and for the first six games of 1974, he was backing up Joe Gilliam. But when Chuck Noll turned to Bradshaw in Week 7, a Hall of Fame career kicked into gear.

5. **Max McGee, WR, Packers, I:** In January 1967, McGee was two years removed from his last good season and playing out the string of a fine career. Then Boyd Dowler got hurt and "Maxie the Taxi" entered football lore.

6. **Corey Webster, CB, Giants, XLII:** Benched three weeks into the season and inactive for two more games, Webster got his chance after injuries struck the Giants. When the playoffs began, he suddenly played like a shut-down corner.

7. **Ottis Anderson, RB, Giants, XXV:** Twice a Pro Bowl pick in St. Louis, Anderson was on the backside of his career and losing playing time until rookie Rodney Hampton broke his leg in the playoff opener. Anderson was named Super Bowl MVP.

8. **Vince Ferragamo, QB, Rams, XIV:** The Super Bowl was only the eighth start of Ferragamo's erratic career. After starter Pat Haden went down, Ferragamo was the Rams' third option. He then directed two playoff victories and nearly notched a third against the vaunted Steelers.

9. **Bruce Wilkerson, LT, Packers, XXXI:** Wilkerson was handed the starting job in Week 16 when top pick John Michels flopped. Protecting Brett Favre's blindside, he allowed only one sack in his four starts.

10. **Larry Brown, CB, Cowboys, XXX:** A backup in his fifth season, Brown became the starter when injuries and a suspension gave him an opening. After intercepting two passes and being named MVP, Brown signed a five-year, $12.5 million deal with the Raiders.

XXIII

SAN FRANCISCO 49ERS 20, CINCINNATI BENGALS 16

January 22, 1989
Joe Robbie Stadium, Miami, Florida

Joe Montana threw the winning touchdown pass to John Taylor with 34 seconds remaining. Jerry Rice was the MVP. Roger Craig touched the ball 25 times and gained 172 yards.

Those were the stars in Super Bowl XXIII, a pulsating 20–16 victory for the San Francisco 49ers over the Cincinnati Bengals at Joe Robbie Stadium in Miami, but in many ways the ultimate hero was Bill Walsh. The 49ers had to go 92 yards in the last three minutes to earn their third Super Bowl championship in eight years and their designation as NFL "team of the 1980s." They were able to do that under suffocating pressure largely because Walsh had, over the previous 10 years, prepared them beautifully for this very moment.

The West Coast system that Walsh used to revolutionize the way offenses performed and quarterbacks functioned in pro football got its start when he was coaching quarterbacks and receivers for the Bengals. Greg Cook, the team's brilliant young quarterback, suffered a career-ending shoulder injury before the opener in 1970. Forced to start Virgil Carter, a smart but limited third-year man, Walsh devised concepts so an offense lacking a strong-armed quarterback could move the ball without taking undue risks.

It worked in Cincinnati with Carter and Ken Anderson. When Walsh became coach of the 49ers in 1979, the offense also succeeded for a time under Steve DeBerg. It wasn't, however, until the athletic, resourceful Montana came of age in his third season (1981) that Walsh's ball-control attack became fully dimensional.

The 49ers defeated the Bengals in Super Bowl XVI, but it was mostly a matter of hanging on at the end, unlike Super Bowl XIX, in which they crushed Miami with an exquisite performance almost from start to finish. This Super Bowl was different as well. The 49ers' backs were against the wall most of the

Attendance: 75,129
Conditions: 76 degrees, partly cloudy, winds SW 10–25
Time of kickoff: 5:18 p.m. (EST)
Length of game: 3 hours, 24 minutes
Referee: Jerry Seeman

MVP: Jerry Rice, WR, 49ers

season. After being penalized for an illegal block, the 49ers were down by 3 points when they took over at their 8 with 3:10 remaining. A 7-point favorite, they were in serious danger of losing.

"The last drive was a culmination of many years of establishing not only our system of football but a style that emphasized precision and skill to reduce the risk factor," Walsh said years later. "The bottom line was: Could we execute a series of plays almost flawlessly? If any one play had been disastrous, it would have cost us the game and the championship. . . . In that kind of situation, with the pressure that's on the team, you want to have familiar plays that men are confident they can execute, rather than trying high-risk plays and depending on great individual effort."

Across the field stood Dick LeBeau, Cincinnati's fifth-year defensive coordinator, who was finishing his 30th season as an NFL player and coach. He noted that the Bengals had stopped the 49ers on 9 of 12 third-down situations. "I thought this was going to be pretty much a third-down situation [on every down] because they had to get the ball upfield," said LeBeau. "Because our third-down defense had held up so well, I thought we had a real good chance of winning it. But you knew with Montana on the other side there were no guarantees."

This wasn't the first time these 49ers had faced such a desperate situation. In the NFC Championship Game leading to their first Super Bowl, the 49ers started from their 11 with 4:54 left, trailing the Dallas Cowboys, 27–21. On the 13th play, Dwight

	1	2	3	4	Final
Cincinnati Bengals	0	3	10	3	16
San Francisco 49ers	3	0	3	14	20

SCORING SUMMARY

1st Quarter
SF   Cofer, 41-yd. FG
2nd Quarter
CIN   Breech, 34-yd. FG
3rd Quarter
Cin   Breech, 43-yd. FG
SF   Cofer, 32-yd. FG
CIN   Jennings, 93-yd. kickoff return (Breech kick)
4th Quarter
SF   Rice, 14-yd. pass from Montana (Cofer kick)
CIN   Breech, 40-yd. FG
SF   Taylor, 10-yd. pass from Montana (Cofer kick)

Clark made "the Catch" for a 6-yard touchdown and one of the most dramatic victories in playoff history. "This reminded me of that drive," said Clark, a year into his retirement. He happened to be standing on the sideline only a few feet from where Taylor snared the 10-yard touchdown. "Not much time, coming from behind. It was a nerve-wracking drive, but I knew Joe was going to get it done."

At first, Montana and Walsh surprised the Bengals by throwing into the middle of the field. Montana found Craig inside for 8 yards and tight end John Frank inside for 7. With the clock running, Montana fired a 7-yard out to Rice in front of soft coverage by cornerback Lewis Billups. Craig gained 1 on a run, setting up third and 2 after the two-minute warning. Craig burst off tackle for 4 and the 49ers called their first timeout.

"I had to call it because Joe was about to faint," Walsh said. "He was so excited, and his adrenaline was pumping so hard, he was hyperventilating." Montana hadn't eaten enough before the game and became dizzy as he screamed out plays at the line over the roaring crowd.

The 49ers moved to the Bengals' 35 after Rice made a 17-yard catch in front of cornerback Eric Thomas, and Craig caught a check-down for 13. After the only incompletion of the drive, Walsh went for broke on second and 10. "There was one bad call I made that almost cost us," he said. "'Fake

Screen, Left Halfback, Check Middle.' I told the coaches on the phone to hold your left one because this is either going to go all the way or we could get in trouble." He noted that two problems arose: first, Craig's release was ruined because he was knocked off balance by the defensive end. At the same instant, center Randy Cross was knocked across the line by the Cincinnati nose tackle and couldn't get back. When the ball was finally thrown to Craig for 5 yards, the head linesman spotted that Cross was still downfield. Walsh had no problem accepting the penalty for ineligible receiver downfield.

The drive, which actually was 102 yards long, resumed with second and 20. "Early in the game Jerry Rice had said, 'I can run the deep over because they're playing me outside. I can get in front of the safeties,'" Walsh said. "I told him, 'We'll do that.' That was the time to call it." Montana took a five-step drop and delivered the ball to Rice a split-second before nose tackle David Grant knocked Montana down.

The Bengals were in a coverage called "One Lurk" that was designed to prevent crossing routes. Billups was locked on Rice in man coverage, with one safety high and the other safety near the line of scrimmage. Rice caught the ball 12 yards downfield, was able to elude both nickel back Ray Horton, who took an improper angle, and the diving David Fulcher, and broke loose for a 27-yard gain to the Cincinnati 18. "That was the play of the game," Horton said, "because we were in the perfect defense for it. I blew it. I should have had the interception and I ended up missing the tackle."

Calling the next play at the line, Montana had just enough time to hit Craig for 8 before defensive end Jason Buck beat left tackle Bubba Paris around the corner and flattened Montana.

San Francisco called its second timeout. It was second down, the ball was resting at the 10, and 39 seconds remained.

On the sidelines, Walsh told Montana they would go for the end zone twice before attempting the tying field goal. The play they used was called "20 Halfback Curl X-Up," which was designed specifically for the Bengals' coverage. "Inside their 15, they locked their linebackers on the tight end and running backs and had their safeties double-cover the wide receivers in combination with the cornerbacks," Walsh said. "They did that every down, every game. So I knew exactly what they were going to do. The whole idea was Jerry Rice would come in motion past John Taylor. John would start up, bend out and then go back up."

The primary target would be Craig on the same route that he had just run for a gain of 8. When fullback Tom Rathman lined up on the wrong side, Craig switched gears quickly and set up on the other side of the backfield. The linebackers responded to his impromptu route just as scheduled, however, and Rice attracted two defenders on the left outside. Horton suddenly had more area to cover because of the motion and widened somewhat toward Rice, who had 11 catches for 215 yards, and away from Taylor, who had been shut out. Taylor faked outside, then cut hard back to the post. Montana, off a five-step drop, delivered a tight, sure spiral that beat the diving Horton. "Actually, [Horton] didn't miss the ball by more than 3 inches," LeBeau said. "If he's got 3-inch longer arms or Montana leads the receiver 3 more inches inside, it goes to the next down. But he didn't and we didn't, and they won."

Boomer Esiason, the NFL's MVP in 1988, dropped back four times in the closing seconds, but the Bengals flopped before time expired. Bengals coach Sam Wyche, who played and coached under Walsh, walked to midfield and told his mentor, "I'm happy for you like I've never been. Congratulations. You deserve it."

Fighting back tears during post-game interviews, Walsh did everything but announce his retirement. At a joint press conference four days later, owner Eddie DeBartolo introduced defensive coordinator George Seifert as Walsh's successor.

Some hailed this as the most exciting Super Bowl to date, and given the ending and a history of blowouts, it might have been. For almost three

CINCINNATI BENGALS (AFC, 12–4)		SAN FRANCISCO 49ERS (NFC, 10–6)	
	Offense		
85	Tim McGee (5-10, 175)	WR	82	John Taylor* (6-1, 185)
78	Anthony Muñoz* (6-6, 278)	LT	74	Steve Wallace (6-5, 276)
75	Bruce Reimers (6-7, 280)	LG	61	Jesse Sapolu (6-4, 260)
64	Bruce Kozerski (6-4, 275)	C	51	Randy Cross (6-3, 265)
65	Max Montoya* (6-5, 275)	RG	62	Guy McIntyre (6-3, 265)
74	Brian Blados (6-5, 295)	RT	79	Harris Barton (6-4, 280)
82	Rodney Holman* (6-3, 238)	TE	86	John Frank (6-3, 225)
81	Eddie Brown* (6-0, 185)	WR	80	Jerry Rice* (6-2, 200)
7	Boomer Esiason* (6-5, 225)	QB	16	Joe Montana (6-2, 195)
21	James Brooks* (5-10, 182)	RB	33	Roger Craig* (6-0, 224)
30	Ickey Woods (6-2, 234)	RB I FB	44	Tom Rathman (6-1, 232)
	Defense		
70	Jim Skow (6-3, 255)	LE	91	Larry Roberts (6-3, 275)
69	Tim Krumrie* (6-2, 268)	NT	95	Michael Carter* (6-2, 285)
99	Jason Buck (6-5, 265)	RE	75	Kevin Fagan (6-3, 260)
51	Leon White (6-3, 245)	LOLB	94	Charles Haley* (6-5, 230)
91	Carl Zander (6-2, 235)	LILB	55	Jim Fahnhorst (6-4, 230)
58	Joe Kelly (6-2, 231)	RILB	99	Michael Walter (6-3, 238)
57	Reggie Williams (6-1, 232)	ROLB	58	Keena Turner (6-2, 222)
24	Lewis Billups (5-11, 190)	LC	22	Tim McKyer (6-0, 174)
22	Eric Thomas* (5-11, 181)	RC	29	Don Griffin (6-0, 176)
33	David Fulcher* (6-3, 228)	SS	49	Jeff Fuller (6-2, 216)
41	Solomon Wilcots (5-11, 185)	FS	42	Ronnie Lott* (6-0, 200)

* Pro Bowl selection

SUBSTITUTIONS

Cincinnati

Offense: WR - 80 Cris Collinsworth, 89 Ira Hillary, 86 Carl Parker; TE - 87 Jim Riggs; T - 77 Dave Rourke, 60 Dave Smith; QB - 15 Turk Schonert; RB - 36 Stanford Jennings, 23 Marc Logan. **Defense:** DE - 73 Eddie Edwards, 72 Skip McClendon; DT - 98 David Grant; LB - 53 Leo Barker, 55 Ed Brady, 90 Emanuel King; CB - 29 Rickey Dixon, 20 Ray Horton, 25 Daryl Smith; S - 27 Barney Bussey. **Specialists:** K - 3 Jim Breech; P - 11 Lee Johnson. **DNP:** 12 Mike Norseth (QB). **Inactive:** 67 David Douglas (T), 32 Stanley Wilson (RB), 96 Curtis Maxey (DE).

San Francisco

Offense: WR - 83 Terry Greer, 85 Mike Wilson; TE - 89 Ron Heller, 84 Brent Jones; T - 77 Bubba Paris; G - 69 Bruce Collie; C - 60 Chuck Thomas; RB - 35 Del Rodgers, 24 Harry Sydney. **Defense:** DE - 78 Pierce Holt, 67 Pete Kugler, 72 Jeff Stover, 96 Danny Stubbs; LB - 50 Riki Ellison, 57 Sam Kennedy, 53 Bill Romanowski; CB - 26 Darryl Pollard, 21 Eric Wright; S - 38 Greg Cox, 46 Tom Holmoe. **Specialists:** K - 6 Mike Cofer; P - 9 Barry Helton. **DNP:** 8 Steve Young (QB). **Inactive:** 32 Terrence Flagler (RB), 54 Ron Hadley (LB).

quarters, however, there wasn't much to quicken the pulse. In fact, Walsh couldn't bring himself to watch the tape for more than a year because of the 49ers' offensive failings.

At least the 49ers, which were second-ranked in total offense, moved the ball for 453 yards. The Bengals, possessors of the league's top-ranked attack, had to settle for 229. "That was probably the worst game that Esiason and everybody else around him played," offensive coordinator Bruce Coslet said. "Boomer was a gunslinger. We had a good running game, a very, very good line, deep threats at wide receiver, and Rodney Holman at tight end. It was just one of those moments in the passing game where it just doesn't click. Coaches go through that at some point, but we never did. It hit us in the Super Bowl."

At least the Bengals had a marvelous regular season, their 12–4 record representing a quantum leap from 4–11 in strike-shortened 1987. In contrast, the regular season for the 49ers had been one crisis after another. Following back-to-back defeats, they found themselves 6–5 heading into a Monday night game against defending-champion Washington. "I remember there was a sense among us that this might be our last year as coaches in San Francisco," Seifert said. "We were not doing as well as expected." DeBartolo was willing to outspend most other owners, but patience wasn't one of his long suits.

The 49ers caught fire to overtake the Rams

and win the NFC West, but entering the playoffs it seemed possible that the team was headed for a fourth straight one-and-out. Yet with Montana and safety Ronnie Lott fitter than they had been in weeks, the 49ers played superlatively to crush Minnesota (34–9) in a revenge game and then overwhelm Chicago (28–3) in arctic conditions at Soldier Field.

One reason for the imprecise play on both sides in the Super Bowl was the woeful condition of the grass field at Joe Robbie. On Saturday, NFL groundskeeper George Toma activated the suction system beneath the field to remove some rainfall from late in the week. Someone forgot to flip the suction switch off later that night. When Toma returned Sunday, the field was bone dry, contributing to injuries left and right. On the third play from scrimmage, left tackle Steve Wallace suffered a fractured fibula in his left leg and had to be replaced by Paris. On the 14th play, all-pro nose tackle Tim Krumrie of Cincinnati went down with a double fracture of his leg and had to be replaced by Grant. "It was like playing on Miami Beach with a carpet over it," said Coslet. "I still think that's the reason Krumrie got his leg broken. It was the worst field I've ever seen."

It was a rough week all around for the Bengals. Six days before kickoff, players and coaches looked down from the balconies at their Omni International Hotel as sections of the city burned a half mile away. "Man, I just came out of [seeing the movie] *Mississippi Burning* and came to see Miami burning," safety Solomon Wilcots said. Violence had erupted when a Hispanic police officer shot a black motorcyclist. "We had FBI protection and they wouldn't let us leave the hotel," Coslet said.

After 24 to 48 hours of unrest, the Bengals were back to thinking football. On Saturday, however, running back Stanley Wilson didn't show up for a seven o'clock meeting. "We go look for him and he's in his room naked in a bathroom cocained out of his mind," remembered Coslet. "So the doctors got him dressed and were going to take him to the hospital and that's when he ran away. Nobody heard from him for like 4 or 5 days. Stanley was a big part of our game plan."

Not only was Wilson the club's short-yardage back, but he also had a low style of running that might have worked well on the rough track. "I think he would have made people miss and would not have been affected by the turf," said Wyche. "I remember when I broke the news, several players slammed their playbooks on the floor and others put their heads in their hands. Everybody was upset, but for different reasons. Some were upset because Stanley was a good guy and had lost to drugs. Some were mad because he'd just hurt their chances to win the Super Bowl."

The 49ers scored first on Mike Cofer's 41-yard field goal, but the kick came only after wide receiver Mike Wilson dropped a 22-yard post pattern at the Bengals 2. Walsh basically blamed himself for having played the more experienced Wilson over the more gifted Taylor. "I'll always wonder if John could have made it," he said. Early in the second quarter, the 49ers drove 68 yards to the Cincinnati 2 before deciding to kick on fourth and 1. "In retrospect, I should have run Roger Craig on the same counter play on which he'd gone 80 yards to score against Minnesota in our playoff game," Walsh said. "We would have scored the touchdown." Walsh's decision looked even worse when the snap from Cross, who retired after the game, was low and led to Cofer's misfire from 19 yards.

Taylor's 45-yard punt return gave the 49ers their third opportunity inside Bengals' territory. Two botched plays lost 12 yards, and on third and 22, Fulcher stripped Craig on a 13-yard run and defensive end Jim Skow recovered. "The Bengals were really a good team, and all Sam Wyche's strategies and tactics were excellent," Walsh said, "but we had better personnel than the Bengals. We outgained them 2–1, but we almost squandered that game."

Elbert "Ickey" Woods, a rookie running back from the University of Nevada–Las Vegas, used his size (5-foot-11½, 234) and speed (4.5) to gain 1,066 yards in the regular season and 228 in the first two playoff games. Woods' end-zone gyrations—demonstrated after most of his 18 rushing touchdowns—became known famously as the "Ickey Shuffle." With Esiason's production waning down the stretch due in part to nagging injuries, the Bengals turned more and more to Woods. In the Super Bowl, he pounded for 27 yards in his first four carries. On number five, a 2-yard gain, he turned up into the hole going full speed and ran into Lott coming full speed, bent on a collision. "Whew!" 49ers defensive line

TEAM STATISTICS

CINCINNATI		SAN FRANCISCO
13	Total First Downs	23
7	Rushing	6
6	Passing	16
0	Penalty	1
229	Total Net Yardage	453
58	Total Offensive Plays	67
3.9	Avg. Gain per Offensive Play	6.8
28	Rushes	27
106	Yards Gained Rushing (Net)	112
3.8	Average Yards per Rush	4.1
25	Passes Attempted	36
11	Passes Completed	23
1	Passes Intercepted	0
5	Tackled Attempting to Pass	4
21	Yards Lost Attempting to Pass	16
123	Yards Gained Passing (Net)	341
4/13	Third-Down Efficiency	4/13
0/1	Fourth-Down Efficiency	0/0
5	Punts	4
44.2	Average Distance	37
2	Punt Returns	3
5	Punt Return Yardage	56
3	Kickoff Returns	5
132	Kickoff Return Yardage	77
0	Interception Return Yardage	0
1	Fumbles	4
1	Own Fumbles Recovered	3
1	Opponent Fumbles Recovered	0
7	Penalties	4
65	Yards Penalized	32
1	Touchdowns	2
0	Rushing	0
0	Passing	2
1	Returns	0
1	Extra Points Made	2
3	Field Goals Made	2
3	Field Goals Attempted	4
0	Safeties	0
16	Total Points Scored	20
32:36	Time of Possession	27:24

coach Bill McPherson said. "Ronnie was really PO'd because our guys weren't tackling him. I mean, it was an explosion. It got our guys going, and [Woods] didn't run very well after that."

There were good reasons why the Bengals' offense never got going. The 49ers' defense had ranked third in yards allowed in 1988. Charles

CINCINNATI

Passing	CP/ATT	YDS	TD	INT	RAT
Esiason	11/25	144	0	1	46.1

Rushing	ATT	YDS	AVG	TD	LG
Woods	20	79	4.0	0	10
Brooks	6	24	4.0	0	11
Jennings	1	3	3.0	0	3
Esiason	1	0	0.0	0	0

Receiving	NO	YDS	AVG	TD	LG
Collinsworth	3	40	13.3	0	23
Brown	3	32	10.7	0	17
Brooks	2	32	16.0	0	20
McGee	2	23	11.5	0	18
Hillary	1	17	17.0	0	17

Interceptions	NO	YDS	LG	TD
None	--	--	--	--

Punting	NO	AVG	LG	BLK
Johnson	5	44.2	63	0

Punt Ret.	NO/FC	YDS	LG	TD
Horton	1/0	5	5	0
Hillary	1/0	0	0	0

Kickoff Ret.	NO	YDS	LG	TD
Jennings	2	117	93t	1
Brooks	1	15	15	0

Defense	SOLO	AST	TOT	SK
Williams	9	1	10	1
Wilcots	7	0	7	0
Bussey	5	1	6	0
Billups	5	0	5	0
Fulcher	5	0	5	1
Horton	4	0	4	0
Zander	4	0	4	0
Buck	3	1	4	1
Barker	3	0	3	0
Grant	3	0	3	0
Thomas	2	1	3	0
McClendon	2	0	2	0
Parker	2	0	2	0
Brady	1	0	1	0
Dixon	1	0	1	0
Holman	1	0	1	0
Dar. Smith	1	0	1	0
White	1	0	1	0
TOTAL	59	4	63	3

SAN FRANCISCO

Passing	CP/ATT	YDS	TD	INT	RAT
Montana	23/36	357	2	0	115.2

Rushing	ATT	YDS	AVG	TD	LG
Craig	17	71	4.2	0	13
Rathman	5	23	4.6	0	11
Montana	4	13	3.3	0	11
Rice	1	5	5.0	0	5

Receiving	NO	YDS	AVG	TD	LG
Rice	11	215	19.5	1	44
Craig	8	101	12.6	0	40
Frank	2	15	7.5	0	8
Rathman	1	16	16.0	0	16
Taylor	1	10	10.0	1	10t

Interceptions	NO	YDS	LG	TD
Romanowski	1	0	0	0

Punting	NO	AVG	LG	BLK
Helton	4	37	55	0

Punt Ret.	NO/FC	YDS	LG	TD
Taylor	3/1	56	45	0

Kickoff Ret.	NO	YDS	LG	TD
Rodgers	3	53	22	0
Taylor	1	13	13	0
Sydney	1	11	11	0

Defense	SOLO	AST	TOT	SK
Haley	7	0	7	2
Fagan	6	0	6	1
McKyer	6	0	6	0
Lott	5	0	5	0
Fuller	4	1	5	0
Griffin	4	0	4	0
Carter	3	0	3	1
Roberts	3	0	3	0
Fahnhorst	1	1	2	0
Cox	1	0	1	0
Holmoe	1	0	1	0
Holt	1	0	1	0
Romanowski	1	0	1	0
Stubbs	1	0	1	1
Turner	1	0	1	0
TOTAL	45	2	47	5

Haley became a starter for the first time and had 15 sacks, including the playoffs. Nose tackle Michael Carter went to the Pro Bowl, and defensive end Kevin Fagan probably should have, based on how well he played in the Super Bowl against franchise left tackle Anthony Muñoz. Strong safety Jeff Fuller became an imposing presence opposite the incomparable Lott.

Cincinnati's two longest plays, a 23-yard pass to a diving Cris Collinsworth and a 20-yard screen to running back James Brooks, set up the second of Jim Breech's three field goals and gave the Bengals a 6–3 lead late in the third quarter. In turn, the 49ers tied the game on Cofer's 32-yard field goal. It was set up when rookie linebacker Bill Romanowski jumped up into a throwing lane, tipped Esiason's pass to Tim McGee high into the air, and intercepted at the Bengals 23. "I don't think he ever saw me," Romanowski said.

Fifty seconds remained in the third quarter when Stanford Jennings, the Bengals' fifth-year running back, fielded the kickoff. "We had a return called 'Wedge on the Ball,'" special-teams coach Mike Stock remembered. "As the blocks were made there was a seam. It was a footrace because Stanford wasn't a speed demon." The 49ers' Ron Heller was muscled out of the lane that Jennings burst through. Jennings then avoided Brent Jones and Sam Kennedy. Terry Greer chased down Jennings, but it was too late and he tumbled into the end zone for a 93-yard touchdown. "I just stood there and watched as nobody even came close to laying a hand on him," said Walsh. The Bengals now led, 13–6.

Each of the four plays in the 49ers' ensuing possession was critical. First, Rice shook off Billups' tackle along the sideline and turned an intermediate pass into a 31-yard gain. Second, Craig got free behind the linebackers on the right side, and Montana found him for 40 yards to the Bengals 14. Third, Montana threw a slant pass to Taylor in the end zone that should have been a routine interception for Billups, who had the ball in his hands but dropped it. "We had a cold dropped interception right in the guy's belly," said Coslet. "It was the easiest catch a defensive back will ever have. It was a mistake that Montana does not make, but he made it. As soon as [Billups] dropped it I said, 'Oh s---. We're in trouble.'" Fourth, Rice ran a quick out against the shell-shocked Billups and maneuvered the ball inside the pylon for a 14-yard touchdown.

A short time later, Rice's acrobatic 44-yard reception on a jump ball over Billups enabled the 49ers to cross the 50 for the seventh time. On third down, Taylor dropped a pass with Fulcher in tight coverage, and Cofer's 49-yard field goal sailed wide right. Starting from their 32, the Bengals moved 46 yards to the San Francisco 24 before center Bruce Kozerski drew his second false-start penalty of the second half. The drive bogged down, and on came Breech to kick a 40-yard field goal through the swirling wind. "That was one of the great pressure kicks in football," said LeBeau, "but it came in a losing effort and nobody remembered it." It was one of the only times in Stock's long career as a special-teams coach that he remembered one of his kickers actually directing the ball outside the upright and then letting the wind blow it in.

With his team leading, 16–13, Wyche worked the bench area. "Play like you're world champions," he implored of his players. "All you got on defense. Play all you got. Give it everything." Wyche knew what he was up against in Montana. Collinsworth, an eight-year veteran, had already been beaten by him in a Super Bowl. "Somebody came over to me on the bench and said, 'We're in good shape. Three minutes left and they've got 90 yards to go,'" said Collinsworth. "I asked him if No. 16 was still on the field. I think I would have been more surprised if Joe Montana did not score that TD. He is not human out there. When you come right down to it, one of the greatest players in the game did it."

The same could be said for Jerry Rice, not to mention the silver-haired gentleman wearing the head set and waving his expressive hands. He has gone down as one of the greatest coaches in NFL history.

Seifert described the 49ers of 1988 as a "struggling" team, and that certainly included the Super Bowl. The 49ers had the poorest regular-season record (10–6) of any team to win the NFL championship since the New York Giants (8–5) in 1934. Their point differential (plus-75) was the lowest of any team in San Francisco during its 18-year span of excellence from 1981 to 1998, with the exception of 1982 when NFL teams played just nine games.

"The character, the inner confidence that had been developed and cultivated over 10 years had been the difference," Walsh wrote in his book, *Building a Champion*. "We'd been written off by many people and had struggled to overcome our earlier frustrations. But we had conditioned ourselves to deal with adversity and, when it hit, we overcame it. We arrived at and won this game so differently from the other two. We played the season our way and reached the summit."

XXIV

SAN FRANCISCO 49ERS 55, DENVER BRONCOS 10

January 28, 1990
Louisiana Superdome, New Orleans, Louisiana

The acclaim for the San Francisco 49ers was universal. So, too, was the ridicule for the Denver Broncos. Super Bowl XXIV, with its big, boxcar score of 55–10, established all kinds of records for one team's domination over another.

As years pass, football historians have come to label the 1989 Broncos as perhaps the worst team ever to reach the Super Bowl. In turn, the 49ers' performance at the Louisiana Superdome has become a bit undervalued by what is viewed as the utter lack of opposition.

In truth, Denver was a worthy foe. The Broncos' regular-season record of 11–5 was one and one-half games better than any other team in the AFC. Their defense, coordinated for the first season by Wade Phillips, permitted the fewest points (226) in the league. Their offense was led by John Elway, coming off one of his greatest games ever against Cleveland in the conference championship game. Under coach Dan Reeves, they had beaten the 49ers in all three of their regular-season meetings, including an overtime affair in 1988 at Candlestick Park.

The 49ers, however, were a juggernaut. With a salary cap still four years away, Eddie DeBartolo's commitment was unsurpassed, outspending every owner in the business. Carmen Policy ran the front office, and two wise old hands, John McVay and Tony Razzano, ran the personnel department and the draft. George Seifert provided the ideal coach in his first year replacing Bill Walsh as head coach. The staff on offense featured coordinator Mike Holmgren, line coach Bobb McKittrick, and receivers coach Sherman Lewis. The staff on defense featured coordinator Bill McPherson, line coach John Marshall, and secondary coach Ray Rhodes. The starting lineup read like an all-star team, and among the reserves, six would make Pro Bowl at least once in their careers, including future Super Bowl MVP Steve Young as backup quarterback.

Attendance: 72,919
Conditions: 72 degrees, indoors
Time of kickoff: 4:23 p.m. (CST)
Length of game: 3 hours, 21 minutes
Referee: Dick Jorgensen

MVP: Joe Montana, QB, 49ers

San Francisco went 14–2 during the regular season. The 49ers crushed the Minnesota Vikings (41–13) and the Los Angeles Rams (30–3) en route to New Orleans, successfully defended their Super Bowl crown by a record score, and joined the Pittsburgh Steelers as the first franchise to win four Super Bowls. They ranked first in total offense and fourth in total defense, as well as leading the NFL in points (442) and finishing third in points allowed (253). Their turnover differential was plus-12.

"The 49ers had the same, identical team as the year before," Walsh said years later, "but they were a year older and were just at their very best. That team, to me, along with the '84 team, were two of the four or five greatest teams of all time. That Super Bowl was just an incredible demonstration of football in every facet of the game. No one could have come close."

Certainly the Broncos didn't. Reeves, participating in his eighth Super Bowl as player, assistant, and head coach, tried to play humble pie in his public pronouncements. "This could be the second-greatest

> "In much of our preparation for that period of time you obviously scouted and would attack the opposing team, but the whole idea was our execution and what we do best. You almost didn't pay attention to the other people."
>
> *George Seifert, 49ers head coach*

	1	2	3	4	Final
San Francisco 49ers	13	14	14	14	55
Denver Broncos	3	0	7	0	10

SCORING SUMMARY

1st Quarter
SF Rice, 20-yd. pass from Montana (Cofer kick)
DEN Treadwell, 42-yd. FG
SF Jones, 7-yd. pass from Montana (kick failed)
2nd Quarter
SF Rathman, 1-yd. run (Cofer kick)
SF Rice, 38-yd. pass from Montana (Cofer kick)
3rd Quarter
SF Rice, 28-yd. pass from Montana (Cofer kick)
SF Taylor, 35-yd. pass from Montana (Cofer kick)
DEN Elway, 3-yd. run (Treadwell kick)
4th Quarter
SF Rathman, 3-yd. run (Cofer kick)
SF Craig, 1-yd. run (Cofer kick)

upset in sports history," he said. "We could do what the American hockey team did against the Russians." The Broncos, a lopsided loser in three other Super Bowls, went in as an 11½-point underdog. The best that Elway could offer was, "I guarantee we'll cover the spread."

Years later, Reeves remembered having been buoyed by having beaten the 49ers in close games in 1982 (24–21), 1985 (17–16), and 1988 (16–13, in overtime). "I had not lost a regular-season game to San Francisco," he said. "I was kind of surprised when they came out such a heavy favorite. I thought it was going to be a great football game but it was just total domination. Joe Montana was a surgeon and he worked his wonders. They were an offensive football team but their defense never got enough credit for how good they were, in my opinion. They played really, really well in that game."

The 49ers played mostly three-deep zone, pressured Elway without doing much blitzing, and contained 1,000-yard rusher Bobby Humphrey. Denver gained 167 yards, committed four turnovers, and had the ball for merely 20 minutes, 29 seconds.

On the first play from scrimmage, Elway threw a 13-yard comeback on the right sideline to Mark Jackson against off coverage played by cornerback Darryl Pollard. "John took the snap and turned with

authority like he always did and threw a pass out there that bounced halfway to the receivers," Denver secondary coach Charlie Waters recalled years later. "I turned around and got into contact with Wade [Phillips] and we went, 'Oh my God. Is this a sign?' You're not supposed to think that way as a coach. One play does not a game make, as we know. But it was kind of an omen of what was getting ready to happen. All of us, even the coaches, had a bad game. We just couldn't perform."

Little was mentioned during the week about Elway's physical condition, but when McPherson was asked years later what the key to the game was, the first thing out of his mouth was the health of Elway. "We were fortunate that Elway was sick," McPherson said. "If Elway had been healthy I think it would have been really a tough game. But, by a long shot, you could see that he wasn't well. . . . We had heard he was sick. When we went to church that morning we said, 'Please let him be sick.'"

Elway repeatedly had to excuse himself during his post-game press conference because of a nasty cough. Trainer Steve Antonopulos, however, said Elway had no fever. Cornerback Tyrone Braxton said he had no recall of Elway being ill. Reeves didn't remember anything about it, either. "But all of us [assistant coaches] knew he was sick all week," Waters insisted. "He was listless. But that guy's a gamer. He did everything he could. If it hadn't been

COACHING STAFFS

San Francisco
Head Coach: George Seifert. *Offense:* Mike Holmgren (coordinator, quarterbacks), Sherman Lewis (receivers), Lynn Stiles (tight ends, special teams), Bobb McKittrick (offensive line), Al Lavan (running backs). *Defense:* Bill McPherson (coordinator), John Marshall (defensive line), Bob Zeman (linebackers), Ray Rhodes (defensive backs). *Strength:* Jerry Attaway.

Denver
Head Coach: Dan Reeves. *Offense:* Chan Gailey (wide receivers, quarterbacks), Pete Mangurian (tight ends, assistant offensive line), George Henshaw (offensive line), Mo Forte (running backs). *Defense:* Wade Phillips (coordinator), Earl Leggett (defensive line), Mike Nolan (linebackers), Charlie Waters (defensive backs). *Special Teams:* Harold Richardson. *Strength:* Al Miller. *Special Assistant:* Marvin Bass.

Super Bowl I don't know if he would have been able to play. He was that weak."

Before being replaced by Gary Kubiak with nine minutes left, Elway completed 10 of 26 passes for 108 yards. His passer rating was 19.4, he turned the ball over three times, and he was sacked four times. His longest completion was a 27-yard shovel pass to Humphrey that set up David Treadwell's 42-yard field goal in the first quarter. Among his completions, four were screen passes and another was a swing pass. The first ball that he completed downfield went for 6 yards to tight end Clarence Kay with two and one-half minutes left in the first half and Denver down, 20–3. He also hit a 12-yard hook to Steve Sewell and two slants for 21 yards to Vance Johnson. "I played lousy," Elway said after the game. "All I can do is the best I can do. Today, it wasn't any good. And, even if it was, I don't know if we could have beaten San Francisco."

Having replaced Walsh as the offensive maestro and play caller, Holmgren attacked the Broncos from his script of 15 opening plays. Roger Craig immediately tore around the left end for 18 yards. On third and 9, Montana threw a screen to Craig for 9. Two plays later, Montana converted on third and 4 with a 10-yard scramble through the middle. The touchdown, from 20 yards out, was vintage Montana-to–Jerry Rice. Montana looked first to fullback Tom Rathman, then to tight end Brent Jones, then to Rice, then to John Taylor and back again to Rice. Neither Braxton nor inside linebacker Karl Mecklenburg could keep up with Rice, given the fact that Montana had all day to work through his progression. When Rice made the catch at the 8, he was in a vulnerable position with rookie safety Steve Atwater coming over fast. "It was a chance of a lifetime," said Atwater. "I tried to take him out." The 217-pound

SAN FRANCISCO 49ERS (NFC, 14–2)		DENVER BRONCOS (AFC, 11–5)	
	Offense		
82	John Taylor* (6-1, 185)	WR	82	Vance Johnson (5-11, 185)
77	Bubba Paris (6-6, 306)	LT	60	Gerald Perry (6-6, 305)
62	Guy McIntyre* (6-3, 265)	LG	66	Jim Juriga (6-6, 269)
61	Jesse Sapolu (6-4, 260)	C	72	Keith Kartz (6-4, 270)
69	Bruce Collie (6-6, 275)	RG	67	Doug Widell (6-4, 285)
79	Harris Barton (6-4, 280)	RT	76	Ken Lanier (6-3, 269)
84	Brent Jones (6-4, 230)	TE	89	Orson Mobley (6-5, 256)
80	Jerry Rice* (6-2, 200)	WR	80	Mark Jackson (5-9, 180)
16	Joe Montana* (6-2, 195)	QB	7	John Elway* (6-3, 210)
33	Roger Craig* (6-0, 224)	RB	30	Steve Sewell (6-3, 210)
44	Tom Rathman (6-1, 232)	RB	26	Bobby Humphrey (6-1, 201)
	Defense		
78	Pierce Holt (6-4, 280)	LE	92	Alphonso Carreker (6-5, 268)
95	Michael Carter (6-2, 285)	NT	71	Greg Kragen* (6-3, 265)
75	Kevin Fagan (6-3, 260)	RE	90	Ron Holmes (6-4, 261)
94	Charles Haley (6-5, 230)	LOLB	56	Michael Brooks (6-1, 235)
54	Matt Millen (6-2, 250)	LILB	55	Rick Dennison (6-3, 220)
99	Michael Walter (6-3, 238)	RILB	77	Karl Mecklenburg* (6-3, 240)
58	Keena Turner (6-2, 222)	ROLB	73	Simon Fletcher (6-5, 240)
26	Darryl Pollard (5-11, 187)	LCB	34	Tyrone Braxton (5-11, 174)
29	Don Griffin (6-0, 176)	RCB	24	Wymon Henderson (5-9, 181)
31	Chet Brooks (5-11, 191)	SS	49	Dennis Smith* (6-3, 200)
42	Ronnie Lott* (6-0, 200)	FS	27	Steve Atwater (6-3, 217)

* Pro Bowl selection

SUBSTITUTIONS

San Francisco
Offense: WR - 88 Mike Sherrard, 85 Mike Wilson; TE - 89 Wesley Walls, 81 Jamie Williams; T - 74 Steve Wallace; G - 66 Terry Tausch; C - 60 Chuck Thomas; QB - 8 Steve Young; RB - 32 Terrence Flager, 24 Harry Sydney, 23 Spencer Tillman. *Defense:* DE - 91 Larry Roberts, 96 Danny Stubbs; NT - 64 Jim Burt, 67 Pete Kugler; LB - 59 Keith DeLong, 56 Steve Hendrickson, 53 Bill Romanowski; CB - 22 Tim McKyer, 21 Eric Wright; S - 40 Johnny Jackson. *Specialists:* K - 6 Mike Cofer; P - 9 Barry Helton.

Denver
Offense: WR - 84 Ricky Nattiel, 83 Michael Young; TE - 87 Paul Green, 88 Clarence Kay; G - 65 Monte Smith; C - 54 Keith Bishop; QB - 8 Gary Kubiak; RB - 35 Ken Bell, 32 Melvin Bratton, 23 Sammy Winder. *Defense:* DE - 91 Warren Powers, 61 Andre Townsend; NT - 68 Brad Henke; LB - 58 Scott Curtis, 97 Bruce Klostermann, 59 Tim Lucas, 51 Marc Munford; CB - 29 Darren Carrington, 36 Mark Haynes; S - 25 Kip Corrington, 48 Randy Robbins. *Specialists:* K - 9 David Treadwell*; P - 2 Mike Horan.

Atwater, who had enjoyed an exceptional rookie season, slammed into the 200-pound Rice. Rice, however, shrugged him off, eluded Braxton inside the 5, and scored standing up.

"Jerry seemed almost inhuman to me," said linebacker Matt Millen, who was cut by the Raiders on the eve of the regular season and then signed by San Francisco on September 14. "No one could push himself like that. He had great impact on young players because he was the greatest receiver ever, yet was outworking everybody on the field."

Later in the first quarter, defensive end Kevin Fagan, a determined performer with five tackles and one sack, stripped the ball from Humphrey, who was playing with broken ribs suffered during the AFC Championship Game against Cleveland, and safety Chet Brooks recovered. Twice on the ensuing drive, Rice found himself open inside for completions of 20 and 21 yards. The 10-play, 54-yard drive ended when Jones caught a short rollout pass, ran over strong safety Dennis Smith inside the 5, and scored a 7-yard touchdown.

The 49ers seized command of the game at 20–3 early in the second quarter with a 14-play, 69-yard drive. The weapons at Holmgren's disposal made the rest of the league envious. Rathman, a complete fullback if there ever was one, reached behind his body to make a one-handed catch for 9 yards on third and 10. He bulled for 1 on fourth and 1, then went another yard for the touchdown. San Francisco extended its lead to 24 points at halftime on Montana's 38-yard strike to Rice. On the play, Craig motioned from left to right and was picked up by nickel back Mark Haynes, who shifted off of Rice. With no help, Smith couldn't stay with Rice in the middle of the field, and Montana lobbed the ball to him at the 4 for another touchdown.

"Haynes was supposed to bump Rice before he switched coverage," said Montana. "He didn't. He gave him a clean release. I faked a slant pattern to John Taylor on the other side and that froze the free safety, Steve Atwater. That was the thing about them. They kept following my eyes. Every time I looked somewhere, they overplayed. They showed that on film, and they never changed."

In the second quarter, the Broncos had the ball four times, ran 15 plays for 36 yards, picked up two

TEAM STATISTICS

SAN FRANCISCO		DENVER
28	Total First Downs	12
14	Rushing	5
14	Passing	6
0	Penalty	1
461	Total Net Yardage	167
77	Total Offensive Plays	52
6.0	Avg. Gain per Offensive Play	3.2
44	Rushes	17
144	Yards Gained Rushing (Net)	64
3.3	Average Yards per Rush	3.8
32	Passes Attempted	29
24	Passes Completed	11
0	Passes Intercepted	2
1	Tackled Attempting to Pass	6
0	Yards Lost Attempting to Pass	33
317	Yards Gained Passing (Net)	103
8/15	Third-Down Efficiency	3/11
2/2	Fourth-Down Efficiency	0/0
4	Punts	6
39.5	Average Distance	38.5
3	Punt Returns	2
38	Punt Return Yardage	11
3	Kickoff Returns	9
49	Kickoff Return Yardage	196
42	Interception Return Yardage	0
0	Fumbles	3
0	Own Fumbles Recovered	1
2	Opponent Fumbles Recovered	0
4	Penalties	0
38	Yards Penalized	0
8	Touchdowns	1
3	Rushing	1
5	Passing	0
0	Returns	0
7	Extra Points Made	1
0	Field Goals Made	1
0	Field Goals Attempted	1
0	Safeties	0
55	Total Points Scored	10
39:31	Time of Possession	20:29

first downs, and went to the locker room hopelessly behind, 27–3. The 49ers didn't have the front seven personnel to crush a team the way that the 1985 Bears or the 1986 Giants did. Instead, they were seven-deep in the defensive line, athletic and smart at outside linebacker, physically strong at inside linebacker, three or possibly four cover players deep

INDIVIDUAL STATISTICS

SAN FRANCISCO

Passing	CP/ATT	YDS	TD	INT	RAT
Montana	22/29	297	5	0	147.6
Young	2/3	20	0	0	85.4

Rushing	ATT	YDS	AVG	TD	LG
Craig	20	69	3.5	1	18
Rathman	11	38	3.5	2	18
Montana	2	15	7.5	0	10
Flagler	6	14	2.3	0	10
Young	4	6	1.5	0	11
Sydney	1	2	2.0	0	2

Receiving	NO	YDS	AVG	TD	LG
Rice	7	148	21.1	3	38t
Craig	5	34	6.8	0	12
Rathman	4	43	10.8	0	18
Taylor	3	49	16.3	1	35t
Sherrard	1	13	13.0	0	13
Walls	1	9	9.0	0	9
Jones	1	7	7.0	1	7t
Sydney	1	7	7.0	0	7
Williams	1	7	7.0	0	7

Interceptions	NO	YDS	LG	TD
Brooks	1	38	38	0
Walter	1	4	4	0

Punting	NO	AVG	LG	BLK
Helton	4	39.5	47	0

Punt Ret.	NO/FC	YDS	LG	TD
Taylor	3/2	38	17	0

Kickoff Ret.	NO	YDS	LG	TD
Fragler	3	49	22	0

Defense	SOLO	AST	TOT	SK
Fagan	6	0	6	1
Millen	5	1	6	0
Romanowski	5	0	5	0
Walter	5	0	5	0
Kugler	3	0	3	1
Flagler	2	0	2	0
Griffin	2	0	2	1
Hendrickson	2	0	2	0
Holt	2	0	2	0
Jackson	2	0	2	0
Stubbs	2	0	2	2
Wilson	2	0	2	0
Walls	1	1	2	0
Brooks	1	0	1	0
Haley	1	0	1	0
Lott	1	0	1	0
Rathman	1	0	1	0
Roberts	1	0	1	1
Turner	0	1	1	0
TOTAL	**44**	**3**	**47**	**6**

DENVER

Passing	CP/ATT	YDS	TD	INT	RAT
Elway	10/26	108	0	2	85.4
Kubiak	1/3	28	0	0	68.8

Rushing	ATT	YDS	AVG	TD	LG
Humphrey	12	61	5.1	0	34
Elway	4	8	2.0	1	3t
Winder	1	-5	-5.0	0	-5

Receiving	NO	YDS	AVG	TD	LG
Humphrey	3	38	12.7	0	27
Sewell	2	22	11.0	0	12
Johnson	2	21	10.5	0	13
Nattiel	1	28	28.0	0	28
Bratton	1	14	14.0	0	14
Winder	1	7	7.0	0	7
Kay	1	6	6.0	0	6

Interceptions	NO	YDS	LG	TD
None	--	--	--	--

Punting	NO	AVG	LG	BLK
Horan	6	38.5	43	0

Punt Ret.	NO/FC	YDS	LG	TD
Johnson	2/1	11	7	0

Kickoff Ret.	NO	YDS	LG	TD
Carrington	6	146	39	0
Bell	2	41	24	0
Bratton	1	9	9	0

Defense	SOLO	AST	TOT	SK
Braxton	9	0	9	1
Atwater	4	4	8	0
Dennison	7	0	7	0
Munford	5	1	6	0
Fletcher	5	0	5	0
Henderson	5	0	5	0
Curtis	4	1	5	0
Kragen	4	0	4	0
Holmes	3	1	4	0
Smith	1	3	4	0
Brooks	3	0	3	0
Carrington	3	0	3	0
Carreker	2	1	3	0
Lucas	2	1	3	0
Townsend	2	1	3	0
Corrington	2	0	2	0
Powers	2	0	2	0
Jackson	1	0	1	0
Juriga	1	0	1	0
Mecklenburg	1	0	1	0
Sewell	1	0	1	0
TOTAL	**67**	**13**	**80**	**1**

at cornerback, and had one of the great safeties in NFL history in Ronnie Lott.

Elway's scatter-shot pegs ruined many of the passing attempts, but the 49ers made some extraordinary plays as well. Three second-quarter punts by Denver's Mike Horan were preceded by a wonderful breakup by Lott on a well-thrown pass to Kay, a sensational tackle by Millen against Humphrey for minus-3, and a difficult deflection by backup cornerback Tim McKyer against Jackson.

Reeves had fired venerable defensive coordinator Joe Collier after the 1988 season and replaced him with Phillips, the son of Bum Phillips and a former coordinator at New Orleans from 1981 to 1985 and at Philadelphia from 1986 to 1988. About the only similarity between Collier and Phillips was their use of the 3-4 base alignment. Whereas Collier's units had been diverse and based on finesse, Phillips' trademarks were simplicity and power. "Joe Collier's defense was calculus," Mecklenburg said. "Wade's was algebra. Wade got the best players and let them play." Only two defensive starters, nose tackle Greg Kragen and Smith, manned the same positions that they had in Super Bowl XXII.

Alphonso Carreker, a semi-bust in Green Bay, had his best season as the Broncos' left defensive end. The right end, Ron Holmes, was acquired from Tampa Bay and played well that season with 9 sacks. Phillips moved Simon Fletcher from left to right outside linebacker and watched him register 12 sacks. Talented Michael Brooks developed into a solid starter on the left outside. After two down seasons, Smith returned to his previous Pro Bowl form. Atwater had been superb. There were tangible reasons why the Broncos ranked second in third-down conversion rate, third against the pass, fourth in sack percentage, and sixth against the run.

"We were really a good defensive team," Waters said. "The thing that was so strange about it was we never blitzed. . . . That's because we'd get pressure other ways. We had great schemes. We had players executing our coverages perfectly. We put together our plan for San Francisco and didn't change one thing. We went into the game pretty confident."

At halftime, Waters said to Phillips, "Wade, what do you think about doing something different? What do you think about blitzing Montana?"

To which Phillips replied, "What? And lose by 100 points?" Said Waters, "We were way past the laughing stage. We weren't laughing. We were dying. I had never experienced a loss like that. Ever. High school, college, or pros. As a player or coach."

In the first 16:13 of the second half, the 49ers struck for four more touchdowns. Two of the drives consisted of one play and another had two plays. After Elway fired an interception directly into the midsection of inside linebacker Michael Walter, Montana threw a deep post to Rice for a 28-yard touchdown over Braxton. "I missed it by a damn fingernail," said Braxton. "I turned early and was watching the ball come. If I had just drove full speed and looked two steps later I would have had a pick."

When the Broncos got the ball back, Elway found himself with ample time but delivered a woefully overthrown ball to wide receiver Michael Young that was intercepted by Chet Brooks and returned 38 yards to the Denver 37. On second down, Taylor ran a post pattern behind cornerback Wymon Henderson for an easy 35-yard touchdown.

Rathman's second score, a 3-yard run, capped an 11-play, 75-yard drive. When cornerback Don Griffin stripped the ball from a scrambling Elway, Stubbs returned the recovery 15 yards to the 1. Craig powered across to make it 55–10 with 13:47 remaining. For the final two series, Young replaced Montana, who finished with a 147.6 passer rating.

Shortly before the game, Millen asked Montana, "Joe, how many points are we going to get?" Montana had been red-hot in practice all week. "I'll never forget that he answered, 'A hundred, if they'll let me,'" Millen said. "He said, 'If they play their safeties the way they've been playing them, we'll eat 'em alive.'"

The more Holmgren studied the Broncos, the more he saw two- and three-deep zone coverage with Atwater and Smith extremely outside conscious. "That's the defense that Bill Walsh designed his whole offensive scheme for when he first came to San Francisco, the static base 3-4," Holmgren said. "I remember Bill saying one day, 'Doesn't anybody play the old-style 3-4 anymore?' Well, these guys do."

According to Braxton, the coverage plan changed on game day. "I think it was the damn coaches who panicked and got scared and played into what San Francisco really wanted," the third-year cornerback said. "We had been practicing man-to-man and three-deep zone. The three-deep zone would have eliminated the run and put more pressure on the corners, but we all talked about it all week. We said we're going to have to do it until they burn us—have somebody in the post and then have the corners locked up out wide. We came out and played two-deep. Of course, Montana and his guys ran up the seams and the middle on us. Against that offense, that wasn't the answer. If they know it's coming, you better change up and get out of there."

It's unlikely that the Denver secondary could have held up if asked to play extensive man coverage. Henderson was the weak link of that defense, Braxton was smart as a whip but lacked true burst, and Haynes was over the hill.

The 49ers also rushed for 144 yards, including 69 by Craig and 38 by Rathman. "Bobb basically designed the running game," Seifert said. "That was his bailiwick. Mike Holmgren would call the runs but many, many times during the course of a game someone would say, 'Ask Bobb what should we be running now.' Bobb was one of our top secrets, I guess you would say. He developed these players and their skills as well as anybody I had ever seen at any coaching position."

Seifert had few concerns that his players might take the Broncos too lightly. Some of them wanted to win for him, but indirectly, many wanted to demonstrate that their past success didn't necessarily revolve around Walsh. "A lot of guys were driven to show that Bill wasn't the only genius around here," said Wright. "He had a good supporting cast of athletes."

Seifert maintained the status quo, which players appreciated. "The system was in place and we were probably even more of a confident team," Seifert said. "I can't say it was the best team the 49ers ever had . . . but it was probably as in-sync of a team that I ever was involved with." Was it an easy act to follow? "No, no, no, it was not," said Seifert, "but I wouldn't trade it for anything. I was following Bill and I was working for Eddie and I had to win the game. I had grown up in San Francisco. I was the right man for that particular moment."

Another motivating factor was the words of Tom Jackson, the Denver linebacker from 1973 to 1986 who later went into broadcasting. In the days leading up to the game, Jackson had been less than complimentary about the 49ers. "What really fueled the fire that year was Tommy Jackson," Wright said. "He pissed us off. We went in with a chip on our shoulder. That was our driving force for the game."

In the grand scheme of things, coaches can only do so much, and inflammatory remarks can only inspire so far. Holmgren often would say that the effect of words would last only for a play or two. After that, the outcome of almost every football game was decided by the men who played it. At the most important position, the 49ers had Montana.

Montana underwent what, at the time, was regarded as delicate back surgery in September 1986. Following an astonishingly short convalescence, he looked infirm if not feeble in playoff losses to the Giants in 1986 and the Vikings in 1987. In 1989, Montana missed three games and halves of two others with knee, elbow, and rib injuries. More injuries were to dog Montana after his trade to Kansas City before his retirement following the 1994 season.

Clearly, though, this was his finest hour. Check out the numbers: a passer rating of 112.8 in the regular season, a passer rating of 146.4 in the playoffs, and a passer rating of 119.4 in 16 games overall. That January, Walsh described the 49ers' offense as "poetry in motion . . . this is *Star Wars*." The 49ers took the game to new heights, and Montana, honored as the regular-season MVP for the first time and Super Bowl MVP for the third time, had reached the pinnacle of his profession.

"Joe is one guy who could have broken this up many moons ago," Lott said before the Super Bowl. "He could have spun away from us, gone on to be rich and famous, more important. He hasn't changed a bit since 1981. He's extraordinary, but ordinary. A normal guy. He's got to be the most unselfish player in the history of the game."

Certainly, this 49er team had proved its point as one of the finest ever assembled.

XXV

NEW YORK GIANTS 20, BUFFALO BILLS 19

January 27, 1991

Tampa Stadium, Tampa, Florida

Buffalo Bills fans will forever remember Super Bowl XXV with a heavy heart. It was the first of the Bills' four consecutive chances to win the NFL championship, and probably their best. The difference between victory and defeat was the margin of a few feet.

In the end, Scott Norwood's field-goal attempt from 47 yards that sailed just wide to the right with four seconds remaining enabled the New York Giants to prevail, 20–19. Set against the backdrop of the first U.S. war in the Persian Gulf, this was one of the most fiercely fought and evenly contested games in Super Bowl history.

Norwood stood in the Bills' cramped locker room for an hour at Tampa Stadium that night answering every last question from wave after wave of reporters and television people. "A lot of other players didn't make plays, but that doesn't excuse me," Norwood said years later. "I'm a player and I'm paid to perform, and I failed in that instance." Norwood's life would never be the same, but eventually he was able to move on, finding happiness and success as a family man and financial planner.

Those who condemned Norwood as a choker or worse were off the mark. Many of his teammates had much easier responsibilities than Norwood and failed. The Giants, according to coach Bill Parcells, "played as well as we could." The Bills, as a 6½-point favorite, surely did not, and so the Super Bowl had its greatest upset since Kansas City ambushed Minnesota 21 years earlier.

If overcoming adversity is the mark of a champion, the Giants couldn't have been more deserving. After starting 10–0, they lost three of their next four games and then limped into the playoffs with 3-point victories over tail-enders Phoenix and New England. "They were saying that the Giants were done, they're backing into

Attendance: 73,813
Conditions: 71 degrees, mostly cloudy, wind SE at 5 mph
Time of kickoff: 6:19 p.m. (EST)
Length of game: 3 hours, 19 minutes
Referee: Jerry Seeman

MVP: Ottis Anderson, RB, Giants

the playoffs," defensive coordinator Bill Belichick remembered. "The whole thing was how bad we sucked."

More importantly, three integral players were no longer available. Quarterback Phil Simms, who was having a much better regular season than he did in 1986 when he led the Giants to victory in Super Bowl XXI, suffered a season-ending foot injury in Week 14 during a 17–13 loss to the Bills. Rodney Hampton, a dynamic rookie running back who stole most of Ottis Anderson's thunder in the final month of the season, suffered a fractured fibula on his second carry of a 31–3 divisional playoff victory over Chicago and was finished. In Week 3 dependable kicker Raul Allegre went down with a season-ending groin injury.

Under Parcells' dynamic leadership, the Giants built an offense to suit backup quarterback Jeff Hostetler's movement skills and saw him come through with the game of his life. They also punched all the right buttons so that 34-year-old Anderson could flourish as the featured back and carry 21 times for 102 yards to emerge as MVP. Additionally, they signed the right kicker off the street in aging Matt Bahr, who made 17 of 23 field goals in the regular season and 8 of 9 in the playoffs.

The Giants reached the Super Bowl by defeating the San Francisco 49ers at Candlestick Park, holding hands as Bahr kicked a field goal from 42 yards as time expired for a 15–13 victory. "That NFC Championship Game was the greatest game I ever

	1	2	3	4	Final
Buffalo Bills	3	9	0	7	19
New York Giants	3	7	7	3	20

SCORING SUMMARY

1st Quarter
NY   Bahr, 28-yd. FG
BUF   Norwood, 23-yd. FG
2nd Quarter
BUF   D. Smith, 1-yd. run (Norwood kick)
BUF   Safety, B. Smith sacked Hostetler in end zone
NY   Baker, 14-yd. pass from Hostetler (Bahr kick)
3rd Quarter
NY   Anderson, 1-yd. run (Bahr kick)
4th Quarter
BUF   Thomas, 31-yd. run (Norwood kick)
NY   Bahr, 21-yd. FG

layed in because of the stakes and the competitive-ess and the greatness of the opponent," legendary inebacker Lawrence Taylor said. "Everyone ex-ected the 49ers to beat us and then three-peat as hampions until Erik Howard jarred the ball loose rom [Roger] Craig with 2½ minutes left." In the Su-er Bowl, the Giants again held hands as Norwood nisfired by what onlookers estimated as a distance f three to five feet.

"Parcells' team in 1986 had all the pieces in lace," Anderson said. "It was a team that expected o win sooner or later. That team had a name, a urpose. This 1990 team had no true identity."

Not only were the Bills a healthy football eam, but they were also an immensely talented ne. General manager Bill Polian, who joined he organization in 1985, and director of player ersonnel John Butler resurrected the franchise vith superb drafting. After coming close in 1988 nd 1989, the Bills worked past the bickering among heir star players and emerged as a dominating orce. Ten players from Buffalo made the Pro Bowl n 1990, including NFL defensive player of the year 3ruce Smith and quarterback Jim Kelly, who had his est season ever with a passer rating of 101.2.

What the Bills didn't get on Super Sunday was championship performance from coach Marv evy, offensive coordinator Ted Marchibroda, and efensive coordinator Walt Corey. The most telling

statistic was the Giants' advantage in time of posses-sion, 40:33 to 19:27. Despite the fact that Thurman Thomas ripped apart the Giants for 135 yards in 15 carries, the Bills called just 19 runs compared to 37 passes. "I always felt that we did not run the ball enough against the Giants during the early stages of that game," Bills offensive line coach Tom Bresnahan said years later. "Whether we were successful on a drive or not, we were on and off the field too quickly. The other issue is we couldn't get off the field." On defense, the Bills proved wholly incapable of contain-ing Hostetler's bootleg passing game, which Giants offensive coordinator Ron Erhardt parlayed into a 9-for-16 conversion rate on third down.

"There is no question we got outcoached in that game," one of the Bills assistant coaches said. "I can see exactly what Parcells tried to do. If we had just run the ball rather than trying to throw it all the time, we probably would have won. If we had Bill Belichick and they had Walt Corey, we would have destroyed them. No question in my mind we had a better team."

Neither team had a turnover. New York set an NFL regular-season record for fewest giveaways with 14, and had only one in the playoffs. The Giants rushed for 172 yards and passed for 214; the Bills rushed for 166 and passed for 205. Buffalo just didn't have the ball enough. "It was the ball control," Giants offensive line coach Fred Hoaglin said. "The way Buffalo was moving the ball at the end of the game, if they would have had 10 more seconds we would have lost."

The dramatic finish began for Buffalo with 2:16 and one timeout remaining after Sean Landeta's 38-yard punt required a fair catch by Al Edwards at the Bills 10. Two runs by Kelly gained 9 yards, and then the Bills converted on third down for the only time in eight attempts, when Thomas scooted through the middle for 22 on a shotgun draw play. "He broke it out of there and Everson Walls, who's not really a very good tackler, made a great tackle," Belichick said. "It probably saved the game."

Kelly found Andre Reed for 4, scrambled for 9 to the New York 46, and called the Bills' final timeout with 48 seconds left. Tight end Keith McKeller made a shoestring catch for 6, and then Thomas bolted inside for 11 to the 29. "Our thing was, let's make Kelly beat us, but Thurman Thomas almost beat us on those two draw plays," said Belichick. "We see the ball handed off; it's not like we got our back turned. But Thomas was a damn good runner."

With the clock running, Kelly spiked the ball. When Norwood took the field, the Giants made him think about it by calling their final timeout. "The drive would have been the memorable thing had the kick gone in," Levy said. "It was a great drive to get us there with 8 seconds left."

But had Kelly really done enough to help Norwood? It's a reasonable question to ponder. The Bills squandered a ton of time during that drive just on his three scrambles alone. On the entire march, Kelly completed just two passes for a mere 10 yards. It wasn't exactly what one would expect from a quarterback destined for the Hall of Fame.

Norwood, 30, had been the Bills' kicker since 1985. He went to the Pro Bowl in 1988, his finest season, after making 86.5 percent of his field goals. His marksmanship dipped to 76.7 percent in 1989 and 69 percent in 1990, which ranked 23rd in the NFL. In that year, Norwood made five of nine attempts, or 55.6 percent, between 40 and 49 yards; the NFL average from that distance in 1990 was 62.1 percent.

"I would guess, at that distance and in that situation, Scottie makes it 50 percent—at most," said Bruce DeHaven, who coached special teams in Buffalo from 1987 to 1999. "He had everything working against him. . . . You've got a right-footed kicker kicking from the right hash with a left to right wind. All three of those things make it a tougher kick."

In those days, Rich Stadium in Buffalo had artificial turf. By mid-October, the Bills could almost never practice on grass. Not once in Norwood's career in Buffalo had he made a kick

BUFFALO BILLS (AFC, 13–3)	Offense	NEW YORK GIANTS (NFC, 13–3)	
80	James Lofton (6-3, 195)	WR	82	Mark Ingram (5-10, 188)
69	Will Wolford* (6-5, 295)	LT	76	John Elliott (6-7, 305)
51	Jim Ritcher (6-3, 275)	LG	66	William Roberts* (6-5, 280)
67	Kent Hull* (6-5, 275)	C	65	Bart Oates* (6-3, 265)
65	John Davis (6-4, 310)	RG	60	Eric Moore (6-5, 290)
75	Howard Ballard (6-6, 325)	RT	72	Doug Riesenberg (6-5, 275)
84	Keith McKeller (6-4, 245)	TE	89	Mark Bavaro (6-4, 245)
83	Andre Reed* (6-1, 190)	WR	85	Stephen Baker (5-8, 160)
12	Jim Kelly* (6-3, 218)	QB	15	Jeff Hostetler (6-3, 212)
41	Jamie Mueller (6-1, 224)	RB	44	Maurice Carthon (6-1, 225)
34	Thurman Thomas* (5-10, 198)	RB	24	Ottis Anderson (6-2, 225)
		Defense		
96	Leon Seals (6-5, 270)	LE I DT	74	Erik Howard* (6-4, 268)
91	Jeff Wright (6-2, 270)	NT I DT	70	Leonard Marshall (6-3, 285)
78	Bruce Smith* (6-4, 275)	RE I LLB	58	Carl Banks (6-4, 235)
97	Cornelius Bennett* (6-2, 238)	LOLB I MLB	52	Pepper Johnson* (6-3, 248)
58	Shane Conlan* (6-3, 230)	LILB I RLB	56	Lawrence Taylor* (6-3, 243)
50	Ray Bentley (6-2, 235)	RILB I CB	21	Reyna Thompson* (6-0, 193)
56	Darryl Talley* (6-4, 235)	ROLB I CB	23	Perry Williams (6-2, 203)
47	Kirby Jackson (5-10, 180)	LCB	25	Mark Collins (5-10, 190)
37	Nate Odomes (5-10, 188)	RCB	28	Everson Walls (6-1, 194)
46	Leonard Smith (5-11, 202)	SS	47	Greg Jackson (6-1, 200)
38	Mark Kelso (5-11, 185)	FS	29	Myron Guyton (6-1, 205)

* Pro Bowl selection

SUBSTITUTIONS

Buffalo
Offense: WR - 85 Al Edwards, 89 Steve Tasker*; TE - 88 Pete Metzelaars, 87 Butch Rolle; G - 74 Glenn Parker, 59 Mitch Frerotte; C - 63 Adam Lingner; QB - 14 Frank Reich; RB - 23 Kenneth Davis, 35 Carwell Gardner, 30 Don Smith. *Defense:* DE - 73 Mike Lodish, 94 Mark Pike; NT - 92 Gary Baldinger; LB - 54 Carlton Bailey, 99 Hal Garner; CB - 27 Clifford Hicks, 31 James Williams; S - 45 Dwight Drane, 22 John Hagy. *Specialists:* K - 11 Scott Norwood; P - 10 Rick Tuten. *DNP:* 7 Gale Gilbert (QB). *Inactive:* 57 Matt Monger (LB), 29 David Pool (CB).

New York
Offense: WR - 84 Troy Kyles, 81 Stacy Robinson; TE - 87 Howard Cross, 80 Robert Mrosko; G - 61 Bob Kratch; C - 59 Brian Williams; RB - 30 Dave Meggett. *Defense:* DE - 77 Eric Dorsey, 93 Mike Fox, 73 John Washington; LB - 51 Bobby Abrams, 98 Johnie Cooks, 99 Steve DeOssie, 57 Lawrence McGrew, 55 Gary Reasons; CB - 46 Roger Brown; S - 26 Dave Duerson, 43 David Whitmore. *Specialists:* K - 9 Matt Bahr; P - 5 Sean Landeta*. *DNP:* 6 Matt Cavanaugh (QB). *Inactive:* 64 Tom Rehder (T).

Buffalo

Head Coach: Marv Levy. *Offense:* Ted Marchibroda (passing game coordinator, quarterbacks), Nick Nicolau (receivers), Don Lawrence (tight ends, quality control), Tom Bresnahan (offensive line), Elijah Pitts (running backs). *Defense:* Walt Corey (coordinator, linebackers), Chuck Dickerson (defensive line), Dick Roach (defensive backs), Chuck Lester (assistant). *Special Teams:* Bruce DeHaven. *Strength:* Rusty Jones.

New York

Head Coach: Bill Parcells. *Offense:* Ron Erhardt (coordinator), Tom Coughlin (wide receivers), Mike Pope (tight ends), Fred Hoaglin (offensive line), Ray Handley (running backs). *Defense:* Bill Belichick (coordinator, defensive backs), Romeo Crennel (defensive line), Al Groh (linebackers). *Special Teams:* Mike Sweatman. *Strength:* Johnny Parker.

s long as 47 yards on grass. "So we asked him to o something in the Super Bowl that he had never one before," DeHaven said. Belichick, an old pecial-teams coach, said, "It was a tough kick, a ery tough kick."

The kick has taken on a life of its own. The ball as placed down only a few inches from the NFL mblem that had been spray-painted on the field. im Rooney, the Giants' director of pro personnel, as heard from several Giants over the years that was not an ideal spot from which to kick, but eHaven didn't put any stock in that. Levy, who ad begun his NFL career as a special-teams coach, nd DeHaven both described the snap by Adam ingner and the hold by Frank Reich as perfect. Punter John Kidd held for Norwood from 1985 o 1989 before he signed with San Diego in March 990 and was replaced by Reich.) However, New rleans kicker Morten Anderson, providing ommentary for a European telecast of the game, etected that the rotation of the laces by Reich :ft them pointing to the side in a less-than-ideal osition for Norwood.

Based on what Norwood said after the game, he vas concerned about the distance and went at the all in overly aggressive fashion. Unfortunately for Norwood, the ball started out right and, given the light wind and his tendency to kick a straight ball, t had no chance to drift back in.

"Frank Reich came off the field and said, 'He crushed it, he absolutely crushed it,'" DeHaven recalled. "The thought that Scottie Norwood was this schlub kicker that choked on his big chance in the Super Bowl couldn't be further from the truth. The guy hit a 47-yard field goal that probably would have been good from 60. It was three-quarters of the way up the crossbar and it was about 4 feet outside. . . . The guy had been a great pressure kicker up until that point. I've never felt like he failed in terms of not putting a good stroke on the ball. He just failed because it was a long kick."

The next day, a crowd estimated at 25,000 to 30,000 packed Niagara Square in downtown Buffalo. As Polian spoke, a chant grew louder and louder: "We want Scottie, we want Scottie." DeHaven's voice quavered as he remembered the moment. Norwood cried, too. "They wouldn't stop until Scottie got up there on the stage," DeHaven said. "I'm sure Buffalo fans say, 'If he had made that kick we might have won two or three of those Super Bowls rather than lose all four.' But certainly there was none of that sentiment the next day." The Bills released Norwood after the 1991 season, during which he converted just 18 of 29 field goals. No other team ever gave him a chance.

Before leaving the East Coast for San Francisco and the NFC Championship Game, Parcells had told his players to pack for two weeks. Both teams had to fly directly to Tampa after the conference title games because the Super Bowl was played seven days later. When the Giants, an 8-point underdog in San Francisco, arrived at the hotel in Tampa at about 5:30 a.m. Monday, they found the lobby decorated in 49ers' colors and a large supply of sourdough bread already in stock. Soon enough, movers were scurrying through the lobby, pushing 49er-rented copy machines and office equipment out the door.

When it came time to game plan for the Bills, Parcells was on the mark again. "Basically, we were just trying to let the air out of the ball," Erhardt said. "We felt we had to do something to slow this outfit down. We said, 'Let's make this a ball-control game.' And we did."

One key would be Anderson, five times a 1,000-yard rusher in St. Louis from 1979 to 1984, but a forgotten backup in New York from 1986 to 1988. He had been exposed by the Giants in Plan B free agency in both 1989 and 1990 when they didn't include him on their 37-man protected list. The running back came through for the team when the championship was on the line.

"I've got to admit, Parcells and Erhardt came up with a heck of a strategy [in the Super Bowl]," Anderson said.

"Boy, he was something," Hoaglin said. "Ottis is one of the few backs that I ever saw who was able to change his running style through his career and still be effective at the end. When he came to New York, he knew he was losing his speed, so he went in the weight room and got stronger and bigger. He got up to 235 and was very, very strong."

The other key to victory against the Bills would be playing to Hostetler's strengths. A third-round draft choice from West Virginia in 1984, Hostetler didn't start his first game until 1988. In fact, he caught a pass, partially blocked a punt, and ran the ball on a fake before he even completed a pass in the regular season. But when Simms went down, he was more than prepared for his opportunity.

According to Hoaglin, during the offseason Parcells came into the meeting room and said, "I don't think that Simms is going to make it through the year. So I want you guys to find out the best way to get the quarterback out of the pocket. Look at college tape, whatever. Spend the whole offseason and find something."

"We came up with this bootleg," Hoaglin recalled. "We called it a naked and we used it a lot. Belichick couldn't stop it in training camp. We'd go to the team part of practice and he'd say, 'OK, why don't you guys just run the bootleg three or four times and get that out of your system so we can play football the rest of the day.'"

New York opened the game by driving 58 yards in 10 plays, scoring on a short field goal by Bahr. Norwood tied the game from 23 yards after Giants cornerback Perry Williams, who had minimal ball skills and struggled playing the ball in the air, panicked on a long pass to James Lofton, batted it straight up into the air, and watched Lofton haul it in for a 61-yard gain. Operating their no-huddle to perfection, the Bills came back to cover 80 yards in 12 plays, scoring on Don Smith's 1-yard plunge. Buffalo had experimented with the no-huddle

BUFFALO	TEAM STATISTICS	NEW YORK
18	Total First Downs	24
8	Rushing	10
9	Passing	13
1	Penalty	1
371	Total Net Yardage	386
56	Total Offensive Plays	73
6.6	Avg. Gain per Offensive Play	5.3
25	Rushes	39
166	Yards Gained Rushing (Net)	172
6.6	Average Yards per Rush	4.4
30	Passes Attempted	32
18	Passes Completed	20
0	Passes Intercepted	0
1	Tackled Attempting to Pass	2
7	Yards Lost Attempting to Pass	8
205	Yards Gained Passing (Net)	214
1/8	Third-Down Efficiency	9/16
0/0	Fourth-Down Efficiency	0/1
6	Punts	4
38.8	Average Distance	43.8
0	Punt Returns	2
0	Punt Return Yardage	37
6	Kickoff Returns	3
114	Kickoff Return Yardage	48
0	Interception Return Yardage	0
1	Fumbles	0
1	Own Fumbles Recovered	0
0	Opponent Fumbles Recovered	0
6	Penalties	5
35	Yards Penalized	31
2	Touchdowns	2
2	Rushing	1
0	Passing	1
0	Returns	0
2	Extra Points Made	2
1	Field Goals Made	2
2	Field Goals Attempted	2
1	Safeties	0
19	Total Points Scored	20
19:27	Time of Possession	40:33

before unleashing it against Cleveland in the 198 playoffs. The Bills lost, 34–30, when running bac Ronnie Harmon dropped a touchdown pass, bu they still piled up 453 yards.

"We had a lot of weapons offensively Bresnahan said, "but we were essentially the sam as every other offense. Whenever we would ge

INDIVIDUAL STATISTICS

BUFFALO

Passing	CP/ATT	YDS	TD	INT	RAT
Kelly	18/30	212	0	0	81.5

Rushing	ATT	YDS	AVG	TD	LG
Thomas	15	135	9.0	1	31t
Kelly	6	23	3.8	0	9
K. Davis	2	4	2.0	0	3
Mueller	1	3	3.0	0	3
D. Smith	1	1	1.0	1	1t

Receiving	NO	YDS	AVG	TD	LG
Reed	8	62	7.8	0	20
Thomas	5	55	11.0	0	15
K. Davis	2	23	11.5	0	19
McKeller	2	11	5.5	0	6
Lofton	1	61	61.0	0	61

Interceptions	NO	YDS	LG	TD
None	--	--	--	--

Punting	NO	AVG	LG	BLK
Tuten	6	38.8	47	0

Punt Ret.	NO/FC	YDS	LG	TD
Edwards	0/3	0	--	0

Kickoff Ret.	NO	YDS	LG	TD
D. Smith	4	66	24	0
Edwards	2	48	33	0

Defense	SOLO	AST	TOT	SK
J. Williams	1	0	1	0
Odomes	5	0	5	0
Kelso	4	2	6	0
Drane	1	0	1	0
L. Smith	8	0	8	0
K. Jackson	2	1	3	0
Bentley	3	1	4	0
Bailey	2	1	3	0
Talley	2	2	4	0
Conlan	8	0	8	0
Lodish	2	0	2	0
B. Smith	3	0	3	1
Wright	6	1	7	1
Baldinger	2	0	2	0
Seals	5	0	5	0
Bennett	4	1	5	0
Tuten	1	0	1	0
Gardner	1	0	1	0
Mueller	1	0	1	0
Tasker	2	0	2	0
TOTAL	63	9	72	2

NEW YORK

Passing	CP/ATT	YDS	TD	INT	RAT
Hostetler	20/32	222	1	0	93.5

Rushing	ATT	YDS	AVG	TD	LG
Anderson	21	102	4.9	1	24
Meggett	9	48	5.3	0	17
Carthon	3	12	4.0	0	5
Hostetler	6	10	1.7	0	5

Receiving	NO	YDS	AVG	TD	LG
Ingram	5	74	14.8	0	22
Bavaro	5	50	10.0	0	19
Cross	4	39	9.8	0	13
Baker	2	31	15.5	1	17
Meggett	2	18	9.0	0	11
Anderson	1	7	7.0	0	7
Carthon	1	3	3.0	0	3

Interceptions	NO	YDS	LG	TD
None	--	--	--	--

Punting	NO	AVG	LG	BLK
Landeta	4	43.8	54	0

Punt Ret.	NO/FC	YDS	LG	TD
Meggett	2/3	37	20	0

Kickoff Ret.	NO	YDS	LG	TD
Meggett	2	26	16	0
Duerson	1	22	22	0

Defense	SOLO	AST	TOT	SK
Howard	6	1	7	0
Collins	6	0	6	0
Reasons	6	0	6	0
G. Jackson	4	0	4	0
Thompson	4	0	4	0
Banks	3	1	4	0
Johnson	3	0	3	0
Walls	2	1	3	0
Bahr	2	0	2	0
Guyton	2	0	2	0
Marshall	2	0	2	1
Rouson	2	0	2	0
Taylor	2	0	2	0
R. Brown	1	0	1	0
Tillman	1	0	1	0
Washington	1	0	1	0
P. Williams	0	1	1	0
TOTAL	47	4	51	1

into a 2-minute situation, to win a game or finish a half, we would suddenly become electric. . . . The catalyst of the whole deal was Jim Kelly. On some totally incongruous down and distance he would call a play that no coach in the world would call, like a reverse, and it would end up going for 20 yards. . . .To me, the guy had a brilliant instinct for what was happening on the field and what to attack the defense with. He had unbelievable self-confidence and he's the world's toughest guy. I've got to say in my career as a college and pro coach, Jim Kelly was the finest football player I was ever around."

Preparing to meet the NFL's leading offense in points scored (428), Belichick had little time to ponder his game plan. Raiders coach Art Shell had called his team's defense probably the finest in franchise history before the Bills decimated the Raiders, 51–3, in the AFC Championship Game.

The Bills' no-huddle was like a fast break, with no more than 20 seconds between plays. Belichick found the coaches' tape all but useless because the time between plays was eliminated. Thus, for the first time in his career, he used nothing but television tapes of the Bills, which gave his players more of a feel for the Bills' tempo. The Giants played a strange 2-3-6 configuration on defense, hoping to encourage the Bills to run and keep the ball out of the air. "I remember saying that if Thomas rushed for 100 yards we would probably win," Belichick said. "If we just stopped them cold, then it would be all passing, and we really felt they were a pretty good passing team."

At halftime, anticipating that the Bills would try to run more, the Giants played a 3-3 defense with defensive end Eric Dorsey replacing dime back Reyna Thompson. "You couldn't run the regular 3-4 against them," Tim Rooney said. "They would have killed you. We were matching up."

The Bills' offense really took off that season when Lofton was fully integrated alongside Reed. Afforded excellent protection most of the day, Kelly kept trying to find Reed on shallow crossing routes. Reed had four of his eight catches and 44 of his 62 yards in the 80-yard drive for a 10–3 lead. His troubles started on the next series when he was wide open but dropped an easy pass on third and 1 at midfield. "Our linebackers, especially [Carl]

Banks but Pepper [Johnson], too, did a really good job of hitting Reed on those crossing patterns," said Belichick. "I mean, they blew him up a couple times. Our thing was, we're going to play a lot of Cover 2 and split-safety coverage, and we're going to tattoo you when you catch them."

The Giants kept pounding on Reed until he wasn't even a factor in the second half. "No other team ever hit me this hard," Reed said. "You can't even compare this to anything I've ever been through. They bruised up my whole body."

Midway through the second quarter, one of the defensive ends in Corey's 3-4, Leon Seals, leveled Hostetler. Though rubbery-legged, he made it off the field under his own power but needed smelling salts on the sidelines. On the Giants' next possession, Anderson inadvertently tripped Hostetler as he dropped back inside his own 5. Grasping the ball in his right hand as he staggered backward, Hostetler felt his right wrist grabbed by onrushing defensive end Bruce Smith. He reacted quickly, clutching the ball to his chest with his left arm before being snowed under for a safety by Bruce Smith, nose tackle Jeff Wright, and linebacker Ray Bentley. "If he fumbles and we recover it for a touchdown, they're down enough where they're not going to be able to sit on the ball and we might beat them, 40–14," said DeHaven. "I've always thought that play right there could have been the difference between us winning two or three Super Bowls."

Late in the first half, the Giants got back into the game on Hostetler's 14-yard touchdown pass to diminutive Stephen Baker on a corner route against cornerback Nate Odomes. The drive consumed three and a half minutes and covered 87 yards in 10 plays. With that, it was time for a patriotic halftime show that was even longer than most Super Bowl extravaganzas. The Giants then ate up 9:29 to open the second half with a 14-play, 75-yard march capped by Anderson's 1-yard touchdown. "Kelly wasn't on the field for an hour and a half," said Rooney. "He could have gone out and played 9 holes. That's a long time to be off the field."

That drive did far more than just idle the Bills' offense. It made something of a hero out of wide receiver Mark Ingram, established Anderson and left tackle John "Jumbo" Elliott as dominant forces in he game, and illustrated the shrewdness of Erhardt. The Giants converted four third downs on the drive, starting with an 11-yard dump pass to Dave Meggett on which linebacker Darryl Talley and nickel back Clifford Hicks missed the tackle. "We waited until the worst time of the season to have our worst game of the year as far as missing tackles and dropping balls," linebacker Cornelius Bennett said.

Three plays later, Anderson took advantage of Elliott's seal block on Bruce Smith for a 24-yard burst around left end. Smith registered a few pressures in the first half, but like many of his teammates, he wore down badly in the second half. "In the playoffs against Chicago, Jumbo took Richard Dent and mopped the field with him," Hoaglin said. "He did the same thing pretty much to Bruce Smith. Bruce Smith had grass stains all over the back of his pants and his jersey."

On third and 13 from the Bills 32, Hostetler hit Ingram at the 26 on a crossing pattern. Safety Greg Jackson bounced off Ingram, and Talley overran him. Then safety Mark Kelso whiffed on the tackle, and dime back J. D. Williams couldn't wrestle Ingram down until he had the first down by a yard. "Ingram was not a great wide receiver, but he was a real competitive guy," said Rooney. "That was the biggest play offensively in the entire game."

Finally, on third and 4, Hostetler bootlegged left and found tight end Howard Cross for 9. "We tried it the other side in the first half and Bennett must have knocked down about four or five of them," Hoaglin said. "We flipped it over the whole second half and must have hit eight or nine of those plays. Smith and Talley weren't as disciplined as Bennett was."

The Bills regained the lead, 19–17, on the first play of the fourth quarter when Thomas scored on a 31-yard draw play. The play underscored just how vulnerable the Giants had made themselves with their unorthodox defenses. Their two linemen, Leonard Marshall and Howard, were blown out of the picture. Guard Jim Ritcher got just enough of linebacker Gary Reasons so he wasn't able to tackle Thomas, who ducked under free safety Myron Guyton, made Thompson miss, and was off to the races behind Reed's cleaving downfield block against Walls. Walls, a cornerback by trade, spent most of the game calling the defenses from the middle of the field.

Starting from their 23, the Giants drove 74 yards to set up Bahr's game-winner from 21 yards. Seven of the plays were rushes, gaining a total of 24 yards, and Hostetler completed four of six passes for 50 yards. Mark Bavaro, no longer the prototypical tight end because of bad knees, slipped behind inside linebacker Shane Conlan for 17 and then beat Bentley for 19. Norwood could have lived his life in blissful anonymity if the Giants had finished the drive with a touchdown and taken a 5-point lead. Instead, center Bart Oates enabled Wright to penetrate and tackle Anderson for minus-4 on first and goal from the 3. "There was a hole there a mile wide but we had a bust," Erhardt said. "I wanted to throw it on that next down. Bill said, 'Let's make sure we get three out of this.' He was about as conservative as you could get." Seven and a half minutes remained, but Bahr's 21-yard field goal ultimately would stand as the difference.

Due to NFL's cutbacks involving Desert Storm, the Giants had no post-game party. Parcells quit in June, and the Giants struggled for most of the ensuing decade under Ray Handley, Dan Reeves, and Jim Fassel.

In Buffalo, Levy was just getting revved up. That night in the locker room, he quoted from a sixteenth century Scottish poem in which Sir Andrew told his troops: "Fight on my men, a little I'm hurt, but not yet slain. I'll just lie down and bleed a while, then I'll rise to fight again." The Bills would be back not once, but three more times, but they would never come as close to winning as this.

"I don't think anyone in Buffalo will ever forget that," said Kelly, referring to Norwood's wayward field goal. "It was a heartbreak because we were the best team in the NFL that year and we were the best team that day."

"Norwood was a very quiet, professional kid. Now he's got to live with that the rest of his life. Just like the Red Sox guy [Bill Buckner]. Even after he dies, they'll still be talking about it."

Nick Nicolau, Bills wide receivers coach

XXVI
WASHINGTON REDSKINS 37, BUFFALO BILLS 24

January 26, 1992

Hubert H. Humphrey Metrodome, Minneapolis, Minnesota

The Washington Redskins, a team in the truest sense of the word, covered themselves in glory at Super Bowl XXVI. The Buffalo Bills, a collection of individuals, covered themselves in shame.

Not one segment of the Redskins' roster suggested they were capable of forging the NFL's best record (14–2) during the regular season, polishing off Atlanta and Detroit in the playoffs by a combined score of 65–17, and then running roughshod over the Bills, 37–24. It was the combination of good players, superior coaching, and a current of unselfishness that made these Redskins one of the more underrated championship teams in Super Bowl history.

"We knew we weren't a great team and that we'd have to play hard and together to win," coach Joe Gibbs said, "and that's what we did. I never enjoyed coaching a team more. I really believe it was a well-balanced team with great team chemistry and great team leadership. I was along for the ride."

The win marked the eighth straight Super Bowl victory for the NFC, and the fourth in six years by a team from the NFC East. Gibbs, 51, won his third Super Bowl in nine years, each with a different quarterback and featured running back. The constants were the magnificent offensive line known as "the Hogs," wide receiver Art Monk, top defensive aides Richie Petitbon and Larry Peccatiello, and owner Jack Kent Cooke.

In Super Bowl XVII, Gibbs had surprised Miami with his new "Explode" package of five shifting wide receivers that he utilized on a pair of touchdown passes. In this Super Bowl, he gave the Bills a steady diet of their own no-huddle offense, something the Redskins had only tinkered with in the past. "We used the no-huddle for only two or three series," Mark Rypien said. "But I think it wore Buffalo down a little bit and worked to our advantage."

The score wasn't indicative of the lopsided tenor of play. "We were dominated," Bills coach Marv Levy would say years later.

Attendance: 63,130
Conditions: 73 degrees, indoors
Time of kickoff: 5:25 p.m. (CST)
Length of game: 3 hours, 43 minutes
Referee: Jerry Markbreit

MVP: Mark Rypien, QB, Redskins

Washington led 17–0 at halftime, 31–10 after three quarters, and 37–10 early in the fourth quarter before Jim Kelly passed for two consolation touchdowns. One year after performing honorably in their upset loss to the New York Giants, the Bills humiliated themselves both on and off the field. Running back Thurman Thomas, the NFL's MVP, lost some of his public appeal through his own arrogance, and then he lost his helmet. Defensive line coach Chuck Dickerson eventually lost his job for an unforgivable slip of the tongue. Andre Reed lost his cool. And the Bills lost the ball five times.

"It was a catastrophe," Bills offensive line coach Tom Bresnahan said years later. "I can't really pin down why except we just got our butts beat. The '91 team had the best statistics of our four Super Bowl teams. . . . But the Redskins were a great team and were perfectly prepared for what we were doing. I'd have to say they were the best team that we played in a Super Bowl, but that may not be fair to Dallas."

The Bills were on the wrong side of a 7-point spread, but talked confidently, if not brashly, in the days leading up to the game. Afterward, they were humbled. "We're falling into the category of the Minnesota Vikings and Denver Broncos," Thomas said. "Once we get to the big games, we don't play as well."

"This is hard to take because we have such a good team," Kelly said. "We've come a long way. You hate to say, 'There's always next year.'" Unbeknownst to him at the time, the painful pattern would continue for two more Super Bowls.

	1	2	3	4	Final
Washington Redskins	0	17	14	6	37
Buffalo Bills	0	0	10	14	24

SCORING SUMMARY

2nd Quarter
WAS Lohmiller, 34-yd. FG
WAS Byner, 10-yd. pass from Rypien (Lohmiller kick)
WAS Riggs, 1-yd. run (Lohmiller kick)
3rd Quarter
WAS Riggs, 2-yd. run (Lohmiller kick)
BUF Norwood, 21-yd. FG
BUF Thomas, 1-yd. run (Norwood kick)
WAS Clark, 30-yd. pass from Rypien (Lohmiller kick)
4th Quarter
WAS Lohmiller, 25-yd. FG
WAS Lohmiller, 39-yd. FG
BUF Metzelaars, 2-yd. pass from Kelly (Norwood kick)
BUF Beebe, 4-yd. pass from Kelly (Norwood kick)

Although Rypien outpolled ball-hawking free safety Brad Edwards, 11–2, to win MVP honors in the vote of media representatives, his was a good—but certainly not great—performance. Wide receivers Gary Clark and Monk basically had their way with the Bills' shaky secondary; Clark caught seven passes for 114 yards and Monk had seven for 113. Rotating running backs Ricky Ervins and Earnest Byner ran hard and well, combining for 121 yards in 27 carries.

Overall, the lion's share of the credit belonged to the collective efforts of the Redskins along both sides of the line of scrimmage.

Petitbon out-schemed the Bills' offensive coordinator, Ted Marchibroda, just as his underrated defensive line outplayed the Bills' highly regarded offensive line and his defensive backs pounded the Buffalo wideouts into submission. In fact, the Redskins' defense was downright nasty in the way it hit anyone who touched the ball, especially Kelly.

When defensive tackle James "Jumpy" Geathers bull-rushed through guard Jim Ritcher to sack Kelly on the third play of the game, the tone was set. Kelly was sacked five times in all, about three more than average during the regular season, and knocked down about 11 more times. He paid a severe physical price for the 283 yards the Bills recorded. One of

the Redskins' most punishing hitters, cornerback Martin Mayhew, actually knocked Kelly out at the end of a scramble early in the fourth quarter. Kelly returned after sitting out a play, but his memory afterward was spotty.

Not even a first-quarter performance filled with uncharacteristic mistakes by the Redskins could inspire the Bills to make a spirited underdog's bid. With their offensive line becoming more and more dominant and their defensive front seven controlling the line of scrimmage, the Redskins were never really challenged by their opponent, which had the next-best record (13–3) in the NFL that season.

If the Bills had done anything at all offensively in the first quarter they might have made a game of it. With Monk catching four passes for 79 yards, the Redskins moved from their 11 to the Buffalo 2 on their second possession. From there, the Bills rose up to deny 245-pound Gerald Riggs on a pair of goal-line thrusts. Rypien's pass to Monk that was ruled a 2-yard touchdown on the field was overturned by replay official Cal Lepore, who ruled that Monk had stepped on the end line. Then Jeff Rutledge, the holder for one of the best special-teams groups in the NFL, dropped the snap from center and Chip Lohmiller's field-goal attempt from 21 yards never even took flight.

Shortly thereafter, the Redskins had another red-zone chance but again came away empty. On third and 9 from the 11, nose tackle Jeff Wright batted a pass high into the air that fell to cornerback Kirby Jackson for an interception. "I see Ricky Ervins break free and he has a gut-cinch touchdown," Rypien said. "You had a reversal on a touchdown, you missed a field-goal opportunity, and now you get this interception on a sure touchdown. So you're kind of thinking maybe this isn't the Redskins' day."

When the Redskins did break through and score, it was only a 34-yard field goal by Lohmiller. A 19-yard run by Byner and Rypien's 41-yard strike to Ricky Sanders behind free safety Mark Kelso got the Redskins to the Bills 17, but center Jeff Bostic was penalized for holding defensive end Bruce Smith on a first-down running play, and the drive bogged down.

Buffalo's defense, which ranked 27th during

the regular season, had been without Smith for 11 games and Wright for 7 because of knee injuries. Although Smith's limited mobility rendered him merely a shadow of himself in the Super Bowl, at least the Bills had him in the lineup. Defensive coordinator Walt Corey used a variation of th[e] Bears' 46 defense in an effort to stop the run, an[d] he structured his aggressive pass rush aroun[d] blitzing linebacker Cornelius Bennett. "He playe[d] like a savage that afternoon," Redskins offensiv[e] line coach Jim Hanifa[n] said, referring to Bennet[t.] "He played his heart out. A[t] the end of the game he wa[s] totally exhausted."

With Corey committed t[o] blitzing, Bennett and outsid[e] linebacker Darryl Talley led [a] charge that resulted in seve[n] knockdowns but no sacks. Mos[t] of the heat came early. "Th[is] burst of adrenaline by the Buffa[lo] defense was the most incredibl[e] thing I'd ever seen, being in m[y] first Super Bowl," Rypien sai[d.] "I was getting hit and it wasn['t] characteristic of our guys to le[t] that happen. Jeff Bostic come[s] over and says, 'Calm dow[n,] weather the storm. These guy[s] are throwing everything the[y] have at us now, but they're goin[g] to tire themselves out.'"

It had taken five posses[s]ions, but by early in the secon[d] quarter the Redskins' fourth[-] ranked offense was rolling[.] Washington moved 51 yards i[n] five plays, taking a 10–0 lea[d] when Jackson got caught up in[-] side and wasn't able to preven[t] Byner from diving into the en[d] zone on a 10-yard pass in th[e] flat. Then the Redskins wen[t] 55 yards in five to set up Riggs[']s 1-yard scoring plunge for [a] 17–0 lead. The big play came o[n] third and 9 when Clark caugh[t] a 15-yard crossing route, juke[d] cornerback Nate Odomes, an[d] stretched it into a 34-yard gain[.]

With 30 seconds remainin[g]

WASHINGTON REDSKINS (NFC, 14–2)		Offense		BUFFALO BILLS (AFC, 13–3)	
84	Gary Clark* (5-9, 173)	WR	80	James Lofton* (6-3, 195)	
87	Ron Middleton (6-2, 270)	TE	88	Pete Metzelaars (6-7, 250)	
79	Jim Lachey* (6-6, 294)	LT	69	Will Wolford (6-5, 295)	
63	Raleigh McKenzie (6-2, 279)	LG	51	Jim Ritcher* (6-3, 273)	
53	Jeff Bostic (6-2, 278)	C	67	Kent Hull (6-5, 275)	
69	Mark Schlereth* (6-3, 283)	RG	74	Glenn Parker (6-3, 301)	
66	Joe Jacoby (6-7, 314)	RT	75	Howard Ballard (6-6, 325)	
85	Don Warren (6-4, 242)	TE	84	Keith McKeller (6-4, 245)	
81	Art Monk (6-3, 210)	WR	83	Andre Reed* (6-2, 190)	
11	Mark Rypien* (6-4, 234)	QB	12	Jim Kelly* (6-3, 218)	
21	Earnest Byner* (5-10, 218)	RB	23	Kenneth Davis (5-10, 209)	
		Defense			
71	Charles Mann* (6-6, 272)	LE	96	Leon Seals (6-5, 270)	
75	Eric Williams (6-4, 290)	LT ǀ NT	91	Jeff Wright (6-3, 270)	
78	Tim Johnson (6-3, 283)	RT ǀ RE	78	Bruce Smith (6-4, 275)	
60	Fred Stokes (6-3, 274)	RE ǀ LOLB	97	Cornelius Bennett* (6-2, 236)	
58	Wilber Marshall (6-1, 231)	LLB ǀ LILB	58	Shane Conlan (6-3, 230)	
54	Kurt Gouveia (6-1, 228)	MLB ǀ RILB	54	Carlton Bailey (6-3, 235)	
55	Andre Collins (6-1, 233)	RLB ǀ ROLB	56	Darryl Talley* (6-4, 235)	
35	Martin Mayhew (5-8, 172)	LCB	47	Kirby Jackson (5-10, 180)	
28	Darrell Green* (5-8, 170)	RCB	37	Nate Odomes (5-10, 188)	
26	Danny Copeland (6-2, 213)	SS	45	Dwight Drane (6-2, 205)	
27	Brad Edwards (6-2, 207)	FS	38	Mark Kelso (5-11, 185)	

* Pro Bowl selection

SUBSTITUTIONS

Washington

Offense: WR - 86 Stephen Hobbs, 83 Ricky Sanders; TE - 82 John Brandes, 88 James Jenkins, 89 Terry Orr; T - 76 Ed Simmons; G - 61 Mark Adickes, 68 Russ Grimm; QB - 10 Jeff Rutledge; RB - 32 Ricky Ervins, 30 Brian Mitchell, 37 Gerald Riggs. **Defense:** DE - 99 Jason Buck; DT - 97 Jumpy Geathers, 94 Bobby Wilson; LB - 50 Ravin Caldwell, 51 Monte Coleman; CB - 47 A. J. Johnson, 45 Sidney Johnson, 20 Alvoid Mays; S - 34 Terry Hoage. **Specialists:** K - 8 Chip Lohmiller*; P - 2 Kelly Goodburn **Inactive:** 16 Stan Humphries (QB), 57 Matt Millen (LB).

Buffalo

Offense: WR - 82 Don Beebe, 85 Al Edwards, 89 Steve Tasker*; TE - 87 Butch Rolle; T - 79 Joe Staysniak; G - 59 Mitch Frerotte; C - 63 Adam Lingner; QB - 14 Frank Reich; RB - 35 Carwell Gardner, 34 Thurman Thomas*. **Defense:** DE - 90 Phil Hansen, 94 Mark Pike; NT - 73 Mike Lodish; LB - 50 Ray Bentley, 99 Hal Garner, 53 Marvcus Patton; CB - 26 Chris Hale, 27 Clifford Hicks, 31 James Williams; S - 20 Henry Jones. **Specialists:** K - 11 Scott Norwood, 5 Brad Daluiso; P - 9 Chris Mohr. **Inactive:** 64 Mike Brennan (T), 7 Gale Gilbert (QB).

in the first half and the ball at the Washington 28, Reed flew into a rage when Edwards wasn't called for interference against him. Reed slammed down his helmet, the ear pads went flying, an unsportsmanlike conduct penalty was called, and the Bills suddenly were out of field-goal range.

Rypien, a sixth-round draft choice in 1986, had been stashed on injured reserve for two years before starting 30 games over the next three seasons. Gibbs kept drafting quarterbacks in the middle rounds (Stan Humphries, Jeff Graham, and Cary Conklin) to challenge Rypien, who fumbled 14 times in 1989 and couldn't hold the job in 1990. No one ever made more of his last chance than Rypien. "Mark had a tremendous, tremendous season," Hanifan said. "I'm talking every day in practice. He was so accurate on his deep balls. The mark of a Joe Gibbs team was a lot of shifting, a lot of motion. Each week it was a different deal, but we'd go out there on Wednesday morning and Ryp knew it better than anybody. He was so bright."

Gibbs hastened Rypien's development by exposing him to such top-caliber quarterbacks coaches as Jerry Rhome, Dan Henning, and Rod Dowhower. In similar fashion, when prized offensive line coach Joe Bugel left for Phoenix in 1990, Gibbs brought in the no-less-highly regarded Hanifan

from Atlanta.

In 1991, the Hogs included Jim Lachey at left tackle, Raleigh McKenzie at left guard, Bostic, Mark Schlereth at right guard, and Joe Jacoby at right tackle. In 19 games, the Redskins outscored their opponents 587–265 and allowed merely 9 sacks (and registered 64 sacks of their own). Jacoby started the season at left guard and McKenzie was on the bench, but when right tackle Ed Simmons went down in Week 2 with a knee injury, Jacoby moved back to tackle. Lachey entered the NFL as a first-round pick but Jacoby and Bostic were free agents, Schlereth was a 10th-round pick, and McKenzie was selected in the 11th round. In the Super Bowl, Lachey neutralized Smith. "That was probably the best game Jimmy ever played in his life," said Hanifan. "We knew Bruce was a great, great player but I also thought that Jimmy Lachey was an outstanding player and that we didn't have to give him any help."

Byner, 29, spearheaded the NFL's seventh-best ground game with 1,048 yards. He entered the league as Cleveland's 10th-round pick in 1984, but it wasn't until the Redskins acquired him in a trade for halfback Mike Oliphant in April 1989 that his career really took off. He made the Pro Bowl both in 1990 and 1991. "He'd get you 4 yards all the time," said Hanifan. "I remembered thinking, 'We blocked that play really good. We should have got more yardage out of that.' Then I'd go, 'Wait a minute. We didn't block that play worth a hoot and Earnest still made 5 yards.' It evened out. Our players would really go to battle with this guy. Then we'd pop Ricky Ervins in there and he gave us a nice change of pace."

The Redskins didn't have an abundance of great players on defense, either, though no one would know it by their level of performance. Defensive end Charles Mann and cornerback Darrell Green were the only Pro Bowl selections, although outside linebacker Wilber Marshall had a big year and probably deserved to go. Defensive tackles Eric Williams and Tim Johnson were acquired in 1990 trades for fourth-round draft choices. Five other starters—end Fred Stokes, middle linebacker Matt Millen, safeties Danny Copeland and Brad Edwards, and Mayhew—arrived during the watered-down version of early free agency known as Plan B.

For the Super Bowl, Millen was deactivated

because it was decided that Kurt Gouveia had better range in coverage. The nickel back was A. J. Johnson until he suffered a sprained knee in the first half and was replaced by Alvoid Mays. Petitbon's plan was to blitz more than usual early, hopeful of stealing running lanes from Thomas and planting seeds of uncertainty in Kelly. Geathers, another Plan B acquisition, led the team in pressures during the season with 27 to go with four and a half sacks. "'Jumpy' was at least as valuable as anybody we had on defense," Peccatiello said. "He could take the guard and literally walk him back to the quarterback."

For years, the Bills had made a living running Thomas toward the strong side of the formation because Reed, the slot receiver in their three-wide receiver attack known as the "K-Gun," usually was able to overpower the nickel back lined up over him. According to Bresnahan, the major reason why Thomas gained a scant 13 yards in 10 carries in the Super Bowl was the decision by the Redskins to move Green to a safety position about 10 yards across from Reed. By doing so, the Redskins felt comfortable moving either linebacker Andre Collins or Monte Coleman immediately across from Reed in the slot.

"To my knowledge, no one had ever done that before," Bresnahan said. "They could stay in regular defensive personnel and they could line the third linebacker up on Andre and let Darrell play safety over the top. Or they could fake that linebacker being out there and then bring him in at the last second to play the run. It was a mismatch between [the linebacker] and Andre, especially when he was working inside and giving Andre a bad angle. All of a sudden one of Jim's best weapons, running toward the slot, was no longer available. The reason why the no-huddle was so good was because we could pass and run with equal effectiveness. That really narrowed our running game."

Just 16 of the Bills' 82 snaps were runs, an imbalance that contributed heavily to Kelly's meager passer rating of 44.8. So, too, did the fact that the Bills dropped an estimated nine passes, including two touchdown passes by Don Beebe and a long pass by tight end Keith McKeller.

Kelly's four interceptions led to 17 points.

WASHINGTON	TEAM STATISTICS	BUFFALO
24	Total First Downs	25
10	Rushing	4
12	Passing	18
2	Penalty	3
417	Total Net Yardage	283
73	Total Offensive Plays	82
5.7	Avg. Gain per Offensive Play	3.5
40	Rushes	18
125	Yards Gained Rushing (Net)	43
3.1	Average Yards per Rush	2.4
33	Passes Attempted	59
18	Passes Completed	29
1	Passes Intercepted	4
0	Tackled Attempting to Pass	5
0	Yards Lost Attempting to Pass	46
292	Yards Gained Passing (Net)	240
6/16	Third-Down Efficiency	7/17
0/2	Fourth-Down Efficiency	2/2
4	Punts	6
37.5	Average Distance	35.0
0	Punt Returns	3
0	Punt Return Yardage	9
1	Kickoff Returns	4
16	Kickoff Return Yardage	77
79	Interception Return Yardage	4
1	Fumbles	6
1	Own Fumbles Recovered	5
1	Opponent Fumbles Recovered	0
5	Penalties	6
82	Yards Penalized	50
4	Touchdowns	3
2	Rushing	1
2	Passing	2
0	Returns	0
4	Extra Points Made	3
3	Field Goals Made	1
3	Field Goals Attempted	1
0	Safeties	0
37	Total Points Scored	24
33:43	Time of Possession	26:17

Two occurred in long-yardage situations when h had time and decided to take a shot deep despit double coverage. Another came on a blitz whe Thomas failed to do his job in pass protection. I didn't lead to points, but it exposed Thomas' half hearted approach in this Super Bowl. Mann beat h man inside and was able to slam into Kelly just a

WASHINGTON

Passing	CP/ATT	YDS	TD	INT	RAT
Rypien	18/33	292	2	1	92.0

Rushing	ATT	YDS	AVG	TD	LG
Ervins	13	72	5.5	0	21
Byner	14	49	3.5	0	19
Riggs	5	7	1.4	2	4
Sanders	1	1	1.0	0	1
Rutledge	1	0	0.0	0	0
Rypien	6	-4	-0.7	0	2

Receiving	NO	YDS	AVG	TD	LG
Clark	7	114	16.3	1	34
Monk	7	113	16.1	0	31
Byner	3	24	8.0	1	10t
Sanders	1	41	41.0	0	41

Interceptions	NO	YDS	LG	TD
Edwards	2	56	35	0
Gouveia	1	23	23	0
Green	1	0	0	0

Punting	NO	AVG	LG	BLK
Goodburn	4	37.5	45	0

Punt Ret.	NO/FC	YDS	LG	TD
Mitchell	0/2	0	**	0

Kickoff Ret.	NO	YDS	LG	TD
Mitchell	1	16	16	0

Defense	SOLO	AST	TOT	SK
Marshall	8	3	11	1
Mayhew	6	0	6	0
Stokes	5	1	6	1
Collins	5	0	5	0
T. Johnson	3	2	5	0
Edwards	3	1	4	0
Gouveia	3	1	4	0
Mays	3	1	4	1
Geathers	2	1	3	1
Caldwell	2	0	2	0
Green	2	0	2	0
Hoage	2	0	2	0
Hobbs	2	0	2	0
Buck	1	0	1	1
Coleman	1	0	1	0
Jacoby	1	0	1	0
S. Johnson	1	0	1	0
Lohmiller	1	0	1	0
E. Williams	1	0	1	0
Mann	0	1	1	0
TOTAL	52	11	63	5

BUFFALO

Passing	CP/ATT	YDS	TD	INT	RAT
Kelly	28/58	275	2	4	44.8
Reich	1/1	11	0	0	112.5

Rushing	ATT	YDS	AVG	TD	LG
K. Davis	4	17	4.3	0	13
Kelly	3	16	5.3	0	9
Thomas	10	13	1.3	1	6
Lofton	1	-3	-3.0	0	-3

Receiving	NO	YDS	AVG	TD	LG
Lofton	7	92	13.1	0	18
Reed	5	34	6.8	0	12
Beebe	4	61	15.3	1	43
K. Davis	4	38	9.5	0	12
Thomas	4	27	6.8	0	8
McKeller	2	29	14.5	0	21
Edwards	1	11	11.0	0	11
Metzelaars	1	2	2.0	1	2t
Kelly	1	-8	-8.0	0	-8

Interceptions	NO	YDS	LG	TD
Jackson	1	4	4	0

Punting	NO	AVG	LG	BLK
Mohr	6	35.0	53	0

Punt Ret.	NO/FC	YDS	LG	TD
Hicks	3/0	9	7	0

Kickoff Ret.	NO	YDS	LG	TD
Edwards	4	77	24	0

Defense	SOLO	AST	TOT	SK
Bailey	7	4	11	0
Talley	5	3	8	0
Bennett	6	1	7	0
Kelso	4	2	6	0
Seals	3	3	6	0
K. Jackson	5	0	5	0
Odomes	3	1	4	0
Drane	3	1	4	0
Bentley	3	0	3	0
Wright	2	1	3	0
Garner	2	0	2	0
B. Smith	2	0	2	0
Jones	1	0	1	0
Lofton	1	0	1	0
Thomas	1	0	1	0
Ritcher	1	0	1	0
J. Williams	1	0	1	0
TOTAL	50	16	66	0

he released the ball because Thomas made almost no effort to slide over and pick him up. Green made a great play underneath, tipping the pass away from Reed so it could be intercepted by Edwards in center field.

The most critical of the interceptions happened on the opening play of the third quarter. It was just another example of the Redskins outwitting the Bills. During the pre-game meal, and again on the bus ride to the stadium, Peccatiello discussed with Petitbon the idea of letting Collins join Marshall at times as the fifth rusher, replacing Stokes. "We said, 'This is going to be good, but let's save it for the second half,'" Peccatiello said. "We called that 'ammo.' Ammo was something to save in case you needed it." As Kelly backed away from center, Collins shot clean through the center-left guard gap. The pass was rushed and the ball ended up behind McKeller, where it was picked off by Gouveia. He returned 23 yards to the 2. Then the stunned Bills didn't lay a glove on Riggs as he cut back into the end zone behind Schlereth's pancake block on linebacker Carlton Bailey.

Washington's linebackers were able to time many of their blitzes perfectly after noticing that when Kelly put his hands out in the shotgun formation, he would then lower them just before the ball was snapped. They also detected that when McKeller came across the formation on a shallow crossing route, Reed would work behind him on an inside route in the opposite direction. "So we passed off different people and always had a guy in position to take away that route from Reed," Peccatiello said. "The Bills did not use a lot of motion. Even though they had very formidable offensive personnel, they never varied from their three–wide receiver formation. But we knew exactly what they'd be in and we had some reads that turned out to be very good. I can't tell you how smart our kids were."

Down by 24 points and with six first downs to show for nine possessions, the Bills took advantage of a Redskins' defense that was missing Green (calf), Johnson (knee), and Coleman (groin) to make it 24–10. Beebe's 43-yard catch behind Edwards set up Scott Norwood's 21-yard field goal. Then Mayhew's 29-yard interference penalty set up Thomas' 1-yard touchdown run. "We knew that if this game was going to be won," Rypien said, "it was going to be on our next drive."

Starting from their 21, the Redskins moved 49 yards using their no-huddle before the coaches decided to signal in a third-and-10 play. The Bills went with a safety blitz even though their best blitzer in the secondary, strong safety Leonard Smith, was on crutches because of an infected knee. On the right side, Clark escaped cornerback James Williams at the line, beat him easily to the corner, and hauled in Rypien's 30-yard touchdown pass.

"Basically, we were more of a man coverage team," said Corey. "We had some great players. Cornelius Bennett—God, he was quick and fast. Shane Conlan. Darryl [Talley] was extremely smart and tough. I used to tell Darryl, 'You're responsible for Bruce [Smith]. You let Bruce do what he wants to do and you make sure you pick up his responsibility as a contain guy.' Bruce was the best defensive lineman I ever had. . . . As long as I could keep Bruce moving I could get by with average linemen. And then we had some people that were just very average. The secondary was very suspect. Good guys and worked hard, but none of them will ever get into the Hall of Fame."

The last thing that the Bills needed leading up to the game was to motivate the Redskins or rekindle their own internal squabbles that undermined them in the late 1980s. But that's exactly what happened. Dickerson, an administrative assistant promoted to defensive line coach by Levy in 1990 after Ted Cottrell took a job with the Phoenix Cardinals, offered what he considered to be a humorous analysis of the Hogs. Adding "oink-oinks" for effect, Dickerson referred to Jacoby as a "Neanderthal," said Bostic was "ugly like the rest of them," and described Lachey as "a ballerina in a 310-pound body."

Sure enough, Gibbs obtained tapes of Dickerson and played them at the Saturday night team meeting. "It upset our players and it upset Marv," Corey said. "Chuck Dickerson. That's a different cat. Not one of my favorite people." Peccatiello ran into Levy in the offseason not long after Dickerson had been fired. "[Levy] said, 'Larry, that was not the straw that broke the camel's back,'" Peccatiello said. "He said, 'That was the girder that brought down the building.'"

As if that wasn't enough, Levy had to deal with revelations by Bruce Smith during Super Bowl week that he was receiving racist hate mail in Buffalo from people telling him to get out of town. Then Thomas took umbrage to remarks made by Marchibroda in Minneapolis that Kelly was the "Michael Jordan" of the Bills, and he blew off a mandatory media session after reading about it the next day at breakfast. A day later, Thomas told the press, "I think I am the Michael Jordan of this team." Said tackle Will Wolford, "You have to understand Thurman. If you don't know him, you'd think he was an idiot. We've known him for two or three years and now we know he's an idiot."

Earlier, Thomas had suffered the eternal embarrassment of not being in the lineup for the first two plays because he couldn't find his helmet. "I'll tell you the story," said Levy. "When they played the national anthem, Thurman set down his helmet and so did a defensive player next to him. The other player picked up Thurman's helmet and walked down to the end of the bench. It's a good story, but it had no impact on the outcome. How we played is what counted."

The Bills bitched about who was going to get the credit and ended up being discredited. "They talked a good game," said Jacoby, "but we played a good game." The Redskins were an aging team with aging ownership and staff, and after finishing a disappointing 9–7 in 1992, the first Joe Gibbs era in D.C. was history. The ledger from Gibbs' 12 seasons showed 140 victories against 65 defeats, four Super Bowl appearances, and three Super Bowl rings. This game, and indeed this team, was Gibbs' ultimate triumph.

Top Ten Coaching Goats

1. **Chuck Dickerson, Bills, XXVI:** Buffalo's defensive line coach mocked "the Hogs" during midweek interviews, and the Redskins used his words to their advantage. Fired shortly after the Super Bowl, Dickerson did sports talk radio in Buffalo for a decade but never coached again.

2. **Bill Parcells, Patriots, XXXI:** Blew a chance for a third Super Bowl championship by kicking off to Desmond Howard just when the Packers were feeling the heat. Spent much of the week on the phone with the Jets and was hired as their head coach five days later.

3. **George Allen, Redskins, VII:** The stage was too big for him. Left the best of the Redskins on the practice field and couldn't handle the national attention.

4. **Andy Reid, Eagles, XXXIX:** Allowed offense to operate at a snail's pace on final scoring drive when every tick of the clock helped the Patriots.

5. **Mike Holmgren, Packers, XXXII:** Suffered through the worst week of his career, failing to adjust to the Broncos' blitzes and losing track of the down with the game on line.

6. **Mike Martz, Rams, XXXVI:** Gave short shrift to his exceptional running game and then didn't go hurry-up until the bitter end.

7. **Dick Vermeil, Eagles, XV:** Team was tight as a drum all week, then played like it and were mauled by the Raiders.

8. **Bill Belichick, Patriots, XLII:** Ended up losing by 3 points after he decided to go for it on fourth and 13 instead of having Stephen Gostkowski attempt a 49-yard field goal.

9. **Raymond Berry, Patriots, XX:** Didn't even try to run the ball, which is what got the Patriots there. Instead, he offered up QBs Tony Eason and Steve Grogan to the Bears' voracious pass rush.

10. **Bud Grant, Vikings, XI:** The Raiders rushed for most of their 266 yards to the weak side, and the "Ice Man" never made a single adjustment.

Dishonorable Mentions: Tom Landry, Cowboys, XIII; Joe Gibbs, Redskins, XVIII; Marv Levy, Bills, XXVIII; John Fox, Panthers, XXXVIII; Jim Caldwell, Colts, XLIV.

XXVII
DALLAS COWBOYS 52, BUFFALO BILLS 17

January 31, 1993
Rose Bowl, Pasadena, California

The majestic San Gabriel Mountains towering above the Rose Bowl made a fitting backdrop for what a magnificent football team accomplished in Super Bowl XXVII and would accomplish in the future.

Coronation or coming-out party? Nobody at the time knew for sure what the Dallas Cowboys' 52–17 annihilation of the Buffalo Bills meant. But the 'Boys most assuredly were back, and it didn't seem like they'd be going away any time soon.

Assembled by the management team of coach Jimmy Johnson and owner Jerry Jones, the "JJs," that was initially reviled in Dallas, this Cowboys team was not only the best team in the NFL but also the youngest. It won the toughest division in the league, the NFC East, defeated probably the second-best team in the league, the 49ers, in the NFC Championship Game, and manhandled the best that the AFC could send its way, a Buffalo team with 11 Pro Bowl players and matchless experience from having played in the previous two Super Bowls.

"I don't know about dynasty," Johnson said after the mismatch. "You don't know what will happen before the start of next year. But we had a great, great year, and I think we'll have a very good football team."

By the time of the Super Bowl, the JJs had made 46 trades in their never-a-dull-moment first four years. None could compare with the October 1989 heist when the Cowboys sent running back Herschel Walker to Minnesota for three first-round draft choices, three second-round draft choices, one third-round draft choice, and five players.

Johnson and Jones treated 1989 like a mass audition, and the club went 1–15. The Cowboys almost qualified for the playoffs in 1990, reached the divisional round in 1991, and then went 13–3 in 1992 when several of the stockpiled draft choices blossomed into impact players. Wide receiver Michael Irvin, in his fifth season, was 26,

Attendance: 98,374
Conditions: 61 degrees, sunny, wind SW at 10 mph
Time of kickoff: 3:25 p.m. (PST)
Length of game: 3 hours, 23 minutes
Referee: Dick Hantak

MVP: Troy Aikman, QB, Cowboys

as was quarterback Troy Aikman, in his fourth season. Running back Emmitt Smith, in his third season, was 23. Other key players who had yet to reach their 27th birthday were wide receiver Alvin Harper; tackle Erik Williams; center Mark Stepnoski; fullback Daryl Johnston; defensive linemen Leon Lett, Russell Maryland, and Tony Tolbert; linebacker Ken Norton; cornerbacks Kevin Smith and Larry Brown; and safety Darren Woodson. The team's oldest starter, left tackle Mark Tuinei, was 32.

"We were such a talented team that we were able to overcome our youth and inexperience," Aikman said. "Our youth was a big reason we were underdogs [by 4 points] against San Francisco, but I think it really was to our advantage because our attitude was to just play. That team, more than any other I was on, just went onto the field and played. Before we knew it we were in the Super Bowl and nobody could believe it."

Not one member of the Cowboys' top-ranked defense was selected to the Pro Bowl. "We had kind of a no-name defense," secondary coach Dave Campo said. "We were a hungry, young football team that people might have taken a little bit for granted.... I'm not sure we got quite as much respect as we probably deserved given the players we had." In 1991, the Cowboys ranked 17th in both yards and points allowed. Ten days before the 1992 opener they traded second- and third-round picks to the 49ers for talented but troubled defensive end Charles Haley. "That was a tremendous front four, but Haley

	1	2	3	4	Final
Buffalo Bills	7	3	7	0	17
Dallas Cowboys	14	14	3	21	52

SCORING SUMMARY

1st Quarter
BUF Thomas, 2-yd. run (Christie kick)
DAL Novacek, 23-yd. pass from Aikman (Elliott kick)
DAL J. Jones, 2-yd. fumble return (Elliott kick)
2nd Quarter
BUF Christie, 21-yd. FG
DAL Irvin, 19-yd. pass from Aikman (Elliott kick)
DAL Irvin, 18-yd. pass from Aikman (Elliott kick)
3rd Quarter
DAL Elliott, 20-yd. FG
BUF Beebe, 40-yd. pass from Reich (Christie kick)
4th Quarter
DAL Harper, 45-yd. pass from Aikman (Elliott kick)
DAL E. Smith, 10-yd. run (Elliott kick)
DAL Norton, 9-yd. fumble return (Elliott kick)

put us over the top," said Campo. "He knew how to win. He was a tough guy. . . . Then we had enough speed inside with Lett and Jimmie Jones."

The Cowboys faced what was supposed to have been a grittier Bills team. The defense was better now that safety Henry Jones, defensive end Phil Hansen, and inside linebacker Marvcus Patton had become starters in their second years, and the great Bruce Smith was back healthy. The offense wasn't quite as prolific, with offensive line coach Tom Bresnahan having been promoted to replace departed Ted Marchibroda as coordinator. Still, Buffalo led the league in rushing and was second in yards. Perhaps most importantly, the Bills had overcome a 35–3 deficit in a wild-card battle with Houston.

"The fact that we had to struggle to get here, after getting in the so-called easy way the last two times," said Marv Levy, the Bills' scholarly 64-year-old coach, "the result is a well-earned sense of self-esteem. I told the players, 'You're a team that's been a bit of a punching bag in the past. Now you've earned people's respect. What you do on Sunday will be what you'll have to live with.'"

Some experts believed the Bills, 6-point underdogs, were ready to win, especially given that the Cowboys' last Super Bowl appearance had been

14 years ago. But Johnson certainly wasn't one of them. "I truthfully can say that I don't know that I've ever been as confident in a big game as I was in that one," he said years later. "I just thought that we were far and away the better team. The night before the game I said, 'We've got this game won. All we have to do is play it a little bit close to the vest and protect the football early and eventually Buffalo will turn it over.' "

The crowd of 98,374 was just getting settled on a 60-degree day when Buffalo's Steve Tasker broke through and blocked a punt by Mike Saxon out of bounds at the Dallas 16. The Bills were able to time their rush because Cowboys long snapper Dale Hellestrae had snapped for them in the late 1980s, so they had his pre-snap routine down pat. Not only was Tasker able to anticipate the count, but he also found a one-on-one matchup to his liking across from rookie linebacker Robert Jones, who was substituting for injured linebacker Dixon Edwards. "I think Tasker blocked seven punts during his career and I know of at least three or four that he tipped," said Bruce DeHaven, the Bills' special-teams coach. "I don't know if a special-teams player deserves to go into the Hall of Fame, but none could do the things that he could."

Haley's third-down sack of Jim Kelly was for naught when Brown was penalized for holding. With the ball on the 5, Thurman Thomas powered to the 2 on first down and into the end zone on second down.

Walt Corey, the Bills defensive coordinator, began the game in a two-deep zone. He was hoping to protect his suspect cornerbacks by keeping the safeties back, gambling that his front seven could contain Emmitt Smith reasonably well. The Cowboys picked up two first downs on their second possession but had to punt when Aikman was pressured into back-to-back incompletions. "They were bringing both inside linebackers and it really surprised us," said Johnson. Then Lett drew a 15-yard penalty for roughing Kelly on a third-and-16 incompletion, and Andre Reed followed with a 21-yard reception to midfield. "Nobody wants to hear this," Cowboys offensive line coach Tony Wise said, "but at that point everybody on that sideline was worried about the game turning into a blowout for them."

Johnson felt great about the machine-gun style practices he conducted to prepare for the Bills' no-huddle, but this was the real thing. "We talked to the players that playing against Buffalo was similar to playing against a super-talented wishbone team in college where there was a transition to get a feel for the pace of the game," Dallas defensive line coach Butch Davis said. "The Bills had great, great skilled athletes, and at first it appeared that we weren't going to come close to slowing them down."

BUFFALO BILLS (AFC, 11–5)			DALLAS COWBOYS (NFC, 13–3)	
		Offense		
80	James Lofton (6-3, 190)	WR	80	Alvin Harper (6-3, 207)
69	Will Wolford* (6-5, 297)	LT	71	Mark Tuinei (6-5, 298)
51	Jim Ritcher* (6-3, 273)	LG	61	Nate Newton* (6-3, 332)
67	Kent Hull (6-5, 278)	C	53	Mark Stepnoski* (6-2, 269)
74	Glenn Parker (6-5, 305)	RG	63	John Gesek (6-5, 282)
75	Howard Ballard* (6-6, 325)	RT	79	Erik Williams (6-6, 321)
88	Pete Metzelaars (6-7, 250)	TE	84	Jay Novacek* (6-4, 231)
83	Andre Reed* (6-2, 190)	WR	88	Michael Irvin* (6-2, 199)
12	Jim Kelly* (6-3, 218)	QB	8	Troy Aikman* (6-4, 222)
34	Thurman Thomas* (5-10, 198)	RB	22	Emmitt Smith* (5-9, 209)
82	Don Beebe (5-11, 184)	WR I FB	48	Daryl Johnston (6-2, 238)
		Defense		
90	Phil Hansen (6-5, 275)	LE	92	Tony Tolbert (6-6, 265)
91	Jeff Wright (6-3, 270)	NT I LT	75	Tony Casillas (6-3, 273)
78	Bruce Smith* (6-4, 273)	RE I RT	67	Russell Maryland (6-1, 275)
97	Cornelius Bennett* (6-2, 236)	LOLB I RE	94	Charles Haley (6-5, 245)
58	Shane Conlan (6-3, 230)	LILB I LLB	98	Godfrey Myles (6-1, 242)
53	Marvcus Patton (6-2, 225)	RILB I RLB	51	Ken Norton (6-2, 241)
56	Darryl Talley (6-4, 235)	ROLB I CB	29	Kenneth Gant (5-11, 191)
29	James Williams (5-10, 178)	LCB	26	Kevin Smith (5-11, 177)
37	Nate Odomes* (5-10, 188)	RCB	24	Larry Brown (5-11, 185)
20	Henry Jones* (5-11, 197)	SS	27	Thomas Everett (5-9, 183)
38	Mark Kelso (5-11, 185)	FS	37	James Washington (6-1, 203)

* Pro Bowl selection

SUBSTITUTIONS

Buffalo
Offense: WR - 81 Brad Lamb, 89 Steve Tasker*; TE - 86 Rob Awalt, 84 Keith McKeller; T - 70 John Fina; G - 65 John Davis, 59 Mitch Frerotte; C - 63 Adam Lingner; QB - 14 Frank Reich; RB - 23 Kenneth Davis, 35 Carwell Gardner. *Defense:* DE - 94 Mark Pike; NT - 73 Mike Lodish; LB - 54 Carlton Bailey, 95 Keith Goganious, 55 Mark Maddox; CB - 26 Chris Hale, 27 Clifford Hicks, 47 Kirby Jackson; S - 43 Matt Darby. *Specialists:* K - 2 Steve Christie; P - 9 Chris Mohr. *DNP:* 93 Keith Willis (DE). *Inactive:* 7 Gale Gilbert (QB), 24 Kurt Schulz (S).

Dallas
Offense: WR - 83 Kelvin Martin, 82 Jimmy Smith; TE - 89 Derek Tennell; G - 66 Kevin Gogan; C - 68 Frank Cornish, 70 Dale Hellestrae; QB - 7 Steve Beuerlein; RB - 34 Tommie Agee, 39 Derrick Gainer. *Defense:* DE - 77 Jim Jeffcoat; DT - 95 Chad Hennings, 97 Jimmie Jones, 78 Leon Lett; LB - 58 Dixon Edwards, 55 Robert Jones, 52 Mickey Pruitt, 57 Vinson Smith; CB - 47 Clayton Holmes, 30 Issiac Holt; S - 20 Ray Horton, 28 Darren Woodson. *Specialists:* K - 2 Lin Elliott; P - 4 Mike Saxon. *Inactive:* 76 Alan Veingrad (T), 23 Robert Williams (S).

The game was a little more than 10 minutes old when James Washington intercepted a wayward pass by Kelly, who was pressured by Kenneth Gant. Not many teams blitzed the Bills because their no-huddle kept defenses off balance. Given an extra week to prepare, defensive coordinator Dave Wannstedt renamed his calls using words like "Pittsburgh," "Buffalo," "Bread and Butter," and "Jam," got everyone on the same page, and went after the gimpy Kelly, who had sat out the previous two and a half games with strained knee ligaments. "It kind of caught them by surprise," said Davis. "We pressured maybe more than in any other game that season."

Two plays went for losses, giving the Cowboys third and 16 at their 47. At that point, Aikman was 4 of 7 for 12 yards, but then he fired a dart to Irvin for 20. "That pass really loosened Troy up," offensive coordinator Norv Turner said. Two plays later, the Cowboys inserted speedy Derrick Gainer at fullback for Johnston and sent him on a flat-and-up pattern. As cornerback James Williams bailed out, Gainer's speed opened up a seam for Pro Bowl tight end Jay Novacek. The linebacker jumped Novacek's out route. "Troy threw a perfect ball and the safety [Mark Kelso] couldn't get there," said Turner. The result was a 23-yard touchdown pass to Novacek.

Starting from the 10 after an illegal-block penalty against linebacker Mark Maddox on the kickoff return, Bresnahan called a screen pass. For years, the Bills had been an effective screen team but always ran it away from the tight-end side of their formation. This time, the Bills tried it toward the tight end. With Haley lined up wide left for the first time rather than wide right, it meant right tackle Howard Ballard would be on an island against him as Kelly backpedaled seven steps.

Noticing the Bills were snapping the ball on the first sound almost every time in their no-huddle, Haley beat Ballard badly around the corner and belted the unsuspecting Kelly with full force under the right shoulder. The fumble bounced into the air and defensive tackle Jimmie Jones gathered it in for a 2-yard touchdown. "I blame myself to this day for that idiot play that probably got the whole thing going," Bresnahan said years later. "I just put Howard in an impossible situation. Jim was so pissed off, he was ready to kill Howard. I said, 'Jim, don't blame Howard. It was my fault.' Then he was ready to kill me.'"

That made it 14–7, but the Bills continued to move the ball. Two carries by Kenneth Davis gained 14 yards, and on the first play of the second quarter

Reed worked free of Gant again and the Cowboys couldn't bring him down until the ball was at their 4 after a 40-yard gain. "Andre Reed would stick the inside nickel guy and try to beat him underneath," said Butch Davis. "We always harped that the nickel back can't get beat to the inside. You're just trying to keep that guy from beating you across your face." The Cowboys adjusted their coverage at halftime and shut down the shallow crossing routes to Reed.

On first and goal, fullback Carwell Gardner carried for 3 yards to the 1. On second down, Thurman ran the same counter play with which he had scored in the first quarter, but linebacker Vinson Smith did a much better job than Robert Jones, shedding a block and stacking him up for no gain. Thomas limped off the field and was replaced by Davis. When Davis took the third-down handoff, planted, and cut toward the bubble at left tackle, Kelly actually raised his arms for what he expected would be a touchdown. But instead of getting low and lunging for the goal line, the 208-pound Davis showed little respect for the 241-pound Norton and tried to take him on high. Norton enveloped Davis with his chest a half-yard out and held his ground until help arrived.

Dallas had its goal-line personnel on the field, but Johnson, Davis, and Campo were peering across the field at the Buffalo coaches. Between Johnson and Campo stood Ray Horton, a backup safety who was playing the final game of his 10-year career before beginning a career in coaching. "Ray was watching their signals," Campo recalled. "He saw a long signal and said, 'They're going to throw it.' So right at the last second we ran our regular people out on the field. I'm not positive that we wouldn't have sent them in anyway, but it added some validity to what we were thinking."

With Tolbert lined up outside Ballard, a rollout pass by Kelly to that side was doomed from the get-go. Tolbert shot up the field past Ballard and hit Kelly just as he lobbed a jump ball in the end zone either to Gardner or tight end Pete Metzelaars. Safety Thomas Everett slipped between receivers and intercepted the pass. "I should have called time out," Levy said. "We had a play called but not for that defense."

The Bills forced a punt and ran Davis three more times for 18 yards, an indication that they remained capable of moving the ball. Then, against another blitz, Kelly took a three-step on a quick screen. Davis had moved up to pick up Norton, but the linebacker timed the snap count and vaulted over the running back, who did well just to chop him in the lower legs. Kelly managed to throw the ball away incomplete, but Norton crashed into his right knee, reinjuring his ligaments and ending Kelly's day. Backup Frank Reich, the hero of playoff victories over the Oilers (41–38) and Miami (29–10), immediately found Reed on another crosser for 38 yards. When the Cowboys once again held inside the 5, Levy took the field goal this time and the Bills trailed just 14–10.

On the last play before the two-minute warning, Emmitt Smith sliced inside Bruce Smith on a strong-side lead and raced 38 yards to the Buffalo 19. On the next play, Irvin spun cornerback Nate Odomes around and burst hard inside for the touchdown pass from Aikman. "Those two plays back-to-back were probably our bread-and-butter run and our bread-and-butter pass," Johnston said. "We didn't do a lot of things to trick people. We did a lot of things that we believed in and challenged people to stop us."

Turner, 40, had been hired by Johnson after the 1990 season, when the Cowboys finished 28th and last in total offense under coordinator David Shula. The third-round selection of Williams enabled Nate Newton to move from right tackle to left guard and solidify the offensive line. As Aikman improved under Turner's inspired coaching, the Cowboys' play-action passing game got better and better. "More than anything else, Norv had such a good relationship with Troy," said Johnson.

By this Super Bowl, the Cowboys had become extremely difficult to stop. "I'm sure other teams look at us and say, 'Well, they don't give you a lot of formations and movement. What's the big deal?'" Turner said before the Super Bowl. "They don't figure it out until they're on the plane home. Because of our line, we're a power rushing team that can throw, and that combination is very hard to defend." Turner's offense was based on the Don Coryell–Ernie Zampese model, with a power run game leading to play-action passing and explosive thrusts downfield.

When the Bills took over possession, Reich checked down to Thomas in the right flat on the first

TEAM STATISTICS

BUFFALO		DALLAS
22	Total First Downs	20
7	Rushing	9
11	Passing	11
4	Penalty	0
362	Total Net Yardage	408
71	Total Offensive Plays	60
5.1	Avg. Gain per Offensive Play	6.8
29	Rushes	29
108	Yards Gained Rushing (Net)	137
3.7	Average Yards per Rush	4.7
38	Passes Attempted	30
22	Passes Completed	22
4	Passes Intercepted	0
4	Tackled Attempting to Pass	1
22	Yards Lost Attempting to Pass	2
254	Yards Gained Passing (Net)	271
5/11	Third-Down Efficiency	5/11
0/2	Fourth-Down Efficiency	0/1
3	Punts	4
45.3	Average Distance	32.8
1	Punt Returns	3
0	Punt Return Yardage	35
4	Kickoff Returns	4
90	Kickoff Return Yardage	79
0	Interception Return Yardage	35
8	Fumbles	4
3	Own Fumbles Recovered	2
2	Opponent Fumbles Recovered	5
4	Penalties	8
30	Yards Penalized	53
2	Touchdowns	7
1	Rushing	1
1	Passing	4
0	Returns	2
2	Extra Points Made	7
1	Field Goals Made	1
1	Field Goals Attempted	1
0	Safeties	0
17	Total Points Scored	52
28:48	Time of Possession	31:12

play. Thomas bobbed, weaved, and cut; then, out of nowhere came the 292-pound Lett flying in pursuit to knock the ball from his hands. Jimmie Jones made the recovery at the 18. For the game, the Bills turned the ball over an unconscionable nine times, five of which were the direct result of the pass rush and two were forced from behind by the hustling Lett—a

INDIVIDUAL STATISTICS

BUFFALO

Passing	CP/ATT	YDS	TD	INT	RAT
Reich	18/31	194	1	2	60.4
Kelly	4/7	82	0	2	58.9

Rushing	ATT	YDS	AVG	TD	LG
K. Davis	15	86	5.7	0	14
Thomas	11	19	1.7	1	9
Gardner	1	3	3.0	0	3
Reich	2	0	0.0	0	0

Receiving	NO	YDS	AVG	TD	LG
Reed	8	152	19.0	0	40
Thomas	4	10	2.5	0	7
K. Davis	3	16	5.3	0	13
Beebe	2	50	25.0	1	40t
Tasker	2	30	15.0	0	16
Metzelaars	2	12	6.0	0	7
McKeller	1	6	6.0	0	6

Interceptions	NO	YDS	LG	TD
None	--	--	--	--

Punting	NO	AVG	LG	BLK
Mohr	3	45.3	48	0

Punt Ret.	NO/FC	YDS	LG	TD
Hicks	1/1	0	0	0

Kickoff Ret.	NO	YDS	LG	TD
Lamb	2	49	33	0
K. Davis	1	21	21	0
Hicks	1	20	20	0

Defense	SOLO	AST	TOT	SK
Bennett	8	1	9	0
Conlan	3	5	8	0
Patton	6	0	6	0
Talley	6	0	6	0
B. Smith	4	1	5	1
H. Jones	3	2	5	0
J. Williams	3	2	5	0
Odomes	4	0	4	0
Kelso	2	2	4	0
Darby	3	0	3	0
Pike	3	0	3	0
Wright	3	0	3	0
Hansen	2	1	3	0
Hale	2	0	2	0
Beebe	1	0	1	0
K. Davis	1	0	1	0
Maddox	1	0	1	0
Metzelaars	1	0	1	0
Goganious	0	1	1	0
Tasker	0	1	1	0
Tolbert	1	0	1	0
TOTAL	**57**	**16**	**73**	**1**

DALLAS

Passing	CP/ATT	YDS	TD	INT	RAT
Aikman	22/30	273	4	0	144.2

Rushing	ATT	YDS	AVG	TD	LG
E. Smith	22	108	4.9	1	38
Aikman	3	28	9.3	0	19
Gainer	2	1	0.5	0	1
Beuerlein	1	0	0.0	0	0
Johnston	1	0	0.0	0	0

Receiving	NO	YDS	AVG	TD	LG
Novacek	7	72	10.3	1	23t
Irvin	6	114	19.0	2	25
E. Smith	6	27	4.5	0	18
Johnston	2	15	7.5	0	8
Harper	1	45	45.0	1	45t

Interceptions	NO	YDS	LG	TD
Everett	2	22	22	0
Washington	1	13	13	0
Brown	1	0	0	0

Punting	NO	AVG	LG	BLK
Saxon	3	43.7	57	1

Punt Ret.	NO/FC	YDS	LG	TD
Martin	3/0	35	30	0

Kickoff Ret.	NO	YDS	LG	TD
Martin	4	79	22	0

Defense	SOLO	AST	TOT	SK
Norton	8	1	9	0
Edwards	4	2	6	0
Maryland	4	2	6	0
Washington	4	2	6	0
Haley	5	0	5	1
Casillas	2	3	5	0
Woodson	4	0	4	0
Everett	3	0	3	1
Holmes	3	0	3	0
Lett	3	0	3	1
Gant	2	1	3	0
L. Brown	2	0	2	0
Jeffcoat	2	0	2	1
R. Jones	2	0	2	0
V. Smith	2	0	2	0
Gainer	1	0	1	0
Holt	1	0	1	0
Horton	1	0	1	0
Pruitt	1	0	1	0
K. Smith	1	0	1	0
TOTAL	**55**	**11**	**66**	**4**

seventh-round draft choice in 1991 from Emporia State who represented the Cowboys' stockpile of talent.

It was mainly on defense where the exuberance of youth overwhelmed Buffalo. Dallas started a unit averaging 25.7 years compared to 30 for the Bills' offense. "I think the quickness showed up as the game wore on," said Wannstedt, who 12 days earlier had been hired by the Chicago Bears as their new head coach. "The guys just gave phenomenal effort every play."

The Bills had aged. James Lofton, 36, closed his career by being shut out, including a dropped touchdown pass in the waning seconds. "An earthquake over in Santa Monica tonight—that's the only thing that will stop the Dallas Cowboys," Lofton quipped. Left guard Jim Ritcher, 34, had some terrible plays, and center Kent Hull, 32, was in and out of the lineup with a knee injury that sidelined him for good in the second half.

As for the 32-year-old Kelly, a mannequin might have displayed more escapability against the waves of pass rushers buzzing him from every angle. Dallas amassed four sacks and another dozen knockdowns. "They weren't used to seeing people with the speed that we have," defensive tackle Tony Casillas said.

Aikman watched with both surprise and glee early in the second quarter when the Bills junked their two-deep approach after the Cowboys pulled ahead, 14–7. His guess was that Corey feared the Bills wouldn't be able to control Emmitt Smith with just seven in the box. The problem was that it placed Buffalo's cornerbacks in too many one-on-one matchups against Irvin, Harper, and Kelvin Martin. "To try to stop Emmitt they stopped doing what had been working, and I think that was a mistake," said Aikman. "Had they stayed in the coverages that they were using earlier in the game the game might have stayed close." One play after Thomas' fumble, Irvin beat Williams on a post-corner route for an 18-yard touchdown, and it was 28–10.

Buffalo, which fumbled eight times in all, lost three fumbles and was intercepted once in the second half. The Cowboys' next 24 points came from Lin Elliott's 20-yard field goal, set up by Irvin's 25-reception against the overmatched Williams; Aikman's 45-yard touchdown bomb to Harper behind Williams; a 10-yard touchdown run

by Emmitt Smith in which he broke three tackles and finally Norton's 9-yard touchdown return of a fumbled shotgun snap by Reich.

The Bills' only score, a 40-yard heave to Don Beebe, came only after Reich scrambled beyond the line of scrimmage before releasing the ball. "That was the only irritation I had in the second half," said Johnson. "Reich was obviously across the line, and the league would confirm that we were right."

The Bills' ninth turnover, which came with five minutes left, became one of the more memorable plays in Super Bowl history. It started when defensive end Jim Jeffcoat, the oldest player on the Cowboys' defense at 31, stormed around Ballard to sack Reich. The ball bounced free, and Lett, with remarkable speed for his size, picked it up at the 35 and sprinted down the sidelines with no defender in sight. At the 10, Lett placed the ball in his right hand, extended it away from his body and began showboating. Beebe caught Lett at the 1 and knocked the ball out of his hand and through the end zone for a touchback. Buffalo ball.

Johnson later laughed about it, but he knew full well that Lett's gaffe had cost his team the Super Bowl scoring record of 55 points held by the 49ers. Meanwhile, it gave Levy something to sell going into the offseason.

"That was a signature play of what the nature of those Buffalo Bills teams was," Levy said years later. "We said, 'This is the heart of the Buffalo Bills. Let's try and get back again.' An apparently meaningless play had great meaning.

"Anything we did positive that year was overshadowed by that terrible defeat. . . . I think this was the most resilient group of players that ever played in the league."

Unscathed by injury all season, the Cowboys had won their third Super Bowl in a record sixth appearance. It was time to gloat, and few coaches did that better than Jimmy Johnson.

"It's almost magical, when you look at the score against Buffalo. This might indeed have been the best game that we played," Johnson wrote in his book, *Turning the Thing Around*, published later that year. "When you take control of a Super Bowl in the third and fourth quarters the way we did, it was pretty impressive.

"How 'bout them Cowboys!"

XXVIII

DALLAS COWBOYS 30, BUFFALO BILLS 13

January 30, 1994
Georgia Dome, Atlanta, Georgia

The last thing in the world that the Buffalo Bills needed in their Super Bowl XXVIII rematch against the Dallas Cowboys was their trade secrets being given away before the game. But now the truth can be told. Not only were the Bills facing a superior opponent favored by 10½ points, but they also were meeting a team that had prior knowledge of their newest stratagem on offense.

Trashed by the Cowboys, 52–17, in the previous Super Bowl, the Bills understood how essential it would be to show different looks out of a no-huddle offense that was missing some of its old juice. There was no time to waste. Only one week separated the conference championship games and Super Sunday in 1994. On Wednesday, the first practice day in Atlanta, the Bills installed both a shuffle pass and a direct snap to the running back, hoping they would surprise the Cowboys' fast-flowing defense, create a few big plays, and help them atone for three straight Super Bowl defeats.

At the Super Bowl, only a few television stations are allowed to tape the standard sports-anchor-at-practice bits while players stretch in the background before the workout begins. It so happened that the cameras were rolling when quarterback Jim Kelly and running back Thurman Thomas were using every minute of what time they had to work with center Kent Hull on the timing of the new plays.

That evening, the Cowboys' staff was meeting at the hotel when the local sports came on. Defensive coordinator Butch Davis remembered coach Marv Levy was being interviewed. In the background, it was clear to the Cowboys that Kelly and Thomas weren't just fooling around.

"The 'B roll' was scanning and it went past them and it looked to me that they were practicing a shuffle pass," coach Jimmy Johnson said years later. "I went to Butch Davis and I said, 'Butch, can you check back? Have they run the shuffle pass this year?' He

Attendance: 72, 817
Conditions: 72 degrees, indoors
Time of kickoff: 6:22 p.m. (EST)
Length of game: 3 hours, 16 minutes
Referee: Bob McElwee

MVP: Emmitt Smith, RB, Cowboys

checked our computer printout, and they had not run a shuffle pass all year long. So we actually put it in our practice schedule and worked against the shuffle pass all week. It was a stroke of luck."

The Cowboys noticed on the critical TV footage that Thomas was lined up to Kelly's left when he had almost always been on his right. "Against it," secondary coach Dave Campo said, "we actually set our front the opposite of the way we normally would so that when they ran the shuffle pass they were running into one of our defensive linemen. So instead of them running into kind of a bubble, they ended up running it right into the extra lineman." Campo recalled the previous Super Bowl when backup safety Ray Horton correctly diagnosed a rollout pass from the sidelines and the Cowboys used his tip for an end-zone interception. "Two situations involving fate," said Campo. "You never know what's going to make the difference."

Said Butch Davis: "One of the biggest games of my coaching career hinged on something that we actually saw on practice tape and allowed us to win the Super Bowl."

The Cowboys defeated the Bills, 30–13, after being down, 13–6, at the half. Thomas' fumble on one of those shuffle passes set up the Cowboys' second field goal. When the Bills tried another shuffle pass on third and 7 from the Dallas 9 late in the first half, Thomas was stuffed for no gain.

In all, the Bills ran four shuffle passes plus three direct snaps to running back Kenneth Davis. The

	1	2	3	4	Final
Dallas Cowboys	6	0	14	10	30
Buffalo Bills	3	10	0	0	13

SCORING SUMMARY

1st Quarter
DAL Murray, 41-yd. FG
BUF Christie, 54-yd. FG
DAL Murray, 24-yd. FG
2nd Quarter
BUF T.Thomas, 4-yd. run (Christie kick)
BUF Christie, 28-yd. FG
3rd Quarter
DAL J. Washington, 46-yd. fumble return (Murray kick)
DAL E. Smith, 15-yd. run (Murray kick)
4th Quarter
DAL E. Smith, 1-yd. run (Murray kick)
DAL Murray, 20-yd. FG

longest gain on the seven plays was 11 yards. It ended up being just another futile effort by the Bills, which became the first franchise in professional sports history to reach four title games in four straight seasons and lose every one. They ran 80 plays, a total that usually equates to victory, but their longest gain was a paltry 24 yards. A good gadget play or two might have turned the tide. Unbeknownst to the Bills, their chicanery never had a chance.

"Now that you say that, I do remember there was a fuss about cameras being where they shouldn't have been," Bills offensive coordinator Tom Bresnahan said years later. "Isn't that unbelievable? But it never was anything I ever considered being a problem. I have never thought of it since that day. We had run the shuffle pass, but it was not a major part of our offense, by any means."

Buffalo had beaten Dallas, 13–10, at Texas Stadium in Week 2. "We had a blocking scheme that was very good to us in which we handed the ball off to Thurman but Dallas had played it pretty well," said Bresnahan. "We thought if we ran that play with that blocking scheme but really gave the look of a pass, it would throw off a linebacker and make the tackle being double-teamed react a little differently."

Judged by the final score, Super Bowl XXVIII wouldn't appear to be much of a game. This performance by the Bills, however, more closely resembled their 1-point loss to the New York Giants in Super Bowl XXV than their embarrassing showings against Washington and Dallas the previous two years. On the other hand, the Cowboys might have suffered a letdown after smashing San Francisco 38–21, for the NFC championship. "Beating them [the Bills] so bad the year before was almost like a curse," Butch Davis said. "I don't want to even insinuate that we were lackadaisical, because you never are in a Super Bowl. But you're maybe too cautious."

Whereas the Bills entered as one of the healthiest teams in the NFL, the Cowboys had injury concerns. Quarterback Troy Aikman suffered a concussion against the 49ers and still was suffering headaches a few days before the Super Bowl. "Troy was not at the top of his game," Johnson admitted. "So we were struggling." Mark Stepnoski, the team's Pro Bowl center, suffered a season-ending knee injury in Week 13 and had to be replaced by guard John Gesek. Defensive end Charles Haley played in all but two games, but wasn't himself and underwent surgery for a ruptured disc after the season. "We did not play all that well," said Johnson.

The Dallas offense, which ranked second in points and fourth in yards, found little success against the multiple 3-4 scheme of defensive

COACHING STAFFS

Dallas
Head Coach: Jimmy Johnson. *Offense:* Norv Turner (assistant head coach, coordinator, quarterbacks), Hubbard Alexander (wide receivers), Robert Ford (tight ends), Hudson Houck (offensive line), Joe Brodsky (running backs). *Defense:* Butch Davis (coordinator, linebackers), John Blake (defensive line), Dave Campo (defensive backs), Jim Eddy (assistant). *Special Teams:* Joe Avezzano, Steve Hoffman (kickers, research and development). *Strength:* Mike Woicik.

Buffalo
Head Coach: Marv Levy. *Offense:* Tom Bresnahan (coordinator, offensive line), Charlie Joiner (wide receivers), Don Lawrence (tight ends, quality control), Jim Shofner (quarterbacks), Elijah Pitts (assistant head coach, running backs). *Defense:* Walt Corey (coordinator, linebackers), Dan Sekanovich (defensive line), Dick Roach (defensive backs), Chuck Lester (assistant linebackers, administrative assistant). *Special Teams:* Bruce DeHaven. *Strength:* Rusty Jones.

coordinator Walt Corey. It took a 50-yard return of the opening kickoff by Kevin Williams to set up the Cowboys' first score. With a first down at the Buffalo 28, Aikman threw two bad passes and the Cowboys had to settle for Eddie Murray's 41-yard field goal. When they got the ball back, a first down turned into a punt when Gesek was penalized for holding. Murray converted another first-quarter field goal from 24 yards after a strange call by offensive coordinator Norv Turner on third and 5 at the 10. On Turner's draw play, Emmitt Smith gained just 3.

Thomas, who had killed Kansas City with 186 yards in 33 carries in the AFC Championship Game, made cornerback Larry Brown miss a tackle in the left flat and turned a short pass into a 24-yard gain. Buffalo's first possession ended with Steve Christie's Super Bowl–record field goal of 54 yards.

The Bills began their second possession at their 41. On the first play, Kelly took a step or two back in shotgun formation, then flipped a shuffle pass to Thomas as he moved from left to right. Apparently, Kelly had needed more practice. The toss was slightly behind Thomas, who had to spin completely around to make the catch. As soon as Thomas squared his shoulders and started up the field, nickel safety James Washington knocked the ball from his grasp and strong safety Darren Woodson recovered at the 50. "That play would be their downfall the whole game," said Washington. "It was a slow-developing play. It really wasn't a great play to run against a defense with our quickness and swarming linebackers and defensive backs."

The departure of James

DALLAS COWBOYS (NFC, 12–4)				BUFFALO BILLS (AFC, 12–4)	
		Offense			
80	Alvin Harper (6-3, 208)	WR	82	Don Beebe (5-11, 180)	
71	Mark Tuinei (6-5, 305)	LT	70	John Fina (6-4, 282)	
61	Nate Newton* (6-3, 325)	LG	74	Glenn Parker (6-5, 305)	
63	John Gesek (6-5, 285)	C	67	Kent Hull (6-5, 284)	
66	Kevin Gogan (6-7, 328)	RG	65	John Davis (6-4, 310)	
79	Erik Williams* (6-6, 324)	RT	75	Howard Ballard* (6-6, 330)	
84	Jay Novacek* (6-4, 232)	TE	88	Pete Metzelaars (6-7, 254)	
88	Michael Irvin (6-2, 205)	WR	83	Andre Reed* (6-2, 190)	
8	Troy Aikman* (6-4, 228)	QB	12	Jim Kelly (6-3, 218)	
22	Emmitt Smith (5-9, 209)	RB	34	Thurman Thomas* (5-10, 198)	
48	Daryl Johnston* (6-2, 238)	FB I WR	80	Bill Brooks (6-0, 189)	
		Defense			
92	Tony Tolbert (6-6, 263)	LE	90	Phil Hansen (6-5, 278)	
75	Tony Casillas (6-3, 279)	LT I NT	91	Jeff Wright (6-3, 274)	
78	Leon Lett (6-6, 285)	RT I RE	78	Bruce Smith* (6-4, 273)	
94	Charles Haley (6-5, 250)	RE I LOLB	53	Marvcus Patton (6-2, 243)	
59	Darrin Smith (6-1, 237)	LLB I LILB	97	Cornelius Bennett* (6-2, 238)	
51	Ken Norton (6-2, 240)	RLB I RILB	55	Mark Maddox (6-1, 233)	
28	Darren Woodson* (6-1, 215)	CB I ROLB	56	Darryl Talley (6-4, 235)	
26	Kevin Smith (5-11, 180)	LCB	25	Mickey Washington (5-9, 191)	
24	Larry Brown (5-11, 182)	RCB	37	Nate Odomes* (5-10, 188)	
27	Thomas Everett* (5-9, 184)	SS	20	Henry Jones (5-11, 197)	
37	James Washington (6-1, 209)	FS	38	Mark Kelso (5-11, 185)	

* Pro Bowl selection

SUBSTITUTIONS

Dallas

Offense: WR - 85 Kevin Williams; TE - 89 Scott Galbraith; G - 68 Frank Cornish; C - 70 Dale Hellestrae; QB - 18 Bernie Kosar; RB - 44 Lincoln Coleman, 39 Derrick Gainer. **Defense:** DE - 77 Jim Jeffcoat; DT - 95 Chad Hennings, 97 Jimmie Jones, 67 Russell Maryland*; LB - 58 Dixon Edwards, 55 Robert Jones, 98 Godfrey Myles, 91 Matt Vanderbeek; CB - 43 Elvis Patterson, 41 Dave Thomas; S - 40 Bill Bates, 46 Joe Fishback, 29 Kenneth Gant. **Specialists:** K - 3 Eddie Murray; P - 19 John Jett. **DNP:** 25 Derrick Lassic (RB). **Inactive:** 81 Tim Daniel (WR), 86 Tyrone Williams (WR), 83 Joey Mickey (TE), 65 Ron Stone (T), 62 James Parrish (T), 17 Jason Garrett (QB), 34 Tommie Agee (RB), 31 Brock Marion (S).

Buffalo

Offense: WR - 85 Russell Copeland, 89 Steve Tasker*; TE - 84 Keith McKeller; T - 66 Jerry Crafts; G - 51 Jim Ritcher; C - 62 Mike Devlin; QB - 14 Frank Reich; RB - 23 Kenneth Davis, 35 Carwell Gardner. **Defense:** DE - 77 Oliver Barnett, 94 Mark Pike; NT - 73 Mark Lodish; LB - 96 Monty Brown, 50 Keith Goganious, 52 Richard Harvey; CB - 36 Jerome Henderson, 28 Thomas Smith; S - 43 Matt Darby, 24 Kurt Schulz. **Specialists:** K - 2 Steve Christie; P - 9 Chris Mohr. **DNP:** 21 Nate Turner (RB). **Inactive:** 81 Brad Lamb (WR), 87 Chris Walsh (WR), 68 Corbin Lacina (G), 7 Gale Gilbert (QB), 33 Eddie Fuller (RB), 92 John Parrella (DE), 99 James Patton (NT), 29 James Williams (CB).

Lofton in the offseason left the Bills without a legitimate deep threat. Don Beebe had blinding speed, but his hands were shaky and his routes imprecise. Andre Reed was in his ninth season and beginning to slow up, and former Colt Bill Brooks was crafty but also lacked speed. Thus, Levy and Bresnahan built their game plan around runs by Thomas and short passes by Kelly, who completed 15 of his opening 18 passes (two were dropped by Brooks) for 139 yards.

Using this formula, the Bills went 80 yards in 17 plays on a drive capped by Thomas' 4-yard touchdown. After shedding left tackle John Fina, defensive tackle Leon Lett had Thomas dead to rights in the hole but wound up grabbing nothing but air. The Cowboys had stopped the Bills near midfield, but rookie cornerback Dave Thomas was penalized for roughing punter Chris Mohr, and this time Buffalo went the distance.

Dallas miscues began to add up in the second quarter. One drive bogged down at the Buffalo 44 and led to a punt. A second drive advanced from the 1 to the Buffalo 37 where, on first down, Aikman threw deep to the inside, but Alvin Harper broke to the outside. Cornerback Nate Odomes made the routine interception, which he returned 41 yards to the Dallas 47. That drive ended on Christie's 28-yard field goal as the first half expired, and the Bills led, 13–6. Before the attempt, a third-and-7 shuffle pass to Thomas didn't fool anyone. Haley, Lett, and linebacker Darrin Smith all reacted beautifully, leaving Thomas nowhere to cut and no gain.

As the teams headed for the locker room, Butch Davis was thinking, "We got their best shot in the first half, and somewhat weathered it."

Aikman had this thought: "We played poorly in the first half, Buffalo had played exceptionally well, and I was thinking that it didn't look good for us. But I looked over and saw their players go in and you would have thought they were the team who was behind. At that moment, I kind of thought they were a team that just felt that something bad was going to happen, that they were snakebit in Super Bowls."

Eight of Emmitt Smith's 10 carries in the first half had been for 4 yards or less. The Bills, who ranked merely 21st against the run, were holding him in check using a daring combination of line

TEAM STATISTICS

DALLAS		BUFFALO
20	Total First Downs	22
6	Rushing	6
14	Passing	15
0	Penalty	1
341	Total Net Yardage	314
64	Total Offensive Plays	80
5.3	Avg. Gain per Offensive Play	3.9
35	Rushes	27
137	Yards Gained Rushing (Net)	87
3.9	Average Yards per Rush	3.2
27	Passes Attempted	50
19	Passes Completed	31
1	Passes Intercepted	1
2	Tackled Attempting to Pass	3
3	Yards Lost Attempting to Pass	33
204	Yards Gained Passing (Net)	227
5/13	Third-Down Efficiency	5/17
1/1	Fourth-Down Efficiency	2/3
4	Punts	5
43.8	Average Distance	37.6
1	Punt Returns	1
5	Punt Return Yardage	5
2	Kickoff Returns	6
72	Kickoff Return Yardage	144
12	Interception Return Yardage	41
0	Fumbles	3
0	Own Fumbles Recovered	1
2	Opponent Fumbles Recovered	0
6	Penalties	1
50	Yards Penalized	10
3	Touchdowns	1
2	Rushing	1
0	Passing	0
1	Returns	0
3	Extra Points Made	1
3	Field Goals Made	2
3	Field Goals Attempted	2
0	Safeties	0
30	Total Points Scored	13
34:29	Time of Possession	25:31

stunts and run blitzes. Moreover, they had prevented Smith, the league MVP, from controlling the game even though both safeties had been able to stay back in two-deep coverage. Johnson strode purposefully into the locker room, having seen enough. "They were giving us some problems jumping inside of blocks," he said. "They weren't taking us on. They

DALLAS

Passing	CP/ATT	YDS	TD	INT	RAT
Aikman	19/27	207	0	1	77.2

Rushing	ATT	YDS	AVG	TD	LG
E. Smith	30	132	4.4	2	15t
K. Williams	1	6	6.0	0	6
Aikman	1	3	3.0	0	3
Johnston	1	0	0.0	0	0
Kosar	1	-1	-1.0	0	-1
Coleman	1	-3	-3.0	0	-3

Receiving	NO	YDS	AVG	TD	LG
Irvin	5	66	13.2	0	20
Novacek	5	26	5.2	0	9
E. Smith	4	26	6.5	0	10
Harper	3	75	25.0	0	35
Johnston	2	14	7.0	0	11

Interceptions	NO	YDS	LG	TD
Washington	1	12	12	0

Punting	NO	AVG	LG	BLK
Jett	4	43.8	47	0

Punt Ret.	NO/FC	YDS	LG	TD
K. Williams	1/1	5	5	0

Kickoff Ret.	NO	YDS	LG	TD
K. Williams	1	50	50	0
Gant	1	22	22	0

Defense	SOLO	AST	TOT	SK
Washington	11	0	11	0
Everett	8	0	8	0
Norton	7	1	8	0
Casillas	2	4	6	0.5
K. Smith	5	0	5	0
Lett	3	2	5	0
Tolbert	3	2	5	0.5
L. Brown	4	0	4	0
Haley	2	2	4	0.5
J. Jones	3	0	3	0
Woodson	3	0	3	0
Bates	2	1	3	0
Jeffcoat	2	1	3	1.5
Gant	2	0	2	0
Maryland	2	0	2	0
Fishback	1	0	1	0
Gainer	1	0	1	0
D. Smith	1	0	1	0
D. Thomas	1	0	1	0
Vanderbeek	1	0	1	0
E. Williams	1	0	1	0
Edwards	0	1	1	0
TOTAL	65	14	79	3

BUFFALO

Passing	CP/ATT	YDS	TD	INT	RAT
Kelly	31/50	260	0	1	67.1

Rushing	ATT	YDS	AVG	TD	LG
K. Davis	9	38	4.2	0	11
Thomas	16	37	2.3	1	6
Kelly	2	12	6.0	0	8

Receiving	NO	YDS	AVG	TD	LG
Brooks	7	63	9.0	0	15
Thomas	7	52	7.4	0	24
Reed	6	75	12.5	0	22
Beebe	6	60	10.0	0	18
K. Davis	3	-5	-1.7	0	7
Metzelaars	1	8	8.0	0	8
McKeller	1	7	7.0	0	7

Interceptions	NO	YDS	LG	TD
Odomes	4	41	41	0

Punting	NO	AVG	LG	BLK
Mohr	5	37.6	52	0

Punt Ret.	NO/FC	YDS	LG	TD
Copeland	1/1	5	5	0

Kickoff Ret.	NO	YDS	LG	TD
Copeland	4	82	22	0
Beebe	2	62	34	0

Defense	SOLO	AST	TOT	SK
Bennett	10	3	13	0
Patton	9	0	9	0
Talley	8	1	9	0
Wright	5	0	5	2
B. Smith	4	1	5	0
Odomes	3	2	5	0
Kelso	2	2	4	0
Maddox	2	2	4	0
H. Jones	3	0	3	0
Washington	3	0	3	0
Goganious	1	1	2	0
Lodish	1	1	2	0
Hansen	0	2	2	0
Barnett	1	0	1	0
Darby	1	0	1	0
Fina	1	0	1	0
Harvey	1	0	1	0
Schulz	1	0	1	0
Tasker	1	0	1	0
TOTAL	57	15	72	2

were shooting the gaps and giving us problems. The best thing to do against that is just run right at 'em. And that's what we did."

The Cowboys made good use of the lengthy Super Bowl halftime break. Turner, who admitted that he had called too many passes (18) compared to runs (11) in the first half, was told by Johnson to start running Smith on what the Cowboys called "Power Right." It was a play that they hadn't used in weeks. "It was Jimmy's demeanor at halftime," fullback Daryl Johnston said. "He said we were fine and we've got a good answer to what they were doing. We drew it up and spent quite a bit of time on it. They were stunting their tackles inside and then looping their linebackers to the outside. We down-blocked the strong side and then kicked out with a fullback lead. We were good at coming off and knocking people off the ball, but we had trouble when people stunted right at the snap. You didn't want to line up nose-to-nose with our guys."

Emmitt Smith meant almost everything to the Cowboys. Of their four defeats that season, he missed two because of a holdout, carried one time for 1 yard against Atlanta before leaving with a thigh bruise, and then played hurt four days later to gain just 51 yards in 16 attempts in a Thanksgiving Day loss to Miami. This was his fourth season in the NFL and his third in a row as rushing champion.

Opening the second half, Kelly handed off to Thurman Thomas for 6, then passed to Brooks for 9. On the next play, left guard Glenn Parker pulled right to trap defensive tackle Tony Casillas. The Bills hoped that Parker's movement would cause Lett to hesitate and give Hull time to block back on him. Instead, the lightning-quick Lett shot straight ahead and Hull couldn't quite get enough of him. Just as Thomas took the inside handoff from Kelly, Lett reached around Hull and jarred the ball loose. "Kent Hull said he thought he had a pretty good block on him, but one hand just came free and just hit the ball," Thomas said. "I thought I had a pretty good grip on it. I fumbled. I cost us the game."

The ball bounced and was quickly scooped up on the run by James Washington, a starter from 1990 to 1992 who had lost his job in training camp when the Cowboys decided to go with Woodson. Kelly alertly ran to the boundary, forcing Washington to cut back, but Washington slipped past Fina, patiently allowed Beebe to overrun him at the 20, and then cut back to the corner for a 46-yard touchdown. "That was the crucial play in the game," Levy said. "The ball was just punched out. The other guy was in perfect position to pick it up on the bounce and there was a clear field ahead of him. Away he went."

Buffalo still was in good shape with the score tied 13–13, especially given the fact it had outgained the Cowboys to that point, 234–170. After that fumble, though, the Bills gained just 80 yards in 36 snaps, failing not only to score but to even penetrate the Dallas 40 until the final minute. "I won't say we dominated them, but I would say we were definitely in control of the game," Bresnahan said. "I felt very strong about our chances of winning. Then turnovers just turned the entire game around."

Defensive end Jim Jeffcoat and Haley collaborated for a sack of Kelly on the next series, forcing a punt. Kelly had been knocked down three times in the first half but hadn't been sacked. "We were so concerned with their run that we stayed on the line of scrimmage and looked for it," Butch Davis said. "We felt if we'd turn the game around we'd have to get a pass rush." In the second half, the Cowboys sacked Kelly three times, knocked him down five times, and made him scramble twice.

Shortly after the first sack of Kelly, the Cowboys put together a textbook eight-play touchdown drive with Emmitt Smith rushing seven times for 61 of the drive's 64 yards. It ended with Smith refusing to go down when hit in the backfield by penetrating nose tackle Jeff Wright, then squirting forward for a 15-yard touchdown. Wright writhed on the turf in agony as he watched the consequences of his missed tackle unfold.

Four of the plays on the drive were a power surge to the right side, with left guard Nate Newton pulling to join right tackle Erik Williams and right guard Kevin Gogan in a three-man wedge weighing 977 pounds. "Man, we put a stampede on those buffaloes," said Newton. "We knew if we kept pounding on them they couldn't stop us. It's a 60-minute game. It ain't won in the first half."

On the final two plays of the march, the Bills lost defensive ends Bruce Smith (wrist) and Phil Hansen (groin) to injury. Bruce Smith would return on the

ext series, but Hansen was finished. Two months
ter the Super Bowl, one of the Bills' personnel
eople described the 275-pound Hansen's matchup
gainst the 324-pound Williams: "He literally got
estroyed by a great, great, great player."

On the sidelines, Corey cussed his players,
sing words like "embarrassing" and "pathetic."
e subsequently benched inside linebacker Mark
Maddox in favor of Keith Goganious, moved outside
inebacker Cornelius Bennett inside, and shifted
nside linebacker Marvcus Patton to the outside.
A lot of teams struggle when they try to tackle
mmitt," said Newton.

The Bills began their next two series with
creen passes to Kenneth Davis that were swal-
owed up for losses of 8 and 4 yards. Davis was
n for Thomas, who insisted he was beset by leg
ramps and hadn't been benched for fumbling.

During the long stoppage of play before the
tart of the fourth quarter, Washington prevailed
pon Johnson to give him freedom within the
owboys' trademark "quarters" coverage scheme.
Jimmy is probably the toughest guy to deal with,
ut one thing about him is he listens," Washington
aid. "He ran the coverage, and I'm lucky that he
id." On third and 6, Washington jumped the route
y Beebe and, rather than splatter the receiver, he
ut in front for an interception, which he returned
2 yards to the Buffalo 34.

"That Dallas staff basically brought that
overage into the league," Campo said. "They ran a
quare-in, and we had worked on it a lot. The corner
as over the top of it, James had no threat vertically,
e saw the ball and went and got it."

A few plays later, it was third and 8 at the Buf-
alo 22. Strong safety Henry Jones broke through on
blitz, but Aikman stood tall and rifled a 16-yard
ut to Harper with Odomes in coverage. From the
, Emmitt Smith ran for 2, 3, and no gain before
ohnson decided to go for it on fourth and 1. "Rather
han taking the field goal I just felt we could pick up
he score and put it out of reach," said Johnson.

Then Emmitt Smith scored easily around left
nd. "Great call by Norv," Johnston said, "because
ur predominant play at the time was an inside
oal-line play, a lead. We actually ran to the weak
ide with a toss and Emmitt walked in."

Smith rushed 20 times in the second half for
91 yards, including 15 for 81 to the right side, and
finished with 30 for 132. It was enough for Smith to
be selected as MVP, although Washington's game-
high 11 solo tackles, interception, forced fumble, and
fumble return for a touchdown prompted Smith to
say, "I wish it could have been a 'co-'[MVP]." Campo
said Washington "had a nose for the football."

The Bills made the playoffs twice more with
Kelly, Thomas, and Reed, but failed to advance beyond the divisional round. They would have to live
with the goose egg for the Super Bowl and some awful overall numbers. In those four seasons, the Bills
had a plus-25 turnover differential in the regular
season and plus-14 in playoff games, yet in the four
Super Bowls, they were minus-13. They fumbled 18
times (eight lost) compared to their opponents' five
fumbles (two lost). After rushing for 135 yards and a
9.0-yard average in Super Bowl XXV, Thomas rushed
for 69 yards (1.9) in the last three. Kelly's cumulative
passer rating was 56.9. Reed had 27 receptions for
323 yards in the Super Bowls, but he caught nothing
deep and didn't score a touchdown.

"In retrospect, we felt that maybe in that first
game we were as good or maybe a tick better than
the Giants and lost it," Levy said. "I think that in
the next three the stronger team won the game."
Levy—a Phi Beta Kappa graduate of Coe College in
1950 with a master's degree in English history from
Harvard—was inducted into the Hall of Fame in
2001, one year before Kelly. "Had we won just one of
those games, they'd be talking about us as one of the
greatest teams of all time," Kelly said.

After the Lombardi Trophy was presented
to owner Jerry Jones, he and Johnson hugged and
mugged for the cameras. Fifty-eight days later,
their volatile alliance irrevocably broken, Johnson
departed the Cowboys. Jones went on to hire Barry
Switzer; Johnson went on to live in South Florida
before coaching the Miami Dolphins to a 38–31
record from 1996 to 1999.

"I blame Jimmy and Jerry for not being able to
get that done between the two of them," Johnston
said. "They couldn't put their personal differences
aside to take a shot at making history."

XXIX

SAN FRANCISCO 49ERS 49, SAN DIEGO CHARGERS 26

January 29, 1995

Joe Robbie Stadium, Miami, Florida

San Francisco and Dallas. Dallas and San Francisco. In 1992, 1993, and 1994, they were the only two teams that really mattered when it came to deciding which was the best team in the NFL. Was the Super Bowl anticlimactic after the 49ers-Cowboys NFL Championship Game trilogy? No doubt about it.

Before meeting in the title game for the third straight year, Niners president Carmen Policy actually said, "If we lose, we die." When the 49ers prevailed, 38–28, San Francisco cornerback Deion Sanders said, "I feel, honestly, this was the Super Bowl. I don't mean to take anything away from— whoever won that other damn game."

That was the San Diego Chargers, a club widely picked to finish last in the AFC West. Their reward for shocking the Pittsburgh Steelers on the road for the conference title was a rematch with the 49ers, a team that in mid-December had crushed them in San Diego, 38–15. "Coach [Bobby] Ross and his staff did a great job that year," Chargers general manager Bobby Beathard would say years later. "The Steeler game was one of the best games I've ever been around. But I knew going into the Super Bowl that it was not a good matchup. My feeling was that was where we wanted to get, where the 49ers were. I hate to say it was a mismatch, but it wasn't an even matchup."

Super Bowl XXIX, played at Joe Robbie Stadium in Miami, was over almost before it began, another Super Bowl that in reality was just a glorified scrimmage. The 49ers became the 11th straight Super Bowl champion from the NFC. The final score, 49–26, marked the ninth time in those 11 games in which the Super Bowl had been a rout.

"To be honest, we knew we were in trouble when we lost the coin toss," Billy Devaney, the Chargers director of player personnel, said shortly after the game. "When they got the ball first, we had a feeling we were going to be playing catchup all day."

Attendance: 74,107

Conditions: 76 degrees, cloudy, chance of rain, wind SW at 5 mph

Time of kickoff: 6:21 p.m. (EST)

Length of game: 3 hours, 36 minutes

Referee: Jerry Markbreit

MVP: Steve Young, QB, 49ers

The 49ers struck for two touchdowns on the first two possessions, needing a mere seven play to gain 138 yards. On and on it went, an awesom display by the 49ers' highest-scoring team in th era of the West Coast offense. Quarterback Stev Young, coach George Seifert, and running bac Ricky Watters had replaced great campaigner Joe Montana, Bill Walsh, and Roger Craig, but made no difference. It was a triumph of the 49er system, a fifth Super Bowl triumph in the spa of 16 years, and denial of a three-peat for th despised Cowboys.

"My answer is in no way meant to demean an team that we may have played," Policy said, "but th truth of the matter is that beating the Cowboys i the NFC Championship Game was the ultimate i terms of long-awaited accomplishment. The rus that we got from that victory was just unmatchabl in terms of any victory we had during the regular o postseason. The Super Bowl was the most importan game as a practical matter. But, from an emotiona psychological, and ego standpoint, that NF Championship Game was as high as it gets."

In some ways, the 49ers were an all-star tean with an all-star coaching staff. After being eliminate by the Cowboys the year before, Policy and owner Ed die DeBartolo had their famous meeting of the mind outside an elevator at Texas Stadium. "That was th defining moment," said Policy. "After the game, w had that memorable elevator ride where we looked a

	1	2	3	4	Final
San Diego Chargers	7	3	8	8	26
San Francisco 49ers	14	14	14	7	49

SCORING SUMMARY

1st Quarter
SF Rice, 44-yd. pass from S. Young (Brien kick)
SF Watters, 51-yd. pass from S. Young (Brien kick)
SD Means, 1-yd. run (Carney kick)

2nd Quarter
SF Floyd, 5-yd. pass from S. Young (Brien kick)
SF Watters, 8-yd. pass from S. Young (Brien kick)
SD Carney, 31-yd. FG

3rd Quarter
SF Watters, 9-yd. run (Brien kick)
SF Rice, 15-yd. pass from S. Young (Brien kick)
SD Coleman, 98-yd. kickoff return (Seay, pass from Humphries)

4th Quarter
SF Rice, 7-yd. pass from S. Young (Brien kick)
SD Martin, 30-yd. pass from Humphries (Pupunu, pass from Humphries)

each other, and he made a very simple statement: 'We cannot let this happen again.'"

In the months before the NFL first implemented a salary cap in February 1994, the 49ers negotiated long-term deals with eight players for a total expenditure of about $12 million, a sum wholeheartedly approved by DeBartolo. With their own house in order, the 49ers found the cap room and the persuasiveness to sign free agents such as linebacker Ken Norton Jr. from Dallas, center Bart Oates from the New York Giants, defensive ends Rickey Jackson from New Orleans and Richard Dent from Chicago, and middle linebacker Gary Plummer from San Diego. In August, they signed nickel back Toi Cook from New Orleans. In November, they re-signed pass rusher Tim Harris.

The team's most dramatic move, however, came in mid-September. That's when Deion Sanders agreed to take a one-year deal worth more than $1.3 million, plus a $750,000 bonus if the 49ers won the Super Bowl. Getting Sanders enabled the 49ers to move semi-slow cornerback Merton Hanks to free safety, where he flourished in place of struggling Dana Hall. It was the final piece of the puzzle, somewhat akin to the 49ers' acquisition of

defensive end Fred Dean early in the 1981 season. "Sanders was the best coverage corner in history and he played extremely well," said Bill Walsh, who in 1994 was finishing up his second stint as coach at Stanford. "Now, would the 49ers have won the Super Bowl without him? Oh, of course. It was great having him, but it wasn't as though he made the difference any more than Fred Dean did. During that period of time we had some of the greatest players ever. It was just a beautiful thing to watch. The AFC at that time was just mismatched against NFC teams."

Leading the star-studded squad was Seifert, the defensive genius under Walsh. In his third season as the 49ers' offensive coordinator was Mike Shanahan, whom esteemed offensive line coach Bobb McKittrick said possessed the best football mind of any coach he had ever worked with. Coaching tight ends was the highly regarded Mike Solari, and the first-year quarterbacks coach was Gary Kubiak. Returning from Green Bay in 1994 to coordinate the defense was Ray Rhodes, who was ably supported by assistant head coach Bill McPherson, defensive line coach Dwaine Board, and linebackers coach John Marshall, among others. "So many good coaches," McPherson mused years later.

Before the game, Jerry Rice walked over to Jackson and Plummer, who were understandably anxious about playing in their first Super Bowl, and guaranteed that a ring would soon be theirs. "The moment he said what he said, the feeling of confidence was back," said Plummer. "The borderline arrogance—no, the over-the-top arrogance—was back. At that point, if I could have bet on the game, I'd have put down $1 million that we were going to win."

During his Hall of Fame induction in August 2005, Steve Young recalled his nervousness just before taking the field. "Steve, don't worry," Young remembered being told by Shanahan. "We're going to crush these guys." And they did.

While the 49ers practiced with supreme efficiency in Miami—"I have to say that it was the most phenomenal week of practice ever," said Young—the Chargers were starting to unravel. Two safeties, journeyman Darren Carrington and talented underachiever Stanley Richard, kept spouting off about who would be the star of the game. Neither played another game for San Diego,

Carrington departing via the expansion draft in February and Richard as an unrestricted free agent in March. "That week, some of our younger players

didn't take the game as seriously as they should special-teams coach Chuck Priefer said years later.

Bill Arnsparger, the Chargers' 68-year-o defensive coordinator, retire shortly after the Super Bowl ar was replaced by Dave Adolp "There were a couple peop saying that they could defen [the 49ers'] offense better tha Arnsparger was doing," sa Beathard, "which was a bunc of crap. We had things like th going rather than the team. was, 'Hey, I'm going to be th big man in this game.' That the way the team played Secondary coach Willie Sha was the only position coach o defense in 1994 who wasn't bac on the staff in 1995.

Said Arnsparger, "Wh Bobby said was exactly righ We played our best game a Pittsburgh to get there, and was too much for our grou to get themselves ready to pla again. . . . We just couldn match up with the 49er offens physically or mentally."

Late in the practice wee the Chargers blew a coverag and allowed the scout-tear wide receiver impersonatin Rice to score. "I remember Bot by Ross in the meeting Saturda night asking Bill, 'Are you sur we got that coverage down?' Priefer said. "And Bill sai 'We'll be fine, coach. We're OK That was the coverage we buste on the second play of the game.

Actually, it was the thir play. Steve Young faked a hand off to fullback William Floy and threw down the middle c the field to Rice, who was run ning a post pattern from th

	SAN DIEGO CHARGERS (AFC, 11–5)			SAN FRANCISCO 49ERS (NFC, 13–3)	
		Offense			
80	Shawn Jefferson (5-11, 180)	WR	82	John Taylor (6-1, 185)	
72	Harry Swayne (6-5, 295)	LT	74	Steve Wallace (6-5, 280)	
73	Isaac Davis (6-3, 325)	LG	61	Jesse Sapolu* (6-4, 278)	
53	Courtney Hall (6-1, 281)	C	66	Bart Oates* (6-4, 275)	
68	Joe Cocozzo (6-4, 300)	RG	63	Derrick Deese (6-3, 270)	
67	Stan Brock (6-6, 295)	RT	79	Harris Barton (6-4, 286)	
87	Duane Young (6-1, 270)	TE	84	Brent Jones* (6-4, 230)	
82	Mark Seay (6-0, 175)	WR	80	Jerry Rice* (6-2, 200)	
12	Stan Humphries (6-2, 223)	QB	8	Steve Young* (6-0, 205)	
20	Natrone Means* (5-10, 245)	RB	32	Ricky Watters* (6-1, 212)	
86	Alfred Pupunu (6-2, 265)	TE | RB	40	William Floyd (6-1, 242)	
		Defense			
94	Chris Mims (6-5, 290)	LE	96	Dennis Brown (6-4, 290)	
98	Shawn Lee (6-2, 300)	LT	97	Bryant Young (6-2, 276)	
93	Reuben Davis (6-5, 330)	RT	94	Dana Stubblefield* (6-2, 302)	
91	Leslie O'Neal* (6-4, 265)	RE	57	Rickey Jackson (6-2, 245)	
92	David Griggs (6-3, 250)	LLB	54	Lee Woodall (6-0, 220)	
57	Dennis Gibson (6-2, 240)	MLB	50	Gary Plummer (6-2, 247)	
55	Junior Seau* (6-3, 250)	RLB	51	Ken Norton (6-2, 241)	
21	Darrien Gordon (5-11, 182)	LCB	25	Eric Davis (5-11, 178)	
28	Dwayne Harper (5-11, 175)	RCB	21	Deion Sanders* (6-0, 185)	
29	Darren Carrington (6-2, 200)	SS	46	Tim McDonald* (6-2, 215)	
24	Stanley Richard (6-2, 201)	FS	36	Merton Hanks* (6-2, 185)	

* Pro Bowl selection

SUBSTITUTIONS

San Diego
Offense: WR - 83 Andre Coleman, 81 Tony Martin; TE - 50 David Binn, 89 Shannon Mitchell; T - 74 Eric Jonassen, 70 Vaughn Parker; QB - 13 Gale Gilbert; RB - 32 Eric Bieniemy, 35 Rodney Culver, 33 Ronnie Harmon. *Defense:* DE - 99 Raylee Johnson; DT - 95 Les Miller, 97 John Parrella; LB - 58 Lewis Bush, 34 Steve Hendrickson, 54 Doug Miller; CB - 31 Willie Clark, 25 Sean Vanhorse; S - 44 Eric Castle, 37 Rodney Harrison. *Specialists:* K - 3 John Carney*; P - 9 Bryan Wagner. *DNP:* 64 Curtis Whitley (C). *Inactive:* 85 Johnnie Barnes (WR), 84 Aaron Laing (TE), 71 Joe Milinichik (G), 60 Greg Engel (C), 11 Jeff Brohm (QB), 79 Cornell Thomas (DE), 90 Reggie White (DT), 43 Lonnie Young (S).

San Francisco
Offense: WR - 81 Ed McCaffrey, 88 Nate Singleton; TE - 85 Ted Popson; T - 75 Frank Pollack; G - 67 Chris Dalman, 64 Ralph Tamm; QB - 18 Elvis Grbac, 14 Bill Musgrave; RB - 35 Dexter Carter, 43 Marc Logan, 20 Derek Loville, 27 Adam Walker. *Defense:* DE - 99 Tim Harris, 71 Charles Mann, 92 Troy Wilson; DT - 91 Rhett Hall; LB - 98 Antonio Goss, 90 Darin Jordan, 55 Kevin Mitchell; CB - 41 Toi Cook, 22 Tyronne Drakeford; S - 28 Dana Hall. *Specialists:* K - 4 Doug Brien; P - 10 Klaus Wilmsmeyer. *Inactive:* 86 Brett Carolan (TE), 65 Harry Boatswain (T), 69 Rod Milstead (G), 95 Richard Dent (DE), 58 Todd Kelly (DE), 72 Mark Thomas (DE), 33 Derrick Dodge (S).

right side into the middle of the field. Cornerback Darrien Gordon released Rice inside, but both Richard and Carrington reacted poorly and the result was a 44-yard touchdown. "We were in a man-free zone and I was outside," Richard said. "There's supposed to be a man in the deep middle, and there wasn't." Added Shaw: "I don't think we ever recovered from the shell shock."

When Beathard was with the Redskins, he had drafted quarterback Stan Humphries in the sixth round in 1988. After four spotty seasons, Humphries was acquired by Beathard for the Chargers in exchange for a third-round pick. Then it was Beathard who pushed to re-create the Redskins' one-back set in San Diego using multiple tight ends and a power-based ground game. During the 1993 draft, he gave up a first-round draft choice to move up to select 245-pound running back Natrone Means in the second round. In 1994, Means went to the Pro Bowl after carrying 343 times for 1,350 yards. "He hasn't been in the league as long as [John] Riggins," Beathard said a few days before the game, "but he's every bit as talented."

On the Chargers' opening possession, Humphries brought his club's 11th-ranked offense to the line on third and 1. Humphries had wide receiver Shawn Jefferson wide open on a quick out against Sanders, but threw a bad pass and the Chargers punted away to the San Francisco 21. The tone had been set.

It took the 49ers four plays to score again. Steve Young broke away from heavy pressure led by defensive end Chris Mims on third and 3 and took off for 21 yards, the first of his four rushing first downs. On the next play, Young faked to Floyd again, inducing outside linebacker Junior Seau to come flying up to meet him. With the middle of the field open due to Seau's over-aggressiveness, Watters slipped behind Seau and caught the ball with his fingertips at the San Diego 30. "Ricky was originally supposed to run a corner pattern but I sent him up the middle instead," said Young.

Carrington came roaring up at the 25, made a stab for the ball locked under Watters' arm, and bounced off him. Near the 17, Richard went for the strip as well, but didn't get it and failed to wrap up, leaving Watters to high-step the final 15 yards and complete a backbreaking 51-yard touchdown play. "It was a beautifully executed fake trap up the middle and Ricky split their defense," Walsh said. "It was just embarrassing to San Diego on that play. That play was one we had used over the years. It breaks that defense."

Gasping for breath, the Chargers responded with a 13-play, 78-yard drive that climaxed with Means' 1-yard run. Offensive coordinator Ralph Friedgen mixed eight runs, including six by Means, with five completions by Humphries—a tough, charismatic leader with a tendency to put on weight. It ate up almost seven and a half minutes, trimmed the Chargers' deficit to 14-7, and demonstrated to the crowd of 74,107 how they made it to the Super Bowl for the first time. "That one sustained drive is how we would have liked to play the game," San Diego director of pro personnel Rudy Feldman said, "but they scored on four of their first five possessions." In other words, the Chargers and their 14th-ranked defense proved wholly incapable of stopping the 49ers.

"Nobody on the San Diego defense could walk off that field thinking they played good," said Chargers linebackers coach Dale Lindsey. "We got our butts handed to us. But they [the 49ers] were awesome."

The 49ers turned right around and gained at least 10 yards on four of their next six plays to end the first quarter. Down after down, they were making crisp, exceptional plays. Among those six plays, there was Rice cutting free off motion on a crossing route ahead of Seau for 19 yards and later steaming around end on a reverse for 10. There was John Taylor making a wonderful catch of a shoe-top slant pass for 12. Finally, there was Steve Young scrambling for 15 behind a blind-side block in the open field by tight end Brent Jones that knocked off two pursuing defensive linemen.

The touchdown also came with ridiculous ease. Young looked left for Taylor and Jones, then came back to Floyd on a check-down in the middle. Outside linebacker David Griggs added another missed tackle to the Chargers' growing list, and Floyd plowed across for the 5-yard score. "He hadn't caught a touchdown pass all year," said Young. "So they were covering our wide receivers and he slipped through. That was the time their defense had to make a stand, but they couldn't do it."

San Diego's next two possessions were three-and-out exercises in utter futility. Humphries was sacked by defensive tackle Dana Stubblefield and almost intercepted by dime back Tyronne Drakeford, forcing a punt. Next time up, a run by Means for no gain led to two more incompletions and another punt. As a 9½-point underdog in Pittsburgh, the Chargers had staged the biggest upset in conference title game history by overcoming a 13–3 deficit to win, 17–13. The decisive plays were a pair of 43-yard touchdown passes by Humphries in the second half.

In this case, Sanders' ability to take away half the field allowed the 49ers' other defenders to populate the other half, leaving available targets few and far between. The 49ers' front seven, which spearheaded a run defense ranked second in the league, featured all-rookie picks Bryant Young at defensive tackle and Lee Woodall at left linebacker, proud old ex-Saint Jackson at right end, and the unorthodox but explosive Harris, who had four and a half sacks in the postseason. San Diego settled for 67 yards rushing in 19 attempts and Humphries had a passer rating of just 56.1. "Humphries had some good games but he wasn't very consistent," McPherson said. "Their offense was really geared up to run the

TEAM STATISTICS		
SAN DIEGO		SAN FRANCISCO
20	Total First Downs	28
5	Rushing	10
14	Passing	17
1	Penalty	1
354	Total Net Yardage	455
76	Total Offensive Plays	73
4.7	Avg. Gain per Offensive Play	6.2
19	Rushes	32
67	Yards Gained Rushing (Net)	139
3.5	Average Yards per Rush	4.3
55	Passes Attempted	38
27	Passes Completed	25
3	Passes Intercepted	0
2	Tackled Attempting to Pass	3
18	Yards Lost Attempting to Pass	15
287	Yards Gained Passing (Net)	316
6/16	Third-Down Efficiency	7/13
0/4	Fourth-Down Efficiency	0/0
4	Punts	5
48.8	Average Distance	39.8
3	Punt Returns	2
1	Punt Return Yardage	12
8	Kickoff Returns	4
244	Kickoff Return Yardage	48
0	Interception Return Yardage	16
1	Fumbles	2
1	Own Fumbles Recovered	2
0	Opponent Fumbles Recovered	0
6	Penalties	3
65	Yards Penalized	18
3	Touchdowns	7
1	Rushing	1
1	Passing	6
1	Returns	0
3	Extra Points Made	7
1	Field Goals Made	0
1	Field Goals Attempted	1
0	Safeties	0
26	Total Points Scored	49
28:29	Time of Possession	31:31

football. I think it really made it tough for them when they got behind."

As the game wore on, the 49ers' offense gave the Chargers fits trying to match up with their personnel. Without substituting, it could jump into four-wide sets at a moment's notice by shifting the agile Jones and the multi-talented Watters, both Pro

INDIVIDUAL STATISTICS

SAN DIEGO

Passing	CP/ATT	YDS	TD	INT	RAT
Humphries	24/49	275	1	2	56.1
Gilbert	3/6	30	0	1	25.0

Rushing	ATT	YDS	AVG	TD	LG
Means	13	33	2.5	1	11
Harmon	2	10	5.0	0	10
Jefferson	1	10	10.0	0	10
Gilbert	1	8	8.0	0	8
Bieniemy	1	3	3.0	0	3
Humphries	1	3	3.0	0	3

Receiving	NO	YDS	AVG	TD	LG
Harmon	8	68	8.5	0	20
Seay	7	75	10.7	0	22
Pupunu	4	48	12.0	0	23
Martin	3	59	19.7	1	30t
Jefferson	2	15	7.5	0	9
Bieniemy	1	33	33.0	0	33
Means	1	4	4.0	0	4
D. Young	1	3	3.0	0	3

Interceptions	NO	YDS	LG	TD
None	--	--	--	--

Punting	NO	AVG	LG	BLK
Wagner	4	48.8	55	0

Punt Ret.	NO/FC	YDS	LG	TD
Gordon	3/2	1	1	0

Kickoff Ret.	NO	YDS	LG	TD
Coleman	8	244	98t	0

Defense	SOLO	AST	TOT	SK
Gibson	9	2	11	0
Seau	9	2	11	1
Gordon	5	0	5	0
Mims	5	0	5	0
Griggs	3	2	5	0
Carrington	4	0	4	0
Harper	3	0	3	0
Johnson	2	0	2	2
Lee	2	0	2	0
Richard	1	1	2	0
Clark	1	0	1	0
R. Davis	1	0	1	0
O'Neal	1	0	1	0
Vanhorse	1	0	1	0
Bieniemy	1	0	1	0
Castle	1	0	1	0
Harmon	1	0	1	0
Harrison	1	0	1	0
Hendrickson	1	0	1	0
D. Miller	1	0	1	0
S. Mitchell	1	0	1	0
Pupunu	1	0	1	0
TOTAL	**55**	**7**	**62**	**3**

SAN FRANCISCO

Passing	CP/ATT	YDS	TD	INT	RAT
S. Young	24/36	325	6	0	134.8
Musgrave	1/1	6	0	0	91.7
Grbac	0/1	0	0	0	39.6

Rushing	ATT	YDS	AVG	TD	LG
S. Young	5	49	9.8	0	21
Watters	15	47	3.1	1	13
Floyd	9	32	3.6	0	6
Rice	1	10	10.0	0	10
Carter	1	1	1.0	0	1
Grbac	1	0	0.0	0	0

Receiving	NO	YDS	AVG	TD	LG
Rice	10	149	14.9	3	44t
Taylor	4	43	10.8	0	16
Floyd	4	26	6.5	1	9
Watters	3	61	20.3	2	51t
Jones	2	41	20.5	0	33
Popson	1	6	6.0	0	6
McCaffrey	1	5	5.0	0	5

Interceptions	NO	YDS	LG	TD
Sanders	1	15	15	0
Cook	1	1	1	0
Davis	1	0	0	0

Punting	NO	AVG	LG	BLK
Wilmsmeyer	5	39.8	46	0

Punt Ret.	NO/FC	YDS	LG	TD
Carter	2/0	12	11	0

Kickoff Ret.	NO	YDS	LG	TD
Carter	4	48	18	0

Defense	SOLO	AST	TOT	SK
McDonald	8	1	9	0
Norton	5	2	7	0
E. Davis	6	0	6	0
Drakeford	4	0	4	0
D. Brown	3	1	4	0.5
Cook	3	1	4	0
Plummer	2	2	4	0
Sanders	2	2	4	0
Young	3	0	3	0
Hall	2	1	3	0
Jackson	2	0	2	0
Stubblefield	2	0	2	1
Walker	2	0	2	0
Hanks	1	1	2	0
Harris	1	1	2	0.5
Mann	1	0	1	0
Goss	1	0	1	0
Jordan	1	0	1	0
Loville	1	0	1	0
K. Mitchell	1	0	1	0
Tamm	1	0	1	0
Wilson	1	0	1	0
Woodall	0	1	1	0
TOTAL	**53**	**13**	**66**	**2**

Bowlers, to split-receiver positions. "Shanahan came in and continued that," McKittrick said, referring to the basic principles of the West Coast attack, "but he also went out of his way more to get a matchup. He did more of that than Walsh or [Mike] Holmgren did. I personally think that's why Young is a 70 percent completion passer instead of a 65 percent."

Against such great athletes, the Chargers either had to cover them with safeties or linebackers, or had to substitute an extra cornerback and leave themselves vulnerable to the run if the 49ers stayed in their conventional two-back look. "Ricky Watters is the second-best wide receiver on that team, and if you don't have another cornerback on the field you're in trouble," said Shaw. "But they still run effectively enough if you're in nickel. We tried to change up and play more man-to-man, but when they flex out you can't do that."

Steve Young's fourth touchdown pass, ending a nine-play drive of 49 yards, came on a routine 8-yard swing to Watters. This time, Arnsparger called a pressure and Young lofted a quick-release pass to Watters in the left flat over the blitzing Griggs. "It's an all-out blitz," said Shaw. "At that time you're grabbing for straws."

Now trailing 28–7, the Chargers quickly reached the San Francisco 13 on a 17-yard pass to wide receiver Mark Seay and a 33-yard screen pass to running back Eric Bieniemy. On first down, cornerback Eric Davis made an excellent breakup of an end-zone pass to wide receiver Tony Martin. On second down, Humphries threw a strike to Seay a step ahead of Hanks in the left corner of the end zone. It wasn't an easy play by any means, requiring Seay to dive and stretch out for the ball, but he did have both hands on it before it came free. "It should have been a catch," Beathard said. "That play really did away with our chances."

When Pro Bowl strong safety Tim McDonald broke up a third-down pass to tight end Alfred Pupunu, Pro Bowl kicker John Carney kicked a 31-yard field goal. The first half ended, 28–10, when Humphries underthrew a bomb to Martin in the waning seconds that had 54-yard touchdown written all over it. Instead, Davis came back for the interception.

San Diego opened the second half as it did the first half—going three and out when another third-and-short pass went awry. This time, it was third and 2 when Martin dropped an easy hook in front of Eric Davis. From there, the 49ers were off on consecutive long drives that pushed the score to 42–10. On a 62-yard drive, Steve Young was 3-of-3 for 53 yards before Watters scored on a 9-yard run. Watters was able to cut back when Seau and Richard overran the play. Then, a 67-yard drive was capped when Young, under heavy pressure, stepped up and hit Rice in the clear at the 3 on a crossing route. When Richard missed another tackle, it led to a 15-yard touchdown pass.

Priefer's special teams, which ranked third in a regular-season breakdown of 19 statistical categories compared to 20th for the 49ers, had produced four touchdowns returns during the regular season. They continued their excellence in the Super Bowl when rookie Andre Coleman returned the kickoff for a 98-yard touchdown. It was a wedge return to the left in which Coleman made Adam Walker miss; then he skipped away from Ed McCaffrey and Antonio Goss and made kicker Doug Brien miss badly in the open field.

A 2-point conversion pass made it 42–18. When the 49ers had to punt, Ross made the decision to go for it on fourth and 1 at his 37 in the waning seconds of the third quarter. The give was to Means off right tackle, but there was nowhere to run when Stubblefield penetrated through left guard Isaac Davis and Woodall stuffed the lead block of H-back Shannon Mitchell. That carry for minus-4 led to Young's record sixth touchdown pass, a 7-yarder to Rice on a slant against cornerback Dwayne Harper.

The few plays of note in the fourth quarter were Sanders' interception off a pressure by Cook, a brilliant interception by the wide-ranging Cook on a long ball to Martin, and Humphries' 30-yard touchdown pass when Martin beat Sanders deep, wrapping up the scoring at 49–26.

As one of the NFL's two youngest teams, the Chargers appeared to have a bright future, but after gaining a wild-card playoff berth the next season, they went almost a decade without another postseason appearance. Ross resigned under pressure in January 1997 and Beathard retired under pressure after the 2000 draft. Even as a 19½-point underdog on Super Sunday, this was San Diego's best shot for a title. "We lost that game because we were an immature football team," Priefer said. "We had some super leaders and players in Humphries and Seau, but my belief is San Francisco would have beat the hell out of anybody that day. It didn't matter. We sure could have played better, though."

This also marked the end of a dynasty in San Francisco. Young, the Super Bowl MVP with a passer rating of 134.8, would play effectively and, at times, brilliantly for four more seasons. Try as he might, however, he wouldn't make another Super Bowl appearance under Seifert and, later, Steve Mariucci.

The 49ers' last shining moment was a tribute to Young's impeccable quarterbacking, Policy's scheming, and DeBartolo's largesse, plus one of the greatest collections of players and coaches in the modern era of professional football.

"That team was put together specifically to win a Super Bowl," Seifert said. "We hadn't won the Super Bowl since my first year. It was mandated that we were to win the Super Bowl. It was an all-out vendetta to put that team together. Fortunately, we were able to."

Ten Best Performances by a Defensive Back

1. **Mike Haynes, CB, Raiders, XVIII:** Acquired November 10 from New England, Haynes was the final piece of the puzzle in a formidable defense. Against the Redskins, he intercepted one pass, dropped another, and broke up a third as "the Smurfs" couldn't get off the jam.

2. **Glen Edwards, S, Steelers, X:** Extremely physical member of an extremely physical secondary. Edwards sealed the victory with a late interception, had four tackles, and hammered on Dallas WR Golden Richards with such force that he had to leave the game.

3. **Deion Sanders, CB, 49ers XXIX:** Delivered what he was hired to do: a Super Bowl win. "Neon Deion" had four tackles, an interception, and two passes defensed.

4. **Bob Sanders, S, Colts, XLI:** Forced a fumble from Bears RB Cedric Benson with a crushing hit and later ranged far and deep to intercept a long pass. "There might be two, three players in the league that can make that interception," Colts president Bill Polian said.

5. **Lester Hayes, CB, Raiders, XVIII:** Together with Haynes, the Raider cornerbacks completely shut down an offense that had broken the NFL record for points. Hayes had almost no stats (one tackle), mainly because Redskins QB Joe Theismann didn't even try to do business on his side.

6. **Corey Webster, CB, Giants, XLII:** Lined up across from Randy Moss on 51 of his 66 plays, including 50 with just 3 yards separating them at the snap, Webster held Moss to a long reception of just 18 yards.

7. **LeRoy Butler, S, Packers, XXXI:** Spent much of the game in the box blitzing Patriots QB Drew Bledsoe and had seven tackles plus a sack. In coverage, he made TE Ben Coates work for everything he got.

8. **James Washington, S, Cowboys, XXVIII:** Lost his job to Darren Woodson but got the chance to play extensively against the Bills' spread offense and made the most of it. Forced a fumble, intercepted a pass, and returned a fumble 46 yards for a touchdown.

9. **Steve Atwater, S, Broncos, XXXII:** The Broncos blitzed Packers QB Brett Favre like there was no tomorrow, and Atwater was a major force with six tackles, a sack, a forced fumble, and two passes defensed.

10. **Rodney Harrison, S, Patriots, XXXIX:** Had two interceptions, two passes defensed, a sack, and seven tackles. His second pick with nine seconds left in the game finished off the Eagles.

Honorable Mentions: Alvin Walton, S, Redskins, XXII; Cliff Harris, S, Cowboys, VI; Jake Scott, S, Dolphins, VII; Eric Wright, CB, 49ers, XIX; Tracy Porter, Saints, XLIV.

XXX

DALLAS COWBOYS 27, PITTSBURGH STEELERS 17

January 28, 1996
Sun Devil Stadium, Tempe, Arizona

The two most crucial plays in Super Bowl XXX were passes spun off to the right side by quarterback Neil O'Donnell. There they were intercepted by cornerback Larry Brown, a bit player on a team laden with stars who turned out to be the MVP. Each interception set up two-play touchdown drives that were the difference in the Dallas Cowboys' 27–17 victory over the Pittsburgh Steelers. Thus, the Cowboys, a 13½-point favorite, were able to avert what would have been the biggest upset since the Jets over the Colts in Super Bowl III.

As coach Barry Switzer handed the Lombardi Trophy to Jerry Jones, he seemed to release 12 months of frustration by saying, "We did it our way, baby!" Once described as a "caretaker" coach by Bill Walsh, Switzer had delivered a Super Bowl to Jones that was even more precious to the owner than the first two, because it proved the Cowboys didn't need Jimmy Johnson to win after all.

"This is the best one of all, for all the adversity we've been through, for all the criticism we've taken, about Coach Switzer, that he was dumb, that he had no discipline, that he didn't have control of things," right tackle Erik Williams said. "Whenever you win a Super Bowl, it's great. For me, and I think for this team and this organization, this is the most satisfying."

To Switzer's credit, he recognized that this Dallas team wasn't as dominant as the ones under Johnson that had belted Buffalo in Super Bowl XXVII and Super Bowl XXVIII. The Cowboys' sense of invincibility had ebbed after the crushing 38–28 defeat by San Francisco in the NFC Championship Game the previous year and their 2–2 skid in December 1995. Switzer strived to win with sheer talent as much as any coach, but when he didn't have a significant manpower advantage, he wasn't a coach who viewed chicanery as a sign of weakness.

He approved a play created just for the Super Bowl, which the Cowboys utilized for their first

Attendance: 76,347
Conditions: 68 degrees, clear, wind NW at 5 mph
Time of kickoff: 4:21 p.m. (MST)
Length of game: 3 hours, 24 minutes
Referee: Red Cashion

MVP: Larry Brown, CB, Cowboys

running play of the game. It sprung Emmitt Smith for 23 yards and set up a field goal. He also signed off on utilizing cornerback Deion Sanders on offense, and "Neon Deion" hauled in a 47-yard bomb to position Dallas for its first touchdown. Additionally, he gave defensive coordinator Dave Campo the go-ahead to copy-cat the zone-blitz scheme, using some of the Steelers' own material against them. In fact, O'Donnell's fatal mistake with just more than four minutes remaining occurred when neither he nor wide receiver Andre Hastings reacted properly to one of those zone blitzes, allowing Brown to make his second crucial interception.

"We had the better team, but that doesn't always mean you're going to win the ball game," Switzer said years later. "We were in the middle of our prime right then. This team could have won four in a row, but we lost to San Francisco in my first year. We came that close. Then free agency started siphoning off the players. That was the last team put together that was a dominant football team. We're not ever going to have that myth or lore about us [as a dynasty]. We're the 'Team of the Nineties.' That's what we'll always be."

The Cowboys didn't have an overwhelming defense during the regular season. Defensive end Charles Haley battled back problems, finally had surgery for a ruptured disc on December 6, and was questionable for the Super Bowl (he played about 5 percent of the snaps against Pittsburgh). Linebacker Darrin Smith didn't report until Week 8 because of a

	1	2	3	4	Final
Dallas Cowboys	10	3	7	7	27
Pittsburgh Steelers	0	7	0	10	17

SCORING SUMMARY

DAL   Boniol, 42-yd. FG
DAL   Novacek, 3-yd. pass from Aikman (Boniol kick)
2nd Quarter
DAL   Boniol, 35-yd. FG
PIT   Thigpen, 6-yd. pass from O'Donnell (N. Johnson kick)
3rd Quarter
DAL   E. Smith, 1-yd. run (Boniol kick)
4th Quarter
PIT   N. Johnson, 46-yd. FG
PIT   Morris, 1-yd. run (N. Johnson kick)
DAL   E. Smith, 4-yd. run (Boniol kick)

ontract dispute. Cornerback Kevin Smith ruptured is Achilles tendon in the opener and was done or the year. His replacement, Clayton Holmes, vas suspended for good on November 3 for violating the NFL's substance-abuse policy. Dominating defensive tackle Leon Lett missed four games in November after being suspended also for substance buse. The Cowboys ranked ninth in yards allowed, ncluding an unsightly 16th against the run, and vere merely 26th on third downs.

Campo, the team's secondary coach from 1991 o 1994, was promoted to coordinator in January 995 when Butch Davis left to coach the University f Miami. Recognizing that leaks existed on defense, Campo reached the conclusion that the Cowboys needed a more extensive blitz package. Under Dave Wannstedt and Davis, the Cowboys had been able to generate more than enough pressure with just their ront four.

"At that time, Fritz Shurmur in Green Bay nd Dick LeBeau in Pittsburgh were the zone-blitz guys," Campo said. "We had not been a big zone pressure team. So during the year I took off all of heir zone blitzes and we started running some of hem. In the playoffs, we unleashed the zone blitzes, especially in the Pittsburgh game. In a lot of ways, we used Dick's own stuff against them. We felt their quarterback [O'Donnell] did a great job all year, but ne was not great under pressure. . . . The zone blitzes were a big factor in that game."

The Cowboys led, 13–7, midway in the third quarter, but the momentum was starting to switch. On third and 9 from the Pittsburgh 48, the Cowboys blitzed and defensive tackle Chad Hennings, working against all-pro center Dermontti Dawson, barged into O'Donnell as he threw toward Ernie Mills. The Steelers' two wide receivers on the right side adjusted their routes over the middle, but O'Donnell threw a horrible pass that slipped off his hand high, traveled wide, and went right to Brown.

"Mills ran the right thing and Neil just read it wrong and heaved it right to Brown," Steelers offensive coordinator Ron Erhardt said years later. "Brown didn't do anything but stay back and play his responsibility." Said Mills, "Neil made a bad, bad read." Said O'Donnell, "I just lost the ball out of my hand." Said Pittsburgh safety Rod Woodson: "They were all inside but Larry just stayed outside for whatever reason covering grass. Neil kind of threw it away and didn't see him."

Brown returned the interception 44 yards to the 18. On the Cowboys' first play, guard Nate Newton accompanied Troy Aikman on a bootleg to the right. On the move, Aikman drilled a strike to Michael Irvin in front of safety Darren Perry for a gain of 17. Emmitt Smith plowed over from the 1 on the next play, and it was 20–7.

By the time of Brown's second interception, the game's tenor had changed dramatically. The Cowboys' lead was down to 3 points, 20–17, following Byron "Bam" Morris' 1-yard touchdown run. On second down in the Cowboys' next offensive series, middle linebacker Levon Kirkland vaulted over Emmitt Smith to sack Aikman for minus-8, and Dallas punted two plays later,

"I had to come in and take over a damn coaching staff that wasn't my coaching staff. They all stayed. I didn't hire anybody. Tough-ass job. It was tough managing a lot of egos. I had a lot of things stacked against me when I went there. Ernie [Zampese] was great. I'm glad he was there. We made it happen."

Barry Switzer, Cowboys head coach

giving the Steelers the ball on their 32-yard line with 4:15 remaining. But on Pittsburgh's first play of their possession, Hastings dropped a short pass from O'Donnell.

Yancey Thigpen and Charles Johnson had bee[n] Pittsburgh's starting wide receivers for most of th[e] season, but Mills stepped in late in the year whe[n] Johnson suffered a season-ending knee injur[y]. Then Mills suffered a torn AC[L] early in the fourth quarte[r]. So Hastings, a more-tha[n] capable number three with 4[?] receptions during the regul[ar] season, was on the field wi[th] Thigpen, leaving second-ye[ar] man Corey Holliday as numb[er] three and rookie quarterbac[k] turned-wideout Kordell Stewa[rt] as number four.

On second and 10 followin[g] Hastings' drop, the Steelers line[d] up with Holliday wide rig[ht] and Hastings slot right. Camp[?] called a zone blitz, sendin[g] an additional rusher in th[e] person of safety Bill Bates an[d] dropping Lett into coverag[e]. Hastings hooked inside, bu[t] O'Donnell threw the ball outsid[e], where Brown was squattin[g] waiting for the interception. "W[e] were in some kind of three- o[r] four-wide set," Erhardt sai[d]. "When certain people wer[e] coming off the strong side hi[s] [Hastings'] responsibility was t[o] break it off. If he read man, h[e] did one thing. If he read zone[,] he did another. He didn't brea[k] it off. He kept running his route.[?]"

Under a barrage of ques[-] tions after the game, O'Donne[ll] refused to point the finger a[t] Hastings, a third-round dra[ft] choice in 1993, even thoug[h] most everyone on the tea[m] knew he was the guilty party[.] "There was a miscommunica[-] tion between Andre Hasting[s] and myself," O'Donnell sai[d] years later. "I will never se[ll]

DALLAS COWBOYS (NFC, 12–4)				PITTSBURGH STEELERS (AFC, 11–5)	
		Offense			
85	Kevin Williams (5-9, 194)	WR	82	Yancey Thigpen* (6-1, 205)	
71	Mark Tuinei* (6-5, 314)	LT	65	John Jackson (6-6, 297)	
61	Nate Newton* (6-3, 320)	LG	66	Tom Newberry (6-2, 285)	
60	Derek Kennard (6-3, 333)	C	63	Dermontti Dawson* (6-2, 288)	
73	Larry Allen* (6-3, 326)	RG	68	Brenden Stai (6-4, 297)	
79	Erik Williams (6-6, 324)	RT	72	Leon Searcy (6-3, 304)	
84	Jay Novacek (6-4, 234)	TE	87	Mark Bruener (6-4, 254)	
88	Michael Irvin* (6-2, 207)	WR	89	Ernie Mills (5-11, 192)	
8	Troy Aikman* (6-4, 223)	QB	14	Neil O'Donnell (6-3, 227)	
22	Emmitt Smith* (5-9, 209)	RB	20	Erric Pegram (5-10, 195)	
48	Daryl Johnston (6-2, 242)	RB	22	John L. Williams (5-11, 235)	
		Defense			
92	Tony Tolbert (6-6, 263)	LE	96	Brentson Buckner (6-2, 305)	
67	Russell Maryland (6-1, 282)	LT I NT	93	Joel Steed (6-2, 300)	
78	Leon Lett (6-6, 291)	RT I RE	97	Ray Seals (6-3, 309)	
94	Charles Haley* (6-5, 255)	RE I LOLB	91	Kevin Greene* (6-3, 247)	
58	Dixon Edwards (6-1, 225)	LLB I LILB	99	Levon Kirkland (6-1, 264)	
55	Robert Jones (6-2, 244)	MLB I RILB	94	Chad Brown (6-2, 240)	
59	Darrin Smith (6-1, 230)	RLB I ROLB	95	Greg Lloyd* (6-2, 228)	
21	Deion Sanders (6-1, 190)	LCB	27	Willie Williams (5-9, 180)	
24	Larry Brown (5-11, 186)	RCB	37	Carnell Lake* (6-1, 210)	
28	Darren Woodson* (6-1, 216)	SS	40	Myron Bell (5-11, 203)	
31	Brock Marion (5-11, 193)	FS	39	Darren Perry (5-11, 196)	

* Pro Bowl selection

SUBSTITUTIONS

Dallas

Offense: WR - 87 Billy Davis, 82 Cory Fleming; TE - 86 Eric Bjornson, 83 Kendell Watkins; G - 65 Ron Stone; C - 70 Dale Hellestrae; RB - 38 David Lang. *Defense:* DE - 96 Shante Carver; DT - 99 Hurvin McCormack, 95 Chad Hennings; LB - 98 Godfrey Myles, 52 Jim Schwantz; CB - 23 Robert Bailey, 29 Alundis Brice; S - 40 Bill Bates, 43 Greg Briggs, 25 Scott Case, 42 Charlie Williams. *Specialists:* K - 18 Chris Boniol; P - 19 John Jett. *DNP:* 69 George Hegamin (T), 11 Wade Wilson (QB), 20 Sherman Williams (RB). *Inactive:* 17 Jason Garrett (QB), 36 Dominique Ross (RB), 90 Oscar Sturgis (DE), 91 Darren Benson (DT).

Pittsburgh

Offense: WR - 88 Andre Hastings, 83 Corey Holliday; TE - 85 Jonathan Hayes; T - 79 James Parrish; G - 73 Justin Strzelczyk; C - 60 Kendall Gammon; QB/RB/WR - 10 Kordell Stewart; RB - 34 Tim Lester, 25 Fred McAfee, 33 Byron "Bam" Morris. *Defense:* DE - 76 Kevin Henry; NT - 90 Bill Johnson; LB - 92 Jason Gildon, 54 Donta Jones, 55 Jerry Olsavsky; CB - 21 Deon Figures, 29 Randy Fuller, 24 Chris Oldham, 26 Rod Woodson; S - 41 Lethon Flowers. *Specialists:* K - 9 Norm Johnson; P - 3 Rohn Stark. *DNP:* 18 Mike Tomczak (QB). *Inactive:* 84 Tracy Greene (TE), 69 Ariel Solomon (C), 16 Jim Miller (QB).

COACHING STAFFS

Dallas

Head Coach: Barry Switzer. **Offense:** Ernie Zampese (coordinator), Hubbard Alexander (wide receivers), Robert Ford (tight ends), Hudson Houck (offensive line), Joe Brodsky (running backs). **Defense:** Dave Campo (coordinator), John Blake (defensive line), Jim Eddy (linebackers), Mike Zimmer (defensive backs). **Special Teams:** Joe Avezzano, Steve Hoffman (kickers, research and development). **Strength:** Mike Woicik.

Pittsburgh

Head Coach: Bill Cowher. **Offense:** Ron Erhardt (coordinator), Chan Gailey (wide receivers), Pat Hodgson (tight ends), Kent Stephenson (offensive line), Dick Hoak (running backs). **Defense:** Dick LeBeau (coordinator), John Mitchell (defensive line), Marvin Lewis (linebackers), Tim Lewis (defensive backs). **Special Teams:** Bobby April.

anyone down the river because that's not my style. It was just too bad because we were still right in it."

Studying the tape, Woodson noticed that Holliday was open behind Brown on a sideline go route. The problem was that O'Donnell didn't get that far into his progression. "Larry didn't do a very good job of covering the guy he was supposed to cover," Campo said. "He kind of got beat on the play to the inside and the ball was being thrown to the underneath guy and he just happened to be there to make the play." Three weeks later, Brown cashed in on his Super Bowl success with a five-year, $12.5 million deal ($3.5 million signing bonus) from Oakland in unrestricted free agency.

Brown, who estimated that he dropped nine interceptions as a rookie 13-game starter in 1991, held on to this one and brought it back 33 yards to the Pittsburgh 6. Emmitt Smith ran left for 2 before the Steelers stopped the clock at 3:47. The carry gave Smith a mere 22 yards in his last 16 carries, an infinitesimal average of 1.4 against the stunting Steelers. "We were at our best when people lined up and stayed where they were," fullback Daryl Johnston said. "Pittsburgh played shades, moved at the snap of the ball, and was undersized and quick. Their strengths fit into some of the things we struggled against. They shut down our run."

On the sidelines, LeBeau was confident that his unit would limit Dallas to a field goal. "I didn't

think they could run it in," he said. "They did. They were good." The Cowboys attacked the B gap on the right side behind a double-team block by right guard Larry Allen and right tackle Williams against defensive end Brentson Buckner. With Buckner on the ground, Emmitt Smith followed Johnston off right tackle. Johnston blocked strong safety Myron Bell, leaving Smith one-on-one at the 4 against Kirkland, who scraped behind Buckner and was unblocked.

When Smith planted his foot to cut inside, Kirkland slipped on the slickened turf that O'Donnell claimed had been cut too short by NFL turf managers. Smith ran through Kirkland's feeble arm tackle, slipped under over-pursuing linebacker Chad Brown, and shouldered past Perry into the end zone for the clinching touchdown. The Steelers would advance to the Dallas 40 before losing the ball on downs, and finally O'Donnell's Hail Mary pass as time expired was intercepted by safety Brock Marion.

"We probably weren't prepared for the hype and the distractions," said Tom Donahoe, the Steelers' director of football operations. "We got off to a terrible start and, once we settled that, we played pretty well. We knew we would have to play well, and I think if we had gotten off to a better start we could have won the game. Then our quarterback made a couple just very costly interceptions as we were getting back into the game. Neil had been so consistent all year."

It marked the 12th straight victory for the NFC, but at least it was a competitive game after four blowouts in a row. Under 38-year-old coach Bill Cowher, the Steelers had rallied from a 3–4 start. When O'Donnell came back from a broken hand in mid-October, Cowher and Erhardt threw caution to the wind and finished the regular season passing on an uncharacteristic 55.5 percent of their snaps. "At first we were a running team, but without [Barry] Foster or tight end Eric Green, we just couldn't pound it like we used to," O'Donnell said. "Probably in the fifth or sixth game we started to really spread it out and get the ball to the wideouts. We did a lot of no-huddles and I'd make quick reads and just let it go."

The best part of that Steelers team, according to Donahoe, was the third-ranked defense featuring Pro Bowl linebackers Greg Lloyd and Kevin Greene.

Woodson, who along with Sanders ranked as the top cornerback in the game, tore the ACL in his right knee in the opener. Carnell Lake's subsequent move from strong safety to cornerback was so successful that he made the Pro Bowl. By appearing for about 15 snaps in the Super Bowl, Woodson became the first player in NFL history to undergo reconstructive knee surgery and play in the same season. "We had guys that could really run," Donahoe said. "At linebacker, we were as good as anybody in the league. With Kevin and Greg's pass-rush ability we were always able to get pressure on the quarterback. What hurt us early [in the Super Bowl] is we were just too hyper and got out of position."

Take, for example, the third play of the game, when Emmitt Smith gained 23 of his unseemly total of 49 yards. "That was a new play specifically for that game," Johnston remembered. "We had flow going to our right and got everybody moving that way. Then it was a designed cutback with Larry Allen pulling and kicking out on Greg Lloyd." In the second quarter, Lloyd played through Allen on the exact same play and tackled Smith for no gain. When challenged by the play for the first time, however, Lloyd played it poorly from wide on the left side and was buried by Allen, a second-year phenom from tiny Sonoma State in California. When Bell slipped and whiffed on the tackle, Smith was away for 23 yards to the 10. But the Steelers held, and Chris Boniol had to kick a 42-yard field goal.

When the Cowboys got the ball back, offensive coordinator Ernie Zampese called Sanders' number on a deep post and Aikman hit him for a gain of 47. "That was critical," said Switzer. "We only had certain plays for him. I'd say he played 10 or 15 snaps on offense." This time, Dallas converted when tight end Jay Novacek came free on a drag route to the left and caught a 3-yard touchdown pass. The Steelers argued that he had been freed by an illegal pick by tight end Kendell Watkins against Lloyd and fellow linebacker Jerry Olsavsky.

On the Steelers' next possession, they made a mistake that helped cost them the game. After successfully converting a fourth-and-1 gamble at midfield, the Steelers were forced to punt when Dawson's shotgun snap on first down from the Dallas 36 went awry for minus-13. "We hadn't

TEAM STATISTICS

DALLAS		PITTSBURGH
15	Total First Downs	25
5	Rushing	9
10	Passing	15
0	Penalty	1
254	Total Net Yardage	310
50	Total Offensive Plays	84
5.1	Avg. Gain per Offensive Play	3.7
25	Rushes	31
56	Yards Gained Rushing (Net)	103
2.2	Average Yards per Rush	3.3
23	Passes Attempted	49
15	Passes Completed	28
0	Passes Intercepted	3
2	Tackled Attempting to Pass	4
11	Yards Lost Attempting to Pass	32
198	Yards Gained Passing (Net)	207
2/10	Third-Down Efficiency	9/19
1/1	Fourth-Down Efficiency	2/4
5	Punts	4
38.2	Average Distance	44.8
1	Punt Returns	2
11	Punt Return Yardage	18
3	Kickoff Returns	5
37	Kickoff Return Yardage	96
77	Interception Return Yardage	0
0	Fumbles	2
0	Own Fumbles Recovered	2
0	Opponent Fumbles Recovered	0
4	Penalties	2
25	Yards Penalized	15
3	Touchdowns	2
2	Rushing	1
1	Passing	1
0	Returns	0
3	Extra Points Made	2
2	Field Goals Made	1
2	Field Goals Attempted	1
0	Safeties	0
27	Total Points Scored	17
26:11	Time of Possession	33:49

done anything like that all year," said Erhardt. "The pitfalls of the shotgun. We had something going there, too. We might have thrown it too much, but we were down the whole game and we had to throw to get into the game."

In the second quarter, each team mounted a 13-play scoring drive and had a three-and-out. The

INDIVIDUAL STATISTICS

DALLAS

Passing	CP/ATT	YDS	TD	INT	RAT
Aikman	15/23	209	1	0	108.8

Rushing	ATT	YDS	AVG	TD	LG
E. Smith	18	49	2.7	2	23
Johnston	2	8	4.0	0	4
K. Williams	1	2	2.0	0	2
Aikman	4	-3	-0.8	0	0

Receiving	NO	YDS	AVG	TD	LG
Irvin	5	76	15.2	0	20
Novacek	5	50	10.0	1	19
K. Williams	2	29	14.5	0	22
Sanders	1	47	47.0	0	47
Johnston	1	4	4.0	0	4
E. Smith	1	3	3.0	0	3

Interceptions	NO	YDS	LG	TD
Brown	2	77	44	0
Marion	1	0	0	0

Punting	NO	AVG	LG	BLK
Jett	5	38.2	51	0

Punt Ret.	NO/FC	YDS	LG	TD
Sanders	1/0	11	11	0

Kickoff Ret.	NO	YDS	LG	TD
K. Williams	2	24	18	0
Marion	1	13	13	0

Defense	SOLO	AST	TOT	SK
D. Woodson	7	3	10	0
Marion	7	2	9	0
R. Jones	4	4	8	0
Case	6	1	7	0
L. Brown	5	2	7	0
Edwards	4	1	5	0
Tolbert	4	1	5	1
D. Smith	3	2	5	0
Bailey	4	0	4	0
Bates	3	1	4	0
Carver	3	1	4	0
Haley	3	1	4	1
Hennings	3	0	3	2
Maryland	3	0	3	0
Lett	2	1	3	0
Schwantz	2	1	3	0
Hellestrae	1	0	1	0
Lang	1	0	1	0
Myles	1	0	1	0
C. Williams	1	0	1	0
Briggs	0	1	1	0
TOTAL	67	22	89	4

PITTSBURGH

Passing	CP/ATT	YDS	TD	INT	RAT
O'Donnell	28/49	239	1	3	51.3

Rushing	ATT	YDS	AVG	TD	LG
Morris	19	73	3.8	1	15
Pegram	6	15	2.5	0	4
Stewart	4	15	3.8	0	7
O'Donnell	1	0	0.0	0	0
J. Williams	1	0	0.0	0	0

Receiving	NO	YDS	AVG	TD	LG
Hastings	10	98	9.8	0	19
Mills	8	78	9.8	0	17
Thigpen	3	19	6.3	1	7
Morris	3	18	6.0	0	10
Holliday	2	19	9.5	0	10
J. Williams	2	7	3.5	0	5

Interceptions	NO	YDS	LG	TD
None	--	--	--	--

Punting	NO	AVG	LG	BLK
Stark	4	44.8	55	0

Punt Ret.	NO/FC	YDS	LG	TD
Hastings	2/0	18	11	0

Kickoff Ret.	NO	YDS	LG	TD
Mills	4	79	22	0
McAfee	1	17	17	0

Defense	SOLO	AST	TOT	SK
Kirkland	8	2	10	1
Lloyd	5	3	8	0
Perry	3	3	6	0
Lake	5	0	5	0
W. Williams	4	1	5	0
Steed	3	1	4	0
Bell	2	1	3	0
C. Brown	1	2	3	0
Flowers	2	0	2	0
Greene	2	0	2	0
Olsavsky	1	1	2	0
Buckner	1	0	1	0
McAfee	1	0	1	0
Seals	1	0	1	1
Strzelczyk	1	0	1	0
Thigpen	1	0	1	0
J. Williams	1	0	1	0
Lester	0	1	1	0
TOTAL	42	15	57	2

Cowboys' march of 62 yards ended with Boniol's 35-yard field goal, four plays after Aikman's 24-yard touchdown pass to Irvin was nullified by his penalty for pass interference against Lake. "He did push off," Switzer said. "Hell, all those big receivers push off those corners. But he wouldn't have had to. He could have used his body to make the play. That play bothered me."

The Steelers' march of 54 yards ended when Thigpen caught a 6-yard touchdown pass with 13 seconds remaining in the half. "That was unusual because Deion got beat on a slant," Campo said. "Thigpen made a great move against press coverage." Mills converted two third-and-long situations with leaping catches of inaccurate throws for gains of 7 and 17 yards. As far as Switzer was concerned, however, the most significant play of the drive, if not the entire first half, was the third play. That was O'Donnell's 19-yard pass to Hastings on third and 20, a play made possible by Darrin Smith's blown coverage. The latter preceded Stewart's 3-yard keeper on another successful fourth-and-1 gamble by Cowher. It gave life to the drive as well as the entire Pittsburgh team for the second half.

"Haley sacked O'Donnell for minus-10, it's third and 20 and I said, 'God Almighty, that ought to win the half for us,'" Switzer said. "Then they hit a damn 19-yard crossing route on the next play." The Cowboys had a two-deep double zone, and Darrin Smith took off with the split receiver down the boundary when he already had a safety covering him. Instead of staying in the flat, playing zone, and picking up the shallow crosser, he turned his back and sprinted down the field, giving Hastings an opening to make the reception. "A dumb-ass brain fart," continued Switzer. "Let the guy catch the ball on a 10-yard crossing route. Just come up, we hem him up and get him down, and they punt the football away. Because of that bonehead play right there they get it in the end zone. All of a sudden, we've got some doubt in our mind and I've got the red ass because two plays in the first half hadn't allowed us to get up, 17–0. Instead of us having control of this game going in the locker room and they've got doubt in their mind, same ol' ass-kicking they're going to get, they're back in the game."

In the second half, the Cowboys had the ball six times, ran 19 plays, and gained a mere 61 yards.

"That was a tremendous defensive effort by our guys," LeBeau said. "They had a tremendous offensive team with that line and the great back and a great receiver and a tremendous quarterback in Aikman. They had a field full of guys that probably will be in the Hall of Fame. But after the second drive we completely contained them. We didn't have a weakness on that defense. We won everything but the score. That's all you're going to remember, but as a defensive coach you don't have any problems remembering holding those guys to 254 [yards]."

Late in the third quarter, the Steelers drove 38 yards to a second-and-2 from their 47. Big back Bam Morris failed to gain on second, third, and fourth downs, when Hennings and defensive end Tony Tolbert defeated blocks to foil Cowher's third fourth-down roll of the dice. Of Morris, who bulled 19 times for 73 yards, O'Donnell said, "Sometimes you didn't know if he'd turn it on during a game. But he ran extremely hard that day."

Pittsburgh forced another punt and back came O'Donnell, completing six of seven passes in a 10-play, 52-yard push that was halted by Tolbert's third-down sack. A 46-yard field goal off the foot of 14-year veteran Norm Johnson made it 20–10. On the sidelines, Bobby April, the Steelers' 32-year-old special-teams coach, suggested the idea of an onside kick to Cowher, an old special-teams coach himself. "I'm not leaving anything in the bag," said Cowher, approving the earliest onside kick at that point in Super Bowl history. When linebacker Dixon Edwards vacated his area prematurely, cornerback Deon Figures made a routine recovery. "We didn't anticipate that," Switzer said. "That onside kick made it a tight game."

Mixing short passes with inside thrusts by Morris, the Steelers covered the 52 yards in nine plays. Morris scored on third and goal, walking in from the 1, and it was 20–17 with 6:36 to play. "We had gone the length of the field and then were right back on the field after the onside kick," remembered Campo. "Our guys were shot defensively. That's where they could have taken control of the football game. Then that was the second interception. Once Emmitt put it in, it was over."

The Steelers lost despite piling up almost an eight-minute advantage in time of possession. They found success exploiting the undersized middle of the Cowboys' front seven and found a way to block Lett and Haley, other than for a play here and there. At times, they even got away with throwing at Sanders. Finally, they didn't fumble, which had been one of their season-long problems.

Clearly, one of the main differences was the play of the quarterbacks, illustrated by Aikman's passer rating of 108.8 compared to O'Donnell's 51.3. By this, his seventh season, Aikman had lost some of his movement skills. Yet, after having two of his first three passes dropped, he hit 10 in a row to enable the Cowboys to draw first blood. "His stats weren't big

like he had in other Super Bowls, but the zero picks was the key," said Switzer. "Fifteen out of 23 is not a great day for Troy Aikman. It should have been about 20 out of 23 and 260 and another touchdown."

But Switzer took it, and so did Jerry Jones. The "Goober Hires Gomer" sign that hung over a Dallas highway ramp shortly after the owner summoned the coach from a five-year hiatus was long gone. No Super Bowl–winning coach ever was criticized as much as Barry Switzer and, outwardly at least, had the ability to laugh it off.

"We did it," Switzer, the self-described "Bootlegger's Boy," said, "and we did it my way."

Ten Best Performances by a Defensive Lineman

1. **Reggie White, DE, Packers, XXXI:** Just because his opponent was Patriots RT Max Lane shouldn't detract from White's overwhelming performance. Besides 3 second-half sacks, he had 4 other pressures and sent Lane sprawling 8 times with his famed "hump" move.

2. **Reggie Kinlaw, NT, Raiders, XVIII:** The Raiders moved the undersized Kinlaw back to give him room to work against "the Hogs" of Washington. Owning C Jeff Bostic, Kinlaw was the main reason why John Riggins averaged a mere 2.5 yards per carry.

3. **Manny Fernandez, NT, Dolphins, VII:** Miami FS Jake Scott was the MVP, but many people said Fernandez should have been the choice. He controlled C Len Hauss and the Redskins' vaunted running attack.

4. **Richard Dent, DE, Bears, XX:** Dent's only problem was trying to get to the Patriots' quarterbacks before his teammates did. It was a jailbreak situation down after down, and Dent did more than his fair share, dominating Pro Bowl LT Brian Holloway.

5. **Justin Tuck, DE, Giants, XLII:** New York's pass rushers devoured the acclaimed O-line of New England, and coordinator Steve Spagnuolo said Tuck was the best player on his defense. He had 2 sacks, 5 tackles, 1 forced fumble, and 4½ pressures.

6. **Harvey Martin, DE, Cowboys, XII:** Denver's LT Andy Maurer had no chance against Martin. He had 2 sacks, dominating the right side with DT Randy White.

7. **L. C. Greenwood, DE, Steelers, X:** Greenwood, in the prime of his career at 29, helped make up for the absence of the injured Joe Greene in the second half. Working against Pro Bowl RT Rayfield Wright, Greenwood had 3 sacks.

8. **Darnell Dockett, DT, Cardinals, XLIII:** Dockett exploited the weak middle of the Steelers' line against both run and pass. He posted 3 sacks, 3 tackles for loss, and several pressures in Arizona's losing cause.

9. **Michael Strahan, DE, Giants, XLII:** Strahan had 5½ pressures, one more than Justin Tuck, to go with a sack and a pass defensed. He retired not long after the Giants upset the Patriots.

10. **Kevin Fagan, DE, 49ers, XXIII:** Fagan, a talented technician, played extremely well against the great Bengals LT Anthony Muñoz. He had a sack and 6 tackles as the right end in the 49ers' 3-4 front.

Honorable Mentions: Gary Johnson, DT, 49ers, XIX; Leon Lett, DT, Cowboys, XXVII; Reggie Kinlaw, NT, Raiders, XV; Michael McCrary, DE, Ravens, XXXV; Willie Davis, DE, Packers, II.

XXXI

GREEN BAY PACKERS 35, NEW ENGLAND PATRIOTS 21

January 26, 1997
Louisiana Superdome, New Orleans, Louisiana

This is the story of two football teams. One was unselfishly bent on a return to glory. The other was hopelessly embroiled in a breakup between its owner and coach.

The team in turmoil, the New England Patriots, finally started to play in the second half. With three minutes left in the third quarter, they had trimmed their deficit to 27–21. Momentum was swinging their way. Then the Patriots kicked off and Desmond Howard, the first special-teams player to be named Super Bowl MVP, returned it 99 yards for a touchdown. Pffffft. That was the end of the Patriots, and the scoring. Green Bay 35, New England 21.

The winning team insisted it wasn't quite that way. As general manager of the Packers from 1991 to 2001, Ron Wolf was chiefly responsible for putting in motion one of the greatest rebuilding projects in NFL history. In five years, he resurrected a storied franchise that had been down in the mouth for 25 years and built it into a powerhouse with a sentimental story that played wonderfully from coast to coast. As it turned out, too, one of Wolf's best friends, Bill Parcells, was coaching his final game for New England.

"Bill always thought that the turning point was Desmond Howard's return," Wolf said years later. "That he had us reeling, and if he had made us go another three-and-out it would have been interesting. Obviously, when they kicked it off to Desmond Howard, that was the coup de grace. But I don't think that our team was ever threatened. . . . I didn't think it was anointed that we were going to win the game. But, by the same token, I didn't see how we could lose it."

Eliminated from the playoffs in Dallas after the 1993, 1994, and 1995 seasons, the Packers got several key players back from injury late in the 1996 season and clearly emerged as the finest team in the league. Counting the playoffs, coach Mike Holmgren's club

Attendance: 72,301
Conditions: 67 degrees, indoors
Time of kickoff: 5:25 p.m. (CST)
Length of game: 3 hours, 21 minutes
Referee: Gerald Austin

MVP: Desmond Howard, KR/PR, Green Bay

scored 30 points or more in its final six games; onl once in the club's first 78 years had the Packers ha a longer streak (seven games in 1963). Balance wa the operative word, with an offense ranked fifth i yards, a defense ranked first in yards allowed, an special teams ranked seventh overall. Green Ba was the first team since the 17–0 Miami Dolphin of 1972 to lead the NFL both in most points score (456) and fewest points allowed (210). The Packer were 14-point favorites in the franchise's first Supe Bowl in 29 years.

Quarterback Brett Favre, 27, won his secon straight NFL MVP award after spending 46 days the offseason at a Kansas rehabilitation center for a addiction to the pain-killing drug Vicodin. Antoni Freeman was fast becoming a star and, together wit mid-November waiver acquisition Andre Risor gave Favre exceptional targets at wide receiver.

Tight end Mark Chmura, who made the Pr Bowl in 1995, was joined by Keith Jackson, wh made the Pro Bowl in 1996 despite having less play ing time than Chmura. Workhorse Edgar Benne split carries down the stretch with the emergin Dorsey Levens. The only mediocre group was th offensive line, but at least the insertion of vetera Bruce Wilkerson for struggling rookie John Miche at left tackle in Week 16 and through the playof solidified the pass protection.

The defensive line was much more tha just the incomparable Reggie White at left en Right end Sean Jones, in his final season, was th

	1	2	3	4	Final
New England Patriots	14	0	7	0	21
Green Bay Packers	10	17	8	0	35

SCORING SUMMARY

1st Quarter
GB Rison, 54-yd. pass from Favre (Jacke kick)
GB Jacke, 37-yd. FG
NE Byars, 1-yd. pass from Bledsoe (Vinatieri kick)
NE Coates, 4-yd. pass from Bledsoe (Vinatieri kick)

2nd Quarter
GB Freeman, 81-yd. pass from Favre (Jacke kick)
GB Jacke, 31-yd. FG
GB Favre, 2-yd. run (Jacke kick)

3rd Quarter
NE Martin, 28-yd. run (Vinatieri kick)
GB Howard, 99-yd. kickoff return (Chmura, pass from Favre)

agiest of veterans. Not only was 340-pound nose tackle Gilbert Brown immovable, he also was active and made plays. Three-technique defensive tackle Santana Dotson enjoyed a tremendous first season in Green Bay after having been mostly an underachiever in Tampa Bay. Linebackers Brian Williams, Wayne Simmons, and George Koonce (who missed the Super Bowl due to a blown knee and was capably replaced by former Bear Ron Cox) were top-shelf. The starting secondary of all-pro strong safety LeRoy Butler, wily free safety Eugene Robinson, and clingy cornerbacks Doug Evans and Craig Newsome intercepted 24 passes in 19 games.

The special teams featured Howard, who in 19 games averaged 16.2 yards on punt returns, 23.8 on kickoff returns, brought 5 back for touchdowns, and fielded 116 returns, fumbling just once. Craig Hentrich's net punting average of 36.3 tied for the best in team history, and veteran kicker Chris Jacke was solid.

Besides Holmgren, whose game plans and play-calling were regarded as cutting edge, the staff included coordinators Sherman Lewis and Fritz Shurmur, future NFL head coaches Andy Reid and Marty Mornhinweg, and a slew of trusted position coaches.

"We were on such a roll," Chmura said. "That team seemed to have so much destiny to it and we had so much depth. You got Dorsey and Edgar in the backfield, you got me and Keith at tight end. In today's game, it would have been a recipe for disaster. But no one cared. Everyone just wanted to win a Super Bowl. That was what was so refreshing about that team."

In 1987, the Packers couldn't even compete on the field and were dealing with the scandal of sexual-assault trials involving wide receiver James Lofton (acquitted) and defensive back Mossy Cade (convicted). At the time *Sports Illustrated*'s Frank Deford wrote a lengthy piece, "Troubled Times in Titletown," in which he noted how the NFL landscape was changing and concluded that little Green Bay might never win big again. "Everybody kept saying that the Lombardi era was the end of us," said Bob Harlan, who joined the organization in 1971 and was elected team president in 1988. "Fans had really lost hope. I wasn't sure we'd get back."

Harlan, whose hiring of Wolf as the team's first non-coaching general manager began the resurgence, used to gaze longingly at the oversized inflatable helmets that were rolled out during Super Bowl pre-game festivities each year. "I thought, 'Boy, I wonder if I'll ever see ours there,'" he said. When he finally did, he said, "I left the hotel early in the morning and walked over to the [Superdome] because I wanted my picture taken by that helmet."

With six minutes remaining and the issue all but decided, NFL security came to whisk Harlan and Wolf down to field level for the presentation of the Lombardi Trophy. In the elevator, Chan Tagliabue, the wife of commissioner Paul Tagliabue, reached over, grasped Harlan by the arm and offered her congratulations. "Paul hit her," Harlan recalled. "'We don't say anything until the game is over,' Paul said. And he was stern about it. . . . Then Ron and I went and stood out in the end zone. Boy, it was unbelievable, that feeling."

As the Patriots' hopes flickered away, owner Robert Kraft was in a much different mood. Will Mc-Donough of *The Boston Globe* had reported six days before the game that Parcells was leaving because of irreconcilable differences with Kraft. Phone records from the New Orleans Marriott hotel showed that Parcells had made dozens of itemized phone calls to Hempstead, New York, home of the New York Jets headquarters. When Parcells didn't even fly home with the team, everyone pretty much knew the jig was up. Five days after the game, Parcells was named coach of the Jets and five of his assistant coaches—Bill Belichick, Maurice Carthon, Romeo Crennel, A Groh, and Charlie Weis—wer along with him.

"Yeah, I'd say it was little bit of a distraction all th way around," Belichick sai years later. "I can tell you firs hand, there was a lot of stu going on prior to the gam I mean, him talking to othe teams—which, honestly, I fe was totally inappropriate. Hov many chances do you get t play for the Super Bowl? Te them to get back to you in couple of days. I'm not sayin it was disrespectful to me, bu it was in terms of the overa commitment to the team."

Whatever the reason, th secondary coached by Belichic blew a coverage on the Packer second play from scrimmag Holmgren sent out a double tight end set for a play called "322 Y Stick," a staple of the West Coas offense designed to ease Favre i slowly with an easy 5-yard ou to Chmura. That morning i his hotel room, Favre had see highlights of Super Bowl XXIV when Joe Montana audibled int some huge plays. This time, h called "Black 78 Razor," wit "Black" meaning the play wa being changed, "78" meaning i would be maximum protectio with eight blockers, and "Razor meaning the flanker would run post and the split end would ru a shake route.

Although the Packer were in the wrong formatio because the two wid receivers, Freeman and Rison were both on the left sid

NEW ENGLAND PATRIOTS (AFC, 11–5)		GREEN BAY PACKERS (NFC, 13–3)	
	Offense		
84 Shawn Jefferson (5-11, 180)	WR	86 Antonio Freeman (6-0, 190)	
78 Bruce Armstrong* (6-4, 295)	LT	64 Bruce Wilkerson (6-5, 305)	
76 William Roberts (6-5, 298)	LG	73 Aaron Taylor (6-3, 305)	
64 Dave Wohlabaugh (6-3, 304)	C	52 Frank Winters* (6-3, 295)	
71 Todd Rucci (6-5, 291)	RG	63 Adam Timmerman (6-3, 295)	
68 Max Lane (6-6, 305)	RT	72 Earl Dotson (6-3, 315)	
87 Ben Coates* (6-5, 245)	TE	89 Mark Chmura (6-5, 250)	
88 Terry Glenn (5-10, 188)	WR	84 Andre Rison (5-10, 195)	
11 Drew Bledsoe* (6-5, 233)	QB	4 Brett Favre* (6-2, 222)	
28 Curtis Martin* (5-11, 203)	RB	34 Edgar Bennett (6-0, 217)	
41 Keith Byars (6-1, 255)	RB	30 William Henderson (6-1, 248)	
	Defense		
92 Ferric Collons (6-6, 286)	LE	92 Reggie White* (6-5, 305)	
97 Mark Wheeler (6-3, 285)	LT | DT	71 Santana Dotson (6-5, 285)	
75 Pio Sagapolutele (6-6, 297)	RT | NT	93 Gilbert Brown (6-2, 344)	
55 Willie McGinest* (6-5, 255)	RE	96 Sean Jones (6-7, 283)	
53 Chris Slade (6-5, 245)	LLB	59 Wayne Simmons (6-2, 248)	
52 Ted Johnson (6-3, 240)	MLB	54 Ron Cox (6-1, 239)	
59 Todd Collins (6-2, 242)	RLB	51 Brian Williams (6-1, 235)	
24 Ty Law (5-11, 196)	LCB	21 Craig Newsome (5-11, 190)	
45 Otis Smith (5-11, 190)	RCB	33 Doug Evans (6-0, 190)	
36 Lawyer Milloy (6-0, 208)	SS	36 LeRoy Butler* (6-0, 200)	
32 Willie Clay (5-10, 198)	FS	41 Eugene Robinson (6-0, 195)	

* Pro Bowl selection

SUBSTITUTIONS

New England

Offense: WR - 15 Ray Lucas, 81 Hason Graham, 82 Vincent Brisby; TE - 85 John Burke, 86 Mike Bartrum; G - 61 Bob Kratch; C - 67 Mike Gisler; RB - 22 Dave Meggett*, 35 Marrio Grier. **Defense:** DE - 74 Chris Sullivan, 96 Mike Jones; DT - 90 Chad Eaton; OLB - 95 Dwayne Sabb, 54 Tedy Bruschi; MLB - 58 Marty Moore; CB - 26 Jerome Henderson, 27 Mike McGruder; S - 23 Terry Ray, 25 Larry Whigham, 30 Corwin Brown. **Specialists:** K - 4 Adam Vinatieri; P - 19 Tom Tupa. **DNP:** 21 Ricky Reynolds (CB). **Inactive:** 80 Troy Brown (WR), 83 Dietrich Jells (WR), 48 Lovett Purnell (TE), 62 Dave Richards (T), 63 Heath Irwin (G), 16 Scott Zolak (QB), 31 Jimmy Hitchcock (CB), 72 Devin Wyman (DT).

Green Bay

Offense: WR - 81 Desmond Howard, 82 Don Beebe, 85 Terry Mickens; TE - 83 Jeff Thomason, 88 Keith Jackson*; T - 77 John Michels; G - 65 Lindsay Knapp; C - 67 Jeff Dellenbach; RB - 25 Dorsey Levens, 27 Calvin Jones, 32 Travis Jervey. **Defense:** DE - 95 Keith McKenzie, 98 Gabe Wilkins; DT - 90 Darius Holland; MLB - 55 Bernardo Harris; OLB - 56 Lamont Hollinquest; CB - 37 Tyrone Williams; S - 28 Roderick Mullen, 39 Mike Prior, 40 Chris Hayes. **Specialists:** K - 13 Chris Jacke; P - 17 Craig Hentrich. **DNP:** 9 Jim McMahon (QB). **Inactive:** 80 Derrick Mayes (WR), 68 Gary Brown (T), 62 Marco Rivera (G), 7 Kyle Wachholtz (QB), 18 Doug Pederson (QB), 94 Bob Kuberski (DT), 46 Michael Robinson (CB), 91 Shannon Clavelle (DE).

of the field, Rison took the lead and correctly ran the post. Green Bay picked up the six-man blitz, Rison easily beat slow-footed cornerback Otis Smith into the vacant middle of the field, and Favre hit him with a long pass on the money for a 54-yard touchdown.

"We told our defensive backs in that situation to switch the defense before the snap and get one of our safeties to the deep middle," said Groh, the defensive coordinator, "but the guy making the call froze or forgot. Favre made the most of it. It should have never happened." In 2004, Favre didn't hesitate when labeling it the greatest audible that he had ever called.

"Maybe we gave it away too soon," linebacker Tedy Bruschi said. "But Favre had the talent and the mental ability, even on the second play of the first Super Bowl he ever played in, to recognize something that we usually didn't do and audible to something maybe they hadn't even worked on all week."

When the Patriots took over, quarterback Drew Bledsoe threw the first of his four interceptions, a short sideline pass behind rookie Terry Glenn on which Evans made a juggling interception at the New England 28. Defensive tackle Mark Wheeler beat guard Adam Timmerman, setting up Ferric

Collons' 10-yard sack of Favre on first down, so the Packers had to settle for Jacke's 37-yard field goal and a 10–0 lead.

Then the Patriots went 76 yards in six plays to score on fullback Keith Byars' 1-yard touchdown catch against Butler. This was preceded by Byars' 32-yard gain on a screen pass in which he broke tackles by Butler and Williams, a 20-yard dump into the right flat to Curtis Martin in which he broke a tackle by Simmons, and a 26-yard penalty against Newsome for interfering on a bomb to wide receiver Shawn Jefferson.

Green Bay averaged 114.9 yards rushing in 1996, its best output since 1985, and 151.7 more in three playoff games. In the Super Bowl, the Packers settled for just 115 yards in 36 attempts (3.2 average) as the Patriots frequently stunted their linemen and altered their linebackers' gap responsibilities. When the Packers tried to run wide with Bennett, his seven carries amounted to zero yards.

Late in the first quarter, second-year middle linebacker Ted Johnson beat second-year fullback William Henderson and Collins beat right tackle Earl Dotson on a sweep in which Bennett lost 4. Hentrich punted to midfield, from where Glenn took advantage of an out-of-position Robinson to make a diving catch of a 44-yard bomb. Then tight end Ben Coates maneuvered behind Cox for a 4-yard touchdown and the Patriots led, 14–10.

Both of the touchdown passes and the long pass to Glenn had come off play-action fakes by Bledsoe. "I thought Bledsoe came out playing very well," Butler said. "They had a great running back and a quarterback who loved to go downfield on play-action."

The Patriots called 30 passes compared to seven runs in the first half, almost half of them off run fakes. "We had Curtis Martin, yet we weren't able to dominate people with our running game," said offensive line coach Fred Hoaglin, who had coached for Parcells in two Super Bowls with the Giants. "The line was young and not as overpowering, so we weren't quite able to do it the way we did in New York."

New England's lack of a running dimension ultimately enabled Shurmur to play a nickel defense extensively from the second quarter on and tee off against Bledsoe, mainly with the ubiquitous Butler—but first the Packers had to get moving.

"When I watch the game now, I can't believe we were behind," Chmura said. "There was just absolutely no panic whatsoever. Deep down, we knew before the game that we were going to win it. We probably should have blown them out. In that Super Bowl we were much better than what we showed."

The Patriots' 14–10 lead stood during the Packers' next two three-and-out possessions, each of which featured misfires by Favre. At this point, early in the second quarter, the Packers hadn't laid a glove on Bledsoe. Then Shurmur blitzed Evans from the slot on third and 10 and watched him crash hard into Bledsoe's back as his pass fell incomplete. "That was the start right there," said Butler. "That's when Fritz got a little impatient and said, 'Enough of this bull bleep.' I started coming from different places and we'd blitz different people. We really confused [Bledsoe] because we got very, very aggressive. He had a rifle, but we felt like he'd throw the ball up for grabs if we could just get in his face."

Holmgren sent out Don Beebe as the third wide receiver, but the Patriots didn't respond with their nickel defense. Across from Freeman in the right slot was strong safety Lawyer Milloy, one of four Patriots to make the NFL all-rookie team. The call was "Trips Right All Go." Free safety Willie Clay moved up into a blitz look, leaving Milloy in man coverage on Freeman. "We told [Milloy] to jam [Freeman] hard and don't let him release because we didn't have anyone who could run with him," said Groh. "But just before the snap our guy, instead of jamming him, started backpedaling and Freeman ran right past him for the score. Who knows why he did it? I don't." The result was an 81-yard go-ahead touchdown.

As a safety at the University of Washington, Milloy had played a lot of man-to-man coverage and a lot of blitz-man coverage with no help, so he had experience in man-to-man, with or without help. But, as Belichick pointed out, "Freeman was fast. . . . If [Milloy] had pressed [Freeman] with outside leverage, like he should have, then he would have at least forced the inside release to the safety. But he went up and pressed him head-up, and then on the snap [Milloy] jumped inside—and it was all over. Should he have pressed him at all? Probably not."

TEAM STATISTICS

NEW ENGLAND		GREEN BAY
16	Total First Downs	16
3	Rushing	8
12	Passing	6
1	Penalty	2
257	Total Net Yardage	323
66	Total Offensive Plays	68
3.9	Avg. Gain per Offensive Play	4.8
13	Rushes	36
43	Yards Gained Rushing (Net)	115
3.3	Average Yards per Rush	3.2
48	Passes Attempted	27
25	Passes Completed	14
4	Passes Intercepted	0
5	Tackled Attempting to Pass	5
39	Yards Lost Attempting to Pass	38
214	Yards Gained Passing (Net)	208
4/14	Third-Down Efficiency	3/15
0/2	Fourth-Down Efficiency	0/1
8	Punts	7
45.1	Average Distance	42.7
4	Punt Returns	6
30	Punt Return Yardage	90
6	Kickoff Returns	4
135	Kickoff Return Yardage	154
0	Interception Return Yardage	24
0	Fumbles	0
0	Own Fumbles Recovered	0
0	Opponent Fumbles Recovered	0
2	Penalties	3
22	Yards Penalized	41
3	Touchdowns	4
1	Rushing	1
2	Passing	2
0	Returns	1
3	Extra Points Made	4
0	Field Goals Made	2
0	Field Goals Attempted	0
0	Safeties	0
21	Total Points Scored	35
25:45	Time of Possession	34:15

Belichick, who had been fired as head coach in Cleveland, joined Parcells' staff as assistant head coach and secondary coach. Groh, who had been with Parcells for four seasons, would seek Belichick's counsel at times, but made every call that season. "It was really kind of a dumb call defensively," Chmura said. "If anything, they

NEW ENGLAND

Passing	CP/ATT	YDS	TD	INT	RAT
Bledsoe	25/48	253	2	4	46.6

Rushing	ATT	YDS	AVG	TD	LG
Martin	11	42	3.8	1	18t
Bledsoe	1	1	1.0	0	1
Meggett	1	0	0.0	0	0

Receiving	NO	YDS	AVG	TD	LG
Coates	6	67	11.2	1	19
Glenn	4	62	15.5	0	44
Byars	4	42	10.5	1	32
Jefferson	3	34	11.0	0	14
Martin	3	28	9.3	0	20
Meggett	3	8	2.8	0	5
Brisby	2	12	6.0	0	7

Interceptions	NO	YDS	LG	TD
None	--	--	--	--

Punting	NO	AVG	LG	BLK
Tupa	8	45.1	53	0

Punt Ret.	NO/FC	YDS	LG	TD
Meggett	4/2	30	20	0

Kickoff Ret.	NO	YDS	LG	TD
Meggett	5	117	26	0
Graham	1	18	18	0

Defense	SOLO	AST	TOT	SK
Slade	10	1	11	0
Johnson	9	1	10	0
Milloy	4	4	8	0
McGinest	4	2	6	1
Collins	3	3	6	0
Clay	4	1	5	0
Bruschi	4	0	4	2
Collons	3	1	4	1
Smith	3	0	3	1
Law	2	1	3	0
Ray	2	1	3	0
Wheeler	0	3	3	0
Bartrum	2	0	2	0
Sabb	2	0	2	0
Whigham	2	0	2	0
Henderson	1	1	2	0
M. Jones	1	1	2	0
McGruder	1	1	2	0
C. Brown	1	0	1	0
Jefferson	1	0	1	0
Roberts	1	0	1	0
Rucci	1	0	1	0
Sagapolutele	0	1	1	0
TOTAL	61	22	83	5

GREEN BAY

Passing	CP/ATT	YDS	TD	INT	RAT
Favre	14/27	246	2	0	107.9

Rushing	ATT	YDS	AVG	TD	LG
Levens	14	61	4.4	0	12
Bennett	17	40	2.4	0	10
Favre	4	12	3.0	1	12
Henderson	1	2	2.0	0	2

Receiving	NO	YDS	AVG	TD	LG
Freeman	3	105	35.0	1	81t
Levens	3	23	7.7	0	14
Rison	2	77	38.5	1	54t
Henderson	2	14	7.0	0	8
Chmura	2	13	6.5	0	8
Jackson	1	10	10.0	0	10
Bennett	1	4	4.0	0	4

Interceptions	NO	YDS	LG	TD
Brian Williams	1	16	16	0
Prior	1	8	8	0
Evans	1	0	0	0
Newsome	1	0	0	0

Punting	NO	AVG	LG	BLK
Hentrich	7	42.7	58	0

Punt Ret.	NO/FC	YDS	LG	TD
Howard	6/1	90	34	0

Kickoff Ret.	NO	YDS	LG	TD
Howard	4	154	99t	1

Defense	SOLO	AST	TOT	SK
E. Robinson	6	3	9	0
Butler	7	0	7	1
Newsome	3	3	6	0
B. Williams	4	1	5	0
Gi. Brown	3	2	5	0
Dotson	3	1	4	1
Simmons	3	1	4	0
Evans	2	2	4	0
Cox	1	3	4	0
S. Jones	3	0	3	0
White	3	0	3	3
Harris	2	0	2	0
Jervey	2	0	2	0
McKenzie	2	0	2	0
Prior	1	1	2	0
Hollinquest	1	0	1	0
Mickens	1	0	1	0
Thomason	1	0	1	0
Wilkins	1	0	1	0
T. Williams	1	0	1	0
TOTAL	50	17	67	5

should have had the safety on me."

Said Milloy, "It was a mismatch. We should have checked out of the blitz and didn't. I didn't know where Willie Clay was exactly, but Antonio gets a step on you, you know you're in trouble."

On the Patriots' next possession, Butler fought his way over the top of diminutive third-down back Dave Meggett to sack Bledsoe for minus-9 on third down. Tom Tupa then got off his third 51-yard punt of the first half. Early in the game, Tupa's 51-yard punt tight to the left sideline, with 4.5 seconds of hang time, had been returned 32 yards by Howard. This time, Tupa hit another 51-yarder near the left sideline with not quite as much hang (4.2), and Howard ran it back 34 yards to the New England 47. "They continued to roll the dice by kicking it to me," Howard said. "Again, a few guys missed. I could tell that I could run well all day." That led to a 31-yard field goal by Jacke and the Packers led, 20–14.

"We paid so much attention to the strength of Brett Favre that we didn't pay enough attention to the strength of their return game," said Charley Armey, the Patriots' director of college scouting.

One play after Butler knocked Bledsoe down on another blitz, the quarterback got happy feet in the face of more pressure and flung up an ill-advised rainbow that was picked off by dime safety Mike Prior. With Levens carrying for gains of 9, 6, 8, and 8 yards, the Packers covered 74 yards to set up Favre's 2-yard touchdown run on a bootleg in which he might not have made it inside the left pylon.

New England came out in man-to-man coverage, according to Belichick, "because we wanted to be really close on the receivers and not give Favre a lot of holes to hit." But when Favre burned the one-on-one stuff for 26.6 yards per completion and three touchdowns in the first half, the Patriots made a quantum shift in their defensive strategy.

"At halftime we said, 'We're not doing that anymore. We're just going to play zone and make them earn it.' And we played good the whole second half, we really did," said Belichick. "We gave up 27 points in the first half, and that was a lot to overcome. Everybody felt we were going to score with Curtis. Terry Glenn had a great year. We had [Shawn] Jefferson and [Vincent] Brisby and Coates. We felt like we were going to score in the 20s. But,

defensively, we didn't play good enough."

Green Bay opened the second half by marching 38 yards in eight plays, setting up fourth and 1 at the New England 38. The Patriots overloaded the strong side of the formation, and when Favre failed to check to an inside run, Johnson burst through to smear Levens wide on the right side for a whopping loss of 7. "That was coach Holmgren maybe trying to shut the door on us midway through the third quarter," said Bruschi. "It got our juices flowing."

On third and 5, Butler was all over Coates in coverage, but the lithe tight end still made the catch for 13 to the Green Bay 35. Bledsoe hit Jefferson with a 9-yard curl against nickel back Tyrone Williams, then Martin sliced through left tackle for 8 to the 18. On the next play, the Packers' defense suffered the humiliation of having Martin pound through the middle for a touchdown. Textbook blocking eliminated defensive tackles Darius Holland and Brown, as well as linebackers Williams and Cox, and then Butler missed at the 3. "It was horrible," Chmura said. "I don't even think our defense played that great. We gave up some big plays."

The Superdome, with Packers' fans in the clear-cut majority, came alive. As Howard assumed his position deep alongside Beebe, Parcells instructed special-teams coach Mike Sweatman to have Adam Vinatieri kick away. "I remember no discussion," Bruschi said. "[Parcells] had confidence in us." Said Wolf, "When [the Patriots] got a little momentum going they were going to prove that they were going to out-tough the Packers." Added Armey, "It's a very competitive thing when you get in the Super Bowl. I know they talked about kicking away [from Howard]."

Vinatieri's kick was fine, carrying to the 1 with an ideal 4.3 seconds of hang time. The wedge, consisting of tight end Jeff Thomason, guard Lindsay Knapp, linebacker Lamont Hollinquest, and defensive end Keith McKenzie, held hands and formed up at the 13 before getting the "go" call to advance. Nolan Cromwell had called a "middle return," hoping to catch the Patriots shading outside, and that's what happened.

Green Bay's five-man front pushed its men out, the wedge sprung Howard, and when McKenzie got a piece of the speedy Vinatieri—"If I didn't get held, I'll give you all the money that I own," the rookie kicker said—Howard was off to the races. Two Patriots, linebacker Marty Moore and wide receiver Hason Graham, dived and just missed getting him down. "Bill's a very arrogant guy," said Chmura. "He probably just figured the cover guys could get it done." After the touchdown, a 2-point pass to Chmura extended Green Bay's lead to 14 points.

Howard, a bust in Washington and Jacksonville, had been on the street since mid-February when the Packers signed him on July 11 to a one-year $300,000 contract. "He was as good at what he did as anyone I have ever seen in my life," Wolf said of Howard's performance that season. "That's what happens sometimes when you get a guy off the scrap heap that has to prove to everybody that he can still play."

Before the game, Parcells made the decision to activate Graham as the number four wide receiver over Troy Brown, who was inactive for the first time all season. That disappointed some New England officials, who regarded Brown as a better receiver and a far more effective player on special teams. Brown underwent hernia surgery in April, aggravated it in practice about 10 days before the Super Bowl, and wasn't able to practice again. "I felt like I could have played," Brown said, "but I think [Parcells] was in a situation where if he dresses this guy how long will I have him?"

A major problem for the Patriots on the return was the fact that Graham, who hadn't been active since Week 13, was out of his lane on the kickoff. This was the last NFL game ever for Graham, who finished his two-year career without a tackle on special teams. Brown, who had six special-teams tackles in 1996, was in the early stages of a 15-year career in New England that would run through 2007. Given how effective Brown was late in his career playing on defense, it's a good bet Brown would have made that tackle. "Not only would [Howard] have been tackled, but he would have fumbled, too," said Brown. "No, just kidding. But back then, I was a really, really good kickoff coverage man. [Graham] was put in a position where he had to stop one of the best kickoff returners ever. That's difficult to do."

Although there was still 3:10 left in the third quarter, this game was over. The Patriots' final five possessions resulted in 4 sacks, 3 punts, 2 interceptions, 1 first down, and minus-3 yards. Three of the sacks were by White (his first three-sack game since Week 5 of 1993), and each came against Max Lane, a sixth-round draft choice from Navy in 1994 who was in his second season as the starting right tackle.

At halftime, offensive coordinator Ray Perkins had approached Hoaglin. "He said, 'Ask Max how he's doing against Reggie and whether we need to keep chipping him or not because we'd like to get the tight end [Coates] out a little faster,'" Hoaglin recalled. "I did the wrong thing by asking the player. Any player is going to say, 'Yeah, I don't need help.' So we decided to get Ben out quicker and it beat us. It kept us from being able to move the ball down the field like we had been doing most of the day." On the 41 plays that White rushed Bledsoe, he knocked Lane sprawling an amazing eight times. Besides the three sacks, he also had four pressures.

When the Packers returned to Green Bay (population 102,000) early the next afternoon, it was 20 degrees and snowing. More than 60,000 waited for hours in Lambeau Field when the anticipated hour-long motorcade through city streets turned into a three-hour marathon. At some locations, the buses barely moved as fans pressed close. The outpouring of 150,000 fans had left the weary players frozen, and although some were more than a little perturbed, others basked in the showering of support. "There was nothing like that parade," Reid said years later. "It was magical. It was great."

Six months later, independent scouting analyst Joel Buchsbaum wrote, "The Packers were quite possibly the best single-season NFL team since the great 15–1 Bears team that went on to destroy the Patriots in Super Bowl XX." Its architect, Wolf, offered his final thoughts: "Just like we had hoped, the history of the franchise flowed over. This no longer was considered the outskirts of the league. Instead, America cultivated a love affair with the region. We became sentimental favorites—the smallest city in the league now boasting the most powerful team. We had no major holes in our lineup, we had depth everywhere, and we had a core of stars that we could depend upon to perform under pressure. We matured and peaked at the right time."

It really was Titletown once again.

XXXII

DENVER BRONCOS 31, GREEN BAY PACKERS 24

January 25, 1998
Qualcomm Stadium, San Diego, California

For the Green Bay Packers, Super Bowl XXXII will be forever remembered as an opportunity squandered and a legacy lost.

For the Denver Broncos, it will be forever known as the ultimate triumph for quarterback John Elway and for the superior coaching that Mike Shanahan and his staff turned in on both sides of the ball.

As the NFC had won 13 straight Super Bowls, including 11 by 10 points or more, it was understandable why the Packers entered this one as an 11½-point favorite. They were the defending champions, they came to San Diego on the crest of a seven-game winning streak, and their quarterback was Brett Favre, the league's MVP for the third year in a row.

Bob Harlan, the Packers president, recalled the Sunday before the team left for San Diego, when he and Ron Wolf were having breakfast in the team's gymnasium. Said Harlan, "I remember saying to Ron, 'What do you think of Denver?' He said, 'I've been watching them on film. They're just like New England. We can beat them.' Those were his exact words. I thought, 'Boy, this is great.'"

Wolf wasn't the only confident Packer; just about all of them were. They expected the Broncos to be another passive, finesse team from the AFC. So the Broncos bit their tongues for two weeks, playing along with the perception that the Packers were an unstoppable force and that they were just happy to be on the same field. "Mike Shanahan was perfect in his mental approach to that game," linebacker Bill Romanowski said years later. "It was all about building the Packers up. They were feeling real good about themselves, and we were telling them how great they were. Really, we felt we had them right where we wanted them.

"[Defensive coordinator] Greg Robinson and I talked probably six months after that game. We said, 'You know what the difference was in that game?' We wanted it more. You could hear the difference in

Attendance: 68,912
Conditions: 67 degrees, clear and sunny, wind WSW at 8 mph
Time of kickoff: 3:24 p.m. (PST)
Length of game: 3 hours, 25 minutes
Referee: Ed Hochuli

MVP: Terrell Davis, RB, Broncos

the way we hit them. If you were to close your eyes and just listen to the game, you would hear the fact we wanted it more."

This was a time when precious few Super Bowls lived up to their billing, but no one could say that about this game. Depending on one's frame of reference, Denver's pulsating 31–24 victory could be labeled as one of the most momentous upsets in Super Bowl history or one in which public perception was out in left field.

"I sure didn't feel like an underdog," Broncos owner Pat Bowlen said. "It was a feeling of quiet confidence. I remember going out to practice on Wednesday and thinking, 'These guys are ready.' It wasn't like we thought we were going to go out and kick Green Bay's ass. But I had been through this three times and got blown out basically in all three when I didn't feel all that comfortable. This time, I felt pretty damn comfortable."

The experts had offered little hope of redemption for the 37-year-old Elway, given his pedestrian performances in three Super Bowl defeats and the supposed might of the NFC. And Elway wasn't spectacular, by any means. He passed for only 123 yards, his passer rating was just 51.9, and his five rushing attempts were good for only 17 yards. "This wipes away all the losses," Elway said, his 15-year career now fulfilled. "I guarantee you, it's 10 times better than anything I could have imagined."

On this day, the Broncos' trump cards were the magnificent running back, Terrell Davis, who

	1	2	3	4	Final
Green Bay Packers	7	7	3	7	24
Denver Broncos	7	10	7	7	31

SCORING SUMMARY

1st Quarter
GB   Freeman, 22-yd. pass from Favre (Longwell kick)
DEN   Davis, 1-yd. run (Elam kick)
2nd Quarter
DEN   Elway, 1-yd. run (Elam kick)
DEN   Elam, 51-yd. FG
GB   Chmura, 6-yd. pass from Favre (Longwell kick)
3rd Quarter
GB   Longwell, 27-yd. FG
DEN   Davis, 1-yd. run (Elam kick)
4th Quarter
GB   Freeman, 13-yd. pass from Favre (Longwell kick)
DEN   Davis, 1-yd. run (Elam kick)

sat out the entire second quarter but still gained 157 yards, and the bold, blitzing defense directed by Robinson.

In 2007, when Harlan retired after a 37-year career in the Packers' front office, he placed this defeat atop his personal list of disappointments. It probably ranked as the most devastating loss for the NFL charter franchise up to that time. "I still say it's the worst loss during my years here," Harlan said. "Ron and I talk about it all the time. I almost feel sorry bringing the subject up because I'm afraid he's going to start throwing things. When you look at the material we had, boy, we had so many people in their prime. You bet we were good enough. We just didn't play like we should have. It just hurts so much."

One play by Elway will remain fixed in Super Bowl lore. With the score tied at 17 late in the third quarter, and the Broncos facing third and 6 at the Green Bay 12, Elway scrambled up the middle, veered right, and leaped into the air just as safety LeRoy Butler dived for his legs. As Elway sold out his body, he absorbed another shot from

backup safety Mike Prior before pinwheeling to earth at the 4. His dramatic first down led to the second of Davis' three 1-yard touchdown runs and inspired the Broncos to hang on down the stretch.

"When John made the whirlybird play, I still remember looking down from the press box and seeing our whole team about out [on the field] to the numbers high-fiving," said Mike Heimerdinger, Denver's wide receivers coach. "When he did that it was like, 'OK, we're winning this no matter what.'"

The winning touchdown, the third by Davis from 1 yard out, came with 1:45 remaining. It also might have been the least defended and most scrutinized score in Super Bowl history.

Two penalties against tackle Ross Verba and a poor throw by Favre behind Antonio Freeman on third and 11 forced the Packers to punt. The Broncos took over at the Green Bay 49 with three and a half minutes left. A 23-yard swing pass to fullback Howard Griffith gave the Broncos first and goal at the 8, but then a first-down holding penalty against Shannon Sharpe shoved the Broncos back to the 18.

On the next play, Davis circled the soft left side of the Packers' defense for 17 yards before being pushed out of bounds at the 1. With that, Shanahan called time out.

As Mike Holmgren and defensive coordinator Fritz Shurmur huddled for 45 seconds along the sidelines, they were operating under the assumption that it was first down rather than second down. Holmgren admitted as much the morning after the game, when reporters caught up to him as he was boarding the team bus for the airport. Remarkably, the subject hadn't been brought up amid the hubbub of the post-game press conferences.

Losing track of a down was bad enough, but having it happen late in the Super Bowl with the score tied won't ever be forgotten by some in the NFL's smallest city.

Assuming it still was first down, Holmgren ordered his defense simply to let the Broncos run in for the go-ahead touchdown. There was

> "We had come off two tough, tough road playoff games. Kansas City and Pittsburgh. Really, the Super Bowl was a respite. Not the team [we] played, but the emotional surroundings. The Super Bowl is a corporate crowd, anyway. A little hand-clapping and that's about it. We had just been in two real dog fights."
>
> *George Dyer, Broncos defensive line coach*

GREEN BAY PACKERS
(NFC, 13–3)

		Offense		
86	Antonio Freeman (6-0, 194)	WR	80	Rod Smith (6-0, 195)
78	Ross Verba (6-4, 305)	LT	65	Gary Zimmerman (6-6, 294)
73	Aaron Taylor (6-3, 305)	LG	69	Mark Schlereth (6-3, 287)
52	Frank Winters (6-3, 300)	C	66	Tom Nalen* (6-3, 286)
63	Adam Timmerman (6-3, 295)	RG	75	Brian Habib (6-7, 293)
72	Earl Dotson (6-3, 315)	RT	77	Tony Jones (6-5, 295)
89	Mark Chmura* (6-5, 253)	TE	84	Shannon Sharpe* (6-2, 228)
87	Robert Brooks (6-0, 180)	WR	87	Ed McCaffrey (6-5, 215)
4	Brett Favre* (6-2, 220)	QB	7	John Elway* (6-3, 215)
25	Dorsey Levens* (6-1, 228)	RB	30	Terrell Davis* (5-11, 208)
30	William Henderson (6-1, 249)	FB	29	Howard Griffith (6-0, 232)
		Defense		
92	Reggie White* (6-5, 304)	LE	90	Neil Smith* (6-4, 269)
71	Santana Dotson (6-5, 285)	LT	94	Keith Traylor (6-2, 304)
93	Gilbert Brown (6-2, 345)	RT	98	Maa Tanuvasa (6-2, 267)
98	Gabe Wilkins (6-4, 295)	RE	91	Alfred Williams (6-6, 263)
54	Seth Joyner (6-2, 245)	LLB	51	John Mobley (6-1, 236)
55	Bernardo Harris (6-2, 247)	MLB	57	Allen Aldridge (6-1, 243)
51	Brian Williams (6-1, 240)	RLB	53	Bill Romanowski (6-4, 245)
37	Tyrone Williams (5-11, 192)	LCB	39	Ray Crockett (5-10, 184)
33	Doug Evans (6-0, 190)	RCB	23	Darrien Gordon (5-11, 178)
36	LeRoy Butler* (6-0, 202)	SS	34	Tyrone Braxton (5-11, 185)
41	Eugene Robinson (6-0, 197)	FS	27	Steve Atwater (6-3, 216)

DENVER BRONCOS
(AFC, 12–4)

* Pro Bowl selection

SUBSTITUTIONS

Green Bay

Offense: WR - 80 Derrick Mayes, 85 Terry Mickens; TE - 81 Tyrone Davis, 83 Jeff Thomason; T - 64 Bruce Wilkerson; G - 62 Marco Rivera; RB - 24 Aaron Hayden, 32 Travis Jervey*, 44 Chris Darkins. **Defense:** DE - 95 Keith McKenzie, 90 Darius Holland; DT - 94 Bob Kuberski; LB - 53 George Koonce, 56 Lamont Hollinquest; CB - 26 Mark Collins; S - 28 Roderick Mullen, 39 Mike Prior; CB/S - 42 Darren Sharper. **Specialists:** K - 8 Ryan Longwell; P - 17 Craig Hentrich; LS - 60 Rob Davis. **DNP:** 13 Steve Bono (QB), 67 Jeff Dellenbach (C). **Inactive:** 84 Bill Schroeder (WR), 12 Ronnie Anderson (WR), 77 John Michels (T), 70 Joe Andruzzi (G), 18 Doug Pederson (QB), 97 Paul Frase (DE), 99 Jermaine Smith (DT), 38 Blaine McElmurry (S).

Denver

Offense: WR - 81 Patrick Jeffers, 85 Willie Green; TE - 89 Dwayne Carswell; T - 74 Harry Swayne; C/G - 63 David Diaz-Infante; RB - 22 Vaughn Hebron, 31 Derek Loville; FB - 37 Anthony Lynn, 42 Detron Smith. **Defense:** DE - 96 Harald Hasselbach; DT - 93 Trevor Pryce, 97 Mike Lodish; LB - 56 Keith Burns, 59 Glenn Cadrez; CB - 21 Randy Hilliard, 25 Darrius Johnson, 26 Tim McKyer; S - 32 Tony Veland, 33 Dedrick Dodge. **Specialists:** K - 1 Jason Elam; P - 16 Tom Rouen. **DNP:** 6 Bubby Brister (QB), 86 Byron Chamberlain (TE). **Inactive:** 88 Sir Mawn Wilson (WR), 70 Jamie Brown (T), 62 Dan Neil (G), 8 Jeff Lewis (QB), 72 Ernest Jones (DE), 99 David Richie (DT), 50 Jon Hesse (LB), 58 Steve Russ (LB).

1:47 remaining, and the Packers, with two timeouts left, wanted all the time they could muster to score a tying touchdown. Sure enough, Davis went barreling into the end zone on the next play against token resistance.

If Holmgren had realized it was second down, he might have given a defense featuring enormous (but also poorly conditioned) Gilbert Brown, Reggie White, and Santana Dotson up front the opportunity to stop Davis. Then if it had gotten to third down, the odds of a touchdown would have decreased as pressure and crowd noise mounted. Maybe the Broncos would have false-started; maybe they would have blown an assignment, or settled for a field goal. If so, the Packers wouldn't have had any timeouts left but still would have about a minute to tie or win.

"Because we couldn't shut him [Davis] down, it was probably the best way to go," Wolf, the general manager, said six months later. "People can say all the things that could happen, like a bad snap, or he could fumble the ball. At the same time, that clock was ticking. I can't ever question strategy. That's not my job. I agree that [Holmgren] is the best coach in the league."

Back came the Packers, with Dorsey Levens picking up 35 yards on a pair of screen passes for a first down at the Denver 35 with 1:04 left. A play later, Favre hit Freeman in stride with a bullet pass half a step ahead of cornerback Darrien Gordon at the Denver 15, but the wide receiver suffered the costliest drop of his eight seasons in Green Bay. "That was huge," tight end Mark Chmura said. "Then we could have got into our attack mode in the red zone. We would have had four shots at the end zone."

Having rushed just four defenders on the first five plays of the possession, Robinson sent six on third and 6 and hurried Favre into an incompletion intended for Robert Brooks at the 9. The referee, Ed Hochuli, charged each team with a timeout after the play because both had an injured player. Thus, Holmgren enjoyed almost a football eternity (2:10) to choose a play to call on fourth and 6 at the Denver 31 with 32 seconds left.

"The last call of the game was maybe the dumbest ever," Chmura said years later. "You should have seen the look in the huddle when 'Two Jet Winston' comes in. We had never run this play all year long. We maybe practiced it three times in training camp, and this is the best you can give us? A player knows when his number is called. 'Two Jet Winston' is no one's number called."

"Two Jet" meant a six-man protection, two wide receivers left and two receivers right, one of whom was Chmura in the slot. Having lost a pair of

defensive backs on the previous play, Robinson went for broke with a seven-man rush that outnumbered the six Green Bay blockers. "We had time to think, because of the injuries," said Robinson. "It was like, 'You've got to take a chance right now, to see if we can end it.'"

To Favre's left, the unblocked man, cornerback Tyrone Braxton, slipped through the line untouched. According to Chmura, all four receivers had been coached to run their routes at 12 yards. "If he goes 'Two Jet Double Slant,' the receivers are three steps and cutting in," said Chmura. "He's still got plenty of time. The only thing Brett could have done was check, but that's really not his fault."

Chmura saw seven blitzers coming and decided Favre's only chance would come if he broke off his route at the first-down marker. Linebacker John Mobley, in man-to-man coverage, cut in front of Chmura and broke up the floater from Favre, effectively ending the game.

"I decided I better just give Brett an option, but we were coached we had to get to 12 [yards] so I didn't know what the hell the option was," Chmura said. "He had good coverage on me. It was just a bad call. Even Brett was confused."

Thus, the Broncos became the second wildcard team to win a Super Bowl, joining the Oakland Raiders of 1980 and touching off a wild celebration in Denver. As exhilarating as the victory was for the Broncos, the defeat was equally crushing for Green Bay. Attempting to join the Pittsburgh Steelers as the only franchise to win consecutive Super Bowls twice, the Packers of the 1990s turned out to be a one-ring team, just as their archrivals, the Chicago Bears, had been a decade earlier.

Surrounded by reporters in the locker room, Wolf uttered his unforgettable summation: "We're a one-year wonder, just a fart in the wind." Six months later, still steamed by his team's general collapse in the second half, Wolf would add: "They out-executed us. I never thought that would be possible. But let me say this. We were defeated. There wasn't anything flukish about it."

Before Holmgren even had a chance to address the team, he got locked in his office at the stadium. After rapping on and kicking the door, he finally was freed after about five minutes. "When something like that happens, it seems like it lasts a lot longer than it really does," said Lee Remmel, the Packers' longtime publicist.

Not only did Holmgren permit the winning touchdown without a fight, but he also failed to exploit the Broncos' soft run defense (4.73 yards allowed per rush, worst in the NFL). Levens, a 1,435-yard rusher, had one carry after the eight-minute mark of the third quarter. In all, Levens rushed 19 times for 90 yards (including 42 yards after contact), but was an afterthought on offense as an erratic Favre dropped back 45 times. Adopting the power-football strategy that the NFC had used to dominate the AFC over the years, Shanahan ran Davis 30 times and put Elway in the pocket only 24 times.

"I have not come up with a logical explanation as to why we didn't run the ball in the second half," Levens said years later. "One of the most heart-breaking things Shannon Sharpe has ever said to me was when we got back to Atlanta in the offseason, he was like, 'Tell Mike I said thank you for not running you because we still haven't stopped you yet.' I still can't watch that game. It still bothers me."

Levens had been used by Holmgren often to close out games against tiring defenses, and the big back almost always responded. Despite facing an undersized front seven and the run being one way he could have protected his own crumbling run defense, Holmgren gave the ball to Levens only once in the last four series of a tight game.

"You [could] take some of the pressure off Brett and give our defense a chance to rest and maybe we could shut down Terrell Davis from running all over us," said Levens. "I don't think we helped the defense out with the play-calling in the second half."

Robinson, for his part, said he "didn't really care, to be honest with you," if Levens would have

had a lot more carries. "If they had decided they were going to try to bloody our nose, we were prepared for that," he said. When the Broncos didn't blitz and Favre had time against four-man rushes, he passed for 256 yards and three touchdowns with a passer rating of 91.0.

During the week, Holmgren patiently replied to questions concerning reports that the Seattle Seahawks were to offer him a job as coach and general manager. It would be another 12 months before that offer arrived (and Holmgren accepted), but judging by his performance in San Diego, it's reasonable to wonder where his thought processes were all week and on game day. The Packers became the third double-digit favorite in Super Bowl history to lose. They played a mediocre game, couldn't stop the run, and weren't able to make the blitzing Broncos pay quite enough for playing such a risky defense.

"The Packers were outcoached, pure and simple," Sharpe said. "LeRoy Butler and Reggie White were their two best defensive players. Where were they?"

Davis might have had 250 yards on the ground if he hadn't been kicked in the head by Santana Dotson on a 5-yard burst late in the first quarter and forced to sit out because of blurred vision. His only snap of the second quarter was on the first play; he carried out a fake when Elway kept wide right for Denver's second 1-yard touchdown. Linebacker Lamont Hollinquest blew containment on the play.

The Broncos ran Davis 15 times for 97 yards left of center, where underachieving defensive tackle Darius Holland was forced to move outside and replace injured Gabe Wilkins (knee) at right end after 12 snaps. Pro Bowl left tackle Gary Zimmerman ran both Wilkins and Holland ragged, and the crisp, cut-blocking Broncos offensive line, coached by the esteemed Alex Gibbs, had its way with outside linebackers Seth Joyner and Brian Williams.

"Alex was a special coach," said Bowlen. "The offensive linemen hated him but they loved him. He was on them all the time. He was screaming all the time. But the net result was they were a very good offensive line, especially when Zimmerman was playing. We became infamous for Alex's blocking scheme, which wasn't illegal but caused a lot of complaining about cutting this and that. But it was his design and it definitely worked."

The venerable White, such a force in Super Bowl XXXI, spent too much time on the ground, was credited with merely one tackle and one pressure, and had to come out for breathers on three second-half plays. Wolf referred to the defeat as the day "our defensive line went away."

Davis returned to the field in the second half and kept pounding away at a defense that Shanahan was certain would be vulnerable if the knifing run support of all-pro strong safety Butler could be minimized. Using formation as well as coaching emphasis, the Broncos didn't have a single run ruined by a blitzing Butler.

"The whole game plan was to see if we could get LeRoy out of the run game," said Heimerdinger. "Nobody had done it all year. LeRoy was killing people in the run game, always coming down from up high and becoming the eighth guy in the box and making all kinds of tackles. Mike's idea was to get him isolated and get him out of there. Once we had him on Shannon, we could go the other way and do some things."

Butler did finish with a game-high nine tackles, but most were well downfield, a situation he implored Shurmur to correct schematically early on. Butler told Shurmur, "All we've got to do is go back to our normal eight-man front. Now I don't have to follow Shannon. Let the corners stay out there. I can cover the slot guy, but I have no man responsibilities and I'm still in the box." The Packers ran the scheme twice, and Butler got to Davis for a 2-yard gain and then got a hit on the quarterback. "[Shurmur] never ran it again," Butler recalled. "At halftime, we made no adjustments. We just sat there and drank Kool-Aid, and [the coaches] bitched at us for a while."

On offense, the Packers simply weren't suitably prepared for the Broncos' wholesale blitzing, even though Robinson had been blitzing every game since the regular-season finale against San Diego. Each of Favre's three touchdown passes came against blitzes, including strikes of 22 and 13 yards to Freeman. The first culminated an eight-play, 76-yard drive that opened the game.

Yet, a cornerback blitz prompted Favre to throw into triple coverage for a first-quarter interception

> "When we came out for the second half, I'll never forget they had to walk across the field to get to the bench. Everybody was walking like they were dead tired or something. It was a sick feeling. You just felt it was falling apart."
>
> *Bob Harlan, Packers president*

by Braxton, which led to Elway's touchdown. On that play, Favre faked a second-and-5 handoff on a five-step drop as both running backs went out through the middle. Gordon blitzed off the weak side, forcing Favre to scramble right. Favre overthrew Brooks, and the ball was intercepted by Braxton. The Broncos then drove 45 yards to take a 14–7 lead.

"The problem early was Mike was 'scatting' the backs," Chmura said. "Say we'd have a '22 Scat Texas.' Scat means the back is out right away. If he takes the 'scat' off, then the back checks for the blitz. We got burned on it I don't know how many times. Play-action will freeze that guy for a second, but it's not going to prevent him from blitzing."

The Packers' next possession ended when Favre was sacked in 1.6 seconds on an all-out blitz by safety Steve Atwater, forcing a fumble that set up a Denver field goal. "[Robinson] blitzed us weak [side] all day," Chmura said. "He had a great game plan and just kept coming. He felt that was probably the only way he could beat us. We moved the ball but we just had mistakes and turnovers."

About seven years after the fact, Wolf said he learned from two coaches whom he would not identify that the Packers' inability to handle the kamikaze-type blitzing could be traced back to Holmgren. "Certain calls were to be made that weren't made. Mike Holmgren refused those calls," Wolf said in 2007. "There would have been an adjustment on the blocking scheme and it would have been over. One of the great things about playing the game of football is you have to adjust. When you fail to adjust in critical situations you're going to lose, and that's what happened. To be pig-headed about it, I mean, to have the answer and then not apply it, that's a little different. It's like a dot in history now, and one of the teams was a one-year wonder. But for somebody to bring it up and explain to you what could have been done and what should have been done, it rekindles the fire every once in a while." Wolf retired from the Packers in May 2001, a revered figure for directing one of the most unexpected franchise revivals in NFL history.

Butler said there was no doubt in his mind that the issue was Holmgren's stubborn refusal to keep more blockers in for pass protection. "He's my favorite coach of all time," said Butler. "But he wanted five eligible [receivers] out. Keeping guys in was too boring for him."

The Packers did gain 350 yards and score 24 points. Their deadliest sin was failing to stop the run. Still, the Packers might have been able to outscore the Broncos because of the latter's mostly suspect secondary, had it not been for the four or five plays on offense that went haywire largely due to the Broncos' blitzing. Two of those blitzes caused turnovers, set up 10 first-half points, and put the Packers in a 17–7 hole from which they could never regain the lead.

Many years after the Super Bowl, Robinson said the only other occasion in his career in which he ever blitzed more was one game against New England's Drew Bledsoe. In all, the Broncos rushed five or more on 48.9 percent of the Packers' 45 dropbacks and six or more on 24.4 percent.

"It's all about time," Robinson said. "They didn't have time. Mike Holmgren's a good coach and they were sound, but I don't think they were totally set up for the systematic approach that we took. Later in Mike's career, they changed and we had to do some adapting. That's kind of what his world went to. Protecting instead of letting them get out and trying to let the quarterback get rid of it. Mike [Shanahan] was never involved in any of the [defensive] plans. He might say different, but in the six years I was there he never did."

Years later, Favre said the Broncos "kind of revolutionized the weak-safety or weak-corner blitz. The West Coast had never seen that. Seeing that type of blitz, you had to change your protection totally. Now everyone does it."

On the second play of the game, Robinson brought the house and sent a message to Favre with

TEAM STATISTICS

GREEN BAY		DENVER
21	Total First Downs	21
4	Rushing	14
14	Passing	5
3	Penalty	2
350	Total Net Yardage	302
63	Total Offensive Plays	61
5.6	Avg. Gain per Offensive Play	5.0
20	Rushes	39
95	Yards Gained Rushing (Net)	179
4.8	Average Yards per Rush	4.6
42	Passes Attempted	22
25	Passes Completed	12
1	Passes Intercepted	1
1	Tackled Attempting to Pass	0
1	Yards Lost Attempting to Pass	0
255	Yards Gained Passing (Net)	123
5/14	Third-Down Efficiency	5/10
0/1	Fourth-Down Efficiency	0/0
4	Punts	4
35.5	Average Distance	36.5
0	Punt Returns	0
0	Punt Return Yardage	0
6	Kickoff Returns	5
104	Kickoff Return Yardage	95
17	Interception Return Yardage	0
2	Fumbles	1
0	Own Fumbles Recovered	0
1	Opponent Fumbles Recovered	2
9	Penalties	7
59	Yards Penalized	65
3	Touchdowns	4
0	Rushing	4
3	Passing	0
0	Returns	0
3	Extra Points Made	4
1	Field Goals Made	1
1	Field Goals Attempted	1
0	Safeties	0
24	Total Points Scored	31
27:35	Time of Possession	32:25

a "zero" blitz; referee Hochuli was probably remiss in not throwing a flag for intentional grounding. Green Bay then stormed the length of the field for an opening touchdown, but after that it was a never-ending struggle for its offense.

"Historically, we were pretty damn good at sideline adjustments," Packers guard Aaron Taylor

GREEN BAY

Passing	CP/ATT	YDS	TD	INT	RAT
Favre	25/42	256	3	1	91.0

Rushing	ATT	YDS	AVG	TD	LG
Levens	19	90	4.7	0	16
Brooks	1	5	5.0	0	5

Receiving	NO	YDS	AVG	TD	LG
Freeman	9	126	14.0	2	27
Levens	6	56	9.3	0	22
Chmura	4	43	10.8	1	21
Brooks	3	16	5.3	0	10
Henderson	2	9	4.5	0	7
Mickens	1	6	6.0	0	6

Interceptions	NO	YDS	LG	TD
Robinson	1	17	17	0

Punting	NO	AVG	LG	BLK
Hentrich	4	35.5	51	0

Punt Ret.	NO/FC	YDS	LG	TD
Brooks	0/1	0	0	0

Kickoff Ret.	NO	YDS	LG	TD
Freeman	6	104	22	0

Defense	SOLO	AST	TOT	SK
Butler	7	2	9	0
Robinson	6	2	8	0
Harris	6	1	7	0
Dotson	6	0	6	0
T. Williams	6	0	6	0
B. Williams	5	0	5	0
Brown	3	1	4	0
Joyner	3	0	3	0
Evans	2	1	3	0
Mullins	2	0	2	0
Chmura	1	0	1	0
Darkins	1	0	1	0
Mickens	1	0	1	0
Thomason	1	0	1	0
White	1	0	1	0
TOTAL	**51**	**7**	**58**	**0**

DENVER

Passing	CP/ATT	YDS	TD	INT	RAT
Elway	12/22	123	0	1	51.9

Rushing	ATT	YDS	AVG	TD	LG
Davis	30	157	5.2	3	27
Elway	5	17	3.4	1	10
Hebron	3	3	1.0	0	2
Griffith	1	2	2.0	0	2

Receiving	NO	YDS	AVG	TD	LG
Sharpe	5	38	7.6	0	12
McCaffrey	2	45	22.5	0	36
Davis	2	8	4.0	0	4
Griffith	1	23	23.0	0	23
Hebron	1	5	5.0	0	5
Carswell	1	4	4.0	0	4

Interceptions	NO	YDS	LG	TD
Braxton	1	0	0	0

Punting	NO	AVG	LG	BLK
Rouen	4	36.5	47	0

Punt Ret.	NO/FC	YDS	LG	TD
Gordon	0/2	0	0	0
R. Smith	0/1	0	0	0

Kickoff Ret.	NO	YDS	LG	TD
Hebron	4	79	32	0
Burns	1	16	16	0

Defense	SOLO	AST	TOT	SK
Braxton	6	1	7	0
Atwater	6	0	6	1
Crockett	6	0	6	0
Mobley	6	0	6	0
Romanowski	4	1	5	0
Aldridge	4	0	4	0
Gordon	3	0	3	0
Dodge	2	0	2	0
Lodish	2	0	2	0
Loville	2	0	2	0
Traylor	2	0	2	0
A. Williams	1	1	2	0
Burns	1	0	1	0
Hasselbach	1	0	1	0
Johnson	1	0	1	0
Sharpe	1	0	1	0
Tanuvasa	1	0	1	0
TOTAL	**49**	**3**	**52**	**1**

said. "But I remember the entire game we didn't know where they were coming from. I think because we were so good on adjustments there was an element where we got outcoached."

Early in the second quarter, Robinson rushed seven against a six-man protection, and Atwater drilled Favre just as he was setting up to deliver on his fifth step. Agreeing that the weak-side blitzing in which the brazen Broncos left the middle of the field wide open was unheard of, Chmura still said adjustments should have been made to handle it after the first series.

"It should have been easy," he said. "Our max protections were 24 and 25, which kept two backs in. Seventy-four and 75, we could do that out of two tight ends. And he [Holmgren] just didn't do that. He tried to roll the dice because we had such an explosive offense."

At the NFL owners meetings two months after the Super Bowl, Holmgren was asked about the Denver blitz. "We practiced everything they threw at us," Holmgren said. "And we went over them many times with Brett. We told him, no matter what, when you see them coming, get the ball out of there. Don't hold on to it to make the big play; there were many times he didn't do that in the game, and it cost us. It led to two turnovers. He saw it coming and didn't pay attention to it."

Chmura retorted, "That's a flat-out lie. How can you get rid of the ball when the receiver is running a 15- or 20-yard in or dig? You can't scream to him and tell him, 'Blitz!' We weren't a sight [adjust] blitz team. The receivers weren't responsible for seeing if there's a blitz and breaking their route off accordingly. That's a bunch of crap."

Tom Lovat, the offensive line coach throughout Holmgren's seven-year tenure in Green Bay and his first five in Seattle, said the remarks by Holmgren "pretty well sum up the whole scenario. If the protection didn't fit, rather than audible, which you didn't want to do a lot of, Brett was told to get the ball out. He had outlets."

Later, Holmgren would shorten the drops for Favre and then Matt Hasselbeck, most notably while with Seattle against Pittsburgh in Super Bowl XL. In Super Bowl XXXII, Favre threw 15 times off three steps, 16 times off five steps, and 9 times off seven steps.

Early that next offseason, Lovat recalled Holmgren sitting with the offensive staff watching "that damn Super Bowl film" about 10 times. The Packers devised a 50 protection in which both backs could get to the side of the blitz without weakening the play. "We took it to Seattle with us and it worked well," said Lovat. "You don't see Robinson in the league anymore." (The Broncos' coordinator later became head coach at Syracuse.)

Should Holmgren and his coaches have been able to adjust successfully that day in San Diego?

"No," Lovat replied. "This was an offseason discussion. Plus, the fact if they [the Broncos] hit you once they've got to be right the next time around. If you start on the sidelines pulling your horns in, then you get so conservative you're playing into their hands."

In the final analysis, Shanahan had beat Shurmur when the Broncos were on offense and Robinson had beat Holmgren when the Broncos were on defense. "You try to analyze it," said Wolf. "There's probably never been a greater team in pro football than the 1985 Chicago Bears and they only won it one year. Then I decided, 'Maybe it's a Midwest thing. Maybe we idolize our players too much, give them too much adoration.'

"Suddenly, there was a different kind of focus out there. And just what Romanowski said. We were fat cats. Maybe they did want it more than we did. Winners can say whatever they want. Losers can only lament what might have been."

Favre, at the peak of his game, shrugged off the defeat, saying, "I'm 28. I think I'll be back—hopefully, several times." This was not to be, as he would play another decade in Green Bay and another season for the New York Jets without playing in another Super Bowl.

Elway did return, 12 months later, with another victorious effort. If there was ever a doubt, those results should have told the Packers that it had been no disgrace losing to Denver.

Ten Who Played Hurt

1. **Dwight White, DE, Steelers, IX:** Battling pneumonia, White spent most of the week before the Super Bowl in the hospital, lost 20 pounds, and never practiced. He played the entire game and then went back to the hospital, where he stayed for 10 more days.
2. **Terrell Owens, WR, Eagles, XXXIX:** Owens wasn't cleared to play until Sunday morning, yet he played 63 of 72 snaps just six and a half weeks after surgery on his right leg.
3. **Jack Youngblood, DE, Rams, XIV:** Suffered a hairline fracture of his left fibula in divisional playoffs, but started in the NFC title game and Super Bowl.
4. **John Schmitt, C, Jets, III:** Played with pneumonia, was on the verge of total exhaustion by the fourth quarter, and vomited in the middle of the team prayer after the game.
5. **Charles Haley, DE, Cowboys, XXVIII and XXX:** Played Super Bowl XXVIII with a ruptured lumbar disc, requiring surgery later, and by XXX was reduced to a part-time role due to additional back problems.
6. **Rob Gronkowski, TE, Patriots, XLVI:** Played 43 of 64 snaps with an extensively taped left ankle that he injured two weeks earlier and wasn't close to his normal dominating self. Underwent surgery less than a week later.
7. **Walt Garrison, RB, Cowboys, V:** Suffered ankle and knee injuries in the NFC title game but went the distance two weeks later in the Super Bowl.
8. **Tom Keating, DT, Raiders, II:** Ruled out with an Achilles tendon injury, but played anyway. Keating limped around effectively enough to register two sacks and eight tackles.
9. **Doug Williams, QB, Redskins, XXII:** Hyperextended his post-operative knee late in the first quarter and had to sit out two plays. He came back and finished the game, though he was unable to attend the post-game party after the knee stiffened.
10. **Kurt Warner, QB, Rams, XXXIV:** Suffered separated rib cartilage in the first half. At halftime, offensive coordinator Mike Martz told backup Paul Justin to get ready to play the second half, but Warner returned and led the Rams to victory.

Ten Most Significant Injuries Suffered during the Super Bowl

1. **Tim Krumrie, NT, Bengals, XXIII:** Suffered a broken tibia and fibula early in the first quarter and had to be flown to a nearby hospital via helicopter.
2. **Leslie Frazier, CB, Bears, XX:** Blew out his knee playing special teams in the first half. Frazier never played another game in the NFL.
3. **Steve Wallace, LT, 49ers, XXIII:** With the turf in deplorable condition, Wallace suffered a broken left fibula a few plays before Krumrie went down.
4. **Lin Dawson, TE, Patriots, XX:** On the Patriots' first play from scrimmage, Dawson stretched to haul in a pass at the 8-yard line and ruptured his patellar tendon.
5. **Dave Studdard, LT, Broncos, XXII:** Playing in his ninth season as a starter for Denver, Studdard blew out his ACL early in the second quarter.
6. **Charles Woodson, CB, Packers, XLV:** Fractured his collarbone diving to defend a long pass shortly before halftime. Broke down at halftime trying to tell teammates how much a Super Bowl ring would mean to him.
7. **Jake Ballard, TE, Giants, XLVI:** Planted his left knee running an outside-breaking route against Patriots LB Brandon Spikes early in the fourth quarter and tore his ACL.
8. **Shannon Sharpe, TE, Broncos, XXXIII:** Played two series and caught two of the four passes thrown to him by John Elway before departing with a sprained knee.
9. **Boyd Dowler, WR, Packers, I and II:** Exited Super Bowl I when a calcium deposit in his bad right shoulder broke loose. A year later, Dowler had to sit again, this time with leg cramps.
10. **John Stallworth, WR, Steelers, XIII:** Suffered muscle cramps late in the first half and didn't return.

XXXIII

DENVER BRONCOS 34, ATLANTA FALCONS 19

January 31, 1999
Pro Player Stadium, Miami, Florida

I f only all of America's sports heroes could go out as John Elway did. The only tears he shed were of overwhelming joy and utter jubilation.

Super Bowl XXXIII will perhaps be remembered for some of the worst judgment ever exercised by the underdog team, but it will always be remembered as a fitting farewell for one of the NFL's consummate quarterbacks.

As the final seconds ticked off in the Denver Broncos' 34–19 victory over the Atlanta Falcons, Elway removed his helmet and flung his arms high above his head. He had passed for 336 yards and one touchdown, had run for another score, and was the game's MVP.

At 38, after 16 memorable seasons, Elway departed on his terms. Elway didn't tell anyone of his impending retirement until a press conference three months later. That way, he reasoned, his teammates wouldn't be shortchanged by adulation run amok for him. So he played his fifth Super Bowl the same way he had played the other 255 regular-season and postseason games of his 16-year career, all with the Broncos. The Falcons never had a chance.

"He didn't come up to me after the game and say, 'I'm going to retire,' but he didn't have to tell me," owner Pat Bowlen said years later. "His body language and just the way it was, I knew after he won Super Bowl XXXIII he was done. . . . John was a strong guy but he said his body just couldn't do it anymore. In his mind, in his head, he was finished."

So were the Broncos, at least for the foreseeable future. They crashed to 6–10 in 1999, a staggering fall for a franchise that had just won back-to-back Super Bowls. Elway, however, wasn't the only star missing. The team's extraordinary running back, Terrell Davis, blew out his knee in Week 4 and was never again the same player. The Broncos would have to be content with two championships and an NFL record of 46 victories over a three-year period.

Attendance: 74,803
Conditions: 73 degrees, mostly cloudy, wind E at 10 mph
Time of kickoff: 6:25 p.m. (EST)
Length of game: 3 hours, 18 minutes
Referee: Bernie Kukar

MVP: John Elway, QB, Broncos

"It was different from the San Francisco teams," said Denver linebacker Bill Romanowski, who played for the 49ers in two Super Bowls. "You were talking about Ronnie Lott, Joe Montana, Roger Craig, Jerry Rice. They were big-time athletes and individuals, where we didn't have that many big-time, well-known guys. There was John Elway, and then a group of guys that kicked ass for one another. That's what comes to mind when I think of those two years."

The Falcons, a 7½-point underdog, weren't supposed to be anywhere near Pro Player Stadium on Super Sunday. They had been 7–9 the year before, and *Pro Football Weekly* forecast them to finish 6–10 in 1998. Then, after coach Dan Reeves and his players defied all odds by posting a 14–2 record in the regular season, the Falcons were 10-point underdogs in the NFC Championship Game at the Metrodome against the once-beaten Minnesota Vikings. In an upset for the ages, the Falcons prevailed in overtime, 30–27.

Denver coach Mike Shanahan knew full well the perils of overconfidence. Twelve months earlier, the Green Bay Packers couldn't stop reading their own press clippings and then were ambushed by these same Broncos. "We wanted Minnesota [instead of Atlanta]. They were the big threat offensively; we wanted the competition on defense," said Tyrone Braxton, the Broncos' 12th-year safety. "The difference was we all talked about what happened with Green Bay the year before. That was still fresh in our

	1	2	3	4	Final
Denver Broncos	7	10	0	17	34
Atlanta Falcons	3	3	0	13	19

SCORING SUMMARY

1st Quarter
ATL   Andersen, 32-yd. FG
DEN   Griffith, 1-yd. run (Elam kick)
2nd Quarter
DEN   Elam, 26-yd. FG
DEN   Smith, 80-yd. pass from Elway (Elam kick)
ATL   Andersen, 28-yd. FG
4th Quarter
DEN   Griffith, 1-yd. run (Elam kick)
DEN   Elway, 3-yd. run (Elam kick)
ATL   Dwight, 94-yd. kickoff return (Andersen kick)
DEN   Elam, 37-yd. FG
ATL   Mathis, 3-yd. pass from Chandler (pass failed)

minds. Don't let it happen to us this year. You still gotta come out and produce."

Any chance the Falcons might have had of getting the Broncos to take them lightly vanished three days after the Vikings game, when Reeves elected to reopen old wounds. During a routine press conference with a national contingent of writers, Reeves reasserted his belief that it was Shanahan's insubordination that led Bowlen to fire Reeves as the coach of the Broncos after the 1992 season. According to Reeves, Shanahan had been trying to undermine Reeves' relationship with Elway. Unbeknownst to Bowlen, Reeves had fired Shanahan as his offensive coordinator following the 1991 season. In the middle was Elway, who once described his final years under Reeves as "hell" and later came to view Shanahan as a peacemaker in his relationship with the imperial head coach.

Enraged by Reeves' remarks, especially given Reeves' acts of reconciliation in the previous year, Shanahan attacked his game plan like never before. "For Mike, this game was personal," Elway said. "I've never seen him more ready for a football game. I knew it meant more to him than any game he has ever coached."

In the mass interviews the week of the Super Bowl, the Atlanta defensive players and coaches were asked if it was more prudent trying to stop Davis or Elway. It made sense to say Davis, who after all had rushed for 2,008 yards in the regular season and then 366 more in playoffs romps past Miami (38–3) and the New York Jets (23–10). Elway, on the other hand, had thrown for a mere 123 against the Packers the year before. So when the Falcons all said Davis, they inadvertently made Elway every bit as inspired as his coach. "I knew they were saying, 'Make Elway beat us,'" Elway said. "My thought was, 'Good, let's go.' I was so motivated, it wasn't even funny."

On Saturday night, Shanahan kept his players occupied with dinner and meetings followed by a customary 11 o'clock curfew. All Reeves asked of his players was to be in by midnight. Sometime between 9 and 10 p.m., Falcons free safety Eugene Robinson was arrested not far from the team's downtown hotel for soliciting oral sex from an undercover police officer posing as a prostitute along Biscayne Boulevard. Earlier that day, Robinson had received the Bart Starr Award for "high moral character" from Athletes in Action. "If I had to point to one guy, he probably was the leader on our team," center Robbie Tobeck said. "I thought that was a crushing blow."

Awakened at midnight, defensive coordinator Rich Brooks was delivered the news by Reeves. Robinson was back at the hotel, having been bailed out by a team official. His wife, two children, father, and assorted relatives were with him. It was a terrible scene. "A lot of the players were up half the night, Ray [Buchanan] and William White, trying to calm the situation down," Brooks said. "Then Dan made the decision to play him. I think it was a huge mental distraction, if nothing else. . . . That, I think, took whatever advantage we had away from us." Brooks pointed to Robinson's role as a leader on the team. "I just think it was one of the most unfortunate things to ever happen to a guy. Because, to me, that's not Eugene. Eugene was just a great guy, a smart guy."

Years later, after finishing his career with Carolina in 2000 and then becoming the analyst on the Panthers' radio network, Robinson was asked about that night. "Time has a way of healing stuff," he said. "I wouldn't say it is completely healed, but it has smoothed things out. I am lucky to do color commentary and I am involved in my kids' school. The Lord has thrown me tremendous amounts of favor."

DENVER BRONCOS			ATLANTA FALCONS	
(AFC, 14–2)			(AFC, 14–2)	
		Offense		
80	Rod Smith (6-0, 200)	WR	80	Tony Martin (6-0, 181)
77	Tony Jones* (6-5, 295)	LT	70	Bob Whitfield* (6-5, 310)
69	Mark Schlereth* (6-3, 287)	LG	68	Calvin Collins (6-2, 307)
66	Tom Nalen* (6-2, 286)	C	61	Robbie Tobeck (6-4, 300)
62	Dan Neil (6-2, 281)	RG	69	Gene Williams (6-2, 315)
74	Harry Swayne (6-5, 295)	RT	74	Ephraim Salaam (6-7, 290)
84	Shannon Sharpe* (6-2, 228)	TE	88	O. J. Santiago (6-7, 267)
87	Ed McCaffrey* (6-5, 215)	WR	81	Terance Mathis (5-10, 185)
7	John Elway* (6-3, 215)	QB	12	Chris Chandler* (6-4, 225)
30	Terrell Davis* (5-11, 208)	RB	32	Jamal Anderson* (5-11, 234)
29	Howard Griffith (6-0, 240)	RB	85	Brian Kozlowski (6-3, 255)
		Defense		
90	Neil Smith (6-4, 273)	LE	92	Lester Archambeau (6-5, 275)
94	Keith Traylor (6-2, 315)	LT	98	Travis Hall (6-5, 300)
93	Trevor Pryce (6-5, 295)	RT	75	Shane Dronett (6-6, 295)
98	Maa Tanuvasa (6-2, 277)	RE	90	Chuck Smith (6-2, 265)
53	Bill Romanowski* (6-3, 241)	SLB	94	Henri Crockett (6-2, 251)
59	Glenn Cadrez (6-3, 249)	MLB	58	Jessie Tuggle* (5-11, 230)
51	John Mobley (6-1, 230)	WLB	97	Cornelius Bennett (6-2, 240)
39	Ray Crockett (5-10, 184)	LCB	34	Ray Buchanan* (5-9, 195)
21	Darrien Gordon (5-11, 184)	RCB	23	Ronnie Bradford (5-10, 188)
26	Tyrone Braxton (5-11, 185)	SS	35	William White (5-10, 205)
27	Steve Atwater* (6-3, 217)	FS	41	Eugene Robinson* (6-0, 197)

* Pro Bowl selection

SUBSTITUTIONS

Denver

Offense: WR - 82 Marcus Nash, 85 Willie Green; TE - 86 Byron Chamberlain, 89 Dwayne Carswell; T - 78 Matt Lepsis; G/C - 63 David Diaz-Infante; QB - 6 Bubby Brister; RB - 22 Vaughn Hebron, 31 Derek Loville; FB - 37 Anthony Lynn, 42 Detron Smith. *Defense:* DE - 90 Neil Smith, 91 Alfred Williams; DT - 95 Marvin Washington, 97 Mike Lodish; LB - 56 Keith Burns, 99 Seth Joyner; CB - 20 Tory James, 25 Darrius Johnson, 28 Tito Paul; S - 48 George Coghill. *Specialists:* K - 1 Jason Elam*; P - 16 Tom Rouen. *Inactive:* 83 Justin Armour (WR), 70 Trey Teague (T), 79 Chris Banks (G), 60 K. C. Jones (C), 14 Brian Griese (QB), 73 Cyron Brown (DE), 54 Nate Wayne (LB), 26 Eric Brown (S).

Atlanta

Offense: WR - 82 Ronnie Harris, 83 Tim Dwight; TE - 86 Ed Smith; T - 76 Jose Portilla; G - 64 Bob Hallen; C/G - 67 Adam Schreiber; RB - 28 Harold Green; FB - 45 Gary Downs. *Defense:* DE - 91 John Burrough, 96 Antonio Edwards; DT - 95 Esera Tuaolo; LB - 52 Craig Sauer, 54 Ruffin Hamilton, 56 Keith Brooking, 59 Ben Talley; CB - 20 Michael Booker, 21 Elijah Williams, 29 Randy Fuller; S - 25 Devin Bush. *Specialists:* K - 5 Morten Andersen; P - 4 Dan Stryzinski. *DNP:* 17 Steve DeBerg (QB), 33 Ken Oxendine (RB). *Inactive:* 89 Todd Kinchen (WR), 84 Rodrick Monroe (TE), 79 Dave Widell (G), 13 Tony Graziani (QB), 93 Shawn Swayda (DE), 26 Darren Anderson (CB), 27 Omar Brown (S), 47 Chris Bayne (S).

The Falcons seemed unaffected on their opening possession. Jamal Anderson—who set an NFL record with 410 carries and finished second to Davis with 1,846 yards—carried five times for 24 yards in a 48-yard drive. A seventh-round draft choice from Utah in 1994, Anderson was described by Falcons scout Dick Corrick as "a Jerome Bettis kind of guy. Except this guy isn't a straight-liner. He has halfback running skills. And his thighs are like most people's waists."

From the Denver 8, however, Romanowski pressured quarterback Chris Chandler into a second-down incompletion and then sacked him for minus-8 on third down. "I came right up the A gap and got a hit on Chandler that just rocked his world," said Romanowski. "Either the back was supposed to get me or they slid the wrong way. He got up slow. A lot of power and weight just slammed right down on him. I truly believe it really helped take the wind out of their sails."

Morten Andersen's 32-yard field goal was good, but the Falcons' Pro Bowl quarterback had paid a physical price. "He wasn't no good after that," Braxton said. "He didn't make smart decisions and do much the rest of the game until late, when it was already over."

The Falcons unveiled Brooks' defensive plan when the Broncos took over. "They had everybody within eight yards of the line of scrimmage," Denver wide receivers coach Mike

That was the area Shanahan had planned to exploit with the ever-dangerous Sharpe. "Shannon probably would have been the MVP had he been able to play," said Bowlen. "Losing Shannon was a big problem for Mike at that point. He knew that they couldn't cover him."

Atlanta's next possession ended on a third and 1 when defensive end Alfred Williams played off a feeble attempted block by tight end O. J. Santiago and spilled Anderson for no gain. The Broncos promptly turned it over when Sharpe—the mouth that roared all week—let Elway's sideline pass slip through his hands and into the arms of Bradford for an interception at the Denver 35.

After Anderson again went nowhere on third and 1, Reeves decided to go for it on fourth down at the Denver 26. "Coaches, when they get in the playoffs, they panic," Braxton said. "Kick the field goal and live another day." Using regular personnel, Reeves ran Anderson wide on a toss sweep. Romanowski fought his way past right tackle Ephraim Salaam and into the path of fullback Brian Kozlowski, who was escorting Anderson. Stripped of his blocking, Anderson had nowhere to go but into the arms of middle linebacker Glenn Cadrez and nose tackle Keith Traylor for a loss of 2. "I think that was a big, big point of the game," Denver defensive line coach George Dyer said. "If they get a field goal, at least they're still in the game."

On the Broncos' next possession, they drove 63 yards in 11 plays to set up Jason Elam's 26-yard field goal. The drive included four rushes for 28 yards by Davis, who still found a way to gain 102 yards in 25 carries despite having the Falcons' rugged run defense stacked against him. "That's the other thing we couldn't do against Denver," Brooks said. "They ran the ball better than almost anyone had all year long against us."

Under Brooks, Atlanta's defense had improved from 20th to 8th in yards allowed in 1998, including a ranking of second against the run. The Falcons had played a soft schedule, however, and were almost free of injuries. Some of their defenders, such as defensive end Lester Archambeau (10 sacks, 7 forced fumbles), defensive tackle Shane Dronett (6½ sacks), and cornerbacks Buchanan and Bradford might have had their finest seasons. "I think it was one of

Heimerdinger said years later. "Rich was not going to let the run game beat him. We were fighting uphill with the run. It was a completely different game plan for us from the first Super Bowl. Now it was John throwing it and 'T. D.' being the change-up." On Denver's fifth play, Elway fired a short slant to Rod Smith, who was sprinting from right to left. "They caught us between a rolled-up corner and a safety," recalled Brooks. Cornerback Ronnie Bradford should have had the play corralled after a 15-yard gain, but he blew the tackle and Smith turned it into a gain of 41 yards.

Denver took a 7–3 lead when Shanahan crossed up the Falcons by decoying with Davis and calling on fullback Howard Griffith for the first of his two 1-yard touchdowns. The drive, however, was costly for the Broncos because tight end Shannon Sharpe suffered a sprained knee on a 14-yard reception against Robinson to the 1 and had to leave the game for good late in the first quarter.

Brooks had done a masterful job all season with Atlanta's defense, especially in hiding the glaring lack of speed at safety with White and Robinson.

those aligning-of-the-stars deals," said Brooks. "We were first in the league in takeaways [44]. We didn't have a lot of well-known star players, but we really played well as a unit." The Falcons' extremely physical front four was coached by gung-ho Bill Kollar, one of the NFL's premier position coaches.

The Falcons' offense, which leaped from 23rd in 1997 to 7th in 1998, also led the NFL in time of possession. The line wasn't anything to write home about, but the 235-pound Anderson was so powerful that he often served as his own blocker. In Week 2 of the next season, Anderson blew out his knee and fared no better than Davis in the final two years of his career.

Besides Anderson, the Falcons also got career years on offense from Chandler (100.9 passer rating), wide receiver Terance Mathis (career-high 17.8-yard average), Santiago (career-best 27 catches and 5 touchdowns), and left tackle Bob Whitfield (his only Pro Bowl). "Chandler was a guy who could still move a little bit and Anderson was not an easy bring-down," said Dyer. "We were pretty impressed, but there's no question Green Bay [in the previous Super Bowl] was a much better football team. Green Bay had too many weapons and was so extremely well coached."

Trailing 10–3, Chandler found Mathis twice for 46 yards—against cautious cornerbacks Ray Crockett and Darrien Gordon—on a long drive that reached the Denver 8. Then Chandler threw high and wild on third down in the end-zone corner for Tim Dwight. Andersen, the 38-year-old marvel playing in his first Super Bowl, missed wide right from the 26.

As the Falcons marched, Shanahan, Elway, and offensive coordinator Gary Kubiak sat together scheming for a way to make Atlanta pay for stacking the line of scrimmage. On the play immediately after the missed field goal, they came up with what Bowlen said was an old standby from Shanahan's three seasons (1992–1994) as offensive coordinator in San Francisco—one that the Broncos hadn't used or practiced in weeks.

Elway faked to Davis off left tackle, spun the other way on a half-bootleg, stopped, and threw deep on a post route to Rod Smith, who normally would either block Robinson if it was a run or

TEAM STATISTICS

DENVER		ATLANTA
22	Total First Downs	21
8	Rushing	8
14	Passing	12
0	Penalty	1
457	Total Net Yardage	337
65	Total Offensive Plays	60
7.0	Avg. Gain per Offensive Play	5.6
36	Rushes	23
121	Yards Gained Rushing (Net)	131
3.4	Average Yards per Rush	5.7
29	Passes Attempted	35
18	Passes Completed	19
1	Passes Intercepted	3
0	Tackled Attempting to Pass	2
0	Yards Lost Attempting to Pass	13
336	Yards Gained Passing (Net)	206
6/13	Third-Down Efficiency	5/11
0/1	Fourth-Down Efficiency	1/2
1	Punts	1
35	Average Distance	39
0	Punt Returns	0
0	Punt Return Yardage	0
3	Kickoff Returns	7
44	Kickoff Return Yardage	227
136	Interception Return Yardage	1
0	Fumbles	1
0	Own Fumbles Recovered	0
1	Opponent Fumbles Recovered	0
4	Penalties	0
61	Yards Penalized	0
4	Touchdowns	2
3	Rushing	0
1	Passing	1
0	Returns	1
4	Extra Points Made	1
2	Field Goals Made	2
4	Field Goals Attempted	3
0	Safeties	0
34	Total Points Scored	19
31:23	Time of Possession	28:37

hook if it was a pass. Elway had just enough time to pump fake, allowing Smith to turn Robinson completely around while Griffith slowed down Archambeau's charge just enough with a cut block. Elway's pass was on the mark and Smith caught it at the Atlanta 43. Robinson—who had been let go by Green Bay as an unrestricted free agent in 1998

DENVER

Passing

Passing	CP/ATT	YDS	TD	INT	RAT
Elway	18/29	336	1	1	99.2

Rushing

Rushing	ATT	YDS	AVG	TD	LG
Davis	25	102	4.1	0	15
Griffith	4	9	2.3	2	4
Loville	2	8	4.0	0	6
Elway	3	2	0.7	1	3
R. Smith	1	1	1.0	0	1
Brister	1	-1	-1.0	0	-1

Receiving

Receiving	NO	YDS	AVG	TD	LG
R. Smith	5	152	30.4	1	80
McCaffrey	5	72	14.4	0	25
Chamberlain	3	29	9.7	0	13
Davis	2	50	25.0	0	39
Sharpe	2	26	13.0	0	14
Griffith	1	7	7.0	0	7

Interceptions

Interceptions	NO	YDS	LG	TD
Gordon	2	108	58	0
Johnson	1	28	28	0
Braxton	1	0	0	0

Punting

Punting	NO	AVG	LG	BLK
Rouen	1	35	35	0

Punt Ret.

Punt Ret.	NO/FC	YDS	LG	TD
None	--	--	--	--

Kickoff Ret.

Kickoff Ret.	NO	YDS	LG	TD
Hebron	2	42	26	0
Chamberlain	1	2	2	0

Defense

Defense	SOLO	AST	TOT	SK
Cadrez	4	4	8	0
Atwater	4	3	7	0
Crockett	5	0	5	0
Romanowski	4	1	5	1
Coghill	3	0	3	0
Gordon	2	1	3	0
Tanuvasa	2	1	3	0
Mobley	1	2	3	1
Traylor	1	2	3	0
A. Williams	2	0	2	0
Braxton	1	1	2	0
Hasselbach	1	1	2	0
Burns	1	0	1	0
James	1	0	1	0
Johnson	1	0	1	0
Loville	1	0	1	0
Lynn	1	0	1	0
Washington	1	0	1	0
Pryce	0	1	1	0
N. Smith	0	1	1	0
TOTAL	**36**	**18**	**54**	**2**

ATLANTA

Passing

Passing	CP/ATT	YDS	TD	INT	RAT
Chandler	19/35	219	1	3	47.2

Rushing

Rushing	ATT	YDS	AVG	TD	LG
Anderson	18	96	5.3	0	15
Chandler	4	30	7.5	0	12
Dwight	1	5	5.0	0	5

Receiving

Receiving	NO	YDS	AVG	TD	LG
Mathis	7	85	12.1	1	30
Martin	5	79	15.8	0	23
Anderson	3	16	5.3	0	9
Harris	2	21	10.5	0	13
Santiago	1	13	13.0	0	13
Kozlowski	1	5	5.0	0	5

Interceptions

Interceptions	NO	YDS	LG	TD
Bradford	1	1	1	0

Punting

Punting	NO	AVG	LG	BLK
Stryzinski	1	39.0	39	0

Punt Ret.

Punt Ret.	NO/FC	YDS	LG	TD
Dwight	0/1	0	0	0

Kickoff Ret.

Kickoff Ret.	NO	YDS	LG	TD
Dwight	5	210	94	1
Kozlowski	2	17	16	0

Defense

Defense	SOLO	AST	TOT	SK
White	9	1	10	0
Dronett	6	1	7	0
Robinson	6	0	6	0
Bradford	4	2	6	0
Tuggle	5	0	5	0
Bennett	4	0	4	0
Hall	3	1	4	0
Buchanan	1	2	3	0
Brooking	2	0	2	0
Downs	2	0	2	0
Fuller	2	0	2	0
C. Smith	1	1	2	0
Crockett	0	2	2	0
Booker	1	0	1	0
Chandler	1	0	1	0
Edwards	1	0	1	0
Salaam	1	0	1	0
Santiago	1	0	1	0
TOTAL	**50**	**10**	**60**	**0**

because the club felt he couldn't run anymore—was hopelessly overmatched and the result was an 80-yard touchdown. "That was a killer," said Brooks. "Eugene bit on the run fake a little bit and there it was."

Dwight's second stellar kickoff return of the game, this one for 42 yards, gave the Falcons field position at the Denver 49. Wide receiver Tony Martin, who had been obtained in June from San Diego for a second-round draft choice, caught a pass for 23 yards before Chandler gained 10 on a scramble to the Denver 16 with three minutes left in the half.

On second and 5, Chandler underthrew wide receiver Ronnie Harris in the right corner, enabling dime back Tory James, who was beaten badly, to scramble back into the play and deflect the ball. On the next play, Gordon made a last-ditch deflection of a pass to Martin in the end zone.

Andersen's 28-yard field goal cut the Falcons' deficit to 17–6, but for a team in desperate need of a touchdown, it was little consolation. "If you ask people about that game, they'll say it was because Eugene Robinson had the incident the night before and it was a total distraction," Reeves said. "He didn't play well; that was a part of it. But he didn't play one down offensively. And, to me, on offense, we just didn't get the job done."

Seven different times the Falcons breached the Denver 30, but came away with just one touchdown (with 2:04 left) and a pair of field goals. "It was our inept execution in the red zone," said Reeves. "We were one of the leading teams that year in scoring and we were very effective inside the red zone. John Elway played extremely well and their defense stopped us when we got in the red zone."

The Falcons caught a break in the third quarter when Elam missed a field-goal attempt from the 38 after a seven-minute drive. Chandler gave the ball back four plays later when he forced a ball down the middle and was intercepted by nickel back Darrius Johnson. Elam misfired again, this time from 48, and the Falcons continued to move the ball between the 20s, gaining 43 yards on three plays to reach the Denver 21. "We moved it up and down the field," said Reed Johnson, Atlanta's director of player personnel. "We ran the ball effectively and we

stopped their run effectively enough. But we didn't tackle very well after the ball was caught, we didn't get to Elway, and we lost the turnover ratio."

This push ended when Traylor, a dominating force late in the season, got good penetration against Whitfield and batted a pass high into the air that Gordon intercepted and returned 58 yards to the Atlanta 24. The Broncos finished that drive with Griffith's second touchdown and then scored again on Elway's 3-yard run with 11:20 left. Elway's score was preceded by Gordon's 50-yard interception return of a post pattern to Martin that was tossed prematurely by Chandler due to pressure. "I thought Tony Martin should have come underneath the safety and Chris thought he was going to," said Reeves. "He threw it and Tony broke in behind the safety and the safety intercepted it."

The Broncos' next touchdown drive, which covered 48 yards in three plays, came with ridiculous ease. On first down, Elway scrambled away from defensive tackle Travis Hall and dumped the ball to Davis in the left flat. Robinson had the angle for the tackle, but one juke by Davis and he was off down the sidelines for 39 yards. Backup Derek Loville powered for 6 to the 3 before the Falcons were fooled by Elway's quarterback draw. Dwight brought back the following kickoff 94 yards for a touchdown, but it was too little and too late.

Some of Denver's success on the ground in the face of Atlanta's clog-the-box defensive strategy was a tribute to the offensive line, which was an amalgamation of two seventh-round draft choices, a 10th-round selection, a free agent, and a third-round choice. The unit was tutored by hard-driving Alex Gibbs, a history scholar with a doctorate in education who probably was the Broncos' best position coach ever, according to Bowlen. "We became infamous for his blocking scheme," the owner said. "His impact, especially on the running game, was over the top."

Gibbs overcame the retirement of Hall of Fame left tackle Gary Zimmerman after the 1997 season by moving right tackle Tony Jones to the left side. He compensated for the free-agent departure of right guard Brian Habib by developing second-year man Dan Neil. Both were upgrades for a line that was the lightest in the league, averaging just 288 pounds.

During their championship run, the Broncos were less talented on defense. It was a group cobbled together with aging veterans and free agents, although defensive tackle Trevor Pryce and outside linebacker John Mobley already were becoming standouts. "We had real, real good team speed," said Dyer, "and we had a tremendous closeness about us."

The Super Bowl was the final game in Denver for strong safety Steve Atwater, who made the Pro Bowl in 1998 for the eighth time. "I don't care what they say about him, it's never enough," Dyer said. "He was a great football player, but he was a greater man. Team guy all the way. Tough. Always had a smile on his face."

Winning his fourth Super Bowl ring, the fiercely competitive Romanowski was Denver's other Pro Bowl defender. The unit was coordinated boldly by Greg Robinson, whose gambling schemes still managed to confuse some offenses. "I think Greg did what he had to do with the personnel that he had," said Bowlen. "I'm not saying they weren't good defensive players. But he knew he had to take risks blitzing people. Now that's sort of become vogue."

Braxton's 13-year career included one season (1994) in Miami as an unrestricted free agent. It was there, in the Dolphins' facility, that he gained even greater appreciation for Elway, in roundabout fashion. "[Dan] Marino would sit in the weight room and talk to everybody, but he wasn't doing the work we were doing," Braxton remembered. "One thing I respected about John, he'd be lifting and running, the same stuff we'd do. . . . Dan had better stats. But when I saw the whole picture, I knew why John got better with age and Dan didn't do as well."

What Elway also had that Marino never did was a franchise running back lined up behind him. Davis was a phenomenal talent, as the Broncos would soon discover in his absence, but Elway never had to play second fiddle to anyone, as the Falcons discovered.

"People had said forever that he couldn't win the big one, that he was good but he couldn't win a Super Bowl," said Heimerdinger, the receivers coach during Elway's last five seasons. "This, to me, was the crowning glory for him. I think John's the best to play the game."

Top Ten Goats (Player)

1. **Eugene Robinson, FS, Falcons, XXXIII:** Arrested for soliciting a prostitute not far from the team hotel on the Saturday night before the game.
2. **Barret Robbins, C, Raiders, XXXVII:** Went on a weekend bender in Tijuana and wasn't allowed to play after he got back.
3. **Stanley Wilson, RB, Bengals, XXIII:** News of his cocaine binge was delivered to players at the Saturday night meeting.
4. **Scott Norwood, K, Bills, XXV:** All things considered, he had about a 50-50 shot from 47 yards to win the game. He missed wide right by about 4 feet.
5. **Jackie Smith, TE, Cowboys, XIII:** Smith's drop of a 3-yard pass in the end zone didn't lose it for the Cowboys, but it surely didn't help.
6. **Asante Samuel, CB, Patriots, XLII:** Nobody would have ever heard of David Tyree if the sure-handed Samuel had held on to Eli Manning's wayward sideline pass earlier that drive.
7. **Cliff Harris, FS, Cowboys, X:** By taunting Pittsburgh kicker Roy Gerela after a missed field goal, Harris incited the Steelers to beat his Cowboys.
8. **Earl Morrall, QB, Colts, III:** Everyone could see Jimmy Orr wide open on the fateful flea-flicker play—everyone except Morrall, who threw elsewhere and was picked off.
9. **Thomas Henderson, LB, Cowboys, XIII:** A flag already had been thrown, but Henderson felt compelled to rough Terry Bradshaw and taunt Franco Harris, who turned his rage into a touchdown on the next play.
10. **Troy Polamalu, S, Steelers, XLV:** The NFL Defensive Player of the Year for 2010 took himself out of plays all day long. He never could get a read on Aaron Rodgers and was as ordinary as ordinary can be. A tender Achilles didn't help.

XXXIV

ST. LOUIS RAMS 23, TENNESSEE TITANS 16

January 30, 2000
Georgia Dome, Atlanta, Georgia

"Is he in? Did he get in?" At first, more than 72,000 at the Georgia Dome and tens of millions more watching at home couldn't tell if Kevin Dyson had tumbled into the end zone or not. The outcome of Super Bowl XXXIV, up till then perhaps the greatest ever played, hung in the balance.

On one sideline, Tennessee coach Jeff Fisher shot upward in a halting leap filled with hope. Across the way, St. Louis coach Dick Vermeil stood transfixed, peering from beneath his headset. The clock read 0:00. From the bench area, no one knew for sure exactly where Rams linebacker Mike Jones

Attendance: 72,625
Conditions: Indoors
Time of kickoff: 6:25 p.m. (EST)
Length of game: 3 hours, 28 minutes
Referee: Bob McElwee

MVP: Kurt Warner, QB, Rams

Tennessee wide receiver Kevin Dyson stretches to full extension to reach for the end zone as time expires, but defensive tackle Mike Jones' firm grasp leaves Dyson a foot short and gives the Rams a Super Bowl championship. *Paul Spinelli/Getty Images*

had tackled Dyson, the Titans wide receiver who still was crawling into the end zone with the ball outstretched.

Wired for sound, the 63-year-old Vermeil could be heard murmuring to himself, "Didn't make it. Didn't make it." Then: "No. No." Finally: "That's it. We win. That's the game. It's over. We're world champions."

An official stood over the football, having marked it halfway between the goal line and the 1. After a pregnant pause of maybe 10 seconds, he kicked the ball away with his left foot. Fireworks burst forth. Confetti filtered down. The Rams raced to midfield in ecstasy. Quarterback Steve McNair covered his ears in despair and began trudging away with the rest of his teammates

St. Louis 23, Tennessee 16.

If Dyson's reception had been 10 yards instead of 9, and assuming Al Del Greco's extra point had been true, the first overtime in Super Bowl history would have been played. As it was, the NFC team with the worst record in the 1990s won the Super Bowl with a 16–3 mark after finishing 4–12 the year before. Tennessee, as the successor to the Houston Oilers, became the last of the eight original AFL teams to play in the Super Bowl. The Titans earned universal praise for its 16–4 season and gutsy comeback.

For two and a half quarters, the "Greatest Show on Turf" Rams had dominated. Then the Titans pulled an about-face and performed in equally dominating fashion. No team in Super Bowl history

	1	2	3	4	Final
St. Louis Rams	3	6	7	7	23
Tennessee Titans	0	0	6	10	16

SCORING SUMMARY

1st Quarter
STL   Wilkins, 27-yd. FG
2nd Quarter
STL   Wilkins, 29-yd. FG
STL   Wilkins, 28-yd. FG
3rd Quarter
STL   Holt, 9-yd. pass from Warner (Wilkins kick)
TEN   George, 1-yd. run (pass failed)
4th Quarter
TEN   George, 2-yd. run (Del Greco kick)
TEN   Del Greco, 43-yd. FG
STL   Bruce, 73-yd. pass from Warner (Wilkins kick)

ever had won by overcoming a deficit of more than 10 points. The Titans were behind, 16–0, and the third quarter was already half in the books before their stirring charge enabled them to draw even on Del Greco's 43-yard field goal with 2:12 to play.

"We felt like fate was on our side," Dyson said years later. "Look how we got there. We had to go through Jacksonville for the third straight time. We went to Indianapolis and the noise. Before that was the 'Music City Miracle.' We just felt like it was our game to win."

It was a coming-of-age season for first-year starter Kurt Warner, the NFL and Super Bowl MVP who passed for 414 yards, despite suffering rib damage in the first half that left his coaches wondering if he could even play in the second half. It was also a coming-of-age game for McNair, whose season included surgery for a ruptured lumbar disc in September and an almost miraculous return to the lineup just 42 days later.

For football connoisseurs, the matchup between Rams offensive coordinator Mike Martz and Titans defensive coordinator Gregg Williams was one to savor. Martz, 48, took the Don Coryell–Ernie Zampese offensive system to new heights with an amazingly aggressive philosophy. Williams, 41, spent a year under Buddy Ryan and, after being groomed by Fisher, attacked the Rams with numerous all-out blitzes in Ryanesque style. His unpredictable but sound schemes kept the Titans, a 7-point underdog, from being blown out before their offense finally got untracked.

Having the best all-around running back in the game, the Rams' Marshall Faulk, on the same field as the best power back in the game, the Titans' Eddie George, didn't make for bad theater, either.

With the score tied 16–16, two plays determined the outcome. The first was the 73-yard touchdown pass from Warner to wide receiver Isaac Bruce with 1:54 remaining that provided the winning margin. The second was the 9-yard pass from McNair to Dyson that wound up at the Rams' ½-yard line as time expired.

To say the Rams were on their heels at 16–16 would be an understatement. Their offense, having moved the ball well enough through three quarters to have scored four or five touchdowns as opposed to just one, was coming off two consecutive three-and-outs. Their defense, having been pounded by the 240-pound George and worn down by chasing McNair, appeared spent. "We were in a great position," Titans linebacker Eddie Robinson said. "Their defense was so tired. If we could get a three-and-out there's no doubt in my mind our offense would score again." It seemed appropriate that Martz would attempt to rest the defense, pick up some first downs, and let kicker Jeff Wilkins try to win it in the final seconds.

"There was a timeout and the place was going nuts and we were going to go into two-minute," Martz recalled. "All we needed to do was go down and get a field goal." He explained how he spoke to Vermeil on the sideline about the "Twins" formation, which involved three wide receivers to one side and one to the other. Martz noticed that whenever they had been in that formation on third down, the Titans had doubled everybody except Bruce, who was singled up. "We told Kurt we were going to

> "Everyone thinks that the tackle at the end was to save the game. That would have tied the game. It doesn't mean they were going to win the game."
>
> *Charley Armey, Rams director of personnel*

ST. LOUIS RAMS (NFC, 13–3)		TENNESSEE TITANS (AFC, 13–3)
	Offense	
88 Torry Holt (6-0, 190)	WR	87 Kevin Dyson (6-1, 201)
76 Orlando Pace* (6-7, 320)	LT	72 Brad Hopkins (6-3, 306)
61 Tom Nutten (6-4, 300)	LG	74 Bruce Matthews* (6-5, 305)
60 Mike Gruttadauria (6-3, 297)	C	60 Kevin Long (6-5, 296)
62 Adam Timmerman* (6-3, 300)	RG	75 Benji Olson (6-3, 315)
73 Fred Miller (6-7, 315)	RT	69 Jon Runyan (6-7, 320)
86 Roland Williams (6-5, 269)	TE	89 Frank Wycheck* (6-3, 250)
80 Isaac Bruce* (6-0, 188)	WR	83 Isaac Byrd (6-1, 188)
13 Kurt Warner* (6-2, 220)	QB	9 Steve McNair (6-2, 225)
28 Marshall Faulk* (5-10, 211)	RB	27 Eddie George* (6-3, 240)
25 Robert Holcombe (5-11, 220)	FB	41 Lorenzo Neal (5-11, 240)
	Defense	
93 Kevin Carter (6-5, 280)	LE	90 Jevon Kearse* (6-4, 262)
99 Ray Agnew (6-3, 285)	LT	91 Josh Evans (6-2, 288)
75 D'Marco Farr* (6-1, 280)	RT	97 Jason Fisk (6-3, 295)
98 Grant Wistrom (6-4, 267)	RE	99 Kenny Holmes (6-4, 270)
52 Mike Jones (6-1, 240)	LLB	55 Eddie Robinson (6-1, 243)
59 London Fletcher (5-10, 241)	MLB	52 Barron Wortham (5-11, 244)
54 Todd Collins (6-2, 248)	RLB	58 Joe Bowden (5-11, 235)
41 Todd Lyght* (6-0, 190)	LCB	25 Denard Walker (6-1, 190)
21 Dexter McCleon (5-10, 198)	RCB	21 Samari Rolle (6-0, 175)
22 Billy Jenkins (5-10, 205)	SS	23 Blaine Bishop (5-9, 203)
35 Keith Lyle (6-2, 210)	FS	33 Anthony Dorsett (5-11, 205)

* Pro Bowl selection

SUBSTITUTIONS

St. Louis

Offense: WR - 81 Az-Zahir Hakim, 82 Tony Horne, 87 Ricky Proehl; TE/LS - 45 Jeff Robinson, 84 Ernie Conwell; T/C - 50 Ryan Tucker; G - 64 Andy McCollum; RB - 31 Amp Lee; FB - 42 James Hodgins. *Defense:* DE - 96 Jay Williams; DT - 90 Jeff Zgonina, 95 Nate Hobgood-Chittick; LB - 51 Lorenzo Styles, 56 Charlie Clemons, 57 Leonard Little, 58 Mike Morton; CB - 32 Dre' Bly; S - 23 Devin Bush, 38 Rich Coady. *Specialists:* K - 14 Jeff Wilkins; P - 2 Mike Horan. *DNP:* 16 Paul Justin (QB), 20 Taje Allen (CB). *Inactive:* 83 Chris Thomas (WR), 77 Matt Willig (T), 71 Cameron Spikes (G), 9 Joe Germaine (QB), 36 Justin Watson (RB), 92 Lionel Barnes (DE), 91 Troy Pelshak (LB), 24 Ron Carpenter (S).

Tennessee

Offense: WR - 81 Chris Sanders, 85 Derrick Mason, 86 Joey Kent; TE - 84 Larry Brown, 88 Jackie Harris; G - 66 Jason Layman; RB - 20 Rodney Thomas. *Defense:* DE - 92 Henry Ford, 96 Mike Jones; DT - 78 John Thornton, 95 Joe Salave'a; LB - 50 Terry Killens, 51 Greg Favors, 59 Doug Colman; CB - 30 Donald Mitchell, 37 Dainon Sidney, 38 George McCullough; S - 24 Steve Jackson, 35 Perry Phenix. *Specialists:* K - 3 Al Del Greco; P/KO - 15 Craig Hentrich. *DNP:* 14 Neil O'Donnell (QB), 76 Jason Mathews (T). *Inactive:* 82 Yancey Thigpen (WR), 71 Zach Piller (G), 62 Craig Page (C), 13 Kevin Daft (QB), 26 Spencer George (RB), 94 Mike Frederick (DE), 54 Phil Glover (LB), 31 Marcus Robertson (S).

throw four go routes and that if he got that coverage we'd get Isaac isolated on the corner and to take a shot," Martz said. "It was the only time to take a shot because everybody would have been gassed and there's a chance you can come back to the two-minute warning where you can recover."

On the snap, sensational rookie Jevon Kearse bull-rushed right tackle Fred Miller back toward Warner, who had taken a five-step drop. "Freddie kind of opened up a little," Rams offensive line coach Jim Hanifan said. "It was real close to him getting a sack, and [then] maybe that ball doesn't get down the field."

On the far right, Bruce took an outside release against cornerback Denard Walker and went deep down the sideline. "We were playing a four-man rush and single coverage, then we decided we were going to bring the blitz," Titans secondary coach Jerry Gray said. "We actually brought five guys and had one free safety in the hole."

Just a step or two from the sideline, Bruce came back to make the catch at the Tennessee 40. Reacting late, Walker lost his footing. "Bruce saw the ball underthrown and had it in his sights the whole time," said Martz. "It wasn't like he beat the coverage or anything like that, but the corner didn't see the ball." Safety Anthony Dorsett was starting only because Marcus Robertson—described by Robinson as "the super-smart, cerebral guy in the secondary"—had suffered a broken ankle in the AFC Championship Game.

Moving over from center field, Dorsett was in ideal position to limit the damage to about 35 yards. "Once he caught it we were like, 'Just make the tackle,'" said Robinson, who blitzed and was watching from 40 yards away. "Had his timing been a little bit better he probably could have taken the guy's head off. In a worst-case scenario, it should have been a big hit." Dorsett, the son of Hall of Fame running back Tony Dorsett, was the Titans' sixth-round draft choice in 1996 and had started just one game before the Super Bowl; this would be his final game for Tennessee. Dorsett had exceptional athletic ability but minimal instincts. When Bruce stopped and cut back, Dorsett went whizzing by and fanned on the tackle completely.

That left cornerback Samari Rolle as the last defender with a chance, but he was eliminated when wide receiver Az-Zahir Hakim got away with an illegal shove in his back.

"Kurt was under an extreme amount of duress when he threw that ball," said Charley Armey, the Rams' vice president of player personnel. "Then Isaac's ability to turn that into a touchdown was just incredible. I think, more than anything, the difference in this ball game was the fact that Isaac Bruce had that competitive edge." It had been Armey's near magical touch in personnel upon arriving from New England in May 1997 that had provided Vermeil with the players.

Were the Titans shaken? Hardly. As Titans director of player personnel Rich Snead said, it would have been worse if Dorsett had made the tackle because then the Rams would have milked the clock down to nothing before probably kicking the winning field goal. Besides, the Titans had gone down swinging, just the way Gregg Williams had wanted. "Gregg's thing in two-minute defense was to blitz and put pressure on them," said Robinson. "If they score, they score quick. Kind of a weird way to look at it but, in actuality, it makes a lot of sense." Plus, the Titans had been unstoppable since the middle of the third quarter on, amassing 173 yards in three straight scoring drives.

But let's also be realistic. In his fifth season, and third as a starter, McNair was anything but a polished passer. According to George, McNair had almost no successful comebacks in two-minute situations on his résumé. Then linebacker Joe Bowden was penalized for holding on the kickoff return, forcing the Titans to start from the 12 with 1:48 and one timeout left. "I'm sure everybody in the country was thinking, 'The chances of this happening aren't very good,'" Titans wide receivers coach Steve Walters said. "The one thing I remembered thinking is I wouldn't put anything past this guy [McNair] even if he has to run it down there himself."

McNair found Derrick Mason for 9 and Frank Wycheck for 7, stopping the clock. On second down, he scrambled left for 12, and rookie cornerback Dre' Bly was penalized an additional 15 yards for grabbing McNair's facemask. Two more completions and another Rams' penalty produced a first down at the 31, where McNair spiked the ball with 31 seconds remaining. By this time, Martz had his head down preparing for overtime and was looking up only when the ball was snapped. "McNair was running around back there and the defensive line was just absolutely gassed by the time they got out to midfield," he said. "If you go back and look at some of those third-down plays he made, it's obnoxious. He was phenomenal."

With 22 seconds showing, McNair made his most phenomenal play of all. Facing third and 5 at the St. Louis 26, he had nothing available as the Rams rushed three and dropped eight into coverage. As McNair drifted to his right, defensive ends Kevin Carter and Jay Williams gave one last chase. McNair accelerated but Carter grabbed him around the waist while Williams grabbed his back from behind. With the ball held out in his right hand, McNair jammed his left hand into the turf for balance and skipped out of the clutches of his fallen foes. "I'm sitting down there just saying, 'He's going down and we better get back to the huddle,'" said Dyson.

All of a sudden, McNair straightened up and fired a strike to Dyson, who was promptly tackled at the 10 as the Titans called their last timeout with 6 seconds showing. "He wouldn't be tackled," said Walters. "He was beyond what you could believe physically. Just a horse. That was the game that vaulted him into being an elite player."

In the press box, third-year offensive coordinator Les Steckel told Fisher it was too risky to count on getting two shots in the end zone. "We had to get a play which we thought gave us the best chance to score," said Walters, who was upstairs next to Steckel. The call was a common red-zone pass that the Titans practiced often but hadn't used that night. To the right side, Wycheck was in the slot flanked by Dyson. To the left, Mason was in the slot flanked by Chris Sanders. "It was a man-zone route," said Dyson. "Their side was a man route and my side was a zone route. They ran a zone so I knew it was coming to me."

The Rams countered with Jones opposite Wycheck, cornerback Todd Lyght opposite Dyson, and safety Billy Jenkins behind them. "We run Wycheck down the seam and Dyson underneath on like a short in or a shallow cross," Walters said. "Either the linebacker sits on the shallow route and you throw it to Wycheck in the end zone, or he sinks off and you hit Dyson coming under and he can run it in." The Rams rushed four, more interested in containing McNair than pressuring him. McNair took the shotgun snap at the 15, backed up to the 18, and then threw the ball on time into the stomach of Dyson,

TEAM STATISTICS

ST. LOUIS		TENNESSEE
23	**Total First Downs**	27
1	Rushing	12
18	Passing	13
4	Penalty	2
436	**Total Net Yardage**	367
59	Total Offensive Plays	73
7.4	Avg. Gain per Offensive Play	5.0
13	**Rushes**	36
29	Yards Gained Rushing (Net)	159
2.2	Average Yards per Rush	4.4
45	**Passes Attempted**	36
24	Passes Completed	22
0	Passes Intercepted	0
1	Tackled Attempting to Pass	1
7	Yards Lost Attempting to Pass	6
407	Yards Gained Passing (Net)	208
5/12	**Third-Down Efficiency**	6/13
0/1	**Fourth-Down Efficiency**	1/1
2	**Punts**	3
38.5	Average Distance	43.0
2	**Punt Returns**	1
8	Punt Return Yardage	-1
4	**Kickoff Returns**	5
55	Kickoff Return Yardage	122
0	**Interception Return Yardage**	0
2	**Fumbles**	0
0	Own Fumbles Recovered	0
8	Opponent Fumbles Recovered	0
8	**Penalties**	7
60	Yards Penalized	45
2	**Touchdowns**	2
0	Rushing	2
2	Passing	0
0	Returns	0
2	**Extra Points Made**	1
3	**Field Goals Made**	1
4	Field Goals Attempted	3
0	**Safeties**	0
23	**Total Points Scored**	16
23:34	**Time of Possession**	36:26

who had motioned down and then back out before beginning his route at the 12 from a location immediately behind Wycheck.

What happened next became one of the most unforgettable moments in Super Bowl history.

Using inside-out technique, Jones ran back with Wycheck until his rear foot hit the 2. Then he broke

ST. LOUIS

Passing	CP/ATT	YDS	TD	INT	RAT
Warner	24/45	414	2	0	99.7

Rushing	ATT	YDS	AVG	TD	LG
Faulk	10	17	1.7	0	4
Holcombe	1	11	11.0	0	11
Warner	1	1	1.0	0	1
Horan	1	0	0.0	0	0

Receiving	NO	YDS	AVG	TD	LG
Holt	7	109	15.6	1	32
Bruce	6	162	27.0	1	73
Faulk	5	90	18.0	0	52
Hakim	1	17	17.0	0	17
Conwell	1	16	16.0	0	16
Proehl	1	11	11.0	0	11
R. Williams	1	9	9.0	0	9
Holcombe	1	1	1.0	0	1
Miller	1	-1	-1.0	0	-1

Interceptions	NO	YDS	LG	TD
None	--	--	--	--

Punting	NO	AVG	LG	BLK
Horan	2	38.5	47	0

Punt Ret.	NO/FC	YDS	LG	TD
Hakim	2/0	8	10	0

Kickoff Ret.	NO	YDS	LG	TD
Horne	4	55	25	0
Morton	0	0	0	0

Defense	SOLO	AST	TOT	SK
Jenkins	9	3	12	0
Fletcher	9	2	11	0
M. Jones	7	2	9	0
McCleon	5	1	6	0
Lyght	4	2	6	0
Collins	2	3	5	0
Little	4	0	4	0
Carter	3	0	3	1
Farr	3	0	3	0
Wistrom	3	0	3	0
Zgonina	3	0	3	0
Bush	2	0	2	0
J. Williams	1	1	2	0
Agnew	1	0	1	0
Bly	1	0	1	0
Clemons	1	0	1	0
Horne	1	0	1	0
Holcombe	0	1	1	0
TOTAL	59	15	74	1

TENNESSEE

Passing	CP/ATT	YDS	TD	INT	RAT
McNair	22/36	214	0	0	77.8

Rushing	ATT	YDS	AVG	TD	LG
E. George	28	95	3.4	2	13
McNair	8	64	8.0	0	23

Receiving	NO	YDS	AVG	TD	LG
Harris	7	64	9.1	0	21
Wycheck	5	35	7.0	0	13
Dyson	4	41	10.3	0	16
George	2	35	17.5	0	32
Byrd	2	21	10.5	0	21
Mason	2	18	9.0	0	9

Interceptions	NO	YDS	LG	TD
None	--	--	--	--

Punting	NO	AVG	LG	BLK
Hentrich	3	43.0	49	0

Punt Ret.	NO/FC	YDS	LG	TD
Mason	1/0	-1	-1	0

Kickoff Ret.	NO	YDS	LG	TD
Mason	5	122	35	0

Defense	SOLO	AST	TOT	SK
Sidney	5	0	5	0
Bishop	4	1	5	0
Dorsett	1	4	5	0
Kearse	4	0	4	0
E. Robinson	3	1	4	0
Evans	3	0	3	0
Walker	3	0	3	0
Bowden	2	1	3	0
Mitchell	2	1	3	0
Fisk	2	0	2	1
Wortham	2	0	2	0
Jackson	2	0	2	0
Favors	1	0	1	0
Killens	1	0	1	0
McCullough	1	0	1	0
Phenix	1	0	1	0
Rolle	1	0	1	0
TOTAL	38	8	46	1

up toward Dyson and was two steps away as the wideout made the catch at about the 4½ in the middle of the field with no other players within 5 yards. Jones

made a lunge for Dyson, managing to get his right hand around his waist and then his left hand around his left knee. Contact was made at the 2. Dyson,

6-foot-1 and 197, worked to extend his body as he was falling to the artificial turf. His reach extended only to the ½-yard line.

"At that instant, I looked at the clock and it read 0:00," George said. "I look back at the field and there was confetti everywhere. At that moment, you just don't believe that you went through a game like that. The more I think about it, it almost hurts. We were so close."

Jones, 6-foot-1 and 240, was an unlikely hero. He had been a running back and later a fullback at Missouri, but when the Raiders signed him as an undrafted rookie in April 1991, they converted him to linebacker. He played on passing downs and special teams for four seasons, became a starter in 1995, and then inked a four-year contract worth $6 million with St. Louis in March 1997. Starting every game over those four seasons, he more than earned his $2 million signing bonus. Although he wasn't highly touted when he first entered the league, Jones could run and he was smart; he scored 28 on the 50-question Wonderlic intelligence test, 9 points higher than the NFL average and the sixth-best score among the 57 running backs at the 1991 combine. "He was a guy that got it done," said George. "He was a solid football player who played hard and worked hard and did everything right." Jones' career ended after he played a portion of a 12th season with Pittsburgh in 2002.

How good was the play made by Jones? "Well, I've seen it missed many times," said Vermeil. "No play like that, when you're in a one-on-one situation, is easy." Asked how often that exact play in those exact circumstances should produce a touchdown,

George guessed 90 percent, while Robinson said 60 percent. Robinson, who played Jones' position for the Titans and found himself in that same situation countless times during his 11-year career, paid tribute. "He played it just about perfect," said Robinson. "You're stretching the rubber band but you don't want to pop it. He had to get deep enough to let the safety help him with the tight end but still be in position to make the tackle. It's a fine line. I thought it was a well-executed play by us but he just made a great play also."

Steckel believed that the play was poorly executed by Dyson and said as much after the game in an interview with Will McDonough, his old friend from *The Boston Globe*. "He just cut off the route," Steckel said. "If he ran that play the way he was supposed to have run it, we would have had the touchdown. But this is what happens to receivers when they get nervous. They cut the route short." A member of the Titans' front office basically offered the same opinion.

Dyson, a first-round draft choice in 1998, was stunned to learn of Steckel's remarks. "He never expressed that to me," Dyson said years later. "I did exactly what he told me to do in the game plan and how we had been practicing it. It had always been a 5-yard route. . . . The only thing I can think of that I would do different is I would have pushed up just a little bit more and maybe went 6½ and just let Frank carry him a little more. But, as a receiver, my discipline is to do what I've been told and it's supposed to work. It's not something I'm ever going to forget. I have a picture of it in my house."

His position coach, Walters, also said the route had always been run at 5 to 6 yards and couldn't possibly have worked if Dyson had run it at 10. "I'd like to have seen him break the tackle," said Walters, "but that's like faulting a guy for not hitting a home run." Added George, "I don't play the position. From what I hear, he cut the route short or he should have taken an extra step and influenced the linebacker a little bit better than what he did."

The Titans might not have needed that touchdown if they had run the ball more in the early going. George had seven carries (for 18 yards) in the first half, whereas the Titans' other 17 plays were dropbacks. "That still baffles me to this day," said George. "We were a running team. I guess we wanted to come out and do something different."

Often, McNair would be sent to the line with a run-pass check option, and according to both Steckel and George, he called too many passes when he saw the Rams stacking the box with eight or nine defenders. "I told him at the half, 'No matter what we call, don't change it. We need to run,'" Steckel told McDonough. "That's how we got back into the game." The long-striding George rushed 21 times for 77 yards in the second half, showing the awesome athleticism and leg drive that marked him in the prime of his career.

A smart-looking drive to open the third quarter still didn't put Tennessee on the board when Lyght charged free off the right side to block a 47-yard field goal try by Del Greco. A few plays later, strong safety Blaine Bishop suffered a sprained neck from tackling tight end Ernie Conwell, and play was delayed for about 10 minutes before he was driven off on a cart. "He was out and it was a big blow," said Dyson. "Blaine was the leader on the defense." When Warner zipped a 9-yard touchdown pass to Holt a step ahead of nickel back Dainon Sidney, the Rams led, 16–0.

As the Titans milled around on the sidelines preparing for the kickoff, Fisher glanced across the field and saw the Rams rejoicing over finally scoring a touchdown on their sixth drive inside the Tennessee 20. Punching the air with his right index finger for effect, Fisher stood among his players and yelled, "Hey. Last I heard, you had to outscore somebody in four quarters. They're celebratin', they're celebratin'. Right now. Look at 'em. Go win the game! Go win the game!"

Robinson, who played six seasons under Fisher, called these the most important words that the fiery coach had ever told his team. "It was one of the best sideline speeches that I've ever heard," he said. "That got guys to refocus and get back into the game." According to Martz, Fisher also fueled the Titans' comeback by having many players take fluid through IVs at halftime. "Nobody really knows that but it was brilliant on his part," he said. "His guys defensively didn't fall off."

From the Rams' perspective, the first half had been just a continuation of their amazing regular-season exploits on offense. They had 294 yards and 18 first downs, but for a team that had averaged 32.9 points during the regular season, being held to merely nine in the first 30 minutes was a downer.

The electrifying Faulk, obtained from Indianapolis for second- and fifth-round draft choices in April, carried merely 10 times for 17 yards, as Martz was as aggressive, if not more so, on offense than Williams was on defense. "We felt really good about Kurt's ability to deal with pressure," Martz said. "We were not going to worry about how many times we ran or threw. Just attack them in every way we could."

The cat-and-mouse game swung the Titans' way whenever St. Louis would move into scoring range. In the first half, the Rams had first downs at the Tennessee 18-, 14-, 17-, 11-, and 10-yard lines and came away with three made field goals, one missed field goal, and one bungled field goal because of a botched hold by punter Mike Horan. Of the 15 plays immediately before the five attempts, Warner had zero completions out of 11 throws.

"There was an ice storm and we didn't get a chance to do our normal red-zone practice on Friday," Martz said. "We went down to the stadium on Friday but it just didn't make any sense to go through the things we were actually going to do because there were all these people in the stands. You get paranoid. So we walked through it in a ballroom, which absolutely confounded us. We just kind of misfired and probably didn't have a great plan, in some respects. And they did a great job in the red zone mixing up some of the zone and the pressure. They were very, very physical."

Williams and company were so physical that Warner came close to not playing in the second half after suffering what Martz described as broken ribs in the first half. "Plural," he said. "He got two cracked ribs and separated cartilage. I was convinced he wasn't going to come out. They were going to shoot Kurt up and he said, 'No, I can play.' He could hardly breathe. After the first series of the second half, I said to [backup] Paul Justin, 'Just make sure you're ready because I don't think he's going to last a series.'"

Not only did Warner refuse to come out, but he also demonstrated the courage needed to expose his chest to Kearse when the onrushing Titans decked him for the last time. That was the thunderbolt to Bruce that sent Vermeil off to what would be an abbreviated retirement and turned Warner into one of the most unlikely Super Bowl heroes.

XXXV

BALTIMORE RAVENS 34, NEW YORK GIANTS 7

January 28, 2001
Raymond James Stadium, Tampa, Florida

Brian Billick left Minnesota for Baltimore in 1999 hell-bent on leading the Ravens into the modern age of offensive football. He never could get the Ravens over that hump, but when the last ball was snapped in the 2000 season, it made little difference because Baltimore was in possession of the Lombardi Trophy as the winner of Super Bowl XXXV.

Defense was something that Billick never played at Brigham Young, or coached at San Diego State, Utah State, Stanford, or Minnesota with the Vikings. He soon came to the realization that when a team plays defense as magnificently as his Ravens did, the primary function of the head coach is to make sure that the offense doesn't muck it up.

On Super Sunday, the Ravens backed up every boast, met every challenge, and proved beyond a shadow of any doubt that they were the NFL's best team. Their take-no-prisoners march through their four-game run as a wild-card playoff team concluded with a 34–7 flogging of the hapless New York Giants at Raymond James Stadium. By doing so, they supported Billick's contention that the Baltimore defense was quite possibly the finest ever assembled.

"Well, it will be easy to quantify," Billick said several years later. "All you have to do to supersede it is win a Super Bowl and break the all-time scoring record. That's the litmus test. You can break the scoring record, but if you don't win the Super Bowl it's discredited. Now there are those who will debate it, and that's fine. That's what sports is about."

Amazingly enough, Baltimore didn't lead the NFL in fewest yards allowed. First place, by the margin of 154 yards over the No. 2 Ravens, went to the Tennessee Titans, a 13–3 team that won the AFC Central Division by a game over Baltimore. But the Ravens allowed merely 165 points, 26 fewer than the Titans and 22 fewer than the Chicago Bears yielded

Attendance: 71,921
Conditions: 65 degrees, partly cloudy and mild, wind W at 8 mph
Time of kickoff: 6:28 p.m. (EST)
Length of game: 3 hours, 23 minutes
Referee: Gerry Austin

MVP: Ray Lewis, LB, Ravens

in 1986, to set a new record for a 16-game season. In the playoffs, the Ravens' defense was impenetrable. Their four opponents in the postseason scored 23 points (with only one offensive touchdown), averaged 209.3 yards (64.5 rushing), turned the ball over 12 times, converted 20 percent on third down, and had a passer rating of 33.4.

The Ravens won despite an offense that went 21 quarters from late October to early November without scoring a touchdown—one quarter shy of the NFL record in the post-merger era. They won despite the trauma of making a quarterback change at midseason, with journeyman Trent Dilfer replacing error-prone Tony Banks, and without a genuine threat at wide receiver. And they won despite an offensive line that was shaky by NFL standards at three of the five positions.

"That offense, the best thing you can say about it is it filled its role," said Billick. "We had to run the ball effectively, not turn it over, and make one play, maybe two, that could get us an advantage, a touchdown or 10 points. That was usually enough to win the game. Not very ambitious. But that was their role, and that's exactly what they did."

The Giants, the top seed out of the NFC with a 12–4 record, were coming off a 41–0 annihilation of Minnesota in the NFC Championship Game and went to Tampa as merely a 3-point underdog. On this day, the Giants' rugged defense wasn't in top form and their offense was brutally overmatched. The Ravens' fast, physical, smart, and deep defense

	1	2	3	4	Final
Baltimore Ravens	7	3	14	10	34
New York Giants	0	0	7	0	7

SCORING SUMMARY

1st Quarter
BAL Stokley, 38-yd. pass from Dilfer (Stover kick)
2nd Quarter
BAL Stover, 47-yd. FG
3rd Quarter
BAL Starks, 49-yd. interception return (Stover kick)
NY Dixon, 97-yd. kickoff return (Daluiso kick)
BAL Je. Lewis, 84-yd. kickoff return (Stover kick)
4th Quarter
BAL Ja. Lewis, 3-yd. run (Stover kick)
BAL Stover, 34-yd. FG

humiliated quarterback Kerry Collins (7.1 passer rating) and rendered the diversified attack of coach Jim Fassel impotent. In 16 possessions, the Giants crossed midfield only twice, reaching the Ravens' 42- and 29-yard lines on two late second-quarter possessions. They punted a record 11 times, unloaded four interceptions, and ended the game on downs. They had just 152 yards and 11 first downs, including 3 by penalty.

"I thought the game would be different than that, but that's what happened," Fassel said several years later. "We could not block their down people, run or pass. [Tony] Siragusa and those guys just manhandled us. Of all the years I've coached, that front seven was as good as any I've seen. You had the speed off the edges. With Sam [Adams] and Tony inside, they were just hard to move. And then they had linebackers that could run behind them. We weren't able to make any plays. . . . Defensively, we gave up too many big pass plays. That was the bottom line."

For the Giants to have a chance, they needed their defense, ranked fifth in both points and yards allowed, to stifle the Ravens just as it had stifled Randy Moss, Cris

"Honestly, we had no fear of any offense in the National Football League that year. Our goal was to have the first Super Bowl shutout. Once the fourth quarter hit we were trying to figure out our ring sizes and how to ask [owner Art] Modell to add a little pizzazz to the ring."

Rod Woodson, Ravens safety

Carter, Robert Smith, and Daunte Culpepper in the NFC title game. "We knew the battle the offense was facing," middle linebacker Micheal Barrow said. "In one of our team meetings, Jessie [Armstead] said, 'Look, we're going to carry the team. We're going to give you this game. We will put points on the board defensively.' We saw ourselves as just as good as the Baltimore Ravens' defense." Defensive coordinator John Fox was fond of telling his players, "First one to 10 points wins."

Matt Cavanaugh, Billick's play-calling offensive coordinator, came out taking shots downfield, almost like a prizefighter looking to land an early haymaker. Although the Ravens rushed on 62 percent of their plays in the playoffs, they dropped back 20 times compared to 11 rushes up until the waning seconds of the first half. The long-ball strategy was low-risk, reasoned Billick, because even if the passes were intercepted, they would serve as just another punt.

Baltimore's wide-receiver corps of Qadry Ismail, Patrick Johnson, and Brandon Stokley left much to be desired, but Johnson did have blazing speed while Ismail and Stokley each had a knack for getting deep. Besides, Billick figured that all three could run by left cornerback Dave Thomas, the most vulnerable starter on the Giants' defense, and even Jason Sehorn, another big, physical corner who had shut down Moss two weeks before. On the Ravens' second possession, Johnson had Sehorn beat for what would have been a 46-yard touchdown, except Dilfer's perfect pass skipped off his hands in the end zone.

Seven minutes remained in the first quarter when Baltimore started at the New York 41 after a 34-yard punt return by Jermaine Lewis. On second and 7, the Ravens trotted out three wide receivers, with Stokley in the slot to the right. Countering with a nickel package, the Giants had Sehorn on the line across from Stokley and Shaun Williams deep as the single safety. Two linebackers, Barrow and Armstead, were covering tight end Shannon Sharpe, the Ravens' primary threat.

BALTIMORE RAVENS	Offense	NEW YORK GIANTS
(AFC, 12–4)		(NFC, 12–4)

			Offense			
87	Qadry Ismail (6-0, 200)		WR	81	Amani Toomer (6-3, 208)
75	Jonathan Ogden* (6-8, 340)		LT	76	Lomas Brown (6-4, 280)
64	Edwin Mulitalo (6-3, 340)		LG	62	Glenn Parker (6-5, 312)
60	Jeff Mitchell (6-4, 300)		C	52	Dusty Zeigler (6-5, 308)
62	Mike Flynn (6-3, 300)		RG	65	Ron Stone* (6-5, 320)
70	Harry Swayne (6-5, 300)		RT	77	Luke Petitgout (6-6, 310)
82	Shannon Sharpe (6-2, 232)		TE	87	Howard Cross (6-5, 278)
80	Brandon Stokley (5-11, 197)		WR	88	Ike Hilliard (5-11, 195)
8	Trent Dilfer (6-4, 229)		QB	5	Kerry Collins (6-5, 250)
31	Jamal Lewis (5-11, 240)		RB	21	Tiki Barber (5-10, 200)
32	Sam Gash (6-0, 240)		FB	34	Greg Comella (6-1, 248)
			Defense		
90	Rob Burnett (6-4, 270)		LE	92	Michael Strahan (6-4, 275)
95	Sam Adams* (6-3, 340)		LT	97	Cornelius Griffin (6-3, 300)
98	Tony Siragusa (6-3, 340)		RT	75	Keith Hamilton (6-6, 295)
99	Michael McCrary (6-4, 260)		RE	94	Cedric Jones (6-4, 270)
58	Peter Boulware (6-4, 255)		SLB	91	Ryan Phillips (6-4, 252)
52	Ray Lewis* (6-0, 245)		MLB	58	Micheal Barrow (6-2, 238)
55	Jamie Sharper (6-3, 240)		WLB	98	Jessie Armstead* (6-1, 240)
22	Duane Starks (5-10, 170)		LCB	41	Dave Thomas (6-3, 218)
21	Chris McAlister (6-1, 206)		RCB	31	Jason Sehorn (6-1, 215)
20	Kim Herring (6-0, 200)		SS	20	Sam Garnes (6-3, 225)
26	Rod Woodson* (6-0, 205)		FS	36	Shaun Williams (6-2, 215)

* Pro Bowl selection

SUBSTITUTIONS

Baltimore

Offense: WR - 83 Patrick Johnson, 84 Jermaine Lewis, 86 Billy Davis; TE - 81 Ben Coates; T - 71 Spencer Folau; G - 77 Kipp Vickers; QB - 12 Tony Banks; RB - 33 Priest Holmes; FB - 29 Chuck Evans. *Defense:* DE - 93 Keith Washington; DT - 79 Larry Webster, 91 Lional Dalton; LB - 50 Brad Jackson, 51 Cornell Brown, 56 Anthony Davis, 57 O. J. Brigance; CB - 35 Robert Bailey, 38 James Trapp; S - 42 Anthony Mitchell, 45 Corey Harris. *Specialists:* K - 3 Matt Stover*; P - 5 Kyle Richardson; LS - 66 John Hudson. *Inactive:* 11 Marcus Nash (WR), 16 Germany Thompson (WR), 72 Sammy Williams (T), 74 Orlando Bobo (G), 7 Chris Redman (QB), 96 Adalius Thomas (DE), 25 Clarence Love (CB), 43 Anthony Poindexter (S).

New York

Offense: WR - 82 Thabiti Davis, 84 Joe Jurevicius, 86 Ron Dixon; TE - 83 Pete Mitchell, 89 Dan Campbell; T - 78 Mike Rosenthal; G - 66 Jason Whittle; C - 69 Derek Engler; RB - 27 Ron Dayne, 29 Damon Washington, 33 Joe Montgomery. *Defense:* DT - 93 Ryan Hale, 99 Christian Peter; LB - 51 Pete Monty, 53 Brandon Short, 90 Jack Golden; CB - 25 Ramos McDonald, 26 Emmanuel McDaniel; S - 23 Omar Stoutmire, 37 Lyle West. *Specialists:* K - 3 Brad Daluiso; P - 9 Brad Maynard. *DNP:* 17 Jason Garrett (QB). *Inactive:* 67 Chris Bober (T), 18 Mike Cherry (QB), 45 Craig Walendy (FB), 79 Jeremiah Parker (DE), 96 George Williams (DT), 59 Kevin Lewis (LB), 28 Reggie Stephens (CB), 2 Jaret Holmes (K).

At the snap, Dilfer looked left toward Sharpe, and Williams took the bait. In effect, he applied triple-coverage on Sharpe and left Sehorn without the help that he anticipated in the middle against Stokley. When Sehorn gave Stokley an inside release, the latter caught another beautifully thrown ball from Dilfer at the 10 and crashed into the end zone for a 38-yard touchdown.

"Instead of the free safety doubling the slot, [Williams] made a brain fart and came to the tight end," Barrow said. "Sehorn was counting on help inside and he didn't have it, so it was just a straight beeline to the end zone. It was just a blown coverage, but we all make mistakes."

Barrow, who played under Buddy Ryan and Jeff Fisher in Houston, and then Dom Capers in Carolina, said Fox's defense was the most complex that he ever played on. "If you were a student of the game, which I take pride in being, 'Foxie' wanted to teach you everything he could," said Barrow. "If we had kept it simple against them with Cover 2, Cover 3, and Cover 4, basic coverages, then I don't think they could have done anything against us. But when we tried to double this guy and match up this guy and confuse this guy and confuse that guy, what we ended up doing was confusing ourselves."

Both teams knew the critical nature of scoring first, given the advantages both defenses had over the marginal offenses.

COACHING STAFFS

Baltimore

Head Coach: Brian Billick. *Offense:* Matt Cavanaugh (coordinator), Milt Jackson (wide receivers), Wade Harman (tight ends, assistant offensive line), Jim Colletto (offensive line), Matt Simon (running backs). *Defense:* Marvin Lewis (coordinator), Rex Ryan (defensive line), Jack Del Rio (linebackers), Steve Shafer (defensive backs), Donnie Henderson (defensive backs), Mike Smith (assistant). *Special Teams:* Russ Purnell. *Strength:* Jeff Friday, Chip Morton (assistant).

New York

Head Coach: Jim Fassel. *Offense:* Sean Payton (coordinator,quarterbacks), Jimmy Robinson (wide receivers), Mike Pope (tight ends), Jim McNally (offensive line), Jim Skipper (running backs, assistant head coach), Mike Gillhamer (assistant). *Defense:* John Fox (coordinator), Denny Marcin (defensive line), Tom Olivadotti (linebackers), Johnnie Lynn (defensive backs), Dave Brazil (quality control). *Special Teams:* Larry MacDuff. *Strength:* John Dunn, Craig Stoddard (assistant).

"Once we scored, honestly, we looked at each other and said, 'This game's over. They're not going to score on us,'" Ravens free safety Rod Woodson said. "Our main goal was to have the first shutout in Super Bowl history. Unfortunately, we gave up a kickoff return."

Two plays after the touchdown, the horrors of playing against the Ravens' defense really began to register on the Giants. On second and 8, Tiki Barber headed left on a wide stretch play that looked promising. Ray Lewis, the Ravens' middle linebacker who had bulked up to 253 pounds without any appreciable loss of speed, flowed on a perfect angle from the other side of the field and intersected with Barber as he was turning up field. After a thud, the gain was just 2 yards. When a third-down play went nowhere, the Giants were left with just another of their 10 three-and-outs.

"I remember talking to people they had played and everybody's comment was, 'You won't appreciate how fast this team is until you play them. You won't get a feel for their speed off tape,'" Fassel recalled. Asked what would have happened if the two teams had met 10 times, Fassel replied, "Offensively, we'd have to do more. I don't know where it was

going to come from. We weren't going to be able to run the ball real effectively on them. Defensively, we could definitely have done better."

As damaging as Stokley's long touchdown had been to the Giants, what happened next might have been even worse. From the Baltimore 47, Dilfer looked for running back Jamal Lewis on a screen pass to the left. With defensive end Michael Strahan a split-second away from burying him, Dilfer threw without having Lewis in his sights. The boneheaded pass was intercepted by Armstead, who returned 43 yards for an apparent touchdown, but the Giants' spontaneous celebration didn't last long. Defensive tackle Keith Hamilton was penalized for holding Lewis and the play was brought back.

"It was like, c'mon, those calls you just don't make," Barrow said. "He [Hamilton] was breaking through the lineman [guard Edwin Mulitalo], and it was one of those things where he thought the back was running the ball. That call was just pathetic." Whatever Hamilton's intent, he did grab Lewis by the right bicep and interrupt his route. Billick sympathized with Fassel, his good friend, because defensive holding on a screen is rarely called.

"It wasn't holding, and they [the NFL office] told me that later," Fassel said. "They took a lot of criticism for it. Here's the thing that nobody knows. We had played them in the preseason. When we tried to run a screen with Tiki, their front guys tackled him and grabbed him. So when we went to play them in the Super Bowl, I remember telling the officials before the game to watch them holding our running back trying to get out. Well, they did it, but they called it on our guy.

"I thought that might really affect Dilfer and Brian would be upset with Dilfer, that the whole atmosphere on their offense might change and their defense would lose confidence in their offense. It was 34–7, and everybody said that one play couldn't make a difference. Well, it swung a lot of momentum."

A few minutes later, the Ravens again demonstrated how carefree they could be on offense given the suffocating nature of their defense. Backed up at the 20 and facing third and 2, the Ravens figured to pound straight-ahead with Jamal Lewis. Instead, Dilfer took another chance deep up the sideline and Ismail easily beat Thomas. If Thomas' desperate dive for the tackle hadn't been successful, Ismail's 44-yard gain would have been an 80-yard score. "He almost stepped out of it, and the game would have been over at that point," said Billick. "[Thomas] was the guy we were going to try to take advantage of. He didn't have great bump skills." The drive stalled and Matt Stover, the all-pro kicker with 35 field goals in 39 attempts during the regular season, drilled a 47-yard field goal and it was 10–0 with 1:41 left in the half.

The Giants responded to adversity for the only time all night. Collins completed a 16-yard hook pass to rookie speedster Ron Dixon before Barber burst through the middle on a shotgun draw for 27 yards, a play that turned out to be their longest of the game. On the next play, Collins saw Ike Hilliard open near the 15 and wanted to throw, but defensive end Michael McCrary threw up his hands and impeded his vision.

Forced to double pump, Collins made the mistake of throwing to Hilliard anyway, and cornerback Chris McAlister leaped to make a rather routine interception at the 1. "Two weeks before in the championship it was one of the greatest games a quarterback ever played," said Fassel, referring to Collins' 381-yard, five-touchdown, 121.7-passer rating outburst against the Vikings. "Then he comes back with this one."

Collins wasn't the only quarterback under duress. Dilfer had to leave for a series early in the third quarter when he suffered a broken finger on his non-throwing hand. "He blames me for it, and I think I did hit him," said Strahan, who had one and a half sacks. "They let Harry [Swayne] block me, and I don't think he blocked me very much. I got a lot of good hits on Dilfer. We weren't really worried about Dilfer throwing the ball, and then he beats us deep. I'll give him credit. He played well that game when they needed him."

The Ravens had benched quarterback Tony Banks after a Week 8 home loss to the Titans. "Tony had made the same mistake twice of throwing the ball in the middle of the field down in the red zone," general manager Ozzie Newsome said. "You just can't do that. Trent played well enough to not get us

beat." The Ravens had signed Dilfer to a one-year, $1 million contract in March when Tampa Bay let him walk as an unrestricted free agent.

The pressure on Collins, however, was even more intense. Surprisingly, the Ravens ranked just 22nd in sack percentage, but in the postseason McCrary broke loose for six sacks. The other end, Rob Burnett,

TEAM STATISTICS

BALTIMORE		NEW YORK
13	Total First Downs	11
6	Rushing	2
6	Passing	6
1	Penalty	3
244	Total Net Yardage	152
62	Total Offensive Plays	59
3.9	Avg. Gain per Offensive Play	2.6
33	Rushes	16
111	Yards Gained Rushing (Net)	66
3.4	Average Yards per Rush	4.1
26	Passes Attempted	39
12	Passes Completed	15
0	Passes Intercepted	4
3	Tackled Attempting to Pass	4
20	Yards Lost Attempting to Pass	26
133	Yards Gained Passing (Net)	86
3/16	Third-Down Efficiency	2/14
0/0	Fourth-Down Efficiency	1/1
10	Punts	11
43.0	Average Distance	38.4
3	Punt Returns	5
34	Punt Return Yardage	46
2	Kickoff Returns	7
111	Kickoff Return Yardage	170
59	Interception Return Yardage	0
2	Fumbles	2
2	Own Fumbles Recovered	1
1	Opponent Fumbles Recovered	0
9	Penalties	6
70	Yards Penalized	27
4	Touchdowns	1
1	Rushing	0
1	Passing	0
2	Returns	1
4	Extra Points Made	1
2	Field Goals Made	0
3	Field Goals Attempted	0
0	Safeties	0
34	Total Points Scored	7
34:06	Time of Possession	25:54

INDIVIDUAL STATISTICS

BALTIMORE

Passing	CP/ATT	YDS	TD	INT	RAT
Dilfer	12/25	153	1	0	80.9
Banks	0/1	0	0	0	39.6

Rushing	ATT	YDS	AVG	TD	LG
Ja. Lewis	27	102	3.8	1	19
Holmes	4	8	2.0	0	6
Je. Lewis	1	1	1.0	0	1
Dilfer	1	0	0.0	0	0

Receiving	NO	YDS	AVG	TD	LG
Stokley	3	52	17.3	1	38t
Coates	3	30	10.0	0	17
Ismail	1	44	44.0	0	44
Johnson	1	8	8.0	0	8
Je. Lewis	1	6	6.0	0	6
Sharpe	1	5	5.0	0	5
Ja. Lewis	1	4	4.0	0	4
Holmes	1	4	4.0	0	4

Interceptions	NO	YDS	LG	TD
Starks	1	49	49t	1
McAlister	1	4	4	0
Sharper	1	4	4	0
Herring	1	2	2	0

Punting	NO	AVG	LG	BLK
Richardson	10	43.0	53	0

Punt Ret.	NO/FC	YDS	LG	TD
Je. Lewis	3/4	34	34	0

Kickoff Ret.	NO	YDS	LG	TD
Je. Lewis	2	111	84t	1

Defense	SOLO	AST	TOT	SK
Harris	5	1	6	0
Woodson	5	1	6	0
Starks	5	0	5	0
R. Lewis	3	2	5	0
Brigance	4	0	4	0
Washington	4	0	4	1
Burnett	3	1	4	1
McCrary	3	0	3	2
Sharper	3	0	3	0
Trapp	3	0	3	0
Adams	1	0	1	0
Dalton	1	0	1	0
Davis	1	0	1	0
Jackson	1	0	1	0
McAlister	1	0	1	0
Siragusa	1	0	1	0
TOTAL	**44**	**5**	**49**	**4**

NEW YORK

Passing	CP/ATT	YDS	TD	INT	RAT
Collins	15/39	112	0	4	7.1

Rushing	ATT	YDS	AVG	TD	LG
Barber	11	49	4.5	0	27
Collins	3	12	4.0	0	5
Montgomery	2	5	2.5	0	4

Receiving	NO	YDS	AVG	TD	LG
Barber	6	26	4.3	0	7
Hilliard	3	30	10.0	0	13
Toomer	2	24	12.0	0	19
Dixon	1	16	16.0	0	16
Cross	1	7	7.0	0	7
Mitchell	1	7	7.0	0	7
Comella	1	2	2.0	0	2

Interceptions	NO	YDS	LG	TD
None	--	--	--	--

Punting	NO	AVG	LG	BLK
Maynard	11	38.4	46	0

Punt Ret.	NO/FC	YDS	LG	TD
Hilliard	3/1	33	19	0
Barber	2/2	13	9	0

Kickoff Ret.	NO	YDS	LG	TD
Dixon	6	154	97t	1
Washington	1	17	17	0

Defense	SOLO	AST	TOT	SK
Williams	5	2	7	0
Barrow	6	0	6	0
Sehorn	6	0	6	0
Strahan	5	1	6	1.5
Garnes	5	0	5	0
Hamilton	5	0	5	0
Phillips	4	0	4	0
Armstead	2	1	3	0
Peter	2	0	2	0
Griffin	1	1	2	1.5
Dixon	1	0	1	0
Hilliard	1	0	1	0
C. Jones	1	0	1	0
McDaniel	1	0	1	0
McDonald	1	0	1	0
Mitchell	1	0	1	0
Monty	1	0	1	0
Thomas	1	0	1	0
TOTAL	**49**	**5**	**54**	**3**

probably enjoyed his best season in 2000, his 11th year. At left tackle, Adams possessed gap-shooting quickness, despite his girth. On passing downs, lightning-fast outside linebacker Peter Boulware put his hand down, and Burnett kicked inside when Siragusa took a breather, offering additional versatility for this imposing front line. Defensive coordinator Marvin Lewis didn't have to blitz much because his four-man rush was so heavy. "What Marvin learned to do was not to overcomplicate his players with a lot of thinking, play some sound fronts and coverages, and let their instincts and athleticism take over," Newsome said. "We did some zone blitzing out of our 4-3 because McCrary was able to drop. What we could do is rush with four because we had Burnett and McCrary. When we brought five with Boulware off the edge it was tough on people."

"We played a lot of Cover 2," Newsome continued, "but we also could play man-to-man with McAlister and [Duane] Starks and keep a safety in the hole. We could bring five and play man-to-man because Ray [Lewis] was a great cover guy and so was Jamie [Sharper]. And we had Woodson covering the tight end.

"It began and ended with our ability to stop the run. We used to play the front where Burnett would be over the tight end. Not many tight ends could block him. We had two guys 350-plus in the middle. They really freed up Ray to make all the plays."

Opposing this rock-ribbed unit was a Giants' offensive line that basically got overrun. Offensive line coach Jim McNally had done an exceptional job integrating three new starters—37-year-old left tackle Lomas Brown, 34-year-old left guard Glenn Parker, and former Buffalo center Dusty Zeigler—all of whom had been obtained in free agency for a combined total of just $3.05 million in signing bonuses. In this game, however, they failed blocking both for run and pass. "But it didn't matter

who we had because Baltimore's defense was so overwhelming," Strahan said. "We could have had Anthony Muñoz out there and I don't know if that was going to help them."

Another shortcoming of the Giants' offense was the lack of vertical stretch at receiver. The tight ends offered nothing in the passing game, Hilliard and Joe Jurevicius weren't vertical threats, and Amani Toomer, though effective, wasn't a speed receiver, either. "Normally, you sit on the bench and focus on yourself, but we were up because we wanted to see what their defense was doing," said Barrow. "I'm telling you, it's not like people were open. They basically just weren't threatened by our guys."

Woodson, the great old pro who had been cut by San Francisco in February 1998 and signed 11 days later by Baltimore, said the Ravens concentrated on taking away seam routes. "That was Kerry Collins' 'M.O.'," said Woodson. "I don't know if they even caught a seam pass the whole game."

Another enormous factor was Ray Lewis, who kept dropping and reading Collins and wound up deflecting four passes, one of which was intercepted. For his exploits, Lewis was named MVP. The Ravens played simple zone coverages and watched Collins play in a confused, if not somewhat intimidated, state. As the second half wore on and his offense remained in the deep freeze, Fassel had to assume more risk.

Ravens cornerback Duane Starks, the 10th player selected in the 1998 draft, had gambled and lost too many times before he finally stopped biting in mid-2000 and began playing superb football. When the Giants sent out three receivers to the left and Toomer alone to the right, Newsome remembered being confident that Starks knew New York's tendency to throw the slant on the back side. With just less than four minutes remaining in the third quarter, Starks sliced inside of Toomer and brought his interception back 49 yards for a backbreaking touchdown.

"I remember Starks told me after the game that they knew based on Kerry's mechanics when the ball was coming out," said Barrow. "Something he did with his hand. [Starks] wasn't threatened by Toomer's speed, and when he saw the glitch with Kerry he just jumped on the ball."

That was the first of three touchdowns in just 36 seconds. On the kickoff following Starks' interception, Dixon skipped away from linebacker Cornell Brown and raced 97 yards to break the shutout. Then Jermaine Lewis turned around and brought back Brad Daluiso's short kick 84 yards for another Ravens score.

Special teams had been an Achilles' heel for New York all season. "We used to raise money from the vets and say, 'OK, if you get a tackle inside the 20 we'll give you $1,000,'" Barrow remembered. "We used to bribe those guys to make things happen. But then the special teams' bug came back to bite us."

Baltimore's final touchdown came courtesy of Jamal Lewis, who got the best of Barrow by plowing over him on a 3-yard touchdown run around left end in the fourth quarter. That was the 24th of Lewis' 27 carries, which added up to 102 yards and a 3.8-yard average. Using the fifth pick of the 2000 draft to select Lewis was the latest in a string of shrewd first-round selections by Newsome, director of college scouting Phil Savage, and a savvy staff of college scouts. Without Jamal Lewis, the Ravens probably wouldn't have had enough offense.

"He and Micheal Barrow were hitting each other as hard as I've ever seen two players, play after play after play," Strahan said. "The will of those two to want to break the other was absolutely mind-blowing. We had to pull Barrow off him a few times because Barrow was trying to choke him—and Barrow was a Christian man. He said Jamal cussed at him, and he was trying to choke the devil out of him. The size of Jamal was very intimidating, and he was extremely fast. He was hitting those holes with no hesitation, no stutter, thinking, 'If you want to stop me you have to bring all you have.'"

There was little reason for the Giants to be mortified, and most of the Giants weren't. In the wild-card game, previously explosive Denver gained merely 177 yards against Baltimore. In the AFC Championship Game, Oakland's top-ranked ground game settled for 24 yards. "It seemed like all 11 guys were better than your 11," said Strahan. "It was their year. You couldn't deny that." Baltimore's weakest defensive starters probably were outside

> "We knew [Jamal Lewis] wasn't bringing any paper plates to the party. We knew we had to gang-tackle this dude. It was a rumble in the jungle. Choking him in the bottom of the pile. You see fingers in the guy's mouth trying to rip out his braces. . . . And he just took it and wanted more. Boy, he took it personal. He earned a lot of respect that day."
>
> *Micheal Barrow, Giants linebacker*

linebacker Jamie Sharper and strong safety Kim Herring, but within three months each signed big contracts. In other words, there wasn't anything close to a weakness on that defense.

Billick would remain with the Ravens for seven more seasons but won just one more playoff game before being fired. He let Dilfer walk as an unrestricted free agent two months after the Super Bowl and signed Elvis Grbac to a five-year, $30 million contract. Grbac played poorly (71.1 rating) in 2001, his final season, and Dilfer went on to start just 29 games over the next seven seasons as a backup and mentor for young quarterbacks in Seattle, Cleveland, and San Francisco.

"I have absolutely zero desire to talk to Brian Billick," Dilfer said in 2007. "He grossly misunderstood the talent of that football team, myself specifically. Those guys [his teammates] will go to their graves swearing to God that we would have won two, three Super Bowls if they would have kept me. To this day, I am so sad I didn't have the chance to face the challenge of repeating." Years later, Woodson said, "Trent was a gutsy, tough individual who knew his role and didn't play above himself. You make your bed and lay in it. They've been laying in it quite a while now."

The Ravens were a one-shot deal, rare among Super Bowl champions in that they weren't quarterback-driven. Without an accomplished offense, the Ravens had to roll behind their defense. And roll they did, devouring foe after foe until there was no foe left to devour.

XXXVI

NEW ENGLAND PATRIOTS 20, ST. LOUIS RAMS 17

February 3, 2002

Louisiana Superdome, New Orleans, Louisiana

The 72,922 fans in attendance at the Superdome and the estimated 132 million television viewers will remember Super Bowl XXXVI as one of the most remarkable upsets in professional football history. It was the day in which Bill Belichick came to be recognized as a coaching great, Tom Brady came of age, and the New England Patriots demonstrated what 53 players united as one can accomplish, no matter the odds.

It was supposed to be a day in which the St. Louis Rams, a team with the most prolific offense in NFL history and a stingy defense ranked third in the league, would add a second Lombardi Trophy. It was supposed to be the day in which New England, a 5–11 team the year before, would more than meet its match in the form of St. Louis' overwhelming advantage in sheer talent.

"There's a shot of [the Rams'] Ricky Proehl before the game looking into an NFL Films camera saying, 'Today a dynasty is born,'" New England linebacker Tedy Bruschi said several years later. "It's ironic, because that's the day our dynasty was born. He was right. He just had the wrong team."

New England was a 14-point underdog, the third highest spread in the history of the Super Bowl. Only the 1968 New York Jets of "Broadway" Joe Namath, which beat the Baltimore Colts as an 18-point underdog, had won against steeper odds.

Like the Jets, the Patriots controlled the game with an effective, if unspectacular, rushing game and a punishing style of defense that forced multiple mistakes and turnovers. Unlike Super Bowl III, this Super Bowl ended in unforgettable style. Brady, unflappable under fire, drove the Patriots 53 yards into scoring position in the final 1 minute, 21 seconds after Fox broadcaster John Madden advocated playing for overtime. Then Adam Vinatieri crushed a 48-yard field goal dead center perfect as time expired to make the Patriots a 20–17 winner.

Attendance: 79,922	
Conditions: Indoors	
Time of kickoff: 5:40 p.m. (CST)	
Length of game: 3 hours, 24 minutes	
Referee: Bernie Kukar	
MVP: Tom Brady, QB, Patriots	

"I get ticked off every time I think of that New England game," St. Louis offensive line coach Jim Hanifan said a few years later. "I don't like even talking about the damn thing."

The outcome represented a turning point for both organizations. Not until 2008, when he led the Arizona Cardinals to Super Bowl XLIII, would Rams quarterback Kurt Warner approach the form that made him the league's MVP in 1999 and 2001. Running back Marshall Faulk—the Associated Press Offensive Player of the Year in 1999, 2000, and 2001 (and MVP in 2000)—never again rushed for 1,000 yards. Coach Mike Martz also earned just one more victory in the postseason before being released by the Rams in January 2006. In contrast, New England would grow into a championship juggernaut by the middle of the decade under Belichick's incomparable coaching and with Brady's splendid quarterbacking.

For any prohibitive underdog to win the Super Bowl, three things must fall into place. The favored team must begin to have doubts; Belichick's defensive game plan—built around roughing up Faulk—obviously disturbed the Rams. Second, the favored team must make a multitude of mistakes, such as three Rams' turnovers that led to the Patriots' first 17 points. Finally, the favored team must be forced to play from behind, which the Patriots essentially made the Rams do from the middle of the second quarter on.

But football games are four quarters long for good reason. The Rams overcame a 17–3 deficit by

	1	2	3	4	Final
St. Louis Rams	3	0	0	14	17
New England Patriots	0	14	3	3	20

SCORING SUMMARY

1st Quarter
STL Wilkins, 50-yd. FG
2nd Quarter
NE Law, 47-yd. interception return (Vinatieri kick)
NE Patten, 8-yd. pass from Brady (Vinatieri kick)
3rd Quarter
NE Vinatieri, 37-yd. FG
4th Quarter
STL Warner,.2-yd. run (Wilkins kick)
STL Proehl, 26-yd. pass from Warner (Wilkins kick)
NE Vinatieri, 48-yd. FG

scoring a pair of touchdowns in the final 10 minutes as the Patriots went three-and-out twice. Sensing his defensive players were exhausted, Belichick actually used his team's final timeout at the four-minute mark to give the defense a break before the Rams' snapped the ball on third and 25. "By the middle of the fourth quarter we're chasing them around and we're dying," Belichick said. "I made a mistake. I don't think [Chris] Sullivan would have helped us and I'm not saying [David] Nugent would have, but we ran out of defensive linemen." Both those players were left inactive when the Patriots decided to play only four pure defensive linemen; another, Riddick Parker, was active but didn't get in.

Hanifan remembered it this way: "Their defensive linemen and linebackers could barely move. So I'm looking at overtime, and we're going to kick their ass." The Patriots had made a valiant bid and taken the fight to the Rams, but it appeared that they would have to demonstrate staying power and perform in overtime in order to win.

When the Patriots started from their 17 with 1:21 and no timeouts remaining, they had gained merely 214 yards to the Rams' 427. They had converted 2 of 11 third downs, 8 of their first 10 possessions had resulted in punts, and they had been inside the Rams' 25 only once all day.

"I mean, we can't score," Belichick said. "As good as the Rams were on offense, that was a damn good defensive team. Our deal offensively was to run the ball as much as we can, because every time we run it that's one less play they have. . . . In three playoff games we score three offensive touchdowns. Brady scrambles against the Raiders. We hit really a busted coverage against Pittsburgh, and in the St. Louis game we hit [David] Patten on an out-and-up. We made plays in the kicking game and we played pretty good on defense."

After the game, Brady said that Belichick told him before the start of the final drive, "Go out and just sling it. Go win the game." Years later, Belichick confessed that it wasn't him or offensive coordinator Charlie Weis who gave the 24-year-old Brady clearance to go for broke. "Brady is going out on the field and Charlie and I are standing there saying, 'OK, here's what we're going to do. Be careful,'" said Belichick. "On the way out [Drew] Bledsoe grabs him and says, 'F--- that. Just go out there and win it. Don't worry about being careful or whatever.' That's the lore. I don't know. I didn't hear that myself."

Huddled around Brady, a sixth-round draft choice in 2000, was a conglomeration of players who struck almost no fear into NFL defenses. The wide receivers were Troy Brown, who caught 101 passes that season despite being small and not fast enough to suit some scouts, and Patten, a one-time Arena Football League player who had been discarded by the New York Giants and Cleveland Browns. The tight end was Jermaine Wiggins, a former free agent awarded to New England off waivers from the Jets in 2000, and the third-down back was J. R. Redmond, a third-round draft choice that year with little experience.

Matt Light, a godsend as the starting left tackle as a rookie, aggravated an ankle injury in the first half and had to be replaced by Grant Williams, a journeyman whom the Patriots let walk as a free agent a month after the Super Bowl. Making the shotgun snap was Mike Compton, whose $625,000 signing bonus was the largest allocated by Belichick to any of the 17 veteran free agents that he signed in the 2001 offseason. Of those 17 players—10 of whom were unrestricted free agents and 7 of whom were "street" free agents—7 became starters, 5 played as situational substitutes, 3 were integral performers on special teams, and 2 were backups.

"I knew that Bill didn't have a lot of patience for players that didn't view football as being very

ST. LOUIS RAMS
(NFC, 14–2)

Offense

#	St. Louis	Pos	#	New England
88	Torry Holt* (6-0, 190)	WR	80	Troy Brown* (5-10, 190)
76	Orlando Pace* (6-7, 325)	LT	72	Matt Light (6-4, 305)
61	Tom Nutten (6-5, 302)	LG	77	Mike Compton (6-6, 310)
67	Andy McCollum (6-4, 295)	C	65	Damien Woody (6-3, 320)
62	Adam Timmerman* (6-3, 300)	RG	63	Joe Andruzzi (6-3, 315)
60	Rod Jones (6-5, 325)	RT	64	Greg Robinson-Randall (6-5, 322)
84	Ernie Conwell (6-1, 265)	TE	85	Jermaine Wiggins (6-2, 255)
80	Isaac Bruce* (6-0, 188)	WR	86	David Patten (5-10, 193)
13	Kurt Warner* (6-2, 220)	QB	12	Tom Brady* (6-4, 220)
28	Marshall Faulk* (5-10, 211)	RB	32	Antowain Smith (6-2, 230)
42	James Hodgins (6-1, 270)	FB	44	Marc Edwards (6-0, 245)

Defense

#	St. Louis	Pos	#	New England
72	Chidi Ahanotu (6-2, 285)	LE	91	Bobby Hamilton (6-5, 280)
66	Brian Young (6-2, 288)	LT	96	Brandon Mitchell (6-3, 280)
90	Jeff Zgonina (6-2, 300)	RT	93	Richard Seymour (6-6, 305)
98	Grant Wistrom (6-4, 270)	RE	98	Anthony Pleasant (6-5, 280)
58	Don Davis (6-1, 234)	LLB	50	Mike Vrabel (6-4, 250)
59	London Fletcher (5-10, 241)	MLB	54	Tedy Bruschi (6-1, 245)
52	Tommy Polley (6-3, 230)	RLB	95	Roman Phifer (6-4, 240)
35	Aeneas Williams* (5-11, 200)	LCB	24	Ty Law* (5-11, 199)
21	Dexter McCleon (5-10, 195)	RCB	45	Otis Smith (5-11, 196)
31	Adam Archuleta (5-11, 212)	SS	36	Lawyer Milloy* (6-0, 207)
20	Kim Herring (6-0, 200)	FS	34	Tebucky Jones (6-1, 218)

NEW ENGLAND PATRIOTS
(AFC, 11–5)

* Pro Bowl selection

SUBSTITUTIONS

St. Louis

Offense: WR - 81 Az-Zahir Hakim, 83 Yo Murphy, 87 Ricky Proehl; TE/LS - 45 Jeff Robinson; TE - 86 Brandon Manumaleuna; T - 50 Ryan Tucker; G - 73 Cameron Spikes; C - 65 Frank Garcia; RB - 24 Trung Canidate, 25 Robert Holcombe. **Defense:** DE - 77 Sean Moran, 91 Leonard Little; DT - 79 Ryan Pickett, 97 Tyoka Jackson; LB - 55 Mark Fields, 57 O. J. Brigance; CB - 23 Jerametrius Butler, 32 Dre' Bly; S - 30 Willie Gary, 41 Nick Sorenson. **Specialists:** K - 14 Jeff Wilkins; P - 4 John Baker. **DNP:** 12 Jamie Martin (QB). **Inactive:** 70 John St. Clair (T), 71 Kaulana Noa (G), 10 Marc Bulger (QB), 33 Justin Watson (FB), 51 Brian Allen (LB), 56 Dustin Cohen (LB), 38 Rich Coady (S).

New England

Offense: WR - 81 Charles Johnson, 84 Fred Coleman; TE - 83 Rod Rutledge; T - 76 Grant Williams; C/G - 67 Grey Ruegamer; RB - 21 J. R. Redmond, 33 Kevin Faulk; FB - 35 Patrick Pass. **Defense:** DE/LB - 55 Willie McGinest; LB - 51 Bryan Cox, 52 Ted Johnson, 53 Larry Izzo, 58 Matt Chatham; CB - 22 Terrance Shaw, 27 Terrell Buckley; S - 23 Antwan Harris, 26 Matt Stevens, 30 Je'Rod Cherry. **Specialists:** K - 4 Adam Vinatieri; P - 13 Ken Walter; LS - 66 Lonie Paxton. **DNP:** 11 Drew Bledsoe (QB), 97 Riddick Parker (DE). **Inactive:** 15 Jimmy Farris (WR), 48 Arther Love (TE), 61 Stephen Neal (G), 74 Kenyatta Jones (G), 19 Damon Huard (QB), 71 Chris Sullivan (DE), 92 David Nugent (DT), 25 Leonard Myers (CB).

important to them. All those guys were passionate about the game," New England director of player personnel Scott Pioli said. "We didn't win because we had a defense like the Ravens or an offense like the Rams. We won because we put together a football team."

On the first play of the final drive, Brady looked right, felt pressure around the edge from defensive end Leonard Little, ran up in the pocket, and delivered a 5-yard pass to Redmond just as Little was burying him from behind. "He's in the grasp and he makes an incredible throw," said Martz. "I felt like we had a chance of getting them three and out, I really did, because they hadn't moved the ball all game long other than that two-minute at the end of the half. Watching him from the sideline, I was shocked at his calmness. When the pressure of the game was on, it seemed like he was a different guy."

The second-down play was another check-down to Redmond, this time for 8 and a first down. When Brady got up to the line and spiked the ball, there were 41 seconds remaining. "They were playing max coverage and he had nothing but the dumps to the backs," wide receivers coach Ivan Fears said. "Brady took it quickly, which was important."

On second and 10 from the 30, Brady flipped the ball in the left flat to Redmond just behind the line of scrimmage. The Patriots were out of timeouts, so getting out of bounds was

St. Louis

Head Coach: Mike Martz. **Offense:** Bobby Jackson (coordinator, associate head coach, running backs), Al Saunders (receivers), Ken Zampese (wide receivers), Wilbert Montgomery (tight ends), Jim Hanifan (offensive line), John Matsko (offensive line, assistant head coach), John Ramsdell (quarterbacks), Henry Ellard (assistant). **Defense:** Lovie Smith (coordinator), Bill Kollar (defensive line), Mike Haluchak (linebackers), Ron Meeks (defensive backs), Matt Sheldon (quality control). **Special Teams:** Bobby April. **Strength:** Chris Clausen, Dana LeDuc.

New England

Head Coach: Bill Belichick. **Offense:** Charlie Weis (coordinator, running backs, quarterbacks), Ivan Fears (wide receivers), Dante Scarnecchia (offensive line, assistant head coach), Jeff Davidson (assistant offensive line). **Defense:** Romeo Crennel (coordinator), Randy Melvin (defensive line), Pepper Johnson (inside linebackers), Rob Ryan (outside linebackers), Eric Mangini (defensive backs). **Special Teams:** Brad Seely. **Strength:** Mike Woicik, Markus Paul (assistant).

almost as vital as the gain. This is when the Rams made a critical miscue. Nickel back Dre' Bly flat missed the tackle at the 35. Still, there appeared to be no way that Redmond could get out of bounds when rookie linebacker Tommy Polley hustled over and hit him with a clean shot from the side maybe 5 yards from the boundary.

With heroic effort, Redmond kept pumping his legs until he reached the sideline for an 11-yard gain to the 41. "This is a key play," St. Louis general manager Charley Armey said. "A lot of people don't think he went out of bounds. Had we kept him in bounds, it could have changed the whole outcome." Brady then stepped away from a blitz called by first-year defensive coordinator Lovie Smith and threw the ball away, setting up second and 10.

The Rams ran a zone blitz with defensive tackle Jeff Zgonina dropping into coverage. New England had the perfect play on, with Brown slipping across the middle from the back side on a shallow crossing route. When Brady stepped up to escape the rush, Zgonina made the mistake of charging forward 2 or 3 yards instead of holding his ground before falling back. The opening he left in the underneath coverage gave Brown a window to make the catch.

Brown eluded Bly and safety Adam Archuleta, then was able to slip out of bounds at the St. Louis 36.

"They ran a lot of Cover 2, but for some reason they dropped the tackle out and Troy Brown ran right by him," Belichick said. Once the Rams did that, he explained, they had no pass rush. Meanwhile, Brady was standing in the backfield with time, though not much, and gave it to Brown 2 yards downfield, who then turned it into a 23-yard run. "That was our offense," Belichick continued, "Three passes to the back, behind the line of scrimmage on most of them. One pass to Troy Brown 2 yards downfield. And a 5-yard pass to Wiggins. Brady did [well], but J. R. made a great run to get out of bounds. The pass to Troy really is an easy 2-yard pass. It wasn't like it was some in cut between three [defenders]."

Smith tried another blitz with 21 seconds left, but Brady beat it by throwing to Wiggins for a gain of 6. "Just a return route to Wiggins," said Belichick. "We said, 'Look, get it to him quick and go down so we have time to clock it.' That made it a 48 [yard attempt] instead of a 54." Brady marshaled his team at the line and caught the bouncing ball with one hand after his spike. Seven seconds remained and the Rams had no timeouts left to ice Vinatieri, not that it would have done any good.

As Vinatieri lined up for the kick, the Rams didn't have a good feeling. Armey had been scouting director for the Patriots in June 1996 when they signed the free agent out of South Dakota State. "One of the reasons we signed him was the fact he was a pressure kicker," said Armey. "I thought that when he walked on the football field that he would do like he has always done, which is make the kick."

Before the boot, Vinatieri was 24-for-24 in domes and 12-for-13 on game-winning boots, including 4-for-4 in 2001. This kick of 48 yards was 8 yards longer than any of his previous game-winners, but it hardly mattered. After all, he had beaten Oakland in the divisional playoffs at home in Foxborough with a 45-yarder at the end of regulation and a 23-yarder in overtime, both coming with 4 inches of snow on the field. "Adam hit a 59-yarder in warmups," said Belichick. "He was our best player. There's no other player that we would say was better at what they did than Adam was at what he did."

In later years, Belichick would describe the Rams as "certainly one of the great NFL teams of all time." A few months after the 2007 Patriots broke the NFL scoring record with 589 points, Belichick said that St. Louis offense had been every bit as good as the Patriots' juggernaut. His problem in the Super Bowl was figuring out how his defense, which ranked 24th during the regular season, could slow down an offense that had scored more than 500 points for the third year in a row (no other NFL team had scored 500 or more even twice).

Preparation for the Super Bowl had been reduced from two weeks to one due to a reconfigured schedule caused by the terrorist attacks of September 11. Therefore, Belichick drew heavily from the Patriots' 24–17 home loss to the Rams in Week 10. In that game, the Rams "just killed us," recalled Belichick, outgaining the Patriots, 482–230.

"We had 1,000 different blitzes up and we ran them all," Patriots outside linebackers coach Rob Ryan said of their first meeting in which Warner passed for 401 yards and was sacked only once. "So when we got ready to play them again, the Rams prepared for every blitz known to man and we played nothing but zone. Then we blitzed five times, rerouted their receivers, and knocked the crap out of Faulk when he was offset. The one week was to our advantage. Absolutely. If it's two weeks, you can prepare for everything."

Belichick was convinced that if Faulk, who rushed for 1,382 yards and caught 83 passes that season, could be waylaid coming out of the backfield, Warner's rhythm and timing would be knocked off-kilter. "So we set the whole game plan around Marshall Faulk," said Belichick. "Everything." The Patriots decided to play the run and set the edge with outside linebackers to make sure that Faulk didn't get outside on a perimeter run. Any time Faulk was offset or not behind the quarterback, or if Warner was in the shotgun, when Faulk released out of the backfield, they were going to hit him. If Faulk was offset to the side where the defensive ends were rushing, they would come out of their rush and hit him.

All week in practice, Belichick drilled his defenders ad nauseam to make sure they knew exactly where Faulk was on every play. "We put Faulk in a green jersey at practice and everybody else had yellow on. Every play when we came out of the huddle I'd be screaming, 'Where is he? Where is he?'" said Belichick. "By Thursday, [Mike] Vrabel turns around and he says, 'Hey, Bill. The son of a bitch is in a green jersey. Will you shut the f--- up?' said to myself, 'I think I'm getting through.'"

Warner did pass for 365 yards, but his passer rating of 78.3 was a better indicator of his mediocre performance. He was indecisive in the pocket despite having adequate protection and threw some wobbly passes that didn't have much on them, due in part to a right thumb injury that he suffered early in the game. He also missed too many open receivers, given his reputation for being one of the most accurate passers the game has known.

Defensive end Willie McGinest put most of the body shots on Faulk, but everybody on the New England defense participated in the mayhem. In the secondary, Pro Bowl wide receivers Isaac Bruce and Torry Holt were pounded by pesky Patriots. "Early in the game, Ike got slammed to the ground and got cracked ribs," Hanifan said. "He played the whole game. Our slot guys made big-time plays because [the Patriots] were raping the dog crap out of Ike and Torry. Neither one did much. But I don't fault New England one bit for doing what they did. What the hell, they weren't calling it." The Patriots were flagged three times for penalties downfield, one of which was declined.

Before the 2004 season, the NFL cracked down on illegal contact and holding by requiring officials to enforce existing rules more strictly. "I took tape from that game and didn't say anything and just showed it to the Competition Committee," Marti said. "Bill was right. If they're going to let you get away with grabbing the jersey and disrupting the route, as furious as you get, you've got to give him credit. It worked. It was the emergence of a great team. But there's some things that happened, particularly in the red zone, that should never have been allowed and obviously wouldn't work [today]."

Said Bruschi, "You have to realize what crew it is. But, in playoff football, I think there still is opportunity to play that way, even with the rule change."

A week earlier, the Rams had managed to stave off Philadelphia, 29–24, primarily because Faulk rushed for 159 yards and two touchdowns in 31 carries. In the Super Bowl, Faulk carried 17 times for 76 yards. Until the Rams' deficit swelled to 17–3, Martz had called merely eight first-down runs compared to 15 first-down passes.

Should the Rams have rushed more often? Hanifan thinks so, but said the coaches were so crushed that they never even discussed their strategy in the Super Bowl once the game was over. "When you think what they were doing, you say, 'Well, screw it, let's go ahead and give that ball to Marshall and let him take the game over,'" Hanifan said. Faulk wound up with 21 touches, four fewer than his average of 25 in his other 16 games. "The second half we would have given him the ball a lot if the game was in the balance or we were ahead," said Martz. "I thought we had a good game plan everywhere. We should have just executed better. Any time you have three turnovers where they get points, that's the game. It's just kind of the way it is. I've come to grips with that."

Afterward, Belichick acknowledged relief that the Rams didn't quicken the pace until the bitter end. "I made the comment that spring after the game that I kind of regretted not doing it," said Martz. "We were thinking about starting the game with our two-minute drill because every time it had been so successful against them."

St. Louis was leading, 3–0, after Jeff Wilkins' 50-yard field goal midway through the first quarter. The Patriots hadn't advanced beyond the New England 45 on its first four possessions when the Rams moved to a first down at their 39. What followed was the first of the game's red-letter play. "We showed them a front that we had been running and we moved late into the front we really wanted, the '46,' my dad's old defense," said Ryan, the son of Buddy Ryan. "They never noticed Vrabel was in a three-point stance. I believe the Rams made a hard call which slid the line to pick up the blitz and they turned the edge loose."

Vrabel, a linebacker let go in free agency by Pittsburgh that March, had his hand down over Rod Jones, a former part-time starter for the Cincinnati Bengals who had taken over for injured Ryan Tucker in the playoffs. Jones blocked down, leaving Vrabel with no one between him and Warner. Apparently stunned to see Vrabel leaping in his face, Warner threw the ball up for grabs in the vicinity of Bruce on a quick out. Cornerback Ty Law cut in front for the interception and was off for a 47-yard touchdown.

"It was just tragic," Martz said. "Just a one-man dog, something that was very basic and we had worked on. We had a new right tackle, Rod Jones, and he turns the guy loose on Kurt. If [Warner] knew [Vrabel] was hot he wouldn't have made the throw." The only one who might have picked up Vrabel was Faulk, but Bruschi took care of that by moving right, which drew Faulk toward him and away from the blitz. "Maybe it was one of my biggest plays that wasn't noticed," said Bruschi, who had become a starter in Week 11 after injuries knocked out Bryan Cox and Ted Johnson. "Sort of just thinking on the run."

Late in the first half, Warner found the 33-year-old Proehl open inside against nickel back Terrell Buckley for a 15-yard completion. Proehl saw his path impeded by dime safety Antwan Harris and tried to get down, but Harris managed to get even lower and then sprung at the trapped wideout. Out the ball bounced and was tracked down by Buckley, who returned it 15 yards to the St. Louis 40. "After the game Ricky was in tears," remembered Martz. "When you look at it on tape it was just a great play. He put his helmet right on the ball. Nothing you can do."

A 16-yard slip screen to Brown and two 8-yard gains set up first and goal with 36 seconds left in the half. The Patriots liked Patten on square-outs in the red zone, but after watching the St. Louis cornerbacks jump such patterns, the coaches decided to fake them out and have him go up the field. "We're out at practice at Tulane on Friday," Belichick said. "I was standing there talking to [football research director] Ernie Adams and we ran the play in practice. I said to Ernie, 'The way these corners play, they're going to jump that route.'"

Adams told Belichick, "If we're not careful, Aeneas Williams is going to intercept the sumbitch and run it back 100 yards." So Belichick walked over to Weis and said, "Charlie, run the out on the goal line and then turn it up and let's throw it in the back corner."

Patten turned cornerback Dexter McCleon and snared Brady's 8-yard pass with a twisting, acrobatic leap. It was New England's only offensive touchdown of the game. Momentum now was on the side of New England, which led, 14–3. "Even coming down from the press box we just knew, 'Man, we're going to win this thing,'" said Ryan.

From that point on, the Patriots generally played with five, six, and even seven defensive backs, anticipating that Martz still wouldn't run much, and presented faster, more agile athletes in an attempt to corral Faulk. "You think you're going to come out in the second half and run the ball and control it," said Martz. "Now you've got to make something happen."

St. Louis had the ball 11 times in the game, didn't have a single three-and-out, and gained at least 20 yards on every possession, yet five times the Rams crossed the 50 without scoring. On the 15 plays that ended those five possessions, 13 were passes and only two were runs. "We feel we're dominating the game, really, at the half," Hanifan said. "There's a screwup by the tackle and the fumble. I think we felt we were a better team than in '99. They were truly veterans now and in the same offense for three years. [The defeat] just makes you sick."

The Rams' first promising push (four plays, 45 yards) of the second half ended with a punt when Pro Bowl guard Adam Timmerman was trashed one-on-one by rookie defensive tackle Richard Seymour and Warner went down on a sack for minus-7. The second drive (five plays, 35 yards) ended when cornerback Otis Smith returned an interception 30 yards that probably would have been a 63-yard touchdown return if his teammate, Seymour, hadn't gotten in his way downfield. The Patriots had blitzed a fifth defender, strong safety Lawyer Milloy, so Warner was eager to deliver the ball. His target was Holt, on a slant against Smith, a 36-year-old who might have struggled breaking even 4.7 seconds in the 40-yard dash. Martz said Holt was too quick with his feet on the play and slipped on a slick field that had been painted by the NFL for cosmetic reasons. "The corner was off him by 5 yards when the ball gets there," said Martz. "I'm thinking it's going to be a 20- or 30-yard gain."

In Bruschi's view, Holt took a powder. "That was sort of the effect of being physical with them all game," he said. "Otis was about to get his hands on him and Torry basically anticipated that his route was going to be over with and stopped running." That was the third and final critical turnover for St. Louis, a team that won 14 games during the regular season almost in spite of its cavalier approach to a

ST. LOUIS	TEAM STATISTICS	NEW ENGLAND
26	Total First Downs	15
7	Rushing	6
16	Passing	8
3	Penalty	1
427	Total Net Yardage	267
69	Total Offensive Plays	54
6.2	Avg. Gain per Offensive Play	4.9
22	Rushes	25
90	Yards Gained Rushing (Net)	133
4.1	Average Yards per Rush	5.3
44	Passes Attempted	27
28	Passes Completed	16
2	Passes Intercepted	0
3	Tackled Attempting to Pass	2
28	Yards Lost Attempting to Pass	11
337	Yards Gained Passing (Net)	134
5/13	Third-Down Efficiency	2/11
0/0	Fourth-Down Efficiency	0/0
4	Punts	8
39.8	Average Distance	43.1
3	Punt Returns	1
6	Punt Return Yardage	4
4	Kickoff Returns	4
82	Kickoff Return Yardage	100
0	Interception Return Yardage	77
2	Fumbles	0
1	Own Fumbles Recovered	0
0	Opponent Fumbles Recovered	1
6	Penalties	5
39	Yards Penalized	31
2	Touchdowns	2
1	Rushing	0
1	Passing	1
0	Returns	1
2	Extra Points Made	2
1	Field Goals Made	2
2	Field Goals Attempted	2
0	Safeties	0
17	Total Points Scored	20
33:30	Time of Possession	26:30

turnover total of 44, the highest in the league. When Vinatieri kicked a 37-yard field goal, New England had extended its lead to 17–3.

Back came the Rams with a 12-play, 77-yard touchdown drive capped by Warner's 2-yard run on what Martz called "a sucker sneak that we kind of made up on the sideline."

ST. LOUIS

Passing	CP/ATT	YDS	TD	INT	RAT
Warner	28/44	365	1	2	78.3

Rushing	ATT	YDS	AVG	TD	LG
M. Faulk	17	76	4.5	0	15
Warner	3	6	2.0	1	5
Hakim	1	5	5.0	0	5
Hodgins	1	3	3.0	0	3

Receiving	NO	YDS	AVG	TD	LG
Hakim	5	90	18.0	0	29
Bruce	5	56	11.2	0	22
Holt	5	49	9.8	0	18
M. Faulk	4	54	13.5	0	22
Proehl	3	71	23.7	1	30
Robinson	2	18	9.0	0	12
Conwell	2	8	4.0	0	9
Murphy	1	11	11.0	0	11
Hodgins	1	8	8.0	0	8

Interceptions	NO	YDS	LG	TD
None	--	--	--	--

Punting	NO	AVG	LG	BLK
Baker	4	39.8	49	0

Punt Ret.	NO/FC	YDS	LG	TD
Bly	3/2	6	7	0

Kickoff Ret.	NO	YDS	LG	TD
Murphy	3	81	38	0
M. Faulk	1	1	1	0

Defense	SOLO	AST	TOT	SK
Polley	6	2	8	0
Archuleta	4	3	7	0
Fletcher	4	2	6	0
Wistrom	5	0	5	1
Little	4	1	5	1
Herring	3	2	5	0
A. Williams	3	2	5	0
Young	3	1	4	0
Zgonina	3	1	4	0
Ahanotu	2	2	4	0
Bly	3	0	3	0
McCleon	2	0	2	0
D. Davis	0	2	2	0
Canidate	1	0	1	0
Fields	1	0	1	0
Holcombe	1	0	1	0
Holt	1	0	1	0
Moran	1	0	1	0
Robinson	1	0	1	0
Warner	1	0	1	0
T. Jackson	0	1	1	0
TOTAL	49	19	68	2

NEW ENGLAND

Passing	CP/ATT	YDS	TD	INT	RAT
Brady	16/27	145	1	0	86.2
K. Faulk	0/0	0	0	0	0.0

Rushing	ATT	YDS	AVG	TD	LG
A. Smith	18	92	5.1	0	17
Patten	1	22	22.0	0	22
K. Faulk	2	15	7.5	0	8
Edwards	2	5	2.5	0	3
Brady	1	3	3.0	0	3
Redmond	1	-4	-4.0	0	-4

Receiving	NO	YDS	AVG	TD	LG
Brown	6	89	14.8	0	23
Redmond	3	24	8.0	0	11
Wiggins	2	14	7.0	0	8
Edwards	2	7	3.5	0	5
Patten	1	8	8.0	1	8t
A. Smith	1	4	4.0	0	4
K. Faulk	1	-1	-1.0	0	-1

Interceptions	NO	YDS	LG	TD
Law	1	47	47t	1
O. Smith	1	30	30	0

Punting	NO	AVG	LG	BLK
Walter	8	43.1	53	0

Punt Ret.	NO/FC	YDS	LG	TD
Brown	1/1	4	4	0

Kickoff Ret.	NO	YDS	LG	TD
Pass	3	85	35	0
Brown	1	15	15	0

Defense	SOLO	AST	TOT	SK
Law	7	1	8	0
T. Jones	6	1	7	0
Milloy	6	1	7	0
Phifer	5	0	5	0
Pleasant	5	0	5	0
O. Smith	5	0	5	0
Vrabel	3	2	5	0
Bruschi	4	0	4	0
McGinest	3	1	4	1
Hamilton	2	2	4	1
Cherry	3	0	3	0
Buckley	2	1	3	0
Seymour	2	1	3	1
Harris	2	0	2	0
Cox	1	1	2	0
Mitchell	0	1	1	0
TOTAL	56	12	68	3

Said Belichick, "Both guards pulled outside, leaving the center with Warner. Our guys reacted to the pull and he freakin' walked right in. [Martz] got us on it. I'd never seen a play like that before, but damn if he didn't run it again [for Detroit] against us [in 2006]. Two guys hit [Lions quarterback Jon Kitna] and knocked him back about 8 yards."

The score came two plays after Warner fumbled on a fourth-and-goal scramble from the 3 on a great play in long pursuit by linebacker Roman Phifer. The former Ram and Jet arrived August 3 for a modest signing bonus of $43,000 and ended up having a critical role, playing 97 percent of the defensive snaps. Said Belichick, "We would have never won that year without Phifer. He brought speed and athleticism to our linebacker position."

Safety Tebucky Jones returned the fumble 97 yards for a touchdown, but it was called back when McGinest was flagged for a blatant hold on Faulk as he tried to slip into the flat on the other side of the field. "We emphasized having contact on the receivers before they touched the ball and after they touched the ball," inside linebackers coach Pepper Johnson said. "Willie put the little extra into it and it got him in trouble. After that play, our athletes, our defense, it totally drained us."

The Patriots were able to blunt a later 55-yard march by the Rams when Warner held the ball too long after being flushed by Seymour and was sacked for minus-16 by McGinest, which led to a punt. But when the Patriots went three-and-out one more time, the Rams had the ball on their 45 with 1:51 left and trailing, 17–10. Then the Patriots' defense allowed a touchdown in 21 seconds flat.

Vrabel blew a tackle in the flat, enabling Az-Zahir Hakim 18 easy yards on a shallow crossing route. Hakim was injured, but backup wide receiver Yo Murphy then caught a swing pass out of the backfield and had the presence of mind to get out of bounds after a gain of 11. "As hard as we've been chasing those quick receivers and Marshall Faulk around, it's catching up on us," said Bruschi. "We're watching that clock."

On the next play, Proehl found himself wide open on a wheel route, and when Jones and backup cornerback Terrance Shaw missed tackles, he dived into the end zone for a tying 26-yard score.

"There had been a lot of discussion during the wee[k] about how we wanted to play it," Ryan said. "W[e] had worked it one way and then we talked and Bi[ll] wanted to go the other way. That was probably th[e] only mistake he made in the game."

As it turned out, the Rams scored too quickl[y.] There was too much time left, allowing Brady t[o] emulate Joe Montana, the star he had adored grow[-]ing up in San Mateo, California. "I see the sam[e] qualities in Tom that we saw in Joe," former Sa[n] Francisco coach Bill Walsh said. "Certainly wha[t] he did against the Rams is very comparable to any[-]thing else anyone has ever done. There were abou[t] five or six plays that he performed with total pois[e] and presence under the most extreme, severe pres[-]sure of the game. That separates him from just abou[t] every other quarterback."

For the Rams, there would be mostly disap[-]pointment on the horizon. "With the pieces we ha[d] in place and the comfort level we all had together[,] we should have been a dynasty," Warner said i[n] 2005. "As we prepared for that second Super Bowl, [I] think everybody felt we had something special, an[d] we thought we'd keep it together for three, four, o[r] five more years."

In February 2008, the *Boston Herald* reporte[d] that former Patriots video assistant Matt Walsh ha[d] taped the Rams' walk-through on Saturday, one da[y] before the game. The writer, John Tomase, recante[d] the story three months later. The NFL, after an inves[-]tigation, concluded that Walsh had been authorize[d] to be present while setting up equipment at the tim[e] of the walk-through. Walsh told Commissioner Rog[-]er Goodell that he was wearing Patriots' attire and didn't act in a "clandestine manner."

According to Matt Walsh, who was fired i[n] 2003, he did share some of what he saw with Bria[n] Daboll, a coaching assistant on the Patriots staff an[d] later the wide receivers coach. Walsh said he tol[d] Daboll that Faulk lined up as a kickoff returner an[d] how the Rams were using their tight ends, and tha[t] Daboll drew diagrams of formations based on hi[s] information. Daboll told the NFL that he didn't re[-]call the conversation with Walsh, which the leagu[e] said wasn't a rules violation, anyway.

For his part, Martz took the high road and ab[-]solved the Patriots of wrongdoing, saying, "I'm very confident that there was no impropriety. I believed Bill Belichick when he said there wasn't, and I took that at face value." Although acknowledging that there was no proof, at least one Rams official continues to insist that the walk-through had been taped by the Patriots.

For the 49-year-old Belichick, the Super Bowl was the culmination of a coaching career that began in 1975 as a gofer with the Baltimore Colts. At last,

he had stepped out from under the long shadow cast by Bill Parcells. Belichick called it his best single-game coaching job, and colleagues agreed.

"By far," concurred Ryan, his linebackers coach from 2000 to 2003. "Has to be. The Rams were as good as advertised. 'Greatest Show on Turf.' They just couldn't handle getting knocked off their timing, especially Faulk. Belichick put the whole plan together. He deserves all the credit in the world."

Top Ten Super Bowl Upsets

1. **Jets over Colts, III:** The Packers twice had held serve easily against the AFC, and Don Shula's supposed Colts juggernaut had just demolished Cleveland, 34–0, for the NFL crown. But the Jets had Joe Namath, multiple weapons on offense, and an established, resolute defense. Pro football was never the same after the Colts went down in flames.

2. **Giants over Patriots, XLII:** With 18 victories in hand, the Patriots needed one more for a perfect season and claim to the title of greatest team ever. Together with Randy Moss and Wes Welker, Tom Brady had rewritten the NFL record books—but the Giants weren't awestruck. Starting fast and finishing strong, the Giants handed Bill Belichick his most disappointing defeat.

3. **Patriots over Rams, XXXVI:** The Rams appeared to have it all: Kurt Warner, Marshall Faulk, "The Greatest Show on Turf," and a rugged defense. But Belichick found ways to disrupt their passing game, and the youthful Brady didn't make mistakes at the end. These aging, modestly talented Patriots epitomized the meaning of *team*.

4. **Chiefs over Vikings, IV:** The Chiefs waited three years for a chance to avenge their loss in Super Bowl I. Not only was the emotional edge leaning Kansas City's way, but so was the edge in talent. Steeped in the static concepts of the hide-bound NFL, the Vikings never had a chance.

5. **Broncos over Packers, XXXII:** Coach Mike Shanahan and his Broncos set the trap for the overconfident Packers, and they fell right in. Denver's blitzing defense consistently beat Brett Favre, and the Packers'

defense became too exhausted to stop Terrell Davis or John Elway.

6. **Giants over Bills, XXV:** Two words: "wide right." Phil Simms was injured and the Giants had struggled mightily late in the season. The Bills had a galaxy of young stars and were coming off a 51–3 demolition of the Raiders. It came down to a 47-yard field goal, and Scott Norwood's kick sailed right.

7. **Raiders over Redskins, XVIII:** League MVP Joe Theismann and the Redskins had amassed 541 points during the season, a league record that would stand for 15 years. The Raiders, however, could rush and cover with anyone in their era. It was no contest.

8. **Colts over Cowboys, V:** Five times a division winner, the Cowboys made the Super Bowl for the first time with a dynamite roster in 1970. Duane Thomas' fumble at the goal line opened the door for the aging Colts, and then Jim O'Brien kicked it down.

9. **Buccaneers over Raiders, XXXVII:** Raiders C Barret Robbins going off on a bender 48 hours before kickoff didn't help. Neither did the horrendous performance of QB Rich Gannon. Still, Tampa Bay's defense was awfully good, and the offense clicked at just the right time.

10. **49ers over Bengals, XVI:** The 49ers eventually went on to establish themselves as the "team of the 1980s," but in 1981 their 26-year-old quarterback was in just his first full year as a starter. The 49ers and Joe Montana did just enough in the first half to stave off the talented but mistake-prone Bengals. San Francisco's goal-line stand in the third quarter loomed large.

XXXVII

TAMPA BAY BUCCANEERS 48, OAKLAND RAIDERS 21

January 26, 2003
Qualcomm Stadium, San Diego, California

Several years after Super Bowl XXXVII, Jon Gruden was asked if he ever had occasion to discuss the one-sided outcome with Al Davis. "No, I can't say I've had any discussions with him since I was banished from Oakland," Gruden said. "Know what I mean?"

Previously, Davis had been only too happy to pick Gruden's brain in January 1996 during an interview for the Raiders' offensive coordinator job. The same thing happened again in 1997 when the Raiders' boss interviewed him not once, but twice, this time for the head-coaching job that eventually went to Joe Bugel. After Davis finally named Gruden to coach the Raiders in 1998, he gloated that "Chucky" turned out to be a great hire.

"But Al had a problem because Jon had become the face of the Raiders," an Oakland front-office source said. "His picture was all over the billboards in Oakland. The fans loved him. Jon did not want to leave the Raiders. It was just sad."

Despite his 40–28 record over four years and two strong playoff runs, Davis agreed to "trade" Gruden—with one year left on his contract—to the Tampa Bay Buccaneers on February 18, 2002. In return, Bucs owner Malcolm Glazer gave Oakland a pair of first-round draft choices, a pair of second-round draft choices, and $8 million in cash.

Eleven months later, the teams met in the Super Bowl at Qualcomm Stadium. For the first time, Gruden had the opportunity to control his own fate in a transaction with Davis. When the Bucs' 48–21 victory was complete, the 39-year-old whiz kid had put it to the 73-year-old owner and Hall of Famer. Gruden had every reason to gloat after his masterful coaching performance, just as Davis (if he could be honest with himself) might have wondered how he could have ever let a coach this good get away.

"It was the greatest game I ever coached in," Gruden said in 2006. "You're playing against your

Attendance: 67,603
Conditions: 81 degrees, sunny, wind WSW at 8 mph
Time of kickoff: 3:26 p.m. (PST)
Length of game: 3 hours, 50 minutes
Referee: Bill Carollo

MVP: Dexter Jackson, S, Buccaneers

former team and you're playing for a world title. It was certainly the biggest win I was ever associated with. We respected them. In 1999, Oakland beat Tampa Bay 45–0. But we had a great defensive team and we peaked offensively at the right time. We got after them."

The Raiders, a 3½-point favorite, had the league's MVP in quarterback Rich Gannon, four or five dynamic weapons, and a massive and formidable offensive line. While not nearly as good, Oakland's defense was competitive enough to rank 6th in points allowed, 11th in yards allowed, and tied for 8th in takeaways. "We expected to blow Tampa out," the Raiders executive said.

Three of Gannon's five interceptions were returned for touchdowns: 44 and 50 yards by nickel back Dwight Smith, and 44 yards by linebacker Derrick Brooks. Gannon called it the worst game of his long career. His counterpart for Tampa Bay, Brad Johnson, played within himself and didn't make a major mistake. Johnson's poise, as well as the 124 yards in 29 carries gained by journeyman running back Michael Pittman behind a much-maligned offensive line, enabled the Bucs to control the ball for more than 37 minutes.

"I was shell-shocked throughout the whole game," recalled Rod Woodson, the Raiders' veteran free safety. "I truly believe we had a better team, but it was basically a blowout. It was unexpected. Rich had a bad game, but we all had a bad game."

The Raiders played without Pro Bowl center Barret Robbins, a big, smart, and nasty eight-year

	1	2	3	4	Final
Oakland Raiders	3	0	6	12	21
Tampa Bay Buccaneers	3	17	14	14	48

SCORING SUMMARY

1st Quarter
OAK Janikowski, 40-yd. FG
TB Gramatica, 31-yd. FG
2nd Quarter
TB Gramatica, 43-yd. FG
TB Alstott, 2-yd. run (Gramatica kick)
TB McCardell, 5-yd. pass from B. Johnson (Gramatica kick)
3rd Quarter
TB McCardell, 8-yd. pass from B. Johnson (Gramatica kick)
TB Smith, 44-yd. interception return (Gramatica kick)
OAK Porter, 39-yd. pass from Gannon (pass failed)
4th Quarter
OAK E. Johnson, 13-yd. return of blocked punt (pass failed)
OAK Rice, 48-yd. pass from Gannon (pass failed)
TB Brooks, 44-yd. interception return (Gramatica kick)
TB D. Smith, 50-yd. interception return (Gramatica kick)

veteran. He went off on a bender Friday, showed up briefly that night, and then didn't get back to the team hotel again until late Saturday night after being drunk all day in Tijuana. According to one player, Robbins didn't even recognize coach Bill Callahan. On Sunday morning, Raiders assistant coach Willie Brown had Robbins up and in the parking lot running some sprints to see if he could play. A team source said Davis wanted Robbins in the lineup, but after intense discussion, Robbins was suspended by Callahan and spent the game in a San Diego hospital receiving treatment for his bipolar disorder. Adam Treu, a six-year veteran who had started 14 games in 2001, replaced Robbins.

"It hurt us a little bit," Rod Woodson said. "It was an efficient offense no matter who was at center. But when you have a guy who is controlling your offense from center for the whole year and then two days before the Super Bowl he's not going to play, now you've got to change your whole offensive line."

Due to extended pre-game festivities, the teams had to schedule their pre-game warmup 90 minutes before kickoff, about 45 minutes earlier than normal. "Our head coach and our head strength coach, Garrett Giemont, said that when we take the field

in pre-game warmup to really tone it down," linebacker Bill Romanowski said. "The Bucs came out at the same time but they were flying around. We were flat out there, kind of going through the motions. Being a big workout guy and understanding the body, I believe that hurt us. Here we are in the tunnel before the game and [linebacker] Eric Barton yells to Gie, 'Can we get fired up now, Gie?' And if you think about the game, we really didn't start playing until about the third quarter."

Regardless, Romanowski said the team was united behind Callahan. "We all believed in him," he said. "We did not waver at all. Truly, he stood behind us." Callahan, the 46-year-old son of a cop from Chicago's South Side, had been promoted from offensive coordinator in mid-March. Callahan selected the running plays while the new offensive coordinator, Marc Trestman, chose the pass plays standing next to him on the sidelines. Thirteen of Gruden's 17 assistants had remained with Callahan. The only Raider aide that accompanied Gruden to Tampa Bay was administrative assistant Mark Arteaga, and even then the Raiders threatened to file tampering charges with the league office.

Trying to hire a staff late in February was just one of Gruden's many obstacles upon his arrival in Tampa. Yes, he was taking over a veteran team that had reached the playoffs four times in the last five years, but he was replacing Tony Dungy, who had been as close as it gets in the NFL to being a beloved figure among his players. Glazer fired Dungy in January 2002, looking for a spark to ignite an offense that never ranked in the top 20 during his six seasons. Glazer tried and failed to hire Bill Parcells and Steve Spurrier, then was turned down by Jimmy Johnson and Steve Mariucci.

"There was some hostility over the circumstances that created the vacancy in the first place," Gruden said. "The players loved Tony, and it was easy to understand why. That was a very sensitive locker room. At our first team meeting I told the players, 'I'm going to be who I am and I'm going to earn your respect. Tony's done a great job here and he's handed me the torch. I don't know how I got here, but I'm here. We've got a lot in common, men. I have some controversy following me, too. But I know you guys will like this program. I know

OAKLAND RAIDERS (AFC, 11–5)			TAMPA BAY BUCCANEERS (NFC, 12–4)
		Offense	
81	Tim Brown (6-0, 195)	WR	19 Keyshawn Johnson (6-3, 212)
65	Barry Sims (6-5, 300)	LT	72 Roman Oben (6-4, 305)
73	Frank Middleton (6-4, 330)	LG	71 Kerry Jenkins (6-5, 305)
62	Adam Treu (6-5, 300)	C	62 Jeff Christy (6-3, 285)
79	Mo Collins (6-4, 325)	RC	60 Cosey Coleman (6-4, 322)
72	Lincoln Kennedy* (6-6, 335)	RT	67 Kenyatta Walker (6-5, 302)
88	Doug Jolley (6-4, 250)	TE	85 Ken Dilger (6-5, 250)
80	Jerry Rice* (6-2, 195)	WR	87 Keenan McCardell (6-0, 191)
12	Rich Gannon* (6-2, 210)	QB	14 Brad Johnson* (6-4, 226)
25	Charlie Garner (5-10, 190)	RB	32 Michael Pittman (6-0, 218)
32	Zack Crockett (6-2, 240)	FB	40 Mike Alstott* (6-1, 248)
		Defense	
99	DeLawrence Grant (6-3, 280)	LE	94 Greg Spires (6-1, 265)
95	Sam Adams (6-3, 345)	NT	91 Chartric Darby (6-0, 265)
97	John Parrella (6-3, 300)	DT	99 Warren Sapp* (6-1, 303)
91	Regan Upshaw (6-4, 260)	RE	97 Simeon Rice* (6-5, 268)
53	Bill Romanowski (6-3, 245)	SLB	51 Alshermond Singleton (6-2, 228)
58	Napoleon Harris (6-2, 255)	MLB	53 Shelton Quarles* (6-1, 225)
50	Eric Barton (6-2, 245)	WLB	55 Derrick Brooks* (6-0, 235)
24	Charles Woodson (6-1, 200)	LCB	25 Brian Kelly (5-11, 193)
20	Tory James (6-1, 190)	RCB	20 Ronde Barber (5-10, 184)
33	Anthony Dorsett (5-11, 205)	SS	41 John Lynch* (6-1, 220)
26	Rod Woodson* (6-1, 205)	FS	34 Dexter Jackson (6-0, 203)

* Pro Bowl selection

SUBSTITUTIONS

Oakland

Offense: WR - 87 Alvis Whitted, 84 Jerry Porter, 83 Marcus Knight; TE - 49 Jeremy Brigham; T - 66 Langston Walker, 74 Matt Stinchcomb; G - 70 Brad Badger; RB - 28 Randy Jordan, 47 Tyrone Wheatley; FB - 40 Jon Ritchie. ***Defense:*** DE - 75 Chris Cooper; DT - 92 Junior Ioane, 57 Rod Coleman; LB - 41 Eric Johnson, 51 Tim Johnson, 56 Travian Smith; CB - 22 Terrance Shaw, 23 Darrien Gordon, 38 Clarence Love; S - 36 Derrick Gibson. ***Specialists:*** K - 11 Sebastian Janikowski; P - 9 Shane Lechler. ***DNP:*** 3 Rick Mirer (QB), 8 Marques Tuiasosopo (QB). ***Inactive:*** 82 James Jett (WR), 78 Chad Slaughter (T), 63 Barret Robbins* (C), 1 Ronald Curry (QB), 30 Madre Hill (RB), 90 Kenyon Coleman (DE), 44 Keyon Nash (S).

Tampa Bay

Offense: WR - 83 Joe Jurevicius, 86 Karl Williams; TE - 80 Todd Yoder, 88 Rickey Dudley; T - 75 Lomas Brown; G - 74 Cornell Green; C - 77 Todd Washington; RB - 27 Aaron Stecker; FB - 30 Darian Barnes, 43 Jameel Cook. ***Defense:*** DE - 95 Ron Warner, 96 Ellis Wyms; DT - 93 DeVone Claybrooks; LB - 52 Nate Webster, 58 Jack Golden; CB - 26 Dwight Smith, 35 Corey Ivy; S - 23 Jermaine Phillips, 38 John Howell. ***Specialists:*** K - 7 Martin Gramatica; P - 9 Tom Tupa; LS - 66 Ryan Benjamin. ***DNP:*** 11 Rob Johnson (QB). ***Inactive:*** 84 Reggie Barlow (WR), 41 Daniel Wilcox (TE), 89 Casey Crawford (TE), 64 Dan Goodspeed (T), 10 Shaun King (QB), 90 Buck Gurley (DT), 59 Justin Smith (LB), 31 Tim Wansley (CB).

you'll benefit from it. I've seen work, guys, and together we ca do this.'"

Tampa Bay's top-ranke defense forced five turnovers i a 31–6 rout of the 49ers in th divisional playoffs. As a 4-poin underdog at Philadelphia in th NFC Championship Game, th Bucs took advantage of thre takeaways and rolled, 27–10, i spite of the 26-degree weathe. "That game was as big as th Super Bowl," defensive coordi nator Monte Kiffin said. "Whe we came off that win we though 'Wow, there's no way they're go ing to stop us now. If we ca go to Philadelphia and win i cold weather, we can certainl go to San Diego and play th Oakland Raiders.'"

Only one week separated th title games and the Super Bow. Each coach knew the other's of fense intimately, but Gruden' advantage was having coache Gannon. Three days before th Super Bowl, Gruden actuall quarterbacked the scout offens to give his defense the best pos sible simulation of Gannon' mannerisms, snap count, ter minology, hand signals, pum, fakes, and cocksure approach "Take absolutely nothing, noth ing away from the way the player played," Bucs offensive coordi nator and offensive line coac Bill Muir said. "On offense, w played way above anybody' expectations. On defense, w played our game. But mayb they had added confidence i terms of some of the mechanic of the offense that Jon presente to them. Regardless of how

Oakland

Head Coach: Bill Callahan. *Offense:* Fred Biletnikoff (wide receivers), Jay Norvell (tight ends), Aaron Kromer (assistant offensive line), Skip Peete (running backs), Marc Trestman (senior assistant), Jim Harbaugh (assistant), John Morton (quality control), Chris Turner (quality control). *Defense:* Chuck Bresnahan (coordinator), Mike Waufle (defensive line), Fred Pagac (linebackers), Ron Lynn (defensive backs), Chris Griswold (quality control), Don Martin (quality control). *Special Teams:* Bob Casullo. *Strength:* Garrett Giemont. *Squad Development:* Willie Brown.

Tampa Bay

Head Coach: Jon Gruden. *Offense:* Bill Muir (coordinator, offensive line), Richard Mann (wide receivers), Art Valero (tight ends), Michael Christianson (assistant offensive line, quality control), Stan Parrish (quarterbacks), Kirby Wilson (running backs), Jeremy Bates (quality control). *Defense:* Monte Kiffin (coordinator), Rod Marinelli (defensive line, assistant head coach), Joe Barry (linebackers), Mike Tomlin (defensive backs), Raheem Morris (quality control). *Special Teams:* Richard Bisaccia. *Strength:* Johnny Parker, Mike Morris (assistant).

"It's like in a war where guys would die for generals. That was Jon Gruden. Very few people in my life would I follow. I would follow Jon. Intelligence-wise, he's average to a little above. But he just has that something special. Even though he's 5-foot-9, all eyes go to Jon Gruden."

Raiders front-office official

much they changed, Jon knew how the quarterback would think."

Before the game, Gruden told his staff that on the first third-and-medium situation, the Bucs would score a touchdown because Keenan McCardell would burn cornerback Charles Woodson on a double move. Sure enough, McCardell did fool Woodson on a third and 5, but defensive end Regan Upshaw ran over left guard Kerry Jenkins on a tackle-end stunt and drilled Brad Johnson just as he threw deep to McCardell, who was 5 yards behind Woodson. The ball fluttered short to Woodson, whose 12-yard interception return to the Tampa Bay 36 led to Sebastian Janikowski's 40-yard field goal, which opened the scoring. The field goal came after defensive end Simeon Rice, a pass-rushing terror with 19½ sacks and eight forced fumbles in 19 games, beat left tackle Barry Sims inside for a clean 6-yard sack on third and 7.

Chuck Bresnahan, the Raiders' defensive coordinator, played press man coverages with a single safety, but also mixed in some zone blitzes. He was trying to hide weaknesses in his outside rush, where starting defensive ends Trace Armstrong and Tony Bryant were on injured reserve, and at cornerback, where Charles Woodson and Tory James were less than 100 percent. Each played with a surgically inserted steel plate to help heal a broken leg.

Gruden stressed a run-pass blend and unpredictability on his play sheet, fearing that first-rate defensive tackles Rod Coleman and Sam Adams might take advantage of his so-so middle trio of Jenkins, center Jeff Christy, and right guard Cosey Coleman if the Bucs weren't able to keep them honest.

When the Bucs got the ball back, the Raiders paid for the first of what would be their many miscues in coverage. On third and 10, Johnson found Joe Jurevicius running free for a 23-yard completion. "They had a zone blitz called and I don't think they were expecting we were going to pick that blitz up," Gruden said. "[Linebacker] Travian Smith made a mistake on the other side and Jurevicius ran right through a rush zone for a big play."

On the next play, Pittman gained 23 on a toss around left end. "We caught them in man-to-man coverage," said Gruden. "We had a little bunch crunch going and Keyshawn [Johnson] made a key block down on their right end. No one touched Pittman. It was a textbook-executed play." Martin Gramatica's 31-yard field goal tied the score, 3–3.

The Raiders, who rushed only 11 times for 19 yards, kept having protection problems. On their next possession, all-pro right tackle Lincoln Kennedy was knocked off his feet on a club move by left end Greg Spires and the result was another sack. In the waning seconds of the first quarter, Rice killed Sims again with an inside move on third and short, and Gannon had to scramble hard to the right.

Rather than just take the sack or throw the ball away, he made a lousy decision and tossed a floater back inside toward tight end Doug Jolley. Free safety Dexter Jackson cut in front and ran the interception back 9 yards to midfield. Oakland's defense stood firm once more, and Gramatica's field goal of 43 yards made it 6–3.

Just about every one of the Bucs' opponents that season thought it could make hay with the interior running game because Tampa Bay's defensive front seven was probably the smallest in the NFL. The Raiders didn't figure to make a living out of it, but with their wide bodies up front, as well as capable little Charlie Garner and big Tyrone Wheatley in the backfield, it wasn't as if Callahan and Trestman didn't have some options. "I think our game plan was kind of bad," Rod Woodson said. "We should have run the ball more. When you play a team that loves to play Cover 2, you've got to run 'em out of Cover 2. Make one of their safeties come down into the box. Once the safety is in the box, that's when you start throwing."

Raiders' radio analyst Tom Flores, the team's former Super Bowl–winning coach, said, "The game plan just killed them. It played right into their defense's hands."

After picking up just their second first down to start their fifth possession, the Raiders blocked a five-man rush with six and sent three wide receivers out into a secondary with Jackson as the single safety in the middle of the field. Before the ball was snapped, Tampa Bay strong safety John Lynch was calling out to Jackson, "Sluggo Seam," a play for which Gruden had warned them to be on the lookout. As Sluggo Seam unfolded, Gannon took a deep drop and fixed his gaze on Jerry Rice to the left. He pump-faked, shifted his body, and fired a 30-yard pass to Jerry Porter slanting into the numbers on the right side.

"All the big plays the Raiders made in the passing game were Gannon pumping and going back to the middle of the field on seams where the free safety had vacated," Gruden said. Typically in a single-safety scenario, the free safety is taught to overlap and play over the top to protect the corners, but the Tampa Bay defensive backs knew what Gannon was going to do. "We played a little bit

TEAM STATISTICS

OAKLAND		TAMPA BA
11	Total First Downs	24
1	Rushing	6
9	Passing	15
1	Penalty	3
269	Total Net Yardage	365
60	Total Offensive Plays	76
4.5	Avg. Gain per Offensive Play	4.8
11	Rushes	42
19	Yards Gained Rushing (Net)	150
1.7	Average Yards per Rush	3.6
44	Passes Attempted	34
24	Passes Completed	18
5	Passes Intercepted	1
5	Tackled Attempting to Pass	0
22	Yards Lost Attempting to Pass	0
250	Yards Gained Passing (Net)	215
7/16	Third-Down Efficiency	6/15
0/0	Fourth-Down Efficiency	0/1
5	Punts	5
39.0	Average Distance	31
3	Punt Returns	1
29	Punt Return Yardage	25
9	Kickoff Returns	4
149	Kickoff Return Yardage	90
12	Interception Return Yardage	172
1	Fumbles	1
1	Own Fumbles Recovered	1
0	Opponent Fumbles Recovered	0
7	Penalties	5
51	Yards Penalized	41
3	Touchdowns	6
2	Rushing	1
0	Passing	2
1	Returns	3
0	Extra Points Made	6
1	Field Goals Made	2
1	Field Goals Attempted	2
0	Safeties	0
21	Total Points Scored	48
22:46	Time of Possession	37:14

deeper and a little bit more conservative with ou corners. I thought he threw the ball anticipating h had looked the free safety off, but Dexter Jackso never left the middle." Jackson, who was chosen a MVP, streaked in front of Porter as the ball arrive for his second interception and ran it back 25 yard to the Oakland 45.

OAKLAND

Passing	CP/ATT	YDS	TD	INT	RAT
Gannon	24/44	272	2	5	48.9

Rushing	ATT	YDS	AVG	TD	LG
Garner	7	10	1.4	0	4
Crockett	2	6	3.0	0	4
Gannon	2	3	1.5	0	2

Receiving	NO	YDS	AVG	TD	LG
Garner	7	51	7.3	0	9
J. Rice	5	77	15.4	1	48t
Jolley	5	59	11.8	0	25
Porter	4	62	15.5	1	39t
Brown	1	9	9.0	0	9
Ritchie	1	7	7.0	0	7
Wheatley	1	7	7.0	0	7

Interceptions	NO	YDS	LG	TD	
C. Woodson	1	12	12	0	

Punting	NO	AVG	LG	BLK
Lechler	5	39	53	0

Punt Ret.	NO/FC	YDS	LG	TD
Gordon	3/0	29	17	0
Brown	0/1	0	0	0

Kickoff Ret.	NO	YDS	LG	TD
Knight	8	143	29	0
Cooper	1	6	6	0

Defense	SOLO	AST	TOT	SK
Barton	8	5	13	0
T. Smith	7	4	11	0
Romanowski	7	3	10	0
C. Woodson	8	0	8	0
R. Woodson	7	1	8	0
Dorsett	6	2	8	0
Coleman	4	1	5	0
James	4	0	4	0
Parrella	3	1	4	0
Harris	2	1	3	0
Cooper	2	1	3	0
T. Johnson	2	0	2	0
Upshaw	0	2	2	0
T. Brown	1	0	1	0
Crockett	1	0	1	0
Ioane	1	0	1	0
Treu	1	0	1	0
Gordon	0	1	1	0
Grant	0	1	1	0
Middleton	0	1	1	0
TOTAL	64	24	88	0

TAMPA BAY

Passing	CP/ATT	YDS	TD	INT	RAT
B. Johnson	18/34	215	2	1	79.9

Rushing	ATT	YDS	AVG	TD	LG
Pittman	29	124	4.3	0	24
Alstott	10	15	1.5	1	5
B. Johnson	1	10	10.0	0	10
Stecker	1	1	1.0	0	1
Tupa	1	0	0.0	0	0

Receiving	NO	YDS	AVG	TD	LG
K. Johnson	6	69	11.5	0	18
Alstott	5	43	8.6	0	16
Jurevicius	4	78	19.5	0	33
McCardell	2	13	6.5	2	8t
Dilger	1	12	12.0	0	12

Interceptions	NO	YDS	LG	TD
D. Smith	2	94	50t	2
Jackson	2	34	25	0
Brooks	1	44	44t	1

Punting	NO	AVG	LG	BLK
Tupa	4	38.8	43	1

Punt Ret.	NO/FC	YDS	LG	TD
Williams	1/4	25	25	0

Kickoff Ret.	NO	YDS	LG	TD
Stecker	3	67	27	0
D. Smith	1	23	23	0

Defense	SOLO	AST	TOT	SK
Kelly	5	3	8	0
Quarles	7	0	7	0
Rice	5	0	5	2
D. Smith	5	0	5	0
Barber	3	2	5	0
Ivy	4	0	4	0
Spires	3	0	3	1
Wyms	3	0	3	1
Brooks	2	1	3	0
Webster	2	1	3	0
Barnes	2	0	2	0
Howell	2	0	2	0
Jackson	2	0	2	0
Sapp	2	0	2	1
Golden	1	0	1	0
Jurevicius	1	0	1	0
Phillips	1	0	1	0
Singleton	1	0	1	0
Benjamin	0	1	1	0
Lynch	0	1	1	0
TOTAL	51	9	60	5

The Bucs went three and out, then the Raiders did the same. Tampa Bay's Karl Williams returned Shane Lechler's 42-yard punt for 25 yards to the Oakland 27. Then Pittman burst for 19 on a fake reverse to the 2, after which Mike Alstott barged in for the touchdown.

When the Raiders got the ball back, the Bucs misplayed a coverage and Garner was in the clear on the left side. The only problem was that he dropped the ball about 7 yards downfield. Kiffin estimated the gain might have been 40 to 50 yards, but not Gruden. "Knowing Garner like I do," he said, "he probably would have got 15 yards because we were fast as hell on defense."

Tampa Bay assumed command late in the first half with a touchdown drive of 10 plays and 77 yards. "It was as complete a drive as you could have, one of the great drives I've been associated with," said Gruden.

Pittman, an unrestricted free-agent acquisition from Arizona in March, contributed 20 yards in four rushes. "I wouldn't necessarily call him an instinctive runner," Muir said. "He's a very physical runner, sometimes maybe to his detriment because he'd rather try to run over somebody than around him. He plays as hard as any player I've ever been around."

As if the Bucs needed any help, the Raiders gave them 15 yards on three penalties. From the 5, Brad Johnson went to the line and, when Oakland showed press-man coverage, checked to McCardell on a fade-stop against Charles Woodson. Touchdown. "That seems to be a Raider thing, the most penalized team in the NFL," Romanowski said. "It's unacceptable, especially in big games. That drive really took the wind out of our sails."

Sluggish on offense dating all the way back to the 1980s, the Bucs came right back to begin the third quarter with another long (14-play, 89-yard) and exquisitely executed touchdown drive. Brad Johnson, athletic enough once upon a time to have played basketball at Florida State, scrambled for 10 on third and 2. Near midfield, the Bucs finally were able to match Jurevicius against strong safety Anthony Dorsett on a deep over route, and the completion was worth 33 yards. "We were playing man-to-man and [Dorsett] needed to keep inside leverage," Romanowski said. "He let [Jurevicius] beat him underneath and across the field."

A holding penalty on right tackle Kenyatta Walker shoved the ball back from the 1 to the 11, but Pittman gained 3 and then McCardell left Dorsett grasping in vain for his jersey on an 8-yard touchdown catch. "We got Keenan inside against Dorsett with a two-way go," Gruden said. "He ran the route perfectly for a wide-open score. We wanted to try to get after their safetyman, Dorsett. McCardell was a great receiver, he really was."

One play later, the margin swelled to 34–3 when Dwight Smith pilfered a short pass on the left side intended for Rice and went down the sidelines 44 yards to the end zone. "They were in a hurry-up offense and were running a lot of smash patterns," said Gruden. "Dwight Smith baited Gannon into throwing the smash to the wide side of the field. Just a great read. Our guys just made play after play after play."

Forty minutes into the game, Gannon had 72 yards passing and a 14.0 passer rating to show for his 26 dropbacks. In the final 20 minutes he would throw for 200 yards, finishing with a passer rating of 48.9, a dramatic drop from his 18-game rating of 98.7. It was, however, typical of what overmatched opposing quarterbacks were able to do against the Bucs in the regular season (48.4) and postseason (45.9).

"You had to throw Gannon off because Gannon was a great quarterback that year," Kiffin said. "I knew him when he was with the Minnesota Vikings. He was out of football [in 1994], and Jon rejuvenated his career and away he went.

"We were all so keyed in. You watch the tapes, Lynch is calling out some plays before they snapped the ball. I think we got a real good rush that day."

Later, with Warren Sapp clawing at his ankles, Gannon skipped away on third down and found

Porter behind Dwight Smith in the very back of the end zone. Judged an incomplete pass on the field, Oakland's replay challenge worked and it was ruled a 39-yard touchdown. According to Gruden, NFL director of officiating, Mike Pereira, informed him two months after the game that it should have remained an incompletion. How much did Gruden want to beat the Raiders? "That really ticks me off still today," he said.

Tampa Bay's lead fell to 34–15 early in the fourth quarter when a feeble snap by Ryan Benjamin and a lousy block by safety Jermaine Phillips enabled linebacker Tim Johnson to block a punt by Tom Tupa. The ball was recovered for a touchdown by cornerback Eric Johnson. The Bucs ate up more than five minutes with another long drive, but failed to score when Tupa dropped a perfect snap on a short field-goal attempt. Then Nate Webster, subbing for middle linebacker Shelton Quarles, who had suffered a concussion on the previous play, bit on a play fake. Rice got behind him at the 14 to haul in a 48-yard touchdown pass with 6:06 to play.

"You're never supposed to get down the middle against our Tampa 2," said Gruden. "[Webster] just blew the coverage. That's why he's a backup and why we sent him to Cincinnati. It's 34–21 and the crowd's in the game. We all know the Raiders can strike quickly. We got to get something done."

The Bucs made one first down and punted. One play after being sacked by Sapp, Gannon had all day and finally decided to take a shot in the middle to wide receiver Marcus Knight. Brooks, the NFL Defensive Player of the Year, made one of his patented deep Cover 2 drops, swooped in front of Knight to intercept the ball, and rambled down the sideline and into the end zone for a 44-yard touchdown.

With a minute left, the Bucs' defense still had to go back out. Brian Kelly, the left cornerback, was busy behind the bench trying to get his family down on the field, so Kiffin waved in Dwight Smith. On the fifth play, Gannon threw a short sideliner to Knight that was tipped ever so slightly by Spires. Smith's 50-yard interception return with two seconds showing completed the rout.

Not only was the defeat utterly devastating for Oakland, but it also signaled the end for a team that was over the hill. Callahan fell victim to his own onerous negativity in 2003, lost the team, and was pink-slipped after a 4–12 campaign. Gannon, Rice, Garner, Romanowski, Robbins, Kennedy, Rod Woodson, guard Mo Collins, defensive tackle John Parrella, and wide receiver Tim Brown never again played as well as they did in 2002. "That's the way it goes," said Gruden, his voice thick with sarcasm. "My heart is out to them."

Tampa Bay didn't fare much better in the next two seasons, stumbling to 7–9 in 2003 and then 5–11 in 2004. The Bucs did reach the playoffs in 2005 and 2007, but were eliminated at the wild-card level both times. Gruden was fired in January 2009, having not won a playoff game in his last six seasons, yet thanks in large part to him, the Super Bowl victory meant no one could crack jokes about the Bucs anymore.

"The thing I remember most is when we flew back to Tampa, the plane circled over the stadium," said Muir, who had been a scout for the Bucs from 1978 to 1981 under their first coach, John McKay. "All the lights were on in the stadium and the stadium was full. The rush was starting to diminish and all of a sudden we saw this and you go, 'Wow.'

"When we got on the bus, people were lined along the road the whole way to the stadium and traffic on the other side of the road was stopped. For some of the older players, like Brooks and Sapp and Lynch, this was something that had eluded them for a long time. I could see the cornerstone guys of this team really just reveling in it. The reception was just overwhelming."

XXXVIII

NEW ENGLAND PATRIOTS 32, CAROLINA PANTHERS 29

February 1, 2004
Reliant Stadium, Houston, Texas

For 59 minutes just about everything that was supposed to happen in Super Bowl XXXVIII didn't happen. Then Tom Brady and Adam Vinatieri, two of the many players whose miscues contributed to the game's sheer unpredictability and thus made it a joy to behold, did what they usually do in the clutch. Brady passed under pressure, Vinatieri kicked in the clutch, and the New England Patriots won another Super Bowl in the closing seconds.

How could anyone have known on a 59-degree night in Houston that both defenses would have been just trying to survive physically? Sweltering conditions took hold inside Reliant Stadium after NFL officials decided to shut the retractable roof about an hour before kickoff.

Would anyone suspect that Carolina's Jake Delhomme, after a horrendous start, would pick apart a heretofore impenetrable unit coached by defensive wizards Bill Belichick and Romeo Crennel that had mystified quarterback Peyton Manning and the Indianapolis Colts two weeks before?

Did people foresee New England's offensive line—with free-agent backups opposing Panther studs Julius Peppers and Kris Jenkins—not allowing a sack?

In the frantic fourth quarter, when the teams went back and forth to score on six of seven possessions, the only misfire came when Brady, in the red zone of all places, was guilty of a bad read and suffered an interception that could well have snuffed out his team's chances.

> "It almost felt like we were playing in a sauna. I remember throwing my jersey in my bag after the game, and it was just soaking wet, like we played outside in the rain."
>
> *Troy Brown, Patriots wide receiver*

Attendance: 71,525
Conditions: Indoors
Time of kickoff: 5:25 p.m. (CST)
Length of game: 4 hours, 5 minutes
Referee: Ed Hochuli

MVP: Tom Brady, QB, Patriots

In Brady's moment of failure, however, as he left the field after his horrendous throw was picked off in the end zone just when the Patriots were in position to deliver the dagger, Belichick saw something in his quarterback that he will always remember.

"Watch that play and watch Brady coming off the field," Belichick said a few years later. "It's one of the most determined looks of a champion that you'd ever want to see. I'll never forget it. No, he doesn't have his head down. Yes, he's made a mistake. But he's not down, and neither is anybody else. This is what a champion looks like right here at his worst moment, an interception in the Super Bowl."

Vinatieri's first half included a blown field-goal attempt from 31 yards and then another from 36 that was kicked too low and blocked. His Carolina counterpart, John Kasay, might never be forgiven in Charlotte for hooking his kickoff out of bounds at the worst time imaginable, just when it seemed as if the crowd of 71,525 and almost 150 million more watching on television were to experience the first overtime in Super Bowl history.

Of the 2,435 kickoffs during the NFL regular season in 2003, only 45 went out of bounds. Kasay, whose game-winning field goals of 49, 47, 47, and 31 yards were instrumental in the Panthers advancing to Houston, kept 77 of his 78 regular-season kickoffs and his first four on Super Bowl Sunday in the field of play.

Instead of having to start from their 27, as the Patriots had done on average after Kasay's four previous

	1	2	3	4	Final
Carolina Panthers	0	10	0	19	29
New England Patriots	0	14	0	18	32

SCORING SUMMARY

2nd Quarter
NE   Branch, 5-yd. pass from Brady (Vinatieri kick)
CAR   S. Smith, 39-yd. pass from Delhomme (Kasay kick)
NE   Givens, 5-yd. pass from Brady (Vinatieri kick)
CAR   Kasay, 50-yd. FG
4th Quarter
NE   A. Smith, 2-yd. run (Vinatieri kick)
CAR   Foster, 33-yd. run (pass failed)
CAR   Muhammad, 85-yd. pass from Delhomme (pass failed)
NE   Vrabel, 1-yd. pass from Brady (Faulk run)
CAR   Proehl, 12-yd. pass from Delhomme (Kasay kick)
NE   Vinatieri, 41-yd. FG

boots, they began from their own 40 with 1 minute, 8 seconds left and in possession of all three timeouts.

"I think it was overexuberance," Dan Henning, the Panthers' offensive coordinator, said a few years later. "He's trying to kick the ball out of the end zone. Everybody says, 'Well, that cost us the game.' Well, they still had to move the goddamn ball almost 40 yards to be in position to kick the field goal. . . . At the end, when we had moved it, they matched everything that we did. New England just happened to have the ball last."

Kasay, a left-footer kicker, hooked it out of bounds on the fly at the 15. "He was worried about Bethel Johnson," said Belichick. "No doubt about it. He was trying to kick it in the corner to his right, away from the return. Bethel Johnson had a lot of shortcomings, but as a kickoff returner he was dangerous."

The Patriots had few doubts as they ran onto the field to start the decisive drive. In Super Bowl XXXVI, Brady had passed them 53 yards in the final 1:21 to set up Vinatieri's 48-yard field goal that beat the St. Louis Rams, 20–17. "We saw the kickoff go out of bounds and everybody was jacked up," wide receiver Troy Brown said. "We had some of the same plays in our two-minute offense as we did back then, only with more firepower now. And [the Panthers'] defense was reeling at that point because their offense was scoring quick, too."

The last five plays, including a 20-yard completion to Brown that was called back because of his penalty for offensive pass interference, came out of shotgun formation. "We had considered going to a three-man rush because our rushers were tired," Carolina defensive coordinator Mike Trgovac said. "It's tough when he's back there in the gun and can see it all."

The opening play, with Brady under center, was an incomplete pass. Brady's first completion was to Brown, who turned a short pass on the right side into a 13-yard gain by dragging cornerback Ricky Manning Jr. for several yards. Brown was penalized on the next play, but on first and 20, Brady came back to Brown again for 13. "Tom was trying to throw to Deion [Branch] and I don't know if he saw me or not," said Brown. "I saw on the tape that one of their guys was behind me diving in for the interception. It was in my zone and I knew I could get it and I'm glad I did." With the clock running, Brady dumped the ball to tight end Daniel Graham for 4 and promptly called timeout.

Only 14 seconds remained. It was third and 3 at the Carolina 40. Coach John Fox discussed with Trgovac the idea of blitzing. In the end, the decision was made to play Cover 2 and rush four. A short completion would make Vinatieri kick a field goal of 50 yards or more to win. The Panthers would take those odds and the possibility that the crack field-goal unit of special-teams coach Scott O'Brien would block another kick.

Offensive coordinator Charlie Weis called a play the Patriots referred to as "Rock." The Patriots flipped the locations of their wide receivers on the right side, with Branch moving to the slot and Brown shifting outside. They did it hoping to match their best, Branch, on Manning, whom they considered Carolina's most vulnerable cover man, not to mention an annoying big mouth.

Brown ran a few steps at Manning and stopped. The Panthers refer to what the Patriots ran as a "China" route. The slot receiver, Branch, was running a post-corner or "7" route behind Manning and in front of safety Mike Minter, who was responsible for that deep half of the field. Brady wanted Branch because a completion to him would mean a shorter kick for Vinatieri. If Manning stayed back, Brady would have to dump it off short to Brown. Three weeks before, Manning, the rookie from UCLA, made the Panthers' defensive play of the year by intercepting the Rams quarterback Marc Bulger's pass in overtime in Carolina's shocking divisional victory in St. Louis. In the NFC Championship Game, he had intercepted the Eagles' Donovan McNabb three times.

Trgovac estimated that if Manning had played "China 7" properly, the ball would have gone to Brown and the gain would have been about 7 yards, giving Vinatieri about a 51-yard try. Instead, Manning played Brown in the hook zone, Branch made a sharp cut, and Brady put the ball on him for 17 yards before Minter had a chance to arrive. "Our corner kind of bit up on the 'China' route," Trgovac said. "It's a pretty common route that people throw against Cover 2. We really wanted to play that deep to short. He had done it right in that game and games before. . . . He just kind of sucked up on that 'China' route and gave up a deep throw."

Brady's expert 4-for-5 marksmanship gained 47 yards and left Vinatieri with an attempt from 41 yards. Although Vinatieri had made 14 game-winning kicks in addition to the Super Bowl XXXVI decider, there were perils for the South Dakota native to ponder during back-to-back timeouts. O'Brien, whose first NFL job was under Belichick in Cleveland in 1991, was long regarded by many of his peers as the best in the business. "We knew this was a really, really good field-goal rush team," said Brown. "All the guys on the sideline were holding their breath and saying their prayers." Not only that, but also the Patriots' top two long

CAROLINA PANTHERS (NFC, 11–5)		NEW ENGLAND PATRIOTS (AFC, 14–2)
	Offense	
87 Muhsin Muhammad (6-2, 217)	WR	83 Deion Branch (5-9, 193)
75 Todd Steussie (6-6, 308)	LT	72 Matt Light (6-4, 305)
78 Jeno James (6-3, 310)	LG	71 Russ Hochstein (6-4, 305)
60 Jeff Mitchell (6-4, 300)	C	67 Dan Koppen (6-2, 296)
65 Kevin Donnalley (6-5, 310)	RG	63 Joe Andruzzi (6-3, 312)
69 Jordan Gross (6-4, 300)	RT	68 Tom Ashworth (6-6, 305)
84 Jermaine Wiggins (6-2, 260)	TE	82 Daniel Graham (6-3, 257)
89 Steve Smith (5-9, 185)	WR	80 Troy Brown (5-10, 193)
17 Jake Delhomme (6-2, 215)	QB	12 Tom Brady (6-4, 225)
48 Stephen Davis* (6-0, 230)	RB	32 Antowain Smith (6-2, 232)
45 Brad Hoover (6-0, 245)	FB	31 Larry Centers (6-0, 225)
	Defense	
90 Julius Peppers (6-6, 283)	LE	91 Bobby Hamilton (6-5, 280)
99 Brentson Buckner (6-2, 310)	LT I NT	92 Ted Washington (6-5, 365)
77 Kris Jenkins* (6-4, 335)	RT I RE	93 Richard Seymour* (6-6, 310)
93 Mike Rucker* (6-5, 275)	RE I OLB	55 Willie McGinest* (6-5, 270)
53 Greg Favors (6-1, 244)	SLB I ILB	54 Tedy Bruschi (6-1, 247)
55 Dan Morgan (6-2, 245)	MLB I ILB	95 Roman Phifer (6-2, 248)
54 Will Witherspoon (6-1, 231)	WLB I OLB	50 Mike Vrabel (6-4, 261)
24 Ricky Manning Jr. (5-8, 185)	LCB	24 Ty Law* (5-11, 200)
23 Reggie Howard (6-0, 190)	RCB	38 Tyrone Poole (5-8, 188)
30 Mike Minter (5-10, 188)	SS	37 Rodney Harrison (6-0, 220)
27 Deon Grant (6-2, 210)	FS	26 Eugene Wilson (5-10, 195)

* Pro Bowl selection

SUBSTITUTIONS

Carolina
Offense: WR - 81 Ricky Proehl, 85 Kevin Dyson, 88 Karl Hankton; TE - 86 Kris Mangum; T - 71 Matt Willig; G - 72 Bruce Nelson; RB - 20 DeShaun Foster, 32 Rod Smart, 37 Nick Goings. **Defense:** DE - 96 Al Wallace, 97 Kemp Rasmussen; DT - 98 Shane Burton; LB - 50 Vinny Ciurciu, 52 Brian Allen, 57 Lester Towns; CB - 21 Terry Cousin, 29 Dante Wesley; S - 28 Colin Branch, 40 Jarrod Cooper. **Specialists:** K - 4 John Kasay; P - 10 Todd Sauerbrun*; LS - 56 Jason Kyle. **DNP:** 9 Rodney Peete (QB). **Inactive:** 80 Eugene Baker (WR), 47 Marco Battaglia (TE), 76 Tutan Reyes (G), 79 Doug Brzezinski (G), 16 Chris Weinke (QB), 94 Kindal Moorehead (DT), 31 William Hampton (CB), 42 Travares Tillman (S).

New England
Offense: WR - 17 Dedric Ward, 81 Bethel Johnson, 87 David Givens; TE - 88 Christian Fauria; G - 60 Wilbert Brown; RB - 33 Kevin Faulk; FB - 35 Patrick Pass. **Defense:** DE - 94 Ty Warren, 97 Jarvis Green; LB - 48 Tully Banta-Cain, 51 Don Davis, 52 Ted Johnson, 53 Larry Izzo, 58 Matt Chatham; CB - 22 Asante Samuel; S - 30 Je'Rod Cherry, 34 Chris Akins, 39 Shawn Mayer. **Specialists:** K - 4 Adam Vinatieri; P - 13 Ken Walter; LS - 46 Brian Kinchen. **DNP:** 76 Brandon Gorin (T), 19 Damon Huard (QB). **Inactive:** 85 J. J. Stokes (WR), 84 Fred Baxter (TE), 6 Rohan Davey (QB), 21 Mike Cloud (RB), 98 Anthony Pleasant (DE), 96 Rick Lyle (DE), 90 Dan Klecko (DT), 23 Antwan Harris (S).

Carolina

Head Coach: John Fox. *Offense:* Dan Henning (coordinator, quarterbacks), Richard Williamson (wide receivers), David Magazu (tight ends), Mike Maser (offensive line), Jim Skipper (running backs), Mike McCoy (assistant). *Defense:* Mike Trgovac (coordinator), Sal Sunseri (defensive line), Sam Mills (linebackers), Rod Perry (defensive backs), Ken Flajole (assistant). *Special Teams:* Scott O'Brien (assistant head coach), Danny Crossman (assistant). *Strength:* Jerry Simmons.

New England

Head Coach: Bill Belichick. *Offense:* Charlie Weis (coordinator), Brian Daboll (wide receivers), Jeff Davidson (tight ends, assistant offensive line), Dante Scarnecchia (offensive line, assistant head coach), John Hufnagel (quarterbacks), Ivan Fears (running backs). *Defense:* Romeo Crennel (coordinator, defensive line), Pepper Johnson (inside linebackers), Rob Ryan (outside linebackers), Eric Mangini (defensive backs). *Special Teams:* Brad Seely. *Strength:* Mike Woicik, Markus Paul (assistant).

> "All week long Belichick continued to rag our wideouts about not getting off the line. They were ready for that game. Everybody was waiting to line up on that little [Ricky] Manning and whip his ass—and we did. He got exposed."
>
> *Rob Ryan, Patriots outside linebackers coach*

snappers, Lonie Paxton and Sean McDermott, had suffered season-ending injuries in mid-December that led to the signing of Brian Kinchen.

Kinchen, 38, hadn't played in the NFL since he was with Carolina in 2000. When the Patriots didn't much care for several long snappers that had been brought in for a tryout, however, Belichick summoned Kinchen, who had been his starting tight end and snapper for most of his five-year tenure with the Cleveland Browns. "At least I knew he could snap," Belichick said. "But the rest of the year was pretty eventful on all placements."

Early on the afternoon of Super Sunday, Kinchen sliced his hand at the pre-game meal with what linebacker Tedy Bruschi said was a butter knife. "He had been a schoolteacher two months before that," Bruschi said. "We're thinking, 'Goodness gracious.' We went into the game just hoping he'd get it there."

Shortly after the team arrived at the stadium, head trainer Jim Whalen approached the head coach. "I think we have a problem," Belichick recalled Whalen saying. "I said, 'What are you talking about?' He said, 'Kinchen cut his hand at the meal.' I said, 'You've got to be kidding me. Jim, this is the Super Bowl. We don't f--- around here.' He said, 'No,

I'm serious. He's got it wrapped,' and he points over to him in the locker room.

"Kinchen comes over to me and says, 'Look, I'm not sure.' I said, 'You better. I'm going to f---ing kill you.' To me, at that point, you're playing. It's a finger. Stitch it up. Put a tourniquet on it. Whatever you want to do. It's a Super Bowl."

O'Brien massed Matt Willig, Jenkins, Shane Burton, Mike Rucker, and Al Wallace in the middle of the line and told them to push and vault. But there was never a doubt when Kinchen's snap was true— "The one good snap he made was on that winning field goal. The rest were a little shaky," said Belichick—the hold by Ken Walter was on the mark, and the kick by Vinatieri split the uprights on a hard, high trajectory to make the final score 32–29.

"If you've got to have one kick with everything on the line, he's the guy I want kicking it," said Belichick. The boot finished off the 14th game-winning drive of Brady's career and made him an easy choice as MVP. "Who would you rather have running a 2-minute drill in today's football?" Weis said. "I'd take Tom Brady 10 out of 10 times."

This was a game that had almost everything, including highly questionable decisions by Fox to go for 2-point conversions after the first two of the Panthers' three fourth-quarter touchdowns. If the Panthers had gone for extra points and succeeded, they would have been up, 24–21, and so there would have been no reason for the Patriots to go for the 2-point conversion on their next score. With Carolina's final touchdown, the Panthers would have led, 31–28, and Vinatieri's closing field goal would have just sent the game into overtime. "That was controversial," Patriots outside linebackers coach Rob Ryan said. "Why the hell do you go for 2 that early? That cost them the game."

Like Belichick, Fox's area of expertise was defense, and he also loved running tough training camps and contact practices during the season. The Panthers had two good running backs in Stephen Davis and DeShaun Foster, two dynamic wide receivers in Muhsin Muhammad and Steve Smith, one of the game's elite defensive lines, and some excellent athletes in the back seven. There was widespread respect in the league for their coaching staff, which had inherited a 1–15 disaster from George Seifert 24 months earlier. "I didn't think the game would be that close," Bruschi said a few years later. "Looking back, I see how good of a football team they were. I think we did play well just to win that game. If we were the best team in the NFL, there was no doubt that the next best team was them."

A 7-point favorite, New England was riding a 14-game winning streak despite playing a murderous schedule. The victory in the Super Bowl gave the Patriots a 10–0 record against teams that finished with winning records, an NFL record. Players that started for New England missed a total of 103 games due to injury, more than any team in 2003 other than Oakland, Houston, Cleveland, and Atlanta. None of those teams won more than five games, while the Patriots went 14–2.

The Patriots were starting three backups on an offensive line that, even at the beginning of the season, didn't have a player ranked near the top of his position. Antowain Smith probably would have fallen somewhere in the low 20s if you were to rank all featured backs in the NFL. The majority of teams in the league had a wide receiver better than any of the five used by New England. Its tight ends were solid but weren't real weapons.

Brady had physical limitations and was capable of having ordinary games; his passer rating of 85.9 ranked 10th in the NFL. The Patriots' defensive line was fairly strong, but only Belichick would be content with Bobby Hamilton as one of the starters. Their linebackers were broken-down old warriors whom few teams would want. Although the entire league would have killed to have Ty Law playing cornerback, many teams thought strong safety Rodney Harrison was finished before he signed with New England as a "street" free agent in March 2003. Additionally, cornerback Tyrone Poole was old and small, and rookie Eugene Wilson had never played anything except cornerback until he was moved to free safety as the replacement for Pro Bowler Lawyer Milloy, a team leader who was waived September 2.

New England's special teams could have been described as extraordinary, were it not for the fact that Walter was a substandard punter and the long-snapping situation was a mess.

Shortly before kickoff, Belichick turned to his longtime friend and advisor Ernie Adams and said, "Can you believe we're here? We can't run the ball, we can't punt the ball, and we can't snap for field goals."

Experts forecast a defensive struggle, and for good reason. Davis was the only offensive player in the game selected for the Pro Bowl. The Belichick-Crennel duo, which had played almost all nickel against the Colts in the AFC Championship Game, were so determined to stop Davis that the Patriots played base 3-4 almost the entire game. The Patriots, a mere 27th in rushing, had to settle for 26-for-83 yards (3.2) from Antowain Smith.

"What I told the team for two weeks was set the edge in the running game and make the backs run back into Ted Washington," said Belichick. "Henning's a good running coach so we knew they'd have a lot of different running schemes for us, but Ted Washington was the ultimate nose tackle. And don't get beat by Steve Smith over the top. We had a lot of respect for [Muhsin] Muhammad but we felt like Smith was the guy. We played a lot of man-free with a five-man rush and we played two-deep zone. We mixed those coverages probably 80 percent of the time."

The game turned into a spellbinding shootout, with 61 points, 868 yards, 46 first downs, and passer ratings of 113.6 for Delhomme and 100.5 for Brady. What happened? Besides having two hot quarterbacks, many participants later agreed that the insufferable heat inside Reliant took an enormous toll on players, especially those on defense.

Neither team could score until 3:05 remained in the first half, but then 24 points went up by halftime. The Patriots broke the 0–0 tie when linebacker Mike Vrabel beat left tackle Todd Steussie, stripped Delhomme, and defensive end Richard Seymour recovered at the Carolina 20. Brady smartly ran for 12 against a three-man rush on third and 5. On the next play, Brady beat an all-out blitz with a nifty play-fake to Antowain Smith and threw a 5-yard touchdown pass to Branch behind cornerback Reggie Howard.

At this point, Delhomme was 1-for-9 for 1 yard and had been sacked three times. In a word, he looked awful. "Yeah, but he's that way," said Ryan. "We were scared of that guy. We wanted him to stay in the pocket because he's so dangerous on the move." Delhomme's penchant for finding receivers with wobbly passes started with a 13-yarder to Ricky Proehl and a 23-yarder to Muhammad. Then, on third and 10, Delhomme threw a surgically placed takeoff route that Steve Smith flagged down at the 3 for a 39-yard touchdown. "Blew right by Tyrone Poole," Ryan said. "We were trying to give him late help over the top but it was a little too late." Wilson had forgotten one of Belichick's two defensive objectives and was mostly at fault by being out of position.

Only 59 seconds were left in the half, but the Patriots weren't done. On their third play, the Patriots picked up a six-man rush, giving Brady time to reset in the pocket. This time, Minter bit on a curl route by Brown, and Branch made a sensational catch over his head for 52 yards. "It was a zone pressure that we called and we just blew the coverage," Trgovac said. "That play hurt us." The Panthers talked for two weeks about defending New England's play-action passes in the red zone. On third and 1, Brady faked to Kevin Faulk and flipped to David Givens, who was wide open behind a zone for another 5-yard score.

Still, the half wouldn't end. A poor squib kick by Vinatieri was fielded deftly by tight end Kris Mangum and returned 12 yards to the Carolina 47 with 12 seconds showing. When tight end Jermaine Wiggins wham-blocked backup nose tackle Ty Warren and fullback Brad Hoover occupied Bruschi in

the hole, Davis burst through for 21 yards. "The only run they hit on us was when we took Ted Washington out for a play and they hit a wham on us," said Ryan. "Gave them a field goal."

Time expired as Kasay drilled it from 50. "We go in and we're all pissed off we gave up 10 points," said Belichick. "We should have never given that field goal up on that 'wham.' That was so stupid."

By halftime, all the players were sagging. "I remember at halftime, which is longer at the Super Bowl, I barely got to make any adjustments because most of the players were on the IV table," Trgovac said. "That never had happened to us. Part of it was we had a bunch of young guys and they spent a lot of [nervous] energy standing there before the game watching this girl sing and this guy sing."

Energized from the lengthy break (during which pop star Janet Jackson's breast was exposed and a streaker wearing only a jockstrap held up the second-half kickoff), the teams played to a scoreless third quarter, before the 4-hour-plus marathon exhausted the defenses down the stretch. New England, the oldest team in the NFL with 15 players over the age of 30, became so fatigued that its defense allowed touchdown drives measuring 81, 90, and 80 yards in the fourth quarter.

"Once you close a roof in a structure that big the air conditioning has to get going," said Bruschi. "I think they closed the roof because one of the pregame acts, some rock band, wouldn't go out there unless it was closed. In the second half it got downright steamy in there. People were stripping off their clothes. Nobody could stop anybody in the fourth quarter. It just got so hot, so humid for February."

The Patriots' lead remained at 14–10 until Antowain Smith powered behind Seymour's block for a 2-yard touchdown 11 seconds into the fourth quarter, increasing it to 21–10. The Panthers were well aware that New England used just one running play on the goal line, but still they couldn't stop it. Three plays earlier, Graham worked free down the middle behind linebackers Dan Morgan and Will Witherspoon for a 33-yard catch, when Trgovac said the Panthers checked coverages just before the snap though not all of the players picked it up.

Trailing by 11, Fox went to the no-huddle for the first time and Delhomme caught fire. Some of

Delhomme's completions were sloppy throws that inexplicably found their way to receivers when defenders were all around. Other times, he was able to buy time against a rush that had little oomph, and then thread the needle. "I give him a ton of credit," said Belichick. "I'm telling you, our thing was, make Delhomme beat us. He almost did. I gained so much respect for him in that game."

Belichick also blamed himself for not keeping defensive tackle Dan Klecko among his 45 active players. "Truth is, I thought I did a crappy job," said Belichick. "I made a really stupid mistake. I cut corners on how many defensive linemen to carry. I should have known better because it's such a long game because of all the celebration and extravaganza. Your players wear down, especially the defensive linemen. They're the first to go."

After completing three passes for 53 yards, Delhomme handed the ball to Foster from shotgun on second and 10 at the Carolina 33. "We told Jake to go to the line because the base defense was in there against our three-wide package," said Henning. "Against three wides they moved the outside linebackers out. So we took a chance at running this little trap play." It was well blocked at the line, especially by pulling guard Kevin Donnalley against linebacker Roman Phifer. Poole was just about to make the tackle when he was blocked by Steve Smith. When Wilson whiffed at the 25, Foster high-stepped untouched to the end zone. Delhomme's 2-point pass to Muhammad was incomplete and the score remained, 21–16.

New England retaliated with an efficient drive of its own, moving 64 yards to set up a third-and-9 at the Carolina 9. Brady faked a handoff, dropped back five steps, but then couldn't locate his primary receiver. "I was wide open in the back of the end zone in the center of the field," Brown said. "His next read was to go to [Christian] Fauria. As he threw it, it got away from him and kind of floated in the air and came right down in the hands of Reggie Howard. At that point it was like, 'Man, what else can we do wrong?' That interception cost us a chance to close it out." The Panthers had gone against their red-zone tendencies and played zone. Howard baited Brady, then drifted back for the easy interception.

TEAM STATISTICS

CAROLINA		NEW ENGLAND
17	Total First Downs	29
3	Rushing	7
12	Passing	19
2	Penalty	3
387	Total Net Yardage	481
53	Total Offensive Plays	83
7.3	Avg. Gain per Offensive Play	5.8
16	Rushes	35
92	Yards Gained Rushing (Net)	127
5.8	Average Yards per Rush	3.6
33	Passes Attempted	48
16	Passes Completed	32
0	Passes Intercepted	1
2	Tackled Attempting to Pass	0
4	Yards Lost Attempting to Pass	0
295	Yards Gained Passing (Net)	354
4/12	Third-Down Efficiency	8/17
0/0	Fourth-Down Efficiency	1/1
7	Punts	5
44.3	Average Distance	34.6
1	Punt Returns	5
2	Punt Return Yardage	42
6	Kickoff Returns	4
116	Kickoff Return Yardage	78
12	Interception Return Yardage	0
1	Fumbles	1
0	Own Fumbles Recovered	1
0	Opponent Fumbles Recovered	1
12	Penalties	8
73	Yards Penalized	60
4	Touchdowns	4
1	Rushing	1
3	Passing	3
0	Returns	0
2	Extra Points Made	5
1	Field Goals Made	1
1	Field Goals Attempted	3
0	Safeties	0
29	Total Points Scored	32
21:02	Time of Possession	38:58

Just more than seven minutes remained when Delhomme backed out from under center on third and 10. He took a five-step drop and, with the Patriots' rush basically null and void, waited a full 6.2 seconds before putting just about everything he had on a ball to Muhammad on a sideline take-off route. Wilson appeared to have either froze or

CAROLINA

Passing	CP/ATT	YDS	TD	INT	RAT
Delhomme	16/33	323	3	0	113.6

Rushing	ATT	YDS	AVG	TD	LG
Davis	13	49	3.8	0	21
Foster	3	43	14.3	1	33t

Receiving	NO	YDS	AVG	TD	LG
Muhammad	4	140	35.0	1	85t
S. Smith	4	60	15.0	1	39t
Proehl	4	71	17.8	1	31
Wiggins	2	21	10.5	0	15
Foster	1	9	9.0	0	9
Mangum	1	2	2.0	0	2

Interceptions	NO	YDS	LG	TD
Howard	1	12	12	0

Punting	NO	AVG	LG	BLK
Sauerbrun	7	44.3	51	0

Punt Ret.	NO/FC	YDS	LG	TD
S. Smith	1/1	2	2	0

Kickoff Ret.	NO	YDS	LG	TD
Smart	4	74	22	0
S. Smith	1	30	30	0
Mangum	1	12	12	0

Defense	SOLO	AST	TOT	SK
Morgan	11	7	18	0
Minter	9	5	14	0
Witherspoon	7	6	13	0
Cousin	3	4	7	0
Howard	6	0	6	0
Manning	4	2	6	0
Wallace	3	3	6	0
Grant	3	2	5	0
Burton	3	2	5	0
Favors	3	0	3	0
Jenkins	3	0	3	0
Buckner	1	2	3	0
Cooper	1	2	3	0
Peppers	2	0	2	0
Rucker	1	1	2	0
Allen	1	0	1	0
Branch	1	0	1	0
Hankton	1	0	1	0
Hoover	1	0	1	0
Rasmussen	1	0	1	0
Sauerbrun	1	0	1	0
Smart	1	0	1	0
Steussie	1	0	1	0
Ciurciu	0	1	1	0
Wesley	0	1	1	0
Willig	0	1	1	0
TOTAL	68	39	107	0

NEW ENGLAND

Passing	CP/ATT	YDS	TD	INT	RAT
Brady	32/48	354	3	1	100.5

Rushing	ATT	YDS	AVG	TD	LG
A. Smith	26	83	3.2	1	9
Faulk	6	42	7.0	0	23
Brady	2	12	6.0	0	12
Brown	1	-10	-10.0	0	-10

Receiving	NO	YDS	AVG	TD	LG
Branch	10	143	14.3	1	52
Brown	8	76	9.5	0	13
Givens	5	69	13.8	1	25
Graham	4	46	11.5	0	33
Faulk	4	19	4.8	0	7
Vrabel	1	1	1.0	1	1t

Interceptions	NO	YDS	LG	TD
None	--	--	--	--

Punting	NO	AVG	LG	BLK
Walter	5	34.6	51	0

Punt Ret.	NO/FC	YDS	LG	TD
Brown	4/1	40	28	0
Branch	1/0	0	0	0

Kickoff Ret.	NO	YDS	LG	TD
B. Johnson	4	78	29	0

Defense	SOLO	AST	TOT	SK
Harrison	8	1	9	1
Vrabel	4	2	6	2
Law	5	0	5	0
Phifer	4	1	5	0
Hamilton	3	1	4	0
Bruschi	2	2	4	0
McGinest	1	3	4	1
Poole	1	2	3	0
Chatham	2	0	2	0
Seymour	2	0	2	0
Akins	1	0	1	0
Cherry	1	0	1	0
Izzo	1	0	1	0
B. Johnson	1	0	1	0
Koppen	1	0	1	0
Mayer	1	0	1	0
Vinatieri	1	0	1	0
TOTAL	39	12	51	4

underestimated Delhomme's arm strength. Muhammad made the catch 51 yards downfield at the 34, kept running, and stiff-armed Wilson into submission at the 15 for an 85-yard touchdown. Wilson lay writhing on the turf after suffering a torn groin and had to be replaced by Shawn Mayer, a rookie free agent from Penn State with two tackles in 11 games. "Not only did he miss the tackle but he got dragged around, he got stiff-armed, and he got hurt," said Ryan. "We had a million rookies playing for us in that game and every one of them played like s----." Fox attempted to extend his 22–21 lead, but another 2-point pass failed.

Back came the Patriots, and after 11 plays they had regained the lead, 29–22, on Brady's 1-yard pass to Vrabel and a 2-point run by Faulk. The salient play occurred on third and 9 at the Carolina 21 when Givens beat Manning at the line, outmuscled him at the break point, and snatched an 18-yard dart from Brady along the sideline. On second down, Weis inserted Vrabel as a tight end on the left side. Covered man-to-man by Wallace, Vrabel ran a crossing pattern just as Graham crossed with him from the right. When Peppers, who was trying to chase Graham, accidentally crashed into Wallace, Vrabel was left all by himself in the end zone for the touchdown.

Brady acknowledged that the Panthers had harassed him more than any opponent all season. Still, he was not sacked; in fact, he hadn't been sacked during the entire postseason. Season-ending injuries eliminated center Mike Compton in Week 2, right tackle Adrian Klemm in Week 3, and left guard Damien Woody in the divisional playoff game. The replacements were left guard Russ Hochstein, a journeyman with one regular-season start before the AFC title game; center Dan "Kops" Koppen, a fifth-round draft choice who made the all-rookie team; and right tackle Tom Ashworth, a third-year free agent like Hochstein who had never started a game until Klemm went down.

"Remember [Warren] Sapp said Carolina would kick the dog out of Hochstein," running backs coach Ivan Fears said. "He was just a true grunt with a great motor that wouldn't quit. As long as we didn't expose him he was going to be all right. 'Kops' was real good and Ashworth had a very good season."

Starting from its 20, Carolina revisited the end zone 1:43 later and tied the score. On the first play, Harrison suffered a broken right forearm. He stayed in for another snap, but then had to leave in excruciating pain. His replacement, Chris Akins, seldom played from scrimmage for four different teams in a five-year career as a special teamer. In this instance, Belichick, Crennel, and secondary coach Eric Mangini failed to have their backup safeties ready to function properly.

Proehl went in motion and made a 31-yard catch inside when Delhomme had all day with Mayer being the closest defender. "We're standing out there with just a patchwork secondary," Belichick said. "To me, we couldn't stop them. What I was worried about, they hit a couple passes and now it's down to 30 seconds. Either we make a play, or they tie it and we got a chance to come back." He implored Crennel, "All-out blitz 'em. Send everybody we got."

On third and 8, the Patriots blitzed again, and Proehl was wide open in the middle for a 12-yard touchdown. One of the backup safeties got the check on the touchdown, but the other one didn't. Nickel back Asante Samuel and Mayer were the guilty parties. "Lo and behold, there's Ricky Proehl all alone in the end zone," said Bruschi. "He tied the game [Super Bowl XXXVI] up in New Orleans and he tied the game up in Houston. Jake's confidence is sky high and we're scrambling a little bit, holding on."

But in this fourth quarter of no defense, Carolina had left an eternity (1:08) on the clock. When Kasay flubbed the kickoff, Manning made a critical error of judgment in coverage, and none of the Panthers' defenders or coaches could make a play or find a strategic solution, the Patriots became champions once again in wonderful style. Two of the Patriots stalwarts offered far different summations.

First, Bruschi: "There are a number of guys that could have got the MVP in New Orleans but this was Brady's game. He led us down there. This is where he really established himself as being on the threshold of being one of the greatest quarterbacks ever."

Now to you, Brown: "People still talk about this game and they'll probably talk about it 50, 60 years from now. People say it was the best Super Bowl ever and I probably have to agree with them. Whoever got the ball last ended up winning."

XXXIX

NEW ENGLAND PATRIOTS 24, PHILADELPHIA EAGLES 21

February 6, 2005
Alltel Stadium, Jacksonville, Florida

Attendance: 78,125
Conditions: 59 degrees, clear, wind N at 12 mph
Time of kickoff: 6:38 p.m. (EST)
Length of game: 3 hours, 38 minutes
Referee: Terry McAulay

MVP: Deion Branch, WR, Patriots

The New England Patriots didn't give away playoff games. To beat them during the pinnacle of the Bill Belichick era, an opponent needed not only top-shelf players and coaching but also precise execution and nerves of steel. The Philadelphia Eagles simply weren't sharp enough to upset the Patriots in Super Bowl XXXIX. Their 24–21 defeat was the result of making one mistake too many.

They tried. Lord knows, the Eagles tried. Wide receiver Terrell Owens played 63 of 72 snaps only six and a half weeks after undergoing surgery to repair a fractured fibula and torn ankle ligament in his right leg. There was no quit in Philadelphia, which beat the 7-point spread. But a 4-to-1 deficit in turnovers and questionable clock management in the fourth quarter prevented it from beating a team as resourceful as New England and thereby claiming its first Lombardi Trophy.

It was little more than a mundane performance for New England, at least by its impossibly high standards. In truth, the Patriots' red-letter moments in 2004 were their divisional playoff blowout of the prolific Indianapolis Colts and their demolition of the rough-and-tumble, once-beaten Pittsburgh Steelers in the AFC Championship Game at Heinz Field.

"We beat the Colts, Pittsburgh had bombed us earlier in the year and we beat them, and Philadelphia was the best team in the NFC all season," Belichick said. "Even though we lost two games we beat those teams the second time around. We took on all comers. I'll leave the historical comparisons to everyone else."

By winning their third Super Bowl championship in four years (all by the margin of a field goal), the Patriots became just the fourth team since the NFL initiated playoffs in 1933 to do so. The others were the Chicago Bears (1940–1942), the Green Bay Packers (1965–1967), and the Dallas Cowboys (1992,

1993, 1995). The Bears teams played in a league with 10 teams, while the Packers beat out 14, 24, and 25 teams, and the Cowboys outlasted between 28 and 30 teams.

In their era, the Patriots not only had to eclipse more teams (32), but also deal with an NFL system featuring a salary cap and unfettered free agency designed to prevent just such a dynasty from sprouting.

"We've never really self-proclaimed ourselves anything," quarterback Tom Brady said. "We just love playing ball. It sounds cliché-ish, but we're a team."

This was the Patriots' record-tying ninth straight playoff victory, a mark they would break with a victory in the wild-card round a year later. With 17–2 records in both 2003 and 2004, they edged the Denver Broncos from 1997 to 1998 (33–6) for the best two-year mark in NFL history.

"Dynasties are things that are talked about a decade later," offensive coordinator Charlie Weis said. "When you're living it you don't feel it. Maybe they'll talk about this team like we talk about those other teams."

This Super Bowl will be remembered for Owens' courageous showing and the play of another wide receiver, New England's diminutive Deion Branch, who made a cluster of difficult receptions at crucial times and was named MVP of the game. Branch's longest catch was just 27 yards, but it was still the longest gain by New England in 63 plays.

	1	2	3	4	Final
New England Patriots	0	7	7	10	24
Philadelphia Eagles	0	7	7	7	21

SCORING SUMMARY

2nd Quarter
PHI L. J. Smith, 6-yd. pass from McNabb (Akers kick)
NE Givens, 4-yd. pass from Brady (Vinatieri kick)
3rd Quarter
NE Vrabel, 2-yd. pass from Brady (Vinatieri kick)
PHI Westbrook, 10-yd. pass from McNabb (Akers kick)
4th Quarter
NE Dillon, 2-yd. run (Vinatieri kick)
NE Vinatieri, 22-yd. FG
PHI Lewis, 30-yd. pass from McNabb (Akers kick)

Super Bowl XXXIX was a workmanlike affair without many compelling plays or performances.

The Eagles had won 51 games from 2000 to 2003 under their steely coach, Andy Reid, but in the three previous seasons they had been ousted in the NFC Championship Game. After such disappointment, reaching the Super Bowl carried with it immense satisfaction. But the Eagles felt they were good enough to go all the way. After all, they had become just the third team since the 16-game schedule was inaugurated in 1978 to clinch a playoff berth after only 11 games. Buoyed by dominating performances against Minnesota (27–14) and Atlanta (27–10) in the playoffs, the Eagles wanted to believe some of their weak showings in playoffs past were behind them now.

"What it really came down to is when we got to the big games in the playoffs we didn't play well," said tackle Jon Runyan, whose unrestricted free-agent signing in 2000 coincided with the emergence of the Eagles. "It was the same way in the Super Bowl. We played well the week before [against the Falcons], then when we got to the Super Bowl we didn't play well. . . . It was turnovers in the first half that killed us. We should have blown them out of the water."

Despite their imperfections, the Eagles did take possession with 46 seconds to go trailing by just a field goal, but the starting point was their own 4-yard line. The game ended deep in Eagles' territory after safety Rodney Harrison's interception

of a deflected pass thrown by Donovan McNabb. In reality, the Eagles had little chance once their onside kick with 1:48 left was blunted in textbook fashion by the Patriots, with tight end Christian Fauria making the recovery. Although David Akers was known for his excellence on onside kicks, the Patriots still expected Reid to kick away given the fact he had two timeouts remaining. Nevertheless, it was the succeeding series of events that caused the Eagles to have so little time for their final possession and will be chewed on for years in Philly.

Trailing 24–14, the Eagles started from their 21 with 5:40 remaining. On the first 10 plays of the drive, as well as the 12th, the Eagles went with McNabb under center instead of in shotgun formation. Every play was designed to be a pass, yet the team kept huddling as Reid gave the play to assistant head coach Marty Mornhinweg for voice transmission to McNabb.

In the Eagles' radio booth, listeners heard both surprise and concern in the voice of Merrill Reese, their beloved play-by-play man for 28 years, when he said, "Time's a-wasting . . . under 4 minutes left." His analyst, former Eagles wide receiver Mike

COACHING STAFFS

New England
Head Coach: Bill Belichick. ***Offense:*** Charlie Weis (coordinator), Brian Daboll (wide receivers), Jeff Davidson (tight ends, assistant offensive line), Dante Scarnecchia (offensive line, assistant head coach), Josh McDaniels (quarterbacks), Ivan Fears (running backs). ***Defense:*** Romeo Crennel (coordinator), Pepper Johnson (defensive line), Dean Pees (linebackers), Eric Mangini (defensive backs). ***Special Teams:*** Brad Seely. ***Strength:*** Mike Woicik, Markus Paul (assistant).

Philadelphia
Head Coach: Andy Reid. ***Offense:*** Brad Childress (coordinator), David Culley (wide receivers), Tom Melvin (tight ends), Juan Castillo (offensive line), Pat Shurmur (quarterbacks), Ted Williams (running backs), Bill Shuey (quality control). ***Defense:*** Jim Johnson (coordinator), Tommy Brasher (defensive line), Steve Spagnuolo (linebackers), Trent Walters (defensive backs), Sean McDermott (safeties), Mike Reed (quality control). ***Special Teams:*** John Harbaugh, Ted Daisher (quality control). ***Strength:*** Mike Wolf. ***Senior Assistant:*** Marty Mornhinweg.

Quick, quickly added, "I think they're being a little too casual with the time and a little too cavalier."

Some of the Patriots' defenders were also perplexed. "I remember a clear picture of myself looking at McNabb and . . . just seeing the seconds ticking away and wondering what they were doing. Why didn't they have a sense of urgency?" linebacker Tedy Bruschi said. "Maybe they knew something I didn't know. But what I knew was the fourth quarter of the Super Bowl was winding down and they don't have more points than we do."

Wide receiver Troy Brown—pressed into duty as the Patriots' nickel back from Week 8 on because of season-ending injuries to starting cornerbacks Ty Law and Tyrone Poole—was loving it. "They were down by a couple scores and were taking their own sweet time," said Brown. "We were just happy we were getting a breather."

The explanations for why the Eagles operated so deliberately were diverse, to say the least. Center Hank Fraley caused a furor when he told a Philly television station in the days after the game that McNabb had become sick during the drive and was close to throwing up. In 2005, when the relationship between Owens and McNabb soured, Owens said, "It wasn't me who got tired at the Super Bowl."

On the 13th play of the drive, McNabb threw a beautiful 30-yard touchdown pass from an empty formation down the middle of the field to slot receiver Greg Lewis, who was open on a deep post route. The Patriots blitzed unbeknownst to Belichick, who thought defensive coordinator Romeo Crennel had told the players that they weren't blitzing anymore when the Eagles went empty. Backup safety Dexter Reid didn't stay back far enough, leaving Lewis open. "We missed the communication," said Belichick. "In the players' minds, if they were in empty we're going to blitz it just like we did on the first series. We end up blitzing six against five to get the ball out, but the problem was we don't cover [Lewis]. Beyond terrible." Until the glitch-blitz on the touchdown to Lewis, the Patriots played soft zones trying to extend the Eagles' drive.

After the scoring drive, even though the Eagles had two timeouts left, a rugged run defense anchored by middle linebacker Jeremiah Trotter, a dynamic punt returner in Brian Westbrook, and an exceptional field-goal kicker in Akers, Reid said no consideration was given to kicking off deep. Reid might well have played it differently if the Eagles' 79-yard drive hadn't taken an excessive amount of time (3:52).

Interviewed in 2006, Runyan said McNabb hadn't appeared injured or in any way incapacitated in the fourth quarter. It also was true that McNabb had been knocked down on at least four of the first eight plays, including once with minimal contact from defensive end Jarvis Green, but three times with heavy contact from linebacker Roman Phifer, Green, and Bruschi. McNabb told a close friend that he had been shaken up early in the drive and was gasping for air at times because of it.

Nevertheless, Reid offered some regret for not having sped up his offense. "Yeah, I probably should have done that [no-huddle] a little bit more. When your quarterback gets hit, it's hard to get the no-huddle thing going," Reid said in 2006. "He was hurting a little bit but he wasn't coming out of the

game. He got the wind knocked out of him. We were in a hurry-up but not a no-huddle. He was getting everybody in and out of the huddle fast. The end result, which I think people overlooked, was we did score a touchdown and that we had time to score another one. We couldn't get it done."

The NFC was a weak conference in 2004, as evidenced by its 20–44 record against AFC opposition, its worst since 1979. The Eagles barely had to break a sweat many times during the regular season. Although McNabb had by far his best season, with a passer rating of 104.7, the Eagles certainly wouldn't be categorized among the NFL's best in two-minute situations. "Early in the season, we were blowing timeouts because we didn't have the right personnel in the game," said Runyan. Still, he said that he never heard a single teammate criticize Reid's strategy. "T.O. [Owens] was banged up. [Todd] Pinkston was kind of dehydrated and cramping. It kind of handcuffed [Reid] on what he could do," Runyan added. "If a coach makes up his mind early, no matter what happens, that he's going to make sure he gets a score and is going for the onside kick, there's not an urgency there. I think that's really what it was."

After the failed onside kick, Belichick called three running plays, exhausting the Eagles' timeouts, and called on Josh Miller to punt on fourth and 5 at the Philly 36. The Eagles went for the block, but the punt hit at the 15, then rolled dead at the 4. "To me, that was the play of the Super Bowl," Bruschi said. "Our punt coverage was throwing a party around the ball. How much more confidence does an offense feel when they come out on the 20? Now they had to go 60, 70 yards for a field goal, and it wasn't going to happen with that time. That put the nail in the coffin."

With 17 seconds remaining, McNabb took a shot down the middle that glanced off the hands of tight end L. J. Smith and was picked off by Harrison, ending the game. "It was a little high and would have been a tough catch," said Reid. "It was a close game. I thought my guys played their hearts out. We had too many turnovers. Not good."

By the 10-minute mark of the second quarter, the Patriots had twice as many punts (four) and even more false-start penalties (two) than they had first downs (one) in their first four possessions. Belichick attributed some of the Patriots' awful start to Jim Johnson, the Eagles' defensive coordinator throughout the Reid years. "He's the best," Belichick said. "He does a great job of attacking protections in blitz and he's the kind of guy who always holds a couple blitzes back. In critical situations in the fourth quarter he'll spring something on you that you haven't seen and worked on. You better be ready for it."

Conversely, at that point the Eagles had just finished off a nine-play, 81-yard touchdown for a 7-0 lead. Wide receiver Todd Pinkston made a tough catch against Brown for 17 on third and 8, then timed his leap better than rookie cornerback Randall "Blue" Gay and came down with a 40-yard bomb. The score came on third and 6 from the 6 when McNabb had time to find Smith cutting into the middle after Gay knocked down his primary target, Owens, in the corner. "Phifer had him pretty good in man-to-man coverage but you can't cover a guy for that long," Bruschi said. "They were in max protect. Still almost made a play on the ball."

The thrust of the Patriots' defensive game plan was two-fold, according to Belichick. "Set the edge on Westbrook," he said. "Our whole deal was make him run between the tackles. Number two, keep McNabb in the pocket. Do not let him run. We didn't feel like McNabb was going to beat us throwing in the pocket. We were worried about the loose plays, scrambling to pass and hitting plays down the field."

Although the Patriots had played very little 4-3 that year, they junked their usual 3-4/4-3 hybrid for a 4-3 base in which outside linebacker Willie McGinest played down as a left end. Meanwhile, Bruschi and fellow linebacker Mike Vrabel spent a lot of time walking up into the A-gaps and the defensive tackles lined up in the B-gaps. The Patriots called it their "Dolphin" package in which, Belichick explained, they would play a defensive end outside the tight end, and whichever linebacker the center blocked, the other guy would then shoot the gap. If the center reached front side, then that linebacker would pull out, while the other one would shoot behind the center and fill that gap before the guard could come down and get him. "In the passing game, it set the edge on McNabb because he couldn't

scramble outside those wide ends," Belichick said. "And in the perimeter run game it forced Westbrook back inside."

It was a scheme that Belichick hadn't used much in his career. "We played it a lot on early downs when we felt it was a higher percentage [chance] that the Eagles would run the ball," said Bruschi. The tactics worked. Runyan chalked up the three-and-outs on the Eagles' first two possessions to the ongoing adjustments against Patriots' unexpected defenses.

"We spent two weeks preparing for a 3-4 defense and they didn't play a 3-4 defense in the Super Bowl," said Brad Childress, the Eagles' offensive coordinator. "They played an even front with guys in both A gaps. They're smart guys." McNabb was hemmed in and held without a rushing yard, and 22 of Westbrook's 44 rushing yards came on a meaningless draw play to end the first half.

Once the Eagles settled their protection problems, Reid found ways to gain 369 yards by exploiting New England's Achilles' heel—at cornerback. Gay, an undrafted rookie from LSU with marginal speed, had to start for Ty Law; second-year man Asante Samuel was starting for the injured Poole; and the nickel and dime backs were Brown and Hank Poteat, a free agent signed off the street on January 10. Also late in the first half, Dexter Reid had to play when free safety Eugene Wilson suffered a game-ending arm injury covering a kickoff. Still, the Patriots played almost exclusively man-to-man coverage largely because they blitzed as much, if not more than, they had all season. By rushing five, the Patriots were able to reduce by one the scrambling lanes available to McNabb.

In establishing his priorities on defense, Belichick faced a dilemma because he didn't know for sure if Owens would play and, if he did, how effective he might be. Orthopedists were quoted far and wide in the press saying it seemed doubtful that Owens would be ready with less than seven weeks recovery time. "He wasn't a big target in the game plan," Belichick said. "I didn't want to go into the game saying, 'T.O. T.O. T.O. T.O. T.O.' And if he doesn't play, then our guys are all, 'OK, our whole game plan is to stop him and he's not even playing.' I tried to make it about Westbrook and McNabb."

All eyes were on Owens before the game. "He

went out in warmups and didn't do s---," Belichick said. "I'm not really expecting too much out of this guy. Maybe he'll go out and give it a shot, he's a competitive guy. So we go out and on one of the first passes I see him explode off the line of scrimmage. Then maybe the second drive they run a crossing pattern and they pick Randall Gay and they hit Owens coming across and I see him coming to our bench and he's building speed and gaining yards [30 in all]. I'm looking at it going, 'How are we going to get this damn guy down?' I don't know how he did it, but he was a beast. We had nobody that could cover him. The problem wasn't Blue. The problem was we should have given him more help on T.O. Gay has some speed and some quickness, but he's a thin guy. Having him on Terrell Owens was a total mismatch."

Reid, a pass-oriented coach to begin with, started throwing on almost every down beginning with the Eagles' third possession. From the Philly 26, McNabb found Westbrook for 14 on a check-down, Smith for 9 on third and 9, and Owens for 30 on the aforementioned shallow crossing route that ruptured when Bruschi inadvertently knocked Gay off the coverage.

After Vrabel beat left guard Artis Hicks for a 16-yard sack back to the 24, McNabb forced a deep ball to Owens that was intercepted by Samuel. The play was brought back, however, and the Eagles were given a first down when Phifer was penalized for illegal contact with Smith. "We're playing a West Coast [style] team," Bruschi said, referring to the Eagles' offense. "We stressed knocking receivers off their routes. We knew we'd have to take one of those penalties once in a while just by playing the way we did." With the ball on the 19, McNabb floated a weak wobbler in the corner for Westbrook. Bruschi was trailing Westbrook in man coverage, but Harrison had time to range over from the middle of the field and make the interception.

New England didn't go anywhere and punted, enabling the Eagles to start from the Patriots 45. The Patriots' defense made another uncharacteristic blunder when Gay dropped an interception on an underthrown take-off route from NcNabb to Pinkston. On third and 11, Smith was fighting to escape Harrison's clutches and pick up the first

TEAM STATISTICS

NEW ENGLAND		PHILADELPHIA
21	Total First Downs	24
6	Rushing	4
14	Passing	18
1	Penalty	2
331	Total Net Yardage	369
63	Total Offensive Plays	72
5.3	Avg. Gain per Offensive Play	5.1
28	Rushes	17
112	Yards Gained Rushing (Net)	45
4.0	Average Yards per Rush	2.6
33	Passes Attempted	51
23	Passes Completed	30
0	Passes Intercepted	3
2	Tackled Attempting to Pass	4
17	Yards Lost Attempting to Pass	33
219	Yards Gained Passing (Net)	324
4/12	Third-Down Efficiency	9/16
0/0	Fourth-Down Efficiency	0/0
7	Punts	5
45.1	Average Distance	42.8
4	Punt Returns	3
26	Punt Return Yardage	19
4	Kickoff Returns	5
63	Kickoff Return Yardage	114
5	Interception Return Yardage	0
1	Fumbles	2
0	Own Fumbles Recovered	1
1	Opponent Fumbles Recovered	1
7	Penalties	3
47	Yards Penalized	35
3	Touchdowns	3
1	Rushing	0
2	Passing	3
0	Returns	0
3	Extra Points Made	3
1	Field Goals Made	0
1	Field Goals Attempted	0
0	Safeties	0
24	Total Points Scored	21
31:37	Time of Possession	28:23

down when Gay poked the ball from his grasp and Wilson recovered.

Fortunate to be trailing by only 7 points, but unable to solve the interior blitzes of the daring Jim Johnson, Weis then made the decision to use three and four wide receivers as his base formation from the middle of the second quarter on. In turn, Johnson

INDIVIDUAL STATISTICS

NEW ENGLAND

Passing	CP/ATT	YDS	TD	INT	RAT
Brady	23/33	236	2	0	110.2

Rushing	ATT	YDS	AVG	TD	LG
Dillon	18	75	4.2	1	25
Faulk	8	38	4.8	0	12
Pass	1	0	0.0	0	0
Brady	1	-1	-1.0	0	-1

Receiving	NO	YDS	AVG	TD	LG
Branch	11	133	12.1	0	27
Dillon	3	31	10.3	0	16
Givens	3	19	6.3	1	13
Faulk	2	27	13.5	0	14
T. Brown	2	17	8.5	0	12
Graham	1	7	7.0	0	7
Vrabel	1	2	2.0	1	2t

Interceptions	NO	YDS	LG	TD
Harrison	2	5	6	0
Bruschi	1	0	0	0

Punting	NO	AVG	LG	BLK
Miller	7	45.1	50	0

Punt Ret.	NO/FC	YDS	LG	TD
T. Brown	3/1	12	8	0
B. Johnson	1/0	14	14	0

Kickoff Ret.	NO	YDS	LG	TD
B. Johnson	2	44	26	0
Pass	1	17	17	0
Fauria	1	2	2	0

Defense	SOLO	AST	TOT	SK
Gay	11	0	11	0
Harrison	7	0	7	1
Bruschi	6	1	7	1
Samuel	4	0	4	0
Vrabel	2	2	4	1
Phifer	3	0	3	0
Reid	3	0	3	0
Wilson	3	0	3	0
T. Johnson	2	1	3	0
Chatham	2	0	2	0
McGinest	2	0	2	0
Seymour	2	0	2	1
Abdullah	1	0	1	0
Colvin	1	0	1	0
Izzo	1	0	1	0
Poteat	1	0	1	0
Traylor	1	0	1	0
Warren	1	0	1	0
Pass	0	1	1	0
TOTAL	53	5	58	4

PHILADELPHIA

Passing	CP/ATT	YDS	TD	INT	RAT
McNabb	30/51	357	3	3	75.4

Rushing	ATT	YDS	AVG	TD	LG
Westbrook	15	44	2.9	0	22
Levens	1	1	1.0	0	1
McNabb	1	0	0.0	0	0

Receiving	NO	YDS	AVG	TD	LG
Owens	9	122	13.6	0	36
Westbrook	7	60	8.6	1	15
Pinkston	4	82	20.5	0	40
G. Lewis	4	53	13.3	1	30t
Smith	4	27	6.8	1	9
Mitchell	1	11	11.0	0	11
Parry	1	2	2.0	0	2

Interceptions	NO	YDS	LG	TD
None	--	--	--	--

Punting	NO	AVG	LG	BLK
Johnson	5	42.8	52	0

Punt Ret.	NO/FC	YDS	LG	TD
Westbrook	3/0	19	10	0
Sheppard	0/2	--	--	0

Kickoff Ret.	NO	YDS	LG	TD
Reed	4	82	26	0
Hood	1	32	32	0

Defense	SOLO	AST	TOT	SK
Adams	5	1	6	0
Lewis	5	1	6	0
Dawkins	4	1	5	0
Trotter	4	0	4	0
Ware	4	0	4	0
Burgess	3	1	4	1
S. Brown	3	1	4	0
Hood	3	0	3	0
Walker	2	1	3	0
Sheppard	2	1	3	0
H. Thomas	1	2	3	0
D. Jones	2	0	2	0
Labinjo	2	0	2	0
G. Lewis	2	0	2	0
Rayburn	2	0	2	0
Reese	2	0	2	0
Simoneau	2	0	2	0
Kearse	1	1	2	0
Mayberry	1	0	1	0
Mikell	1	0	1	0
Mitchell	1	0	1	0
Owens	1	0	1	0
Reed	1	0	1	0
Simon	1	0	1	0
Thomason	1	0	1	0
TOTAL	56	10	66	1

removed his starting linebackers, including the rampaging Trotter, and inserted dime backer Ike Reese.

"What they did defensively was bring Trotter up the middle a lot," said Belichick. "What that forced us to do was have the center take him." The Eagles' objective, according to Belichick, was to keep the line from sliding one way or the other, trying to make the Patriots' tackles single-block Jevon Kearse and Derrick Burgess. "That was a problem," he said. "Plus, they had [Corey] Simon inside. Not that he was a great pass rusher, but he was a load and it was hard for the quarterback to step up in the pocket, and you had those two guys coming around the edge. That was pretty effective. We had trouble with their pass rush, I know that."

On the first two plays of the Patriots' turnaround possession in the second quarter, the Patriots ran screen passes to Corey Dillon. Each time, Johnson blitzed up the middle, but Dillon found ample room on the left flank for gains of 13 and 16 yards. "I felt like the screens slowed down a little bit of that inside blitzing," Belichick said. But the drive ended at the Eagles 4 when Brady bungled a handoff to Kevin Faulk and defensive tackle Darwin Walker came up with the loose ball that Brady actually had the best chance to recover.

The Patriots finally broke through to tie the score at 7–7 shortly before intermission on David Givens' 4-yard touchdown catch. Brady wanted Fauria inside, but the veteran tight end slipped, and Branch was double-teamed. Brady remained patient. "I always use that play for the quarterbacks, reading the play out and not making up your mind," said Belichick. "They got Fauria singled and Branch doubled, . . . two guys on him shoulder-to-shoulder. Givens goes outside and is coming back in and sees Brady in trouble. Givens kind of uncovers back outside and Brady gives it to him on the sideline."

Without so much as shifting his feet, Brady made the play to Givens against Lito Sheppard, the Eagles' all-pro left cornerback who was caught napping. "Lito normally will make that play all the time," said Johnson, "but I think he misjudged it and kind of got lost when Brady looked off the other way and all of a sudden Givens kind of drifted out."

Branch suffered knee cartilage damage in Week 2 that required arthroscopic surgery, and he didn't return until Week 10. The decision by Belichick not to place him on injured reserve was one of the best that he ever made. Having taken advantage of the long halftime to script the first 10 snaps of the second half, Weis used four wideouts on six straight plays in a nine-play, 69-yard touchdown march to open the third quarter. "Maybe it wasn't the turning point of the game, but now the momentum had switched," said Johnson. "We felt we had momentum the first half. On that drive we had a couple chances on third down and couldn't get off the field. I think we really had control of the game in the first half and didn't take advantage of it."

On the first third down, the Eagles blitzed both Reese and safety Brian Dawkins. Rookie cornerback Matt Ware, the dime back, couldn't keep up with Branch on a third-and-6 crossing route, and it turned into a 27-yard gain. Three plays later, on third and 10, the Eagles rushed just four, and Branch beat cornerback Sheldon Brown inside for a 15-yard completion. After Dillon failed to gain, Johnson blitzed on second down and Branch beat Ware from the left slot on a corner route for 21 yards to the 2. Vrabel, in at tight end on the left side, fought his way off the line against Kearse and made a juggling catch for a 2-yard touchdown.

"The difference in the game for us was Deion was hot," Patriots running backs coach Ivan Fears said. "They couldn't handle him. Brady had guys hanging on him. He knew the blitz was coming but he could throw it at Deion and he was snagging s--- left and right with guys flapping at him and knocking the hell out of him. Deion isn't one of those talkers or hype guys. That boy can play."

Later in the third quarter, the Eagles went 74 yards in 10 plays. Owens had done most of his damage against Gay, but here his two catches (for 15 yards) came against Samuel. Gay, however, did give up three completions worth 23 yards. On third and 3, Westbrook reached behind his back to make a 4-yard reception before Gay could break it up. On the next play, Westbrook lined up in the right slot and ran a slant, and McNabb gunned him the ball as he dove into the end zone between Vrabel and Reid. "Great throw because Vrabel had to be 2 inches from that ball," said Bruschi. "That was one of the better balls McNabb threw that game. That's what we were afraid of, Westbrook's receiving ability out of the backfield. You can only stop a good player so long."

At this point, Weis went back to the running game and three-tight end formation that was such an integral part of the Patriots' success in 2004. Dillon, acquired from Cincinnati on April 19 for a second-round draft choice, gained a franchise-record 1,635 yards as New England improved to seventh in rushing from 27th the year before. Weis called runs on 50.6 percent of the plays, too, an increase from 47.3 percent in 2001, 38.3 percent in 2002, and 45.4 percent in 2003. "He gave us some speed and change of direction that Antowain [Smith] wasn't going to do," said Fears. "Plus, he played with power when we needed him to. He had a great year." The Patriots' nine-play, 66-yard drive contained two more screen passes for 27 yards and was culminated by Dillon's 2-yard touchdown burst off left tackle.

New England then extended its lead to 24–14 on Adam Vinatieri's 22-yard field goal with 8:40 left. The key play was a 19-yard reception by Branch on second and 13 in which cornerback Sheldon Brown appeared just as likely to intercept the ball. The phenomenal catch became even more significant when Simon was penalized 15 yards for roughing Brady after the throw.

The Eagles immediately retaliated by moving into scoring range. Owens caught a 10-yard hook against Gay, stiff-armed the rookie as he spun back toward the sideline, and charged 36 yards before Reid managed to shove him out of bounds. "If he's healthy I think that he takes that to the house," Runyan said. "I think he runs past a couple people and maybe sidesteps somebody and gets in." Owens, who caught nine of the 15 passes thrown in his direction for 122 yards, had been spectacular in his first season for the Eagles before being injured in Week 14.

Owens insisted he would play in the Super Bowl, but it wasn't until Sunday morning when the final decision to play him was rendered by the club's medical staff, according to Reid. "I thought he played a phenomenal game," said Troy Brown, who covered him several times from the slot. "We figured he'd be favoring that leg or not be able to do certain things, but the speed he showed was just unbelievable. Without him, they wouldn't have had much of a chance to even make it competitive."

With first down at the Patriots 36, McNabb dropped back on the next play and threw about 12 yards into the middle of the field. Reid said it was a combination route involving Smith and running back Dorsey Levens. The ball was poorly thrown—too high for Levens and too soft to reach the tight end—and the ever-alert Bruschi came across to cradle the interception. "I was faced the other way at first but I saw McNabb's eyes were fixed on his tight end," said Bruschi. "I sort of flipped to the other side and McNabb underthrew the ball."

It was the Eagles' third turnover inside the New England 40 and was too much to overcome. This was the fifth straight playoff defeat for the Eagles in which McNabb had thrown at least one critical interception. "Donovan battled his heart out," said Andy Reid. "You had two good football teams playing each other and you can't turn the ball over. That's the name of the game." To win their first title since 1960, the Eagles needed more than just a mediocre performance from their quarterback.

In winning their ninth straight playoff game, the Patriots had one turnover. In those nine games, their turnover differential of plus-19 (25 takeaways compared to six giveaways) explained just about everything there was to explain.

New England's roster never wowed many personnel people around the league, but scouts were in agreement that the Patriots' mix of selfless, competitive players and Belichick's magnificent coaching made for one of the most remarkable teams in NFL history.

"I have great respect for two guys," the 63-year-old Johnson said, "Belichick and Brady. I mean, Belichick never leaves anything undone. People credited Charlie Weis for doing a great job and Romeo Crennel, but I always felt you see his hand in everything. And, of course, Tom Brady. He's such a great quarterback."

XL

PITTSBURGH STEELERS 21, SEATTLE SEAHAWKS 10

February 5, 2006
Ford Field, Detroit, Michigan

As the years pass, Mike Holmgren's rebuke of Super Bowl officials, perhaps the harshest criticism in the first 40 years of the event, will eventually fade away. The enduring portrait of Super Bowl XL will be what the Pittsburgh Steelers did just to get there, and the three decisive plays that they made to defeat the Seahawks, 21–10, at Ford Field in Detroit.

This was the story of an organization's stubbornness in the face of fan unrest, a coach's willingness to admit he might have been wrong and the subsequent alteration of his motivational approach, and the belief of 53 players in their coaches, each other, and one special teammate who inspired them all.

For owner Dan Rooney, the Lombardi Trophy was vindication for having given coach Bill Cowher a two-year extension in July 2004 on the heels of a 6–10 season.

For Cowher, it was the crowning achievement of his 14-year career as a head coach and the realization that, in times of adversity, players don't necessarily need to be browbeaten in order to respond.

And for all the Steelers and their passionate fan base, it meant the hunt for the elusive "One for the Thumb" (a fifth Super Bowl title) was over. The sentimental, successful sendoff for Jerome "the Bus" Bettis as he played his final NFL game in his hometown made it all the more sweet.

On December 4, two days after losing at home to the Cincinnati Bengals, the Steelers were 7–5 and situated no better than eighth among the teams battling for the six playoff berths in the AFC. The next day, Cowher made the decision to eradicate everything from the first three months of the season and demand only that his men play each game as if it would be their last. "Clear your mind," Cowher told them. "You'll be amazed— amazed—how fresh you feel when you forget

everything in your life except what you're doing right now."

With the zone-blitzing defense of coordinator Dick LeBeau beginning to flex its muscle and some injured players returning to the lineup, the Steelers won their final four games to claim the sixth playoff seed. In the first three playoff games, Ben Roethlisberger compiled a passer rating of 124.8 and the defense allowed merely 52 points in road victories over Cincinnati, Indianapolis, and Denver. All three teams had offenses ranked among the top six in the league.

Designated as the home team, the Steelers instead chose to wear visiting white uniforms for the fourth straight week. They also decided to let Bettis run out of the tunnel alone at the start of the game and then wave out his teammates that had helped get him there. The Steelers were the first team since the 1985 New England Patriots to win three playoff games on the road, and they became the first six seed to win it all (the previous low was a fourth seed).

"We were a better team than a number six seed and that's why you might not see a number six run the table again," the 68-year-old LeBeau said. "We just got some guys back at the right time and our team played its best at the critical time. We weren't dead in the water, but we were certainly looking at a very daunting task. Our guys just kind of thought at the end that nobody was going to beat them. And that's the way it turned out."

Attendance: 68,206
Conditions: Indoors
Time of kickoff: 6:27 p.m. (EST)
Length of game: 3 hours, 36 minutes
Referee: Bill Leavy

MVP: Hines Ward, WR, Steelers

	1	2	3	4	Final
Seattle Seahawks	3	0	7	0	10
Pittsburgh Steelers	0	7	7	7	21

SCORING SUMMARY

1st Quarter
SEA   Brown, 47-yd. FG
2nd Quarter
PIT   Roethlisberger, 1-yd. run (Reed kick)
3rd Quarter
PIT   Parker, 75-yd. run (Reed kick)
SEA   Stevens, 16-yd. pass from Hasselbeck (Brown kick)
4th Quarter
PIT   Ward, 43-yd. pass from Randle El (Reed kick)

How the Steelers managed to defeat the Seahawks by 11 points in the lowest-scoring Super Bowl in 31 years was hard to figure. The MVP, wide receiver Hines Ward, dropped two passes, including one in the end zone. The winning quarterback, Roethlisberger, had a passer rating of 22.6. And the winning defense played no better than mediocre football, at least by its lofty standards.

"I thought we'd win and I think we played well, other than the drops," said Holmgren, the widely respected coach of the Seahawks. "That hurt us, clearly. We gained a tremendous amount of yardage. We had the leading rusher, the leading passer, and we turned the ball over once. I mean, you look at the numbers and you'd swear we won the game, by normal standards."

Aside from three dropped passes by tight end Jerramy Stevens (a combined 61 yards downfield), the Seahawks lost because their special teams were abominable, just as they were almost all season. Also, Pro Bowl quarterback Matt Hasselbeck played only an average game, and their defense, while rock-solid on 53 of the Steelers' snaps, came apart on the other three.

"I thought defensively we played our tail off. We never got on track offensively but we made the plays on offense when we had to," said Cowher. "I just think it's a sign of a good football team when you don't play your best football game and still win."

For the fifth straight Super Bowl, neither team could score a touchdown in the first quarter. The only points in the first 15 minutes, a 47-yard field goal by Seattle's Josh Brown, held little in the way of satisfaction for Holmgren. A few plays earlier, back judge Bob Waggoner called wide receiver Darrell Jackson for offensive pass interference against safety Chris Hope in the back of the end zone, negating what looked like a 16-yard touchdown pass to Jackson. It was one of six officiating decisions that Holmgren questioned, some more vehemently than others.

"I cannot fault my team," Holmgren said about the outcome of the game. "The players played hard and, for the most part, they played pretty well. But officiating should not be the big story after a Super Bowl or NCAA championship or any championship game. And it was. I don't care what anybody says."

Holmgren's knowledge of the rule book and the time he spent trying to improve the officiating was unchallenged. He was first appointed to the NFL Competition Committee in 1994 and served until 1998, including the last two years as co-chairman. He resigned after leaving Green Bay for Seattle in 1999 but agreed to return in February 2002 at the request of Commissioner Paul Tagliabue. He served through the committee's meeting at the combine in February 2006, and then resigned without comment.

After the Super Bowl, Holmgren scowled his way through a press conference but didn't address the officiating directly. Before departing Detroit on Monday, Holmgren told reporters: "Penalties, as much as anything, were the story of the game. It might be the first time I've said that in my entire life." The next day, during a rally at Qwest Field in Seattle before about 15,000 fans, Holmgren ratcheted his attack up a level when he said, "We knew it was going to be tough going against the Pittsburgh Steelers. I didn't know we were going to have to play the guys in the striped shirts as well."

"We were very much a visiting team. In the five or six Super Bowls I was involved in, that was the first time that ever happened where it was that much of an advantage."

Mike Holmgren, Seahawks head coach

SEATTLE SEAHAWKS (NFC, 13–3)			PITTSBURGH STEELERS (AFC, 11–5)	
		Offense		
84	Bobby Engram (5-10, 188)	WR	82	Antwaan Randle El (5-9, 192)
71	Walter Jones* (6-5, 315)	LT	77	Marvel Smith (6-5, 321)
76	Steve Hutchinson* (6-5, 313)	LG	66	Alan Faneca* (6-5, 307)
61	Robbie Tobeck (6-4, 297)	C	64	Jeff Hartings* (6-3, 299)
62	Chris Gray (6-4, 308)	RG	73	Kendall Simmons (6-3, 319)
75	Sean Locklear (6-4, 301)	RT	78	Max Starks (6-7, 337)
86	Jerramy Stevens (6-7, 260)	TE	83	Heath Miller (6-5, 256)
82	Darrell Jackson (6-0, 201)	WR	86	Hines Ward (5-11, 205)
8	Matt Hasselbeck* (6-4, 223)	QB	7	Ben Roethlisberger (6-5, 241)
37	Shaun Alexander* (6-0, 225)	RB	39	Willie Parker (5-10, 209)
38	Mack Strong* (6-1, 245)	FB	35	Dan Kreider (5-11, 255)
		Defense		
94	Bryce Fisher (6-3, 268)	LE	91	Aaron Smith (6-5, 298)
91	Chuck Darby (6-0, 270)	NT	98	Casey Hampton (6-1, 325)
99	Rocky Bernard (6-3, 293)	DT I RE	67	Kimo von Oelhoffen (6-3, 305)
98	Grant Wistrom (6-5, 272)	RE I LOLB	53	Clark Haggans (6-3, 243)
56	Leroy Hill (6-1, 229)	SLB I LILB	51	James Farrior (6-2, 243)
51	Lofa Tatupu (6-0, 238)	MLB I RILB	50	Larry Foote (6-1, 239)
54	D. D. Lewis (6-1, 241)	WLB I ROLB	55	Joey Porter* (6-3, 250)
21	Andre Dyson (5-10, 183)	LCB	24	Ike Taylor (6-1, 191)
23	Marcus Trufant (5-11, 199)	RCB	26	Deshea Townsend (5-9, 190)
28	Michael Boulware (6-2, 223)	SS	43	Troy Polamalu* (5-10, 212)
33	Marquand Manuel (6-0, 209)	FS	28	Chris Hope (5-11, 206)

* Pro Bowl selection

SUBSTITUTIONS

Seattle

Offense: WR - 18 D. J. Hackett, 81 Peter Warrick, 87 Joe Jurevicius; TE - 83 Ryan Hannam; T/G - 77 Floyd Womack; QB - 15 Seneca Wallace; RB - 20 Maurice Morris, 39 Josh Scobey. **Defense:** DE - 69 Joe Tafoya; DT - 90 Marcus Tubbs, 93 Craig Terrill; LB - 50 Cornelius Wortham, 53 Niko Koutouvides, 57 Kevin Bentley, 58 Isaiah Kacyvenski; CB - 22 Jimmy Williams, 27 Jordan Babineaux, 31 Kelly Herndon; S - 35 Etric Pruitt. **Specialists:** K - Josh Brown; P - 16 Tom Rouen; LS - 52 Jean-Philippe Darche. **DNP:** 65 Chris Spencer (C). **Inactive:** 88 Itula Mili (TE), 74 Ray Willis (T), 73 Wayne Hunter (T), 11 David Greene (QB), 43 Leonard Weaver (FB), 78 Robert Pollard (DE), 95 Rodney Bailey (DT), 25 Michael Harden (CB).

Pittsburgh

Offense: WR - 80 Cedrick Wilson, 81 Sean Morey, 85 Nate Washington; TE - 84 Jerame Tuman; T - 72 Barrett Brooks; C - 56 Chukky Okobi; RB - 34 Verron Haynes, 36 Jerome Bettis. **Defense:** DE - 90 Travis Kirschke, 99 Brett Keisel; NT - 76 Chris Hoke; LB - 57 Clint Kriewaldt, 92 James Harrison; CB - 20 Bryant McFadden, 21 Ricardo Colclough, 29 Chidi Iwuoma; S - 23 Tyrone Carter, 31 Mike Logan. **Specialists:** K - 3 Jeff Reed; P - 17 Chris Gardocki; LS - 60 Greg Warren. **DNP:** 16 Charlie Batch (QB), 22 Duce Staley (RB). **Inactive:** 89 Lee Mays (WR), 79 Trai Essex (T), 68 Chris Kemoeatu (G), 8 Tommy Maddox (QB), 96 Shaun Nua (DE), 46 Arnold Harrison (LB), 54 Rian Wallace (LB), 27 Willie Williams (CB).

Some Steelers officials, media members in Pittsburgh, and Steelers fans just about everywhere categorized Holmgren as just another whining loser. In March, Tagliabue admitted that he had a fine and letter of reprimand for Holmgren drafted, but in the end elected not to send it. Perhaps it was a favor for Holmgren's years of committee service, or possibly it was tacit admission that the officiating had been less than stellar.

On the end-zone play, Jackson broke off his post pattern against Hope when Hasselbeck began to scramble. There was contact between them, initiated by Hope. A step or two later, Jackson put his right hand into Hope's chest and the safety rocked back on his heels before Jackson went the other way and was wide open to make the catch. "That call is not made all season," Holmgren said. "He [Jackson] extended his arm but there was hand checking. They're saying because he broke the pocket the defender can chuck the receiver, which is true. But he can't grab him. That's what was happening."

Countered LeBeau: "That definitely was a push-off. Plus, where it was applied, the ball was maybe 7 yards away from the point of reception. You shove at that point, you're taking away the defender's opportunity to make a play on the ball."

When the slow-to-engage Steelers' offense failed to record a first down for the third straight possession, Pittsburgh had to punt. Peter Warrick brought it back 34 yards on a well-executed "picket-fence" return, only to have it called back when backup safety Etric Pruitt was penalized for holding. It was the first of 10 glitches for Bob Casullo's special teams that ranked a lowly 30th in the NFL.

Four of Tom Rouen's six punts went for touchbacks, although Josh Scobey cost his team by not downing one of them. Kevin Bentley drew a holding penalty on a kickoff return. Field-goal attempts of 50 yards or more certainly aren't gimmes, but in a dome Brown should be expected to make at least one. Instead, he missed from 54 by a few feet to close the first half and then from 50 by a couple more feet to open the second half. Late-arriving coverage enabled Pittsburgh's Antwaan Randle El to make a 20-yard return when Rouen shanked a punt. Also, Warrick gave up 16 yards of roll by not fielding a second-half punt.

The Steelers finally crossed midfield with six and a half minutes left in the second quarter, and then Ward promptly dropped a pass in the right corner of the end zone that should have been a 22-yard touchdown. It was discomforting, to say the least, for Roethlisberger, who had already thrown an easy stop route that was dropped by wide receiver Cedrick Wilson, and who badly underthrew a corner route to Randle El that strong safety Michael Boulware intercepted with a wonderful show of ball skills. One play after the drop by Ward, tight end Heath Miller was penalized for offensive pass interference. Then defensive end Grant Wistrom flew around left tackle Marvel Smith for an 8-yard sack, putting Roethlisberger in a third-and-28 hole at the Seattle 40.

Offensive coordinator Ken Whisenhunt sent in a control-type pass designed to gain a few yards and give kicker Jeff Reed a field-goal try. The Seahawks rushed only three and, when Wistrom circled wide left, Roethlisberger scrambled up and passed him. As he drew within a foot or two of the 40, "Big Ben" sensed the line of scrimmage was near and had the presence of mind to step back to the 41.

When Wistrom dived and just missed tripping him up, Roethlisberger had several seconds to scan the field before he spotted Ward running free near the 10. As the ball arrived, Boulware had his left hand on it, but Ward yanked it away with both arms. "I caught his hand with the ball," said Ward, who took a pain-killing injection in the shoulder that he sprained Friday during practice and also vomited before the game because of nervousness. "I wasn't going to let the ball go." The 37-yard gain advanced the ball to the 3. "I think Michael went for the interception and it got through him," said Seattle acting defensive coordinator John Marshall.

Bettis, less than two weeks shy of his 34th birthday, banged straight-ahead to the 1 on first down. He failed to gain on second down when Wistrom destroyed tackle Barrett Brooks, who was in as an extra blocker on the goal line. Leroy Hill, one of the team's two prized rookie linebackers, helped on the tackle.

After the 2-minute warning, the Steelers decided to decoy with Bettis and have Roethlisberger plunge in behind him on the left side. Bettis got a good block on rookie middle linebacker Lofa Tatupu, the Seahawks' leading tackler, but Hill worked under pulling guard Alan Faneca and took out Roethlisberger's legs just as he began a headlong dive for the goal line. The other linebacker, D. D. Lewis, charged up to prevent the ball from going past the white line.

It was the responsibility of head linesman Mark Hittner to determine whether the ball crossed the plane of the goal line. Hittner immediately raised his right arm and then ran forward five steps toward the pile. As the official ran toward him, Roethlisberger shoved the ball across the line. Between his fifth and sixth steps, Hittner raised his other arm signaling touchdown. The call to review was made upstairs by replay official Bob Boylston because the play occurred in the final 2 minutes of the half. Referee Bill Leavy upheld the touchdown.

"I don't think he got in," Holmgren argued. "Whatever was called on the field was going to be the call. I don't have a qualm with the replay ruling. My only problem was the line judge [head linesman]. He's got one arm up in the air, which is the indicator for ball is down. Now he gets in close to the play, you see that Roethlisberger moves the ball over the goal line, then he changes it and goes, 'Touchdown.' The explanation was he got his mechanics mixed up. Well, hell. It's the Super Bowl, the cream of the crop. That's all he's got to do. Now you don't get your mechanics mixed up." NFL spokesman Greg Aiello said Hittner's initial one-handed signal did not indicate fourth down but that the play was over. Cowher later said he would have gone for it on fourth down.

On Seattle's next possession, Hasselbeck completed three quick passes for 33 yards, putting the Seahawks at the Pittsburgh 40 with one minute left in the half. On first down, Jackson beat cornerback Ike Taylor on a deep sideline route in the right corner. Jackson's left foot was in bounds, but his right foot skimmed the front pylon before landing out of bounds. Tom Hill, the side judge, correctly

ruled no catch because the pylon isn't part of the field of play. Holmgren didn't dispute the call but no doubt cursing his fate, wondered why Boylston didn't insist on a review. "I think it was close," he said. "That's the type of play the guy upstairs must review."

On second down, Holmgren called an off-tackle run by Shaun Alexander that would have gained considerably more than its 4 yards if guard Chris Gray had been able to block defensive end Brett Keisel, who made the tackle. Holmgren then went back to Jackson deep against Taylor, and this time he caught the ball out of bounds at the 4.

At halftime, the Seahawks were lamenting Boulware being inches away from a deflected pass if not an interception, what they considered to be a ticky-tacky penalty on Jackson to wipe out a touchdown, the almost-made long field goal by Brown, Roethlisberger getting into the end zone by inches on a questionable call, and Jackson being out of the end zone by about a foot. "I wasn't unhappy with how we moved the ball against what I thought was a really fine defense," said Holmgren. "The pass to Ward was a huge play in the game. Boulware became the closest guy to the play but it was really inexperience back there that hurt us on the play. That was a throw-up, a knuckleball pass, an ugly pass. But they got it."

Early in the second quarter, the Seahawks lost free safety Marquand Manuel for the game after he suffered a groin injury while tackling Ward out of bounds on a reverse. Initially a backup, Manuel had turned into a reliable starter and leader in Week 7 after the more talented Kenny Hamlin suffered a skull injury in a bar fight. Pruitt, a sixth-round draft choice by Atlanta in 2004, was elevated November 4 from the Seahawks' practice squad to take Hamlin's berth on the 53-man roster. Now he was asked to replace Manuel. Pruitt had spent most of the Super Bowl run-up wearing a red jersey at practice impersonating Pittsburgh's Troy Polamalu. He estimated that his total number of reps with the number one defense during Super Bowl preparation was 15 to 20. This turned out to be the final game of Pruitt's NFL career.

The second half began poorly for Pittsburgh when, on the first snap, Ward dropped another pass.

'Now it's a passing down so I'm thinking they'd be playing coverage to stop the pass," Whisenhunt said. "I thought [the running play on second down] would get us, in worst case, into third and short. We call the play Counter Pike." The Steelers sent out two wide receivers on the left side and Ward on the right; the Seahawks took out Lewis and inserted nickel back Jordan Babineaux.

Just about every team other than the Denver Broncos ran a version of the play. The play-side tackle (in this case, Max Starks) and play-side guard (Kendall Simmons) have good angles to block down, and then the weak-side guard (Faneca) pulls and packs a moving punch at the point of attack. Ward's job was to block the most dangerous defensive back, either the cornerback, Andre Dyson, or the strong safety, Boulware.

With Boulware playing in a two-deep shell alongside Pruitt, Ward went after Dyson. Simmons caved in defensive tackle Rocky Bernard, moving him so easily that Starks had to offer almost no double-team help before moving to the linebacker level and making a key block by cutting off Tatupu. At the point, Miller shoved defensive end Bryce Fisher inside, just where the Steelers wanted him to go. Said Fisher, "I went down a little too far inside."

Faneca swung around Fisher and overwhelmed Hill in the hole. At this point, the Seahawks had a problem because Bernard and Fisher had been knocked so far out of their gaps, but still they had Boulware, the unblocked man. "That's the running back's guy, as they say," said Whisenhunt.

Willie Parker, just the fourth undrafted free agent to start at running back in a Super Bowl, took the handoff and cut between Fisher and the submerged Hill. Boulware flew up from the secondary to make the tackle. Said Holmgren, "I think he'll make that play 8 out of 10 times, 9 out of 10."

Boulware played it outside-in, so when Parker stayed inside, the strong safety lunged and missed. "The linebacker [Hill] got kicked out and you step up inside and you've got to make the tackle," said Will Lewis, the Seahawks' director of pro personnel. "That's the deal."

The only man left to prevent Parker from a 75-yard touchdown was Pruitt, whose 4.55-second clocking in the 40-yard dash was no match for Parker's 4.4. "Once Willie hit the crease and wasn't even slowed down by Boulware, it became a foot race pretty much and Pruitt was going to be outmatched speed-wise," Will Lewis said. Even if Pruitt had taken a perfect angle, it's questionable whether he would have made the tackle. When Pruitt took a flat angle, all he could do was dive at the 50 hoping against hope to clip one of Parker's heels.

"You can say that Boulware should [have tackled Parker], but that's hard," said Whisenhunt. "He's got to run around guys that are making their blocks. The play was blocked so well that he couldn't get to Willie. If Jerome's running it we probably get 15 to 20 yards. When Willie's running it we get a touchdown."

Stevens' second drop came at the Pittsburgh 8 on the next series and wrecked a drive that was culminated by Brown's second missed field goal. Then the Steelers, leading 14–3, marched from their 40 to the Seattle 7 in an attempt to take total command. On third and 6, Ward and Wilson lined up on the right side within a yard of each other. When Ward drove hard into the end zone, Boulware and Babineaux double-covered him. Whisenhunt anticipated that would happen, given Ward's effectiveness in the red zone.

Wilson took a step or two inside and dime back Kelly Herndon jumped inside of him. So Wilson took off to the empty sideline for what he expected to be an easy touchdown. Instead, Roethlisberger threw an awful pass that was intercepted by Herndon, who returned 76 yards to the Pittsburgh 20. "He tried to just lob it out there because Kelly Herndon had been beat so bad," said Whisenhunt. "But Ben just made a bad throw and the ball came up short."

Instead of going up 17–3, the Steelers' lead was cut to merely 14–10 when Stevens caught Hasselbeck's 16-yard pass in the right side of the end zone. Polamalu and Taylor were caught on a crossing route between Jackson and Stevens. "It was one of our two poorest plays," said LeBeau. "It was a common switch play. It's something we actually practiced every week. It was a matter of communication and identifying the threat of the route."

Late in the third quarter, the Seahawks began a 13-play drive from their 2. Alexander, the NFL's

MVP, carried four times for 23 yards. Hasselbeck, whom Holmgren said he had come to trust as much as two of his former charges, Brett Favre and Steve Young, kept for 8 on a bootleg and completed four of five passes for 50 yards. Then Stevens came free down the middle and this time hung on for an 18-yard gain to the 1—or so the Seahawks thought. A flag was down. Right tackle Sean Locklear had been penalized for holding linebacker Clark Haggans.

"Worst call in the game. Absolutely," Holmgren said, his voice rising even when speaking two months after the game. "The other [holds] you could kind of probably say, 'OK, maybe this, maybe that,' although I don't think they should call them in a game like this. This one, there was no penalty. Absolutely no penalty. Behind closed doors, that's been agreed on."

Haggans got a jackrabbit start. Locklear jammed his right hand into Haggans' chest. The pass rusher dipped and fell. "Unquestionably a hold," LeBeau countered. "Every hold they called, I would call them flagrant holds."

After nose tackle Casey Hampton trashed center Robbie Tobeck and sacked Hasselbeck for minus-5, it was third and 18. In the first quarter, Hasselbeck got away with an errant toss to Jackson on third and 16 when Taylor dropped what should have been a routine interception. On what appeared to be the same play, Hasselbeck took a five-step drop against a four-man rush and sailed the ball over Jackson's head into the hands of Taylor. "That was the one throw that he probably shouldn't have done," said Holmgren. "He waited a little long with the throw, and on that throw you can't be late. Then the decision to go to that side of the field was incorrect. Matt's emotional, too. He probably was really pissed about the pass [the nullified completion to Stevens] getting down there."

Taylor made the interception at the 5 and returned 24 yards to the 29. Hasselbeck threw what looked like an old-fashioned cross-body block into Taylor's knees that cut him down. The officials flagged Hasselbeck for an illegal block below the waist, apparently assuming that he was trying to take down the accompanying blocker, corner-back Deshea Townsend. In fact, Hasselbeck never touched Townsend.

TEAM STATISTICS

SEATTLE		PITTSBURGH
20	Total First Downs	14
5	Rushing	6
15	Passing	8
0	Penalty	0
396	Total Net Yardage	339
77	Total Offensive Plays	56
5.1	Avg. Gain per Offensive Play	6.1
25	Rushes	33
147	Yards Gained Rushing (Net)	181
5.5	Average Yards per Rush	5.5
49	Passes Attempted	22
26	Passes Completed	10
1	Passes Intercepted	2
3	Tackled Attempting to Pass	1
14	Yards Lost Attempting to Pass	8
259	Yards Gained Passing (Net)	158
5/17	Third-Down Efficiency	8/15
1/2	Fourth-Down Efficiency	0/0
6	Punts	6
50.2	Average Distance	48.7
4	Punt Returns	2
27	Punt Return Yardage	32
4	Kickoff Returns	2
71	Kickoff Return Yardage	43
76	Interception Return Yardage	24
0	Fumbles	0
0	Own Fumbles Recovered	0
0	Opponent Fumbles Recovered	0
7	Penalties	3
70	Yards Penalized	20
1	Touchdowns	3
0	Rushing	2
1	Passing	1
0	Returns	0
1	Extra Points Made	3
1	Field Goals Made	0
3	Field Goals Attempted	0
0	Safeties	0
10	Total Points Scored	21
33:02	Time of Possession	26:58

"Matt throws the interception and he gets called for a phantom penalty and 15 yards gets tacked on to that. So that's a 50-yard play. Then they throw the flea-flicker," Holmgren said. "The whole thing was too bad."

Just under 11 minutes remained. Defensive tackle Marcus Tubbs of Seattle shed center Jeff

SEATTLE

Passing	CP/ATT	YDS	TD	INT	RAT
Hasselbeck	26/49	273	1	1	67.8

Rushing	ATT	YDS	AVG	TD	LG
Alexander	20	95	4.8	0	21
Hasselbeck	3	35	11.7	0	18
Strong	2	7	3.5	0	7

Receiving	NO	YDS	AVG	TD	LG
Engram	6	70	11.7	0	21
Jurevicius	5	93	18.6	0	35
Jackson	5	50	10.0	0	20
Stevens	3	25	8.3	1	16t
Strong	2	15	7.5	0	13
Hannam	2	12	6.0	0	9
Alexander	2	2	2.0	0	4
Morris	1	6	6.0	0	6

Interceptions	NO	YDS	LG	TD
Herndon	1	76	76	0
Boulware	1	0	0	0

Punting	NO	AVG	LG	BLK
Rouen	6	50.2	57	0

Punt Ret.	NO/FC	YDS	LG	TD
Warrick	4/0	27	15	0

Kickoff Ret.	NO	YDS	LG	TD
Scobey	3	55	25	0
Morris	1	16	16	0

Defense	SOLO	AST	TOT	SK
Tatupu	6	3	9	0
Hill	7	1	8	0
Boulware	2	3	5	0
Pruitt	4	0	4	0
Lewis	2	2	4	0
Babineaux	3	0	3	0
Trufant	3	0	3	0
Bernard	2	0	2	0
Koutouvides	2	0	2	0
Tubbs	2	0	2	0
Wistrom	2	0	2	1
Darby	1	0	1	0
Hasselbeck	1	0	1	0
Kacyvenski	1	0	1	0
Manuel	1	0	1	0
Herndon	0	1	1	0
TOTAL	39	10	49	1

PITTSBURGH

Passing	CP/ATT	YDS	TD	INT	RAT
Roethlisberger	9/21	123	0	2	22.6
Randle El	1/1	43	1	0	158.3

Rushing	ATT	YDS	AVG	TD	LG
Parker	10	93	9.3	1	75t
Bettis	14	43	3.1	0	12
Roethlisberger	7	25	3.6	1	10
Ward	1	18	18.0	0	18
Haynes	1	2	2.0	0	2

Receiving	NO	YDS	AVG	TD	LG
Ward	5	123	24.6	1	43t
Randle El	3	22	7.3	0	8
Wilson	1	20	20.0	0	20
Parker	1	1	1.0	0	1

Interceptions	NO	YDS	LG	TD
Taylor	1	24	24	0

Punting	NO	AVG	LG	BLK
Gardocki	6	48.7	60	0

Punt Ret.	NO/FC	YDS	LG	TD
Randle El	2/0	32	20	0

Kickoff Ret.	NO	YDS	LG	TD
Colclough	2	43	22	0

Defense	SOLO	AST	TOT	SK
Taylor	6	1	7	0
Townsend	5	1	6	1
Farrior	4	2	6	0
Haggans	5	0	5	1
Polamalu	4	1	5	0
Foote	4	1	5	0
Hampton	4	0	4	1
Smith	3	1	4	0
Keisel	3	0	3	0
Porter	3	0	3	0
Carter	2	1	3	0
Harrison	2	1	3	0
Hope	1	2	3	0
McFadden	2	0	2	0
Randle El	2	0	2	0
von Oelhoffen	2	0	2	0
Kriewaldt	1	1	2	0
Colclough	1	0	1	0
Hoke	1	0	1	0
Iwuoma	1	0	1	0
TOTAL	56	12	68	3

> "I kept looking at the scoreboard when the game was over saying, 'I'm not going to wake up here, am I?' I kept staring at it. It was almost hypnotic."
>
> *Dick LeBeau, Steelers defensive coordinator*

Hartings and tackled Parker for 1. In the booth upstairs, Whisenhunt had a plan ready. He would run a speed screen (and make 7 yards) to Randle El and try to set up the reverse pass. "Our wide receivers coach, Bruce Arians, and I talked about it," said Whisenhunt. "He said, 'We're ready to go.'"

When Roethlisberger picked up the first down on a quarterback draw, Whisenhunt sent in one of the Steelers' many gadget plays using the exact same formation as the speed screen. The toss went to Parker heading left, and the Seahawks, in an eight-man front, attacked the run. Randle El, a quarterback at Indiana, was lined up on the left side near Ward. As Parker came around, Randle El doubled back and took the handoff. Boulware came in off the back side just far enough so that when he reacted to the reverse, Roethlisberger could cut-block him and give Randle El ample time to find Ward on his deep over route.

The Seahawks were in a Cover 3 zone with Pruitt lined up 13 yards deep in the middle of the field at the snap of the ball. As Parker headed left, Pruitt came up 3 yards and moved forward, while Ward was crossing his face, headed the opposite way in a hurry. Marcus Trufant, the cornerback to Pruitt's right, reacted almost instantly and gave chase. By the time Randle El's spiral was caught by Ward at the 6, Trufant was a step and a half away and Pruitt was 10 yards farther back. The 43-yard touchdown gave Ward five catches for 123 yards, enough for the MVP award.

According to Whisenhunt, the Steelers still would have run the play if Manuel had been in the lineup. "But we also knew he was out and we were going to try to exploit the backup," he said. "The ball was really well thrown. El throws it well enough to be a competent quarterback in the league. The only issue with him is his size."

The Steelers had shown the play in Week 9 against Cleveland and against the Bengals in the playoffs. Holmgren and Cowher entered the league as head coaches in 1992, were good friends, and had almost identical overall records entering the game but one of their many differences was Cowher's love of trick plays and Holmgren's abhorrence of them.

"It boiled down basically to three plays," said Marshall. "The run that broke out. A scramble we didn't handle correctly. And a trick play that we had practiced. It hurts when you lose a key guy in your secondary in the second quarter. I think if that hadn't happened we would have defended the reverse pass. Other than that, guys played tough and we handled the run game extremely well."

After Seattle received the kickoff, Hasselbeck scrambled 18 yards for one first down and passed 13 yards to Joe Jurevicius for another. On a third and 8 the Seahawks sent out four wide receivers. All game LeBeau had to sit on blitzes because Holmgren kept in more blockers than usual. This time, Townsend tried to appear as inconspicuous as possible in the right slot across from Jurevicius.

On the snap, Townsend shot by two occupied offensive linemen as part of a five-man zone pressure. Hasselbeck looked left, turned back right, and was sacked by Townsend for minus-5. "That was Matt," Holmgren said. "He should have changed the protection. He's changed it every single time on that and he just flat missed it. There's no good reason. It wasn't disguised that much. They had one extra man on that side and he should have changed the protection that way."

Another Seattle punt, another Rouen touchback. In came Bettis, the Detroit Mackenzie High School grad playing in his first Super Bowl and his final game. Bettis ran twice for 4 yards and Roethlisberger passed for the key first down. Then Bettis ran twice for 7 and Roethlisberger ran for another first down. Three more runs by Bettis took it down to the 2-minute warning. Soon enough, Super Bowl XL was over.

As thousands of Steelers fans in the remarkably pro-Pittsburgh crowd cheered, tears were noticeable in Cowher's eye as he hugged his three daughters and kissed his wife, Kaye. He had much to be thankful for, but he had even more reason to be overjoyed. These Steelers, with expectations so much lower than some of Cowher's other top teams, had bought his message and made him, at long last, a Super Bowl winner.

"We've been in Pittsburgh a long time, and people were getting restless," Kaye Cowher said. "You can say you can be fulfilled if you don't win [the Super Bowl], but I saw the look on his face after the game. And I know."

Just about every great coach in the post-merger era has won a Super Bowl. Now Cowher had joined Holmgren and many others on the list.

Top Ten Defensive Coaching Jobs

1. **Steve Spagnuolo, Giants, XLII:** The Patriots had killed teams all season. The Giants and Spanuolo had the perfect antidote.
2. **Bill Belichick and Romeo Crennel, Patriots, XXXVI:** Mug Marshall Faulk wherever he goes. Body Isaac Bruce and Torry Holt. Don't blitz Kurt Warner. The "Greatest Show on Turf" ran aground.
3. **Richie Petitbon and Larry Peccatiello, Redskins, XXVI:** Used a nickel defense most of the way (CB Darrell Green played safety) and kept the Bills' top-ranked offense completely off-kilter.
4. **George Seifert, 49ers, XIX:** Could anybody stop Dan Marino? The 49ers did. In an almost unprecedented move, Seifert played a nickel defense over the last three quarters, and the "Marks Brothers" (Clayton and Duper) never got on track.
5. **Gregg Williams, Titans, XXXIV:** The Titans' 17th-ranked defense held the Rams' top-ranked offense to a standstill until Isaac Bruce escaped with that underthrown pass.
6. **Greg Robinson, Broncos, XXXII:** No one before or since has ever run more zero blitzes in a Super Bowl than Robinson. Brett Favre and the Packers adjusted to weak-side blitzing the next season, just not in time to save their budding dynasty.

7. **Buddy Ryan, Bears, XX:** The Patriots weren't exactly chopped liver, but playing at fever pitch for their departing coordinator, the Bears suffocated Tony Eason and Co.
8. **Bud Carson and George Perles, Steelers, IX:** Using the stunt 4-3 drawn up by defensive-line coach Perles, the Steelers controlled the line of scrimmage and the Vikings in the chill of old Tulane Stadium.
9. **Marvin Lewis, Ravens, XXXV:** In the NFC Championship Game, the Giants ran up 518 yards and 41 points against Minnesota. Against a Ravens' defense that had no weaknesses, the Giants settled for 152 yards and 7 points.
10. **George Seifert, 49ers, XXIII:** With six Pro Bowlers, Cincinnati had one of the league's most prolific offenses. Operating against a 49ers defense that seldom huddled and let LB Riki Ellison communicate the calls, the Bengals had their worst game of 1988.

Honorable Mentions: Ernie Stautner, Cowboys, VI; Dave Wannstedt, Cowboys, XXVII; Charlie Sumner, Raiders, XV; Chuck Studley, 49ers, XVI; Bob Zeman, Raiders, XI; Gregg Williams, Saints, XLIV.

XLI
INDIANAPOLIS COLTS 29, CHICAGO BEARS 17

February 4, 2007
Dolphin Stadium, Miami, Florida

L ate on the afternoon of February 4, 2007, the skies over Dolphin Stadium in Miami turned black. Then a hard, drenching rain began to fall, lasting until just past midnight. Thus, the 41st Super Bowl became the first played in game-long precipitation—some would call it an underdog's rain. It should have been a gift from the heavens for the Chicago Bears, a cold-weather team built to perform best in sloppy conditions. As a touchdown underdog against the Indianapolis Colts, a dome team that had been eliminated in wintry weather by New England in two of the previous three seasons, the Bears had every reason to feel bullish about their upset chances.

Then, with the game just 14 seconds old, the Bears gobbled up the point spread. The Colts elected to kick the ball deep to rookie sensation Devin Hester, from neighboring Riviera Beach, Florida, and he brought back Adam Vinatieri's boot 92 yards for an electrifying touchdown. Colts cornerback Marlin Jackson had Hester dead to rights just 12 yards into the return but fanned on the tackle. None of his teammates got another chance to bring Hester down.

The Bears had been afforded little chance by most of the sporting press beyond the "Land of Lincoln." Combined with the equalizing effect of the weather, it now seemed entirely possible that the upstart team with the inferior quarterback from the weaker of the two conferences would at least be competitive and might just win. That the Colts performed well below par for almost the entire first half only enhanced the chances of a stunning outcome.

With their foe on the ropes and ready to be had, the Bears couldn't have found themselves in a better position. But the return by Hester was as much a finish as a start for Chicago. The Bears were unable to take advantage of their good fortune; slowly and inexorably, the tide turned against them.

Attendance: 74,512
Conditions: 67 degrees, mostly cloudy and rain, wind N at 10 mph
Time of kickoff: 6:27 p.m. (EST)
Length of game: 3 hours, 31 minutes
Referee: Tony Corrente

MVP: Peyton Manning, QB, Colts

The Colts went nowhere fast in the early going. On Peyton Manning's first pass, middle linebacker Brian Urlacher instinctively dropped to a point where tight end Dallas Clark was running a seam route. Urlacher got both hands on the ball near the Indianapolis 40, but wasn't quite able to make the interception. After gaining one first down, the Colts had two offensive linemen penalized for false starts in a span of three plays. Then Manning made an egregious mistake by forcing a long pass into Cover 2 zone coverage, and safety Chris Harris intercepted.

The Bears went three-and-out, but the Colts remained in their funk. On two occasions during their second possession, Manning went to the line with the choice of the customary two runs and one pass, as provided him by offensive coordinator Tom Moore, and promptly handed off to rookie Joseph Addai, who ran straight into the teeth of a Bears' blitz. On one run by Addai for no gain, left tackle Tarik Glenn cried, "No, no, no," as Manning was barking out the play at the line that Glenn recognized had no chance for success. "The system is based on Peyton's ability to get us into the right play at the right time," Colts president Bill Polian would say several months afterward. As rain pelted down and the pro-Chicago crowd roared, things could hardly have been going much worse for Indianapolis.

"We were putting pressure on, moving around, doing a lot of things," said Ron Rivera, the Bears' defensive coordinator. "We wanted to attack and

	1	2	3	4	Final
Indianapolis Colts	6	10	6	7	29
Chicago Bears	14	0	3	0	17

SCORING SUMMARY

1st Quarter
CHI   Hester, 92-yd. kickoff return (Gould kick)
IND   Wayne, 53-yd. pass from Manning (kick aborted)
CHI   Muhammad, 4-yd. pass from Grossman (Gould kick)
2nd Quarter
IND   Vinatieri, 29-yd. FG
IND   Rhodes, 1-yd. run (Vinatieri kick)
3rd Quarter
IND   Vinatieri, 24-yd. FG
IND   Vinatieri 20-yd. FG
CHI   Gould, 44-yd. FG
4th Quarter
IND   Hayden, 56-yd. interception return (Vinatieri kick)

get after them. We didn't want Manning to get comfortable. He just threw up the first interception. We had Manning out of his comfort zone and we were up, 7–0."

Then it was third and 10. Manning set up under Pro Bowl center Jeff Saturday, went through his typical machinations, and slowly backed up into shotgun position. The Bears were in a nickel defense, with cornerback Ricky Manning Jr. replacing linebacker Hunter Hillenmeyer, against the Colts' one-back slot formation that they employed on almost every snap of the game.

In the two weeks leading up to the Super Bowl, Bears coach Lovie Smith and his defensive staff had devised a system designed to prevent communication foul-ups. Fearful of the Colts deciphering sideline signals from coaches to players, the Bears decided to outfit their linebackers and defensive backs with wristbands on which the defenses were listed in code.

Rivera called for Cover 2 with a four-man rush. Two linebackers and three cornerbacks were spread across the field in intermediate zone coverage while the two safeties, Harris to the left and rookie Danieal Manning to the right, lined up 13 yards deep, each with responsibility for half of the field.

"One of the guys running on the field said to Danieal, '1, 1, 1,'" Rivera said. "On the wristband,

1 meant to play Cover 2. When the guy went, '1, 1, 1,' [Danieal] played Cover 1 instead of going to his wristband, looking at it and saying, 'OK, 1 says I'm playing Cover 2.'"

The Bears' expectation was that Peyton Manning, given his rocky start, would be hesitant to throw downfield, and if he did check down, the gain would be fewer than 10 yards, thus forcing the Colts to punt. Odds are Manning would have dumped the ball to Addai if Danieal Manning hadn't come charging up in what he thought was man-to-man coverage on tight end Ben Utecht, the slot receiver on his half of the field who was running a shallow crossing route. The cornerback on that side, Charles Tillman, correctly dropped 12 to 15 yards when the wide receiver to the outside of Utecht, Reggie Wayne, released hard inside.

Although Wayne was now sprinting deep into the wide-open sector vacated by Danieal Manning, Peyton Manning had to fight just to get the ball off. Defensive tackle Tank Johnson trashed left guard Ryan Lilja and bore in for the sack, but the best that Johnson could do was swing an arm around the quarterback's waist. With a 10-mile-per-hour wind at his back, Manning had more than enough arm strength to get the ball to Wayne, who hauled it in at the 18 without a defender within 10 yards of him.

Wayne's 53-yard touchdown failed to draw the Colts even because holder Hunter Smith dropped the snap on the extra point. Shortly thereafter, the Bears went ahead, 14–6, on a 57-yard scoring drive, which was set up when a missed block by Glenn enabled defensive end Alex Brown to force a fumble by Addai. The Colts' defense then gave up a 52-yard run by Jones, leading to Rex Grossman's 4-yard touchdown pass to Muhsin Muhammad and the Bears' largest lead. On Jones' slant off left tackle, the Bears caught the Colts in one of their frequent stunts. "Nick Harper should have made that tackle," coach Tony Dungy said. "We were a little antsy early and Antoine [Bethea] just overran it a little bit. But part of that you have to give to Thomas Jones for making a good run and cutting back against the grain." Harper, who spent the second half on crutches with a sprained ankle that had prevented him from practicing all week, was beaten by Muhammad on a delay route for the score.

INDIANAPOLIS COLTS
(AFC, 12–4)

		Offense
87	Reggie Wayne* (6-0, 198)	WR
78	Tarik Glenn* (6-5, 332)	LT
65	Ryan Lilja (6-2, 291)	LG
63	Jeff Saturday* (6-2, 290)	C
73	Jake Scott (6-5, 291)	RG
71	Ryan Diem (6-6, 330)	RT
44	Dallas Clark (6-3, 252)	TE
88	Marvin Harrison* (6-0, 185)	WR
18	Peyton Manning* (6-5, 230)	QB
29	Joseph Addai (5-11, 214)	RB
86	Ben Utecht (6-6, 251)	TE I FB
		Defense
98	Robert Mathis (6-1, 231)	LE
92	Anthony McFarland (6-0, 300)	LT
79	Raheem Brock (6-4, 274)	RT
93	Dwight Freeney (6-1, 268)	RE
94	Rob Morris (6-2, 243)	SLB
58	Gary Brackett (5-11, 235)	MLB
59	Cato June (6-0, 227)	WLB
25	Nick Harper (5-10, 182)	LCB
42	Jason David (5-8, 177)	RCB
41	Antoine Bethea (5-11, 203)	SS
21	Bob Sanders (5-8, 206)	FS

* Pro Bowl selection

CHICAGO BEARS
(NFC, 13–3)

		Offense
87	Muhsin Muhammad (6-2, 215)	WR
76	John Tait (6-6, 312)	LT
74	Ruben Brown (6-3, 300)	LG
57	Olin Kreutz* (6-2, 292)	C
63	Roberto Garza (6-2, 305)	RG
69	Fred Miller (6-7, 314)	RT
88	Desmond Clark (6-3, 249)	TE
80	Bernard Berrian (6-1, 185)	WR
8	Rex Grossman (6-1, 217)	QB
20	Thomas Jones (5-10, 215)	RB
37	Jason McKie (5-11, 243)	FB
		Defense
93	Adewale Ogunleye (6-4, 260)	LE
99	Tank Johnson (6-3, 295)	LT
95	Ian Scott (6-3, 302)	RT
96	Alex Brown (6-3, 260)	RE
92	Hunter Hillenmeyer (6-4, 238)	SLB
54	Brian Urlacher* (6-4, 258)	MLB
55	Lance Briggs* (6-1, 240)	WLB
33	Charles Tillman (6-1, 196)	LCB
31	Nathan Vasher (5-10, 180)	RCB
46	Chris Harris (6-0, 205)	SS
38	Danieal Manning (5-11, 196)	FS

SUBSTITUTIONS

Indianapolis
Offense: WR - 10 Terrence Wilkins, 85 Aaron Moorehead; TE - 81 Bryan Fletcher; T - 74 Charlie Johnson; C/G - 57 Dylan Gandy; RB - 30 DeDe Dorsey, 33 Dominic Rhodes. *Defense:* DE - 64 Bo Schobel, 91 Josh Thomas; DT - 61 Dan Klecko, 95 Darrell Reid; LB - 50 Rocky Boiman, 53 Keith O'Neil, 54 Freddy Keiaho, 56 Tyjuan Hagler; CB - 26 Kelvin Hayden, 28 Marlin Jackson; S - 36 Dexter Reid, 43 Matt Giordano. *Specialists:* K - 4 Adam Vinatieri; P - Hunter Smith; LS - 48 Justin Snow. *DNP:* 12 Jim Sorgi (QB). *Inactive:* 11 Ricky Proehl (WR), 84 John Standeford (WR), 76 Dan Federkeil (T), 69 Matt Ulrich (G), 99 Ryan LaCasse (DE), 51 Gilbert Gardner (LB), 27 Tim Jennings (CB), 34 T. J. Rushing (CB).

Chicago
Offense: WR - 81 Rashied Davis; TE - 82 Gabe Reid, 85 John Gilmore; T - 78 John St. Clair; G - 60 Terrence Metcalf; RB - 29 Adrian Peterson, 32 Cedric Benson. *Defense:* DE - 97 Mark Anderson; DT - 70 Alfonso Boone, 71 Israel Idonije; LB - 53 Leon Joe, 58 Darrell McClover, 94 Brendon Ayanbadejo*; CB - 21 Dante Wesley, 23 Devin Hester*, 24 Ricky Manning Jr; S - 35 Todd Johnson, 44 Cameron Worrell. *Specialists:* K - 9 Robbie Gould*; P - 4 Brad Maynard; LS - 65 Patrick Mannelly. *DNP:* 14 Brian Griese (QB), 16 Mark Bradley (WR). *Inactive:* 12 Justin Gage (WR), 68 Anthony Oakley (C/G), 18 Kyle Orton (QB), 48 J. D. Runnels (FB), 90 Antonio Garay (DT), 59 Rod Wilson (LB), 22 Tyler Everett (S), 27 Nick Turnbull (S).

Although a Vinatieri field goal early in the second quarter cut their deficit, the Colts didn't overtake the Bears until the midpoint of the quarter, when Dominic Rhodes went over for a 1-yard touchdown.

Some maintain that the 56-yard interception return for a touchdown by Colts cornerback Kelvin Hayden in the fourth quarter was the decisive play. It did, after all, turn a 5-point margin into the final count of 29–17. Yet, even though the Colts were behind for long stretches of the first half, it never felt like they were overmatched. Blessed with superior personnel and schemes, it always seemed just a matter of time before the Colts would win. Their dominating play in the second half was more than enough to dispatch the Bears, which never came close to overcoming the ineptness of Rex Grossman at quarterback and perhaps an overall "C" performance.

"We were dictating early in the game," said Bobby DePaul, the Bears' director of pro personnel. "We had all the confidence and the mojo. Peyton wasn't off to a good start. Then we had that mistake. You can't give a guy like Peyton Manning his confidence back. The momentum shifted and we could never get it back. I just think they beat us mentally more than anything."

The Colts—who gave Indianapolis its first pro sports championship since the Indiana Pacers won the American Basketball Association championship in 1973—climaxed a gritty playoff run as the third seed in the AFC, the better conference by far in 2006. After defeating Kansas City (23–8) and Baltimore (15–6) in defensive playoff struggles, the Colts overcame a 21–3 first-half deficit to stun the Patriots, 38–34, in the greatest come-from-behind effort in championship-game history. They triumphed despite having many more games (49) lost by starters to injury than most Super Bowl champions. Then they lost two starters (Harper and right tackle Ryan Diem) to injury in the second quarter of the Super Bowl and another (Utecht) early in the third.

This was also one of the most socially significant moments in the annals of professional team sports in that, in one year, two African American coaches, Dungy and Smith, brought teams to the Super Bowl, in which no black head coach ever had appeared before. Smith, who got his first NFL assistant position from Dungy in 1996 as linebackers coach at Tampa Bay, and Dungy also struck a blow for a modernistic, less confrontational style of coaching.

"The head coach of a successful team, to many people, looked like Vince Lombardi," Dungy said a few days before the Super Bowl. "It was a white, middle-aged coach who screamed fire and brimstone. That's what we saw on NFL Films, and it was a great picture. The thing we didn't see is there were a lot of other people who were successful. I happened to grow up under Bud Grant and he was just as successful in a completely different way. I don't think there was ever a picture of somebody who was not white.

"I think now, over the years and with this happening and two guys coming to the Super Bowl with maybe different personalities than most people perceive of an NFL head coach, a different value system maybe, a different way of expressing themselves, people say, 'You know what? Anything can work if you get the right person.'"

Dungy, fired by the Buccaneers in January 2002 after a six-year record of 56–46, wasn't the only key figure in Indianapolis with demons to cast aside. Polian, five times NFL executive of the year, had been 0–3 in Super Bowls as general manager of the Buffalo Bills. Peyton Manning, the first player drafted by Polian for the Colts in 1998, had been stigmatized as a quarterback who couldn't win the big one, with a 3–6 playoff record as the leader of six teams that won at least 10 games in the regular season.

Amazingly, the Colts lost their last four road games of the 2006 season. The low point came on December 10 in Jacksonville when they yielded 375 rushing yards in a 44–17 drubbing. That night even Polian admitted to considerable doubt about whether the team could find a way to handle the run sufficiently in the postseason against the power run teams of the AFC. "But after looking at the tape Tony said, 'Hey, it's fixable,'" Polian recalled, "and we got it fixed."

The return of free safety Bob Sanders in the playoff opener after a 12-game absence due to a knee injury was monumental. The decision by Dungy in Week 14 to start 245-pound backup middle linebacker Rob Morris on the strong side rather than 225-pound Gilbert Gardner was significant as well. Defensive tackle Anthony "Booger" McFarland, obtained by Polian from Tampa Bay at the trading

> "[Manning] stunk early, but he regrouped because it's Peyton Manning. He played an excellent second half. Everybody's good when you've got a quarterback, for God's sake. Let's be honest. That was a tale of two quarterbacks."
>
> *Bobby DePaul, Bears director of pro personnel*

deadline for a second-round draft choice, played better as the season progressed and was the first defensive player whom Dungy cited for meritorious performance in the Super Bowl. Another important adjustment was that Dungy, who established the team's defensive philosophy but allowed coordinator Ron Meeks to call the game, decided in the playoffs to align ends Dwight Freeney and 231-pound Robert Mathis in the 7-technique location rather than wider in their customary 9-technique position.

Seldom, if ever, has a Super Bowl team made more dramatic improvement in such a red-letter category as the Colts. After ranking last in the regular season with a yield of 173 rushing yards per game, including 202.8 in their last six games, the Colts allowed merely 82.8 in four playoff games, even though the opposing running backs were such outstanding players as Larry Johnson, Jamal Lewis, and Laurence Maroney.

In September, the NFL's annual examination of 53-man rosters revealed that Indianapolis fielded both the lightest (237.7 pounds per man) and shortest (6-foot-1.1) team in the league. Few squads, if any, in Super Bowl history were less imposing stepping off the bus than the 2006 Colts. "Ugly looking," said one personnel man for a team in the Colts' division, "and really small."

Any number of Colts' players and coaches conceded that if football were a contest measuring size and athletic ability, they wouldn't even be in the playoffs. "I know," said John Teerlinck, the Colts' garrulous defensive line coach. "They look worse than you. Our midgets and our runts and our misfits. We laugh about it all the time—after we kick your ass."

The matchup that Dungy said caused him the most concern was the Colts' smallish offensive line against the front seven of the Bears' fifth-ranked defense. "When their front four really controlled things, got the quarterback off rhythm, got you out of your running game, that's when they were really tough," Dungy said.

Under Howard Mudd, the Colts' esteemed position coach, the team's offensive linemen had other ideas. "Just the way the playoffs had played out, that confidence running the ball just began to breed in us," said Saturday, a Colts' starter since 2000. "Then it started raining, so you knew it was going to be hard to throw. Guys just had that mentality, 'Hey, we're going to try to knock guys on the ground, open up big holes, and let our running backs do the work.' I don't think, as a group, we could have played any better." Regarded for years as a finesse team, the Colts smashed the stereotype with 191 yards on the ground, the most against the Bears all season.

On the Colts' first running play, Addai made one cut and pounded through a hole created by Lilja's crushing block against Johnson. When Urlacher made the tackle 14 yards downfield after being shoved aside by Saturday, the die was cast. "When that happened, I said, 'Yes, I think that's what we were looking for,'" Mudd said. "We thought we could run right at 'em between the tackles. In that game we ran slant, belly, trap, sprint draw, and one more. That's it. Five different plays."

After losing Diem to an ankle injury, the Colts had to play with rookie Charlie Johnson, a sixth-round pick from Oklahoma Stat e with just 131 regular-season snaps under his belt. "Under the circumstances, I thought our best [lineman in the Super Bowl] was Johnson," said Dungy. "He was blocking their best defensive lineman [Adewale Ogunleye] and we didn't have to give him any extra help."

Other than a missed block by Saturday on a third-and-2 late in the first half, Mudd thought Saturday dominated Urlacher. Said Rivera, "Brian's problem on occasion is he tends to look for the ball a little bit too soon before he defeats the blocker. He was looking for the ball instead of working against Saturday."

"They really kicked their ass is what they did," said Mudd, referring to his line. "But they didn't have one of their good players [Tommie Harris], and that was good for us." Not only had the Bears been without their best defensive lineman, Harris, since

Week 13 with a hamstring injury, they also lost their exceptional safety and team leader, Mike Brown, to a foot injury in Week 6. "No Tommie Harris, they lost the safety, and Tank Johnson was obviously distracted," said Polian. "They were a depleted defense coming into the Super Bowl and that's a bad matchup. Just as it was a bad matchup for us early in the year when we were depleted. . . . If you don't have all your guns, you're not the same team."

Wayne's long first-quarter touchdown served to awaken the Colts' offense, while the clarion call for the Indianapolis defense, according to Dungy, came a few plays after the Bears' second touchdown, with the Bears leading by 8 and poised to take real command. From the Chicago 48, backup tailback Cedric Benson took a first-down handoff off right guard and was met head-on by Sanders. Benson wound up flat on his back, the ball came loose, and the Colts recovered. "Put his hat right on the ball," Bears general manager Jerry Angelo said of Sanders' hit.

Again the Colts couldn't move, however, and the Bears went back on offense. Benson had to leave with a sprained medial collateral knee ligament when his leg hit the helmet of linebacker Cato June on a 4-yard carry. "We lost our 1-2 combination, Jones and Benson, which had been working pretty good the latter part of the season," said Angelo. "I don't think it played a big part in our [ineffective] running game, but it probably played something."

The Bears failed to make a first down on the final four possessions of the first half and went to the locker room trailing 16–14. Their play-caller, coordinator Ron Turner, tried forcing the issue on the ground with Jones but made little headway. Late in the first quarter, Turner ran Jones on third and 6, gained 4, and punted, giving the Colts a short field en route to a field goal. Late in the second quarter, he ran Jones on a third-and-3 counter to the strong side, with tight end Desmond Clark and pulling guard Ruben Brown double-teaming Mathis at the point of attack. The Bears were forced to punt again when linebacker Gary Brackett got to Jones and stopped him a yard short. Dungy called it "a huge play."

The Bears were trailing 19–14 by their first possession of the second half. Turner pulled an about-face and called four straight passes. Second and 1 has always been a heavy running down in the NFL, but for this one from the Colts 45, Turner went with a drop-back pass. Right guard Roberto Garza lunged and whiffed against McFarland, enabling the Colts tackle to blow by on a spin move and sack Grossman for a loss of 11.

On third and 12, Grossman fumbled for the second time on what the Bears said was a clean exchange from center Olin Kreutz. Eleven more yards were lost in the ugly scramble that ensued before Grossman recovered. "I don't think we stayed as committed to our running game as we had in the past," Muhammad said. "But I don't make those decisions."

On defense, the Bears also strayed from their game plan after Wayne's touchdown. Rivera blitzed six men on six of the Colts' first 20 dropbacks, but then didn't rush more than five on their final 19. The Bears' blitzing tactics came to a screeching halt midway through the second quarter after two bad plays. Against a five-man pressure, Peyton Manning found Marvin Harrison on a shallow crossing route for 22 yards, with linebacker Lance Briggs mismatched in coverage. On the next play, the Bears sent two extra rushers up the middle, and Manning broke containment right and found Clark for 17. "All the left defensive end [Israel Idonije] has to do is stay outside and contain and Manning runs right to him for the sack," Rivera said. "The main reason we lost the game defensively was we made too many basic mistakes." He added, "The biggest thing was, we didn't tackle very well."

The Bears missed 15 tackles on defense and 2 on special teams (the Colts' totals were 5 and 3). Chicago's linebackers accounted for seven of the misses, including three by Urlacher. Two plays after the 17-yard completion to Clark, Rhodes broke the tackle of cornerback Nathan Vasher on third and 2 and advanced 3 yards to the Chicago 8. "We had Rhodes hit at or behind the line and we fricking miss the tackle," Rivera said. "They should have had to kick a field goal." Instead, on first and goal Rhodes roared for 7 yards on a trap of Johnson behind textbook blocking from the guards and center, and then he scored easily from the 1 on the next play.

Chicago dodged further damage in the final two minutes of the half when tight end Bryan Fletcher lost a fumble inside the Chicago 40 after a hit by Tillman, who recovered the ball. After Grossman botched another exchange and defensive tackle Raheem Brock recovered the fumble for Indianapolis at the Chicago 35, Urlacher worked behind Saturday to drill Addai for no gain on a third and 2 at the Chicago 17. The half ended when Vinatieri's kick was wide left from 36 yards. "It was a little demoralizing," said Russ Purnell, the Colts' special-teams coach. "We had controlled the football but it was 16–14. [Vinatieri] just pulled it a little bit. It didn't miss by much."

The Bears opened the second half in Cover 2, according to Rivera, hoping that Peyton Manning could be coaxed into making another mistake downfield. Instead, he completed six of six short passes for 31 yards as the Colts consumed seven and a half minutes in a 13-play, 56-yard drive to set up Vinatieri's 24-yard field goal, increasing their advantage to 19–14. Four of the receptions were by Addai, who caught all 10 of the passes thrown to him in the game for 66 yards. Of Addai's 143 total yards, 64 came after contact. Of Rhodes' 121 yards, 85 came after contact. Said Polian, "Certainly in the playoff run, the combination of Joseph Addai and Dominic Rhodes was every bit as good as Thurman Thomas and Kenny Davis during those great years in Buffalo."

Manning never came close to an interception after the second series. "I really didn't think he was going to be patient enough to just work underneath us," said Rivera, "but he came out in the third quarter and did just that. I take my hat off to him. Then our seam players in Cover 2 didn't react as quickly as you need them to."

Danieal Manning missed two tackles and the other safety, Harris, was exposed on the first play of the Colts' second possession in the third quarter. The Colts ran the same sprint draw to Rhodes that had resulted in the first-quarter fumble when Glenn had failed to block Alex Brown. This time Brown stunted hard inside, with Hillenmeyer scraping behind to fill the vacant C-gap. Rhodes took the handoff, froze Hillenmeyer dead in his tracks, and then shrugged off the linebacker's desperate lunge.

TEAM STATISTICS

INDIANAPOLIS		CHICAGO
24	Total First Downs	11
12	Rushing	3
11	Passing	8
1	Penalty	0
430	Total Net Yardage	265
81	Total Offensive Plays	48
5.3	Avg. Gain per Offensive Play	5.5
42	Rushes	19
191	Yards Gained Rushing (Net)	111
4.5	Average Yards per Rush	5.8
38	Passes Attempted	28
25	Passes Completed	20
1	Passes Intercepted	2
1	Tackled Attempting to Pass	1
8	Yards Lost Attempting to Pass	11
239	Yards Gained Passing (Net)	154
8/18	Third-Down Efficiency	3/10
0/1	Fourth-Down Efficiency	0/1
4	Punts	5
40.5	Average Distance	45.2
3	Punt Returns	1
42	Punt Return Yardage	3
4	Kickoff Returns	6
89	Kickoff Return Yardage	138
94	Interception Return Yardage	6
2	Fumbles	4
0	Own Fumbles Recovered	1
3	Opponent Fumbles Recovered	2
6	Penalties	4
40	Yards Penalized	35
3	Touchdowns	2
1	Rushing	0
1	Passing	1
1	Returns	1
2	Extra Points Made	2
3	Field Goals Made	1
4	Field Goals Attempted	1
0	Safeties	0
29	Total Points Scored	17
38:04	Time of Possession	21:56

"Hunter was right there to make the tackle for no gain and he just missed the tackle," Rivera said. "He's a lot more reliable than that."

Saturday locked up Urlacher for three full seconds before the all-pro tried to escape by spinning off in the improper direction. By then, Rhodes was flying down the left side. Harris came over and

INDIANAPOLIS

Passing	CP/ATT	YDS	TD	INT	RAT
P. Manning	25/38	247	1	1	81.8

Rushing	ATT	YDS	AVG	TD	LG
Rhodes	21	113	5.4	1	36
Addai	19	77	4.1	0	14
Dal. Clark	1	1	1.0	0	1
P. Manning	1	0	0.0	0	0

Receiving	NO	YDS	AVG	TD	LG
Addai	10	66	6.6	0	12
Wayne	2	61	30.5	1	53
Harrison	5	59	11.8	0	22
Dal. Clark	4	36	9.0	0	17
Fletcher	2	9	4.5	0	6
Rhodes	1	8	8.0	0	8
Utecht	1	8	8.0	0	8

Interceptions	NO	YDS	LG	TD
Hayden	1	56	56	1
Sanders	1	38	38	0

Punting	NO	AVG	LG	BLK
Smith	4	40.5	50	

Punt Ret.	NO/FC	YDS	LG	TD
Wilkins	3	14	18	0

Kickoff Ret.	NO	YDS	LG	TD
Wilkins	4	89	28	0

Defense	SOLO	AST	TOT	SK
Brackett	6	2	8	0
June	5	2	7	0
Hayden	4	1	5	0
Bethea	4	0	4	0
Morris	4	0	4	0
Harper	3	0	3	0
Mathis	2	1	3	0
Sanders	2	1	3	0
David	2	0	2	0
Jackson	2	0	2	0
McFarland	2	0	2	1
Boiman	1	0	1	0
Diem	1	0	1	0
Fletcher	1	0	1	0
Keiaho	1	0	1	0
Moorehead	1	0	1	0
Dar. Reid	1	0	1	0
Dex. Reid	1	0	1	0
Brock	0	1	1	0
TOTAL	43	8	51	1

CHICAGO

Passing	CP/ATT	YDS	TD	INT	RAT
Grossman	20/28	165	1	2	68.3

Rushing	ATT	YDS	AVG	TD	LG
Jones	15	112	7.5	0	52
Grossman	2	0	0.0	0	0
Benson	2	-1	-0.5	0	4

Receiving	NO	YDS	AVG	TD	LG
Des. Clark	6	64	10.7	0	18
Berrian	4	38	9.5	0	14
Muhammad	3	35	11.7	1	22
Jones	4	18	4.5	0	14
McKie	2	8	4.0	0	4
Davis	1	2	2.0	0	2

Interceptions	NO	YDS	LG	TD
Harris	1	6	6	0

Punting	NO	AVG	LG	BLK
Maynard	5	45.2	58	

Punt Ret.	NO/FC	YDS	LG	TD
Hester	1/0	3	3	0

Kickoff Ret.	NO	YDS	LG	TD
Davis	1	15	15	0
Gilmore	2	6	9	0
Hester	1	92	92	1
Peterson	1	10	10	0
G. Reid	1	9	9	0

Defense	SOLO	AST	TOT	SK
Briggs	11	2	13	0
Tillman	7	4	11	0
Urlacher	7	3	10	0
D. Manning	7	1	8	0
Vasher	4	2	6	0
Hillenmeyer	1	5	6	0
Ta. Johnson	4	1	5	0.5
I. Scott	4	0	4	0
Harris	3	1	4	0
Brown	2	0	2	0
R. Manning	2	0	2	0
Ogunleye	2	0	2	0
Anderson	1	1	2	0.5
To. Johnson	1	1	2	0
Ayanbadejo	1	0	1	0
Boone	1	0	1	0
Garza	1	0	1	0
Grossman	1	0	1	0
Jones	1	0	1	0
Peterson	1	0	1	0
Mannelly	0	1	1	0
TOTAL	62	22	84	1

whiffed on the tackle, enabling Rhodes to race 20 more yards (for 36 in all) to the Chicago 28. Two more booming blocks by Saturday sprung Rhodes on a pair of 8-yard bursts before Vinatieri's 20-yard field goal made it 22–14.

At this point, with three minutes remaining in the third quarter, the Colts had run 63 plays to the Bears' 23. Another squib kick by Vinatieri (who kicked long to Hester only to start the game) and a 15-yard unnecessary roughness penalty on Mathis enabled the Bears to start from the Indy 40. On third and 8, Grossman did well to elude a sack and might have run for the first down. Instead, he threw rashly into traffic and was fortunate the pass was not intercepted by cornerback Jason David. Robbie Gould then kicked a 44-yard field goal.

When the Bears next got the ball back, there were 13½ minutes remaining and they still were down just 22–17. Muhammad worked inside, reached for a pass thrown behind him, and held on for a 22-yard gain. On the next play, Muhammad flanked wide right against Hayden, a one-time wide receiver at Illinois who had been converted to cornerback in 2004 when Turner was the head coach of the Fighting Illini. "I was trying to make a double move and get behind the defender," said Muhammad. "We had a lot of success with that particular play."

The problem for Muhammad was that the Colts were in an eight-man front, and Hayden was playing well off Muhammad in deep-third coverage. "Ron Turner had played against our defense a ton when he was with the Bears [1993–1996]," Dungy said. "They knew we jump things and we read the quarterback. They had tried three or four double moves, and a lot of them had come in that midfield area. Kelvin just did a good job of being aware of it."

Grossman pump-faked once hoping Hayden would come up, but he kept drifting back. Meanwhile Muhammad had no choice but to run the route anyway, all the while thinking that Grossman surely would recognize there was no chance for a completion and would check down or throw the ball away. Grossman stayed with it, however, throwing a floater from a stiff-legged base. Muhammad didn't appear even to see the ball until it was too late. Hayden made a leaping interception tight

to the sideline, eluded Muhammad, and weaved 56 yards to the end zone as his teammates turned into marvelous blockers. A replay challenge from Chicago showed that Hayden's left foot was just inches from being out of bounds at the start of his return.

Two minutes later, Grossman faked a handoff to Jones off right tackle as rookie safety Antoine Bethea flew up into the box. "That was the one time they actually got us," Dungy said. "Antoine was supposed to be deep. We were two scores ahead but the play-action caught him and they had a shot with it."

Speedy wide receiver Bernard Berrian ran a deep over route from out of the left slot into the sector vacated by Bethea. June chased but couldn't keep up. In ideal weather, it would have been a relatively easy 50-yard throw for an NFL quarterback. "Normally, that's the best thing he does is throw deep balls," said Dungy, referring to Grossman. In the rain, however, Grossman delivered a ball that was horribly off line, perhaps 10 yards short and 10 yards inside. So, Sanders had time to range from the other half of the field and make a sensational interception, which he returned 38 yards.

The rest, as they say, was academic. Grossman was able to pad his statistics, completing 9 of 11 passes in the final seven and a half minutes for 73 yards to finish with a passer rating of 68.3. That placed him in the same ballpark as Manning's 81.8, yet in the final analysis, the play of the quarterbacks was dramatically different. "As a young guy with ability who's coming on, everything has to work properly for Rex to have a good day," said Polian, "whereas Peyton, with nine years of experience, can shrug off an interception. In the end, when you compare the two, obviously there's no comparison." Grossman fell apart against a defense that didn't find it necessary to blitz him even once on a pass all day.

Indianapolis' superiority was evident in yardage (430–265) and time of possession (38:04–21:56). Angelo pointed out that even though the Bears, in his judgment, had played poorly in all three phases, they did remain in contention until the fourth quarter. As one of the Colts' coaches suggested, the game might well have been a rout given typically ideal Super Bowl weather. Moreover, the Colts turned the ball over three times and were guilty of seven other glaring

Top Ten Kick Returns

1. **Desmond Howard, Packers, XXXI:** Late in the third quarter, the Patriots have just cut the lead to 27–21. Adam Vinatieri's boot hangs for 4.3 seconds, but the coverage is late in arriving. Howard takes it right back up the middle and goes 99 yards for a clinching touchdown.

2. **Fulton Walker, Dolphins, XVII:** With the score tied at 10, punter Jeff Hayes kicks off for Washington. Walker receives the kick, eludes Otis Wonsley, and then outruns LeCharls McDaniel. When Hayes falls, the last 60 yards of Walker's 98-yard return are easy.

3. **Devin Hester, Bears, XLI:** Vinatieri's opening kickoff has 4.13 seconds of hang time. Marlin Jackson has a bead on Hester, but is faked out badly and never even touches him. Matt Giordano makes a great chase and overhauls Hester, but it's in the end zone after a 92-yard run.

4. **Stanford Jennings, Bengals, XXIII:** After San Francisco ties the game at 6 late in the third quarter, Jennings receives the ensuing kick and bursts through the coverage. Terry Greer eventually catches up to him inside the 5, but they tumble into the end zone to complete a 93-yard touchdown.

5. **John Taylor, 49ers, XXIII:** Early in the second quarter, Taylor fields a 63-yard punt by Lee Johnson. Putting together a string of moves, he makes three tacklers miss and runs it back 45 yards.

6. **Rick Upchurch, Broncos, XII:** With the Broncos down 20–3 in the third quarter, Upchurch returns a kickoff 67 yards and sets up Denver's lone touchdown.

7. **Jermaine Lewis, Ravens, XXXV:** After the Giants score their first (and only) points of the game on a return by Ron Dixon, Lewis receives Brad Daluiso's short kickoff at the 16. He eludes two cornerbacks and finishes off an 84-yard run for a touchdown.

8. **Ron Dixon, Giants, XXXV:** Immediately before Lewis' return, Dixon uses his sprinter's speed to go 97 yards for a touchdown. He skips past Cornell Brown and is gone.

9. **Tim Dwight, Falcons, XXXIII:** Early in the fourth quarter, the Broncos score to make it 31–6. Dwight fields the ensuing kickoff and takes advantage of a missed tackle by Tory James to complete a 94-yard touchdown return.

10. **Andre Coleman, Chargers, XXIX:** Trailing 42–10 late in the third quarter, the Chargers run a wedge return to their left, and Coleman hits the crack. After Coleman eludes several tacklers, he jukes kicker Doug Brien and is off for a 98-yard touchdown.

---

mistakes in the first half before they came through with an almost flawless second half.

"It wasn't a great game for us," said Dungy. "We were probably an 8 [on a scale of 1 to 10]. We did a lot of things well, especially in the front [lines]. Given the weather conditions and the emotion, it was pretty good on our part."

Clearly, the Colts didn't have to be operating at peak efficiency to dispatch the best team from the NFC, just as New England and San Diego probably wouldn't have needed to, either. Still, that didn't detract from their accomplishment.

The Colts joined the Dallas Cowboys of 1992 as the only Super Bowl champion without a single player on defense selected for the Pro Bowl. Dungy and his exceptional coaching staff found ways within their fully dimensional system to play championship defense when it counted most. The offense had been Super Bowl caliber most of the decade.

"Last year's team was healthier and had more talent on it," Polian said, "but this one was more resilient and tough-minded. I'm a personnel man, but I can tell you that it isn't personnel that wins. The people who tell you that are dead wrong. What wins is team chemistry, leadership, character, hard work. We've had more talented teams than this team, but this team is the world champion and there's a reason why."

XLII

NEW YORK GIANTS 17, NEW ENGLAND PATRIOTS 14

February 3, 2008
University of Phoenix Stadium, Glendale, Arizona

After the fact, the New York Giants could easily be portrayed as a supremely confident David that found a way to slay Goliath. Truth be told, however, the underdog squad in Super Bowl XLII had little to no idea if it had enough nerve or manpower to contain the highest-scoring offense in the history of the NFL.

"I thought New England had a juggernaut, I really did," Steve Spagnuolo, the Giants' defensive coordinator, said several months after the game. "In my days here on earth, it was the most prolific offense I had ever seen with the best quarterback ever to play the game, in my opinion. In a lot of ways I'm in awe of their offense and the people that coach them and what they do. Now that didn't mean I didn't think we could win. Our guys were confident they could compete, especially coming off that Game 16. But I thought if we could hold them under 30 we were doing a decent job. That's how much respect I had for them."

Game 16 was a matchup between the Giants and the undefeated Patriots in the regular-season finale. With a wild-card playoff berth secure and nothing material to be gained, Giants coach Tom Coughlin stood up for integrity and went all-out to win in what turned out to be a 38–35 defeat for the 10–6 Giants and a 16–0 season for New England. In that game, many of the Giants proved to themselves and their teammates that the Patriots weren't invincible. Even more important was the stubborn performance of Spagnuolo's defense and the message that the first-year coordinator received from defensive lineman Justin Tuck as they walked off the field that night at Giants Stadium.

"Believe it or not, Justin said to me, 'Coach, if we get the chance to play them again, just let us get after them.' What he was saying was to let the four down guys do it," Spagnuolo said. "I remembered that conversation. There were moments in the

Attendance: 71,101	
Conditions: Indoors	
Time of kickoff: 4:30 p.m. (MST)	
Length of game: 3 hours, 35 minutes	
Referee: Mike Carey	
MVP: Eli Manning, QB, Giants	

[Super Bowl] when I said, 'I'm just going to let the front four take care of this.'"

Of the unit versus unit matchups in this Super Bowl, only the Giants' defensive line against the Patriots' offensive line turned into a mismatch. The Giants shut down the Patriots' solid running game and contained Tom Brady. Final numbers on the New York pass rush showed 5 sacks (against an offense that allowed an average of 1.3 sacks in the first 18 games), 8 knockdowns, 5 hurries, and 2 batted passes. With heavy pressure from his front four, Spagnuolo could get away with blitzing an abnormally low 26 percent. Thus, Spagnuolo was able to roll coverage at times behind cornerback Corey Webster's matchup against the great Randy Moss and limit Brady to a long completion of merely 19 yards.

"Their front rushed well. [Guard] Chris Snee is a good player," said Patriots coach Bill Belichick when asked months later if any of the Giants had really impressed him. "I respect what the Giants did, but I'm not sure either team played their best game. They were a little better than we were on that day. . . . There were five plays at the end of the game that very easily could have gone the other way and the game's over. That's really what it came down to."

Trying to become the first 19–0 team in pro football history, the Patriots lost, 17–14, after quarterback Eli Manning's 13-yard touchdown pass to wide receiver Plaxico Burress with 35 seconds left culminated a 12-play, 83-yard drive. Gone was the Patriots'

	1	2	3	4	Final
New York Giants	3	0	0	14	17
New England Patriots	0	7	0	7	14

SCORING SUMMARY

1st Quarter
NY   Tynes, 32-yd. FG
2nd Quarter
NE   Maroney, 1-yd. run (Gostkowski kick)
4th Quarter
NY   Tyree, 5-yd. pass from Manning (Tynes kick)
NE   Moss, 6-yd. pass from Brady (Gostkowski kick)
NY   Burress, 13-yd. pass from Manning (Tynes kick)

place in the conversation as greatest team ever, as was their bid for a fourth championship in seven years. "Was it disappointing to lose?" Belichick said. "Yeah. Will I remember it? I mean, yeah. It was a great accomplishment by the team. Not easy to do."

The second of a Super Bowl–record three lead changes in the fourth quarter transpired on Brady's 6-yard touchdown pass to Moss. All but 71 of the 80 yards in the drive came through the air. On the march, the Patriots began to max protect for the first time, while the Giants' four-man rush, by Spagnuolo's admission, began to show telltale signs of fatigue. "It was max protection; they kept the tight end in and there was a lot of play-action," he said. "They were just being the 18–0 Patriots. They were in a pressure situation needing to score and they executed their offense. I'd love to have that series back. . . . We should have pressured more."

On third and 6, middle linebacker Antonio Pierce made a call when Wes Welker crossed the formation in motion but Tuck didn't pick it up. Instead of being the fourth rusher, Tuck dropped into coverage, leaving an insufficient three-man rush. The Giants made another mistake on the outside, where safety Gibril Wilson double-covered Welker inside with help from linebacker Kawika Mitchell. The coverage was designed for Wilson and Webster to double Moss outside. Falling back on his haunches, Webster reacted poorly, failed to get his hands on Moss, and went sprawling as Moss scored easily on a soft inside cut. "That was one of the few times in the playoffs where I thought Corey did not continue

to play aggressive," said Spagnuolo. "We had a miscommunication inside and we really had a safety not executing the right defense. Usually when that happens against good teams, they find a way to score."

Webster, a second-round draft choice in 2005, had come to symbolize the rise of the Giants late in the season. Not only had he been benched by midseason, but he was inactive for two games when the Giants were playing Sam Madison and R. W. McQuarters, two aging players with minimal speed. When injuries struck, however, Coughlin gave Webster what was in effect one last chance, and in the four playoff games he played almost to the level of a shut-down corner, especially against Terrell Owens in the divisional upset of Dallas. In the Super Bowl, Webster covered Moss on 51 of the receiver's 66 plays, including 39 snaps with just 2 yards or less separating them across the line of scrimmage. Moss caught 5 of 12 targeted passes for 62 yards, but his only catch with Webster in coverage was the touchdown.

"You couldn't ask for anything more than the way Corey played Moss," said Marc Ross, the Giants' director of college scouting. "Corey was a perfect example of just everything coming together at the right time. . . . When Corey stepped up it took the pressure off everybody and made everyone better. Where that confidence came from at that time, I have no idea."

Stephen Gostkowski's 67-yard kickoff, which hung in the air almost forever (4.28 seconds), was fielded by Domenik Hixon. He accelerated ahead to the 17 and was blown up by safety Ray Ventrone, a free agent from Villanova. It was Ventrone's first tackle in three years. "He went down and just splattered the kid and it was like, 'Man, this guy could be one of the heroes of the Super Bowl,'" said Brad Seely, the Patriots' special-teams coach from 1999

> "The Giants got hot at the end and were really playing good, kind of like we were in 2001. I thought they were better from the last game of the season to the Super Bowl even."
>
> *Brad Seely, Patriots special-teams coach*

NEW YORK GIANTS (NFC, 10–6)				NEW ENGLAND PATRIOTS (AFC, 16–0)	
		Offense			
17	Plaxico Burress (6-5, 232)	WR	83	Wes Welker (5-9, 185)	
66	David Diehl (6-5, 319)	LT	72	Matt Light* (6-4, 305)	
69	Rich Seubert (6-2, 310)	LG	70	Logan Mankins* (6-4, 310)	
60	Shaun O'Hara (6-2, 303)	C	67	Dan Koppen* (6-2, 296)	
76	Chris Snee (6-3, 317)	RG	61	Stephen Neal (6-4, 305)	
67	Kareem McKenzie (6-6, 327)	RT	77	Nick Kaczur (6-4, 315)	
89	Kevin Boss (6-6, 253)	TE	84	Benjamin Watson (6-3, 255)	
81	Amani Toomer (6-3, 203)	WR	81	Randy Moss* (6-4, 210)	
10	Eli Manning (6-4, 225)	QB	12	Tom Brady* (6-4, 225)	
27	Brandon Jacobs (6-4, 264)	RB	39	Laurence Maroney (5-11, 220)	
39	Madison Hedgecock (6-3, 266)	FB	44	Heath Evans (6-0, 250)	
		Defense			
92	Michael Strahan (6-4, 255)	LE	94	Ty Warren (6-5, 300)	
96	Barry Cofield (6-4, 306)	DT I NT	75	Vince Wilfork* (6-1, 335)	
98	Fred Robbins (6-4, 317)	DT I RE	93	Richard Seymour (6-6, 310)	
72	Osi Umenyiora* (6-3, 261)	RE I OLB	50	Mike Vrabel* (6-4, 261)	
53	Reggie Torbor (6-2, 250)	SLB I ILB	55	Junior Seau (6-2, 250)	
58	Antonio Pierce (6-1, 238)	MLB I MLB	54	Tedy Bruschi (6-1, 247)	
55	Kawika Mitchell (6-1, 253)	WLB I OLB	96	Adalius Thomas (6-2, 270)	
31	Aaron Ross (6-0, 197)	LC	22	Asante Samuel* (5-10, 185)	
23	Corey Webster (6-0, 202)	RC	27	Ellis Hobbs (5-9, 195)	
37	James Butler (6-2, 215)	SS	37	Rodney Harrison (6-0, 220)	
28	Gibril Wilson (6-0, 209)	FS	36	James Sanders (5-10, 210)	

* Pro Bowl selection

SUBSTITUTIONS

New York

Offense: WR - 12 Steve Smith, 85 David Tyree, 87 Domenik Hixon; TE - 88 Michael Matthews; T - 79 Guy Whimper; G - 77 Kevin Boothe; C/G - 67 Grey Ruegamer; RB - 22 Reuben Droughns, 44 Ahmad Bradshaw. **Defense:** DE - 71 Dave Tollefson, 91 Justin Tuck; DT - 93 Jay Alford; LB - 51 Zak DeOssie, 52 Tank Daniels, 57 Chase Blackburn, 59 Gerris Wilkinson; CB - 25 R. W. McQuarters, 29 Sam Madison, 35 Kevin Dockery; S - 43 Michael Johnson. **Specialists:** K - 9 Lawrence Tynes; P - 18 Jeff Feagles. **DNP:** 2 Anthony Wright (QB). **Inactive:** 83 Sinorice Moss (WR), 86 Jerome Collins (TE), 61 Adam Koets (T), 13 Jared Lorenzen (QB), 26 Danny Ware (RB), 75 Manny Wright (DT), 99 Russell Davis (DT), 33 Geoffrey Pope (CB).

New England

Offense: WR - 10 Jabar Gaffney, 15 Kelley Washington, 18 Donte' Stallworth; TE - 88 Kyle Brady; T - 68 Ryan O'Callaghan; G - 71 Russ Hochstein; RB - 33 Kevin Faulk; FB - 38 Kyle Eckel. **Defense:** DE - 90 Le Kevin Smith, 97 Jarvis Green; NT - 95 Rashad Moore; LB - 52 Eric Alexander, 53 Larry Izzo, 58 Pierre Woods; CB - 21 Randall Gay; S - 23 Willie Andrews, 26 Eugene Wilson, 41 Ray Ventrone; CB/S - 31 Brandon Meriweather. **Specialists:** K - 3 Stephen Gostkowski; P - 6 Chris Hanson; LS - 66 Lonie Paxton. **DNP:** 16 Matt Cassel (QB). **Inactive:** 80 Troy Brown (WR), 17 Chris Jackson (WR), 82 Stephen Spach (TE), 65 Wesley Britt (T), 74 Billy Yates (G), 7 Matt Gutierrez (QB), 92 Santonio Thomas (NT), 28 Antwain Spann (CB).

to 2008. "It was like, 'OK, now we're going to start playing like we're supposed to be playing. This is our game to win.'" Joel Collier, the Patriots' secondary coach, said, "We all thought we had the momentum. Eighty-three yards they'd have to go to try and win the football game. That's pretty good odds right there."

Manning, ranked merely 25th in passer rating at 73.9 during the regular season, had played his best regular-season game in more than two seasons (118.6 rating), statistically speaking, five weeks earlier against New England. What Collier remembered most from the first meeting was Manning's proficiency in two-minute situations. "Considering what we had given up to them in that game (395 yards), our defense played pretty well in the Super Bowl," said Collier. "We did a pretty decent job of shutting down the run game and giving Manning some trouble. We took care of Plaxico, for the most part. But as it turned out, the two-minute is what got us in the end from a defensive perspective."

The Giants started from their 17 with 2:39 and three timeouts left. With 1:40 remaining, they were facing fourth and 1 at their 37. The Patriots played the down tough with four linemen, four linebackers, and a safety in a nine-man box. Although rookie running back Ahmad Bradshaw had been outperforming starter Brandon Jacobs, Coughlin went with his jumbo back. Rashad Moore, a

New York

Head Coach: Tom Coughlin. *Offense:* Kevin Gilbride (coordinator), Mike Sullivan (wide receivers), Mike Pope (tight ends), Pat Flaherty (offensive line), Dave DeGuglielmo (assistant offensive line), Chris Palmer (quarterbacks), Jerald Ingram (running backs), Sean Ryan (quality control). *Defense:* Steve Spagnuolo (coordinator), Mike Waufle (defensive line), Bill Sheridan (linebackers), Peter Giunta (secondary, cornerbacks), David Merritt (secondary, safeties), Andre Curtis (assistant). *Special Teams:* Tom Quinn, Thomas McGaughey (assistant). *Strength:* Jerry Palmieri, Markus Paul (assistant).

New England

Head Coach: Bill Belichick. *Offense:* Josh McDaniels (coordinator, quarterbacks), Nick Caserio (wide receivers), Pete Mangurian (tight ends), Dante Scarnecchia (offensive line, assistant head coach), Ivan Fears (running backs), Bill O'Brien (assistant). *Defense:* Dean Pees (coordinator), Pepper Johnson (defensive line), Matt Patricia (linebackers), Joel Collier (defensive backs). *Special Teams:* Brad Seely. *Strength:* Mike Woicik, Harold Nash (assistant).

reserve defensive tackle, displaced left guard Rich Seubert just enough so the Patriots had a chance to stop the 264-pound Jacobs. But Jacobs was able to squirt through right guard and, with a late fall forward, gained the first down by about a foot. It was hardly a powerful run by Jacobs, and it almost cost New York the game.

On the next play, Adalius Thomas—an outside linebacker in New England's 3-4 base defense but the right end on passing downs—beat left tackle David Diehl badly and forced Manning to scramble. It was the first of Thomas' four pressures in a span of five plays; he would finish with six and a half in all, including a pair of sacks. Other than him, the Patriots' pass rushers were basically shut out, with neither Mike Vrabel nor Ty Warren recording a pressure.

Desperate to harass Manning, Belichick and coordinator Dean Pees wound up blitzing five or more on 44.7 percent of the Giants' dropbacks. "I just think our two lines asserted themselves physically," Giants offensive coordinator Kevin Gilbride said. "Certainly, our defensive line was spectacular, and I think our offensive line was

solid." When the Giants decided to release left tackle Luke Petitgout in February 2007, they were fortunate that Diehl, primarily a starting guard from 2003 to 2006, proved capable of at least functional play at left tackle.

Following a timeout, the Patriots blitzed safety Rodney Harrison, and Manning sailed a pass high over the head of wide receiver David Tyree, who was open on a sideline comeback. The ball went directly to cornerback Asante Samuel near the boundary. Samuel, whose 10 interceptions in 2006 tied for the league lead, later said he misjudged his leap and should have jumped even higher. As the ball glanced off his gloved hands, New England's best chance for victory went with it. "Biggest play, or non-play, in the drive," said Collier, "because that shuts it down. You're talking 95 percent of the time he catches that. Through the time [three years] I was with him he had maybe three drops. He's a Pro Bowl player who should make a play like that."

Wide receiver Amani Toomer viewed it as an auspicious omen for New York. "I was like, 'You know what? We have a shot because that's how they usually finish teams off,'" he said.

On third and 5 at their 44, the Giants deployed Tyree wide right, Steve Smith slot right, Toomer slot left, and Burress wide left. The defenders on the Tyree-Smith side, safety James Sanders and Samuel, blew their assignments in zone coverage, leaving Tyree open to the post and Smith open to the corner. "The bottom line was, the coverage broke down as the play extended, not at the beginning," Belichick said. "If you're a safety like Harrison, and you're the last guy, your job is to prevent the play from going further than that. And that's what he did. But it should have never come to that."

As the play unfolded, Gilbride's eyes were downfield, where he could see Tyree open inside and Smith open outside. Gilbride was thinking, "Throw the ball, throw the ball." Then he looked back and saw why Manning hadn't thrown it.

The Patriots rushed only four, but Thomas abused Diehl around the corner in 2.4 seconds, forcing Manning to step up from 9-yard depth in shotgun formation. Over the next 3.1 seconds, Manning was under siege from not only Thomas, but also Richard Seymour and Jarvis Green, who

> "Obviously, Eli had an up and down year, but people still believed in him. Just the way he handled things and his demeanor, his calmness, his poise, not getting pissed off at anybody. If the guy could go through that, you believe he won't be intimidated by any situation."
>
> *Marc Ross, Giants director of college scouting*

ran a successful inside twist. Green placed his left arm around Manning's waist, but Seubert recovered and pushed Green away. Seymour wheeled around center Shaun O'Hara and bore down on Manning when Snee reacted too late to pick him up. "We're upstairs going, 'Yeah!'" said Collier. "We were just waiting for him to go down and the whistle to blow."

Green got his left hand on Manning and then his right, but never both at the same time. Seymour grabbed the No. 10 white jersey with his left hand, pulling and stretching it. The referee, Mike Carey, peered in from a couple of yards away, preparing to blow the play dead. "It was like a scene out of the *Planet Earth* or *National Geographic*, where it's a lion jumping on the back of a wild horse," said Carey. "You could see him desperately trying to pull out, and somehow he did." O'Hara laughingly suggested that it was the first time Manning ever broke a tackle.

Manning found himself spit back out to the 33, suddenly with time to gather himself and the presence of mind to look downfield. Seymour, Thomas, and Vrabel all were running straight toward the quarterback when he released the pass. The ball was in the air for 2.3 seconds. "When I saw how high it was, I said, 'That's good, we'll knock this down,'" Collier said. "The percentages were so low."

Sanders was too deep and still out of position, but Harrison had ample time to come across from the other hash mark. He was standing next to Tyree when the ball was coming back down at the 25. Tyree was the first to the ball, just a split-second before Harrison got his right hand on it. As Tyree fell backward, the ball remained semi-secure in his right hand and he managed to press the ball to the

back of his helmet while getting his left hand onto the ball. Tyree's left foot hit the ground, supporting his weight, as he crashed onto the inside of Harrison's left leg. Over his head, the ball came within inches of touching the ground, which would have meant incomplete pass.

Harrison, a 14-year veteran, clawed at the ball as Smith rushed in. From his knees, Smith began pulling at Harrison's neck and shoulders. Smith walked away, then took the very real risk of incurring what might have been a catastrophic penalty for taunting by coming back and screaming at Harrison once again. Harrison, who a few months later said he had no regrets because "not in a million years does he make that catch again," was exonerated by Belichick. "Harrison made as good a play as he could have made on it," the coach said. "I don't think there's anything else he could have done."

Said Seely, "Obviously, you're going to carry that with you the rest of your life because of what we were playing for. The guy makes a catch of forever in Super Bowls, and it's a guy that besides coaches and players in the league you've never heard of. As the guys that lost the game, that's one of the ways we try to justify it. That wouldn't happen again. Well, it did that day, and they won the game."

Tyree, a sixth-round pick in 2003 from Syracuse, had carved out a niche in the NFL mostly by contributing on special teams. "The velocity of the throw, the defender draped all over me, the curved surface of the ball against a round helmet, the way we came down to the ground," Tyree said. "It just doesn't make sense."

Said Ross, "When it's your fifth receiver against a Pro Bowl safety, the odds aren't good. But it was just a game where everything went our way. Afterward, the kid just said he wanted it, so he did. And on that play Eli said, 'This is my destiny. I'm going to make it happen.'"

Alertly, Coughlin called for a timeout, his second. With 59 seconds showing, the 32-yard gain left New York with a first down at the 24. When play resumed, Manning held the ball too long (five seconds) and went down in Thomas' grasp for a 1-yard sack. On second down, Smith and Tyree were open on the left side, but Thomas collapsed the pocket against Diehl again, and Manning sent up a floater that fluttered 6 yards downfield near Tyree and dime safety Brandon Meriweather. The Patriot had the best shot at it but couldn't make the interception. "Brandon actually was in pretty good position and should make the play," said Collier. "He had dropped far too many during the season, but that was within his range."

Issued another reprieve, Gilbride on third and 11 ran the same play but to the right side, which in this case was the short side of the field. He also had Jacobs remain in as the sixth blocker to chip Thomas, helping Diehl. The Patriots rushed four for the fourth snap in a row, and this time Manning found Smith in the clear cutting from the slot toward the sideline. Meriweather, the defender on Smith, allowed himself to get bumped off by Toomer and was late getting to the flat. "It hadn't happened to us in a long time," said Collier. "We worked on that a lot."

Smith, a clutch possession receiver in the playoffs after returning from an 11-week absence due to a fractured scapula, turned neatly up the field for 4 yards after the catch before slipping out of bounds. Meriweather's sloppy coverage had given the Giants another first down, this time at the 13.

Given the Patriots' inability at this point to rush or cover effectively, Gilbride called the same play from the same formation for the third snap in a row. "I didn't think they'd blitz zero," he said. "I thought they'd play the same coverage and the ball would go back to Steve Smith again." The Patriots did have a history of bringing the house in the red zone. With Vrabel having no luck against right tackle Kareem McKenzie and double-teams finally slowing Thomas, New England dialed up a seven-man blitz for the only time in the game.

Collier, whose contract wasn't renewed by Belichick shortly after the Super Bowl, wouldn't disclose if Belichick or Pees made the call. "Unfortunately, that's one of them I'll have to go to my grave with," he said. "I have to leave it be. My impression . . . is that both coordinators would bounce things off [Belichick]. Bill would offer, 'That's good, that's good,' or 'I might think this.' But he would never say you have to do this or you have to do that."

Belichick offered nothing specific on whose idea it was to all-out blitz. "In the end, they're all my calls," he said. "I have the final say on all of them. We're blitzing and we should get there. The corner can't sit there and think about the guy running eight moves. You have to think, 'We're blitzing and the ball's going to come out, and I've got to break on it.' Burress double-moved him."

In the Week 16 meeting, the Giants had sent Burress wide left in the red zone against Ellis Hobbs, the right cornerback. Manning had the freedom to read Hobbs' pre-snap position and signal Burress to run either the slant or the fade. Later, Gilbride saw on tape Hobbs breaking up a lot of slants. "So we said, 'Remember. The only play it's going to be is a fade,'" said Gilbride. "I reminded them of that Saturday night in the meeting."

When the Patriots came with seven rushers against six blockers, Jacobs crossed in front of Manning from left to right and smacked Harrison, the most dangerous blitzer. Thomas, who would have been unblocked on the play side, aborted his rush after two or three steps because he was responsible for Jacobs in man coverage if he filtered out on a check-down. "Eli had all the time in the world after that because that defender actually pulled off," Gilbride said.

Hobbs, in his first season as a full-time starter, set up on the 8 and Burress was straddling the 15 when the ball was snapped. "I had to play him inside," Hobbs said. "What you hope is we can get to the quarterback so he doesn't have time to throw it." Burress took three hard strides, jabbed inside, and ran the slant-and-go to the corner. Manning comfortably released the ball in 1.6 seconds and Hobbs had no chance to recover. "Part of me says it's our fault for putting him in that situation," said Collier. "I feel bad for the kid because [Burress is] not an easy guy to cover. . . . It's the kind of matchup that we spent the whole game trying to avoid." Collier added, "But when it comes down to it, defensive backs have to cover. Sometimes they have to cover all by themselves."

Still, there were 29 seconds remaining when the Patriots started from their 26, down by 3 points and with three timeouts left. On the first play, Brady was pressured and threw incomplete on a deep seam route to Welker. On second down, he was sacked for minus-10 when rookie defensive tackle

Jay Alford beat right guard Russ Hochstein in 2.5 seconds. "Another example of a guy stepping up in the playoffs," said Ross. "By far his best play of the year."

On the next play, Brady dashed right to buy time and flung a 65-yard bomb for Moss, who was a step or two behind Webster and Wilson. The ball grazed Webster's outstretched fingers at the 19 an instant before Moss touched it with both hands, but he couldn't quite hang on. "Corey made a hell of a play," said Spagnuolo. "I guess if Tom throws it five yards deeper you could make the argument that Moss is going to catch it." Brady's fourth-down prayer carried 64 yards toward Moss on the left side, but Webster was in perfect position and the ball fell incomplete.

The scoreboard read 0:01. Manning would be required to field the snap and take a knee. Suddenly, Belichick came jogging across the field to shake hands with Coughlin, his old friend and colleague. With officials trying to clear the field, Belichick set sail for the far tunnel and the Patriots' locker room, leaving his players and coaches to stand alone in defeat.

For Belichick, it was another brush with controversy. In September 2007, he was fined $500,000 and the Patriots were fined $250,000 by NFL Commissioner Roger Goodell for illegally taping the signals of opposing coaches. New England was also made to forfeit its first-round draft choice in 2008. Hall of Fame coach Don Shula, whose 1972 Dolphins thus remained the only undefeated team (17–0) in the Super Bowl era, compared the Patriots' three Super Bowl triumphs to Barry Bonds' home-run record that was tainted by alleged steroid abuse.

"The 'Spygate' thing has diminished what they've accomplished," Shula said. "You would hate to have that attached to your accomplishments. They've got it."

Owner Robert Kraft called the 2007 Patriots the best of his many great teams, apparently based on the Patriots' prodigious statistical achievements. Their 589 points established an NFL record, as did Brady's 50 touchdown passes and Moss' 23 touchdown receptions. They had a point differential of plus-315, widest in NFL history, and turned the ball over a league-low 15 times. Their turnover-differential of plus-16 also included 31 takeaways by the defense.

Yet, in the Super Bowl, New England's defense failed on six of seven excellent chances to take the ball away. Besides the dropped interceptions by Samuel and Meriweather in the final drive, Sanders and nickel back Randall "Blue" Gay couldn't come up with potential interceptions. In the second quarter, backup linebacker Pierre Woods appeared to be on top of a botched handoff between Manning and Bradshaw before the running back inexplicably was able to rip the fumble recovery away from Woods. On the next series, the Patriots had the chance to recover a sack-fumble by Manning, but Smith beat them to it. "It would have been nice if we could have caught any of those," said Belichick. "We had our chances."

The Giants' lone turnover, one of just two in four playoff games, occurred on an early second-quarter short pass from Manning to Smith on a pivot route that might well have gone for a 14-yard touchdown had it not been dropped. When Manning threw the ball a tad early, it ricocheted off Smith's hands to Hobbs for the interception. "That was the other time they blitzed," said Gilbride. "There was a little pressure but Eli had enough time to hang in there another half count. Steve usually makes the play. Hit him right in the hands."

New York had set the physical tone on the game-opening series, eating up a Super Bowl–record 9:59 before settling for Lawrence Tynes' 32-yard field goal. Urged by Coughlin and Gilbride to let the game come to him, Manning completed a pair of third-down passes against Gay, a defender whose coverage from the slot was successfully exploited by the Giants. The opening sequences also showed that Bradshaw, a seventh-round draft choice from Marshall, wouldn't be intimidated. First, he ran over Meriweather, and two plays later he ran over Samuel, bouncing up to trash-talk Harrison.

"I had talked to Ahmad and Steve Smith all week that you had to treat Rodney Harrison for what he was, which was a bully," Gilbride said. "You have to stand up to him and back him down. If you go back through the game, the two of them are constantly going after Harrison."

When it was the Patriots' turn, they opened with a delayed screen to Laurence Maroney off deliberate play-action fakes. When Brady turned around to release the ball, defensive ends Osi Umenyiora and Michael Strahan were right there to grind him into the ground as the pass fell incomplete. Due in large part to a 16-yard interference penalty against Pierce on an end-zone seam route to tight end Ben Watson, the Patriots were able to take the lead, 7–3. Until New England's 80-yard drive late in the fourth quarter, the Giants' defense yielded just 11 first downs and nary a point in the Patriots' next six possessions.

A third-and-1 carry by Maroney lost 2 in the second quarter when Umenyiora beat left tackle Matt Light off the ball. Brady then absorbed back-to-backs sacks: the first when left guard Logan Mankins blew a blitz pickup against a newly installed delayed rush by Pierce, and the second when Tuck beat Mankins up the field. Late in the first half, Tuck caused Brady to fumble after slipping past Mankins one more time, and the Giants recovered for their only takeaway.

Playing the final game of his brilliant 15-year career, Strahan led the onslaught with 5½ pressures. Tuck contributed 4½ and Umenyiora had 3½. Two of Spagnuolo's blitzers, Mitchell and Wilson, each had two pressures. "Our defensive MVP would have been Tuck," said Spagnuolo. "We had what we called an 'Okie offset' to put Justin on Mankins. Justin felt he could get after him. Our guys were possessed, no question."

Mankins, Light, and center Dan Koppen all made the Pro Bowl for a New England line expertly coached by Dante Scarnecchia since 1999. Mankins allowed 5½ pressures, while Light and right tackle Nick Kaczur allowed 4 each, Hochstein (who replaced injured Stephen Neal late in the second quarter) allowed 2½, and Koppen allowed ½. "Trust me, I know [Scarnecchia] is still sick about it," Seely said several months later. "That wasn't the way we play. I mean, who's counting on that happening to a guy like Logan Mankins? Tom was running for his life. He was just trying to buy a little time to get guys open and he didn't have it."

The sheer dominance of the Giants' front four against the Patriots' line was no surprise to Ross, however. "A lot of [the Patriots'] notoriety came from Brady making quick reads and getting the ball away so quick," he said. "We had better players up front—better athletes, better pass rushers than they were blockers. Moss is superior. Brady is superior. The rest of their guys, that O-line and those old line-backers, and their secondary are just average—we matched up well against them."

Until their final possession, the Patriots basically stayed with what worked for them all season. That is, they sent out five receivers and relied on Brady to find the open man. Should the Patriots have made the adjustment to six- and even seven-man protections sooner? "If you asked those [offensive coaches] today they'd probably say, 'Yes,'" Seely said. "But I think it comes down to, what worked to get you there? You played 18 games and were very successful, as successful as anyone has ever been in this league."

Four of the Giants' 5 sacks came with 4 rushers opposed by 5 blockers. Of Brady's 8 knockdowns, 4 came with 4 rushers working against 5 blockers, and another with 3 rushers opposing 5. As well as Strahan, Tuck, and Umenyiora performed, the Patriots couldn't double all three, so they essentially decided to double none. "Keep them in? For who? They didn't blitz," said Belichick. "You can [chip], but then who are you going to throw to? You'd have one, two guys going out. It very easily could have turned out differently. In the end, it turned out the way it did."

If the Patriots did have plans to balance their offense, those plans quickly went awry. Maroney, who had rushed for 100 yards or more in four of the previous five games, settled for 36 yards in 14 carries. In all, New England rushed 16 times, and seven resulted in no gain or negative yardage. The tight ends, Kyle Brady and Watson, were responsible for three and a half of those poor runs when they couldn't handle Umenyiora and Tuck on the edges. "They were such a prolific passing team that our guys just didn't get so geared up about that and have them gash us for a bunch of runs," said Spagnuolo. "Our guys did a picture-perfect job of filling in their gaps."

Brady had suffered an injury to his right ankle in the AFC Championship Game that landed him in a protective boot and kept him from practicing in the days before the Patriots left for Phoenix. During game week, however, he participated fully in practice and wasn't even listed on the team's official injury report. According to Belichick and several of his coaches, Brady didn't appear hampered by the ankle in the Super Bowl.

"After I looked at the tape—maybe he wasn't quite as good," said Gilbride. "He missed a lot of passes and he usually doesn't do that. There were guys wide open. Was that the ankle or was that the pressure, or a combination of the two? I don't know."

Early in the third quarter, the Giants committed one of their four penalties when linebacker Chase Blackburn was a step late getting off the field before a punt on fourth and 2. No flag was thrown, but Seely mentioned it to Belichick. Because of the lengthy commercial break, the Patriots had time to look at the sideline photo, which confirmed their suspicion, and Belichick tossed the red challenge flag. "It was a possession play," said Belichick. "That was a turnover."

On third and 13, running back Kevin Faulk displayed remarkable second effort to turn a routine flat pass into 14 yards and a first down at the New York 28. Backup safety Michael Johnson overran the play, one of the Giants' six missed tackles (the Patriots had three). With the Patriots primed for at least a field-goal attempt, Strahan beat Kaczur off the ball on third and 7 and sacked Brady in 3.2 seconds for minus-6. That set up what would have been a 49-yard try for Gostkowski, whose longest field goal in 18 games had been 45 yards. In Seely's opinion, he had at least a 50 percent chance to make it.

"In that week's practice at Arizona State, Stephen had struggled a little bit off the left hash from long yardage," said Seely. "Hindsight is 20–20. Looking back on it, well, we should have kicked it. But as prolific as our offense was, we had gone for it on fourth down a bunch of times. Even on our sidelines it wasn't that big a deal. I've never asked Bill why he didn't do it."

Said Belichick, "I just thought it was the best thing for us at that time. If we miss a field goal, we give up a lot of field position. Losing yardage on the play before probably didn't help."

From the shotgun on fourth and 13, Pierce cheated on the coverage and was out of position, enabling Watson to come open on a seam route to the

right. But Brady didn't have time to wait for Watson because Umenyiora and Tuck executed a successful tackle-end stunt against Mankins and Koppen. Umenyiora flattened Brady just after he rushed a long pass over the head of Jabar Gaffney deep on the left side.

Nonetheless, the Patriots' defense had gone

TEAM STATISTICS

NEW YORK		NEW ENGLAND
17	**Total First Downs**	22
4	Rushing	3
13	Passing	17
0	Penalty	2
338	**Total Net Yardage**	274
63	Total Offensive Plays	69
5.4	Avg. Gain per Offensive Play	4.0
26	**Rushes**	16
91	Yards Gained Rushing (Net)	45
3.5	Average Yards per Rush	2.8
34	**Passes Attempted**	48
19	Passes Completed	29
1	Passes Intercepted	0
3	Tackled Attempting to Pass	5
8	Yards Lost Attempting to Pass	37
247	Yards Gained Passing (Net)	229
8/16	**Third-Down Efficiency**	7/14
1/1	**Fourth-Down Efficiency**	0/2
4	**Punts**	4
39.0	Average Distance	43.8
3	**Punt Returns**	1
25	Punt Return Yardage	15
2	**Kickoff Returns**	4
39	Kickoff Return Yardage	94
0	**Interception Return Yardage**	23
2	**Fumbles**	1
2	Own Fumbles Recovered	0
1	Opponent Fumbles Recovered	0
4	**Penalties**	5
36	Yards Penalized	35
2	**Touchdowns**	2
0	Rushing	1
2	Passing	1
0	Returns	0
2	**Extra Points Made**	2
1	**Field Goals Made**	0
1	Field Goals Attempted	0
0	**Safeties**	0
17	**Total Points Scored**	14
30:27	**Time of Possession**	29:33

NEW YORK

Passing	CP/ATT	YDS	TD	INT	RAT
Manning	19/34	255	2	1	87.6

Rushing	ATT	YDS	AVG	TD	LG
Bradshaw	9	45	5.0	0	13
Jacobs	14	42	3.0	0	7
Manning	3	4	1.3	0	5

Receiving	NO	YDS	AVG	TD	LG
Toomer	6	84	14.0	0	38
S. Smith	5	50	10.0	0	17
Boss	1	45	45.0	0	45
Tyree	3	43	14.3	1	32
Burress	2	27	13.5	1	14
Bradshaw	1	3	3.0	0	3
Hedgecock	1	3	3.0	0	3

Interceptions	NO	YDS	LG	TD
None	--	--	--	--

Punting	NO	AVG	LG	BLK
Feagles	4	35.3	55	0

Punt Ret.	NO/FC	YDS	LG	TD
McQuarters	3/0	25	16	0

Kickoff Ret.	NO	YDS	LG	TD
Hixon	2	39	25	0

Defense	SOLO	AST	TOT	SK
Butler	10	1	11	0
Pierce	8	3	11	0
Mitchell	3	5	8	1
Tuck	5	1	6	2
G. Wilson	3	2	5	0
Dockery	4	0	4	0
Umenyiora	3	1	4	0
Robbins	3	0	3	0
Strahan	2	1	3	1
Alford	2	0	2	1
Madison	2	0	2	0
Torbor	2	0	2	0
Blackburn	1	1	2	0
Johnson	1	1	2	0
Ross	1	1	2	0
Webster	1	1	2	0
Bradshaw	1	0	1	0
Cofield	1	0	1	0
DeOssie	1	0	1	0
Wilkinson	0	1	1	0
TOTAL	54	19	73	5

NEW ENGLAND

Passing	CP/ATT	YDS	TD	INT	RAT
T. Brady	29/48	266	1	0	82.5

Rushing	ATT	YDS	AVG	TD	LG
Maroney	14	36	2.6	1	9
Faulk	1	7	7.0	0	7
Evans	1	2	2.0	0	2

Receiving	NO	YDS	AVG	TD	LG
Welker	11	103	9.4	0	19
R. Moss	5	62	12.4	1	18
Faulk	7	52	7.4	0	14
Stallworth	3	34	11.3	0	18
Maroney	2	12	6.0	0	8
K. Brady	1	3	3.0	0	3

Interceptions	NO	YDS	LG	TD
Hobbs	1	23	23	0

Punting	NO	AVG	LG	BLK
Hanson	4	32.5	49	0

Punt Ret.	NO/FC	YDS	LG	TD
Welker	1/1	15	15	0
Faulk	0/1	0	0	0

Kickoff Ret.	NO	YDS	LG	TD
Maroney	4	94	43	0

Defense	SOLO	AST	TOT	SK
Harrison	11	1	12	0
Bruschi	5	3	8	0
Seymour	3	4	7	0
Warren	4	2	6	0
A. Thomas	5	0	5	2
Wilfork	4	1	5	0
Sanders	3	1	4	0
Meriweather	3	0	3	0
Woods	3	0	3	0
Seau	2	0	2	0
Alexander	1	1	2	0
Samuel	1	1	2	0
Vrabel	1	1	2	0
Green	1	0	1	1
Izzo	1	0	1	0
Koppen	1	0	1	0
Ventrone	1	0	1	0
Hobbs	0	1	1	0
TOTAL	50	16	66	3

two and a half quarters without allowing a point, maintaining the 7–3 lead entering the fourth quarter. One of the Patriots' effective coverages had been a "quarter-quarter-half" look, made highly unusual because Harrison was dropping down within 4 yards of the line rather than playing the standard depth of 9 to 10 yards. "In an unorthodox way, they had what amounted to double coverage on each of the wideouts but still having the eighth guy in the box," said Gilbride. "It made the running game tougher sleddin'. It's not a sound coverage, but if you don't exploit it, it is sound. They were getting rolled-up coverage on 'Plax' and an extra guy down on the line of scrimmage."

The way to beat the coverage, said Gilbride, was with the tight end on an inside-breaking route or the outside receiver on a post. That's what the Giants had done in the third quarter, but Vrabel had other ideas, tying up tight end Kevin Boss at the line and preventing him from getting into his route. Thus, Manning had to throw it away.

"I finally went to the sidelines," recalled Gilbride, "and said, 'Here's what we're going to do. No matter what the coverage, you [Boss] are going to run a seam because there's nobody deep.'" To help Boss obtain a clean release, Gilbride added return motion for the rookie so he could start farther away from a defender. "The problem is he got so wide that Harrison actually saw him and fell back outside-in," said Gilbride, "but there was nobody deep and he caught the ball."

The 45-yard completion to Boss, the longest play of the game, came on the first play from scrimmage of the fourth quarter and positioned the Giants at the New England 35. Boss, who replaced Jeremy Shockey in Week 15 when the Pro Bowl player went on injured reserve with a broken leg, made the catch 20 yards downfield. He shook off Harrison initially before the veteran recovered, dived at him, and clipped his heels. "Two guys covered the back and nobody covered the tight end," Belichick said. "We obviously blew the communication on the play. Coaching. Playing. At this level that shouldn't happen. It wasn't a hard play."

The Giants converted a third-and-4 when Smith beat Gay on an inside route from the right slot for 17 yards. Then on second down from the 5, Gilbride flanked Tyree wide right against Samuel, hoping the Patriots might think it was a run. "We were trying to play a little outside technique and have the safeties be in position to discourage the inside throw," Collier said. "The play-action fake got Junior [Seau] and the safety [Sanders] on that side, which created a lane." Tyree slashed down inside ahead of Samuel, and Manning's pass whizzed past umpire Tony Michalek so fast that Seau could only wave at the ball

before it was caught by Tyree for the touchdown. The Giants had regained the lead, 10–7.

"I'll tell you what the game plan was in the passing game," Belichick said. "Play the receivers from the inside out. Let them throw the ball in the flat, throw the ball to the sideline. Don't let them in the middle."

And so, when both teams struck for their touchdowns in the final 3 minutes, New York's 3-point margin remained for what Giants' co-owner John Mara called "the greatest victory in the history of this franchise. Without question." Retired Giants' general manager Ernie Accorsi said, "In perspective, this was almost as historic as Super Bowl III."

Throughout New England, shock and sorrow walked hand in hand. Two days before the Super Bowl, all 12 sportswriters from *The Boston Globe* predicted a Patriots victory, by the average score of 35–21. The night before the game, Spagnuolo said the players were informed about a forthcoming Boston Globe book, *19–0: The Historic Championship Season of New England's Unbeatable Patriots*, which was being sold in advance through online booksellers. "We came within 30 seconds of having an unbelievable season, something that probably won't be duplicated again in my lifetime," said Kraft. "But in the last minute and a half, what [the Giants] did was amazing. Either you win or you don't win, then you've got to carry on. On that day, the Giants were a better team."

Favored in all 19 of its games, the Patriots won all but one. A playoff underdog against Tampa Bay, Dallas, and Green Bay, the Giants established an NFL record by winning 11 straight games on the road, counting the Super Bowl.

"I think people underrated severely the players we had," said Ross. "We had a quarterback who had the ability and it came together for him. We had a running game and a good offensive line. We had playmakers at receiver and tight end. We had a great defensive line. The linebackers flew around. The secondary was probably the weak point, but we had a safety who made a lot of plays and the corners stepped up.

"It may sound a little cliché but sometimes people don't really think they're going to win. But with each round that we played, our guys really believed in each other. They were never intimidated by the situation. Our guys were on such a roll of confidence."

Ten Best Plays by a Wide Receiver

1. **David Tyree, Giants, XLII:** Tyree's astonishing catch was "one in a million." With 1:15 left in the game and facing extreme pressure, Eli Manning throws a rainbow to Tyree. He leaps and traps the ball against his helmet for a 32-yard gain. Four plays later, the Giants notch the game-winner.

2. **Lynn Swann, Steelers, X:** It's one of the best known catches, even though it didn't lead to any points. Covered man-to-man by Cowboys CB Mark Washington, Swann leaps for the pass from Terry Bradshaw, tips the ball up in mid-air, and then cradles it to his chest as he crashes to the turf for a gain of 53 yards.

3. **Santonio Holmes, Steelers, XLIII:** Second and goal at the 6 with 42 seconds remaining and Arizona ahead 23–20, Holmes runs a corner route. QB Ben Roethlisberger guns a high pass that barely clears three defenders. Holmes extends, snatching the ball with both hands as his toes stay down before he falls out of bounds on the game-winning score.

4. **Lynn Swann, Steelers, XIII:** With the Steelers leading 28–17 late in the game, Swann is double-covered deep in the end zone. He leaps as high as he can and snags the pass from Terry Bradshaw with his fingertips. It turns out to be the winning score.

5. **Butch Johnson, Cowboys, XII:** By the seven-minute mark of the third quarter, Johnson has already fumbled on a reverse and a kickoff, but he finally redeems himself. On a deep post pattern, he catches a long pass from Roger Staubach in his outstretched fingertips at the 1 and crashes into the end zone— despite playing with a broken thumb.

6. **Jerry Rice, 49ers, XXIV:** In the midst of a long first-quarter drive, Joe Montana throws inside to Rice, who is his third read. Rice makes the catch at the 8, fights off two defenders, and finishes the 20-yard touchdown for the game's first points.

7. **John Stallworth, Steelers, XIV:** It's not looking good for Pittsburgh early in the fourth quarter, trailing 19–17 and Lynn Swann sidelined with blurred vision.

On third and 8, John Stallworth breaks free from coverage and hauls in Terry Bradshaw's throw before striding into the end zone for a 73-yard touchdown.

8. **Mario Manningham, Giants, XLVI:** The Giants started from their 12-yard line with 3:46 left and trailing 17–15. On the first play, Manningham ran a take-off route and made a spectacular 38-yard catch tight to the sideline before being smashed by two defenders.

9. **Otis Taylor, Chiefs, IV:** With their lead cut to 16–7 after a Vikings score early in the third quarter, the Chiefs come right back. Against an eight-man blitz on first down, Len Dawson connects with Taylor on a hitch, who then sails past two defensive backs to complete the clinching 46-yard touchdown.

10. **Max McGee, Packers, I:** On third and 3 late in a scoreless first quarter, Bart Starr audibles to a skinny post route to McGee. The pass is behind McGee, but he reaches back and pulls it in with his right arm. With no defenders left, McGee does a fast jog in for a 37-yard touchdown and the first ever Super Bowl points.

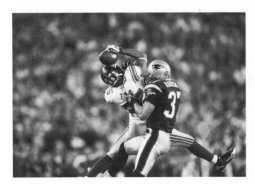

Trapping the ball against his helmet, David Tyree makes a miraculous catch of Eli Manning's pass late in Super Bowl XLII as he fights off Patriots safety Rodney Harrison. Tyree's grab set up the game-winning score and catapulted the Giants to one of the greatest upset victories in Super Bowl history. *Damian Strohmeyer/ Sports Illustrated/Getty Images*

XLIII

PITTSBURGH STEELERS 27, ARIZONA CARDINALS 23

February 1, 2009
Raymond James Stadium, Tampa, Florida

The margin between Ben Roethlisberger and Kurt Warner was as narrow as the one between the Pittsburgh Steelers and the Arizona Cardinals. But in a Super Bowl differentiated by powerless running games and the fourth-quarter collapse of two defenses, the outcome ultimately came down to the play of the quarterbacks.

Each player was superb. Their combined passer rating (104.4) ranked fourth in Super Bowl history, with the losing Warner's rating of 112.3 almost 20 points better than Roethlisberger's 93.2. Still, passer ratings never tell the complete story, and they certainly didn't here. In an epic contest that wasn't decided until the last five seconds, Roethlisberger's near-flawless performance carried the day in the Steelers' 27–23 victory.

Roethlisberger didn't win the most valuable player award. That went to Santonio Holmes, whose four receptions for 73 yards in a last-chance drive included the game-winner deep in the right corner from 6 yards out with 35 seconds remaining. But as spectacular as the finger-tip, toe-dragging catch by Holmes was, the pass by Roethlisberger, which came just one play after Holmes dropped the same type of laser-like toss deep in the left corner, was one for the books, too.

"Everybody talks about the catch, but I still think the throw was unbelievable," said Bruce Arians, the Steelers' offensive coordinator. "He made a throw that I don't know anyone else can make to win that ball game. . . . He just was unbelievable in the last drive. Santonio is very good, and he can be great. But there's no doubt Ben is a great player now."

Larry Fitzgerald's 64-yard touchdown sprint through the heart of the NFL's top-ranked defense gave Arizona the fourth-quarter lead, at 23–20, and might have been as awe-inspiring as any reception in football annals. But the Cardinals left 2½ minutes

Attendance: 70,774	
Conditions: 68 degrees, mostly cloudy, wind NNW at 3 mph	
Time of kickoff: 6:31 p.m. (EST)	
Length of game: 3 hours, 38 minutes	
Referee: Terry McAulay	
MVP: Santonio Holmes, WR, Steelers	

for the Steelers, who already had come from behind five times in the fourth quarter or overtime to tie or win during the season. "They're going to score, that's how you want 'em to score, huh?" 36-year-old coach Mike Tomlin told his offensive linemen as they waited to take the field. "Quick."

The Cardinals knew the Steelers' modus operandi. As it turned out, holding them to a field goal, which would have forced the first Super Bowl overtime, would have been a blessing. "The first thing I did was look at the clock and say, 'Oh, s---, how are we going to hold on?'" said Todd Haley, the Cardinals' offensive coordinator. "I was scared to death. Everybody was celebrating. I took Larry on the side and tried to temper everybody. I said, 'Hey, start prayin' right now.' I thought overtime at worst. But the quarterback and Holmes just made a couple phenomenal plays."

Eleven months earlier, the Steelers had given Roethlisberger a $25.2 million signing bonus as part of a six-year extension worth more than $100 million. "He earned his $100 million right there with that one drive," Fitzgerald said.

After winning four Super Bowls in the 1970s with Terry Bradshaw behind center, the Steelers went to the playoffs 11 times in the 20-year span from 1983 to 2002. Their tried-and-true formula was to be physical, run the ball, and blitz out of a 3-4 defense. Until Roethlisberger arrived with the 11th overall draft selection in 2004, the Steelers never fully trusted their passing game.

	1	2	3	4	Final
Pittsburgh Steelers	3	14	3	7	27
Arizona Cardinals	0	7	0	16	23

SCORING SUMMARY

1st Quarter
PIT   Reed, 18-yd. FG
2nd Quarter
PIT   Russell, 1-yd. run (Reed kick)
ARI   Patrick, 1-yd. pass from Warner (Rackers kick)
PIT   Harrison, 100-yd. interception return (Reed kick)
3rd Quarter
PIT   Reed, 21-yd. FG
4th Quarter
ARI   Fitzgerald, 1-yd. pass from Warner (Rackers kick)
ARI   Safety, holding penalty on Hartwig in end zone
ARI   Fitzgerald, 64-yd. pass from Warner (Rackers kick)
PIT   Holmes, 6-yd. pass from Roethlisberger (Reed kick)

In 2008, the Steelers rushed on merely 45 percent of their plays, and their rushing average of 105.6 yards per game was the lowest of any playoff team in franchise history. A large part of the problem was the patchwork offensive line that ranked as one of Pittsburgh's poorest in years. Somewhat surprisingly, the Cardinals proved to be a physical match for the Steelers; six of running back Willie Parker's 19 carries went for loss or no gain, including three that were the direct result of blocks missed by tight end Matt Spaeth. But, insisted Arians, these Steelers shouldn't be summarily excluded from the list of the NFL's greatest teams just because they ranked 23rd in rushing during the regular season and averaged 2.9 per carry in three playoff games. The NFL game evolved, and so did the Steelers.

"When you think back to the Super Bowl teams," Arians said, "it was Bradshaw to Swann and Stallworth. It was a great defense, great quarterbacks and receivers, and a solid running game. When we won Super Bowl XL we didn't run the ball worth a crap in the playoffs. It was Ben. Going into the Seattle game we knew we could win if he just didn't lose it, and he made enough plays for us to win it. But on that team he was just a young kid. This team was totally different. We were a much better passing team, and our quarterback was a veteran and a

leader. Against Arizona, the quarterback was going to win the game for us."

Roethlisberger made the Pro Bowl for the first time in 2007 when his passer rating of 104.7 ranked second behind Tom Brady. He slipped to 24th (80.1) in 2008 due in part to the Week 1 right shoulder injury that had him operating at about 65 percent until about Week 12, according to Arians. "Late December—whoa—the 55-, 60-yard balls were back," said Arians, "which he couldn't throw [previously]." Then, in the AFC Championship Game victory over Baltimore, Roethlisberger was speared in the back. He remained in the game and practiced all week in Tampa, but three days before the Super Bowl Arians saw Roethlisberger in pain. "He cut one loose and went, 'Oooooooh,'" said Arians. "I knew something grabbed him and he couldn't breathe. He said, 'It's my ribs.' I said, 'Take a deep breath and don't throw the ball hard anymore.' Whether they were cracked, shadows, whatever." Listed as probable on the injury report, Roethlisberger showed no signs of physical impairment during the game, Arians said. Several days after the game, Roethlisberger said an MRI revealed two small rib fractures.

After the bolt out of the blue from Warner to Fitzgerald put Arizona in front with 2:37 left in the game, the Steelers didn't exactly take the field on a high note. Their only score of the second half had been Jeff Reed's 21-yard field goal that capped a 16-play, 79-yard push. The biggest plays, however, were three penalties for 35 yards against the Cardinals. The march ended terribly when, on third and goal at the 2, Roethlisberger lost a yard on a quarterback draw when left guard Chris Kemoeatu and center Justin Hartwig failed to block defensive tackle Gabe Watson. "It was a gimme [touchdown]," said Arians. "I think Chris thought the center was going to help him more, but then the center stepped away and went for the linebacker. One looks more glaring than the other but they're both at fault."

Pittsburgh's first two possessions of the fourth quarter were even more disappointing. The offensive linemen simply could not handle defensive tackle Darnell Dockett. On the first series, right tackle Willie Colon missed a cut-off block and Dockett smeared Parker for minus-4, and then Dockett split Hartwig and right guard Darnell Stapleton for a

PITTSBURGH STEELERS
(AFC, 12–4)

#	Player		Pos	#	Player
		Offense			
86	Hines Ward (5-11, 205)		WR	11	Larry Fitzgerald* (6-3, 220)
78	Max Starks (6-7, 345)		LT	69	Mike Gandy (6-4, 316)
68	Chris Kemoeatu (6-3, 344)		LG	74	Reggie Wells (6-3, 308)
62	Justin Hartwig (6-4, 312)		C	63	Lyle Sendlein (6-4, 300)
72	Darnell Stapleton (6-3, 305)		RG	76	Deuce Lutui (6-3, 332)
74	Willie Colon (6-3, 315)		RT	75	Levi Brown (6-5, 322)
83	Heath Miller (6-5, 256)		TE	82	Leonard Pope (6-8, 258)
10	Santonio Holmes (5-10, 192)		WR	81	Anquan Boldin* (6-1, 217)
7	Ben Roethlisberger (6-5, 245)		QB	13	Kurt Warner* (6-2, 209)
49	Sean McHugh (6-5, 265)		TE I RB	32	Edgerrin James (6-0, 219)
39	Willie Parker (5-10, 209)		RB I FB	45	Terrelle Smith (6-0, 250)
		Defense			
91	Aaron Smith (6-5, 305)		LE I LE	94	Antonio Smith (6-3, 285)
98	Casey Hampton (6-1, 340)		NT	97	Bryan Robinson (6-4, 300)
99	Brett Keisel (6-5, 295)		RE I DT	90	Darnell Dockett (6-3, 285)
56	LaMarr Woodley (6-1, 265)		LOLB I RE	55	Travis LaBoy (6-3, 250)
51	James Farrior* (6-1, 215)		SILB I SLB	56	Chike Okeafor (6-4, 251)
50	Larry Foote (6-1, 239)		WILB I MLB	54	Gerald Hayes (6-1, 249)
92	James Harrison* (5-11, 250)		ROLB I WLB	58	Karlos Dansby (6-3, 250)
24	Ike Taylor (6-0, 195)		LCB	26	Roderick Hood (5-11, 198)
20	Bryant McFadden (5-11, 190)		RCB	29	Dominique Rodgers-Cromartie (6-1, 182)
43	Troy Polamalu* (5-10, 207)		SS	24	Adrian Wilson* (6-2, 230)
25	Ryan Clark (5-11, 205)		FS	21	Antrel Rolle (6-0, 208)

ARIZONA CARDINALS
(NFC, 9–7)

* Pro Bowl selection

SUBSTITUTIONS

Pittsburgh

Offense: WR - 14 Limas Sweed, 85 Nate Washington; TE - 89 Matt Spaeth; RB - 21 Mewelde Moore, 33 Gary Russell; FB - 38 Carey Davis. *Defense:* DE - 90 Travis Kirschke, 93 Nick Eason; DT - 76 Chris Hoke; LB - 54 Andre Frazier, 55 Patrick Bailey, 57 Keyaron Fox, 94 Lawrence Timmons; CB - 22 William Gay, 26 Deshea Townsend, 37 Anthony Madison; S - 23 Tyrone Carter. *Specialists:* K - 3 Jeff Reed; P - 17 Mitch Berger; LS - 61 Jared Retkofsky. *DNP:* 79 Trai Essex (T), 65 Jeremy Parquet (G), 4 Byron Leftwich (QB). *Inactive:* 66 Tony Hills (T), 69 Jason Capizzi (T), 2 Dennis Dixon (QB), 71 Scott Paxson (DE), 96 Orpheus Roye (DE), 53 Bruce Davis (LB), 31 Fernando Bryant (CB), 27 Anthony Smith (S).

Arizona

Offense: WR - 15 Steve Breaston, 85 Jerheme Urban, 87 Sean Morey*; TE - 89 Ben Patrick; G - 61 Elton Brown; RB - 28 J. J. Arrington, 34 Tim Hightower. *Defense:* 91 Kenny Iwebema, 92 Bertrand Berry, 93 Calais Campbell; DT - Gabe Watson; LB - 51 Pago Togafau, 52 Monty Beisel; CB - 20 Ralph Brown, 27 Michael Adams; S - 22 Matt Ware, 47 Aaron Francisco. *Specialists:* K - 1 Neil Rackers; P - 5 Ben Graham; LS - 48 Nathan Hodel. *DNP:* 80 Early Doucet (WR), 70 Pat Ross (C), 7 Matt Leinart (QB). *Inactive:* 84 Jerame Tuman (TE), 68 Elliot Vallejo (T), 72 Brandon Keith (T), 2 Brian St. Pierre (QB), 46 Tim Castille (FB), 78 Alan Branch (DT), 57 Victor Hobson (LB), 25 Eric Green (CB).

12-yard sack. When the Steelers got the ball back, Dockett bull-rushed over Stapleton on an inside stunt for a 10-yard sack, forcing another punt.

"I thought [Dockett] did play a great game," said Clancy Pendergast, the coordinator of the Cardinals' 4-3 "under" defense that ranked 19th in the regular season before soaring to force 12 turnovers in playoff victories over Atlanta (30–24), Carolina (33–13), and Philadelphia (32–25). "He was disruptive in the running game, and with his three sacks was able to put a lot of pressure on Ben. We did a good job at the line of scrimmage. The guys tackled well and we flew to the football. They had [205] yards of total offense until the last drive. We just didn't control the last drive."

The Steelers' offensive malaise intensified on the three-play series just before the strike to Fitzgerald. Pinned down at the 1, Hines Ward dropped a first-down pass near the 7, Parker did well to get out of the end zone for no gain after defensive end Antonio Smith stuffed Stapleton, and then Hartwig was flagged for holding outside linebacker Chike Okeafor in the end zone, which by rule was a safety. "They rushed seven and it was all picked up, but then Justin got hit on the stunt, lost his balance, and just got run over," Arians said. "Justin played on one leg. He sprained his MCL in the San Diego playoff game and really probably shouldn't have been playing in the Baltimore game brought the house even though unpredictability and risk-taking had been his trademark as a coordinator. A week later, Pendergast was fired.

At first, the Cardinals' approach paid off. On the first play of the drive, Smith beat Kemoeatu so badly that the 350-pound offensive guard was penalized for holding him. On first and 20 from the 12, Arizona ran end-tackle twists on each side. The right tackle, Smith, came free on the outside and Roethlisberger barely was able to step up and away from him at the 2. Stunting wide on the other side, Dockett reached to knock the ball out but barely missed. As Roethlisberger bought time to the right, he found the uncovered Holmes for 14 yards with Dominique Rodgers-Cromartie (DRC) in coverage.

"Ben can do so many more things to beat you," said Arians, who coached quarterbacks in Indianapolis during Peyton Manning's first three seasons. "A sack there and the game's probably over. He's going to get sacked a lot more than most people because he's not going to throw the ball away like Peyton. He will extend the play."

As the clock wound down toward the 2-minute warning, none of the Cardinals appeared ready when the ball was snapped on second and 6. Roethlisberger pumped, then let it go deep up the right sideline to Nate Washington. The dime safety on that side, Aaron Francisco, had a legitimate chance for the interception. Partially due to his sloppy start, however, he wasn't in good position when the ball arrived, and Washington was able to tip it away. Then Holmes snagged a third-down curl against linebacker Karlos Dansby for 13; Rodgers-Cromartie had a clean shot to strip the ball from the side but didn't attack the receiver with any aggression.

Playing a Tampa 2 scheme, cornerback Roderick Hood was late arriving on a curl to Washington and the reception gained 11 to the 50. Washington suffered a separated shoulder on the play; although he stayed in, he was in pain and a non-factor thereafter. The other wideout, Hines Ward, played his normal complement of snaps despite a two-week-old sprained MCL that curtailed his ability to block and cut.

or the Super Bowl. He didn't practice at all." Adding insult to injury, Roethlisberger had thrown a gutsy third-down strike from eight yards deep in the end zone to Holmes for 19 on a skinny post. Interestingly, Tomlin told Arians before the third down that if they didn't get the first down, punter Mitch Berger was going to take an intentional safety.

In the bench area, offensive line coach Larry Zierlein didn't mince words: either get Dockett blocked or the Steelers were kaput. "There was a little challenging going on," Arians said. "Larry did a great job getting his guys ready for that drive." The key against any formidable interior rusher is the first few plays when the player is fresh and explosive. Dockett, who to that point had been on the field for 44 of 53 snaps, lined up six times over Stapleton and three times over Kemoeatu during the nine-play drive. The Steelers kept two blockers on Dockett for the opening six snaps, three of which he stunted. As he tired, the Steelers were able to single block him.

Pendergast, who rushed six or more on just 3 of the Steelers' 38 dropbacks in the game, sent four men seven times and five twice in the game's last drive. In other words, he never switched up and

After Roethlisberger scrambled for 4, the Steelers called their second timeout with 1:02 left. On the next play, Pendergast zone-blitzed with five, but the protection was firm. Roethlisberger wanted to throw left against a soft Cover 2 but had time to come back right, where Mewelde Moore was available in the flat. Rodgers-Cromartie had no choice but to come up and take Moore. When Roethlisberger pumped and brought the ball down, Holmes was left one-on-one in the half field against Francisco in an athletic mismatch that offensive coordinators seldom get because defensive coordinators work so hard to hide them. When Francisco left Brigham Young in 2005, his time in the 40-yard dash was 4.75 seconds. When Holmes left Ohio State in 2006, his 40 time was 4.44. "Francisco is a very heady player," Arians said, "always in the right position. Just limited speed-wise."

To his credit, Holmes stayed with his curl route despite Roethlisberger's pump and then made the catch 11 yards downfield with his back to Francisco. As Francisco angled in to make the tackle, his feet slipped out from underneath him. In a flash, Holmes was off down the sideline before being dragged down by the hustling Francisco at the 6 after a gain of 40. "I think God coaches that," said Arians. "You just have to have a good feel where to spin out. [Holmes is] such a good open-field runner, being a punt returner." The Steelers called their last timeout with 49 seconds remaining.

The duel between Holmes and Rodgers-Cromartie, the 16th pick in the 2008 draft out of Tennessee State, was completely one-sided. Coach Ken Whisenhunt didn't make Rodgers-Cromartie a starter until Week 8, and after a slow start he played so well that Pendergast was able to match him all over the field in the postseason. "There's a good chance we wouldn't even have been there if Dominique hadn't made some of the plays he did," Whisenhunt said. "We did some things defensively putting him on an island [in the Super Bowl] in order to try to get some of those negative plays or pressure the quarterback."

During the buildup to the game, Holmes eagerly awaited being matched by Rodgers-Cromartie. "Santonio was talking all week, 'This guy is good but he's still a rookie,'" linebacker James Farrior said. "And he said a rookie can't cover him." As it turned out, Holmes was right. Rodgers-Cromartie played with too much cushion, wasn't assertive, and made mistake after mistake, almost as if the game was too big for him. His inability even to compete proved too much of an obstacle for Arizona's defense to overcome.

On first and goal, the Steelers emptied the backfield and the Cardinals played four-across ("quarters") coverage behind a four-man rush. The Steelers' play was designed to go right, but Roethlisberger didn't like what he saw. He pump-faked again and looked back left, where Holmes came off the line lazily and then broke his route hard to the corner. Rodgers-Cromartie got caught watching the quarterback's eyes and broke up toward the flat, where Dansby was in the neighborhood covering Moore. It was a mistake, but a mistake that many rookie cornerbacks would make. Holmes was about as open as a receiver can get in the red zone. The pass from Roethlisberger was perfect but the leaping Holmes let it go through his outstretched hands. "That was an easier throw and catch than the next one," said Arians. "Totally a drop. He was worried about his feet and not catching the ball. All we preach is, catch the ball and drag your toe."

On second down, again the call from Pendergast was quarters coverage with a four-man rush. "At this point I thought they'd sell out," said Arians. "We tried to free-release the halfback [Moore] in the flat with Hines hooked up short and 'Tone' going over the top of him. A traditional route. Again, they stayed in zone. Ben went through his progression."

On the right side, Holmes stumbled coming off the slot after a jam by nickel back Ralph Brown but put his hand up anyway. Ward came down in short motion, hooked at the 3, and was jumped neatly by Dansby. Moore circled into the flat and was checked by Brown. On the left, tight end Heath Miller was working inside into the end zone, and Washington, with his damaged shoulder, slipped down in the middle of the field trying to evade safety Antrel Rolle.

The Cardinals were in excellent shape as long as Rodgers-Cromartie remained in his outside quarter of the field and mirrored Holmes in double coverage with Francisco, who was coming over from the middle. But, perhaps anticipating a pivot back toward the outside by Ward, DRC stepped toward him and ended up losing all contact with Holmes, who cut to the corner. "My read was bad," Rodgers-Cromartie said after the game. "I got taken out of my zone."

Afforded excellent protection, Roethlisberger was able to scan the entire field before releasing the ball in 3.9 seconds. Holmes had sprinted hard off the line, then gathered himself in the corner. Brown, a nine-year veteran, saw the route develop and rather heroically raced back to the spot where Rodgers-Cromartie was supposed to have been. Holmes was open but Brown was closing in, although Roethlisberger probably never even saw Brown before he gunned it high and hard to Holmes. Brown started to reach with his right hand, overran the ball slightly, and then reached up with his left hand. He missed deflecting the ball by a matter of inches.

About 8½ yards deep and a step or two from out of bounds, Holmes snared the ball with both hands, put it away with his right, and braced his fall with his left while dotting the red-painted end zone with both toes. The play was reviewed upstairs. The touchdown was confirmed.

"That's how you be great! That's how you be great!" Holmes shouted after reaching the bench area.

Officials watched for quite a while as teammates hugged Holmes. When they left to set up the extra-point attempt with a kicking ball, Holmes unbuckled one of the straps on his helmet and began to impersonate LeBron James. More than 20 seconds had elapsed, enough time for NFL supervisor of officials Mike Pereira not to classify it as a taunt. Two weeks later, Holmes was fined $10,000 for using the ball as a prop. Holmes also had risked a penalty by removing his helmet, but Pereira said that happened when he was out of bounds and walking back to the bench area.

Down 27–23 and needing a touchdown, the Cardinals began from their 23 with two timeouts and 29 seconds remaining. "My thoughts were to get it over the 50 so we'd have two shots at the end zone," Whisenhunt said. "I felt we had a chance." With eight Steelers in coverage, Warner still managed to find an opening in the zone created when linebacker James Harrison moved up to cover running back J. J. Arrington in the flat. Warner's precise throw to Fitzgerald on a deep crossing route picked up 20 yards. "I told James Harrison to go deep because we had been practicing against that play all week," said Farrior. "He wasn't quite deep enough. I was getting nervous." The Cardinals called their final timeout with 15 seconds left after a check-down to Arrington gained 13 to the Pittsburgh 44.

"Kurt's max is about 55 yards," said Haley. "There was a little bit of a breeze so I felt we had to get somewhere inside the 50 to have a legit shot to get a throw to the end zone." Some expected Arizona to throw a deep out for 15 or 20 yards to the Pittsburgh 25 or 30, setting up a more reasonable shot at the end zone. But the Cardinals went with a Hail Mary, which with Fitzgerald on their side they surely didn't consider an act of desperation.

"As crazy as it sounds, I don't have any doubt that if Kurt gets that throw off, Larry's catching it," Haley said. "He was clearly playing better than anyone else has at that position. The statistics pretty much state that. The zone Larry was in, I think he's making the play."

Fitzgerald, who surpassed Jerry Rice's postseason records after three games before finishing with 30 catches for 546 yards and seven touchdowns in four, ran down the right side with Anquan Boldin. "Honestly, I was pretty open," said Fitzgerald, "but it doesn't matter what they were doing. I would have been able to get to that football. I know me."

The Steelers had safety Troy Polamalu stationed on the numbers to Fitzgerald's side of the field and cornerback Ike Taylor nearby. "Obviously, it would have been a jump ball, and we would have had three guys for their two," Pittsburgh secondary coach Ray Horton said. Arians feared the worst. "[Fitzgerald] had braced himself up," he said. "He was surrounded, but nobody can jump as high as he can."

As defensive coordinator Dick LeBeau rushed three, Warner waited with the shotgun snap for Fitzgerald and others to get downfield. To the quarterback's right, linebacker LaMarr Woodley knocked right tackle Levi Brown off balance. Warner appeared to have some room to duck left but instead remained in the pocket. Finally, the persistent Woodley came free and, after 6.4 seconds, grabbed Warner's right hand and arm just as his motion was starting. The ball bounced free and was recovered by defensive end Brett Keisel at the Pittsburgh 49 with 5 seconds left.

According to Haley, Polamalu came up to Dick LeBeau when everybody was getting ready to celebrate and told him, "Coach, when Warner was winding up Larry was five feet in front of me, and I'm thinking to myself, 'I'm about to be on the wrong end of a highlight right here.'"

The Cardinals howled for Bob McGrath, the replay assistant, to permit referee Terry McAulay to review it on the field. "Certainly, it was reviewed," said Pereira, who from his seat in the operations booth had the same equipment as McGrath. "I ran it slow and saw him lose possession on the initial contact. To me, it was a no-brainer that it was a fumble."

And so, one of the most entertaining Super Bowls was over, a fight to the finish pitting the Steelers, a seven-point favorite and possessors of five Lombardi trophies, against the Cardinals, historically the NFL's most futile franchise, with one playoff victory in the previous 51 years.

"It would have gone down as one of the great sports stories of all time given the history of the Cardinals and the ineptitude," said Haley, who five days later was hired to coach the Kansas City Chiefs. "To do things that had never been done in an organization, to do things when nobody thinks you can do it, is just so fulfilling. It was a very emotional, touching year. It's just unfortunate that those last 2:34 didn't go our way."

Nearly all the participants agreed that the most significant play of the game occurred in the closing seconds of the first half when Harrison blew his assignment, dropped into coverage instead of rushing as he had been schooled to do, and wound up with a 100-yard interception return for a touchdown as time expired. It was the longest play in Super Bowl history and one of the most bizarre. "We're going in to score a touchdown to put us up, 14–10, and we were going to get the ball to start the second half," said Haley. "Instead of it being 14–10 Arizona, it's 17–7 Pittsburgh. In my mind, we had kind of taken control of the game. It just was really a crushing play for us. Crushing."

Arizona had taken over at the Steelers' 34 with 2 minutes remaining after defensive tackle Bryan Robinson batted a pass by Roethlisberger at the line and it was intercepted by Dansby. On third

and 10 for the Cardinals, Tim Highsmith gained 10 yards on a check-down thanks to a missed tackle by Taylor, and Warner followed with consecutive first-down completions to Fitzgerald and Boldin. Arizona called its final timeout with 18 seconds showing. The ball officially was on the 1-yard line but the spot was much closer to the 2. It rested on the right hash mark.

Haley instructed Warner to call two plays. The first was a run-pass option to be verbalized by Warner at the line, depending on the defense. The formation was termed Split Right, meaning Boldin would line up on the left two yards outside the numbers and Fitzgerald would be inside him in the slot. "It's just a formation call that we've called a thousand times," said Haley. If the Cardinals failed to score and the clock was running, the second-down play was to be a fade to Fitzgerald.

As the players took their positions, Haley was horrified to see Boldin three or four yards *inside* the numbers. "He's eight yards out of position potentially," said Haley. "I'm on the sidelines screaming but the walkie-talkie communication cuts off at 15 seconds so there was no way for me to relay the information. If we had a timeout, we could have called timeout right there on the sideline. It was a worst-case scenario." If Boldin had lined up properly, Fitzgerald said he would have widened with him.

Because it was only first down, Warner could have taken the shotgun snap and spiked the ball or even just thrown it away. Had Warner been more aware, he could have gestured for Boldin to go wider, but according to Whisenhunt, Warner's first responsibility was to check the defense and see if the run is there. "He's got a lot of other things he's trying to accomplish besides worrying about where the split of the receivers is," continued Whisenhunt. "We hadn't run that exact play a million times, but we've run the scheme of play where the splits and the way they align are very important to the success of the play, especially the run-pass checks, which that was."

According to LeBeau, his call was a "maximum blitz" in which everyone not involved in coverage was to rush.

LeBeau later told some of his coaching colleagues that Harrison's job was to rush. "James is blitzing," said Horton, adding that he had no latitude to alter his assignment. "Later on that hurts us because he starts doing that the rest of the game. We called a couple more blitzes and he started just dropping on his own. First time he did that. This is one of those things you put down to fate."

The call by Warner was described by Fitzgerald as a "rub" play. In man coverage, Taylor went with Fitzgerald on a vertical route into the end zone. Boldin then slanted inside behind Fitzgerald and had clear separation from Deshea Townsend, the trailing nickel back. "It was an all-out blitz and that was the correct way for [Warner] to go," said Whisenhunt. "James was supposed to blitz. When he didn't blitz, he was standing there and just broke on the ball. Had the split been a little bit wider, James would not have gotten there."

Harrison jab-stepped forward with his left foot, quickly brought it back, and then made four steps to his right. Just 1.4 seconds elapsed between the shotgun snap by Lyle Sendlein and the toss by Warner from the 9. Two players, the unblocked Woodley and linebacker Lawrence Timmons, were bearing down on him. Timmons was so quick off the ball that left guard Reggie Wells had all he could do just to get his left arm into Timmons' face. Immediately, McAulay threw a flag penalizing Wells for grabbing the facemask. Thus, even if Boldin had lined up correctly, caught the ball, and scored, the play would have been brought back to the 16 with about 14 seconds left. Then figure one, maybe two throws into the end zone, and if the Cardinals were unsuccessful, Neil Rackers would have attempted a 34-yard field goal.

With Boldin's course underneath him, Harrison's path intersected with the ball at the goal line. He cradled the ball to his chest, tucked it under his right arm, bumped into Townsend, and was off on his 15½-second journey to eternal fame. "He did something that, as a linebacker, he's not trained to do," Haley said. "He made a fantastic play, probably one of the greatest plays of all time, in the Super Bowl."

Obviously, most of the fault fell on Boldin. Haley accepted responsibility as well, pondering if he got greedy. "I put blame on myself for maybe asking them to do too much by calling two plays in the huddle, and one of them was a check-with-me," he said. "That's a lot, but that's the trust I had in

Kurt." And right there was the one killer mistake by Warner, something that Roethlisberger never came close to doing in the game. "Boldin lined up wrong, no doubt about it, but Kurt has got to recognize that's happened," Haley said. "He's always responsible in the end for not throwing it to their guy. Kurt said after the fact that it felt like something was wrong but there was so much going on at that time he couldn't quite process it to move Boldin out or throw the ball to Larry in the back of the end zone."

Fitzgerald absolved Haley of blame and, when asked about Boldin's miscue, said, "Mistakes are just part of being human, the nature of the beast." What galled Fitzgerald more than anything was the Cardinals' inability to stop Harrison, until he and wide receiver Steve Breaston dragged him down almost precisely on the goal line (a booth replay confirmed he was in). "From day one after we came back last season, the biggest point of emphasis as an offensive team was, even though turnovers were inevitable, you can't allow teams to score touchdowns," he said. "Whenever we had an interception in practice, guys were running as fast as they could to make the tackle. The Steelers did a hell of a job going down there and making some blocks, but a defensive end able to run 100 yards without being tackled, I felt, was a little disappointing."

Only a few yards from Harrison, Boldin first made contact at the 2 with Farrior, who admitted that he played the Super Bowl at "no more than 215 pounds" (his program weight was 243). They continued to jostle until Boldin lost his composure, grabbed Farrior around the shoulders, and hurled him to the ground near the sideline at the 18. After that, Boldin just jogged down the field and wasn't a factor. A video analysis showed that, if Boldin had hustled, there was a good chance Harrison wouldn't have scored.

"After he threw me down I was pretty much a spectator after that," said Farrior. "I happened to look up at the clock and it was maybe 4, 5 seconds left and I was thinking to myself, 'He needs to go out of bounds so we can at least kick a field goal.' But I think his determination and his will just got him into the end zone."

Many other Cardinals had chances, too. Tight end Leonard Pope was able to catch up at about the 40-yard line, in part because Warner managed to slow Harrison down, but Pope ill-advisedly hurled himself toward Harrison and wound up grabbing Taylor instead. Highsmith, tackle Mike Gandy, and Breaston were among the others giving maximum effort.

Besides Breaston, who sprinted almost 150 yards on the play, Fitzgerald was the most distant of the Cardinals when Harrison intercepted. Fitzgerald trotted from six yards deep in the end zone until the 17, where he broke into a dash before being shoved out of bounds by Polamalu near the Arizona 45.

As Fitzgerald ran out of bounds in the Arizona bench area, he crashed hard into Rolle, who had his helmet off and was standing near the back portion of the six-foot white border of the field. Rolle had been the closest Cardinal to the field when the ball was snapped and only began to step back when Harrison was about 10 yards away. That area is supposed to be kept clear so officials can operate effectively. Rolle was the only Cardinal player in the white. According to Haley, there's no doubt that Fitzgerald would have caught Harrison if not forced to restart his run because of Rolle. "He was apologetic," said Fitzgerald of Rolle. "He was frustrated, he was sorry. Things like that happen."

Signed by the Steelers as a free agent from Kent State in 2002, Harrison was released twice. "When he got here, he was a knucklehead that didn't know the plays," said Farrior. "We didn't think he could be coached." Signed by Baltimore in January 2004, Harrison was cut five months later without ever putting on pads for the Ravens. "One of our coaches thought he was surly and a real hard-ass," a member of Brian Billick's staff said. "Didn't like the way he'd be standing out at practice." Harrison finally became a starter in his sixth season (2007), then ascended to become NFL Defensive Player of the Year in 2008. When several of his more celebrated teammates kept wanting Harrison to relax and go out for drinks with them at the Pro Bowl, he stayed behind all week to lift and work out. "Pound for pound, James Harrison is the strongest guy on the team," said Marcel Pastoor, one of the Steelers' strength coaches. "There's no amount of weight that he can't lift. There's nobody that can go one-on-one with him."

Harrison, the youngest of 14 children, was rewarded in April 2009 with a six-year, $52.5 million

TEAM STATISTICS

PITTSBURGH		ARIZONA
20	Total First Downs	23
4	Rushing	2
12	Passing	20
4	Penalty	1
292	Total Net Yardage	407
58	Total Offensive Plays	57
5.0	Avg. Gain per Offensive Play	7.1
25	Rushes	12
58	Yards Gained Rushing (Net)	33
2.3	Average Yards per Rush	2.8
30	Passes Attempted	43
21	Passes Completed	31
1	Passes Intercepted	1
3	Tackled Attempting to Pass	2
22	Yards Lost Attempting to Pass	3
234	Yards Gained Passing (Net)	374
4/10	Third-Down Efficiency	3/8
0/0	Fourth-Down Efficiency	0/0
3	Punts	5
46.3	Average Distance	36.0
2	Punt Returns	2
5	Punt Return Yardage	34
4	Kickoff Returns	5
80	Kickoff Return Yardage	91
100	Interception Return Yardage	-1
0	Fumbles	2
0	Own Fumbles Recovered	1
1	Opponent Fumbles Recovered	0
7	Penalties	11
56	Yards Penalized	106
3	Touchdowns	3
1	Rushing	0
1	Passing	3
1	Returns	0
3	Extra Points Made	3
2	Field Goals Made	0
2	Field Goals Attempted	0
0	Safeties	1
27	Total Points Scored	23
33:01	Time of Possession	26:59

contract, the largest ever for a defensive player in Pittsburgh.

After Whisenhunt had deferred to the Steelers upon winning the coin toss, Roethlisberger came out blazing on the opening drive, and the Steelers moved 71 yards. Perhaps expecting a defensive struggle, Tomlin took the field goal rather than

PITTSBURGH

Passing	CP/ATT	YDS	TD	INT	RAT
Roethlisberger	21/30	256	1	1	93.2

Rushing	ATT	YDS	AVG	TD	LG
Parker	19	53	2.8	0	15
Moore	1	6	6.0	0	6
Roethlisberger	3	2	0.7	0	4
Russell	2	-3	-1.5	1	1

Receiving	NO	YDS	AVG	TD	LG
Holmes	9	131	14.6	1	40
Miller	5	57	11.4	0	21
Ward	2	43	21.5	0	38
Washington	1	11	11.0	0	11
C. Davis	1	6	6.0	0	6
Spaeth	1	6	6.0	0	6
Moore	1	4	4.0	0	4
Parker	1	-2	-2.0	0	-2

Interceptions	NO	YDS	LG	TD
Harrison	1	100	100	1

Punting	NO	AVG	LG	BLK
Berger	3	35.0	49	0

Punt Ret.	NO/FC	YDS	LG	TD
Holmes	2/1	5	4	0

Kickoff Ret.	NO	YDS	LG	TD
C. Davis	2	38	21	0
Russell	2	42	24	0

Defense	SOLO	AST	TOT	SK
Taylor	5	3	8	0
Farrior	6	1	7	0
Timmons	5	0	5	0
Keisel	4	1	5	0
Clark	2	3	5	0
Harrison	3	1	4	0
Woodley	3	1	4	2
McFadden	3	0	3	0
Townsend	2	1	3	0
Carter	2	0	2	0
Foote	2	0	2	0
Gay	2	0	2	0
Madison	2	0	2	0
Hampton	1	1	2	0
Polamalu	0	2	2	0
Bailey	1	0	1	0
C. Davis	1	0	1	0
Kirschke	1	0	1	0
Moore	1	0	1	0
Russell	1	0	1	0
Holmes	0	1	1	0
Aa. Smith	0	1	1	0
TOTAL	47	16	63	2

ARIZONA

Passing	CP/ATT	YDS	TD	INT	RAT
Warner	31/43	377	3	1	112.3

Rushing	ATT	YDS	AVG	TD	LG
James	9	33	3.7	0	9
Arrington	1	0	0.0	0	0
Hightower	1	0	0.0	0	0
Warner	1	0	0.0	0	0

Receiving	NO	YDS	AVG	TD	LG
Fitzgerald	7	127	18.1	2	64
Boldin	8	84	10.5	0	45
Breaston	6	71	11.8	0	23
Arrington	2	35	17.5	0	22
James	4	28	7.0	0	11
Urban	1	18	18.0	0	18
Hightower	2	13	6.5	0	10
Patrick	1	1	1.0	1	1

Interceptions	NO	YDS	LG	TD
Dansby	1	-1	-1	0

Punting	NO	AVG	LG	BLK
Graham	5	35.0	45	0

Punt Ret.	NO/FC	YDS	LG	TD
Breaston	2/0	34	34	0

Kickoff Ret.	NO	YDS	LG	TD
Arrington	4	82	23	0
Breaston	1	9	9	0

Defense	SOLO	AST	TOT	SK
Dansby	5	3	8	0
Hayes	4	3	7	0
Wilson	7	0	7	0
Dockett	5	1	6	3
Hood	5	1	6	0
Okeafor	6	0	6	0
Rodgers-Cromarti	5	0	5	0
Beisel	2	3	5	0
Rolle	1	2	3	0
R. Brown	2	0	2	0
Campbell	2	0	2	0
Ant. Smith	1	1	2	0
Adams	1	0	1	0
L. Brown	1	0	1	0
Francisco	1	0	1	0
Hightower	1	0	1	0
Iwebema	1	0	1	0
LaBoy	1	0	1	0
Morey	1	0	1	0
Watson	1	0	1	0
TOTAL	53	14	67	3

go for it on fourth down from the 1. When the Steelers got the ball back, Roethlisberger made his only poor throw of the game on a first down from the Arizona 44. After Washington ran right past Rodgers-Cromartie into the middle of the field after a play-action fake, Roethlisberger underthrew him so badly that DRC was able to make up his five-yard deficit and tip the ball away. "We had a wide-open touchdown pass and he just hung it," said Arians. Of Roethlisberger's other eight incompletions, three were dropped, two were batted, one was thrown away, and two others were on target deep but defensed. He also had three completions for 43 yards wiped out by holding penalties.

On defense, the Steelers stifled the Cardinals' 32nd-ranked ground game that had been an asset in the playoffs behind a rejuvenated Edgerrin James. Even though the flow of the game limited prized nose tackle Casey Hampton to merely 14 snaps, defensive ends Aaron Smith (53) and Keisel (55) along with the linebackers proved to be immovable. "The key in the game was we were not able to run it when they were playing pass as well as we had in the playoffs," said Haley. "Those backers and that front three is really, really a good group, clearly as good as we had seen."

Not only did the Steelers shut down the ground game, they applied constant pressure on Warner. He was sacked twice, knocked down after eight other passes, and hurried six times. Gandy was responsible for 6½ of the 16 pressures, and Woodley and Harrison each had 5. The Cardinals also hurt themselves with 11 penalties for 106 yards; 4 of the penalties interrupted drives and led to punts.

To thwart Fitzgerald, LeBeau played Cover 2 with a twist: After rerouting the wide receiver at the line, Taylor, the cornerback assigned to Fitzgerald, stayed on him instead of giving way at 15 yards and assuming responsibility for the flat. That essentially provided a double-team with the safety (usually Polamalu, although a few times Polamalu and Taylor switched positions) at the cost of leaving the flat open. The Cardinals did have some success exploiting the void in the flat, but not to the extent Haley thought was possible.

Although Fitzgerald didn't even have a pass thrown his way until 2 minutes remained in the half, the well-rounded Cardinals rode Warner's patience to a mid-second quarter touchdown on tight end Ben Patrick's 1-yard catch over clingy coverage by linebacker Larry Foote. On the previous play, Boldin beat cornerback Bryant McFadden on a tendency-breaking inside-outside route for 45 yards. "It was designed for a big play to Larry, but they were doubling Larry almost the first three, three and a half quarters," said Haley. "Anquan ran what we call a deep pivot. I think McFadden was just playing a route combination that he had seen us run a bunch."

Fitzgerald said he went to the coaches at some point in the first half and advocated a four-wide-receiver set with or without a huddle. "Their front seven is what makes them so tough to deal with," he said. "When you spread them out and get their four cornerbacks on the field, I think that puts them at a disadvantage, especially against us. If we would have gone to that a little earlier, Kurt probably could have thrown for 500 yards."

Fitzgerald maintained that the Cardinals' system of hot reads would have been sufficient for Warner to get the ball out and mitigate wholesale protection breakdowns. "I was really churning about it," said Haley. "I was fearful to go to it too early because if it hadn't worked . . . then we would have had nowhere to turn. Now, it didn't. Our guys held up when they had to."

Trailing 20–7 with 11½ minutes left in the game, Arizona went four wides against a 4-1 defense that had Townsend and dime back William Gay in for Hampton and Foote. After catching one of two targeted passes for 12 yards through three quarters, Fitzgerald beat Taylor four times in match-up coverage for 31 yards in an eight-play, 87-yard drive. The long gain was a 22-yard check-down to Arrington when Keisel botched a coverage and vacated the middle of the field. Taylor had his body on Fitzgerald and his hand on the ball but still couldn't defend the 1-yard fade to Fitzgerald for a TD.

A few minutes later, the Cardinals were back at their 26 when Gay allowed Breaston inside and Warner found him for 23 yards. This time, the Steelers held, thanks to three straight pressures from Woodley and Harrison. The punt by Arizona and then the safety by Arizona led to the 64-yard pass to the amazing Fitzgerald.

"It was sick," Farrior said. "He almost won the game by himself."

From their four-wide formation, the Cardinals sent Fitzgerald wide right against Taylor and Boldin slot right against Townsend. Polamalu, who was on that side, and free safety Ryan Clark were 21 yards deep. LeBeau's call was "Cover 2 Man," meaning the four cornerbacks were in man-to-man coverage with the two safeties behind them. Reading the coverage correctly, Boldin ran a 12-yard out leaving Fitzgerald to beat Taylor inside.

According to Fitzgerald, being able to cross the face of a cornerback who is playing with inside leverage is "very rare." But he did. "Ike has good feet," he said. "So I just tried to mash him, tried to monster him to get my leverage." The throw from Warner was on target seven yards downfield. A step behind, Taylor compounded his mistake by leaping for Fitzgerald's heels. He missed. "What really hurt him is he dove instead of just trying to stay on his feet," Farrior said. "I'm pretty sure Ike is faster than Fitzgerald. He definitely could have got him."

As Fitzgerald turned right between the hash marks and headed for the goal line 55 yards away, Polamalu and Clark were trying to make a sudden change in direction; both of them were covering the same route, by Boldin on the right and by Jerheme Urban on the left. "Both safeties are exactly three yards outside the numbers when they should be three yards inside the numbers," according to Horton. "I'm sure they thought the route was a deep corner route. They're anticipating getting to the deep sideline. But the route is just a short out so that's covered by the guys who are on them. Ike was wrong for letting the guy in there and he should have made the tackle, but it's on [the safeties] to stop it from being a touchdown."

In their preparation, Warner and Haley hadn't been quite sure how to cope with Polamalu. "We called him the wild card because he's a very unpredictable player," Haley said. "That's what scared us.

There are times he comes out of the scheme and just uses his ability or instincts to make plays. He makes a lot of them, obviously. But that one hurt him." Farrior said that Polamalu "does a lot of things we don't understand. . . . He's got an extra vision we don't have. I don't even know if he knows where he's going to be." Farrior estimated that Polamalu was right "probably 85 percent of the time." Said Horton: "I'd say a little bit higher than that."

Neither Polamalu nor Clark could draw within 5 yards of Fitzgerald before he crossed majestically into the end zone, giving Arizona its short-lived lead. In 16 games, one of the most accomplished defenses in Steelers' history had allowed an NFL-low two passes of 40 yards or more. Fitzgerald and Boldin each did it in this one game. In just 27 minutes of possession time, the Cardinals gained 407 yards against a unit that had yielded more than 300 just once (322 at Tennessee) in the first 18 games. Arizona was 2½ minutes away from scoring the biggest come-from-behind victory in Super Bowl history.

"When Larry scored, to me, it was a triumph of our football team to come back against the No. 1 defense in the league," said Whisenhunt, who along with five of his assistants once served under coach Bill Cowher in Pittsburgh. "To put up those points in that short of a span on that team in a situation that was the most critical in the history of this franchise—you can't lose sight of celebrating what we accomplished."

After dealing with the loss of 12 starters for 56 games in the regular season due to injury and facing the seventh most difficult schedule and the hardest of the 12 playoff teams, it was a season filled with do-or-die comeback opportunities for the Steelers.

As Tomlin put it on Super Bowl night, "We've been in some pretty bleak situations. The guys don't blink. They deliver. That's how we play."

It wasn't defense and it wasn't the ground game that won the Steelers their sixth Super Bowl crown. Primarily, it was "Big Ben."

"Something different from what you're used to seeing from the Pittsburgh Steelers," said Farrior, the team's undisputed leader. "But we never had a $100 million quarterback before, either."

1. **Mike Jones, LB, Rams, XXXIV:** Jones hits Titans WR Kevin Dyson at the 2 as he strains to score on a reception as time expires. Jones' tackle is secure; Dyson can stretch no farther than the 1/2-yard line. The Rams win.

2. **James Harrison, LB, Steelers, XLIII:** Eighteen seconds remain in the first half with Arizona perched on the Pittsburgh 1. Kurt Warner throws a quick inside pass to Anquan Boldin from shotgun formation. Harrison sinks back into the throwing lane, makes the interception, and rolls 100 yards for a touchdown.

3. **Dan Bunz, LB, 49ers, XVI:** Late in the third quarter, Cincinnati has the ball third and goal at the 1. QB Ken Anderson fakes a handoff, rolls right, and throws in the flat to RB Charles Alexander, who is covered man-to-man by Bunz. When Alexander turns up field, Bunz meets him full force at the 1 for the tackle. When a fourth-down run fails, the 49ers find the key to victory.

4. **Tracy Porter, CB, Saints, XLIV:** Three minutes remained as the Colts drove for the tying touchdown. Then Porter undercut the great Reggie Wayne, picked the great Peyton Manning, and jetted 74 yards for the clinching score.

5. **Jack Lambert, LB, Steelers, XIV:** With five minutes left and the Steelers leading 24–19, it's first down for the Rams at the Pittsburgh 32. Rams QB Vince Ferragamo doesn't see Billy Waddy open on the sideline and throws in the middle to Ron Smith. Lambert uses his great speed to make the interception, effectively securing victory.

6. **Clay Matthews, LB, and Ryan Pickett, DE, Packers, XLV:** It was the first play of the fourth quarter and the Packers were on the ropes. Then Matthews played a hunch, Pickett spilled inside, and together as one, they knocked the ball loose from Steelers RB Rashard Mendenhall.

7. **Ty Law, CB, Patriots, XXXVI:** On first down from the St. Louis 39 in the second quarter, the Patriots shift late into their "46" defense with Mike Vrabel lining up outside of backup LT Rod Jones. Jones blows his assignment, giving Vrabel a straight shot at QB Kurt Warner, who hurries a quick out to Isaac Bruce that Law intercepts and returns 47 yards for a touchdown.

8. **Kelvin Hayden, CB, Colts, XLI:** Down 22–17, the Bears have a first down at their 38. Receiver Muhsin Muhammad runs a double move on Hayden, who is playing off. Instead of selecting another receiver or throwing the ball away, QB Rex Grossman tries a sideline floater. Hayden leaps for the interception, manages to stay in bounds by inches, and dashes 56 yards for a touchdown.

9. **Leon Lett, DT, Cowboys, XXVIII:** With the Bills leading 13–6 early in the third quarter, Lett beats C Kent Hull and punches the ball out of the hands of RB Thurman Thomas. It bounces to FS James Washington, who returns the recovery 46 yards for a touchdown.

10. **Charles Haley, DE, Cowboys, XXVII:** Starting from their 10 with the score tied at 7, the Bills try a strong-side screen pass to Thurman Thomas. On the play side, Haley beats RT Howard Ballard off the ball and slams into the unsuspecting Jim Kelly. The ball pops into the air and DT Jimmie Jones gathers it in for a 2-yard touchdown.

XLIV

NEW ORLEANS SAINTS 31, INDIANAPOLIS COLTS 17

February 7, 2010
Sun Life Stadium, Miami Gardens, Florida

Attendance: 74, 059
Conditions: Clear
Time of kickoff: 6:31 p.m. (EST)
Length of game: 3 hours, 14 minutes
Referee: Scott Green

MVP: Drew Brees, QB, Saints

	1	2	3	4	Final
New Orleans Saints	0	6	10	15	31
Indianapolis Colts	10	0	7	0	17

SCORING SUMMARY

1st Quarter
IND   Stover, 38-yd. FG
IND   Garcon, 19-yd. pass from Manning (Stover kick)
2nd Quarter
NO   Hartley, 46-yd. FG
NO   Hartley, 44-yd. FG
3rd Quarter
NO   P. Thomas, 16-yd. pass from Brees (Hartley kick)
IND   Addai, 4-yd. run (Stover kick)
NO   Hartley, 47-yd. FG
4th Quarter
NO   Shockey, 2-yd. pass from Brees (Moore, pass from Brees)
NO   Porter, 74-yd. interception return (Hartley kick)

The majority of Super Bowls have been won because one of the teams was superior, both in personnel and performance. Other games were lost largely because one of the teams picked a bad time to lay an egg.

As Super Bowl XLIV dawned, the Indianapolis Colts were a 5-point favorite to defeat the New Orleans Saints. In truth, that was more a nod by oddsmakers to the vast disparity in pedigree than the caliber of the players on each 53-man roster. From their respective bunkers, Colts president Bill Polian and Saints general manager Mickey Loomis crunched numbers and tape during the two-week run-up and concluded that little separated the two clubs.

Peyton Manning was fresh off a regular season in which he led the Colts to a 14–0 start and earned a record fourth MVP award. Nevertheless, Drew Brees paced all quarterbacks in passer rating (109.6) and completion percentage (NFL-record 70.6 percent) as the Saints opened 13–0. Neither team possessed anything resembling that type of horsepower on defense, and as for special teams, both clubs ranked near the bottom of the league.

"You had two teams that were pretty evenly matched," Loomis said. "Without something extraordinary happening, whoever had the last possession would end up winning. Yet, something extraordinary did happen. We got an interception for a touchdown on a game-winning drive by the Colts."

Indeed, Tracy Porter's 74-yard return of Manning's pass to Reggie Wayne with about three minutes remaining did clinch victory for the Saints, 31–17. New Orleans, one of five franchises never to have played in the Super Bowl, became perhaps the NFL's unlikeliest champion ever. Two days later, a deliriously happy crowd estimated at 800,000 lined the parade route in a city that had been ravaged by the floodwaters of Hurricane Katrina in August 2005.

"These were the people we'd been playing for—people who'd lost so much and struggled so valiantly, literally crying tears of joy," coach Sean Payton said in his book, *Home Team*. "We had been lifted by our city, and we had lifted it, too. We had been the tragic Saints from tragic New Orleans, but neither of us was tragic anymore."

Some of the Colts, including Polian, insisted that they had beaten themselves, citing not only the bad interception but also the failure of wide receiver Hank Baskett to recover the Saints' shocking onside kickoff at the onset of the second half that turned the game around. As damaging as those plays were, the Colts certainly didn't just give the game away. The interception was the Colts' only turnover, and they didn't yield a sack. Five penalties for 45 yards in a clean, crisply played game—3 hours, 14 minutes made it the shortest Super Bowl in 25 years—were more than manageable. And they piled up 432 yards to 332 for the Saints.

But New Orleans didn't turn the ball over all day, was penalized just three times for 19 yards, and took just one sack. Ultimately, this game was settled on defense, where the two teams could hardly have played the game with more different game plans, and on special teams. In each of these phases, the Saints took chances that the Colts were not willing to take.

That onside kick wouldn't have happened if Payton wasn't a creative thinker, unencumbered by typical NFL coaching strategy. That interception wouldn't have happened if Gregg Williams wasn't willing to risk a six-man pressure on the play, all the while imploring Porter to trust his tape study and sit on Wayne's route. Payton approved of Williams' daring game plan, which included 16 blitzes on pass plays compared to only 3 for Larry Coyer, the Colts defensive coordinator.

Payton took another enormous gamble, going for it on fourth and goal from the Indianapolis 1. It failed, but the alternative—kicking a field goal with 1:55 left in the second quarter and giving Manning the ball with two timeouts—wasn't overly appealing, either. When the Colts subsequently tried to extricate themselves from a hole on third and 1, their dive play by little Mike Hart was stymied, and the Saints were the ones kicking a field goal to end the first half trailing 10–6.

If the Saints played the 44th Super Bowl as if they were rolling dice back home on Bourbon Street, the Colts played it true to their conservative rural roots in Indiana.

"When you're playing in the playoffs against good teams," said Loomis, "you have to go win the games. You can't just sit back and expect the other teams to lose it. Sean does have a lot of guts."

Brees was chosen MVP, completing a Super Bowl–record 32 passes that didn't include a completion to Lance Moore on a 2-point conversion that extended New Orleans' lead to 24–17 late in the fourth quarter. "He's very much like Peyton Manning," Coyer said. "It's his offense, and he knows how to use motions and shifts to make you declare your intentions. Quick in, quick out. He was great, I thought." His otherworldly 29-of-32 marksmanship (90.6 percent) in the final three quarters was preceded by 3-of-7 in the first quarter.

The longest pass play by the Saints was for merely 27 yards. On the third play of the game, Brees overthrew one of his two deep threats, Robert Meachem, who was open on a go pattern against cornerback Jacob Lacey. "We wanted to send a message early," said Curtis Johnson, who coached the Saints wide receivers. "The message was, if you play us man-to-man, we're going to run by you." As it turned out, the Colts played cornerbacks Kelvin Hayden (47 snaps), Tim Jennings (35), Lacey (59), and Powers (15) well off receivers in either Cover 2 or Cover 3 zones. In simplistic terms, Brees threw the ball inside and on checkdowns against Cover 2, then outside against Cover 3 and man-to-man.

"We tried to take away their running game and protect ourselves deep," Coyer said. "Their success through the year had been play-action deep balls. We did that, but still [Brees] made plays. . . . They isolated [Reggie] Bush by using motion and did it twice for real good plays. They out-tempo'd us."

Defensive end Dwight Freeney suffered ligament damage in his ankle in a 30–17 victory over the New York Jets in the AFC Championship Game and didn't practice at all for two weeks. Playing without a pain-killing injection, he had more snaps (25) than any Colts' defensive lineman in the first half before settling for merely 13 in his increasingly futile second-half showing. His only pressure was a bull-rushing sack against left tackle Jermon Bushrod midway in the second quarter. Robert Mathis had the only other knockdown of Brees, as well as the team's only two hurries. The Saints were overjoyed when Freeney kept trying spin moves against Bushrod because they recognized his weakness was against power rushes.

"Really, from the mid-point of the second quarter on, [Freeney] was no factor," Polian said. "If you can't rush, you can't play zone. Plus, we didn't match up. We were [a sitting duck]."

An even 6 feet tall, Brees compensated with a high release point and by moving so well laterally in the pocket that he was able to throw around rushers. After a drop by Marques Colston left the Saints with one first down and two punts for their opening two possessions, Indianapolis safety Melvin Bullitt told his teammates in the bench area, "Keep that pressure up the middle. He's nervous. He can't even see over y'all." The Saints never even had to punt after that as Brees joined Len Dawson, Joe Theismann, and Steve Young as the shortest quarterbacks to win a Super Bowl.

"There has to be true greatness to play as well as he plays with that kind of a handicap," said Polian. "It sounds as though I'm denigrating him by saying handicapped, but it is. It's hard to play quarterback and not be 6-4 in today's game. He's done it as well as anyone has ever done it."

The Saints were coming off playoff victories over Arizona (45–14) and Minnesota (31–28 in overtime) in which Gregg Williams' relentless blitzing battered quarterbacks Kurt Warner and Brett Favre. But Williams understood that Manning's ability to get rid of the ball on time, blended with the tried-and-true protection packages of long-time Colts offensive line coach Howard Mudd, would require restraint on his part. "At noon the day of the Super Bowl, I got a call from Jeff Fisher, my best friend in coaching," Williams said. "The first thing he said was, 'I know your impatient ass, and you've got to be patient today. Don't let him throw over the top of you in a hurry.'"

Until Austin Collie beat fellow rookie Malcolm Jenkins for a 40-yard bomb in the final minutes, the Saints defense hadn't allowed a play longer than 27 yards. Williams never did sack Manning, but the pressure was steady, yielding five knockdowns and six hurries. He rushed five or more on 43 percent of passes and six or more on 19 percent before the Saints lead swelled to 14 points at the end. "You can't get to Peyton Manning if he doesn't want you to," said Williams. "The only way you have a chance is if you disrupt the stem and timing of the route, as opposed to the quarterback himself. We were pretty effective in that." The cornerback position had killed New Orleans for years, but decisions by Loomis to draft Porter in the second round in 2008 and to sign unrestricted free agent Jabari Greer in March 2009 turned a weakness into a relative strength.

Whereas the Colts spent the entire game in a four-man front, the Saints came out in a 3-4 defense before shifting to their more customary 4-3 in the second quarter. With Indianapolis aligned in three-wide receiver sets about 85 percent of the time, the Saints were in their base defense on just 14 snaps. Other than at the bitter end, Williams decided to match up against the Colts with a 3-3 nickel package in which outside linebackers Scott Fujita and Scott Shanle kept bouncing around before the snap. "It's no secret that throughout his career, Peyton Manning

has struggled against three-man front defenses," said Fujita. "That wasn't really our forte, but we featured that throughout the game. Three-man fronts have a tendency to maybe create some more confusion. . . . We wanted to bring five or six guys from all different angles to keep him constantly uncertain."

Mixing 14 passes with seven runs in the first quarter, the Colts marched 53 yards for a field goal and then a Super Bowl–tying 96-yard drive for a touchdown and a 10–0 lead. The touchdown drive included carries by Joseph Addai for 16, 11, and 26 yards. Last in the NFL in rushing, the Colts' ground game was "tremendous" in the Super Bowl (99 yards, 5.2 average), according to Polian. Yet, the Saints were confident the run wouldn't beat them. "We were able to invite them to run the ball at times when they did not want to but felt they had to," said Williams. "I know that we controlled the line of scrimmage."

Greer suffered a bruised leg bringing down Addai after the 26-yard run, Addai's longest since 2006. Safety Usama Young replaced Greer at left corner, and Manning struck with a 19-yard touchdown pass to Garcon just one play later. From a press position, Young bailed back outside without so much as touching Garcon, who headed vertically into the end zone. Young's non-bump led some to heap criticism upon him, but what few knew is that a pre-snap call by safety Roman Harper told Young to do just that. "The huddle call was an over-and-under double to protect Usama Young, not a side-to-side double," Williams said. "Roman just froze. He called a side-to-side double which allowed [Garcon] to run through and tells Usama not to jam him. I wanted to strangle [Harper]. Ten years ago, in Super Bowl XXXIV, maybe I do. Basically, I put my arm around Roman and went through the thought process. He said, 'Coach, I just brain-farted.' I said, 'We've got three quarters to go. Let's go.'"

The Saints awakened on their third possession. A 15-yard penalty on linebacker Phillip Wheeler for roughing Bush out of bounds saved New Orleans from a third-and-1 situation. Running back Pierre Thomas inspired his team when he broke tackles by linebackers Clint Session and Gary Brackett as well as Hayden to gain nine on a pass in front of the Saints' bench. "We missed like 25 tackles," said Coyer. "Had we been a great tackling team, we might have been

NEW ORLEANS SAINTS
(NFC, 13–3)

Offense

11	Marques Colston (6-5, 221)	WR
74	Jermon Bushrod (6-4, 315)	LT
77	Carl Nicks (6-5, 353)	LG
76	Jonathan Goodwin (6-3, 318)	C
73	Jahri Evans* (6-4, 335)	RG
78	Jon Stinchcomb* (6-5, 315)	RT
88	Jeremy Shockey (6-4, 251)	TE
19	Devery Henderson (5-11, 203)	WR
17	Robert Meachem (6-2, 210)	WR
9	Drew Brees* (6-0, 209)	QB
25	Reggie Bush (5-11, 203)	RB

Defense

93	Bobby McCray (6-6, 260)	LE
98	Sedrick Ellis (6-0, 307)	LT
69	Anthony Hargrove (6-3, 285)	RT
91	Will Smith (6-2, 282)	RE
55	Scott Fujita (6-5, 250)	LB
51	Jonathan Vilma* (6-0, 230)	MLB
58	Scott Shanle (6-2, 245)	WLB
32	Jabari Greer (5-9, 180)	LC
22	Tracy Porter (5-11, 186)	RC
41	Roman Harper (6-0, 200)	SS
42	Darren Sharper* (6-1, 210)	FS

INDIANAPOLIS COLTS
(AFC, 14–2)

Offense

87	Reggie Wayne* (5-11, 198)	WR
74	Charlie Johnson (6-4, 308)	LT
65	Ryan Lilja (6-3, 285)	LG
63	Jeff Saturday* (6-2, 290)	C
66	Kyle DeVan (6-1, 300)	RG
71	Ryan Diem (6-6, 320)	RT
44	Dallas Clark* (6-3, 252)	TE
85	Pierre Garcon (6-0, 210)	WR
17	Austin Collie (6-1, 200)	WR
18	Peyton Manning* (6-5, 230)	QB
29	Joseph Addai (5-11, 214)	RB

Defense

98	Robert Mathis* (6-0, 235)	LE
90	Daniel Muir (6-1, 313)	LT
99	Antonio Johnson (6-3, 340)	RT
93	Dwight Freeney* (6-1, 265)	RE
50	Philip Wheeler (6-2, 240)	LB
58	Gary Brackett (5-11, 235)	MLB
55	Clint Session (5-11, 235)	WLB
26	Kelvin Hayden (5-10, 195)	LC
27	Jacob Lacey (5-10, 177)	RC
33	Melvin Bullitt (6-1, 201)	SS
41	Antoine Bethea (5-11, 203)	FS

* Pro Bowl selection

SUBSTITUTIONS

New Orleans
Offense: WR - 15 Courtney Roby, 16 Lance Moore; TE - 85 David Thomas; T - 64 Zach Strief; C - 60 Nick Leckey; QB - 11 Mark Brunell; RB - 21 Mike Bell, 23 Pierre Thomas; FB - 36 Kyle Eckel. *Defense:* DE - 97 Jeff Charleston; DT - 92 Remi Ayodele; LB - 50 Marvin Mitchell, 52 Jonathan Casillas, 54 Troy Evans; CB - 20 Randall Gay, 27 Malcolm Jenkins; S - 28 Usama Young, 31 Pierson Prioleau, 39 Chris Reis. *Specialists:* K - 5 Garrett Hartley; P - 6 Thomas Morstead; LS - 57 Jason Kyle. *DNP:* 90 DeMario Pressley (DT). *Inactive:* 87 Adrian Arrington (WR), 80 Darnell Dinkins (TE), 84 Tory Humphrey (TE), 67 Jamar Nesbit (G), 10 Chase Daniel (QB), 30 Lynell Hamilton (RB), 96 Paul Spicer (DE), 59 Anthony Waters (LB).

Indianapolis
Offense: WR - 81 Hank Baskett; TE - 47 Gijon Robinson, 84 Jacob Tamme; T - 67 Tony Ugoh; G - 61 Jamey Richard; RB - 31 Donald Brown, 32 Mike Hart, 35 Chad Simpson. *Defense:* DE - 96 Keyunta Dawson; DT - 68 Eric Foster, 79 Raheem Brock; LB - 52 Cody Glenn, 54 Freddy Keiaho, 59 Ramon Humber; CB - 20 T. J. Rushing, 23 Tim Jennings, 25 Jerraud Powers; S - 40 Jamie Silva, 43 Aaron Francisco. *Specialists:* K - 3 Matt Stover; P - 1 Pat McAfee; LS - 48 Justin Snow. *DNP:* 7 Curtis Painter (QB). *Inactive:* 14 Sam Giguere (WR), 46 Colin Cloherty (TE), 75 Michael Toudouze (T), 78 Mike Pollak (G), 94 Ervin Baldwin (DE), 69 John Gill (DT), 95 Fili Moala (DT), 4 Adam Vinatieri (K).

really good. But I thought the Saints played at a different speed than we played, I really did."

On third and 3 from the Colts 22, Coyer deviated from his standard four-man rushes by sending three for the only time all day. That's when Freeney walked back Bushrod into the pocket and Brees brought the ball down before being sacked in 3.2 seconds. "That's the one time we fooled Brees in the game," Coyer said. "We had a three-man rush, and he thought we were blitzing. He held the ball just a second, and Freeney got him."

No doubt mortified, Bushrod was halfway to the sideline when New Orleans coaches screamed at him to get back on the field to join the field-goal protection team. Despite the distraction, 23-year-old free agent kicker Garrett Hartley pounded a high, soaring kick from 46 yards dead center through the uprights. Later, he connected off the left hash from 44 and 47 yards, both attempts high and right down the middle. "Pretty impressive," said Fujita. "If you had told me that the outcome of that game would almost depend on him, I might have told you I was nervous about our chances. Unbelievable. He's got a little bit of a swagger, which almost irritated a lot of us in the locker room being older guys."

Holding a 10–3 lead, the Colts had chances to take command in the final nine minutes of the first half but failed to gain even a first down and had to punt twice. On a second and 1, the Colts jumped into a double–tight end formation and ran Addai wide for minus-3 when tackle Ryan Diem and tight end Gijon Robinson decided not to cross block. Then on third down, Garcon dropped an inside-breaking route 16 yards downfield. Had he made the catch, the second-year receiver from Haiti had only to outrun Sharper for what might have been a 72-yard touchdown. Polian insisted it was a much harder catch than it looked because Garcon's vision was impeded. Fujita was able to pressure Manning on a six-man rush when left tackle Charlie Johnson turned him loose on a stunt. "Big, big play," Williams said. "They slowed their momentum on that drop."

Later in the second quarter, the Saints rolled from their 28 to a third and goal at the Indianapolis 1. Following the 2-minute warning, Payton sent out three tight ends and tried to run Mike Bell off the right side. "They're a small team by NFL standards," Curtis Johnson said. "We planned it all week that we were going to get down there and out-tough 'em." When defensive tackle Daniel Muir beat guard Jahri Evans and Wheeler stoned a lead block by fullback

Kyle Eckel, Bell had to widen his track and slipped for no gain. Payton yelled at Bell as he came off for not wearing the proper cleats. It was the last snap of the game for Bell.

The Colts called their first timeout, giving Payton another stoppage to ponder fourth and 1—he decided against the field goal. Given a run-pass option at the line, Brees went with a run to Thomas off right tackle. Once again, the Colts responded. Mathis stunted inside and sacrificed his 235-pound body to use up right tackle Jon Stinchcomb and prevent Evans from getting off on Brackett. It was the clean-charging Brackett who took a good angle and made a strong tackle at the 1, with help from Session and Jennings. "They had too many guys for what we ran," Curtis Johnson said. "So we got hit in the mouth."

One minute, 48 seconds were left in the half. Hart slammed inside for 4 on first down, then Addai ripped through the middle for 5. The Saints called their first timeout before the third-and-1.

When Manning got to the sidelines, coach Jim Caldwell, offensive coordinator Tom Moore, and Mudd told him it was their preference to throw the ball. But when Manning voiced dissent, the coaches went along with the quarterback. The play would be a quick hitter to Hart on a play similar to the one that worked on first down. "A lot of us expected a quick play-action and Peyton fitting in a quick slant," said Fujita. "That's not the most physical offensive line in the world. I don't think they had a shot running the ball against us on that play."

The dive to Hart, who lined up three yards off the line between DeVan and Diem on the right side, had proved to be the Colts' best short-yardage play. Manning was awful on sneaks, and with none of the three tight ends capable of moving defenders off the ball, Indianapolis had limited options.

With New Orleans in a 4-3 front and sending a run blitz on, Hart's aiming point was the soft spot in the defense between DeVan and center Jeff Saturday. Left guard Ryan Lilja and Saturday got enough of defensive tackle Anthony Hargrove so Hart might have made it. However, on the left, Charlie Johnson was beaten badly when defensive end Will Smith slammed across his face. Hart tried hitting the gap but never went anywhere after basically being stopped cold by the back end of Johnson. The measurement came out a full yard short. "I remember Hargrove actually played a little high," Saints defensive line coach Bill Johnson said. "But he just country-stronged it. And Smith got off and hit that [hard-charge] technique good." Polian heartily approved of the call. "There's a situation in every game where you've got to make a yard," he said. "A pass is not as high percentage a play. That's a finesse defense. Block somebody. We got no movement at the point of attack, and somebody got beat on the back side."

After being torched for nine yards in two carries, the Saints had risen up and made the stop. Following the Colts' punt, Brees threw a dig route to Devery Henderson against Cover 2 for 19 yards, and Hartley banged his second field goal. "It's one of the two plays that changed the game," said Polian. "If we make it, we can choose whether we want to try to score by using our timeouts or simply run the clock out."

The other pivotal play, the successful onside kick, was the byproduct of Payton's belief that the Saints had to do something to steal a possession from Manning. In effect, piling up Hart on third down had cost the Colts a chance to score. The onside kick would be the other.

Payton's first idea was a fake punt. When aides cautioned against it, he began thinking about an onside kick. In Payton's first four seasons, the team's only surprise onside had been in 2007. Moreover, during the 2009 regular season, just 10 onside kicks had been tried in the entire league before the 5-minute mark of the fourth quarter. The fact that just one had been successfully recovered didn't deter Payton, who said, "We knew we had to do something to rattle these Colts. Plus, I liked the unspoken message such a bold call sent to our team."

In April, the Saints had traded up into the fifth round to select Thomas Morstead, a punter who also kicked off at Southern Methodist. Morstead had improved dramatically late in the season, but still the fact remained that he had never even attempted an onside kick in competition. Nevertheless, when the Saints' special-teams coaches began working with Morstead in the practices leading to the Super Bowl, they discovered him to be a natural. The extended halftime wasn't too far along when Payton announced to the entire team that the Saints would open the second half with the onside kick.

Morstead placed the ball upright on the tee along the right hashmark, advanced 10 yards and kicked the outside quarter of the ball across his body to the left. Lined up to Morstead's left from the outside in were Harper, wide receiver Courtney Roby, linebacker Marvin Mitchell, safety Chris Reis, and linebacker Troy Evans. The Colts were aligned in a six-man front, with Hank Baskett on the outside across from Roby. Spread out to Baskett's left, in order, were linebacker Cody Glenn, linebacker Ramon Humber, linebacker Freddy Keiaho, tight end Jacob Tamme, and safety Aaron Francisco.

In practice, Morstead had been placing the ball almost exactly the necessary 10 yards before it would hook back for an easy recovery by a Saint. "Our guys were able to beat the return guy to it every single time. It was just flawless," said Fujita. "We were convinced there would be no problems whatsoever."

The play wasn't exactly flawless, but it worked. Roby and Mitchell were supposed to block Baskett and Glenn, leaving Harper for the recovery. But not only did Roby and Mitchell miss their blocks, Morstead's boot landed 13 yards downfield and bounced ahead two more yards to the 45. Of the six Colts up front, Baskett was the only one to back up prematurely, moving from the 46 to 50 before he came back for the ball.

At the 45, Baskett went for the ball. But instead of trying to make the recovery with his hands, he tried to fall on it. The ball appeared to carom off his facemask, and it bounced ahead to the 42. "One, Baskett must stay where he is and not back up," Polian said. "Two, he has to catch the ball. That's what he gets paid to do. Simple as that. End of story."

Reis, the fourth Saint down, had the next chance at the ball. He reached for it, slipped onto his back, lifted his head, reached under his right buttocks and at least partially secured it with one hand against his body just as Baskett arrived grabbing for it on all fours. Baskett was at an excellent angle to rip the ball away from Reis when linebacker Jonathan Casillas, the second player to Morstead's right, slammed into Baskett. In effect, Casillas became Reis' personal protector, pushing Baskett's hands and arms off him and using his body to cut off Tamme and Humber as well.

Just eight seconds after the kick, Payton had the temerity to saunter onto the field close to the scrum where at least a dozen bodies were piled on top of each other. There were screams of "Blue ball!" followed by shouts of "White ball!" until finally, 1:03 after the ball had been put into play, referee Scott Green signaled New Orleans' possession. "The things that went on in the bottom of that pile will be legendary," Gregg Williams said. "Chris Reis looked like he had been in a fistfight gangster brawl. Scratches and cuts all over him. At any point in time he could have said, 'Uncle,' and not come out with that ball. But that kid is a tough kid."

It took the Saints just six plays to take a 13–10 lead. Thomas broke three more tackles, this time by Session, Brackett, and safety Antoine Bethea, to gain 12 yards on the first play. The 16-yard touchdown came on a screen pass, one of Payton's pet calls in the red zone. Thomas cut behind blocks by Goodwin and Evans and worked inside of Brackett. Muir had a chance to make the tackle from behind but gave half-hearted effort. Jennings turned down the chance to make the tackle near the 10. Bethea missed at the 5. "We had three guys there, and we just didn't do it," said Coyer. "I don't think we were the same team between the first half and the second half. We dropped off."

Back came Indianapolis to cover 76 yards in 10 plays, including five-of-six passing by Manning for 52 yards. Addai spun away from Vilma in traffic for a 4-yard touchdown four plays after Dallas Clark beat bracket coverage by Shanle and Fujita on a 27-yard reception. The Saints responded with Hartley's 47-yard field goal, making him the first kicker in Super Bowl history to make three of 40 yards or more, trimming the Colts' lead to 17–16.

On the sixth play of another sustained drive, the Colts finally found the deep matchup they wanted with Wayne against Porter on the left side. But just as the ball was about to be released, Smith came off Lilja in a five-man pressure and crashed into Manning, and the ball fluttered a few yards short of Wayne near the Saints 20. "I'll see that play until my dying day," said Polian. Still, a 14-yard slant to Wayne against Porter on fourth and 2 sustained the drive at the Saints 32. After Addai gained 2 on first down, the next three plays became the beginning of the end for Indianapolis.

At the line, Manning smelled a blitz coming and checked to a bubble screen to Collie on the right side. Collie spun outside and was smothered for a 3-yard loss. If Collie had cut up inside, as expected, he would have picked up blocks from Diem, DeVan, and Saturday and probably gained at least 10 yards. "[Collie] ran the wrong way," said Mudd. Diem, Johnson, and Manning each gave Collie one of those "what are you doing?" kind of looks.

Mudd believes that the hangover from the blatant error by Collie, particularly on the part of Manning, might well have contributed to what happened next. On third and 11, Vilma checked from an overload blitz involving Fujita and Jenkins into a no-blitz Cover 2. When Fujita saw that Jenkins had missed the check and was going to blitz anyway from the slot, he left his underneath zone to cover Jenkins' deeper seam drop. By vacating his zone to cover for Jenkins, Fujita left an underneath route wide open for Clark. Fujita estimated that a pass to Clark would have resulted in about a 10-yard gain.

Instead, Manning looked the safeties off and went deep down the middle to Collie, who was being covered man-to-man by Vilma. "Huge play by Vilma," said Fujita. "In Cover 2, he's got the deep middle. He defended it better on that play than I've ever seen him defend it before." Vilma was step for step with Collie when the pass fell incomplete at the 3.

Manning's decision to go for it all with a wide receiver matched against a middle linebacker wasn't a bad bet. Still, a pass to an open Clark at the very least would have shortened the distance for kicker Matt Stover. According to Mudd, the decision by Manning was out of character and might have stemmed from his disgust at how the second-down screen unfolded.

At 42, Stover was the oldest player ever in a Super Bowl. Caldwell sent him out to try from 51 yards even though he hadn't made a kick that long since 2006. His boot had the distance but missed to the left. "Poor decision to kick it," said Polian. "Every statistical piece of information indicated that nine in 10 he's going to miss."

Starting from their 41, the Saints went the distance in nine plays, including seven completions by Brees to seven different receivers measuring 5, 6, 8, 8, 6, and 9 yards before the 2-yard touchdown to tight end Jeremy Shockey on a split-receiver slant against the overmatched Lacey. The pass for 2 points was good to an eighth receiver, Moore, after Payton's successful replay challenge overturned the incomplete call on the field.

The Colts trailed 24–17, but they weren't finished. From their 30, Manning hit Garcon twice for 27 yards and then Wayne twice for 17 more. With 3:24 remaining, they faced third and 5 at the 31. It would be up to Gregg Williams' defense to seal the game for the Saints.

A quarterback himself during his college days at Northeast Missouri State, Williams was finishing his 20th year as an NFL coach. Over time, he had reached the conclusion that if the quarterback had freedom to change the play at the line, then someone on his defense needed to have the same freedom. "Similar to what Tom Moore does with Peyton Manning, I do the same thing when I have a London Fletcher or a Jonathan Vilma, someone of that cerebral magnitude," he said. "It's very challenging to coach it, but there's big dividends when you let those players make those decisions they see are happening on the field when I'm on the sideline guessing."

In the Super Bowl, Williams estimated that on 35 of the Colts' 59 plays, Vilma changed his sideline call. In effect, Williams gave Vilma command of the entire defense on the field, and throughout the playoffs, Fujita was given command of the rush. The fluid, united front enabled the Saints to counteract Manning's advantage at the line. Disguise had been the hallmark of the New Orleans' defense all season.

"A lot of people think Gregg's a big X's and O's guy and scheme guy, but that really couldn't be further from the truth," Fujita said. Said Williams, "My specialty is dealing with people, especially difficult people. I have a way of getting to them."

Porter became an instant starter as a rookie, but Fujita felt the effort of the rookie from Indiana was lacking. Several times, he grabbed Porter on the field, screaming at him to finish plays. When Williams was hired to replace Gary Gibbs before Porter's second season, he sized up the atmosphere in the locker room and recognized that the Saints had to get more out of Porter. "I was on his ass," Williams said. "Confidence is a fragile thing. We had to get him to try to be more resilient. Now I can't shut the kid up. He is a shit-talking machine."

TEAM STATISTICS

NEW ORLEANS		INDIANAPOLIS
20	Total First Downs	23
3	Rushing	6
16	Passing	16
1	Penalty	0
332	Total Net Yardage	432
58	Total Offensive Plays	64
5.7	Avg. Gain per Offensive Play	6.8
18	Rushes	19
51	Yards Gained Rushing (Net)	99
2.8	Average Yards per Rush	5.2
39	Passes Attempted	45
32	Passes Completed	31
1	Passes Intercepted	1
1	Tackled Attempting to Pass	0
7	Yards Lost Attempting to Pass	0
281	Yards Gained Passing (Net)	333
3/9	Third-Down Efficiency	6/13
0/1	Fourth-Down Efficiency	1/2
2	Punts	2
44.0	Average Distance	45.0
1	Punt Returns	1
4	Punt Return Yardage	0
4	Kickoff Returns	5
102	Kickoff Return Yardage	111
74	Interception Return Yardage	0
0	Fumbles	0
0	Own Fumbles Recovered	0
0	Opponent Fumbles Recovered	0
3	Penalties	5
19	Yards Penalized	45
3	Touchdowns	2
0	Rushing	1
2	Passing	1
1	Returns	0
3	Extra Points Made	2
3	Field Goals Made	1
3	Field Goals Attempted	2
0	Safeties	0
31	Total Points Scored	17
30:11	Time of Possession	29:49

As trainers attended to an injured Anthony Hargrove, Williams moved out almost to the numbers of the field. Half a dozen plays before that, the Saints had almost gotten to Manning on an inside blitz after having used edge and overload pressures most of the game. Fujita happened to run past Williams after that play, suggesting he come

NEW ORLEANS

Passing	CP/ATT	YDS	TD	INT	RAT
Brees	32/39	288	2	0	114.5

Rushing	ATT	YDS	AVG	TD	LG
Thomas	9	30	3.3	0	7
Bush	5	25	5.0	0	12
Bell	2	4	2.0	0	4
Brees	1	-1	-1.0	0	-1
Henderson	1	-7	-7.0	0	-7

Receiving	NO	YDS	AVG	TD	LG
Colston	7	83	11.9	0	27
Henderson	7	63	9.0	0	19
Thomas	6	55	9.2	1	16t
Bush	4	38	9.5	0	16
Moore	2	21	10.5	0	21
Shockey	3	13	4.3	1	7
Thomas	1	9	9.0	0	9
Meachem	2	6	3.0	0	6

Interceptions	NO	YDS	LG	TD
Porter	1	74	74	1

Punting	NO	AVG	LG	BLK
Morstead	2	44.0	46	0

Punt Ret.	NO/FC	YDS	LG	TD
Bush	1/1	4	1	0

Kickoff Ret.	NO	YDS	LG	TD
Roby	4	102	34	0

Defense	SOLO	AST	TOT	SK
Vilma	7	0	7	0
Harper	6	1	7	0
Shanle	5	1	6	0
Jenkins	4	0	4	0
Porter	4	0	4	0
Ellis	3	0	3	0
Fujita	3	1	4	0
Greer	3	1	4	0
Gay	2	0	2	0
Hargrove	2	1	3	0
McCray	2	0	2	0
Sharper	2	1	3	0
Charleston	1	0	1	0
Smith	1	0	1	0
TOTAL	45	6	51	0

INDIANAPOLIS

Passing	CP/ATT	YDS	TD	INT	RAT
Manning	31/45	333	1	1	88.5

Rushing	ATT	YDS	AVG	TD	LG
Addai	13	77	5.9	1	26
Brown	4	18	4.5	0	5
Hart	2	4	2.0	0	4

Receiving	NO	YDS	AVG	TD	LG
Clark	7	86	12.3	0	27
Collie	6	66	11.0	0	40
Garcon	5	66	13.2	1	19t
Addai	7	58	8.3	0	17
Wayne	5	46	9.2	0	14
Brown	1	11	11.0	0	11

Interceptions	NO	YDS	LG	TD

Punting	NO	AVG	LG	BLK
McAfee	2	43.0	46	0

Punt Ret.	NO/FC	YDS	LG	TD
Rushing	1/0	0	0	0

Kickoff Ret.	NO	YDS	LG	TD
Simpson	5	111	29	0

Defense	SOLO	AST	TOT	SK
Brackett	12	1	13	0
Lacey	6	0	6	0
Bullitt	5	0	5	0
Hayden	5	1	6	0
Bethea	4	0	4	0
Jennings	3	0	3	0
Session	3	2	5	0
Foster	2	0	2	0
Brock	1	0	1	0
Freeney	1	0	1	1
Johnson	1	1	2	0
Muir	1	0	1	0
Powers	1	1	2	0
Dawson	0	1	1	0
TOTAL	45	7	52	1

back with that inside blitz, which the Saints called "Ram Single." Williams gestured that he would.

Now Williams told his players, "We had a free runner the last time and they can't block this. The ball is going to come out in 1.9 [seconds], otherwise he's rocked. So everybody sit on their routes. If they double move us, you point at me. It's my fault. But, please,

don't cushion those routes. We've got him hit. It's got to come out quick." His call was a six-man pressure, with man coverage underneath and Sharper in the deep middle. All three linebackers were to blitz the A and B gaps on the right side of the Indianapolis line.

When the Colts came out in a formation with Collie wide left, Wayne slot left, Clark tight on the right side, and Garcon wide right, Porter later would say he knew what was coming. "We know they only run one or two route combinations on third down," said Williams. "That's what they do on third and 4 to 6. Tracy Porter knew, beyond the shadow of a doubt, because I'm screaming at him what route he's going to get. He kind of made a hand gesture like he's got it, stop yelling at me."

Collie motioned down and then broke inside of Wayne, ending up man-to-man against Jenkins. Clark ran a vertical route on the backside. The idea of the play is that Porter will be maintaining outside leverage on Wayne, which was true at first, and that Wayne will be open after a sharp cut to the inside. Wayne drove straight ahead five steps covering a distance of six yards, and Porter worked inside to a head-up position over Wayne.

At the top of the route, Wayne either was slow coming out of his break or stumbled. Shanle was coming to his right and Manning could feel it. The ball was thrown in precisely 1.9 seconds to the inside, where Manning expected Wayne to be. The rest is history. Porter undercut the route, intercepted the ball, and ran it back straight down the field for a touchdown.

Manning said little after the game. Wayne didn't, either. "It was a perfect storm," said Polian. "Reggie's timing is off. They've got enough pressure to make him get the ball out. And he jumps the route. The fact that he stumbled threw the timing off. The whole thing is timed precisely. It's nobody's fault, really. If the guy doesn't jump the route, it's nothing more than incompletion."

Porter, said Fujita, deserved to be the hero. "To be that young and step up in the clutch and take that kind of gamble, to make the biggest play in Saints' history, I think he gets all the credit."

Could Manning have gone to Collie, who had a step on Jenkins? Polian said timing prevented that throw. Both Williams and Fujita said yes (assuming Shanle didn't get to Manning first), even though the presence of Sharper breaking toward Collie would have made it a dangerous throw. After reviewing the tape, Mudd said it was a throw Manning should have made. "But, in his mind, I guess, once the ball is snapped he knew he had man coverage and, if he could set his feet, he was just going to throw it to Reggie, his money guy," said Mudd. "I don't think he was going to

read it out. . . . If I was Peyton, I'd like to have the ball back. I don't believe he will ever blame Reggie. Now or ever. Maybe there isn't a clear answer."

In the end, the Colts had just eight possessions, and six were disappointments due largely to a total of 10 plays. Four of those plays were bad runs. Three were dropped passes. After Manning marshaled his team one final time, he called a trap on third and goal from the New Orleans 3. Once again, the redoubtable Smith, who played all of the 65 snaps, beat Johnson across his face, and Addai had nowhere to run, losing 2 yards. On fourth down from the 5 with 50 seconds left on a running clock, Manning took a shotgun snap and fired between the hashmarks to Wayne, who had the ball skim right through his hands at the 2. If the catch had been made, Wayne would have been hit hard but may have ricocheted into the end zone. "I've run it back a lot," said Williams. "Whether Reggie heard footsteps or whatever, it was a legitimate drop."

For a record seventh season in a row, the Colts posted at least 12 victories in the regular season. They did it with a hand-picked rookie coach, Caldwell, keeping the team on track following the retirement of the beloved Tony Dungy and overcoming a rash of injuries. Victory in the 44th Super Bowl would have placed Indianapolis in the conversation with New England as the team of the decade. Defeat meant that honor would go to the Patriots, by acclamation.

"We won the [playoff] games handily but took a physical beating in the Baltimore and Jet games on defense," Bill Polian said in his summation. "It took its toll in the Super Bowl. It was a very, very memorable season. We came up a little short."

Three years earlier, it had been Peyton Manning who was named MVP of the first Super Bowl in Indianapolis history. This time, the MVP was Drew Brees, also his team's undisputed leader, for bringing the first championship to New Orleans.

Born on All Saints Day in 1966, the Saints had won the Lombardi Trophy for a city, a state, and a region that probably would cherish it more than any other place in America. "It was an amazing symbol of triumph over adversity, a reminder of how far this team and this city had come," wrote Sean Payton. "Their courage inspired a football team of perennial losers all the way to the Super Bowl."

XLV

GREEN BAY PACKERS 31, PITTSBURGH STEELERS 25

February 6, 2011
Cowboys Stadium, Arlington, Texas

Standing against Aaron Rodgers in Super Bowl XLV were the Pittsburgh Steelers, the NFL's best all-around defense in 2010. For two weeks, Hall of Fame defensive coordinator Dick LeBeau, his superb staff of assistant coaches, and safety Troy Polamalu, the NFL defensive player of the year, plotted ways to confuse and unnerve Rodgers, who had entered his third season as Brett Favre's successor for the Green Bay Packers without a playoff victory on his resume.

In winning eight of their previous nine games, the Steelers' patented 3-4 defense had limited opposing quarterbacks to a combined passer rating of just 60.9. Realizing that running extensively against Pittsburgh's base personnel would be difficult, coach Mike McCarthy concluded that his offense must live and die with Rodgers and the passing game. "We were going to put the ball in Aaron's hands and put it on his shoulders," McCarthy said. "We knew he would produce."

When historians reflect on the 45th Super Bowl, they will remember the ice storm that froze Dallas and the structural snafus at Cowboys Stadium that left hundreds of seatless fans furious. When it came to the game itself, the performance of Rodgers in the Packers' 31–25 victory should only grow in luster.

"Aaron did some great things in this game as far as winning one-on-one battles with his eyes," McCarthy said several months later. "And he had some drops. It may have been the all-time greatest quarterback performance in the history of the Super Bowl. I'm just telling you, as a quarterback guy, he played extremely well."

Rodgers posted a rating of 111.5, passing for 304 yards and three touchdowns in his MVP effort. The five passes that his wide receivers dropped had a combined total of 87 yards at the drop point. Given the fact that Jordy Nelson dropped what probably would have been a 51-yard touchdown in the first quarter, James Jones dropped what probably would

Attendance: 103,219
Conditions: Indoors
Time of kickoff: 5:34 p.m. (PST)
Length of game: 3 hours, 32 minutes
Referee: Walt Anderson

MVP: Aaron Rodgers, QB, Packers

have been a 75-yard touchdown in the third quarter, and Nelson dropped what might have been a 40-yard touchdown in the fourth quarter, Rodgers' yardage total would have shattered the Super Bowl record of 414 set by Kurt Warner.

Indeed, Rodgers very well could have had another touchdown pass on his final throw, but Nelson, playing with a ruptured bursa sac in his left knee, didn't have enough left to go up and get another Rodgers strike in the right corner of the end zone. After Mason Crosby followed with a field goal, the Packers' defense rose up to prevent Ben Roethlisberger from leading a trademark last-ditch touchdown drive.

"Rodgers was outstanding," said Kevin Colbert, the Steelers' director of football operations. "He had three pin-point passes where our coverage was pretty good, and he put it where it needed to be. He made special throws. When you make special throws in a special game, and you win the Super Bowl, you cement your place as an elite quarterback, which we felt he was."

LeBeau rushed five or more on 59 percent of Rodgers' dropbacks, and Rodgers was knocked down 11 times, including three sacks. But Rodgers refused to buckle, secured the ball when under siege, and never even came close to throwing an interception.

The Packers went down as one of the most richly deserving championship teams of the Super Bowl era. After an injury-free training camp, the youthful Packers were a popular pick to win it all.

Then the regular season started, and good players began going down. Running back Ryan Grant in Week 1. Linebacker Nick Barnett, safety Morgan Burnett, and tackle Mark Tauscher in Week 4. Tight end Jermichael Finley and defensive end Mike Neal in Week 5. All were lost for the year.

In the Super Bowl, the Packers lost wide receiver Donald Driver early in the second quarter with an ankle injury and all-pro cornerback Charles Woodson late in the second quarter with a broken collarbone, leaving them without 8 of their 22 preferred starters. One play before Woodson's departure, rookie nickel back Sam Shields suffered a shoulder separation. "That's the way it was the whole year," defensive coordinator Dom Capers said. "Nobody used injuries as an excuse. Guys went down, we put in guys and expected them to make plays."

The Packers were 8–6 before they massacred the New York Giants in the finest game played by a McCarthy-coached team and then held off Chicago in week 17. The 10–6 finish enabled Green Bay to edge Tampa Bay and the Giants based on the fourth tiebreaker, strength of victory, and qualify for the playoffs as the No. 6 seed. Ultimately, the Packers joined the Steelers of 2005 as the only title teams to win three straight road games in the playoffs.

"They were on a roll very similar to what we were in Super Bowl 40 coming in as a wild card," Steelers offensive coordinator Bruce Arians said. "They had a rash of injuries like we had, but both those teams had a resolve to get there and beat good teams along the way. I thought the guys might have been a little too amped up for this one."

At the Steelers' subdued post-game dinner, clusters of players tried to make sense of a subpar showing when a third Super Bowl victory in six years would have warranted the label "second dynasty" in Pittsburgh. Nothing was more costly than their 3–0 deficit in turnover differential, but the first series spoke volumes about the readiness of coach Mike Tomlin's team. After a 4-yard pass to the Green Bay 40, guard Chris Kemoeatu was beat off the ball by nose tackle B. J. Raji, and Rashard Mendenhall was smeared for minus-4. On third down, wide receiver Antonio Brown blew his route on the sideline, and Roethlisberger's on-target pass sailed incomplete. On the punt, Shields lost all awareness of where he

	1	2	3	4	Final
Pittsburgh Steelers	0	10	7	8	25
Green Bay Packers	14	7	0	10	31

SCORING SUMMARY

1st Quarter
GB   Nelson, 29-yd. pass from Rodgers (Crosby kick)
GB   Collins, 36-yd. interception return (Crosby kick)
2nd Quarter
PIT   Suisham, 33-yd. FG
GB   Jennings, 21-yd. pass from Rodgers (Crosby kick)
PIT   Ward, 8-yd. pass from Roethlisberger (Suisham kick)
3rd Quarter
PIT   Mendenhall, 8-yd. run (Suisham kick)
4th Quarter
GB   Jennings, 8-yd. pass from Rodgers (Crosby kick)
PIT   Wallace, 25-yd. pass from Roethlisberger (Randle El run)
GB   Crosby, 23-yd. FG

was in relation to returner Tramon Williams, backing into him and causing a fumble. Steeler gunner Keenan Lewis had the first and probably best shot at making the recovery. Official Walt Anderson and his crew needed 33 seconds to clear players off the pile and rule that the ball had been recovered by Williams. It was the closest the Steelers would come to a takeaway all day.

"I feel like they wanted it more than we did," wide receiver Mike Wallace said. "I don't feel like we had a good game. At all. Offense. Defense. Special teams. Nobody really did what they're used to doing."

Green Bay's first series also was revealing. On McCarthy's opening play, he sent out five split receivers (running back James Starks also flanked wide) with Rodgers in shotgun formation. The next two plays also were from shotgun with three and four wide receivers. In effect, McCarthy was letting LeBeau's defense know that the Packers intended to attack. Of the Packers' 56 snaps, 68 percent came with either three (21 plays), four (16), or five (1) wide receivers on the field. The Packers had a fullback in the lineup on only 17 plays and ended up rushing just 13 times.

Even though the Steelers' defensive coaches praised the effectiveness of the Packers' rushing attack behind Starks, McCarthy didn't want to get bogged down against the most dominant run defense in Pittsburgh history. The Packers respected cornerback Ike Taylor, who spent most of the game matched against Greg Jennings. On the other hand, the Packers remembered how they had torched the other cornerback, Bryant McFadden, for gains of 27, 44, 30, 28, and 22 yards when he was starting for Arizona in the Cardinals' 51–45 wild-card victory over Green Bay in January 2010. They viewed nickel back William Gay and dime back Anthony Madison as vulnerable too.

"Last year, McFadden struggled against us and that's where we felt comfortable again," Nelson said. "We wanted to have them in nickel as much as possible. We believe our top four guys are No. 1 and No. 2 receivers all over the league."

The Packers' opening possession ended with a punt after Nelson beat McFadden on a sideline go route but dropped the ball 33 yards downfield at the Pittsburgh 18. "We liked the matchup, and we wanted to be aggressive," said McCarthy. "If they were going to bump us, we were going to take a shot as much as we could. Our plan was to go get 'em."

On the ensuing Steelers drive, Mendenhall reeled off gains of 15 (safety Charlie Peprah had the first of the Packers' nine missed tackles) and 9 yards, but a false-start penalty against fullback David Johnson on second and 1 stalled the drive, and the Steelers punted.

A mix of five passes and three runs gained 51 yards and moved the Packers to the Pittsburgh 29, where Rodgers lobbed deep to Nelson once more on the right sideline for a touchdown.

It was third and 1. The play was a "bluff" screen, with tight end Andrew Quarless on a corner route as No. 1 in the progression, fullback John Kuhn to the short flat as No. 2, and third-down back Brandon Jackson on the screen as No. 3. "That's my triangle," McCarthy said. "I try to build triangles to help the quarterback." Nelson, the sole wide receiver, also was on the strong side covered by Gay. "In a normal situation, this route by Nelson would be a clear [out]," said McCarthy. "If Gay plays off him, the ball will go to the screen. It would have been a big play."

Gay, however, was in press coverage. Even though there was just one yard to go, McCarthy had given Rodgers the green light to take a shot against bump and run. "There haven't been too many times

in my career that you give your quarterback that option unless you believe in him," McCarthy said. "No. 12, he is a hell of a player now." As Nelson peered inside, Rodgers touched the right side of his helmet with his right hand. Said Nelson, "It was the same route. It was more of an alert saying, 'If you beat him, or if you don't, I'm still going to throw it to you.'" Gay was right next to Nelson but never turned back for the ball. "Gay was in great shape," Steelers secondary coach Ray Horton said. "I'd like Gay to knock the ball down. That's how close he was."

Two plays later, the bungling Steelers found themselves in a 14–0 hole. Brown returned the kickoff to the Pittsburgh 42, but Ryan Mundy's illegal block sent the Steelers back to their own 7. On first down, Arians called a five-step drop by Roethlisberger in which he would pump fake on a curl route to Wallace and then hit him deep on a double move. Expecting a run by the Steelers in their double tight-end formation, Capers placed eight in the box with Nick Collins sitting between the hash marks as the lone safety.

"They would notoriously jump 14-yard routes on the quarterback's action," Arians said. "They are coached extremely well, but we thought we had set them up. We would have liked to have had better field position to run it. I think Mike had him by a step. It would have been either a long incompletion, pass interference, or a 93-yard touchdown."

From left to right, the Packers rushed Ryan Pickett, Raji, Howard Green, and Frank Zombo. Green, a 360-pounder cut 10 times in his long career, used his power and leverage to beat the 344-pound Kemoeatu, shoving him straight back and slamming Roethlisberger's right shoulder as his arm came forward. The pass fluttered well short of Wallace and into the hands of Collins, who made an excellent break on the ball. "On the play-action, we were looking to draw that safety up," Colbert said. "I give Collins more credit than Green because he stayed in position. He never really bit." Catching the ball 2 yards from the sideline, Collins used blocks by Zombo and Pickett and vaulted into the end zone for a 37-yard touchdown return.

The Packers intercepted eight passes in the postseason, each one almost more electrifying than the other. Besides Collins, Williams returned

PITTSBURGH STEELERS
(AFC, 12–4)

Offense

#	Pittsburgh	Pos	#	Green Bay	

GREEN BAY PACKERS
(NFC, 10–6)

Pos			
Offense			

Pittsburgh			Green Bay
17 Mike Wallace (6-1, 201)	WR	85	Greg Jennings* (5-11, 198)
72 Jonathan Scott (6-6, 318)	LT	76	Chad Clifton* (6-5, 326)
68 Chris Kemoeatu (6-3, 344)	LG	73	Daryn Colledge (6-4, 306)
64 Doug Legursky (6-1, 315)	C	63	Scott Wells (6-2, 290)
73 Ramon Foster (6-5, 345)	RG	71	Josh Sitton (6-3, 313)
71 Flozell Adams (6-7, 350)	RT	75	Bryan Bulaga (6-5, 316)
83 Heath Miller (6-5, 253)	TE	81	Andrew Quarless (6-4, 243)
86 Hines Ward (5-11, 205)	WR	80	Donald Driver (5-11, 195)
88 Emmanuel Sanders (5-11, 180)	WR	87	Jordy Nelson (6-2, 217)
7 Ben Roethlisberger (6-5, 250)	QB	12	Aaron Rodgers (6-2, 225)
34 Rashard Mendenhall (5-10, 225)	RB	44	James Starks (6-2, 222)
Defense			
96 Ziggy Hood (6-3, 303)	LE	79	Ryan Pickett (6-2, 338)
98 Casey Hampton (6-1, 345)	NT	90	B. J. Raji (6-1, 337)
99 Brett Keisel (6-5, 285)	RE	77	Cullen Jenkins (6-3, 298)
56 LaMarr Woodley (6-1, 265)	LOLB	52	Clay Matthews* (6-3, 257)
51 James Farrior (6-1, 232)	SILB	50	A. J. Hawk (6-1, 247)
94 Lawrence Timmons (6-1, 234)	WILB	55	Desmond Bishop (6-2, 240)
92 James Harrison* (5-11, 260)	ROLB	58	Frank Zombo (6-3, 248)
20 Bryant McFadden (5-11, 190)	LC	21	Charles Woodson* (6-1, 202)
24 Ike Taylor (6-0, 195)	RC	38	Tramon Williams (5-11, 186)
43 Troy Polamalu* (5-10, 207)	SS	26	Charlie Peprah (5-11, 203)
25 Ryan Clark (5-11, 205)	FS	36	Nick Collins* (5-11, 207)

* Pro Bowl selection

SUBSTITUTIONS

Pittsburgh

Offense: WR - 84 Antonio Brown, 82 Antwaan Randle El, 81 Arnaz Battle; TE - 89 Matt Spaeth; T - 66 Tony Hills; G - 79 Trai Essex; FB - 85 David Johnson; RB - 21 Mewelde Moore, 33 Isaac Redman. *Defense:* DE - 93 Nick Eason; NT - 76 Chris Hoke; ILB - 50 Larry Foote, 57 Keyaron Fox, 55 Stevenson Sylvester; CB - 22 William Gay, 37 Anthony Madison, 23 Keenan Lewis; S - 26 Will Allen, 29 Ryan Mundy. *Specialists:* K - 6 Shaun Suisham; P - 13 Jeremy Kapinos; LS - 60 Greg Warren. *DNP:* 4 Byron Leftwich (QB). *Inactive:* 61 Chris Scott (T), 77 Dorian Brooks (C), 16 Charlie Batch (QB), 27 Jonathan Dwyer (RB), 91 Aaron Smith (DE), 69 Steve McLendon (NT), 97 Jason Worilds (OLB), 28 Crezdon Butler (CB).

Green Bay

Offense: WR - 89 James Jones, 16 Brett Swain; TE - 83 Tom Crabtree, 86 Donald Lee; T - 70 T. J. Lang; G - 72 Jason Spitz; FB - 30 John Kuhn, 35 Korey Hall; RB - 32 Brandon Jackson. *Defense:* DE - 95 Howard Green, 98 C. J. Wilson, 94 Jarius Wynn; OLB - 53 Diyral Briggs, 49 Robert Francois; ILB - 57 Matt Wilhelm; CB - 37 Sam Shields, 24 Jarrett Bush, 22 Pat Lee; S - 20 Atari Bigby. *Specialists:* K - 2 Mason Crosby; P - 8 Tim Masthay; LS - 61 Brett Goode. *DNP:* 10 Matt Flynn (QB). *Inactive:* 67 Nick McDonald (G), 62 Evan Dietrich-Smith (C), 6 Graham Harrell (QB), 45 Quinn Johnson (FB), 23 Dimitri Nance (RB), 93 Erik Walden (OLB), 28 Brandon Underwood (CB), 40 Josh Gordy (CB).

an interception 70 yards for a touchdown in the 48–21 divisional rout in Atlanta, and Raji brought back another 18 yards for a clinching score in the title game at Soldier Field. Ninety-eight interceptions have been returned for touchdowns in NFL playoff history; the Packers became the first team to return one in three straight playoff games. "The big difference in the game," said Capers, "is we had three takeaways that accounted for 21 points."

One reason LeBeau blitzed so often was to contain Rodgers, who ranked third in rushing yards (356) by a quarterback during the regular season before adding 56 more in the first three playoff games. Hemmed in by the disciplined rush of the Steelers, Rodgers was forced for the first time all season to make all his plays from the pocket. Although Capers' blitz numbers (31 percent) ran about normal, the crux of his game plan hinged on keeping Roethlisberger from buying time and then beating the scheme with his arm and his feet.

"The first thing we did back in Green Bay was put up eight to 10 plays of Roethlisberger making plays off improvising," Capers said. "His game, once he feels the rush, is to duck his shoulder and come out of there. He and Hines Ward just play off each other. So it was a different type of game plan. The worst thing we could do was fly up the field and be out of control. Many times, we were bull-rushing and mirroring. We really preached that this was not about sacking the quarterback."

Thus, the Packers weren't disappointed when outside linebacker Clay Matthews, their elite pass rusher, was held without a sack, knockdown, or hurry for the first time all season. "Clay was given specific instructions not necessarily to go wild with the pass rush," said Raji. "We all made a commitment to each other. Thank God he's a great teammate and he's not selfish."

Still, Arians had reason to salute the play of his patchwork offensive line, which had been without right tackle Willie Colon (Achilles) since July and left tackle Max Starks (neck) since Week 8. More damaging was the major ankle injury suffered in the AFC Championship Game by center Maurkice Pouncey, a Pro Bowl selection as a rookie. Neither Flozell Adams, the longtime Cowboy who started at right tackle, nor journeyman left tackle Jonathan Scott gave up a single pressure, and third-year backup Doug Legursky, starting his first game at center, yielded merely one-half pressure. "Flozell played

great on Matthews—he never really got near the quarterback," said Arians. "I thought Legursky played extremely well. Run blocking, I thought they [the line] were outstanding."

Held to 29 yards and one first down in their first three possessions, the Steelers scored early in the second quarter on Shaun Suisham's 33-yard field goal. The long gain was an 18-yard scramble through a five-man rush by a limping Roethlisberger. After that, Capers said, the Packers instructed linebacker A. J. Hawk or whoever else was the fifth man in the pressure to "spy" Roethlisberger before committing to the rush.

On the play before Roethlisberger's longest jaunt of the game, tight end Heath Miller found himself wide open near the Green Bay 30 against a blown coverage. However, Roethlisberger's front foot gave out on the Sportfield Softtop surface, and the pass skidded short of Miller. "He almost blew his [left] knee out," said Arians. "The foot just came out from under him. It was an easy 30-yard gain, and the ball bounces to him."

A few plays later, rookie Emmanuel Sanders planted his right foot on a 13-yard curl that he caught for a first down. He limped off, returned after one play, and then was shut down with a fracture that required surgery. Afterward, the Steelers complained about the rock-hard condition of the field to the league office but received little satisfaction. The Packers agreed. "Jordy Nelson's knee was awful," said McCarthy. "He had to come off the plane in a wheelchair, his knee was that big. He did it on that long catch in the fourth quarter. Charles [Woodson] broke his collarbone in the same area."

Each team incurred additional blows in the next few minutes. Pittsburgh's Arnaz Battle suffered a broken rib covering the ensuing kickoff and, other than covering one more punt, didn't play again. Without Sanders, their No. 3, and Battle, their No. 6, the Steelers were down to four wide receivers. The Packers lost Driver, and McCarthy had to play mediocre Brett Swain as his No. 4 wide receiver and junk plans for his five-receiver sets.

Soon thereafter, the Steelers committed their second turnover on an interception that Arians chalked up both to attrition and bum luck. On second and 11, Arians called "Steelhead," a play designed to spread the Packers' 4-1 defense with five wideouts. On the left, Wallace lined up outside across from Shields, Ward was in the middle across from Woodson, and Miller was inside across from dime back Jarrett Bush.

As Woodson, who Capers said should have been deeper, moved up to press Ward on his inside route, the veteran cornerback sensed that Peprah also was out of position and peeled off to chase the tight end. Still, Woodson was at least five yards behind Miller, and at the same time, Ward now was free in the middle. "It was a busted coverage, but sometimes you blow them in the right way," said Arians. "Heath Miller was uncovered running down the field for a touchdown, and that would have been the first read had it been Emmanuel Sanders. But it being a tight end running a deep route, Ben didn't look to him."

Instead, after 2.6 seconds against moderate pressure, Roethlisberger threw the 4-yard crosser to Wallace, who had a step on Shields. Bush, who had just one previous interception in five seasons as a Packer, broke hard and snatched the ball from Wallace's grasp. It was by far the biggest play of Bush's modest career. "Huge, huge play," said McCarthy. "Jarrett Bush is a warrior and gives you everything he's got."

From the Pittsburgh 47, it took Green Bay just four plays to score a third touchdown and assume a 21–3 lead. With the Steelers playing Cover 3 behind a fire zone, McFadden was giving too much cushion isolated on the left against Nelson. When Nelson planted and worked back to the sideline, Rodgers zinged the comeback route to him for 16 yards. James Starks, a sixth-round draft choice who wasn't activated until Nov. 9 because of a hamstring injury, ran for 12 yards on the next play.

As Rodgers broke the huddle on first down from the 21, both he and McCarthy wondered how Polamalu would react to the coming play. On the Packers' third play of their opening series, McCarthy had sent three wide receivers right and one to the left. When Nelson, the inside man on the right, broke into the middle, Rodgers hitched and came back to Driver, the middle receiver, for a gain of 24. Polamalu, the safety to the strong side, broke to cover Nelson, and Driver was wide open.

This time, McCarthy flanked Jones and Nelson left with Jennings and Quarless right before Jennings motioned across and set up just inside of Nelson. Pittsburgh was in a two-safety shell with Polamalu over the top on the strong side, just as he had been on Driver's 24-yard reception. With Jones, Nelson and Jennings all running vertical routes on Polamalu's side, this time Polamalu jumped to cover Nelson, the middle receiver, instead of splitting Nelson and Jennings. "Polamalu clearly played No. 2 [Nelson], and I'm sure Aaron's eyes had a bunch to do with it," said McCarthy. "This is the game within the game. Who are you moving? The back-side safety [Ryan Clark] or the near safety [Polamalu]?"

Now across from Jennings, linebacker James Farrior hesitated for a split-second as his much speedier opponent was bursting behind him down the seam. "If James had just gone with him a couple more yards, he would have been deep enough and then Aaron has to hold the ball and throw it a little bit later and we have a chance to intercept," linebacker coach Keith Butler said. "That's one of those mistakes that we had not made before. You always hear this is a game of inches, and here it really was."

Given the fact that Polamalu had been looked off, the touchdown pass figured to be easy. But what the Packers didn't expect was for Clark to leave Taylor in one-on-one coverage on Quarless and break hard toward Jennings. According to Nelson, Rodgers said he never saw Clark.

The ball left Rodgers' hand 2.40 seconds after it had been snapped, and his pass was in the air 0.85 seconds. Fully extended near the 4, Clark came within inches of tipping it away from Jennings. Jennings displayed extraordinary concentration and courage, making the catch and holding on after taking a whack in the back from Polamalu. Mobbed by teammates in the end zone, Jennings pantomimed slipping on his Super Bowl ring.

As the game unfolded, Polamalu was victimized several more times. For the second Super Bowl in three years, he gave up big plays and didn't make any. Despite an Achilles-related injury that Horton indicated bothered him for several months and caused him to sit out two late-December games,

Polamalu said his leg felt better in the Super Bowl than it had since mid-season.

A week before the Super Bowl, McCarthy said he expected Polamalu to be used more in pressure than coverage. LeBeau, however, rushed him on merely two plays, a decision Horton said was based on his reduced movement ability and not out of respect for the Packers' passing game. "He couldn't run," said Arians. "You never saw him near the ball. For the whole playoffs, he was one-legged playing deep rather than the short safety. He just gutted it out for his teammates."

The elation on the Packers' sideline didn't last long. Antwaan Randle El, a nine-year veteran subbing for Sanders, beat Shields on a deep sideline route and, when Shields couldn't corral him, broke free for 37 yards to the Green Bay 40 at the two-minute mark. Shields suffered his shoulder injury at the end of the play, and then on the next snap, Woodson snapped his collarbone defending a take-off route to Wallace. After finding Ward for gains of 14 and 17 yards, Roethlisberger eluded the bull-rushing Raji and, 4 seconds after the snap of the ball, flipped it to Ward in the corner for an 8-yard touchdown. In man coverage, Bush looked back for the ball and then lost contact with Ward. "We had the initial break covered and then Hines just adjusted off it," said Capers. "It was classic Roethlisberger and Hines Ward." It also was 21–10.

Just before the Packers went out for the second half, Woodson tried to tell his assembled teammates just how much the Super Bowl meant to him. He was too choked up to speak, but his teammates understood their leader. Running backs coach Edgar Bennett said that, like Reggie White, "[Woodson] just has the ability to reach guys."

On the first third down of the second half, McCarthy sent Jennings, Nelson, and Jones to the right side. With Jennings double-covered inside, Rodgers went to Jones outside on a slant with Gay in close coverage. When Gay tried to undercut the route, Jones didn't extend his arms properly and dropped the ball when it got into his body. Because Polamalu, the last defender, wasn't taking a good angle, it's likely Jones would have been off for a 75-yard touchdown. In the previous five games, Jones also had dropped almost-certain scoring strikes of

71 and 67 yards. "The pass was on the money," said Butler. "That was one that went our way. That was part of the momentum change."

It didn't take long for the Steelers' comeback to gain steam. Beginning at midfield, the Steelers went back to basics. "It was time to buckle it up and go get 'em," Arians said. "We went into the game with the idea of running on them, and we weren't going to leave it yet." First, Matthews lost outside leverage when blocked by tight end Matt Spaeth, and Mendenhall circled right for 17 yards. Two plays later, on third and 1, Collins lost outside leverage on the other side, and Isaac Redman went wide for 16 to the Green Bay 8.

Arians went back to the weak-side counter with the pulling Kemoeatu leading the way off the right side on first down, and Mendenhall surged across for the touchdown. "They ran that same 'Counter-O' play, wedged us out of there, and got a vertical seam," said Capers. "We led the league over two years in [fewest] TD runs allowed."

It was 21–17. Momentum had shifted. "I could sense it. I could feel it," Capers said. "The crowd really got into it. My concern is we were down some players and we had to change our game plan." Nelson dropped another pass, linebacker James Harrison scrambled off the turf against center Scott Wells to sack Rodgers as he tried to escape, and the Packers had to punt again.

After picking up one first down at the Green Bay 44, the Steelers deployed in a running formation, and the Packers trotted out their 4-4 "hippo" defense. As Roethlisberger faked a handoff to Mendenhall and began a seven-step drop, Williams read run and let Wallace release without jamming him. It left Wallace one-on-one with Peprah, the matchup the Steelers had been trying to obtain throughout the game. Wallace's assignment was to head for the back pylon in the left corner of the end zone. Instead, he was headed more toward the 10 when the unhurried Roethlisberger released the ball from the Pittsburgh 47. "He beat the safety so clean he just ran away from him instead of going higher," said Arians. "We had a wide-open touchdown, and Mike Wallace took a little different angle than Ben was expecting. Ben was expecting him deeper, and Mike came a little flat." Said Wallace, "We hit that nine out of 10. Eight out of 10, for sure."

Pittsburgh advanced to the Green Bay 29, but the Packers held fast. On fourth and 15 from the 34, Tomlin made a decision that he would quickly regret, waving out Suisham for a 52-yard attempt. The kick missed far to the left. "There was no reason not to believe he wouldn't make it," Arians said. "Shaun had been banging it all year, and he was banging it easy in pre-game."

Following another lousy three-and-out and a special-teams penalty during Tim Masthay's mediocre punt, the Steelers were in business once again at the Green Bay 41. On the final play of the quarter, Mendenhall barged for 8 yards on a counter. "The momentum was in their favor at certain points in the third quarter," said McCarthy. "The third quarter was not our finest moment. But that's why you play 60 minutes."

The Steelers came out with two tight ends left, Wallace wide right, tight end David Johnson as the fullback offset left, and Mendenhall behind Roethlisberger. Green Bay countered with its 4-4.

During the break, Matthews told players in the huddle that based on his film study, he expected another counter to be coming at him and Pickett, the left end. With the Steelers at the line, Matthews screamed, "Spill it, Pickett! Spill it!" All day long, Pickett had locked horns with Adams at the point of attack. This time, Pickett would fire inside Adams and, if it was the counter that Matthews anticipated, attempt to use up both the pulling lineman and Johnson, the lead blocker. "You're either a contain team or spill team," said Arians. "Very seldom do they switch during a game. It was a good play for them to spill it and scrape it because we were blowing them up pretty good with the [contain]."

Regarded as a top-notch blocker, Johnson was "a little bit fooled" by Pickett's sudden penetration and Matthews' position outside, according to Arians. Instead of covering up Matthews, Johnson almost didn't touch him. Johnson had gotten too high, and there was Matthews, bending in classic football-strike pose, prepared to uncoil on the ball carrier.

Shortly after receiving the handoff, Mendenhall was sandwiched almost simultaneously between Pickett and Matthews. "There was no loose carrying of the ball," said Arians. "I think Clay just totally surprised Rashard." Driving forward, Matthews lifted Mendenhall off the ground and planted him on his back as the ball popped loose. Johnson, the closest player to the ball, didn't react until it was too late. Inside linebacker Desmond Bishop hustled off a block by Adams and recovered the ball shin-high on the second bounce back at the Green Bay 45.

TEAM STATISTICS

PITTSBURGH		GREEN BAY
19	Total First Downs	15
8	Rushing	4
11	Passing	11
0	Penalty	0
387	Total Net Yardage	338
64	Total Offensive Plays	55
6.0	Avg. Gain per Offensive Play	6.1
23	Rushes	13
126	Yards Gained Rushing (Net)	50
6.0	Average Yards per Rush	3.8
40	Passes Attempted	39
25	Passes Completed	24
2	Passes Intercepted	0
1	Tackled Attempting to Pass	3
2	Yards Lost Attempting to Pass	16
261	Yards Gained Passing (Net)	288
7/13	Third-Down Efficiency	6/13
0/1	Fourth-Down Efficiency	0/0
3	Punts	6
51.0	Average Distance	40.5
4	Punt Returns	1
5	Punt Return Yardage	0
6	Kickoff Returns	3
111	Kickoff Return Yardage	63
0	Interception Return Yardage	38
1	Fumbles	0
0	Own Fumbles Recovered	0
0	Opponent Fumbles Recovered	1
6	Penalties	7
55	Yards Penalized	67
3	Touchdowns	4
1	Rushing	0
2	Passing	3
0	Returns	1
3	Extra Points Made	4
1	Field Goals Made	1
2	Field Goals Attempted	1
0	Safeties	0
25	Total Points Scored	31
33:25	Time of Possession	26:35

PITTSBURGH

Passing	CP/ATT	YDS	TD	INT	RAT
Roethlisberger	25/40	263	2	2	77.4

Rushing	ATT	YDS	AVG	TD	LG
Mendenhall	14	63	4.5	1	17
Roethlisberger	4	31	7.8	0	18
Redman	2	19	9.5	0	16
Moore	3	13	4.3	0	7

Receiving	NO	YDS	AVG	TD	LG
Wallace	9	89	9.9	1	25
Ward	7	78	11.1	1	17
Randle El	2	50	25.0	0	37
Sanders	2	17	8.5	0	13
Miller	2	12	6.0	0	15
Spaeth	1	9	9.0	0	9
Mendenhall	1	7	7.0	0	7
Brown	1	1	1.0	0	1

Interceptions	NO	YDS	LG	TD

Punting	NO	AVG	LG	BLK
Kapinos	3	44.3	56	0

Punt Ret.	NO/FC	YDS	LG	TD
Brown	4/0	4	2	0
Randle El	1/0	0	0	0

Kickoff Ret.	NO	YDS	LG	TD
Brown	4	88	38	0
Redman	1	12	12	0
Moore	1	11	11	0

Defense	SOLO	AST	TOT	SK
Clark	6	2	8	0
McFadden	4	0	4	0
Taylor	4	0	4	0
Polamalu	3	0	3	0
Timmons	3	0	3	0
Woodley	3	0	3	1
Gay	2	0	2	0
Keisel	2	1	3	0
Farrior	1	1	2	0
Hampton	1	0	1	0
Harrison	1	0	1	1
Hood	1	0	1	1
Madison	1	0	1	0
TOTAL	**32**	**4**	**36**	**3**

GREEN BAY

Passing	CP/ATT	YDS	TD	INT	RAT
Rodgers	24/39	304	3	0	111.5

Rushing	ATT	YDS	AVG	TD	LG
Starks	11	52	4.7	0	14
Rodgers	2	-2	-1.0	0	-1.0

Receiving	NO	YDS	AVG	TD	LG
Nelson	9	140	15.6	1	38
Jennings	4	64	16.0	2	31
Jones	5	50	10.0	0	21
Driver	2	28	14.0	0	24
Jackson	1	14	14.0	0	14
Quarless	1	5	5.0	0	5
Hall	1	2	2.0	0	2
Crabtree	1	1	1.0	0	1

Interceptions	NO	YDS	LG	TD
Collins	1	37	37	1
Bush	1	1	1	0

Punting	NO	AVG	LG	BLK
Masthay	6	40.5	51	0

Punt Ret.	NO/FC	YDS	LG	TD
Williams	1/0	0	0	0

Kickoff Ret.	NO	YDS	LG	TD
Lee	2	44	28	0
Nelson	1	19	19	0

Defense	SOLO	AST	TOT	SK
Peprah	9	1	10	0
Bishop	6	2	8	0
Zombo	5	0	5	1
Collins	4	0	4	0
Matthews	3	0	3	0
Williams	3	3	6	0
Bush	2	1	3	0
Hawk	2	3	5	0
Pickett	2	0	2	0
Shields	2	0	2	0
Woodson	2	1	3	0
Lee	1	0	1	0
TOTAL	**41**	**11**	**52**	**1**

"Coaches can't pick everything up," said Raji. "I guess Clay looked at the amount of times they ran from that formation. Pickett, trusting his teammate, made the play. He easily could have said, 'No, they're not running that, let's do this.' Understanding our defense, I'd definitely split [the credit] 50-50. Pickett swallowed up some blockers and gave a playmaker the opportunity to cause a fumble."

Jones made an exceptional catch for 12 yards on a low sideline pass on third and 7. One play later,

LeBeau zone-blitzed, leaving Nelson matched inside against Clark. "That is exactly what we wanted," said McCarthy. With the Steelers out of position and an open field ahead, Nelson dropped the pass.

Now it was third and 10, and LeBeau dialed up the "Cobra" fire-zone blitz that Capers had tried hundreds of times on the Packers' practice field against Rodgers with little success. When Rodgers and Wells recognized the corner blitz was coming, they adjusted the protection, and Brandon Jackson moved outside to pick up McFadden. Nelson stayed with his crossing route, an almost identical pattern to his drop on the previous play. Dropping down to replace McFadden against Nelson, Clark gave too much cushion. Nelson caught the ball at the 28, skipped away from Clark, and outflanked Farrior before Polamalu pushed him out at the 2 after a gain of 38.

Horton said Clark, whom he described as a "great tackler," should have stopped Nelson immediately. Polamalu accepted blame as well. "He shouldn't get any yards after the catch on that," said Butler. "We were out of position. We guessed on a couple things, and our guessing was wrong. He made some good moves and got around us."

On first and goal, the Packers tried to sneak tight end Tom Crabtree out from the protection and into the flat. Defensive end Brett Keisel smelled out the play and, failing to spot an open Quarless in the end zone, Rodgers wisely absorbed a 6-yard sack by LaMarr Woodley after 5.1 seconds. Two weeks earlier, Rodgers had been intercepted by Chicago's Brian Urlacher after forcing a pass over the middle in a similar situation.

Facing second and goal from the 8, McCarthy went back to the 1 by 3 set with Jennings, Nelson, and Swain aligned to the right. "We had done so much vertical," said McCarthy. "Greg already had caught a touchdown. They had been seeing a lot of

> "It was really like a normal game for our guys. I didn't see any big eyes. They went out and played their asses off and enjoyed themselves."
>
> *Mike McCarthy, Packers head coach*

post. So this is the play that marries it. One is called 'Indy,' and this is called 'Colt,' where Greg goes to the corner. Jordy and Swain are running 5-yard ins. If Aaron gets any pressure, he just takes the three-step stick route."

During the two-week run-up, Horton and the Pittsburgh defensive staff had watched every one of the Packers' 19 games. "This is a play we practiced the heck out of," said Horton. "This play, that coverage. That play was no surprise. We expected it. We had the defense we wanted. And they scored without anyone being around the guy." Horton never did find out what happened. All he saw was Farrior, Madison, and Polamalu, three of the four defenders across from Jennings, milling about looking at each other when the play got underway.

Once again, Polamalu took himself out of a crucial play. "Earlier in the game, they ran Jennings down the middle," he said. "I was anticipating that same pass play, and I guessed wrong." When Rodgers looked left, Polamalu reacted to the quarterback's eyes. As he did so, Jennings broke to the corner and routinely gathered in the pass from Rodgers seven or eight yards ahead of Polamalu.

It took the Steelers 4½ minutes to cover 66 yards, slicing a 28–17 deficit to 28–25. They kept running the "tear" screen to Wallace in which Roethlisberger would take one step and fire to the flat when he read blitz. The touchdown came on third and 3 when Shields, isolated on the left side pressing Wallace, peeked in the backfield and was beat down the sideline. "I took one step inside, he bit on it, and then I went back outside," Wallace said. For the two-point conversion, Arians selected the read option that Roethlisberger had executed at Miami (Ohio) but the Steelers had never shown with him. Still, Shields was in position to tackle Randle El at the 2 but dipped his bad shoulder and missed. It was the final play for Shields.

Half of the fourth quarter remained, an eternity in the NFL, and the Packers' lead of three points was as slim as it had been. Starting from the 25, McCarthy did what he had done for the entire game. He attacked.

On first down, he sent out three wide receivers, hoping to match Nelson against Clark on a wheel route behind a seven-man protection. The play unfolded downfield as it had been drawn up, with Nelson open deep behind Clark. On the outside, however, Timmons beat Starks as part of a five-man pressure, and Rodgers flushed before being sacked by defensive end Ziggy Hood. "We weren't happy about that," said McCarthy, referring to Starks' feeble block.

So the Packers went to four wides on second and 14, and Nelson got 9 yards back on another in-breaking route against Clark. Third and 5 became third and 10 after a false start by Daryn Colledge. The clock was stopped at 5:59. The crowd of 103,219, the first of over 100,000 for a Super Bowl in 24 years, was as noisy as it had been. Horton thought the Packers to be in big trouble. "We had a chance to win if we stop that particular play," said Butler.

McCarthy stayed true to form, placing Jennings on the inside left of a 3 by 1 formation. Jones was outside, Swain in the middle, and Nelson alone on the right opposite McFadden. "I'm expecting two deep, either Tampa 2 or Cover 2, or [Cover] 2 Man," said McCarthy. "The defensive coach has help over the top and a call he can win with. But I'd much rather go down throwing this ball than trying to run an option route for five yards and hope the guy gets 10. I have tremendous confidence in Greg and Aaron on that route. This is what we do."

Having rushed at least five on eight of the Packers' first 10 plays of the fourth quarter, LeBeau changed up and elected to play coverage. For only the second time in the game, he rushed with just three. Harrison dropped over center, spying Rodgers. Across from Jennings was Taylor, easily the Steelers' best cover corner. Polamalu, the safety to that side, perhaps was positioned a bit too deep at 20 yards. Rodgers stood in shotgun formation.

Jennings began his seam route by accelerating off the line. Taylor made it somewhat easy for him by turning his hips prematurely and playing the pattern more with his ability than his technique. There was little doubt that Taylor anticipated the route. The 2009 meeting between the two teams was less than five minutes old when Rodgers threw the same pass to the same receiver in the same set on the same side and Jennings took it 83 yards for a touchdown. Only in that situation, the Steelers were in a zone, with Timmons walked out across from Jennings.

In trail technique, Taylor was trying to use his long arms and good speed to reduce the throwing window available to Rodgers so that only an exceptional pass could be completed. Jennings was trying to get on top of Taylor as quickly as possible, giving Rodgers a target before one of the safeties could enter the picture.

Jennings' first look back at Rodgers was at the 35, 10 yards downfield. From Wells' snap to Rodgers' throw, 2.25 seconds elapsed. The ball was in the air for another 1.05. The catch was made at the 45, maybe a yard beyond Taylor's outstretched left arm. At that point, Polamalu still was eight yards distant. Jennings snatched the ball in stride and burst between the hash marks for 11 more yards before Polamalu's low-block sent him pin-wheeling after a gain of 31. It was, said McCarthy, the play of the game.

"How many quarterbacks have the arm and the courage to throw that pass?" Butler asked. "One. The guy that did it." He added, "A lot of guys, when they lose the Super Bowl, they say they gave them the game. It's very hard for somebody to say we gave that game away. We didn't. They took it."

The longest rush by Starks, 14 yards, pushed the Packers down to the 30, and then on second and 9, Rodgers and Jones connected on a back-shoulder pass against Gay for 21 yards to the 8.

Having squandered two timeouts in the third quarter, Tomlin decided not to stop the clock by using his final timeout after two short completions drained off 90 seconds. With 2:15 left, the Packers were in a 2 by 2 formation, and LeBeau came with a six-man pressure, although Polamalu contributed nothing as he raced frantically from right to left behind the line and then slipped as he started his rush.

McCarthy had given Rodgers a run or pass option at the line, as he did most of the game. Rodgers chose Nelson, who had a physical advantage on Madison in the right slot. Nelson was open in the corner, but the ball skipped off his fingertips. "I was so pissed after this," McCarthy said. "Then I saw Jordy's knee after the game. I think it was because he was hurt. Jordy will make that play every day of the week."

The 23-yard field goal by Crosby extended the Packers' lead to 31–25. Redman returned the kickoff to the 26, but the Steelers' starting point was pushed back to the 13 when linebacker Keyaron

Fox was penalized half the distance to the goal for unnecessary roughness against Crabtree. "That was just so stupid," Butler said.

Thus, the Steelers would have to travel 87 yards with 1:59 and one timeout remaining. "I had been part of a great drive the year before [against Green Bay] in the same type of situation, and I felt we could do it again," said Wallace. "Ben is one of the best in the game when it comes to that."

Roethlisberger opened with a completion to Miller against a three-man rush. "[Zombo] missed the tackle, and they got 15 yards, and I said, 'That's it,'" recalled Capers. "So we five-man rushed the rest of the game."

Ward caught a 5-yard pass, but with the clock running, the Steelers blew at least 10 seconds when Randle El lined up on the wrong side and had to hurriedly switch. Even with the clock stopped after A. J. Hawk's pressure forced Roethlisberger to throw the ball away, the Steelers still looked out of sorts. On third and 5, Roethlisberger sailed a pass that wasn't close to a receiver. "We had some guys in different spots where they had never practiced," said Arians. "We did have some guys out of position because of the injuries, which ate up some clock. And we didn't hit the passes we needed to hit."

Astonishingly, the Steelers seemed confused coming out of the huddle before fourth down too. Wallace ran a 12-yard curl against tight coverage by Williams, there was some contact, and the pass fell incomplete. On all five plays, the Packers had exercised rush discipline, refusing to allow Roethlisberger to ad lib. Said B. J. Raji, "When he gets outside the pocket, he's one of the best in the league. Inside the pocket, we didn't think he could beat us."

As confetti rained down, Pam Oliver of Fox TV asked Jennings about the many hurdles the Packers had cleared to win their fourth Super Bowl and record 13th NFL championship. In his response, Jennings bemoaned the losses of Woodson and then Driver, whom he matter-of-factly referred to as "our No. 1 receiver." Anyone who followed the Packers would know that the 36-year-old Driver hadn't been the go-to man in Green Bay for two, arguably three seasons. But the grace shown by one of the team's stars to show respect for the club's senior-most member exemplified the unselfish attitude that permeated the locker room.

At the Packers' team meeting the night before the Super Bowl, McCarthy stunned some of his players by having representatives on hand to take their ring sizes. It wasn't an act of braggadocio since the players would be receiving NFC championship rings even if they were to lose the next day, although the rookie Zombo referred to the gambit as "a little awkward and weird, actually." Woodson labeled it as a "vote of confidence" by McCarthy.

When players began shuffling into their meeting room at the Omni Mandalay Hotel that Saturday night, Jennings spotted a baby grand piano just outside. It wasn't long before rookie defensive end C. J. Wilson began to play. An accomplished musician, Wilson had the lobby jumping in no time.

"Next thing you know, there's 30 guys over there," said McCarthy. "He's banging on the keys, they're signing songs." Kevin Elko, the sports psychologist who would address the team, had never seen anything like it.

Camaraderie, of course, only goes so far. Given their onslaught of injuries, the worst to hit the Packers since 1979, the championship became the ultimate triumph for McCarthy and general manager Ted Thompson. Then there was Aaron Rodgers. In his superlative, turnover-free performance against a formidable defense, only 2 or 3 of his 15 incomplete passes could be attributed to mis-reads or mis-throws. Rodgers completed his third season as a starter ranked No. 1 all-time in post-season passer rating (112.6) and regular-season passer rating (98.4). Rodgers had stepped from under the shadow of Brett Favre forever.

Just two other Super Bowl champions had lost as many games (10) as the Packers. Those six defeats, however, were by a total of 20 points. Furthermore, the Packers never trailed by more than seven points in any of their 20 games.

"To say we lost six games, that's fine," said McCarthy, the son of a Pittsburgh firefighter and tavern owner. "We had a lot of transition and challenge. We played good football from start to finish. I kept telling them to believe that our performance was as good as anybody in the league.

"I think it's premature to even answer if we were a great team. I think we had a great year. In 2010, we achieved greatness, and we were a special team."

XLVI

NEW YORK GIANTS 21, NEW ENGLAND PATRIOTS 17

February 5, 2012
Lucas Oil Stadium, Indianapolis, Indiana

To suggest that Tom Coughlin was in the same strata as Bill Belichick or, for that matter, that Eli Manning was in the same league as Tom Brady, would have been considered heresy among the pro football intelligentsia five years ago. After a pair of eye-opening Super Bowls, there no longer is any doubt. They most assuredly are.

When Coughlin, Manning, and the New York Giants defeated Belichick, Brady, and the New England Patriots in Super Bowl XLII in February 2008, it rivaled the New York Jets' win over Baltimore in January 1969 as the greatest upset in Super Bowl history. Even though the Patriots were favored by a field goal in Super Bowl XLVI in 2012, many football people recognized the rematch for what it was. Despite a 9–7 record in the regular season, the Giants by the time of the playoffs were the more complete and probably better team.

By virtue of their three Super Bowl championships and legendary level of performance, Belichick and Brady will one day be enshrined in the Pro Football Hall of Fame. Now, having twice vanquished what some regard as the finest coach and quarterback in NFL history, Coughlin and Manning could end up in Canton too.

Once again, it was Coughlin's indefatigable leadership and Manning's end-of-game magnificence that brought the Lombardi Trophy to New York and New Jersey. Manning was voted most valuable player in the Giants' 21–17 triumph, but Coughlin, who at age 65 surpassed Dick Vermeil (63) as the oldest Super Bowl–winning coach, was most responsible for turning a team with a 7–7 record and lack of identity into a force that simply could not be stopped.

"It's amazing," said Giants defensive coordinator Perry Fewell, who had never beat a Belichick-coached team as the Bills coordinator from 2006 to 2009. "Coaching in Buffalo for four years, watching

Attendance: 68,658
Conditions: Indoors
Time of kickoff: 6:30 p.m. (EST)
Length of game: 3 hours, 23 minutes
Referee: John Parry

MVP: Eli Manning, QB, Giants

how explosive that team [the Patriots] could be in their heyday and the adjustments their coaching staff would make. But Tom has a formula for his team. He gets his men to buy into his formula. That's what separates Tom. He doesn't get enough credit for developing his formula and his football teams. At 65, he's just hitting his peak."

The Super Bowl ended in excruciating fashion for the Patriots. Brady's 63-yard Hail Mary pass into the middle of the end zone hung in the air seemingly forever before it was tipped by safety Kenny Phillips and came down maybe a half-second away from being caught by onrushing Rob Gronkowski. If the all-pro tight end hadn't suffered the ankle injury in the AFC Championship Game victory over Baltimore, which required surgery five days after the Super Bowl, he might have been in position to get that ball.

"I'm telling you," Patriots offensive coordinator

"We had a veteran coach that had coached in a Super Bowl, fifteen veteran players that had played in the game, and Eli Manning leading us and setting the tone for our conduct when we started our practices in New Jersey. That set the tone for us winning that game."

Perry Fewell, Giants defensive coordinator

	1	2	3	4	Final
New York Giants	9	0	6	6	21
New England Patriots	0	10	7	0	17

SCORING SUMMARY

1st Quarter
NY   Safety, penalty in end zone on Brady
NY   Cruz, 2-yd. pass from Manning (Tynes kick)
2nd Quarter
NE   Gostkowski, 29-yd. FG
NE   Woodhead, 4-yd. pass from Brady (Gostkowski kick)
3rd Quarter
NE   Hernandez, 12-yd. pass from Brady (Gostkowski kick)
NY   Tynes, 38-yd. FG
NY   Tynes, 33-yd. FG
4th Quarter
NY   Bradshaw, 6-yd. run (run failed)

Bill O'Brien said, "that was as close as you can get to a Hail Mary without catching it. But, at the end of the day, they made plays or better coaching decisions than we did. . . . In a game that's so very closely played, those things are going to win and lose you the game."

As Coughlin extended his hand near midfield after the game, Belichick waded in and bear-hugged his former colleague from Bill Parcells' staff in New York. At last letting go, Belichick kept speaking to Coughlin for what seemed an eternity by NFL post-game standards before hugging the victor again and finally walking away.

Neither party would discuss the theme of Belichick's message, but Giants guard Chris Snee had an idea. "Coach had said prior to the game that the only way you earn New England's respect is by being physical with them," said Snee. "Every time we play them, it's a four-quarter game, a physical game. This was no different."

Kevin Gilbride, the Giants offensive coordinator since 2007, said Coughlin was most appreciative of Belichick's comments. "Whatever it was, Belichick was very effusive in the things he was saying, and Tom seemed genuinely moved by it."

There was much to respect about these fourth-seeded Giants, who became the fifth champion in seven years to win without benefit of a first-round bye. Remarkably, they trailed entering the fourth

quarter in 11 of their 20 games. The Super Bowl marked the eighth time the Giants had come from behind to win in the fourth quarter or overtime.

Through the ups and downs of a trying regular season, the Giants finished 27th in the league on defense and 32nd—dead last—in rushing. Injuries were a factor, with two defensive starters—cornerback Terrell Thomas and middle linebacker Jonathan Goff—blowing out knees in the preseason and left tackle Will Beatty suffering a season-ending detached retina in the 10th game. Still, this was an underachieving club most of the season.

The Giants expanded their deep talent base with the rise of defensive end Jason Pierre-Paul and wide receiver Victor Cruz, both in just their second seasons. Even though the Giants' front four, with standbys Justin Tuck and Osi Umenyiora, could be overpowering at times, many scouts said the extremely athletic Pierre-Paul was New York's best player on defense. Together with Hakeem Nicks, the speedy, shifty Cruz gave the Giants the most productive pair of wideouts in the league.

On defense, Fewell said the key to the turnaround was the decision by general manager Jerry Reese to re-sign middle linebacker Chase Blackburn on November 30, two days after the Giants hemorrhaged 577 yards in a 49–24 loss at New Orleans. A six-year veteran of Giants' special teams, Blackburn was sitting home in Marysville, Ohio, preparing to find work as a substitute teacher. Despite the fact Blackburn hadn't played football in 11 months, Coughlin played him extensively five days later in a 38–35 loss to unbeaten Green Bay (he intercepted Aaron Rodgers) and then started him ahead of rookies Greg Jones and Mark Herzlich the rest of the way.

Safety Antrel Rolle and others had been guilty of countless mental mistakes that not even the formidable four-man rush could hide. With his encyclopedic knowledge of Fewell's defense, ability to communicate, and respect throughout the locker room, Blackburn is credited with helping a disjointed unit become a cohesive one.

Facing the prolific passing attacks of Atlanta, Green Bay, and New England in the playoffs, the Giants incredibly did not allow a wide receiver to catch a pass for more than 21 yards. Even though Matt Ryan, Rodgers, and Brady were throwing to the likes of Roddy White, Julio Jones, Greg Jennings, Jordy Nelson, and Wes Welker, the wideouts for the Giants' four playoff opponents averaged merely 107.5 yards per game and scored one touchdown.

"We went through a tough time in four or five games where we just got the hell beat out of us," Fewell said. "We found who we were in the Green Bay game [December 4] when they beat us on the last drive. We had to put some veteran players in there, and we didn't have the 'Mike' backer. With Chase, we gained a lot of confidence and found out who we were."

As the 27th-ranked defense, the Giants eclipsed the 25th-ranked Saints of 2009 as the worst statistical defense of any Super Bowl champion. However, there was nothing shabby about a unit that reduced its regular-season yields of 25 points and 376.4 yards to 14 and 328.0 in the postseason.

"Whenever you play them, the first three hours of your game-plan meeting is about how you're going to handle their pass rush," O'Brien said of the Giants defense. "You've got to get the ball out quickly. Even if you're double-teaming guys, they're so big and athletic, they're hard to keep out all day. They're a very physical defense. They've got big corners and big safeties, and they disrupt your passing game with how they play you. It's very difficult to [expose coverage] because of that pass rush."

The 2011 Patriots sent eight players to the Pro Bowl, six more than the Giants, en route to the No. 1 seed in the AFC. Belichick's decision to sign former Chiefs guard Brian Waters off the street in early September saved the offensive line when veteran center Dan Koppen was lost for the year after suffering a leg injury in the season opener a week later. Guard Dan Connolly shifted inside, the 34-year-old Waters turned in another Pro Bowl season, and New England's offense, unconventionally built around multi-talented tight ends Aaron Hernandez and Gronkowski, was dominant once again.

Defensively, it was a different story. Of the 24 defensive players on New England's 53-man Super Bowl roster, a total of 13 had been cut, 9 more than once. Belichick made a league-high 36 roster moves after the opening game, and the revolving door swung mostly on the 31st-ranked defense. In all, 22 of the 53 Patriots had known the agony of being released, including 8 starters.

"To me, they're all castoffs," one scout said with exaggeration before the Super Bowl. "So it's a hell of a coaching job. They've done more with less."

Another personnel man added, "That's not a very good team. I don't know anyone who could take that team and go win seven, eight games. If this guy [Belichick] wins the Super Bowl with this team, it's unbelievable."

Other than defensive tackle Vince Wilfork, inside linebackers Jerod Mayo and Brandon Spikes, and safety Patrick Chung, Belichick was playing guys on defense that few teams would even want on their rosters.

"The national tone was that we were underdogs, and it was a positive thing," said Brian Ferentz, the Patriots tight ends coach. "That's right where Coach likes us. There really wasn't a lot of pressure on our football team because people felt our personnel was shaky. The Giants were playing their best football, which was parallel to the '07 season, but we thought we were playing pretty good football too."

Nevertheless, when Manning trotted onto the field with 3 minutes, 46 seconds remaining in the Super Bowl, the Giants had scored merely 15 points and found themselves trailing by two. They had controlled the ball using passes underneath and into the flats, plus the 1-2 rushing punch of Ahmad Bradshaw and 270-pound Brandon Jacobs. But due largely to Belichick's bend-don't-break defense, there had been very few down-the-field completions. No team had ever won a Super Bowl without a reception of at least 20 yards, and considering the Giants' longest pass through the first 56 minutes had been 19 yards, they were facing considerable odds starting from their 12-yard line with one timeout remaining.

"There wasn't any question in my mind that they were going to struggle to hold us in check," Gilbride said of New England's defense. "But I thought they actually did a terrific job just playing very conservatively the entire game. They were two-high, whether it was two-deep or four-deep. They were not letting us get any one-on-one matchups with our outside guys. They were challenging us to prove we could run the ball, which we hadn't done real well all year, and show the discipline to string out [long] drives and put it in the end zone. Somewhere along the line, we were going to need a big play, and we wound up getting it right away."

NEW YORK GIANTS (NFC, 9–7)		Offense	NEW ENGLAND PATRIOTS (AFC, 13–3)	
88	Hakeem Nicks (6-1, 207)	WR	84	Deion Branch (5-9, 195)
66	David Diehl (6-5, 307)	LT	72	Matt Light (6-4, 305)
77	Kevin Boothe (6-5, 305)	LG	70	Logan Mankins* (6-4, 305)
64	David Baas (6-4, 307)	C	63	Dan Connolly (6-3, 313)
76	Chris Snee (6-2, 309)	RG	54	Brian Waters* (6-2, 320)
67	Kareem McKenzie (6-5, 320)	RT	76	Sebastian Vollmer (6-7, 315)
85	Jake Ballard (6-6, 271)	TE	87	Rob Gronkowski* (6-6, 260)
80	Victor Cruz (6-0, 202)	WR	83	Wes Welker* (5-8, 185)
10	Eli Manning* (6-4, 220)	QB	12	Tom Brady* (6-4, 225)
45	Henry Hynoski (6-0, 261)	FB I TE	81	Aaron Hernandez (6-2, 242)
44	Ahmad Bradshaw (5-9, 217)	RB	39	Danny Woodhead (5-7, 195)
		Defense		
91	Justin Tuck (6-5, 267)	LE	98	Gerard Warren (6-4, 325)
97	Linval Joseph (6-4, 317)	LT I NT	74	Kyle Love (6-1, 310)
99	Chris Canty (6-7, 315)	RT I RE	75	Vince Wilfork* (6-1, 324)
90	Jason Pierre-Paul* (6-4, 284)	RE I SOLB	50	Rob Ninkovich (6-3, 250)
93	Chase Blackburn (6-3, 243)	MLB I SILB	55	Brandon Spikes (6-3, 250)
59	Michael Boley (6-2, 235)	WLB I WILB	51	Jerod Mayo (6-1, 245)
26	Antrel Rolle (6-0, 203)	SLOT I WOLB	95	Mark Anderson (6-4, 255)
23	Corey Webster (6-0, 197)	LC	32	Devin McCourty (5-10, 186)
31	Aaron Ross (6-0, 192)	RC	24	Kyle Arrington (5-9, 196)
34	Deon Grant (6-1, 215)	SS	44	James Ihedigbo (6-0, 214)
21	Kenny Phillips (6-2, 209)	FS	25	Patrick Chung (5-11, 212)

* Pro Bowl selection

SUBSTITUTIONS

New York

Offense: WR - 82 Mario Manningham, 15 Devin Thomas, 12 Jerrel Jernigan; TE - 86 Bear Pascoe, 47 Travis Beckum; T - 70 Tony Ugoh; G - 62 Mitch Petrus; RB - 27 Brandon Jacobs, 28 D. J. Ware. *Defense:* DE - 72 Osi Umenyiora, 71 Dave Tollefson; DT - 95 Rocky Bernard; OLB - 57 Jacquian Williams, 94 Mathias Kiwanuka, 55 Spencer Paysinger; MLB - 53 Greg Jones; CB - 20 Prince Amukamara, 36 Will Blackmon; S - 22 Derrick Martin, 39 Tyler Sash. *Specialists:* K - 9 Lawrence Tynes; P - 5 Steve Weatherford; LS - 51 Zak DeOssie. *DNP:* 8 David Carr (QB). *Inactive:* 13 Ramses Barden (WR), 79 James Brewer (T), 63 Jim Cordle (C), 33 Da'Rel Scott (RB), 69 Justin Trattou (DE), 73 Jimmy Kennedy (DT), 58 Mark Herzlich (MLB).

New England

Offense: WR - 85 Chad Ochocinco, 11 Julian Edelman, 18 Matthew Slater*; T - 77 Nate Solder, 61 Marcus Cannon; C - 62 Ryan Wendell; RB - 42 BenJarvus Green-Ellis; FB - 36 Lousaka Polite. *Defense:* DE - 94 Shaun Ellis, 71 Brandon Deaderick; OLB - 58 Tracy White, 52 Dane Fletcher; ILB - 90 Niko Koutouvides; CB - 29 Sterling Moore, 27 Antwaun Molden, 41 Malcolm Williams; S - 31 Sergio Brown. *Specialists:* K - 3 Stephen Gostkowski; P - 14 Zoltan Mesko; LS - 48 Danny Aiken. *DNP:* 8 Brian Hoyer (QB), 22 Stevan Ridley (RB), 69 Alex Silvestro (DE), 23 Nate Jones (CB). *Inactive:* 64 Donald Thomas (G), Nick McDonald (C), 15 Ryan Mallett (QB), 33 Kevin Faulk (RB), Shane Vereen (RB), 97 Ron Brace (NT), 59 Gary Guyton (ILB).

In a memorable game that had few memorable plays, the first snap of New York's nine-play, 88-yard winning touchdown drive will live on in Super Bowl lore.

Mario Manningham, the Giants' No. 3 wideout, flanked left about two yards outside the numbers as Cruz and Nicks set up wide right. After taking the shotgun snap, Manning recognized the Cover 2 defense and looked toward Nicks, who was open at the 15 on a return route. Manning apparently thought nickel back Kyle Arrington was in play on Nicks, and so decided to look back left toward Manningham, who was running a take-off route down the sideline.

The cornerback across from Manningham, free agent Sterling Moore, had saved the AFC title game by dislodging an end-zone pass from the hands of Ravens wideout Lee Evans in the final seconds. This time, Moore wasn't as fortunate after being beat again.

As Manningham took an outside release, Moore's job was to ride him off the route, ideally right out of bounds. Because the Giants were using maximum protection with seven blockers against four rushers, there was no flat receiver to occupy any of Moore's attention. Moore, who was playing too soft five yards away at the snap, let Manningham escape down the sideline without laying a glove on him.

"Maybe Sterling could have done more," said Devin McCourty, who was playing

New York

Head Coach: Tom Coughlin. **Offense:** Kevin Gilbride (coordinator), Sean Ryan (wide receivers), Mike Pope (tight ends), Pat Flaherty (offensive line), Mike Sullivan (quarterbacks), Jerald Ingram (running backs), Jack Bicknell (assistant offensive line), Kevin Gilbride Jr. (assistant). **Defense:** Perry Fewell (coordinator), Robert Nunn (defensive line), Jim Herrmann (linebackers), Peter Giunta (secondary, cornerbacks), David Merritt (secondary, safeties), Al Holcomb (assistant). **Special Teams:** Tom Quinn, Larry Izzo (assistant). **Strength:** Jerry Palmieri, Markus Paul (assistant).

New England

Head Coach: Bill Belichick. **Offense:** Bill O'Brien (coordinator, quarterbacks), Chad O'Shea (wide receivers), Brian Ferentz (tight ends), Dante Scarnecchia (assistant head coach, offensive line), Ivan Fears (running backs), George Godsey (assistant), Josh McDaniels (assistant). **Defense:** Matt Patricia (de facto coordinator, safeties), Pepper Johnson (defensive line), Patrick Graham (linebackers), Josh Boyer (defensive backs), Brian Flores (assistant). **Special Teams:** Scott O'Brien. **Strength:** Harold Nash, Moses Cabrera (assistant).

safety on the other side. "But I watched it in slow motion. I thought Sterling did a pretty good job of carrying it and making it a tough throw. If you were a betting man, you wouldn't bet your house on Eli making a throw that perfect and that Manningham could catch it on that sideline and keep his feet in bounds."

Chung, the safety on the play side, backpedaled 11 yards to the 37 and squared his body ever so slightly as Manning tried to look him off. He then used his low 4.5-speed and made a strong break on the ball. At the same time, Moore showed a good burst and was whacking the top of Manningham's right shoulder pad when the ball arrived.

Back at the line, left guard Kevin Boothe drew the short straw—one-on-one with Wilfork—while his teammates double-teamed the other three Patriots pass rushers. "It was more about being able to withstand his initial surge," said Boothe. "He's such an explosive player. I gave Eli enough time, but if he pump fakes one more second, then I think he'd have to move or he couldn't follow-through."

The fact that Wilfork had his arms up and was shoving Boothe deeper and deeper so that Manning

wasn't able to step freely with his front foot made the 38-yard pass into such a tiny window at the 50-yard line all the more heroic.

Manning's arcing throw, in the air 2.3 seconds, sailed just over Manningham's right shoulder and into his waiting hands. What made the catch was the skill and presence of mind by Manningham to jump with both feet slightly into the field just as the ball came down and a split-second before Chung arrived. All three players crashed down right in front of Belichick, clad in khakis and a gray hoodie chopped off at the elbow. He never even unfolded his arms, then asked for a perfunctory replay challenge that upheld the catch call by side judge Laird Hayes.

"That's a play that you make to win the Super Bowl," Patriots linebacker Rob Ninkovich said. "That's like the [Santonio] Holmes catch in the back of the end zone versus Arizona. That's what everybody dreams of as a kid."

Immediately, the play brought back memories of the 32-yard reception by New York's David Tyree during the touchdown drive that upended New England four years earlier.

"But it wasn't like Tyree," said Marc Ross, the Giants' director of college scouting. "That was just a once in a lifetime, almost fluke kind of deal. This was something you teach a receiver to do. It was the perfect throw and a perfect catch."

Manningham blew his route on the next play, failing to come back for a back-shoulder sideline throw that Manning had placed on target. He made amends on second down, catching a curl route for 16 yards to the 34. At this point, Belichick and his de facto coordinator, Matt Patricia, had rushed either three or four men on 35 of 37 dropbacks (the other two were five-man pressures). In the first half, the Patriots didn't play a single snap with a safety in the box.

> "What makes you think you can get the ball in there? I've seen Eli make so many plays, you just grow to expect it. But I still can't believe the pass and the catch."
>
> *Kevin Boothe, Giants guard, on the Manning-to-Manningham fourth-quarter pass play*

Now, with the clock ticking below 3 minutes, the Patriots blitzed six on the next two plays as the Giants were approaching field-goal range. Each time, Manning read the Patriots like a first-grade primer.

On first down, Manning audibled to a go screen to Manningham that would have gained substantially more than 2 yards if Cruz had picked up the check and blocked Moore, who made the tackle.

Then the offensive coordinator took the play-calling out of Eli's hands.

"I called two plays, a run and a pass," Gilbride said. "I didn't call the previous one because they had been all two-deep. He [Manning] saw the blitz again and went to the pass alert. If it's blitz man, you just take the best-look side. Hakeem was wide open. It's what you're hoping for, that you can trust your quarterback. And I do."

With dime back Antwaun Molden playing well back to protect against a big play, Nicks slanted in front of him for 14 yards to the 18 at the two-minute warning.

All game, the 250-pound Spikes had been a one-man wrecking crew, slamming into and then shedding blockers to prevent runs of two and three yards from rupturing into nine or ten.

"He is probably the most physical linebacker I have played in the last year or two, if not longer," Boothe said.

On the next play, Spikes and Mayo blasted into the A gaps, Snee came off Gerard Warren to pick Spikes up, and Bradshaw had room to burst for 7 yards to the 11. When the Patriots pressured again, Manning calmly flipped it out to Nicks on a hitch for 4 and a first down at the 7.

At this point, Belichick had made up his mind to allow the go-ahead touchdown in order to preserve time and a second timeout for the offense. Yet even with the clock stopped at 1:09 because Nicks had gone out of bounds, the Patriots were unable to transmit those instructions to Mayo. Having halted Bradshaw after a gain of 1, the Patriots had to expend their second timeout, during which the defense was told not to contest the touchdown. Bradshaw took the bait and scored, and the Giants' lead was four after a two-point conversion run failed.

The Patriots had calculated the odds of Lawrence Tynes making a chip-shot field goal as time expired at about 97 percent. Their kick-blocking unit didn't inspire confidence even though it was coached by Scott O'Brien, who in two decades as an NFL special-teams coach had come up with more than his share of clutch blocks, including one in Super Bowl XXXVIII for Carolina against New England.

The decision to allow the touchdown rather than take the chance with a last-second field goal was made even though Tynes had been extremely fortunate on his 38-yard field goal in the third quarter, which barely slipped inside the left upright. Two weeks earlier, a 32-yard miss by Baltimore's Billy Cundiff with 11 seconds left prevented the Ravens from carrying the Patriots into overtime.

New England, which took over at its own 20-yard line with 0:57 left on clock, had blistered Fewell's defense for a 14-play touchdown drive to close the first half when Brady hit 10 of 10 passes for 98 yards. "We had been virtually unstoppable all year in two-minute at the end of the half," Bill O'Brien said.

According to cornerbacks coach Peter Giunta, in the final minute of the game, the Giants switched from what they had done at the end of the first half to a form of Cover 2 with a Cover 3 element, as linebacker Jacquian Williams kept running back to play the post.

"Perry did a great job changing it up," Giunta said of his defensive coordinator. "We had them a little out of whack. Plus, we got the great pass rush."

Bill Walsh used to speak on the impact of a heavy pass rush in the fourth quarter. He would have liked these Giants who, even without blitzing on any of Brady's final eight dropbacks, still managed to register one sack, one knockdown, and four hurries.

In all, the Giants had two sacks, six knockdowns, and eight hurries in the game, a total of 16 pressures compared to the Patriots' 9. Tuck led with five pressures, Pierre-Paul had four, and Umenyiora and tackle Linval Joseph, who played an exceptional game, each had three.

"I thought our rush was good, not great," said Fewell. "We touched him 15 times. We were able to make him move the launch point more often than not. But I have never seen Tom Brady move and escape like he did in this football game."

On the first play of the final series, Phillips got antsy sitting in a two-deep shell and moved up to

> "Gronkowski played ninety-six percent of the snaps because I used to say every week, 'Why would we ever take this guy off the field? For what reason other than maybe to rest him?' He was an extremely important member of that offense."
>
> *Bill O'Brien, Patriots offensive coordinator*

help cover Welker. It created an open half of the field that Brady, unhurried by the rush, might have exploited if he had waited a half-count longer on his deep crossing route to Deion Branch.

"The only person over there was [Corey] Webster," Fewell said. "It could have been a bad situation. Webster may tackle him at the 50 or the 45."

But when Brady unloaded somewhat prematurely, the out-of-position Phillips happened to be in his throwing lane and with a leap tipped the ball so it bounced harmlessly off Branch's hands.

The sack, by Tuck, came on a stunt against guard Logan Mankins, and on fourth and 16, the game almost ended on another sack when Pierre-Paul shot by right tackle Sebastian Vollmer on an inside charge. Somehow, Brady eluded both Pierre-Paul and Umenyiora, fled left, squared up, and gunned a sideline bullet to Branch for 19 yards and a first down.

"That's what makes Tom Brady a great quarterback," Ferentz said. "He just has an uncanny feel, then he turns around and fires a great ball."

After one more first down, the Giants pressured Brady into two more incompletions. The Patriots were 51 yards away, and five seconds remained. It was time for a Hail Mary, the kind like Manning had completed to Nicks at the end of the first half against Green Bay in the divisional playoff game.

Gronkowski, who played 96.3 percent of the Patriots' snaps in the regular season, was feeling the effects of the ankle injury and had stood on the sidelines for the previous eight plays. Now he joined Hernandez on the right side, with Branch and Welker split wide left. "Usually when we throw them in practice, Rob just goes up and catches them," said Ferentz. "He does a nice job of judging the ball and he's a big, tall guy."

But with Gronkowski gimpy, he flipped assignments with Hernandez. "Aaron became the

designated jumper," O'Brien said. "Either go up and catch it, or bat it forward or backward to somebody. Then 'Gronk' would be there to try to catch the tip."

Fewell wanted Phillips, Grant, and Williams going up against the jumper, while Webster and cornerback Prince Amukamara would hover behind the pack and everyone else would block out their man.

After Gronkowski set sail past Michael Boley, the linebacker inexplicably began jogging and was 15 yards behind the tight end when Brady uncorked his perfectly placed heave in 5.3 seconds against a three-man rush. Not only was Gronkowski unchecked charging from the right of the scrum, Welker had outhustled Rolle and was running in free on the left.

"You'd like to coach it a hell of a lot better than how we coached it," said Fewell. "Boley doesn't turn and run fast enough, as well as Antrel. You've got to continue to box out the receivers so they don't have a shot at it, either."

Phillips was the only one of the five players who vaulted to actually touch the ball, which then began its slow descent in front of the pack right where Gronkowski was angling fast.

"The thing I'm most concerned about is [pass interference]," Fewell said. "Because the game can't end on a defensive penalty. On the sideline, I was just watching the official. When he did his safe sign, that's when we erupted."

In the deathly quiet of the Patriots' locker room, Gronkowski approached Ferentz and asked if he could have caught it. "He didn't realize that it had bounced," Ferentz said. "He was about two feet away from it before it bounced."

Belichick has said championships in the NFL often come down to a matter of inches. The unanswered Hail Mary wasn't the Patriots' only close call. "We had three balls out that we could have recovered, but it just didn't bounce our way," said Ninkovich. "A fumble was our opportunity to change that whole game around."

In the first quarter, Gilbride sent in receiving-type tight end Travis Beckum for fullback Henry Hynoski to give the Giants one back, two tight ends, and two wideouts for a third and 3 at the New England 11. The Patriots had been late substituting earlier in the drive, and now they were again. From a 3-4 defense, three defensive linemen trotted off and four players—including two linemen, Moore and

Molden—ran on to give the Patriots a total of 12 men on the field.

"I remember just before the snap seeing Antwaun come on the field," McCourty recalled. "I'm not sure if he heard someone say the package or someone say, 'Go out.' We just know there was some type of confusion on the sidelines."

On his head set, Gilbride was able to alert Manning to the snafu and urge him to snap the ball quickly before his transmission cut off at the 15-second mark. As Molden scampered aimlessly in the secondary, Ninkovich remembered thinking, "What's going on? We should take a timeout." Then the ball was snapped.

Manning threw on the right side to Cruz, who had the ball stripped by Sparks and recovered by Moore. Instead, the penalty gave the ball back to the Giants, and one play later, Cruz caught a 2-yard touchdown.

Ultimately, the responsibility for bad football such as that rests with Belichick, then Patricia, then the players. According to Ninkovich, it was the defense's only such penalty of the season.

"It was a fluke mistake that was on more than one individual, I can tell you that," said Ferentz. "I think it was a team mistake, and obviously, we paid the price for it."

In the third quarter, Nicks had fumbled for the first time in his 19 games when Mayo stripped him from behind after a 17-yard catch. Six Patriots were closer to the ball than any other Giant, and it was loose for almost 2 seconds. But when the ball bounced back toward the line, Hynoski easily made the recovery.

Finally, in the fourth quarter, the Giants were coming out of their end when Bradshaw was hit from the side by Spikes and fumbled for the second time in his 16 games. Diving at Bradshaw, safety James Ihedigbo had the ball bounce off his facemask and back to Snee, who recovered at the New York 11 as four Patriots crashed on top of him. "'Digs' [Ihedigbo] was so mad," recalled McCourty. "He said to me, 'I was already in mid-air, and I couldn't adjust.' Nothing you can do about that. You've got to make sure of the tackle."

Ihedigbo and defensive lineman Shaun Ellis reacted by grabbing their helmets with both hands and looking to the heavens as if to say, "What next?"

This was the second to last of the Giants' eight legitimate possessions, and like all the rest, they picked

up at least two first downs and crossed midfield. This drive, one of four to end with a punt, died on two incomplete passes to Manningham around a false-start penalty on Boothe, his second costly infraction.

On second and 5 from the New England 38, the Giants were in a little-used two-back, three-wideout set because tight ends Jake Ballard and Beckum had been

TEAM STATISTICS

NEW YORK		NEW ENGLAND
26	Total First Downs	21
7	Rushing	6
18	Passing	15
0	Penalty	0
396	Total Net Yardage	349
71	Total Offensive Plays	62
5.6	Avg. Gain per Offensive Play	5.6
28	Rushes	19
114	Yards Gained Rushing (Net)	83
4.1	Average Yards per Rush	4.4
40	Passes Attempted	41
30	Passes Completed	27
0	Passes Intercepted	1
3	Tackled Attempting to Pass	2
14	Yards Lost Attempting to Pass	10
282	Yards Gained Passing (Net)	276
5/11	Third-Down Efficiency	6/12
0/0	Fourth-Down Efficiency	1/1
4	Punts	3
40.8	Average Distance	41.0
1	Punt Returns	0
10	Punt Return Yardage	0
4	Kickoff Returns	3
75	Kickoff Return Yardage	73
0	Interception Return Yardage	0
2	Fumbles	0
2	Own Fumbles Recovered	0
0	Opponent Fumbles Recovered	0
4	Penalties	5
24	Yards Penalized	28
2	Touchdowns	2
1	Rushing	0
1	Passing	2
0	Returns	0
2	Extra Points Made	2
2	Field Goals Made	1
2	Field Goals Attempted	1
1	Safeties	0
21	Total Points Scored	17
37:05	Time of Possession	22:55

NEW YORK

Passing	CP/ATT	YDS	TD	INT	RAT
Manning	30/40	296	1	0	103.8

Rushing	ATT	YDS	AVG	TD	LG
Bradshaw	17	72	4.2	1	24
Jacobs	9	37	4.1	0	11
Ware	1	6	6.0	0	6
Manning	1	-1	-1.0	0	-1

Receiving	NO	YDS	AVG	TD	LG
Nicks	10	109	10.9	0	19
Manningham	5	73	14.6	0	38
Pascoe	4	33	8.3	0	12
Cruz	4	25	6.3	1	8
Hynoski	2	19	9.5	0	13
Bradshaw	2	19	9.5	0	11
Ballard	2	10	5.0	0	9
Ware	1	8	8.0	0	8

Interceptions	NO	YDS	LG	TD
Blackburn	1	0	0	0

Punting	NO	AVG	LG	BLK
Weatherford	4	40.8	51	0

Punt Ret.	NO/FC	YDS	LG	TD
Blackmon	1/0	10	10	0

Kickoff Ret.	NO	YDS	LG	TD
Jernigan	3	71	34	0
Blackmon	1	4	4	0

Defense	SOLO	AST	TOT	SK
Boley	9	1	10	0
Grant	5	1	6	0
Phillips	5	1	6	0
Blackburn	4	2	6	0
Tuck	3	0	3	2
Rolle	3	0	3	0
Williams	2	1	3	0
Ross	2	1	3	0
Pierre-Paul	2	0	2	0
Bernard	2	0	2	0
Paysinger	1	1	2	0
Joseph	1	1	2	0
Amukamara	1	0	1	0
Webster	1	0	1	0
Canty	1	0	1	0
Umenyiora	0	1	1	0
TOTAL	**42**	**10**	**52**	**2**

NEW ENGLAND

Passing	CP/ATT	YDS	TD	INT	RAT
Brady	27/41	276	2	1	91.1

Rushing	ATT	YDS	AVG	TD	LG
Green-Ellis	10	44	4.4	0	17
Welker	2	21	10.5	0	11
Woodhead	7	18	2.6	0	6

Receiving	NO	YDS	AVG	TD	LG
Hernandez	8	67	8.4	1	12
Welker	7	60	8.6	0	19
Branch	3	45	15.0	0	19
Woodhead	4	42	10.5	1	19
Gronkowski	2	26	13.0	0	20
Ochocinco	1	21	21.0	0	21
Green-Ellis	2	15	7.5	0	8

Interceptions	NO	YDS	LG	TD

Punting	NO	AVG	LG	BLK
Mesko	3	41.0	48	0

Punt Ret.	NO/FC	YDS	LG	TD

Kickoff Ret.	NO	YDS	LG	TD
Edelman	3	73	31	0

Defense	SOLO	AST	TOT	SK
Mayo	8	3	11	0
Spikes	8	3	11	0
McCourty	6	1	7	0
Molden	5	0	5	0
Arrington	4	1	5	0
Anderson	3	2	5	1.5
Ninkovich	3	1	4	0.5
Moore	3	0	3	0
Wilfork	3	0	3	0
Chung	2	4	6	0
Ihedigbo	2	3	5	0
Slater	2	0	2	0
Warren	1	1	2	0
Deaderick	1	0	1	1
Fletcher	1	0	1	0
Love	1	0	1	0
Gronkowski	1	0	1	0
Ellis	0	2	2	0
White	0	2	2	0
Gostkowski	0	1	1	0
TOTAL	**54**	**24**	**78**	**3**

lost during the game with torn ACLs. Manningham ran by Moore on a take-off route, but the pass was a tad long, and Manningham's footwork wasn't as precise as it would be a few minutes later. "That was foreshadowing," Ross said with a laugh. "We'd rather have the one that he caught later than that one."

Just a few plays earlier, Boothe had reminded Snee not to jump if the Patriots shifted their line late. "They did and, of course, I jumped," said the mortified Boothe, who hadn't been penalized all season. "We come off the field, and Chris says, 'Oh, you mean like that?'"

On third down, the Giants howled for pass interference against Moore on a comeback route but didn't get it.

Beginning from the 8-yard line with 9:30 remaining, the Patriots took advantage of a blown coverage by Pierre-Paul for a 19-yard gain in the flat by Danny Woodhead on third and 5. When Welker gained 11 on a reverse and the Patriots converted another third down, they were ready to expand their 17–15 lead. Just five minutes were left.

On its previous possession, New England had a promising drive thwarted when Brady, flushed by Joseph, saw Gronkowski matched one-on-one with the slow-footed Blackburn 50 yards downfield. Brady decided to take a jump-ball shot to his massive tight end, even though it was first down. Getting no deep help from Grant, who froze on the play, Blackburn was alone as he gave chase. When the pass came up short, Blackburn was able to turn back and make a falling-down interception as Gronkowski, unable to change directions sharply, could do little more than watch. "That was the big play in the game," said Giunta. "Chase just made a great play on the ball."

But now the Patriots were driving again. "We get tough starting field position, but we're moving the ball down the field," said Ferentz. "We knew, just like everyone in the stadium knew, that we could win the game on that drive." With a touchdown, the Giants would have been two scores down.

From the New York 43, O'Brien went to a power set with fullback Lousaka Polite, in for his third and last snap of the game, and tackle Nate Solder operating as a second tight end. A 4-3 base defense,

the Giants played 59 snaps in the Super Bowl in their 4-2 nickel, four snaps in their 4-1 dime, and none in the 4-3. Even here against the Patriots' big lineup, the Giants played their nickel. Attempting to follow Polite through the B gap on the left side, BenJarvus Green-Ellis was jarred in the backfield by defensive tackle Chris Canty and smothered for minus-1.

"I wish I had that call back," said O'Brien, who left the next morning to assume his duties as Joe Paterno's successor at Penn State. "We were on a roll doing other things. In college football, you might have 80 to 85 plays in a game. In the NFL, you only have, at the most, maybe 70 plays. Every single play counts. That was nobody's fault but mine. If you get off rhythm one bit in a game like that, you're going to have trouble."

What happened? Canty, set up in the A gap between Mankins and Connolly, decided to charge into the B gap and worked free outside of Mankins, who was expecting to double-team Canty in the A gap with Connolly. At the same time, Boley covered for Canty by moving from the B to the A gap.

"Chris told me he heard the call by the center saying they were going to double-team him and knew exactly what was coming," said Fewell. "I loved it. Hey, as a ball coach, you say, 'If you do that, you've got to make the play. If not, your ass is mine.'"

On second and 11, the Giants stayed in their nickel against two wideouts left and three receivers right. Concerned about Blackburn one-on-one against Hernandez on the right, Fewell made a call to double Hernandez while using man coverage against the four other receivers and keeping Phillips in the deep middle. It left Rolle matched on Welker in the left slot.

"Well, we played the 'Man Free,' and Rolle did not get the call," said Fewell. "It's made throughout the secondary and the linebackers. He should have known exactly what that call was, or anticipated it. But I may not have emphasized it enough."

Welker, the NFL leader with 122 receptions that year, cleared Rolle after 10 yards and was alone sprinting to his landmark, the left edge of the numbers, as Brady watched him all the way. Webster, the cornerback to that side, was busy with Branch near the sideline. Phillips, the single safety, had no chance to break up the pass even if it had been thrown inside, according to Fewell.

"Tom Brady gave New England a chance to win both Super Bowls. Kenny Phillips knocked the ball down in the end zone, and Corey Webster knocked the ball away from Randy Moss in Arizona [in Super Bowl XLII]."

Peter Giunta, Giants secondary coach

"He's trying to paint Wes' outside shoulder with the ball to keep it away from Phillips," O'Brien said. "I would never doubt Tom and his judgment on where to throw the ball. It's been proven over time that he knows what he's doing. That's a very, very difficult throw and a very, very difficult catch."

Perhaps because Welker was so wide open, Brady put considerable air under the ball. Looking over his inside shoulder, Welker had to twist his body back to the inside as he faded away. He had both hands on the ball. Afterward, Welker took full responsibility for the misconnection.

"I'd say 99 out of 100 times we complete that ball, and I might be understating it," Ferentz said. "Then we would be in a mode to grind the clock a little bit. We would have felt like we were in pretty good position to win the game."

Fewell didn't disagree, even suggesting it might have been a 44-yard touchdown for Welker because Phillips' angle wasn't ideal. "I think that was the ball game right there," said Ross. "We still could have held them to a field goal and then go win it, but that was gigantic."

On third down, Brady faked to Woodhead, took a seven-step drop against three-deep coverage, and 5.1 seconds after the snap, gunned another dig route to Branch at 18-yard depth. "There was a defender [Boley] in front of Branch, or a defender that he thought was going to be able to break it up," said O'Brien. "So he's trying to slow Branch down with the ball, basically."

Branch, whose feet were just outside the hash mark, had to stop and come back for the ball. Moving with Branch, Webster then had time to break it up. Fewell said it's 20-20 hindsight to say Brady should have tried to lead Branch on the throw. "Call it a critical mistake or call it just not connecting," said Ferentz. "We didn't make the plays when we had to make plays. That's how you lose close games."

Brady's day began with a safety when back judge Tony Steratore whistled him in the end zone for heaving the ball away in the middle of the field 20 yards away from the nearest receiver. Tuck pressured Brady, but Fewell credited Boley and Blackburn most for scrambling back and choking off the Patriots' passing lanes. Blackburn made the same type of instinctual drop to force a second-and-8 incompletion in the third quarter, a play that led to a three-and-out and was characterized by Bill O'Brien as the beginning of the end for New England.

Before the misfire, Brady had completed a Super Bowl–record 16 passes in a row. Of his 3 misfires in 23 attempts, one was the safety and two others were swatted away by Pierre-Paul. Brady's passer rating through two and a half quarters was 132.1. From that point on, he completed just 7 of 18 for 75 yards and a rating of 28.7.

It didn't help Brady that none of his receivers other than Woodhead did much after the catch. Welker averaged 3.9 YAC on his seven receptions, and Hernandez was even lower, at 2.6 on his eight. The Giants missed just five tackles all day.

"We played well all year offensively," said Gilbride. "Defensively, from the Jet game [December 24] on, we played really good football. Those guys came on like gangbusters. That really, really made a big difference."

Wilfork had been dominating in the AFC title game, but in the Super Bowl, he failed to generate a pressure and had only three tackles. In 68 snaps, Wilfork lined up 47 times on the Giants' left side over or near Boothe. "Kevin Boothe played great," Gilbride said. "He actually may have been our MVP all year."

Forgive Gilbride for his unintentional omission of Manning, who outplayed the great Brady and found ways to defeat Belichick in a second Super Bowl. No matter that the Giants were the first team in history to reach the Super Bowl despite having been outscored by their opponents (400–394) in the regular season.

When you break the game down, said Marc Ross, the outcome was due mostly to Manning.

"It's close, but I think we're better now than in '07 just because the quarterback is so much better," Ross said. "I don't know how you can say it any other way. The guy is great. Two fourth-quarter drives to win Super Bowls. There's not anybody else that you'd rather have than him."

THE HALL OF SHAME

Ten Costliest Fumbles from Scrimmage

1. **Duane Thomas, RB, Cowboys, V:** Thomas' third-quarter fumble at the goal line, and the disputed recovery by Colts DT Billy Ray Smith, killed Dallas.
2. **Oscar Reed, RB, Vikings, VIII:** Down by 17 at the end of the first half, Reed got the call on fourth and 1. LB Nick Buoniconti drilled him, FS Jake Scott recovered, and Minnesota was finished.
3. **Brent McClanahan, RB, Vikings, XI:** Once again, the Vikings were denied at goal line. This time, from the 2, LB Phil Villapiano put his helmet on the ball, and LB Willie Hall recovered.
4. **Chuck Foreman, RB, Vikings, IX:** From the Steelers' 5, Fran Tarkenton's reverse-pivot handoff was placed too high for Foreman to handle cleanly, and DT Joe Greene recovered.
5. **Rashard Mendenhall, RB, Steelers, XLV:** TE David Johnson missed the block, LB Clay Matthews and DE Ryan Pickett made the play, and Mendenhall made his turning-point fumble.
6. **Thurman Thomas, RB, Bills, XXVII:** On a swing pass, DT Leon Lett swooped in to force the fumble, and DT Jimmie Jones recovered. Then the rout was really on.
7. **Craig James, RB, Patriots, XX:** On a pitchout, James was stripped deep in the backfield by DE Richard Dent, and LB Mike Singletary recovered. It got real ugly after that.
8. **Tom Matte, RB, Colts, III:** Matte gave it up on the opening play of the second half when DE Verlon Biggs jumped him from behind and LB Ralph Baker jumped on the ball.
9. **Cris Collinsworth, WR, Bengals, XVI:** Collinsworth had advanced on a 19-yard reception to the 49ers' 8 when CB Eric Wright made the strip and CB Lynn Thomas made the recovery.
10. **Ricky Proehl, WR, Rams, XXXVI:** Trying to get down, Proehl didn't get quite low enough to prevent S Antwan Harris from jarring the ball loose. CB Terrell Buckley recovered the ball.

Ten Costliest Dropped Passes

1. **Jackie Smith, TE, Cowboys, XIII:** Smith slipped on wet turf in the end zone. Roger Staubach threw a bit too early. The veteran TE tried to body-catch it but couldn't make the play.
2. **Antonio Freeman, WR, Packers, XXXII:** Green Bay was driving for the tying TD in the final minute when Freeman dropped Brett Favre's sizzling throw at the Denver 15. The costliest drop of Freeman's eight seasons as a Packer.
3. **Preston Dennard, WR, Rams, XIV:** The underdog Rams had a chance for a 17–17 tie at halftime when Dennard couldn't make what would have been a tough catch in the back of the end zone.
4. **John Mackey, TE, Colts, III:** What looked like a 58-yard TD pass from Earl Morrall went for naught when the great TE Mackey dropped it in the clear.
5. **Wes Welker, Patriots, XLVI:** No, it wasn't easy trying to torque his body to adjust to Tom Brady's mediocre throw. But this late chance for Welker is a play he would almost always make.
6. **Don Beebe, WR, Bills, XXVI:** Buffalo closed the first half scoreless when Beebe failed to catch what should have been a 20-yard TD pass from Jim Kelly.
7. **Charlie Garner, RB, Raiders, XXXVII:** The speedy Garner had 50 yards of wide-open green grass ahead

of him in the second quarter against a blown coverage but dropped this routine check-down.

8. **Patrick Johnson, WR, Ravens, XXXV:** Early on, Johnson ran a take-off route past CB Jason Sehorn but couldn't haul in Trent Dilfer's beautiful long pass.

9. **Mark Seay, WR, Chargers, XXIX:** San Diego's last chance to make it a game went awry late in the first half. That's when Seay couldn't make a tough catch in the corner of the end zone.

10. **Charley Taylor, WR, Redskins, VII:** In a game of precious few big plays, Taylor had a chance to make one at the Miami 3 in the second quarter but dropped the ball.

Ten Worst Blown Coverages

1. **Eddie Brown, S, Rams, XIV:** The Rams were leading the favored Steelers, 19–17, early in the fourth quarter and had them in a third-and-8 hole at their 27. Brown took the blame for leaving the middle of the field and giving WR John Stallworth room to haul in a 73-yard touchdown pass from Terry Bradshaw.

2. **Dominique Rodgers-Cromartie, CB, Cardinals, XLIII:** In the final minute, Rodgers-Cromartie short-circuited and vacated the left corner of the end zone, but Steelers WR Santonio Holmes dropped the ball. On the very next play, the rookie made an even more egregious error and left Holmes open again. This time, Holmes made the game-winning catch.

3. **Danieal Manning, FS, Bears, XLI:** On third and 10 with the Bears up, 6–0, Manning surged forward in man coverage on TE Ben Utecht when everyone else was correctly playing zone. That enabled WR Reggie Wayne to be wide open deep for a 53-yard touch-down pass from Peyton Manning.

4. **Aaron Kyle, CB, Cowboys, XIII:** Kyle lined up across from John Stallworth on the Steelers' first possession, but permitted Stallworth to take an outside release when his help from FS Cliff Harris was sitting inside. Harris had no chance to get over, and the result was a 28-yard touchdown.

5. **Shaun Williams, FS, Giants, XXXV:** On second and 7 in a scoreless first quarter, Williams was supposed to help CB Jason Sehorn double-cover WR Brandon Stokley in the slot. When Williams jumped TE Shannon Sharpe, Stokley was wide open for a 38-yard touchdown pass from Trent Dilfer.

6. **Etric Pruitt, FS, Seahawks, XL:** Early in the fourth quarter and Pittsburgh leading 14–10, WR Antwaan Randle El moved from left to right and then threw deep to Hines Ward. Pruitt, an injury fill-in, had no clue and let Ward cross his face flying in the other direction. Ward's 43-yard touchdown catch completed the scoring.

7. **Kent McCloughan, CB, and Rodger Bird, S, Raiders, II:** Early in the second quarter, Boyd Dowler ran a quick post, caught Bart Starr's pass 20 yards downfield, and strode in for a 62-yard touchdown. The plan was to switch off the coverage, but neither McCloughan nor Bird played it properly.

8. **Ricky Manning Jr., CB, Panthers, XXXVIII:** With the score tied at 29, the Patriots had the ball at the Carolina 40 with 14 seconds left. On the right side, Manning was playing Cover 2 with a receiver in front of him and another receiver, Deion Branch, behind him. Manning moved up, giving the more dangerous receiver, Branch, ample room to catch Tom Brady's pass for 17 yards. As a result, Adam Vinatieri's game-winning kick was from 41 and not 51 yards.

9. **Eugene Robinson, FS, Falcons, XXXIII:** Leading 10–3 with 5:07 left before halftime, the Broncos ran a deep bootleg pass off a play-action fake by John Elway. When Elway pump-faked, Robinson got turned around and was burned deep by Rod Smith for an 80-yard touchdown.

10. **Bernard Jackson, FS, Broncos, XII:** On third and 10 in the third quarter, the Cowboys were leading, 13–3. Roger Staubach had seen Jackson take chances and leave the middle of the field. When Jackson crept in too shallow, Butch Johnson ran by him for a 45-yard touchdown pass.

Top Ten Special Teams Blunders

1. **Garo Yepremian, K, Dolphins, VII:** The Dolphins were dreaming about their ring sizes when Howard Kindig's snap was low, as was Yepremian's 49-yard field goal attempt, which was blocked by Washington's Bill Brundige. The ball bounced back to Yepremian, who attempted to pass it. Mike Bass leapt to make the interception and returned it 49 yards for a touchdown.

2. **John Kasay, K, Panthers, XXXVIII:** The Panthers were coming off a tying touchdown with 1:08 left when Kasay, one of the NFL's most reliable kickers, hooked the kickoff, and it went out of bounds on the fly at the 15. By rule, the Patriots were allowed to start from the 40. Six plays later, Adam Vinatieri's 41-yard field goal won the game.

3. **Bill Brown, FB, Vikings, IX:** On the second-half kickoff, Roy Gerela slipped and sent a skidder to the 28. Brown, playing in his final game, picked it up but fumbled, and Pittsburgh's Marv Kellum recovered at the Minnesota 30. Four plays later, the Steelers extended their lead from 2–0 to 9–0. Steelers defensive coordinator Bud Carson said it was the turning point of the game.

4. **Randy White, DT, Cowboys, XIII:** Roy Gerela slipped on another kickoff, this time with seven minutes left in the game. The ball bounced to the wedge and was fielded by White, who was playing with a cast on his broken left thumb. Just as White was switching the ball from one hand to the other, Tony Dungy hit him. The ball came free and Pittsburgh's Dennis Winston recovered. Lynn Swann caught the winning touchdown pass on the next play.

5. **Charlie West, S, Vikings, IV:** Midway in the second quarter, the Vikings were trailing, 9–0. West ran up to field Jan Stenerud's kickoff at the 11. The ball bounced off West's left thigh and was recovered by Kansas City's Remi Prudhomme at the 19. The Chiefs scored their first touchdown six plays later.

6. **Hank Baskett, WR, Colts, XLIV:** The entire game turned when S Chris Reis recovered the Saints' shocking onside kick to open the second half. It was Baskett's play to make. The former Eagle failed.

7. **Rodger Bird, S, Raiders, II:** With 23 seconds left in the first half, Bird fumbled Donny Anderson's high left-footed punt, and Dick Capp recovered for Green Bay at the Oakland 45. The Packers added a field goal in the closing seconds for a 16–7 lead.

8. **Robert Jones, LB, Cowboys, XXVII:** The game was just three minutes old when Steve Tasker beat Jones inside and blocked Mike Saxon's punt out of bounds at the Dallas 16. The Bills scored a touchdown four plays later. Jones had replaced an injured Dixon Edwards.

9. **Archie Griffin, RB, Bengals, XVI:** Just 15 seconds remained in the Bengals' horrible first half against the 49ers. Griffin fielded Ray Wersching's squib kick on the third bounce, was hit by Rick Gervais, and fumbled. Milt McColl recovered at the Cincinnati 4, and Wersching's ensuing 26-yard field goal made it 20–0.

10. **Bobby Walden, P, Steelers, X:** Walden fumbled the snap on a punt, and the Cowboys took over 11 yards behind the line at the Dallas 29. Roger Staubach passed to Drew Pearson for a touchdown on the next play to secure a 7–0 lead. As the holder in Super Bowl IX, Walden had botched a snap on an aborted field goal.

APPENDIX
SUPER BOWL RECORD BOOK

PLAYER RECORDS

SERVICE

Most Games, Player	6 - Mike Lodish, Bills (XXV–XXVIII)/Broncos (XXXII, XXXIII)
Most Games, Winning Team	5 - Charles Haley, 49ers (XXIII, XXIV)/Cowboys (XXVII, XXVIII, XXX)
Most Games, Winning Team, Quarterback	4 - Terry Bradshaw, Steelers (IX, X, XIII, XIV); Joe Montana, 49ers (XVI, XIX, XXIII, XXIV)
Most Games, Coach	6 - Don Shula, Colts (III)/Dolphins (VI–VIII, XVII, XIX)
Most Games, Winning Team, Coach	4 - Chuck Noll, Steelers (IX, X, XIII, XIV)
Most Games, Losing Team, Coach	4 - Bud Grant, Vikings (IV, VIII, IX, XI); Don Shula, Colts (III)/Dolphins (VI, XVII, XIX); Marv Levy, Bills (XXV–XXVIII); Dan Reeves, Broncos (XXI, XXII, XXIV)/Falcons (XXXIII)

SCORING

Most Points, Career	48 - Jerry Rice, 49ers, Raiders, 4 games (8 TD)
Most Points, Game	18 - Roger Craig, 49ers, XIX (3 TD); Jerry Rice, 49ers, XXIV (3 TD), XXIX (3 TD); Ricky Watters, 49ers, XXIX (3 TD); Terrell Davis, Broncos, XXXII (3 TD)

TOUCHDOWNS

Most Touchdowns, Career	8 - Jerry Rice, 49ers/Raiders, 4 games (8 rec.)
Most Touchdowns, Game	3 - Roger Craig, 49ers, XIX (1 rush, 2 rec.); Jerry Rice, 49ers, XXIV (3 rec.), XXIX (3 rec.); Ricky Watters, 49ers, XXIX (1 rush, 2 rec.); Terrell Davis, Broncos, XXXII (3 rush)

POINTS AFTER TOUCHDOWN

Most (One-Point) PATs, Career	13 - Adam Vinatieri, Patriots/Colts, 5 games (13 att.)
Most (One-Point) PATs, Game	7 - Mike Cofer, 49ers, XXIV (8 att.); Lin Elliott, Cowboys, XXVII (7 att.); Doug Brien, 49ers, XXIX (7 att.)
Most Two-Point Conversions, Game	1 - Mark Seay, Chargers, XXIX; Alfred Pupunu, Chargers, XXIX; Mark Chmura, Packers, XXXI; Kevin Faulk, Patriots, XXXVIII; Moore, Saints, XLIV; Randle El, Steelers, XLV

FIELD GOALS

Most Field Goals Attempted, Career	10 - Adam Vinatieri, Patriots/Colts, 5 games
Most Field Goals Attempted, Game	5 - Jim Turner, Jets, III; Efren Herrera, Cowboys, XII
Most Field Goals, Career	7 - Adam Vinatieri, Patriots/Colts, 5 games (10 att.)
Most Field Goals, Game	4 - Don Chandler, Packers, II; Ray Wersching, 49ers, XVI
Longest Field Goal	54 yds. - Steve Christie, Bills, XXVIII

SAFETIES

Most Safeties, Game	1 - Dwight White, Steelers, IX; Reggie Harrison, Steelers, X; Henry Waechter, Bears, XX; George Martin, Giants, XXI; Bruce Smith, Bills, XXV

RUSHING

Most Attempts, Career	101 - Franco Harris, Steelers, 4 games
Most Attempts, Game	38 - John Riggins, Redskins, XVII
Most Yards Gained, Career	354 - Franco Harris, Steelers, 4 games
Most Yards Gained, Game	204 - Timmy Smith, Redskins, XXII
Longest Run From Scrimmage	75 - Willie Parker, Steelers, XL (TD)
Highest Average Gain, Career (20 att.)	9.6 - Marcus Allen, Raiders, 1 game (20–191)
Highest Average Gain, Game (10 att.)	10.5 - Tom Matte, Colts, III (11–116)
Most Touchdowns, Career	5 - Emmitt Smith, Cowboys, 3 games
Most Touchdowns, Game	3 - Terrell Davis, Broncos, XXXII

PASSING

Highest Passer Rating, Career (40 att.)	127.8 - Joe Montana, 49ers, 4 games
Most Passes Attempted, Career	197 - Tom Brady, Patriots, 5 games
Most Passes Attempted, Game	58 - Jim Kelly, Bills, XXVI
Most Passes Completed, Career	127 - Tom Brady, Patriots, 5 games
Most Passes Completed, Game	32 - Tom Brady, Patriots, XXXVIII; Drew Brees, Saints, XLIV
Most Consecutive Completions, Game	16 - Tom Brady, Patriots, XLVI
Highest Completion Pct, Career (40 att.)	70.0 - Troy Aikman, Cowboys, 3 games, (80–56)
Highest Completion Pct, Game (20 att.)	88.0 - Phil Simms, Giants, XXI (25–22)
Most Yards Gained, Career	1,277 - Tom Brady, Patriots, 5 games
Most Yards Gained, Game	414 - Kurt Warner, Rams, XXXIV
Longest Pass Completion	85 - Jake Delhomme (to Muhammad), Panthers, XXXVIII (TD)
Most 300-Yard Passing Games, Career	3 - Kurt Warner, Rams (XXXIV, XXXVI), Cardinals (XLIII)
Highest Average Gain, Career (40 att.)	11.10 - Terry Bradshaw, Steelers, 4 games (84–932)
Highest Average Gain, Game (20 att.)	14.71 - Terry Bradshaw, Steelers, XIV (21–309)
Most Touchdown Passes, Career	11 - Joe Montana, 49ers, 4 games
Most Touchdown Passes, Game	6 - Steve Young, 49ers, XXIX
Lowest Interception Pct., Career (40 att.)	0.00 - Jim Plunkett, Raiders, 2 games (46 att.)
Most Attempts, Without Interception, Game	48 - Tom Brady, Patriots, XLII
Most Passes Had Intercepted, Career	8 - John Elway, Broncos, 5 games
Most Passes Had Intercepted, Game	5 - Rich Gannon, Raiders, XXXVII

PASS RECEIVING

Most Receptions, Career	33 - Jerry Rice, 49ers/Raiders, 4 games
Most Receptions, Game	11 - Dan Ross, Bengals, XVI; Jerry Rice, 49ers, XXIII; Deion Branch, Patriots, XXXIX; Wes Welker, Patriots, XLII

Most Yards Gained, Career	589 - Jerry Rice, 49ers/Raiders, 4 games
Most Yards Gained, Game	215 - Jerry Rice, 49ers, XXIII
Longest Reception	85 - Muhsin Muhammad (from Delhomme), Panthers, XXXVIII
Highest Average Gain, Career (8 rec.)	24.4 - John Stallworth, Steelers, 4 games (11–268)
Highest Average Gain, Game (3 rec.)	40.33 - John Stallworth, Steelers, XIV (3–121)
Most Touchdowns, Career	8 - Jerry Rice, 49ers/Raiders, 4 games
Most Touchdowns, Game	3 - Jerry Rice, 49ers, XXIV, XXIX

INTERCEPTIONS BY

Most Interceptions By, Career	3 - Chuck Howley, Cowboys, 2 games; Rod Martin, Raiders, 2 games; Larry Brown, Cowboys, 3 games
Most Interceptions By, Game	3 - Rod Martin, Raiders, XV
Most Yards Gained, Career	108 - Darrien Gordon, Chargers/Broncos/Raiders, 4 games
Most Yards Gained, Game	108 - Darrien Gordon, Broncos, XXXIII
Longest Return	100 - James Harrison, Steelers, XLIII
Most Touchdowns, Game	2 - Dwight Smith, Buccaneers, XXXVII

PUNTING

Most Punts, Career	17 - Mike Eischeid, Raiders/Vikings, 3 games; Mike Horan, Broncos/Rams, 4 games
Most Punts, Game	11 - Brad Maynard, Giants, XXXV
Longest Punt	63 - Lee Johnson, Bengals, XXIII
Highest Average, Career (10 punts)	46.5 - Jerrel Wilson, Chiefs, 2 games (11–511)
Highest Average, Game (4 punts)	50.2 - Tom Rouen, Seahawks, XL (6–301)

PUNT RETURNS

Most Punt Returns, Career	8 - Troy Brown, Patriots, 3 games
Most Punt Returns, Game	6 - Mike Nelms, Redskins, XVII; Desmond Howard, Packers, XXXI
Most Fair Catches, Game	4 - Jermaine Lewis, Ravens, XXXV; Karl Williams, Buccaneers, XXXVII
Most Yards Gained, Career	94 - John Taylor, 49ers, 3 games
Most Yards Gained, Game	90 - Desmond Howard, Packers, XXXI
Longest Return	45 - John Taylor, 49ers, XXIII
Highest Average, Career (4 ret.)	15.7 - John Taylor, 49ers, 3 games (6–94)
Highest Average, Game (3 ret.)	18.7 - John Taylor, 49ers, XXIII (3–56)
Most Touchdowns, Game	None

KICKOFF RETURNS

Most Kickoff Returns, Career	10 - Ken Bell, Broncos, 3 games
Most Kickoff Returns, Game	8 - Andre Coleman, Chargers, XXIX; Marcus Knight, Raiders, XXXVII
Most Yards Gained, Career	283 - Fulton Walker, Dolphins, 2 games

Most Yards Gained, Game	244 - Andre Coleman, Chargers, XXIX
Longest Return	99 - Desmond Howard, Packers, XXXI (TD)
Highest Average, Career (4 ret.)	47.5 - Fulton Walker, Dolphins, 1 game (4–190)
Highest Average, Game (3 ret.)	47.5 - Fulton Walker, Dolphins, XVII (4–190)
Most Touchdowns, Game	1 - Accomplished 8 times

FUMBLES

Most Fumbles, Career	5 - Roger Staubach, Cowboys, 4 games
Most Fumbles, Game	3 - Roger Staubach, Cowboys, X; Jim Kelly, Bills, XXVI; Frank Reich, Bills, XXVII
Most Fumbles Recovered, Career	2 - Shared by 13 players
Most Fumbles Recovered, Game	2 - Jake Scott, Dolphins, VIII (1 own, 1 opp.); Roger Staubach, Cowboys, X (2 own); Randy Hughes, Cowboys, XII (2 opp); Butch Johnson, Cowboys, XII (2 own); Mike Singletary, Bears, XX (2 opp.); Jimmie Jones, Cowboys, XXVII (2 opp.)
Most Yards Gained, Game	64 - Leon Lett, Cowboys, XXVII (opp.)
Longest Return	64 - Leon Lett, Cowboys, XXVII
Most Touchdowns, Game	1 - Mike Bass, Redskins, VII (opp., 49 yds.); Mike Hegman, Cowboys, XIII (opp., 37 yds.); Jimmie Jones, Cowboys, XXVII (opp., 2 yds.); Ken Norton, Cowboys, XXVII (opp., 9 yds.); James Washington, Cowboys, XXVIII (opp., 46 yds.)

COMBINED NET YARDS GAINED

(Rushing, receiving, interception returns, punt returns, kickoff returns, and fumble returns)

Most Attempts, Career	108 - Franco Harris, Steelers, 4 games
Most Attempts, Game	39 - John Riggins, Redskins, XVII
Most Yards Gained, Career	604 - Jerry Rice, 49ers/Raiders, 4 games
Most Yards Gained, Game	244 - Andre Coleman, Chargers, XXIX; Desmond Howard, Packers, XXXI

SACKS

| Most Sacks, Career | 5.0 - Willie Davis, Packers, 2 games |
| Most Sacks, Game | 3.0 - Willie Davis, Packers, II; L. C. Greenwood, Steelers, X; Dwight White, Steelers, X; Reggie White, Packers, XXXI; Darnell Dockett, Steelers, XLIII |

TEAM RECORDS

GAMES, VICTORIES, DEFEATS

Most Games	8 - Cowboys (V, VI, X, XII, XIII, XXVII, XXVIII, XXX)
Most Consecutive Games	4 - Bills (XXV–XXVIII)
Most Games Won	6 - Steelers (IX, X, XIII, XIV, XL, XLIII)
Most Consecutive Games Won	2 - Packers (I–II); Dolphins (VII–VIII); Steelers (IX–X, XIII–XIV); 49ers (XXIII–XXIV); Cowboys (XXVII–XXVIII); Broncos (XXXII–XXXIII); Patriots (XXXVIII–XXXIX)
Most Games Lost	4 - Vikings (IV, VIII, IX, XI); Broncos (XII, XXI, XXII, XXIV); Bills (XXV–XXVIII); Patriots (XX, XXXI, XLII, XLVI)
Most Consecutive Games Lost	4 - Bills (XXV–XXVIII)

SCORING

Most Points	55 - 49ers, XXIV
Fewest Points	3 - Dolphins, VI
Most Points, Both Teams	75 - 49ers (49) vs. Chargers (26), XXIX
Fewest Points, Both Teams	21 - Redskins (7) vs. Dolphins (14), VII
Largest Margin of Victory	45 - 49ers (55) vs. Broncos (10), XXIV
Most Points, 1st Half	35 - Redskins, XXII
Most Points, 2nd Half	30 - Giants, XXI
Most Points, 1st Quarter	14 - Dolphins, VIII; Raiders, XV; Cowboys, XXVII; 49ers, XXIX; Patriots, XXXI; Bears, XLI; Packers, XLV
Most Points, 2nd Quarter	35 - Redskins, XXII
Most Points, 3rd Quarter	21 - Bears, XX
Most Points, 4th Quarter	21 - Cowboys, XXVII
Most Points, Both Teams, 1st Half	45 - Redskins (35) vs. Broncos (10), XXII
Most Points, Both Teams, 2nd Half	46 - Buccaneers (28) vs. Raiders (18), XXXVII
Fewest Points, Both Teams, 1st Half	2 - Vikings (0) vs. Steelers (2), IX
Fewest Points, Both Teams, 2nd Half	7 - Dolphins (0) vs. Redskins (7), VII; Broncos (0) vs. Redskins (7), XXII
Most Points, Both Teams, 1st Quarter	24 - Patriots (14) vs. Packers (10), XXXI
Most Points, Both Teams, 2nd Quarter	35 - Redskins (35) vs. Broncos (0), XXII
Most Points, Both Teams, 3rd Quarter	24 - Redskins (14) vs. Bills (10), XXVI
Most Points, Both Teams, 4th Quarter	37 - Panthers (19) vs. Patriots (18), XXXVIII

TOUCHDOWNS

Most Touchdowns	8 - 49ers, XXIV
Fewest Touchdowns	0 - Dolphins, VI
Most Touchdowns, Both Teams	10 - 49ers (7) vs. Chargers (3), XXIX
Fewest Touchdowns, Both Teams	2 - Colts (1) vs. Jets (1), III

POINTS AFTER TOUCHDOWN

Most (One-Point) PATs	7 - 49ers, XXIV; Cowboys, XXVII; 49ers, XXIX
Most (One-Point) PATs, Both Teams	9 - Steelers (5) vs. Cowboys (4), XIII; Cowboys (7) vs. Bills (2), XXVII
Fewest (One-Point) PATs, Both Teams	2 - Colts (1) vs. Jets (1), III; Colts (1) vs. Cowboys (1), V; Vikings (0) vs. Steelers (2), IX
Most Two-Point Conversions	2 - Chargers, XXIX
Most Two-Point Conversions, Both Teams	2 - Chargers (2) vs. 49ers (0), XXIX

FIELD GOALS

Most Field Goals Attempted	5 - Jets, III; Cowboys, XII

Most Field Goals Attempted, Both Teams	7 - Jets (5) vs. Colts (2), III; 49ers (4) vs. Bengals (3), XXIII; Rams (4) vs. Titans (3), XXXIV; Broncos (4) vs. Falcons (3), XXXIII
Fewest Field Goals Attempted, Both Teams	1 - Vikings (0) vs. Dolphins (1), VIII; 49ers (0) vs. Broncos (1), XXIV; Eagles (0) vs. Patriots (1), XXXIX; Patriots (0) vs. Giants (1), XLII
Most Field Goals	4 - Packers, II; 49ers, XVI
Most Field Goals, Both Teams	5 - Bengals (3) vs. 49ers (2), XXIII; Cowboys (3) vs. Bills (2), XXVIII
Fewest Field Goals, Both Teams	0 - Dolphins vs. Redskins, VII; Steelers vs. Vikings, IX

SAFETIES

Most Safeties	1 - Steelers, IX; Steelers, X; Bears, XX; Giants, XXI; Bills, XXV; Cardinals, XLIII; Giants, XLVI.

FIRST DOWNS

Most First Downs	31 - 49ers, XIX
Fewest First Downs	9 - Vikings, IX; Dolphins, XVII
Most First Downs, Both Teams	50 - 49ers (31) vs. Dolphins (19), XIX; Titans (27) vs. Rams (23), XXXIV
Fewest First Downs, Both Teams	24 - Cowboys (10) vs. Colts (14), V; Giants (11) vs. Ravens (13), XXXV
Most First Downs, Rushing	16 - 49ers, XIX
Fewest First Downs, Rushing	1 - Patriots, XX; Rams, XXXIV; Raiders, XXXVII
Most First Downs, Rushing, Both Teams	21 - Redskins (14) vs. Dolphins (7), XVII
Fewest First Downs, Rushing, Both Teams	6 - Cardinals (2) vs. Steelers (4), XLIII
Most First Downs, Passing	20 - Cardinals, XLIII
Fewest First Downs, Passing	1 - Broncos, XII
Most First Downs, Passing, Both Teams	33 - Giants (18) vs. Patriots (15), XLVI
Fewest First Downs, Passing, Both Teams	9 - Broncos (1) vs. Cowboys (8), XII
Most First Downs, Penalty	4 - Colts, V; Dolphins, VIII; Bengals, XVI; Bills, XXVII; Rams, XXXIV; Steelers, XLIII
Most First Downs, Penalty, Both Teams	6 - Bengals (4) vs. 49ers (2), XVI; Rams (4) vs. Titans (2), XXXIV
Fewest First Downs, Penalty, Both Teams	0 - Cowboys vs. Dolphins, VI; Dolphins vs. Redskins, VII; Cowboys vs. Steelers, X; Dolphins vs. 49ers, XIX; Steelers vs. Seahawks, XL; Packers vs. Steelers, XLV

NET YARDS GAINED RUSHING AND PASSING

Most Yards Gained	602 - Redskins, XXII
Fewest Yards Gained	119 - Vikings, IX
Most Yards Gained, Both Teams	929 - Redskins (602) vs. Broncos (327), XXII
Fewest Yards Gained, Both Teams	396 - Giants (152) vs. Ravens (244), XXXV

RUSHING

Most Attempts	57 - Steelers, IX
Fewest Attempts	9 - Dolphins, XIX
Most Attempts, Both Teams	81 - Redskins (52) vs. Dolphins (29), XVII
Fewest Attempts, Both Teams	38 - Cardinals (12) vs. Steelers (26), XLIII

Most Yards Gained	280 - Redskins, XXII
Fewest Yards Gained	7 - Patriots, XX
Most Yards Gained, Both Teams	377 - Redskins (280) vs. Broncos (97), XXII
Fewest Yards Gained, Both Teams	91 - Cardinals (33) vs. Steelers (58), XLIII
Highest Average Gain	7.00 - Raiders, XVIII (33–231); Redskins, XXII (40–280)
Lowest Average Gain	0.64 - Patriots, XX (11–7)
Most Touchdowns	4 - Bears, XX; Broncos, XXXII
Fewest Touchdowns	0 - Accomplished 29 times
Most Touchdowns, Both Teams	4 - Dolphins (3) vs. Vikings (1), VIII; Bears (4) vs. Patriots (0), XX; 49ers (3) vs. Broncos (1), XXIV; Broncos (4) vs. Packers (0), XXXII
Fewest Touchdowns, Both Teams	0 - Steelers vs. Cowboys, X; Raiders vs. Eagles, XV; Bengals vs. 49ers, XXIII

PASSING

Most Passes Attempted	59 - Bills, XXVI
Fewest Passes Attempted	7 - Dolphins, VIII
Most Passes Attempted, Both Teams	93 - Chargers (55) vs. 49ers (38), XXIX
Fewest Passes Attempted, Both Teams	35 - Dolphins (7) vs. Vikings (28), VIII
Most Passes Completed	32 - Patriots, XXXVIII; Saints, XLIV
Fewest Passes Completed	4 - Dolphins, XVII
Most Passes Completed, Both Teams	63 - Saints (32) vs. Colts (31), XLIV
Fewest Passes Completed, Both Teams	19 - Dolphins (4) vs. Redskins (15), XVII
Highest Completion Percentage (20 att.)	88.0 - Giants, XXI (25–22)
Lowest Completion Percentage (20 att.)	32.0 - Broncos, XII (25–8)
Most Yards Gained	407 - Rams, XXXIV
Fewest Yards Gained	35 - Broncos, XII
Most Yards Gained, Both Teams	649 - Patriots (354) vs. Panthers (295), XXXVIII
Fewest Yards Gained, Both Teams	156 - Dolphins (69) vs. Redskins (87), VII
Most Touchdowns	6 - 49ers, XXIX
Fewest Touchdowns	0 - Accomplished 19 times
Most Touchdowns, Both Teams	7 - Steelers (4) vs. Cowboys (3), XIII; 49ers (6) vs. Chargers (1), XXIX
Fewest Touchdowns, Both Teams	0 - Jets vs. Colts, III; Dolphins vs. Vikings, VIII; Bills vs. Cowboys, XXVIII
Most Times Sacked	7 - Cowboys, X; Patriots, XX
Fewest Times Sacked	0 - Accomplished 10 times
Most Times Sacked, Both Teams	10 - Patriots (7) vs. Bears (3), XX; Packers (5) vs. Patriots (5), XXXI
Fewest Times Sacked, Both Teams	1 - Eagles (0) vs. Raiders (1), XV; Broncos (0) vs. Packers (1), XXXII

INTERCEPTIONS BY

Most Interceptions By	5 - Buccaneers, XXXVII
Most Interceptions By, Both Teams	6 - Colts (3) vs. Cowboys (3), V; Buccaneers (5) vs. Raiders (1), XXXVII
Fewest Interceptions By, Both Teams	0 - Bills vs. Giants, XXV; Rams vs. Titans, XXXIV
Most Yards Gained	172 - Buccaneers, XXXVII
Most Yards Gained, Both Teams	184 - Buccaneers (172) vs. Raiders (12), XXXVII
Most Touchdowns	3 - Buccaneers, XXXVII

PUNTING

Most Punts	11 - Giants, XXXV
Fewest Punts	1 - Falcons, XXXIII
Most Punts, Both Teams	21 - Giants (11) vs. Ravens (10), XXXV
Fewest Punts, Both Teams	2 - Falcons (1) vs. Broncos (1), XXXIII
Highest Average (4 punts)	50.17 - Seahawks, XL (6–301)
Lowest Average (4 punts)	31.00 - Buccaneers, XXXVII (5–155)

PUNT RETURNS

Most Punt Returns	6 - Redskins, XVII; Packers, XXXI
Fewest Punt Returns	0 - Vikings, VIII; Bills, XXV; Redskins, XXVI; Broncos, XXXII; Packers, XXXII; Falcons, XXXIII; Broncos, XXXIII; Patriots, XLVI
Most Punt Returns, Both Teams	10 - Packers (6) vs. Patriots (4), XXXI
Fewest Punt Returns, Both Teams	0 - Broncos vs. Packers, XXXII; Falcons vs. Broncos, XXXIII
Most Yards Gained	90 - Packers, XXXI
Fewest Yards Gained	−1 - Cowboys, VI; Titans, XXXIV
Most Yards Gained, Both Teams	120 - Packers (90) vs. Patriots (30), XXXI
Fewest Yards Gained, Both Teams	0 - Broncos vs. Packers, XXXII; Falcons vs. Broncos, XXXIII
Highest Average Gain (3 ret.)	18.7 - 49ers, XXIII (3–56)
Most Touchdowns	None

KICKOFF RETURNS

Most Kickoff Returns	9 - Broncos, XXIV; Raiders, XXXVII
Fewest Kickoff Returns	1 - Jets, III; Raiders, XVIII; Redskins, XXVI
Most Kickoff Returns, Both Teams	13 - Raiders (9) vs. Buccaneers (4), XXXVII
Fewest Kickoff Returns, Both Teams	5 - Jets (1) vs. Colts (4), III; Dolphins (2) vs. Redskins (3), VII; Redskins (1) vs. Bills (4), XXVI
Most Yards Gained	244 - Chargers, XXIX
Fewest Yards Gained	16 - Redskins, XXVI
Most Yards Gained, Both Teams	292 - Chargers (244) vs. 49ers (48), XXIX
Fewest Yards Gained, Both Teams	78 - Dolphins (33) vs. Redskins (45), VII

Highest Average Gain (3 ret.)	44.0 - Bengals, XXIII (3–132)
Most Touchdowns	1 - Dolphins, XVII; Bengals, XXIII; Chargers, XXIX; Packers, XXXI; Falcons, XXXIII; Ravens, XXXV; Giants, XXXV; Bears, XLI
Most Touchdowns, Both Teams	2 - Ravens (1) vs. Giants (1), XXXV

PENALTIES

Most Penalties	12 - Cowboys, XII; Panthers, XXXVIII
Fewest Penalties	0 - Dolphins, VI; Steelers, X; Broncos, XXIV; Falcons, XXXIII
Most Penalties, Both Teams	20 - Cowboys (12) vs. Broncos (8), XII; Panthers (12) vs. Patriots (8), XXXVIII
Fewest Penalties, Both Teams	2 - Steelers (0) vs. Cowboys (2), X
Most Yards Penalized	133 - Cowboys, X
Fewest Yards Penalized	0 - Dolphins, VI; Steelers, X; Broncos, XXIV; Falcons, XXXIII
Most Yards Penalized, Both Teams	164 - Cowboys (133) vs. Colts (31), V
Fewest Yards Penalized, Both Teams	15 - Dolphins (0) vs. Cowboys (15), VI

FUMBLES

Most Fumbles	8 - Bills, XXVII
Fewest Fumbles	0 - Accomplished 24 times
Most Fumbles, Both Teams	12 - Bills (8) vs. Cowboys (4), XXVII
Fewest Fumbles, Both Teams	0 - Los Angeles vs. Steelers, XIV; Packers vs. Patriots, XXXI; Steelers vs. Seahawks, XL
Most Fumbles Lost	5 - Bills, XXVII
Most Fumbles Lost, Both Teams	7 - Bills (5) vs. Cowboys (2), XXVII
Fewest Fumbles Lost, Both Teams	0 - Accomplished 13 times
Most Fumbles Recovered	8 - Cowboys, XII (4 own, 4 opp.)

TURNOVERS

(Balls lost on interceptions and fumbles)	
Most Turnovers	9 - Bills, XXVII
Fewest Turnovers	0 - Accomplished 18 times
Most Turnovers, Both Teams	11 - Colts (7) vs. Cowboys (4), V; Bills (9) vs. Cowboys (2), XXVII
Fewest Turnovers, Both Teams	0 - Bills vs. Giants, XXV; Rams vs. Titans, XXXIV

MISCELLANEOUS RECORDS

Most MVP Awards	3 - Joe Montana (XVI, XIX, XXIV)
Oldest Winning Head Coach	Tom Coughlin, Giants, XLVI (65 yrs, 158 days)
Youngest Winning Head Coach	Mike Tomlin, Steelers, XLIII (36 yrs, 323 days)
Oldest Player	Matt Stover, Colts, XLIV (42 yrs, 11 days)
Youngest Player	Jamal Lewis, Ravens, XXXV (21 yrs, 155 days)
Longest Game	4:05 - Patriots vs. Panthers, XXXVIII

Largest Attendance	103,985 - Redskins vs. Dolphins, XVII, Rose Bowl Stadium, Pasadena, California				
Highest Television Rating	49.1 - 49ers vs. Bengals, XVI (73% share)				
Most Times Hosting, City	10 - Miami, Florida				
Most Times Hosting, Venue	6 - Louisiana Superdome, New Orleans, Louisiana				

COMPOSITE STANDINGS

Team	W	L	Pct.	Pts.	OP
San Francisco 49ers	5	0	1.000	188	89
Baltimore Ravens	1	0	1.000	34	7
New Orleans Saints	1	0	1.000	31	17
New York Jets	1	0	1.000	16	7
Tampa Bay Buccaneers	1	0	1.000	48	21
Green Bay Packers	4	1	.800	158	101
New York Giants	4	1	.800	104	104
Pittsburgh Steelers	6	2	.750	193	164
Dallas Cowboys	5	3	.625	221	132
Oakland/L.A. Raiders	3	2	.600	132	114
Washington Redskins	3	2	.600	122	103
Baltimore/Indianapolis Colts	2	2	.500	69	77
Chicago Bears	1	1	.500	63	39
Kansas City Chiefs	1	1	.500	33	42
New England Patriots	3	4	.428	138	186
Miami Dolphins	2	3	.400	74	103
Denver Broncos	2	4	.333	115	206
St. Louis/L.A. Rams	1	2	.333	59	67
Arizona Cardinals	0	1	.000	23	27
Atlanta Falcons	0	1	.000	19	34
Carolina Panthers	0	1	.000	29	32
San Diego Chargers	0	1	.000	26	49
Seattle Seahawks	0	1	.000	10	21
Tennessee Titans	0	1	.000	16	23
Cincinnati Bengals	0	2	.000	37	46
Philadelphia Eagles	0	2	.000	31	51
Buffalo Bills	0	4	.000	73	139
Minnesota Vikings	0	4	.000	34	95
NFC/NFL	25	21	.543	1,147	949
AFC/AFL	21	25	.456	949	1,147

BIBLIOGRAPHY

The following is a list of sources used in the compilation of the stories and quotes for each Super Bowl.

SUPER BOWL I

Author Interviews
Bobby Beathard, Tom Bettis, Jerry Burns, Walt Corey, Forrest Gregg, Dave Hanner, Tom Pratt, Johnny Robinson.

Books and Articles
Lewis, Michael. "Are You Ready for Some Super Bowl? First to the Ball." *New York Times Magazine*, Feb. 5, 2006.

MacCambridge, Michael. *America's Game: The Epic Story of How Pro Football Captured a Nation.* New York: Random House, 2004.

Maule, Tex. "Wham, Bam, Stram!" *Sports Illustrated*, Jan. 19, 1970.

McDonell, Chris, ed. *The Football Game I'll Never Forget.* Buffalo, N.Y.: Firefly Books, 2004.

O'Brien, Michael. *Vince: A Personal Biography of Vince Lombardi.* New York: William Morrow, 1987.

Peary, Danny, ed. *Super Bowl: The Game of Their Lives.* New York: Macmillan, 1997.

Stram, Hank, with Lou Sahadi. *They're Playing My Game.* New York: William Morrow, 1986.

SUPER BOWL II

Author Interviews
Jerry Burns, Forrest Gregg, Dave Hanner, Charlie Sumner, Ron Wolf.

Books and Articles
Goska, Eric. *Green Bay Packers: A Measure of Greatness.* Iola, Wis.: Krause Publications, 2003.

Kramer, Jerry. *Instant Replay.* New York: Signet, 1985.

Maule, Tex. "A Romp for the Pack." *Sports Illustrated*, Jan. 15, 1968.

Maule, Tex. "Green Bay, Handily." *Sports Illustrated*, Jan. 22, 1968.

O'Brien, *Vince: A Personal Biography of Vince Lombardi.*

Otto, Jim, and Dave Newhouse. *Jim Otto: The Pain of Glory.* Champaign, Ill.: Sagamore Publishing, 2000.

Peary, *Super Bowl: The Game of Their Lives.*

The Sporting News, Complete Super Bowl Book. St. Louis: The Sporting News, 1995.

SUPER BOWL III

Author Interviews
Bill Arnsparger, Walt Michaels, Buddy Ryan, Don Shula.

Books and Articles
Cimini, Rich. "Jets Feel Super." *New York Daily News*, Jan. 31, 2008.

Evans, Luther. "I Guarantee We'll Win—Namath." *Miami Herald*, Jan. 10, 1969.

Florence, Mal. "Landry: Mental Anxiety Put Pressure on Colts," *Los Angeles Times*, Jan. 13, 1969.

Green, Jerry. *Super Bowl Chronicles: A Sportswriter Reflects on the First 30 Years of America's Game.* 2nd. ed. Grand Rapids, Mich.: Masters Press, 1995.

Hawkins, Alex. *My Story (and I'm Sticking to It).* Reprint ed. Chapel Hill, N.C.: Algonquin Books, 1990.

Koppett, Leonard, ed. *The New York Times at the Super Bowl.* New York: Quadrangle, 1974.

Kriegel, Mark. *Namath: A Biography.* New York: Penguin Books, 2004.

Maule, Tex. "A Go Pattern vs. a Stop Team." *Sports Illustrated*, Jan. 13, 1969.

Maule, Tex. "Say It's So, Joe." *Sports Illustrated*, Jan. 20, 1969.

McDonell, *The Football Game I'll Never Forget.*

Miller, Jeff. *Going Long: The Wild 10-Year Saga of the Renegade American Football League in the Words of Those Who Lived It.* New York: McGraw Hill, 2004.

Peary, *Super Bowl: The Game of Their Lives.*

"*Sport* Interview: Don Shula." *Sport*, Nov. 1984.

Tanton, Bill. "Colt Win Margin Seen Comfortable." *Baltimore Evening Sun*, Jan. 11, 1969.

Zimmerman, Paul. "Revolutionaries," *Sports Illustrated*, Aug. 17, 1998.

SUPER BOWL IV

Author Interviews
Tom Bettis, Jerry Burns, Tom Flores, Tom Pratt, Jerry Reichow, Johnny Robinson.

Books and Articles
Koppett, *The New York Times at the Super Bowl.*

MacCambridge, *America's Game.*

Pasquarelli, Len. "Backup Plan." ESPN.com, July 18, 2005.

Peary, *Super Bowl: The Game of Their Lives.*

Stram and Sahadi, *They're Playing My Game.*

SUPER BOWL V

Author Interviews
Gil Brandt, Ted Hendricks, Dan Reeves, Jerry Tubbs, Charlie Waters.

Books and Articles
Green, *Super Bowl Chronicles.*

Jones, Robert F. "To Kill a Memory That Still Hurts." *Sports Illustrated*, Jan. 11, 1971.

Koppett, *The New York Times at the Super Bowl.*

Maule, Tex. "Eleven Big Mistakes." *Sports Illustrated*, Jan. 25, 1971.

Peary, *Super Bowl: The Game of Their Lives.*

Thomas, Duane, and Paul Zimmerman. *Duane Thomas and the Fall of America's Team.* New York: Warner Books, 1988.

SUPER BOWL VI

Author Interviews
Bill Arnsparger, Gil Brandt, Forrest Gregg, Dan Reeves, Don Shula, Jerry Tubbs, Charlie Waters.

Books and Articles

Golenbock, Peter. *Landry's Boys: An Oral History of a Team and an Era*. Chicago: Triumph Books, 2005.
Koppett, *The New York Times at the Super Bowl*.
Maule, Tex. "A Cowboy Stampede." *Sports Illustrated*, Jan. 24, 1972.
McDonell, *The Football Game I'll Never Forget*.
Peary, *Super Bowl: The Game of Their Lives*.
Thomas and Zimmerman, *Duane Thomas and the Fall of America's Team*.

SUPER BOWL VII

Author Interviews

Bill Arnsparger, Bobby Beathard, Marv Levy, Don Shula, LaVern Torgeson.

Books and Articles

Green, *Super Bowl Chronicles*.
Maule, Tex. "17-0-0." *Sports Illustrated*, Jan. 22, 1973.
McDonell, *The Football Game I'll Never Forget*.
Peary, *Super Bowl: The Game of Their Lives*.
The Sporting News, Complete Super Bowl Book.

SUPER BOWL VIII

Author Interviews

Bill Arnsparger, Bobby Beathard, Jerry Burns, Jerry Reichow, Don Shula, Jeff Siemon.

Books and Articles

Green, *Super Bowl Chronicles*.
Kaufman, Ira. "The Perfect Season." *Tampa Tribune*, Jan. 27, 2009.
Koppett, *The New York Times at the Super Bowl*.
McDonell, *The Football Game I'll Never Forget*.
Peary, *Super Bowl: The Game of Their Lives*.
Reid, Ron. "On to the M&M Bowl." *Sports Illustrated*, Jan. 7, 1974.
Smith, Don. News release. Pro Football Hall of Fame, April 1, 1994.
Zimmerman, Paul. "His Eyes Have Seen the Glory." *Sports Illustrated*, July 27, 1981.

SUPER BOWL IX

Author Interviews

Jerry Burns, Bud Carson, George Perles, Jerry Reichow, Tim Rooney, Jeff Siemon, Lionel Taylor.

Books and Articles

Bradshaw, Terry, with David Fisher. *It's Only a Game*. New York: Simon and Schuster, 2001.
Chastain, Bill. *Steel Dynasty: The Team That Changed the NFL*. Chicago: Triumph, 2005.
Jenkins, Dan. "Pittsburgh Punches It Out." *Sports Illustrated*, Jan. 20, 1975.
Peary, *Super Bowl: The Game of Their Lives*.

SUPER BOWL X

Author Interviews

Gil Brandt, Bud Carson, George Perles, Dan Reeves, Tim Rooney, Lionel Taylor, Jerry Tubbs, Charlie Waters.

Books and Articles

Bradshaw and Fisher, *It's Only a Game*.

Chastain, *Steel Dynasty*.
Golenbock, *Landry's Boys*.
Green, *Super Bowl Chronicles*.
Henderson, Thomas "Hollywood," and Peter Knobler. *Out of Control: Confessions of an NFL Casualty*. New York: Putnam, 1987.
McDonell, *The Football Game I'll Never Forget*.
Peary, *Super Bowl: The Game of Their Lives*.

SUPER BOWL XI

Author Interviews

Jerry Burns, Tom Flores, Ted Hendricks, Jerry Reichow, Buddy Ryan, Jeff Siemon, Ron Wolf.

Books and Articles

Green, *Super Bowl Chronicles*.
Peary, *Super Bowl: The Game of Their Lives*.
The Sporting News, Complete Super Bowl Book.

SUPER BOWL XII

Author Interviews

Gil Brandt, Joe Collier, Dan Reeves, Jerry Tubbs, Charlie Waters.

Books and Articles

Golenbock, *Landry's Boys*.
Green, *Super Bowl Chronicles*.
Jenkins, Dan. "Doomsday in the Dome." *Sports Illustrated*, Jan. 23, 1978.
Marshall, Joe. "The Orange Is Doomed to be Crushed." *Sports Illustrated*, Jan. 16, 1978.
Peary, *Super Bowl: The Game of Their Lives*.
The Sporting News, Complete Super Bowl Book.
Wojciechowski, Gene. "Wheeling and Dealing." *Los Angeles Times*, Jan. 31, 1988.

SUPER BOWL XIII

Author Interviews

Gil Brandt, George Perles, Dan Reeves, Tim Rooney, Jerry Tubbs, Charlie Waters.

Books and Articles

Bradshaw and Fisher, *It's Only a Game*.
Chastain, *Steel Dynasty*.
Golenbock, *Landry's Boys*.
Green, *Super Bowl Chronicles*.
Henderson and Knobler, *Out of Control*.
Jenkins, Dan. "What a Passing Parade." *Sports Illustrated*, Jan. 29, 1979.
Marshall, Joe. "Pouncing on a Championship." *Sports Illustrated*, Jan. 15, 1979.
McDonell, *The Football Game I'll Never Forget*.
Peary, *Super Bowl: The Game of Their Lives*.
Zimmerman, Paul. *The New Thinking Man's Guide to Pro Football*. New York: Simon and Schuster, 1984.

SUPER BOWL XIV

Author Interviews

Bud Carson, George Perles, Lionel Taylor, LaVern Torgeson.

Books and Articles

Bradshaw and Fisher, *It's Only a Game.*
Chastain, *Steel Dynasty.*
Hubbard, Steve. "Tarnished Steel." *The Sporting News*, Nov. 10, 1986.
Johnston, Joey. "Against All Odds, He Played." *Tampa Bay Tribune*, Jan. 29, 2009.
Marshall, Joe. "The Anatomy of a Touchdown." *Sports Illustrated*, Jan. 28, 1980.
Peary, *Super Bowl: The Game of Their Lives.*
The Sporting News, Complete Super Bowl Book.
Zimmerman, Paul. "They Were Just Too Much." *Sports Illustrated*, Jan. 28, 1980.
Zimmerman, Paul. "The Path to Power." *Sports Illustrated*, Aug. 30, 1999.

SUPER BOWL XV

Author Interviews

Bill Bergey, Tom Flores, Ted Hendricks, Charlie Sumner, Dick Vermeil, Jerry Wampfler, Ron Wolf.

Books and Articles

Green, *Super Bowl Chronicles.*
Peary, *Super Bowl: The Game of Their Lives.*
Reese, Merrill, with Mark Eckel. *It's Gooooood!* Champaign, Ill.: Sports Publishing, 1998.
Zimmerman, Paul. "This Was the Time for One Good Man." *Sports Illustrated*, Feb. 2, 1981.

SUPER BOWL XVI

Author Interviews

Bruce Coslet, Forrest Gregg, Dick LeBeau, Bill McPherson, George Seifert, Chuck Studley, Bill Walsh, Eric Wright.

Books and Articles

Peary, *Super Bowl: The Game of Their Lives.*
The Sporting News, Complete Super Bowl Book.
Walsh, Bill, with Glenn Dickey. *Building a Champion: On Football and the Making of the 49ers.* New York: St. Martin's Press, 1992.
Zimmerman, Paul. "X'd, O'd and KO'd." *Sports Illustrated*, Feb. 1, 1982.

SUPER BOWL XVII

Author Interviews

Bill Arnsparger, Bobby Beathard, Dan Henning, Larry Peccatiello, Don Shula, LaVern Torgeson.

Books and Articles

Wulf, Steve. "A Game of Hogs and Goats." *Sports Illustrated*, Jan. 24, 1983.
Zimmerman, Paul. "Hail to the Redskins!" *Sports Illustrated*, Feb. 7, 1983.

SUPER BOWL XVIII

Author Interviews

Bobby Beathard, Ted Hendricks, Larry Peccatiello, Charlie Sumner, LaVern Torgeson, Ron Wolf.

Books and Articles

Neft, David S., and Richard M. Cohen. *The Football Encyclopedia: The Complete History of Professional NFL Football from 1892 to the Present.* New York: St. Martin's Press, 1994.
Zimmerman, Paul. "It'll Be Los Angeles by Three." *Sports Illustrated*, Jan. 23, 1984.
Zimmerman, Paul. "A Runaway for the Raiders." *Sports Illustrated*, Jan. 30, 1984.

SUPER BOWL XIX

Author Interviews

Bill McPherson, George Seifert, Don Shula, Chuck Studley, Bill Walsh, Eric Wright.

Books and Articles

Green, *Super Bowl Chronicles.*
Peary, *Super Bowl: The Game of Their Lives.*
The Sporting News, Complete Super Bowl Book.
Walsh and Glenn Dickey, *Building a Champion.*
Zimmerman, Paul. "The Niners Were Never Finer." *Sports Illustrated*, Jan. 28, 1985.

SUPER BOWL XX

Author Interviews

Raymond Berry, Raymond Clayborn, Mike Ditka, Dan Hampton, Buddy Ryan.

Books and Articles

McMahon, Jim, with Bob Verdi. *McMahon!: The Bare Truth about Chicago's Brashest Bear.* New York: Warner Books, 1986.
Peary, *Super Bowl: The Game of Their Lives.*
The Sporting News, Complete Super Bowl Book.
Zimmerman, Paul. "Up Against It." *Sports Illustrated*, Jan. 27, 1986.
Zimmerman, Paul. "A Brilliant Case for the Defense." *Sports Illustrated*, Feb. 3, 1986.

SUPER BOWL XXI

Author Interviews

Bill Belichick, Joe Collier, Ron Erhardt, Pepper Johnson, Dan Reeves, Tim Rooney.

Books and Articles

O'Connor, Ian. "Giants QB Was Near-Perfect in Super Bowl Win." *Bergen Record*, Jan. 25, 2007.
Peary, *Super Bowl: The Game of Their Lives.*

SUPER BOWL XXII

Author Interviews

Bobby Beathard, Tyrone Braxton, Joe Collier, Dan Henning, Nick Nicolau, Larry Peccatiello, Dan Reeves, LaVern Torgeson.

Books and Articles

Kaufman, Michelle. "Impact Still Resonates 19 Years Later." *Miami Herald*, Feb. 3, 2007.
Peary, *Super Bowl: The Game of Their Lives.*

Zimmerman, Paul. "One Super Show." *Sports Illustrated*, Feb. 8, 1988.

Zimmerman, Paul. "Revolutionaries." *Sports Illustrated*, Aug. 17, 1998.

SUPER BOWL XXIII

Author Interviews

Bruce Coslet, Ray Horton, Dick LeBeau, Bill McPherson, Bill Romanowski, George Seifert, Mike Stock, Bill Walsh, Eric Wright.

Books and Articles

"Handling Pressure." *Miami Herald*, Feb. 3, 2007.

King, Peter. *Football: A History of the Professional Game.* Birmingham, Ala.: Oxmoor House, 1993.

McDonough, Will. "Pressure-Packed with Intrigue." *Boston Globe*, Jan. 28, 2002.

Miller, Ira. "49ers Win 20–16 in Super Thriller." *San Francisco Chronicle*, Jan. 23, 1989.

"South Florida's Four Off-the-Field Super Bowls." *South Florida Sun-Sentinel*, Jan. 30, 2007.

"Stanley Wilson: Drug Relapse." *South Florida Sun-Sentinel*, Jan. 30, 2007.

Walsh and Glenn Dickey, *Building a Champion.*

Zimmerman, Paul. "Revolutionaries." *Sports Illustrated*, Aug. 17, 1998.

SUPER BOWL XXIV

Author Interviews

Tyrone Braxton, Bill McPherson, Dan Reeves, Bill Romanowski, George Seifert, Bill Walsh, Charlie Waters, Eric Wright.

Books and Articles

Green, *Super Bowl Chronicles.*

King, Peter. "Dad's Boy." *Sports Illustrated*, Jan. 29, 1990.

Lieber, Jill. "The Fab 5." *Sports Illustrated*, Jan. 29, 1990.

Peary, *Super Bowl: The Game of Their Lives.*

Zimmerman, Paul. "The Calm, The Storm." *Sports Illustrated*, Feb. 5, 1990.

SUPER BOWL XXV

Author Interviews

Bill Belichick, Tom Bresnahan, Walt Corey, Bruce DeHaven, Ron Erhardt, Fred Hoaglin, Pepper Johnson, Marv Levy, Nick Nicolau, Tim Rooney.

Books and Articles

Greenfeld, Karl Taro. "A Life After Wide Right." *Sports Illustrated*, July 12, 2004.

King, Peter. *Inside the Helmet: A Player's View of the NFL.* New York: Simon and Schuster, 1993.

Maiorana, Sal. *Stadium Stories: Buffalo Bills.* Guilford, Conn.: Globe Pequot, 2005.

Peary, *Super Bowl: The Game of Their Lives.*

Taylor, Lawrence, with Steve Serby. *LT: Over the Edge.* New York: Harper Collins, 2003.

Zimmerman, Paul. "High and Mighty." *Sports Illustrated*, Feb. 4, 1991.

SUPER BOWL XXVI

Author Interviews

Tom Bresnahan, Walt Corey, Bruce DeHaven, Jim Hanifan, Marv Levy, Nick Nicolau, Larry Peccatiello, LaVern Torgeson.

Books and Articles

Maiorana, *Stadium Stories: Buffalo Bills.*

Peary, *Super Bowl: The Game of Their Lives.*

Zimmerman, Paul. "Mission Accomplished." *Sports Illustrated*, Feb. 3, 1992.

SUPER BOWL XXVII

Author Interviews

Tom Bresnahan, Dave Campo, Walt Corey, Butch Davis, Bruce DeHaven, Ray Horton, Jimmy Johnson, Daryl Johnston, Marv Levy.

Books and Articles

Bayless, Skip. *The Boys.* New York: Simon and Schuster, 1993.

Dent, Jim. *King of the Cowboys: The Life and Times of Jerry Jones.* Holbrook, Mass.: Adams Publishing, 1995.

Johnson, Jimmy, as told to Ed Hinton. *Turning the Thing Around: Pulling America's Team Out of the Dumps—And Myself Out of the Doghouse.* New York: Hyperion, 1994.

Peary, *Super Bowl: The Game of Their Lives.*

Zimmerman, Paul. "These Bills Are Due … ." *Sports Illustrated*, Feb. 1, 1993.

SUPER BOWL XXVIII

Author Interviews

Tom Bresnahan, Dave Campo, Walt Corey, Butch Davis, Bruce DeHaven, Jimmy Johnson, Daryl Johnston, Marv Levy.

Books and Articles

Maiorana, Stadium Stories: Buffalo Bills.

Peary, *Super Bowl: The Game of Their Lives.*

SUPER BOWL XXIX

Author Interviews

Bill Arnsparger, Bobby Beathard, John Marshall, Bill McPherson, Chuck Priefer, George Seifert, Bill Walsh.

Books and Articles

Arkush, Dan. "Red-Hot Rivalry." *Pro Football Weekly Preview '95*, June 1995.

Farmer, Sam. "Simply Uncatchable." *Los Angeles Times*, Sept. 6, 2005.

Gosselin, Rick. "How to Build a Super Bowl Team in the 90s." *Ultimate Sports Pro Football '95*, June 1995.

Peary, *Super Bowl: The Game of Their Lives.*

Telander, Rick. "Beaten Deep." *Sports Illustrated*, Jan. 23, 1995.

Telander, Rick. "Superb?" *Sports Illustrated*, Feb. 6, 1995.

Zimmerman, Paul. "What If … ." *Sports Illustrated*, Jan. 30, 1995.

SUPER BOWL XXX

Author Interviews
Dave Campo, Tom Donahoe, Ron Erhardt, Daryl Johnston, Dick LeBeau, Rod Woodson, Barry Switzer.

Books and Articles
Luksa, Frank. "Wrong Side of Red River." *Ultimate Sports Pro Football '96*, June 1996.

Peary, *Super Bowl: The Game of Their Lives*.

Moritz, Carl. "Forget 'Prime Time'—Brown Is 'Right Place at the Right Time.'" *The Sporting News*, Feb. 5, 1996.

SUPER BOWL XXXI

Author Interviews
Charley Armey, Bill Belichick, Troy Brown, Tedy Bruschi, LeRoy Butler, Mark Chmura, Brett Favre, Bob Harlan, Gil Haskell, Fred Hoaglin, Andy Reid, Ron Wolf.

Books and Articles
Buchsbaum, Joel. Green Bay Season Preview. *Pro Football Weekly Preview '97*, June 1997.

Edes, Gordon. "Secondary Can't Pass Favre's Test." *Boston Globe*, Jan. 27, 1997.

Holley, Michael. *Patriot Reign: Bill Belichick, the Coaches, and the Players Who Built a Champion*. New York: HarperCollins, 2004.

Madden, Michael. "They're Left Grasping at Air—And for Answers." *Boston Globe*, Jan. 27, 1997.

McDonough, Will. "Pressure-Packed with Intrigue." *Boston Globe*, Jan. 28, 2002.

Peary, *Super Bowl: The Game of Their Lives*.

Romell, Rick. "Packer Pride." *Milwaukee Journal Sentinel*, Jan. 28, 1997.

Wolf, Ron, and Paul Attner. *The Packer Way: Nine Stepping Stones to Building a Winning Organization*. New York: St. Martin's Griffin, 1999.

Zimmerman, Paul. "Anatomy of a Return." *Sports Illustrated*, Feb. 3, 1997.

SUPER BOWL XXXII

Author Interviews
Pat Bowlen, Tyrone Braxton, LeRoy Butler, Mark Chmura, George Dyer, Bob Harlan, Gil Haskell, Mike Heimerdinger, Dorsey Levens, Sherman Lewis, Tom Lovat, Greg Robinson, Bill Romanowski, Aaron Taylor, Ron Wolf.

Books and Articles
Silver, Michael. "7-Up." *Sports Illustrated*, Feb. 2, 1998.

Silverstein, Tom. "Favre Fails to Deliver Magical Performance." *Milwaukee Journal Sentinel*, Jan. 26, 1998.

Silverstein, Tom. "Levens Remains Bitter Over Loss in Super Bowl." *Milwaukee Journal Sentinel*, Feb. 2, 2005.

SUPER BOWL XXXIII

Author Interviews
Pat Bowlen, Tyrone Braxton, Rich Brooks, Dick Corrick, George Dyer, Mike Heimerdinger, Dan Reeves, Bill Romanowski.

Books and Articles
"Eugene Robinson: Christian Player Finds Himself in Deep Trouble." *South Florida Sun-Sentinel*, Jan. 30, 2007.

Mitchell, Fred. "Super Temptations Abound." *Chicago Tribune*, Jan. 24, 2007.

Reilly, Rick. "Saturday Night Fever." *Sports Illustrated*, Feb. 9, 1999.

Silver, Michael. "The Magnificent 7." *Sports Illustrated*, Feb. 9, 1999.

SUPER BOWL XXXIV

Author Interviews
Charley Armey, Kevin Dyson, Eddie George, Jerry Gray, Jim Hanifan, Mike Martz, Eddie Robinson, Rich Snead, Dick Vermeil, Steve Walters.

Books and Articles
McDonough, Will. "Pressure-Packed with Intrigue." *Boston Globe*, Jan. 28, 2002.

SUPER BOWL XXXV

Author Interviews
Micheal Barrow, Brian Billick, Jim Fassel, Ozzie Newsome, Michael Strahan, Rod Woodson.

Books and Articles
Hensley, Jamison. "QB Would Have Liked to Stay with Ravens." *Baltimore Sun*, Feb. 3, 2007.

SUPER BOWL XXXVI

Author Interviews
Charley Armey, Bill Belichick, Tedy Bruschi, Ivan Fears, Jim Hanifan, Pepper Johnson, Mike Martz, Rob Ryan.

Books and Articles
Halberstam, David. *The Education of a Coach*. New York: Hyperion, 2006.

"Herald's Tomase Says He Will Regret Sypgate Error for Life." Associated Press, May 17, 2008.

Holley, Michael. "Script Casts Coach in New Light." *Boston Globe*, Feb. 4, 2002.

Reiss, Mike. "Daboll Doesn't Recall Talk." *Boston Globe*, May 16, 2008.

Silver, Michael. "Pat Answer." *Sports Illustrated*, Feb. 11, 2002.

Silver, Michael. "Fallen Idols." *Sports Illustrated*, Nov. 21, 2005.

"Tom Brady: The Best Ever?" *Men's Journal*, Dec. 2005.

SUPER BOWL XXXVII

Author Interviews
Jon Gruden, Monte Kiffin, Bill Muir, Bill Romanowski, Rod Woodson.

Books and Articles
Gruden, Jon, with Vic Carucci, *Do You Love Football?!: Winning with Heart, Passion, and Not Much Sleep*. New York: Harper, 2004.

Hirsley, Michael. "'Fearful' Callahan Supports Robbins." *Chicago Tribune*, Jan. 30, 2003.

Silver, Michael. "What a Steal?" *Sports Illustrated*, Feb. 3, 2003.

SUPER BOWL XXXVIII

Author Interviews
Bill Belichick, Troy Brown, Tedy Bruschi, Kevin Dyson, Ivan Fears, Dan Henning, Rob Ryan, Mike Trgovac.

Books and Articles
Halberstam, *The Education of a Coach.*

SUPER BOWL XXXIX

Author Interviews
Bill Belichick, Troy Brown, Tedy Bruschi, Ivan Fears, Jim Johnson, Andy Reid, Jon Runyan.

Books and Articles
Minnesota Vikings press conference transcript, Oct. 26, 2006.
Pompei, Dan. "Another Fine Mess." *The Sporting News*, Feb. 18, 2005.
Zimmerman, Paul. "Point, Counterpoint." *Sports Illustrated*, Feb. 14, 2005.

SUPER BOWL XL

Author Interviews
Gil Haskell, Mike Holmgren, Dick LeBeau, Will Lewis, Marquand Manuel, John Marshall, Ken Whisenhunt.

Books and Articles
Boyle, John. "Explanations of Six Key Plays." *Seattle Times*, Feb. 10, 2006.
Colston, Chris. "Pieces Fall into Place for Cowher." *USA Today Sports Weekly*, Feb. 8–14, 2006.
King, Peter. "Kings of the Road." *Sports Illustrated*, Jan. 30, 2006.
King, Peter. "Match Game." *Sports Illustrated*, Feb. 6, 2006.
King, Peter. "Flag Frenzy." *Sports Illustrated*, Feb. 15, 2006.
Markowski, Tom. "Trick Play Was Steelers' Treat." *Detroit News*, Feb. 6, 2006.
Pompei, Dan. "Big Shoes Left Unfulfilled." *The Sporting News*, Feb. 17, 2006.
Romero, Jose Miguel. "The 'Official' Story of the Super Bowl." *Seattle Times*, Feb. 7, 2006.
Silver, Michael. "Hearts of Steel." *Sports Illustrated*, Feb. 13, 2006.
Silverstein, Tom. "Tagliabue Shows Compassion." *Milwaukee Journal Sentinel*, April 2, 2006.

SUPER BOWL XLI

Author Interviews
Jerry Angelo, Bobby DePaul, Tony Dungy, Howard Mudd, Muhsin Muhammad, Bill Polian, Russ Purnell, Ron Rivera, Jeff Saturday, John Teerlinck.

Books and Articles
"The Polian Corner," Colts.com, Feb. 7, 2007.

SUPER BOWL XLII

Author Interviews
Bill Belichick, Joel Collier, Kevin Gilbride, Marc Ross, Brad Seely, Steve Spagnuolo.

Books and Articles
Borges, Ron. ronborges.com, Nov. 7, 2007.
Layden, Tim. "Remember?" *Sports Illustrated*, Aug. 4, 2008.
MacMullen, Jackie. "Pass and Fail." *Boston Globe*, Feb. 5, 2008.
Reiss, Mike. "'The Catch' Won't Haunt Harrison." *Boston Globe*, June 1, 2008.
Vacchiano, Ralph. "Referee: I Almost Sacked Eli Manning." *New York Daily News*, Feb. 7, 2008.
Vacchiano, Ralph. *Eli Manning: The Making of a Quarterback.* New York: Skyhorse Publishing, 2008.

SUPER BOWL XLIII

Author Interviews
Bruce Arians, James Farrior, Larry Fitzgerald, Todd Haley, Ray Horton, Clancy Pendergast, Mike Pereira, Ken Whisenhunt.

Books and Articles
Finder, Chuck. "Steelers' Harrison Took Circuitous Route to Stardom." *Pittsburgh Post-Gazette*, January 11, 2009.
King, Peter. "Reliving Pittsburgh's Final Drive." SI.com, February 9, 2009.

SUPER BOWL XLIV

Author Interviews
Larry Coyer, Scott Fujita, Bill Johnson, Curtis Johnson, Mickey Loomis, Howard Mudd, Bill Polian, Gregg Williams.

Books and Articles
Finney, Peter. "Win was a Long Time Coming." *New Orleans Times-Picayune.* Jan. 25, 2010.
King, Peter. "Who Dat, Indeed." SI.com, Feb. 8, 2010.
Payton, Sean, and Ellis Henican. *Home Team: Coaching the Saints and New Orleans Back to Life.* New York: New American Library, 2010.
Smith, Jimmy. "An End to Remember." *New Orleans Times-Picayune.* Feb. 3, 2010.

SUPER BOWL XLV

Author Interviews
Bruce Arians, Arnaz Battle, Keith Butler, Dom Capers, Kevin Colbert, Ray Horton, Mike McCarthy, Jordy Nelson, B. J. Raji, Mike Wallace.

SUPER BOWL XLVI

Author Interviews
Kevin Boothe, Brian Ferentz, Perry Fewell, Todd Fuhrman, Kevin Gilbride, Peter Giunta, Devin McCourty, Rob Ninkovich, Bill O'Brien, Marc Ross, Chris Snee.

INDEX